ANTHROPOLOGY
TODAY: *Selections*

CONTRIBUTORS

Erwin H. Ackerknecht

Marston Bates

Ralph Beals

Wendell C. Bennett

David Bidney

William C. Boyd

Alfonso Caso

Pierre Teilhard de Chardin

V. Gordon Childe

J. Grahame D. Clark

Joseph H. Greenberg

A. Irving Hallowell

Harry Hoijer

Clyde Kluckhohn

Claude Lévi-Strauss

Margaret Mead

Hallam L. Movius, Jr.

F. S. C. Northrop

Robert Redfield

Irving Rouse

Meyer Schapiro

William L. Straus, Jr.

Henri V. Vallois

S. L. Washburn

Gordon R. Willey

ANTHROPOLOGY
TODAY: *Selections*

Edited by SOL TAX

THE UNIVERSITY OF CHICAGO PRESS
CHICAGO & LONDON

International Standard Book Number: 0-226-79083-5
Library of Congress Catalog Card Number: 62-17960

THE UNIVERSITY OF CHICAGO PRESS, CHICAGO 60637
The University of Chicago Press, Ltd., London

Preface

In June of 1952, eighty scholars from most parts of the world met at the Wenner-Gren Foundation in New York for a two-week symposium on the state of the sciences of anthropology. The discussions were based on fifty papers prepared in advance for study by all the participants. After the symposium, these papers were published in a book *Anthropology Today*. Since Professor A. L. Kroeber was president of the symposium and wrote an introduction to the book, the volume is usually catalogued under his name as author or editor.

Anthropology Today is subtitled "An Encyclopedic Inventory" because each of the fifty papers in it was designed

agree that the volume is the best existing summation of anthropological thinking. *Anthropology Today* therefore has great vogue as a presentation of anthropology to students, to scholars in other fields, and to the educated layman.

The present selection is designed to increase in two ways the usefulness of the work: first, the price is greatly reduced and, second, it omits articles now outdated by the march of science and of events (e.g., Heizer's and Oakley's articles on methods of dating, Rowe's on technical aids, and all the articles on applied anthropology).

The original organization provided the following grid:

	Problems of the Historical Approach	Problems of Process	Problems of Application
Method........	3	5	....
Results.........	13	11	9
Theory.........	5	3	....

to provide a "systematic overview of the methods deployed and substantive results obtained by research along a particular front—a subject or field or segment of anthropology—as this has developed, particularly in recent years. Each inventory paper takes stock of the methods gradually defined and refined in this subject or field and the principal findings made" (Kroeber, in *Anthropology Today*, p. xv). Most of the papers indeed followed this formula. Some are less inventory-like, more "problem oriented"; yet all reviewers

The rubrics (which do not always distinguish the articles) are dropped now and the articles included in the present selection reordered generally in the more traditional anthropological pattern of biological→historical→sociocultural. Except for relatively minor changes, the articles printed here are exactly as they appeared in the original volume. However, the biographical data have been updated.

Of the fifty original authors (in addition to A. L. Kroeber himself), death has taken Pierre Teilhard de Chardin,

V. Gordon Childe, Wendell C. Bennett, Clyde Kluckhohn, Robert Redfield, and G. Jan Held. Only Held's paper (on applied anthropology in the late Netherlands East Indies) is omitted from the present volume.

Royalties on the original edition of *Anthropology Today* were assigned to the Wenner-Gren Foundation and have returned most of the cost of publica-tion; royalties on the present volume will be assigned in the same manner. It is expected that they will complete the payment and thus make the equivalent of the original sum furnished by the Foundation available to it for anthropological research and for further conferences and publication.

SOL TAX

CHICAGO
February 1962

Contents

The Strategy of Physical Anthropology

By S. L. WASHBURN

THE STRATEGY of a science is that body of theory and techniques with which it attacks its problems. All sciences have their traditional ways of marshaling and analyzing data, and the effectiveness of a science may be judged by the way its strategy actually solves problems and points the way to new research. For many years physical anthropology changed little and was easy to define. Physical anthropologists were those scientists, interested in human evolution and variation, who used measurements as their primary technique. The main training of a physical anthropologist consisted in learning to make a small number of measurements accurately, and one of the great concerns of the profession has been to get agreement on how these measurements should be taken. The assumption seems to have been that description (whether morphological or metrical), if accurate enough and in sufficient quantity, could solve problems of process, pattern, and interpretation.

It was essential to get a general appreciation of the varieties of primates, including man, before the problems of evolution could be understood. As knowledge of the primates increased, the kinds of problems to be solved became more and more defined. Is man's closest living relative an arboreal ape or a tiny tarsier? By what methods could

such a problem be attacked? Should as many characters as possible be compared, or would a few critical ones settle the matter? Should adaptive characters be stressed, or does the solution of the problems of phylogeny lie in nonadaptive features? Does the body evolve as a unified whole, or may different parts change at different times?

The general understanding of the primates and of human races proceeded rapidly and productively in the nineteenth century. The classifications of Flower and Lydekker (1891) and Deniker (1900) are remarkably close to those of today. The principal progress since that time has been in the discovery of fossils, and the quantity and quality of descriptive materials has increased greatly. Many small problems have been clarified, but the main outlines of the classification of the primates were clear more than fifty years ago.

During the last fifty years, although excellent descriptive data were added, techniques improved, and problems clarified and defined, little progress was made in understanding the process and pattern of human evolution. The strategy of physical anthropology yielded diminishing returns, and, finally, application of the traditional method *by experts* gave contradictory results. After more than a century of intensive fact-finding, there is less agreement among

1

informed scientists on the relation of man to other primates than there was in the latter part of the nineteenth century. (Schultz, 1936, 1950*a, b;* Simpson, 1945; and Straus, 1949, have recently summarized many of these conflicting views and the evidence for them.) With regard to race, agreement is no greater, for some recognize a few races based on populations, while others describe a great number, many of which are types and refer to no populations at all.

Difficulties of this sort are by no means confined to physical anthropology but are common in many parts of descriptive zoölogy. The dilemma arises from continuing the strategy which was appropriate in the first descriptive phase of a science into the following analytic phase. Measurements will tell us which heads are long, but they will not tell us whether longheaded people should be put into one biological category. A photograph may show that a person is fat, but it gives no clue to the cause of the fat, and a grouping of fat people may be as arbitrary as one of longheads.

It is necessary to have a knowledge of the varieties of head form, pigmentation, body build, growth pattern, etc., before the problems of evolution, race, and constitution can be clearly stated. But all that can be done with the initial descriptive information is to gain a first understanding, a sense of problem, and a preliminary classification. To go further requires an elaboration of theory and method along different lines. Having passed through its initial descriptive phase, physical anthropology is now entering into its analytic stage. Change is forced on physical anthropology partially by the fact that its own strategy has ceased to yield useful results but, far more, by the rise of modern evolutionary theory (treated elsewhere in this symposium by Carter). The meeting of genetics, paleontology, and evolutionary zoölogy created the new systematics (neozoölogy), just as the impact of the new evolutionary theory is creating a new physical anthropology. Anthropologists are fortunate that their problems are logically and methodologically similar to those which have been debated and largely solved in zoölogy. Therefore, their task is far simpler than that which confronted taxonomists fifteen years ago. The anthropologist may simply adopt the new evolutionary point of view, and his task is primarily one of adapting to this intellectual environment and devising techniques suitable to his particular needs. The nature and implication of the changes will be made clearer by considering the contrast between the old and the new systematically, under the headings of purpose, theory, technique, and interpretation. These comparisons will be made briefly in Table 1, and then each will be considered in some detail. It should be remembered in making the comparisons that the differences are in degree only and that brief contrasts, especially in a table, make them appear unduly sharp. As Stewart (1951) has rightly pointed out, the new physical anthropology has evolved from the old, and there is a real continuity. However, a great change is taking place in a short time. If this is called "evolution," it is evolution of a quantum type. It is a burst of acceleration on the part of a species which had been quiescent for a long period of time. Actually, the physical anthropology of 1950 will seem much more like that of 1900 than it will like that of 1960. Since the transition described in this paper is still taking place, it would be very difficult to discern its magnitude from the anthropological literature. The remarks in this paper are based heavily on the discussions which have been held at the Wenner-Gren summer seminars for physical anthropologists, and those reading only current American physical anthropology would get little idea of the size or importance of these changes. Since the transition in zoölogy is now general and international, that in anthropology soon will be, and it is hoped that the extent and nature of the changes now taking place in other countries may be discussed at length at this conference.

This point can be made clear by examples. It has long been known that browridges vary in size and form. Cunningham (1909) gave a classification into which the majority of browridges can be fitted. The classification of browridges by this or similar schemes is a standard part of traditional physical

TABLE 1

Old	New
Purpose	
Primarily classification	Understanding process
Problems solved by classification and correlation	Classification a minor part, and the *cause* of differences critical
Description of difference enough	
Theory	
Relatively little and unimportant; facts speak for themselves	Theory is critical, and the development of consistent, experimentally verified hypotheses a major objective
Technique	
Anthropometry 80 per cent, aided by morphological comparison	Measurement perhaps 20 per cent, supplemented by a wide variety of techniques adapted to the solution of particular problems
Interpretation	
Speculation	The primary objective of the research is to prove which hypotheses are correct; the major task begins where the old left off

PURPOSE

In commenting on the contrasts between the new and the old physical anthropology outlined in Table 1, it should be stressed that the area of interest or ultimate purposes of the field are the same. The understanding and interpretation of human evolution remains the objective. However, the immediate purpose of most scientific investigations will be but a small step toward the final goal. The investigator will be concerned with race, constitution, fossil man, or some similar problem. In the past the primary purpose of the majority of investigations of this sort was classification rather than the interpretation of any part of the phenomenon being investigated.

anthropology. But what do the differences mean, and to what are they related? The classification gives no answers to these problems. To say that one fossil has browridges of Type II and another of Type III does not give any information on the significance of the difference, nor does it allow any inference to be made concerning relationship. In general, big browridges are correlated with big faces, but the appearance of size is also dependent on the size and form of the braincase. Microcephals appear to have large ridges, but this is due solely to the small size of the brain. In such an extreme case everyone would interpret the difference as being due to the change in size of the brain, but how much of the

difference between the browridge of
Java man and modern man is due to
the difference in the face, and how
much to a difference in the brain? In
the literature a phylogeny of browridges
is presented (Weidenreich, 1947). This
can be interpreted only if the ridges
are sufficiently independent in size and
form that tentative conclusions may be
drawn from the classification and historical sequence. No one doubts the
validity of the descriptive statements,
but there is very real doubt that any
conclusions can be drawn from this sort
of table. This is because the ridge is
anatomically complex and because the
same general form of ridge may be due
to a diversity of different conditions.
For example, the central part of the divided type of ridge may be due to a
large frontal sinus, acromegaly, a deposit of mechanically unoriented bone,
or highly oriented bone. The general
prominence of the region may be due
to a large face or a small brain; but
probably, with faces of equal mass,
those associated with long cranial bases
and large temporal muscles have larger
browridges than those which are associated with shorter bases and larger
masseter muscles. The description of
the differences between an Australian
Aboriginal and a Mongoloid can be
done by the traditional methods, but
it can be interpreted only if the anatomical causes lying behind the differences are analyzed. The description offers no technical difficulty, but analysis
is possible only by the use of a variety
of methods which have not been part
of the equipment of anthropology (see
paper by Rowe in this symposium).

This example shows the way in which
classification was the aim and tool of
physical anthropology. As viewed traditionally, if one was interested in browridges, the procedure was to classify
the structures and then to draw conclusions on the interrelations of races
or fossil men. That is, the classification
gave a tool to be used in the analysis
of evolution and variation. It was, in
this sense, final knowledge. But in a
different sense the classification merely
outlined the problems to be investigated. No description of the types of
browridges gives understanding of the
reasons for any of them. The classifications show what kinds exist, under what
circumstances they are found, and so
pose a series of problems which need
investigation. To traditional physical
anthropology, classification was an end,
something to be used. To the new physical anthropology, classifications merely
pose problems, and methods must be
devised to solve them.

The traditional reliance on classification as a method of analysis produced
two of the characteristics of traditional
zoölogical taxonomy and physical anthropology. (1) If classification is the
primary aim and tool, then agreement
on method is all-important. Therefore,
the efforts of physical anthropologists
have been to get agreements on how to
take measurements and observations.
Introductions to physical anthropology
are largely instructions on how to take
measurements, with little or no indication of what it is that the measurements are supposed to mean. International congresses have ended with pleas
for uniformity, so that classification
might continue. One may hope that this
congress will break with the traditions
of the past and urge that undue emphasis on uniformity is undesirable and
will stress the need for new techniques
for the solution of particular problems.
(2) The second result of the emphasis
on classification is that, when difficulties
arise, they are met by making the classifications more complicated. This may
be illustrated in the study of race. By
the early part of the nineteenth century,
several simple classifications of races
existed, and causal explanations had
been offered. Races were due to climate, isolation, etc. In the meantime,

classifications of races have become vastly more numerous, and many are extremely complex, but explanations of cause and process have remained much as they were. Dobzhansky (1950) points out that the principal task of the anthropologist now should be to try to understand the causes and process of race formation. Dobzhansky's clear and eloquent plea should be read by all anthropologists, and I have only one qualification, or rather explanation. Traditional anthropologists thought that they were dealing with cause and process much more than Dobzhansky thinks they were. The difference really lies in the attitude toward classification. The traditional physical anthropologist thought that classification, if done in sufficient detail, would give the clues to problems of cause and process. Classifications were accompanied by remarks on how they were explained by hybridization, environment, etc. If one believes that classifications alone give understanding, then one will make the classifications more and more complicated, just as anthropologists have been doing. However, if one thinks that classification can do no more than map the results of process, then one will be content with a very rough mapping until the processes have been analyzed. The new physical anthropology is separated from the old, not by any difference in the desire to know causes, but by a very real difference in belief as to the extent to which classification can reveal causes.

Some classification is a necessary first stage in ordering the data in an area of knowledge, but its meaning depends on understanding the processes which produce the variety of form. After the first stage of preliminary description, scientists must turn to problems of process or face an era of futile elaboration of classifications which cannot be interpreted for lack of adequate techniques and theories.

THEORY

It is a characteristic of the first stage of a science that theory is not considered important. If classification can solve problems and if it can be reached by marshaling enough facts, then theory need be of little concern. However, as knowledge increases and problems are more precisely formulated, theory becomes of great importance. For a considerable time after the idea of organic evolution had been accepted, comparisons were made without any general theoretical concern, other than that the parts compared should be homologous. Later, anthropology was particularly disturbed by the controversy as to whether deductions concerning relationship should be made on the basis of adaptive or nonadaptive characters. This, in turn, raised the question of whether it was better to compare many features, or whether the comparison of a few critical ones might not give more reliable results. Parallel evolution became recognized as a complicating feature, but, on the whole, physical anthropology continued to operate without any great concern for its theoretical foundations. It should be stressed that this general point of view was characteristic of much of historical zoölogy, ethnology, and archeology. Theoretical issues were not absent, but they were not deemed very important, and the major effort went into collecting specimens and data and describing facts. The realization has been growing for some years that facts alone will not settle the problems and that even the collection of the "facts" was guided by a complex body of unstated assumptions.

The necessary guiding theories have been recently set forth by numerous zoölogists, and the new zoölogy states simply that evolution is the history of genetic systems. Changes in isolated populations are due to mutation, selection, and accidents of genetic sampling (drift). The major cause of change is selection, which is a simple word covering a vast number of mechanisms (Dobzhansky, 1951). The implications of this theory for physical anthropology are numerous and complicated. The basic issue may be stated as follows: If evolution is governed primarily by adaptation, the demonstration of the nature and kind of adaptation is the principal task of the anthropologist. Evolution is a sequence of more effective behavior systems. To understand behavior, live animals must be studied first, and then, when fossils are found, the attempt can be made to interpret the differences by a knowledge of the living forms. It is necessary to remember that fossils were alive when they were important. They were the living, adapted forms of their day, and they must be understood in that setting. In so far as the record is fragmentary, the task is full of uncertainty; but this is a difficulty inherent in the kind of material and does not alter the logical problem.

Traditional physical anthropology was based on the study of skulls. Measurements were devised to describe certain features of the bones, and, when the technique was extended to the living, the measurements were kept as close to those taken on the skeleton as possible. From a comparative and classificatory point of view this was reasonable, and for a while it yielded useful results, but it brought the limitations of death to the study of the living. Whereas the new physical anthropology aims to enrich the study of the past by study of the present, to understand bone in terms of function and life, the old tried to reduce the living to a series of measurements designed to describe bones. Similarity in measurements or combinations of measurements was believed to show genetic affinity. Although

it is true that humans of similar genotype are metrically similar, it is not true that similar measurements necessarily mean genetic similarity. Boyd (1950) has discussed this in detail. However, the point is so important that one example will be given here. Straus (1927) has shown that the ilium is approximately the same length in males and females, but the upper part is longer in males, and the lower longer in females. It is only an accident that the two different parts happen to give approximately the same total length. The descriptive statement that the ilium length is the same in male and female is correct and could be proved beyond doubt with elaborate statistics. However, the conclusion that the bones are anatomically or genetically similar would be wrong. The basis for dividing the ilium into upper and lower parts is that these have different functions. The upper is concerned primarily with muscle origin and sacral articulation. The lower ilium is an important segment of the pelvic inlet, which grows rapidly at puberty (Greulich and Thoms, 1944), making the large female inlet suitable for childbirth. The understanding of the ilium which leads to the division into upper and lower segments is based on an appreciation of its function in the living, on the different adaptive nature of the two parts. It is in this sense that the understanding of the living enriches and brings life to the study of the bones. The metrical discrimination is based on anatomical understanding which can be partially expressed metrically and given deeper meaning by statistics. But the original discrimination is based on an appreciation of an adaptive complex. After the choice to measure upper and lower ilium has been made, measurements help by showing the degree of difference, the variability and the correlation of parts, and prove that the anatomical judgment was justified. *But no statistical manipulation will make a discrimination which is not inherent in the original measurements.* Statistics may bring out relations which are there but which are not obvious to the investigator, as shown by Howells (1951).

If a measurement is regarded as genetically determined, nonadaptive, and not correlated with others, it might then be used in the comparison of races without further question. This seems to have been the approximate working hypothesis of traditional physical anthropology. However, if traits are anatomically complex, adaptive, and correlated, they will be useful for description, but comparisons will not automatically yield solutions to problems of affinity. Present genetic and evolutionary theory suggests that characters are, for the most part, complex and adaptive, but this does not give information about any particular situation. The theory that the measurements were nonadaptive allowed one to work blindly and with confidence. The traditional measurements, accurately taken and treated with proper statistics, *gave certain answers.* The belief that traits are complex and adaptive means that the metrical comparisons *pose problems,* which must then be investigated by other methods. Measurements tell us that roundheads have become more common (Weidenreich, 1945), but they do not tell us that roundheads are genetically similar or why roundheads have become more common. From an anatomical point of view, is brachycephalization due to changes in the brain, dura, sutures, or base of the skull? From an evolutionary point of view, is the change due to adaptation or genetic drift? It should be stressed that, although all seem agreed that selection is the most important factor in evolution, there is no agreement on the importance of genetic drift (Carter, 1951; Dobzhansky, 1951) or the extent

to which traits of little or no adaptive importance exist or spread.

In the past, investigators have assumed that characters were adaptive or nonadaptive, but this is the very question which needs investigation (as discussed by Dobzhansky, 1950). Further, it should be stressed that it is not a question of one or the other, but of selective pressures varying from very little to very great. Some characteristic features of a race may be due to drift, others to strong selection, others to mild selection, still others to mixture due entirely to cultural factors. Whether a particular trait or gene frequency is highly adaptive or of little importance can be settled only by research, and the answer will surely differ at different times and places.

Closely related to the idea of nonadaptation is the concept of orthogenesis. If evolution is *not* caused by selection, then the long-term changes must be due to some other cause, and change may be accounted for by some inner irreversible force. This general concept has been very common in anthropology. For example, it has been maintained that, since man's arms are shorter than apes', man could not be descended from an ape, as this would reverse the course of evolution. According to the theory that evolution is adaptive, there is no reason why man's ancestors may not have had much longer arms. When selection changed, arms may have become shorter. (Actually, the difference is small; Schultz, 1950a.) According to the irreversible orthogenetic-force theory, man could not be descended from an ape, and a few measurements settle the matter. According to the theory of natural selection, man could be descended from an ape, but the theory does not prove that he was. All it does is indicate the kind of adaptive problem which must be understood before the data of comparative anatomy and the fossil record can be interpreted. Certainly, one of the reasons why the theory of orthogenesis, irreversibility, and the importance of nonadaptive characters was popular is that it allowed conclusions to be drawn by a few rules based on little evidence. The theory of selection offers no simple answers but merely points the direction in which answers must be sought. The successive adaptive radiations of the primates must be understood in terms of the evolution of more efficient behavior. The elucidation of the adaptive mechanisms will require all the help which paleontology, anatomy, archeology, and experiment can give. Far more work will be done to reach less definitive conclusions, but an understanding of the pattern and process of primate evolution will be gained. The belief that selection is the major cause of evolution alters the way evolution should be studied. In so far as anthropological conclusions have been based on the concepts of orthogenesis, irreversibility, and the use of nonadaptive traits, the conclusions need re-examination. Parallelism needs to be interpreted as the result of similar selection on related animals rather than be used as a way of discounting resemblances.

Aside from the concept of selection, there are two other aspects of evolutionary theory which are of the utmost importance for anthropology. These are, first, that descriptions should be based on populations and, second, that genes, or traits, may vary independently. Taken together, these two facts mean that the anthropological concept of type is untenable, and refusal to accept this fact is the main reason why some anthropologists have been reluctant to adopt genetic concepts. Both these points have been elaborated by numerous authors and are discussed in this symposium by Boyd and Carter. The implications for anthropology of the concept of population and independence of genes are best understood by the history of the concept of race (Count, 1950). In the earlier racial classifications a race was a group of people living in one part of the world who were obviously different from other people in physical characters. Thus the peoples of Europe, Africa south of the Sahara, eastern Asia, Australia, and the Americas were early recognized as races. How the peoples of India should be treated was always a problem, for a variety of reasons which lie beyond the scope of this essay. In the main, this classification is the same as that which Boyd (1950) gives on the basis of gene frequencies. Even the difficulty with regard to India is present in Boyd's classification. As knowledge increased, the larger areas were subdivided, and groups such as the Bushmen or Polynesians were recognized. The division of the world into areas occupied by more or less physically distinct groups was completed before 1900. The genetic study of race seems to be substantiating a large part of this general classification of mankind, although parts will surely be changed.

After 1900, to an increasing extent, a fundamentally different kind of "race" came to be used. In this race the group described was not a breeding population but a segment of such a population sorted out by various criteria. This second kind is called "type." Originally the Australoid race meant the populations of aboriginal Australia. By extension, the Australoid type was any skull, whether found in South Africa or America, which had certain morphological features common in the population of Australia. Similarly, the Mongoloid, or Negroid, race applies to groups of populations which have already been found to have genetic individuality. But there is no suggestion that the Mongoloid or Negroid types can be substantiated genetically.

The difficulty with the typological

approach has been recognized by many (especially Huxley and Haddon, 1936; Benedict, 1940; Dahlberg, 1942), who pointed out that the more unrelated characters are used for sorting, the more races (types) there will be. Weidenreich (1946) objected to adding the blood groups to the traditional anthropological characters, on the ground that this would make the theoretical total of races 92,780! With the typological approach, the more that is known, the more types there will be; but, no matter how much is known, the number of populations remains unchanged. However much is ultimately known about the genetics and anatomy of the Australian aborigines, there are still the same tribes living on the same continent. Populations are reproductive groups which are defined by the ethnologist or archeologist, or deduced from the way skeletons are found. The intensity of anatomical and genetical investigation does not increase the number of populations.

A "race" is a group of genetically similar populations, and races intergrade because there are always intermediate populations. A "type" is a group of individuals who are identical in those characters (genetic or phenotypic) by which the type was sorted (but *not* in other features!). The race concept and the type concept are fundamentally different, and modern zoölogical theory is compatible only with the race concept.

If anthropologists should adopt current zoölogical practice, several of the classifications of human races would be discarded, and the strategy of some schools of thought would be entirely abandoned. However, the change may be less than it appears at first sight. The reason for this is that most physical anthropologists simply were not interested in theory. In the majority of classifications, exemplified by that of Hooton (1946), some of the races refer to populations and others to types. Even the type descriptions usually contain data on the whole series, prior to the type analysis. At present *there is no anthropological theory of race,* but two old, incompatible concepts carried along side by side. One of the primary tasks in developing a new physical anthropology is systematically to apply the modern zoölogical concept of race, to discard the types, and to put the traditional information into the form in which it will be most useful for the understanding of race formation.

In summarizing the contrast between the old and the new physical anthropology with regard to theory, the main point to emphasize is that the application of a consistent, experimentally verified, evolutionary theory is the first task of the physical anthropologist. Since investigators were not interested in theory and since there is great diversity in actual practice, no useful purpose would be served by trying to discuss the implications of the new evolutionary theory in more detail. In the past, all the useful ideas were present in traditional physical anthropology, but so were the useless ones.

Boyd (1950) has stressed the break with the past, and Stewart (1951) the continuity with the past. Actually, physical anthropology is in a period of rapid transition in which both continuity and great change are important. At such a time disagreements are to be tolerated and major changes of personal opinion expected. For example, in 1940 Boyd criticized anthropologists for using adaptive characters when he maintained that they should use only nonadaptive ones. In 1950 he was equally vehement in his criticism of anthropologists for not seeking to use adaptive traits. At neither time were anthropologists as a profession doing either consistently, and at both times the real issue was to try to demonstrate which traits were adaptive, an issue which can be settled only by research.

Agreement is needed on the following points: (1) physical anthropology needs a consistent, proved, theoretical framework; (2) the necessary evolutionary and genetic theories are available and should be applied to the problems of human evolution; (3) untenable concepts should be abandoned; (4) a time of transition should be *welcomed* in which great differences in personal opinion are to be expected. These differences should be settled by research and not allowed to become personal or national issues.

TECHNIQUE

A successful scientific strategy depends on theories and techniques adequate to solve problems. As theories change, techniques must alter also, as they exist only to solve problems and not as ends in themselves. Traditional physical anthropology was committed to the view that description alone would solve its problems, and, in practice, description of a very limited kind The same measurements were applied to the solution of problems of the classification of the primates, relations of fossil men, description of race, human growth, and constitution. The technical training of a physical anthropologist was primarily indoctrination in the measurements of a particular school. In spite of the vast progress in biology, the practices of the physical anthropologist remained essentially the same for over one hundred years, although modified in detail and refined. As pointed out earlier, these techniques were an efficient part of the strategy of a descriptive science. They helped to outline the classification of the primates, fossil men, and races. The problems of interpreting human evolution and variation were clarified, but the traditional techniques failed to solve the problems of process. There are more different theories of man's origin and differentia-

tion now than there were fifty years ago, and in this sense the strategy of physical anthropology failed. This was due partly to the theoretical dilemmas outlined before and partly to inadequacy of the techniques.

The reasons why the traditional anthropometric measurements are inadequate to do more than they already have done, that is, outline a rough classification and indicate problems, can be made clear by an example. A variety of measurements and observations are traditionally taken on the nose (length, breadth, shape of profile, form of lower margin). Then these data are compared, on the basic assumption that *nose* is an independent entity which has been described and whose attributes may be compared. But the concept of adaptation suggests that the middle part of the face should be viewed in a very different way. Benninghoff (1925) and recently Seipel (1948) have shown by the use of the split-line technique that the face is highly organized in response to the stresses of mastication. The margins of the piriform aperture are thick in stressed, and thin in unstressed, forms. Further, the breadth of the aperture corresponds approximately to the intercanine distance, or breadth, of the incisor teeth. In man the incisors develop in the subnasal area, and, as Baker (1941) has shown, developing teeth exert a positive force increasing the size of the surrounding bone. Gans and Sarnat (1951) have shown that the growth in the region of the maxillary-premaxillary suture is accelerated at the time of eruption of the permanent canine tooth. This supplements the observations of Seipel (1948) on the way the erupting canine causes the reorganization of a large area of the face in the chimpanzee. Far from being an independent structure which can be described by itself, the nose is an integrated part of the face, and variations in its form can be interpreted only as a part of the functioning face. The form of the nose is the result of a variety of factors. Just how many and how they are interrelated can be discovered only by research, but it seems clear that the most important ones, as far as gross form is concerned, are the teeth and forces of mastication. But these are not included in the traditional descriptions of the nose, nor will looking at skulls or measuring them give this kind of information.

Since the problem of interpreting the form of the nose is part of the problem of understanding the functioning pattern of the face, the methods needed to interpret this form must describe the pattern. The traditional measurements will not do this, and they must be supplemented by techniques which are appropriate to this particular problem. Such methods are the split-line technique of Benninghoff, alizarin vital stain, experimental removal of teeth, marking sutures, etc. Some of these techniques can be applied directly to man. Others require experimental animals, but at least this much is necessary to understand what is done when a simple measurement is taken across the nasal aperture. There is no way of telling in advance what methods, in addition to measurement, will be needed, as these depend on the particular problem to be solved. What is needed in research and in education is an elastic approach, showing the problems which have arisen from the traditional classifications and techniques and encouraging every attempt to develop new and more efficient methods.

INTERPRETATION

The traditional method of interpretation in physical anthropology primarily was speculation. Races, for example, have been attributed to endless mixtures, hormones, minerals, climate, adaptation, isolation, and chance, but little effort has been devoted to proving any of the theories. Similarly, measurements have been claimed to be adaptive or nonadaptive, but detailed proof substantiating either point of view is lacking. Actually, all dimensions of the human body serve functions, and the practical issue is to show what, in an anatomical sense, is being measured and what genetic or environmental factors may modify it. The face as a whole may be highly adaptive, and its main course in human evolution determined by selection, but small differences between races may be due to genetic drift. What is needed is *proof* of adaptation or drift in particular cases.

The point may be made clearer by returning to the example of the nose. It has often been suggested that big noses appear when faces become small. But this theory has many exceptions and gives no idea of the factors actually involved. Since the split-line technique shows that the nasal bones are actually stressed by the forces of mastication, would it be reasonable to suppose that these bones would be bigger if the forces were reduced? If one nasal bone of a rat is removed on the first day of life, the other nasal bone grows to approximately one and a half times normal size. Further comparable removal of interparietal and parietal bones shows that these also grow large if free to do so. It seems to be a general rule that cranial roofing bones will grow bigger if forces normally stopping growth are removed. Schaeffer (1920) pictures skulls in which the nasal bones are entirely absent and the roof of the nose is formed by the maxillae. Piecing these lines of evidence together, it appears that the answer is again a question of pattern. Other things being equal, less pressure may result in more growth of nasal bone, but the actual proportions will depend on the interrelations of the size of the nasals, frontal processes of the maxillae, and the pressures.

Instead of relating nose form to selection or climate, it is necessary to insert an intermediate step, the analysis of the nose. Rather than saying that the pigmy's broad nose is an adaptation to the tropics, it may be that the nose is the result of a short face with large incisor teeth. The short face may be correlated with small total size (stature?), and the big teeth need explanation. Not enough is known about the form of the face to be sure that the racial differences of the nose should be correlated with climate at all.

Perhaps the relation of speculation, proof, and the importance of new methods can be best illustrated by theories concerning race mixture. It has become customary in physical anthropology to account for most of the races of the world by mixture. Of the four interrelated causes of difference recognized by zoölogists (mutation, selection, drift, and migration), only one has been regarded as the principal source of new varieties of man. The absence of evidence for three primary races has been pointed to by Boyd (1950) and numerous others, and it is probably only rarely that mixture has been a major cause of race formation. The differentiation of races, for whatever reasons, must be accounted for on other grounds, as mixture can only make gene frequencies more alike.

If the Indians are a result of Mongoloid and Australian mixture, then they should have high blood group N, and considerable B. Actually they have the least N in the world, and B only among the Eskimo. In other words, the postulated mixture does not explain the facts known about the Indians. The more complicated hypotheses work no better. If Negroids are an important element in the mixture, then Rh° should appear in the Indian, and it does not. If European elements are there, A2 and Rh negative should be present. It is clear that mixture alone will not explain the American Indian blood groups. Drift and/or selection must have operated also to change the gene frequencies, because what is found in the American Indian is something new, not found in the Old World or derivable from Old World frequencies by any mixtures. In spite of all the work that was done by traditional methods, it was possible for competent investigators to hold a number of divergent views as to the origin of the American Indian. The advent of a technique which made it possible to deal with the theories in objective, quantitative terms clearly shows that much of the speculation was unfounded and the role of mixture, as opposed to differentiation, exaggerated. The blood groups provide precise techniques for measuring mixture, provided that the mixture is relatively recent, as Carbon 14 suggests in the case of the American Indian (Johnson, 1951).

In summary, the traditional physical anthropologist thought that his task was finished when he had classified and speculated. This era is past, and there are enough classifications and speculations. Now methods must be developed which will prove which speculations were on the right track. The best of the past should be combined with new techniques to bring proof in the place of speculation.

CONCLUSION

The attempt has been made to consider under the headings of purpose, theory, technique, and interpretation the changes now taking place in physical anthropology. The strategy of the traditional descriptive investigations has been contrasted with the developing analytic strategy, with its emphasis on theory, process, and experiment. The whole change is precisely parallel to that which has taken place in systematics.

The new strategy does not solve problems, but it suggests a different way of approaching them. The change from the old to the new affects the various parts of physical anthropology very differently. In studies of growth and applied anthropology, where the knowledge of dimensions is directly useful, changing theories make little difference. In evolutionary investigations the theoretical changes are of the greatest importance, and much of the anthropological work on race and constitution is eliminated by the rejection of the concept of type. However, one of the main implications of the new point of view is that there is a far more detailed interrelationship between the different parts of anthropology than under the old strategy. A dynamic analysis of the form of the jaw will illuminate problems of evolution, fossil man, race, growth, constitution, and medical application. The unraveling of the process of human evolution and variation will enrich the understanding of other mammalian groups, whereas the detailed description of a fossil has a much more limited utility. By its very nature, the investigation of process and behavior has a generality which is lacking in purely descriptive studies. The problems of human evolution are but special cases of the problems of mammalian evolution, and their solution will enrich paleontology, genetics, and parts of clinical medicine.

But some of the problems of human evolution are unique to man. In so far as man has adapted by his way of life, the study of human evolution is inseparably bound to the study of archeology and ethnology. It is because of the importance of the cultural factor that a separate study of human evolution is necessary. Human migrations, adaptations, mating systems, population density, diseases, and ecology—all these critical biological factors become increasingly influenced by the way of life. If we would understand the process of human evolution, we need a modern dynamic biology and a deep appreciation of the history and functioning of culture. It is this necessity which gives all anthropology unity as a science.

LITERATURE CITED

BAKER, L. W. 1941. "The Influence of the Formative Dental Organs on the Growth of the Bones of the Face," *American Journal of Orthodontics*, XXVII, 489–506.

BENEDICT, R. 1940. *Race: Science and Politics.* ("Modern Age Books.") New York: Viking Press.

BENNINGHOFF, A. 1925. "Spaltlinien am Knochen, eine Methode zur Ermittlung der Architektur platter Knochen," *Anatomischer Anzeiger*, LX, 189–205.

BOYD, W. C. 1950. *Genetics and the Races of Man.* Boston: Little, Brown & Co.

CARTER, G. S. 1951. *Animal Evolution.* London: Sidgwick & Jackson.

COUNT, E. W. 1950. *This Is Race.* New York: Henry Schuman.

CUNNINGHAM, D. J. 1909. "The Evolution of the Eyebrow Region of the Forehead, with Special Reference to the Excessive Supraorbital Development of the Neanderthal Race," *Transcriptions of the Royal Society, Edinburgh*, XLVI, 283–311.

DAHLBERG, G. 1942. *Race, Reason, and Rubbish.* New York: Columbia University Press.

DENIKER, J. 1900. *The Races of Man.* New York: Charles Scribner's Sons.

DOBZHANSKY, T. 1950. "Human Diversity and Adaptation," *Cold Spring Harbor Symposia on Quantitative Biology*, Vol. XV: *Origin and Evolution of Man*, pp. 385–400. Cold Spring Harbor, Long Island, N.Y.: Biological Laboratory.

———. 1951. *Genetics and the Origin of Species.* 3d ed. New York: Columbia University Press.

FLOWER, W. H., and LYDEKKER, R. 1891. *Mammals Living and Extinct.* London: Adam & Charles Black.

GANS, B. J., 'and SARNAT, B. G. 1951. "Sutural Facial Growth of the *Macaca rhesus* Monkey," *American Journal of Orthodontics,* XXXVII, 827–41.

GREULICH, W. W., and THOMS, H. 1944. "The Growth and Development of the Pelvis of Individual Girls before, during, and after Puberty," *Yale Journal of Biology and Medicine,* XVII, 91–97.

HOOTON, E. A. 1946. *Up from the Ape.* Rev. ed. New York: Macmillan Co.

HOWELLS, W. W. 1951. "Factors of Human Physique," *American Journal of Physical Anthropology,* n.s., IX, 159–91.

HUXLEY, J. S., and HADDON, A. C. 1936. *We Europeans.* New York: Harper & Bros.

JOHNSON, F. 1951. *Radiocarbon Dating.* ("Memoirs of the Society for American Archaeology," No. 8.)

SCHAEFFER, J. P. 1920. *The Nose, Paranasal Sinuses, Nasolacrimal Passageways, and Olfactory Organ in Man.* Philadelphia: Blakiston's Son & Co.

SCHULTZ, A. H. 1936. "Characters Common to Higher Primates and Characters Specific for Man," *Quarterly Review of Biology,* XI, 259–83, 425–55.

——. 1950a. "The Physical Distinctions of Man," *Proceedings of the American Philosophical Society,* XCIV, 428–49.

——. 1950b. "The Specializations of Man and His Place among the Catarrhine Primates," *Cold Spring Harbor Symposia on Quantitative Biology,* Vol. XV: *Origin and Evolution of Man,* pp. 37–52. Cold Spring Harbor, Long Island, N.Y.: Biological Laboratory.

SEIPEL, C. M. 1948. "Trajectories of the Jaws," *Acta odontologica Scandinavica,* VIII, 81–191.

SIMPSON, G. G. 1945. *The Principles of Classification and a Classification of Mammals.* (American Museum of Natural History Bull. 85.) New York.

STEWART, T. D. 1951. "Three in One: Physical Anthropology, Genetics, Statistics," *Journal of Heredity,* XLII, 255–56, 260.

STRAUS, W. L. 1927. "The Human Ilium: Sex and Stock," *American Journal of Physical Anthropology,* XI, 1–28.

——. 1949. "The Riddle of Man's Ancestry," *Quarterly Review of Biology,* XXIV, 200–223.

WEIDENREICH, F. 1945. "The Brachycephalization of Recent Mankind," *Southwestern Journal of Anthropology,* I, 1–54.

——. 1946. *Apes, Giants, and Man.* Chicago: University of Chicago Press.

——. 1947. "The Trend of Human Evolution," *Evolution,* I, 221–36.

Primates[1]

By WILLIAM L. STRAUS, JR.

SINCE TYSON (1699) described the anatomy of a young chimpanzee and thus founded the science of Primatology, knowledge of the living primates has greatly increased. Yet, despite this, our knowledge of these animals is woefully incomplete, and numerous important areas of investigation remain unexplored.

The study of living non-human primates has two aspects for the anthropologist: first, to throw light upon the physical, psychological, and social nature of man by studying those animals of the zoological group to which he belongs, and, second, to gain, through study of these animals (especially, although not exclusively, of their skeletons), comparative data which are necessary in any attempt to reconstruct primate, and particularly human, phylogeny (especially, although again not exclusively, as an aid in evaluating and interpreting fossil remains). These two aspects, although in some degree differing in purpose and approach, are so closely related and overlap to such an extent that they actually cannot be considered separately.

ANATOMY

SOMATOMETRY

The bodily dimensions and proportions of most living primates are well known, thanks largely to the pioneer investigations of Mollison (1910) and the later, more extensive studies of Schultz (1926, 1927, 1933, et seq.). For several genera (particularly the anthropoid apes, and also a few of the monkeys) there exists adequate knowledge of the range of variability; for many others, however, measurement has been confined to only a few specimens. Detailed studies of growth changes in the anthropoids and some monkeys, notably the rhesus and proboscis monkeys, have been made by Schultz (1924, 1926, 1927, et seq.); but for many genera information is completely lacking.

In general, however, the gaps in this field of study are relatively minor ones, except for the all-important aspect of growth, particularly prenatal growth. It is largely the lack of material that hinders this latter phase of study, for such material can best be secured from animals collected in their native habitats.

GROSS ANATOMY

Most of our knowledge of non-human primates lies in this field. Yet even here the gaps are little short of appalling. All the anthropoid apes, except the siamang, have received more or less systematic study. Among all the other primates, however, only three Old World monkeys (the rhesus monkey, *Macaca*

---

1. Statements of fact, where not specifically documented, are based upon the texts and bibliographies of publications listed at the end of this paper. Ruch's *Bibliographia primato- logica* is to be especially noted; this includes exhaustive bibliographies of the anatomy, physiology, biochemistry, and psychobiology of Primates, up to the year 1941.

mulatta; the guereza, *Colobus;* and the langur, *Semnopithecus entellus*), one New World monkey (the common marmoset, *Hapale jacchus*), the tarsier (*Tarsius*), a few lemurs, and, if it be included in the order Primates, the pentailed tree shrew (*Ptilocercus*), have been so treated.

Yet for none of these has such study been other than narrowly basic, resting upon a few specimens. Quantitative studies—excepting only certain parts of the skeleton (notably the skull), particularly of the anthropoids (the monograph on the gibbons by Schultz, 1944, is an outstanding contribution)—have been very few, and in most of these there has been no real attempt at statistical analysis. The mean and the range of variation have too often represented the primatologist's concept of ultimate biometrical study. The variance itself has been neglected. The difficulties, temporal and otherwise, of dissecting and studying the soft parts of large series of animals, even on the rare occasions when such series are available, are too obvious to require comment. The literature, of course, contains a number of descriptions of individual specimens, particularly of anthropoid apes, that can be brought together for analysis; but, aside from the difficulties of gaining access to many of these publications, the accounts are of unequal value and often are difficult to assess. Perhaps of greater value are the special studies that deal with specific organs, organ systems, and regions, often embracing many genera, yet again usually only single specimens. The teeth and the skull have received the greatest attention, the muscles and the thoracic and abdominal viscera have had fairly adequate treatment, but the vascular system and the peripheral nerves have fared relatively poorly. Almost nothing is known about the joints.

Another important factor is that of age. For many reasons, fully mature specimens often are not available. Comparisons have frequently been made of animals of different ages. This has sometimes led, as Osman Hill (1950) has recently pointed out, to erroneous concepts, particularly respecting the anthropoid apes. It may be noted, parenthetically, that this sort of error is not confined to a study of living primates, as witness the sanguine comparisons that have been made of juvenile specimens of *Australopithecus* with adult material of other primates, including man.

Even the teeth, which have always assumed a very great importance in both taxonomic and phylogenetic studies, have rarely received quantitative treatment. Aside from the investigations of Remane (1921) and Ashton and Zuckerman (1950) on the anthropoids, and those of the latter authors on the green monkey (1950–51), there has been little work along this line. Indeed, it is not improbable that undue emphasis has often been placed upon slight differences in dental morphology, with consequent taxonomic or phylogenetic interpretations that would not have been drawn had more information regarding the dental variability of the involved form or forms been available.

In short, except for a small number of studies that deal with the skeleton and the dentition, gross-anatomical studies of non-human primates have largely been confined, frequently of necessity, to single or a few specimens. From this there has arisen the concept of the "type" when thinking of animals of different species or even genera—an unfortunate taxonomic concept that has too often plagued anthropology. It is to be admitted that such "type" study is often imposed by paucity of material and, as such, is but a necessary first step in the knowledge of an animal. It will continue to exist respecting many primates until such time as specimens become available in quantity. But, even with due cognizance of its widely distributed nature and hence of its relative inaccessibility, such material does exist for a number of genera or even species. It is to be expected, for at least some of these forms, that future research will gradually substitute a knowledge of population for that of "type."

A great deal of "hole-filling" is needed in straight morphology, particularly in that of the soft parts. But, again, study of practically untouched animals such as *Aotus, Callimico, Cacajao, Theropithecus,* and *Erythrocebus* will depend upon the availability of material, heretofore lacking. To this group may be added the siamang, *Symphalangus,* which has been but little studied, save for the skeleton. There is even a scarcity in museum collections of postcranial skeletal material of this interesting and important anthropoid ape.

Even many of the better-known forms —indeed, practically all of them—need much more study. The recent Raven memorial volume, *The Anatomy of the Gorilla* (Gregory, 1950), is a case in point. Granting its great merits, this volume cannot be said to be either systematic or comprehensive. Yet we have nothing even comparable to this for any of the other anthropoid apes. And the non-hominoid primates are, as noted above, not much better off.

It is possible that interest in straight, descriptive anatomy of primates has passed its peak. Students have become interested in definite problems, and many of the anatomical gaps will probably be bridged incidentally to the solution of such problems. Thus the anatomy of *Callimico* (hapalid in its limb skeleton and cebid in its skull and teeth) will probably become known when someone becomes deeply interested in the exact zoological status of the Hapalidae and makes a real effort to secure embalmed specimens of that rare genus. Erikson (1952) has demonstrated how interest in a specific problem—in this instance the locomotor patterns of the platyrrhines—can be a stimulus for the gathering of material.

HISTOLOGY

Histology has been one of the most neglected fields. Whatever little is known of non-human primates has largely been incidental to other investigations, chiefly in the medical sciences. Hence scattered data exist for only a few forms, such as the rhesus monkey, that have been used as laboratory animals. Even the anthropoid apes have not found their way under the microscope, except on relatively rare occasions. Yerkes (1951) has recently pointed out that histological knowledge of the gorilla is almost nonexistent; and the other anthropoids are scarcely better off in this respect.

Even so obvious an organ as the skin has barely been examined histologically, although its importance is not merely morphological but involves physiological and ecological considerations of the greatest interest. Many, if not most, of the few existing observations have been made on young animals, and animals of different ages have sometimes been compared, with undoubtedly misleading conclusions. For the skin is a structure that assuredly undergoes significant age changes (see Straus, 1950).

Comparative studies of the histology of bone fall into the same category. Indeed, it can hardly be said that even a modest beginning has been made in this field. Such studies would be of great value for eventual correlation with comparative studies of the physical and physiological properties of bone and of bones. It may be that the natural reluctance of museums and other repositories of skeletal material to permit mutilation of bones has been the chief deterrent to such investigations.

The list of comparative-histological hiatuses could be extended almost indefinitely. There is little or no knowledge of the endocrine glands, despite indications of their generic and even specific physiological variability. Even such a tissue as skeletal muscle offers a fruitful field for comparative-histological study.

It is to be doubted whether qualified workers will be sufficiently interested —or, in fact, whether they will find it particularly profitable—to systematically describe conditions over a range of species. Past attempts at broad comparative-histological studies have not gone very far. Probably our histological knowledge will continue to accrue as an accompaniment of other investigations—ecological, physiological, and medical—that embrace microscopic studies. The field is a rich one, however, for anyone with imagination and proper training. The skin, the endocrine glands, the digestive system, to mention only the more obvious, should be figurative gold mines. The nervous system surely needs no comment.

NEUROANATOMY

Discussion of the anatomy of the nervous system as a separate item is justified by the fact that the only feature at all peculiar to the Primates as a zoological order is the unique tendency toward high development of the central nervous system, especially the brain, within a relatively unspecialized body.

A great deal has been done with the brains of primates other than man, largely relative to the fissural patterns of the cerebral cortex (see Connolly, 1950). Indeed, a rather large body of data has been recorded. Cortical cyto-architecture has also received considerable attention, but the gaps here are very great; for such studies are not only extremely laborious but require properly preserved material, which has been available for only a few forms. Hence, despite the classic studies of Brodmann (1905 *et seq.*), the Vogts (1906 *et seq.*), Mott and his co-workers (1908 *et seq.*),

and Campbell (1916 *et seq.*), and those of more recent workers, the number of genera that have been investigated is not large. Moreover, knowledge of this important field necessarily revolves around the "type," since little is known of individual variability. Inasmuch as cortical expansion and differentiation is certainly one of the most distinctive features of primate evolution and radiation, and since it reflects so much in the way of the adaptation and the potentialities of the total organism, the desirability of filling in the major existing gaps in our knowledge can scarcely be overemphasized.

In view of the admittedly predominant role of vision in primate evolution, it is gratifying that we now possess a considerable amount of data relating to the visual apparatus (including the eye, the visual pathways, and the receptive centers; there is a good deal of information about the retina, the lateral geniculate body, and even the visual cortex of a number of genera). Yet conditions are poorly known or even unknown in some of the more important genera. The necessity of a sound morphological background for physiological and psychological studies of vision is too evident to need any special comment.

The cerebellum has fared better than most of the other parts of the brain, due largely to the researches of Bolk (1906). Both the spinal cord and, except for the thalamus, the brain stem (despite the work of Tilney) represent almost untapped sources, however, particularly with respect to internal, microscopic anatomy and projection systems. The little work that has been carried out on these structures leaves no doubt that they would yield much to comparative study.

Despite the considerable neuroanatomical information that has been gathered, it must be noted that an undue proportion of it relates to only a few forms, particularly the more common laboratory types like the macaque and the chimpanzee.

DEVELOPMENT AND GROWTH

As pointed out above, the amount of existing information pertaining to the later, fetal stages of development, although incomplete, is nevertheless large, due chiefly to the continued, systematic investigations of Schultz. Much less is known about the early, embryonic stages that are even more difficult to procure. This is to be greatly regretted, for there is every reason to believe than an understanding of early development, including implantation and membrane formation, is a valuable aid in assessing the phylogenetic relationships of extant forms. Not a little is known about the early stages of development in *Tarsius*, a number of lemurs, platyrrhine and catarrhine monkeys, and the Hylobatinae. Of these, however, the rhesus monkey alone has been intensively studied (see Corner *et al.*, 1941); in fact, in some respects it is better known than man. Very little, however (indeed, almost nothing), is known about the early embryology of the great anthropoid apes. The problem does not appear to be insurmountable, although it is probable that, for some time to come at least, embryologists will have to rely upon the occasional, chance material recovered from animals collected in the wild. Information about the later stages of membrane formation is more plentiful and diverse, and existing studies on placentation embrace a large variety and number of primate genera.

Problems of growth and development in non-human primates will undoubtedly receive much attention, if for no other reason than their obvious bearing upon man. The analysis of primate growth has recently taken on a distinctly experimental tinge. The value of carefully devised experiments in studying growth (e.g., feeding madder or alizarin to study bone growth; cutting muscles to determine their influence upon the developing skeleton) has long been recognized by anatomists, and Washburn (1943 *et seq.*) has recently demonstrated their importance for physical anthropology. Thus it has become apparent that in some instances classical measurement is insufficient by itself and that only properly planned experiments upon growing animals can determine the factors involved in the correlative growth and development of complex mosaics like the skull. Use of experimental methods has hitherto been limited, of necessity, to animals other than primates. The direct application of such methods to primates merely awaits an adequate supply of material.

PHYSIOLOGY

As regards the non-human primates, physiology is largely unexplored territory. What little has been accomplished deals chiefly with one primate, the macaque, particularly the rhesus monkey. The relatively meager existing knowledge of the physiology of the circulatory, respiratory, and digestive systems is almost entirely limited to that animal. This is likewise true of endocrine physiology, which is to be greatly deplored; for studies on the thyroid gland suggest that there can be striking differences in the role of this gland among even closely related species (Fleischmann, Shumacker, and Straus, 1943), and the same is to be suspected of other endocrine organs.

Much more is known about the physiology of reproduction and the physiology of the nervous system. Knowledge of the reproductive physiology of the rhesus monkey rivals that of man. Other macaques and the baboons are rather well understood, but the remaining Cercopithecinae and the Semnopithecinae have had little study. Information about the anthropoid apes is almost entirely restricted to the chimpanzee. The New World monkeys, *Tarsius,* and especially the lemurs, are but poorly known. (See Asdell, 1946.)

There is a large body of literature dealing with the physiology of the nervous system of non-human primates. Most of this concerns the cerebral cortex (chiefly the motor functions), whereas less is known about the brain stem and the cerebellum, little about the spinal cord and the peripheral nerves, and virtually nothing about the autonomic nervous system. Again, however, except for the cerebral cortex (where a wide variety of primates has been investigated), existing knowledge is almost entirely limited to the ubiquitous rhesus monkey. There are a few data relative to the physiology of the eye and the ear in several genera. The physiological maturation of the nervous system has received scant attention; Hines's (1942) careful and thorough study of the development of reflex patterns, posture, and progression in the rhesus monkey is outstanding.

The study of primate muscle physiology has been greatly neglected. When one recalls the striking, unexplained differences in strength between primates of approximately the same weight (as between chimpanzee and man)—differences that cannot be explained on the basis of leverages—the need for such studies is evident.

There are many physiological problems that are particularly pertinent to ecology and psychobiology. Some beginning studies, again largely on the macaque, have been made in the all-important related fields of basal metabolism and temperature regulation. This brings to mind the problem of climatic adaptation. Even excluding man, primates live in very different sorts of climates. This is true not only of different genera and species, but even of members of one and the same species. The

rhesus monkeys offer a challenging problem here. These animals constitute a single species, *Macaca mulatta,* with six recognizable geographical races, that attains a wider distribution in geography and altitude than any other species of monkey—from North India through Burma, Siam, and French Indo-China, well into China (Miller, 1933). It is found from or near sea-level up to 5,000 or 6,000 feet in the Himalayas. And these adaptations to various types of climate have been made without benefit of a culture. Another related case concerns the gorillas, which may constitute two species or only one, depending upon one's taxonomic outlook. The lowland gorilla inhabits the hot, damp, coastal forests of West Africa, whereas the mountain gorilla lives in the mixed bamboo forest of the eastern Congo, ranging in altitude from 7,500 to 12,000 feet (Hooton, 1942). Study of animals from different climatic zones would probably yield rich dividends, particularly if metabolic and other physiological studies were correlated with such anatomical features, for example, as the density of the hair, the character and density of the glands of the skin, and the blood picture. In this connection, the endocrine glands cannot be ignored. The probability of their functional variability in different species has already been mentioned (see also Fleischmann, 1947). Such variability may well have prime adaptive, evolutionary significance.

Modern physiological techniques, however, especially those of neurophysiology, are such that they can be properly used only by those who have special training. To attack many of the problems noted above, the cooperation of primatologists and physiologists is necessary.

Problems of posture and locomotion may be considered here, inasmuch as they are essentially physiological in nature. These problems may be expected to receive a great deal of attention in the future. They can be attacked in two ways: by observation of living animals supplemented by gross-anatomical and metrical studies, and by experimentation in the laboratory. The studies of Pratt (1943) and others on experimentally produced bipedal rats indicate what might be done with primates. The different quadrupedal, pronograde modes of primate locomotion are ripe for analysis. It is clear that to speak of quadrupedal posture and locomotion as if this were a unity, even among primates, is an extreme oversimplification. The same is true of the various types of bimanual locomotion or brachiation. There is ample evidence that the brachiation of *Colobus*, that of the Hylobatinae, that of the great apes, and that of *Ateles* represent different types of adaptations that express themselves in various degrees and kinds of anatomical specializations. Yet these have never been clearly described or properly analyzed. This problem has a great bearing upon that of human evolution. It is probable that at least some of the disagreement about the occurrence or nonoccurrence of a brachiating stage in human phylogeny is due to a lack of clarity about what such a stage would involve, and hence is to a large degree semantic in nature.

Any future studies of posture and locomotion—whether bipedal, bimanual, or quadrupedal—must necessarily be physiological as well as anatomical. Too often have posture and locomotion been thought of in terms of skeleton and muscles alone. Yet these are essentially effector organs, for it has been clearly demonstrated that the central nervous system is the prime controlling agent. Any comparative study of posture and locomotion must consider differences in the latter, as well as differences in the vascular mechanisms that also are largely under neural control.

Other experimental techniques are ready to be utilized for dynamic analyses of functional problems. The recent development of the "stresscoat" deformation method and of the use of strain gauges, for example, opens up new avenues of attack upon various problems related to the primate skeleton.

BIOCHEMISTRY

Biochemical studies of non-human primates have been largely serological in character. The corpus of knowledge regarding both precipitins and blood groups is by no means inconsiderable and includes numerous genera. But even more extensive studies are needed in this important field. It is to be expected that the recent wide recognition of the great importance of blood-group studies in the anthropology of human racial groups and of their aid in assessing group relationships will provide a stimulus for such studies among non-human primates as well. Cooperation not only between the primatologist and the biochemist but also between interested investigators and zoological parks could be very productive.

The rhesus monkey has been employed rather extensively in various vitamin studies, but virtually nothing is known about the vitamin requirements of other non-human primates. A comparative viewpoint is badly needed here and might produce much of interest, for it may well be that there is variability in the vitamin requirements of primates.

A bare start, although embracing a fair number of genera, chiefly catarrhine, has been made in the field of carbohydrate, fat, and protein metabolism. Studies of the various nitrogenous excretory products of primate urine (see Rheinberger, 1936) have yielded such suggestive results that the fertility of this and related fields for systematic exploration is clearly indicated. The probable ecological, taxonomic, and phylogenetic significance is apparent.

Biochemical studies require special techniques, but some of these are relatively simple and can be mastered without too much difficulty by those who possess fundamental chemical training.

PSYCHOBIOLOGY

The literature in the field of psychobiology is truly extensive. A great deal has been done on the experimental side, and a number of non-human primate genera have received at least some study. But, again, as in so many other areas of investigation, the macaque and the chimpanzee—chiefly because they have been easiest to procure —have received the major share of attention. Thanks largely to the extensive, intensive, and continuing studies of the Yale–Harvard–Orange Park group of investigators, our knowledge of the chimpanzee is very considerable.

Less progress has been made in observational psychobiology, and especially in the very difficult and highly important field of observation of primates in their native habitats. Much, however, has been written, but chiefly by unqualified observers. The careful studies of Carpenter on howling monkeys in Central America (1934) and on gibbons in Siam (1940), and those of Nissen (1931–32) on chimpanzees in French Guinea, are outstanding exceptions. To these must be added the classic pioneer investigations of Zuckerman (1932) on baboons, both in their natural environment and in a colony of animals transplanted from their native habitat. More investigations of animals in their native environments are badly needed. Such studies of the gorilla and the orang-utan are particularly desirable; but political considerations will probably be a barrier to any serious study of the latter for some time to come.

GENETICS

Anthropologists have found genetics to be a valuable tool in the study and analysis of human populations, not only in regard to blood groups but also in regard to gross-morphological and even physiological characters. It is to be expected, therefore, that the methods of population genetics, giving due attention to mutation, selection, migration, and genetic drift, will eventually be applied to other primates and that they will produce important information. The application of such methods, however, has distinct limitations at the present time. Investigations of series of living animals from one area, or even of comparable series of embalmed cadavers, is well-nigh out of the question. But something might be done with skeletal material. The museums of America and Europe possess series of skeletons of single species of primates collected at one locality. Such series, it is true, are not too numerous, and they usually consist largely, if not entirely, of skulls, but some of them are of sufficient size to warrant this sort of studies. One major handicap is that but little or nothing is known about the sizes of the populations (not to mention the sizes of the breeding populations) from which such series have been taken. Yet, despite this, some problems could be attacked successfully. The recent illuminating analysis of samples of two geographically isolated populations of the green monkey (*Cercopithecus aethiops sabaeus*), representing the parent-stock from West Africa and the descendants of animals transplanted to the West Indies, by Ashton and Zuckerman (1950–51), is the sole study of this kind for primates.

Experimental hybridization has been carried out in a number of zoological gardens, but the results of such hybridizations of primates have rarely or never been adequately analyzed from the genetic viewpoint (see Zuckerman,

1933). It is important, for example, not only to know whether a certain interspecific or intergeneric cross is possible, yielding viable hybrids, but especially to know whether or not the F_1 hybrids themselves are fertile. If the latter be true, it would follow that the barriers between the crossable forms must have been entirely geographical down to the present date, and it would indicate, moreover, that genetic barriers such as exist in many groups of animals are slow to form in the primates. Especially illuminating would be the genetic analysis of the backcrosses between the F_1 hybrids and the parent-species. In the hybrid only those dominant traits present in either species, plus such characters as give blending or intermediate effects, would show up. But in the backcrosses it would be possible to determine whether particular traits are due to single gene differences or to multiple factors; whether traits are linked or segregate freely; whether the gene interactions are in all cases harmonious or in some combinations produce disharmonies of structure or physiology; etc. A study of the blood antigens like that carried out by Irwin and his colleagues in crosses between different species of doves and pigeons (1947) could scarcely fail to clarify greatly the problem of the closeness of relationship between species, races, and populations of primates. Some of these problems might be successfully attacked by cooperation between primatologists, geneticists, and zoological gardens.

PALEONTOLOGY

Recent years have witnessed numerous and important discoveries of the fossil remains of various primates. Chief interest has naturally centered upon such forms as the Australopithecinae, with their promise of elucidating the later stages of hominid evolution. Other less dramatic but also highly significant material, however, has been brought to light.

The Primates probably arose from some primitive insectivore-like stock, but whether this was proto-erinaceoid or proto-tupaioid remains a question. Prosimians, both lemuroid and tarsioid, were already differentiated in the Paleocene, so that it may be concluded that the divergence of lemuroids and tarsioids occurred before that date. Barth (1950), however, thinks that a strict separation of lemuroids and tarsioids was not present in the Eocene and hence groups all these early prosimian forms together; he cites the great number of unplaceable genera in support of his contention.

The lemuriform lemurs were present in numbers from the Paleocene through the Eocene. They are represented by the Plesiadapidae (Paleocene-Eocene) and the more generalized Adapidae (Eocene). After the Eocene there is a complete break in their fossil record until they reappear in profusion in the Pleistocene.

The precise relationship of the Lorisiformes to other prosimians is unknown; for their paleontological record has been a blank except for a single genus from the Pliocene of India. The recently unearthed remains of galagine lemurs (as yet undescribed) from Lower Miocene deposits in East Africa (Clark and Leakey, 1951) may throw some light on the history of this group.

The history of the Tupaioidea and their relationships to the undoubted primates remains obscure. Whether they are the most primitive of lemuriform lemurs, as claimed by Le Gros Clark (1934) and Simpson (1945), or whether they are to be regarded as primates at all, are questions that await the discovery of additional paleontological material. The gap between *Anagale* of the Lower Oligocene of Mongolia, described by Simpson over twenty years ago, and the living tupaioids is a great one. *Anagale* appears in some ways to be more lemur-like than are the extant tupaioids, and this is the chief reason (although not the only one) for regarding the latter as true lemuriforms; but this important matter is far from being settled.

Numerous Tarsioidea have been found in the Paleocene and Eocene of North America and in the Eocene of Europe. But they disappear from the fossil record in the Lower Oligocene and are represented in Recent times by only a single genus, *Tarsius,* that ranges from the East Indies to the Philippines. No new fossil material has appeared in recent years to elucidate their phylogenetic relationships to the lemuriform and lorisiform lemurs, on the one hand, and to the simian primates (Anthropoidea or Pithecoidea), on the other hand. Their probable origin from a more generalized, more lemur-like stock which also gave rise to the Lemuriformes and the Lorisiformes is indicated, as has been ably discussed by Simpson. Some workers, such as Le Gros Clark, however, believe that the lemurs and the tarsiers originated independently from the basal primate stock and that the latter did not pass through a lemuroid stage in their evolution.

Many students derive the simian primates from essentially generalized tarsioids; but the evidence for this is derived chiefly from the comparative study of living forms rather than from the fossil record. The presence of certain tarsioid-like characters in the mandible of *Parapithecus,* a catarrhine primate from the Lower Oligocene of Egypt, has been advanced in support of this view. *Pondaungia* and *Amphipithecus,* from the Upper Eocene of Burma, each represented by a single mandibular fragment containing teeth, have been regarded by some investigators as representing a transitional stage from a tarsioid to a simian phase (Pilgrim, 1927; Clark,

1950). Indeed, these specimens have even been advanced as evidence of the origin of the anthropoid ape line of evolution directly from tarsioids without the intervention of a monkey-like phase; and Le Gros Clark thinks it probable that both the cercopithecoid and hominoid sequences may have separated at a stage of evolution represented by *Amphipithecus.* Beyond this, the supposed tarsioid ancestry of the simian primates remains unsupported by concrete evidence. It has been suggested that the simian characters of fossil and living Tarsioidea may well have arisen as parallel developments independently of their counterparts in the Anthropoidea. Indeed, the possible derivation of the latter from a more generalized, more lemur-like prosimian stock, such as the Adapidae, rather than from true tarsioids, certainly cannot be excluded (see Simpson, 1945). In this connection, it may be recalled that *Notharctus,* an adapid of the North American Eocene, has been regarded by some workers as ancestral to the New World monkeys.

The phylogenetic history of the New World monkeys or platyrrhines is quite unknown. Save for a single Miocene genus, *Homunculus,* the fossil record of this group does not extend back beyond the Pleistocene. Not only are these Pleistocene forms similar to extant platyrrhines of the same areas, but even *Homunculus* resembles the living subfamily Aotinae. It is still an open question whether the platyrrhine and catarrhine simians were derived from a single or from separate ancestral prosimian stocks. Nor is there any fossil evidence bearing on the moot question of the exact zoological status of the Hapalidae (marmosets and tamarins)— whether they are truly the most primitive of all living platyrrhines or whether much of their apparent primitiveness represents a specialized retrogression from more generalized cebid ancestors.

The origins of the catarrhine or Old World Anthropoidea are not much clearer. As noted above, Le Gros Clark thinks that the catarrhines may have arisen from tarsioids via a transitional stage resembling *Amphipithecus*. The latter, however, is so fragmentary that it is open to diverse interpretations. It has even been classified (together with the equally obscure *Pondaungia*) as a possible pongid of uncertain affinities (Simpson, 1945). *Parapithecus*, a Lower Oligocene genus represented by a single lower jaw with teeth, has been variously regarded as a primitive Old World monkey, as a primitive anthropoid ape, and as a proto-catarrhine from which all existing catarrhine primates (monkey, apes, man) could have been derived (see Gregory, 1922). Obviously, more material belonging to this highly important genus is badly needed.

The matter of a possible tarsioid origin for the catarrhines has already been discussed. Granting its probability, it remains a question whether any or all of the Anthropoidea of the Old World arose as such directly from prosimian ancestors or whether they first passed through a "platyrrhine" stage more or less resembling the more generalized of the living New World monkeys. Each of these suppositions has its advocates. The many remarkable morphological resemblances between the more advanced platyrrhines and some of the catarrhines bear upon this question. It remains to be determined whether these are merely evolutionary parallelisms or are evidences of an even closer relationship. At the moment, the former interpretation appears to be the more reasonable one.

The history of the Old World monkeys is fragmentary. A number of remains of undoubted cercopithecoids (both cercopithecine and semnopithecine) have been found in Pliocene deposits of the Old World, including Europe; and they have recently been reported, with the characteristic cercopithecoid dental specializations, as occurring in the Lower Miocene of East Africa. If *Moeripithecus* and *Apidium*, both from the Lower Oligocene of Egypt, are accepted as true cercopithecoids, the Old World monkeys had already begun their separate course of evolution at this early date, and the contemporary *Parapithecus* could be regarded as a primitive anthropoid ape. But, as Simpson (1945) has pointed out, the allocation of these two fragments to the Cercopithecidae is dubious. The better-known *Oreopithecus* of the Lower Pliocene, however, is generally regarded as a cercopithecoid, although of uncertain position, for its teeth exhibit peculiarities not found in undoubted Cercopithecidae. All three of these forms (*Moeripithecus*, *Apidium*, *Oreopithecus*) are known only from fragments of jaws and teeth, and none of them exhibits the distinct bilophodontism of the molars that is characteristic of the Cercopithecidae. This specialized tendency toward extreme bilophodontism, it must be noted, seems to be the chief taxonomic criterion of a cercopithecoid. It is a criterion that stems from paleontological necessity, since usually only jaws and teeth are preserved as fossils. The question arises as to whether a catarrhine primate can be regarded as a cercopithecoid in the absence of bilophodont molars, even if the rest of its body is truly cercopithecoid. The same sort of problem arises in dealing with the fossils of other catarrhine primates. However, as noted above, the paleontological record has granted the dentition priority in assessing relationships. Hence it is well to recognize that the vertical taxonomy of mammals, and thus of primates, is primarily based upon the teeth and, it may be added, is likely to remain so, at least for a long time. Nevertheless, it should also be recognized that such a taxonomy is inevitably prone to a certain despotism and artificiality, for it tends to ignore the fact that the dentition does not always completely characterize the total animal (a notable example of this among living primates is the lemuriform lemur, *Daubentonia*) and that teeth, moreover, are subject to the same biological variability as other parts of the body.

Recent years have brought highly significant additions to our knowledge of the history of the Hominoidea (anthropoid apes, man). The important group of Lower Miocene apes collected in East Africa by Leakey and the remarkable and rich discoveries of the Australopithecinae in South Africa by Dart and Broom, particularly by the latter, are bringing about a rewriting of the phylogenetic history of the hominoids.

Leaving aside not only ambiguous *Amphipithecus* and *Pondaungia* but also *Parapithecus,* a line of evolution for the Hylobatinae (gibbons, siamang) may now be reasonably postulated on the basis of existing evidence. This would run from *Propliopithecus* of the Lower Oligocene of Egypt to *Limnopithecus* of the Lower Miocene of East Africa, and, from some of the less specialized representatives of the latter genus, to the modern gibbon and siamang. Le Gros Clark also regards *Pliopithecus* of the European Miocene and Lower Pliocene as an offshoot of the *Limnopithecus* stock; but whether *Pliopithecus* is to be viewed as directly ancestral to the modern Hylobatinae or as an independent collateral branch of hylobatine evolution is by no means clear.

This current appraisal of hylobatine phylogeny is founded primarily on characters of the jaws and teeth. Fortunately, recent discoveries of limb-bone material, by no means inconsiderable in nature, of both *Limnopithecus* and *Pliopithecus*, are of great value in helping to elucidate one of the more vexed problems of hominoid evolution. The known limb bones of *Limnopithecus,* although they possess certain hylobatine features, also exhibit definite monkey-like characters and are distinctly cercopithecoid in their proportions (Clark and Thomas, 1951). Much the same is true of *Pliopithecus* (Zapfe, 1952). The hindlimb of *Pliopithecus* is essentially gibbon-like, but some parts of the forelimb skeleton exhibit characters that must be regarded as primitive and which find their counterparts in lemurs. Furthermore, the forelimb is not lengthened as in modern Hylobatinae, the intermembral index being similar to those found among living baboons. Available evidence thus suggests that the precursors of the extant Hylobatinae, at least as late as the Miocene, and perhaps the Pliocene, may well have been quadrupedal animals, and that the striking brachiating specializations so characteristic of the modern gibbons and siamang appeared late in their evolutionary history.

The other known representatives of the East African Lower Miocene Hominoidea belong to two genera, *Proconsul* and *Sivapithecus,* both assigned to that far-flung and heterogeneous group, the Dryopithecinae, hitherto found only in Europe (Middle Miocene through Pliocene) and India (Pliocene) and hitherto known almost entirely from teeth and jaws. *Proconsul,* which is of especial interest, has been described in detail by Le Gros Clark and Leakey (1951), who would derive it from some advanced, *Limnopithecus*-like hylobatine type.

The genus *Proconsul* is represented not only by jaws and teeth, described as three species that exhibit a most remarkable range in size, but also by an invaluable, uniquely preserved skull of the smallest species, *P. africanus,* and by a number of limb bones assigned to the intermediate-sized species, *P. nyanzae*. These present an exceptionally significant combination of characters. In brief, the teeth of *Proconsul* are distinctly of an anthropoid ape type and even show certain specializations in the direction of the living African great apes. The skull, however, definitely approximates those of the smaller cercopithecoid monkeys in its general morphology; and it has a number of primitive features not found in existing great apes. Its endocranial cast, moreover, indicates a brain that was cercopithecoid, rather than anthropoid, in pattern. The limb bones parallel the skull in their many cercopithecoid, nonanthropoid characters. In fact, they strongly suggest that these early Miocene dryopithecines were cursorial quadrupeds, and they provide no indications of a brachiating mode of locomotion as found in the living anthropoids. On the evidence of the teeth —and despite the rest of the skeleton— these creatures have been classified as anthropoid apes, although of a very primitive type. This would seem to be an almost inevitable procedure in view of the dental nature of current primate taxonomy, as already noted above. Save for those who are imbued with awe for the canons of taxonomy, however, it is not of paramount importance whether we regard *Proconsul* as a generalized anthropoid ape or as a somewhat advanced monkey. Of much greater importance is the fact that from animals possessing extremities of this type (but not necessarily from animals of the *Proconsul* group itself, with their distinct dental specializations), as Le Gros Clark and Leakey have pointed out, there could have developed, in one direction, the modern anthropoid apes with their highly specialized limbs adapted to brachiation and, in another direction, the immediate forerunners of the Hominidae. The implication here is that the line leading directly to man never passed through a brachiating phase. This is in accord with other recent assessments of evidence bearing upon this problem (see Straus, 1949).

It should also be noted that the recently unearthed fossil evidence suggests that the gibbons developed their characteristic brachiating specializations independently of the great apes. This finds support from studies of living hylobatines and pongines. For comparisons of the skeleton and muscles of the upper extremities of gibbons and great apes, and of their modes of locomotion, make it evident that the adaptations to a bimanual, brachiating mode of locomotion are different in these two groups of hominoids (Straus, 1940, 1941, 1942). However, as pointed out earlier, the several types of primate brachiation constitute a subject in need of further investigation.

The Australopithecinae will not be discussed at any length here. It is sufficient to note that it is generally recognized that, whatever their precise zoological affinities, they are of the greatest importance for the light that they throw, directly or indirectly, upon certain critical phases in the evolution of the Hominidae. The several different views respecting their exact phylogenetic status and relationships cannot be considered here. But it may be pointed out that these divergent views are possible because certain important problems remain unsettled (see, e.g., Zuckerman, 1950). Their geological age is highly uncertain. The exact character of their habitat has not been established. To some students their posture remains a reasonable point of doubt. The phylogenetic significance of some of their morphological characters is open to different interpretations. The view has been expressed that much of the material needs to be more thoroughly studied and evaluated, particularly by comparison with statistically significant series of other primates. The meaning of the curious giant forms is quite obscure. The enthusiastic attempts to reconstruct the social life of the Australopithecinae have not been calculated to inspire confidence. In short, many important questions remain to be answered. The great quantity of Australopithecine material thus far uncovered, and the prospect of still more to come, betokens years of careful study. The discoverers of this material have accomplished an amazing and highly praiseworthy job under great difficulties. But the lack of adequate comparative material is often all too evident. It would be a great aid in the solution of at least some of the problems relating to the Australopithecinae if casts could be made available to workers in other countries after the original descriptions and analyses of the specimens have been published.

LIST OF REFERENCES

ASDELL, S. A. 1946. *Patterns of Mammalian Reproduction.* Ithaca, N.Y.: Comstock Publishing Co.

ASHTON, E. H., and ZUCKERMAN, S. 1950. "Some Quantitative Dental Characteristics of the Chimpanzee, Gorilla and Orang-outang," *Philosophical Transactions of the Royal Society of London,* ser. B, CCXXXIV, 471–84.

———. 1950–51. "The Influence of Geographic Isolation on the Skull of the Green Monkey (*Cercopithecus aethiops sabaeus*), I–IV," *ibid.,* CXXXVII, 212–38; CXXXVIII, 204–13, 213–18, 354–74.

BARTH, F. 1950. "On the Relationships of Early Primates," *American Journal of Physical Anthropology,* n.s., VIII, 139–49.

BOLK, L. 1906. *Das Cerebellum der Säugetiere.* Jena: Gustav Fischer.

BRODMANN, K. 1905. "Beiträge zur histologischen Lokalisation der Grosshirnrinde. Dritte Mitteilung. Die Rindenfelder der niederen Affen," *Zeitschrift für Psychologie und Neurologie,* IV, 177–226.

CAMPBELL, A. W. 1906. *Histological Studies on the Localisation of Cerebral Function.* Cambridge: At the University Press.

CARPENTER, C. R. 1934. *A Field Study of the Behavior and Social Relations of Howling Monkeys (Alouatta palliata).* ("Comparative Psychology Monographs," No. 48.)

———. 1940. *A Field Study in Siam of the Behavior and Social Relations of the Gibbon (Hylobates lar).* ("Comparative Psychology Monographs," No. 84.)

CLARK, W. E. LE GROS. 1934. *Early Forerunners of Man.* London: Ballière, Tindall & Cox.

———. 1950. "New Palaeontological Evidence Bearing on the Evolution of the Hominoidea," *Quarterly Journal of the Geological Society of London,* CV, 225–64.

CLARK, W. E. LE GROS, and LEAKEY, L. S. B. 1951. *The Miocene Hominoidea of East Africa.* ("Fossil Mammals of Africa," No. 1.) London: British Museum of Natural History.

CLARK, W. E. LE GROS, and THOMAS, D. P. 1951. *Associated Jaws and Limb Bones of Limnopithecus macinnesi.* ("Fossil Mammals of Africa," No. 3.) London: British Museum of Natural History.

CONNOLLY, C. J. 1950. *External Morphology of the Primate Brain.* Springfield, Ill.: Charles C. Thomas.

CORNER, G. W., et al. 1941. *Embryology of the Rhesus Monkey (Macaca mulatta).* ("Carnegie Institution of Washington Publications," No. 538.) Washington, D.C.

ERIKSON, G. E. 1952. "Locomotor Types and Body Proportions in the New World Primates," *Anatomical Records,* CXII, 24. (65th Annual Session of the American Association of Anatomists.) (Abstract.)

FLEISCHMANN, W. 1947. "Comparative Physiology of the Thyroid Hormone," *Quarterly Review of Biology,* XXII, 119–40.

FLEISCHMANN, W.; SHUMACKER, H. B., JR.; and STRAUS, W. L., JR. 1943. "Influence of Age on the Effect of Thyroidectomy in the Rhesus Monkey," *Endocrinology,* XXXII, 238–46.

GREGORY, W. K. 1922. *The Origin and Evolution of the Human Dentition.* Baltimore: Williams & Wilkins Co.

—— (ed.). 1950. *The Anatomy of the Gorilla* (The Henry Cushier Raven Memorial Volume). New York: Columbia University Press.

HILL, W. C. OSMAN. 1950. "Man's Relation to the Apes," *Man,* No. 257.

HINES, MARION. 1942. "The Development and Regression of Reflexes, Postures, and Progression in the Young Macaque." In *Contributions to Embryology,* No. 30, pp. 153–209. ("Carnegie Institution of Washington Publications," No. 196.)

HOOTON, E. 1942. *Man's Poor Relations.* Garden City, N.Y.: Doubleday, Doran & Co.

IRWIN, M. R. 1947. "Immunogenetics," *Advances in Genetics,* I, 133–59. New York: Academic Press.

MILLER, G. S., JR. 1933. "The Groups and Names of Macaques." In HARTMAN, C. G., and STRAUS, W. L., JR. (eds.), *The Anatomy of the Rhesus Monkey,* chap. i, pp. 1–9. Baltimore: Williams & Wilkins Co.

MOLLISON, T. 1910. "Die Körperproportionen der Primaten," *Morphologisches Jahrbuch,* XLII, 79–304.

MOTT, F. W., and KELLEY, AGNES M. 1908. "Complete Survey of the Cell Lamination of the Cerebral Cortex of the Lemur," *Proceedings of the Royal Society of London,* ser. B, LXXX, 488–506.

NISSEN, H. W. 1931–32. *A Field Study of the Chimpanzee.* ("Comparative Psychology Monographs," No. 36.)

PILGRIM, G. E. 1927. "A Sivapithecus Palate and Other Primate Fossils from India," *Palaeontologica Indica,* XIV, 1 ff.

PRATT, L. W. 1943. "Behavior of Bipedal Rats," *Bulletin of the Johns Hopkins Hospital,* LXXII, 265–73.

REMANE, A. 1921. "Beiträge zur Morphologie des Anthropoidengebisses," *Archiv für Naturgeschichte,* LXXXVII A, 1–179.

RHEINBERGER, MARGARET B. 1936. "The Nitrogen Partition in the Urine of Various Primates," *Journal of Biological Chemistry,* CXV, 343–60.

RUCH, T. C. 1941. *Bibliographia primato-logica.* Springfield, Ill., and Baltimore: Charles C. Thomas.

SCHULTZ, A. H. 1924. "Growth Studies on Primates Bearing upon Man's Evolution," *American Journal of Physical Anthropology,* VII, 149–64.

——. 1926. "Fetal Growth of Man and Other Primates," *Quarterly Review of Biology,* I, 465–521.

——. 1927. "Studies on the Growth of Gorilla and of Other Higher Primates," *Memoirs of the Carnegie Museum, Pittsburgh,* XI, 1–87.

——. 1933. "Die Körperproportionen der erwachsenen catarrhinen Primaten, mit spezieller Berücksichtigung der Menschenaffen," *Anthropologischer Anzeiger,* X, 154–85.

——. 1933. "Observations on the Growth, Classification and Evolutionary Specialization of Gibbons and Siamangs," *Human Biology,* V, 212–55, 385–428.

——. 1944. "Age Changes and Variability in Gibbons: A Morphological Study on a Population Sample of a Man-like Ape," *American Journal of Physical Anthropology,* n.s., II, 1–129.

SIMPSON, G. G. 1945. "The Principles of Classification and a Classification of Mammals," *Bulletin of the American Museum of Natural History,* LXXXV, 1–350.

STRAUS, W. L., JR. 1940. "The Posture of the Great Ape Hand in Locomotion and Its Phylogenetic Implications," *American Journal of Physical Anthropology,* XXVII, 199–207.

——. 1941. "The Phylogeny of the Human Forearm Extensors," *Human Biology,* XIII, 23–50, 203–38.

——. 1942. "Rudimentary Digits in Primates," *Quarterly Review of Biology,* XVII, 228–43.

——. 1949. "The Riddle of Man's Ancestry," *ibid.,* XXIV, 200–223.

——. 1950. "The Microscopic Anatomy of the Skin of the Gorilla." In GREGORY, W. K. (ed.), *The Anatomy of the Gorilla,* Part IV, pp. 213–26. New York: Columbia University Press.

TILNEY, F. 1928. *The Brain from Ape to Man: A Contribution to the Study of the Evolution and Development of the Hu* man Brain. 2 vols. New York: Paul B. Hoeber.

TYSON, E. 1699. *Orang-utang, sive Homo sylvestris: or, the Anatomy of a Pygmie Compared with that of a Monkey, an Ape, and a Man. To which is Added, a Philological Essay Concerning the Pygmies, the Cynocephali, the Satyrs, and Sphinges of the Ancients. Wherein it will Appear that they are all either Apes or Monkeys, and not Men, as Formerly Pretended.* London: Thomas Bennet.

VOGT, O. 1906. "Ueber strukturelle Hirncentra, mit besonderer Berücksichtigung der strukturellen Felder des Cortex pallii," *Anatomischer Anzeiger,* XXIX, Erg. H, 74–114.

WASHBURN, S. L. 1951. "The New Physical Anthropology," *Transactions of the New York Academy of Sciences,* ser. II, XIII, 298–304.

WASHBURN, S. L., and DETWILER, S. R. 1943. "An Experiment Bearing on the Problems of Physical Anthropology," *American Journal of Physical Anthropology,* n.s., I, 171–90.

YERKES, R. M. "Gorilla Census and Study," *Journal of Mammology,* XXXII, 429–36.

ZAPFE, H. 1952. *Die Pliopithecus-Funde aus der Spaltenfüllung von Neudorf an der March (CSR),* pp. 1–5. ("Verhandlungen der Geologisches Bundesanstalt 1952," Sonderheft C.)

ZUCKERMAN, S. 1932. *The Social Life of Monkeys and Apes.* London: Kegan Paul, Trench, Trubner & Co.

——. 1933. *Functional Affinities of Man, Monkeys, and Apes.* New York: Harcourt, Brace & Co.

——. 1950. "Taxonomy and Human Evolution," *Biological Reviews,* XXV, 435–85.

The Idea of Fossil Man

By PIERRE TEILHARD DE CHARDIN

I. BIRTH

THE IDEA of the existence of a man who[1] can be regarded as the precursor, both chronologically and morphologically, of the builder of historical civilization—this idea, I submit, represents a surprisingly recent conquest of the modern mind. Today no one any longer questions it or even wonders at it. And yet only a little more than a century ago it would have been as impossible and as shocking for the serious scientist to speak (or even think!) in terms of "fossil man" as it still was, fifty years ago, for official science to suggest the mutability of the atom.

In his classic *Les Hommes fossiles*,[2] Professor M. Boule vividly pictured prehistory's heroic days (in and around 1850), when the best brains of France and England fought hard to break the philosophico-scientific spell which made it almost impossible for the ordinary mind of that time (and this in spite of Buffon, Cuvier, and Lamarck) to conceive of man (or even of apes) as a part of the so-called "extinct world."

Nowadays everyone has heard of the bitter discussions provoked by the first Chelleo-Acheulean hand-axes collected by Boucher de Perthes (1846) in the Pleistocene gravel of the Somme River, a find which coincided with Lartet's discovery of the Miocene *Pliopithecus* and *Dryopithecus* in southern France. Today we smile as we think of the thrills and triumphs experienced by our great predecessors[3] when in 1864 they first observed, on a fragment of mammoth tusk,[4] the carved outline of the mammoth itself—definite testimony, over man's own signature, that man (at that time still believed to have been "created" in 4000 B.C.) had known and hunted the fabulous and (to the scientist of the period) fabulously ancient animal.

These are well-known facts. But they must be remembered and borne in mind if we are to understand fully the many painstaking efforts, both of excavation and of discussion, which the idea of fossil man was destined to undergo before it reached the modern (and probably still immature) version that is commonly accepted today.

II. GROWTH

The fact that they had established beyond doubt man's contemporaneous existence with an extinct Pleistocene fauna did not lead the paleontologists of the 1860's to conclude that man, even at that early stage, could have differed appreciably, either anatomically or mentally, from what we ourselves are at the present day.

1. Judging from the anatomical characteristics, geological horizon, chemical transformation, and faunistic association of his bones.
2. Paris: Masson, 1923.
3. A triumph which resulted in occasional outbursts of an excessive belief in the existence of a "Tertiary man."
4. Unearthed in the Upper Paleolithic cave of La Madeleine, France.

31

But after overcoming the initial difficulty of visualizing man's high antiquity, the early prehistorians still had to surmount another mental hurdle, namely, a reluctance even to imagine a representative of the human race who would exhibit, osteologically, any prehuman features. Long after Boucher de Perthe's victory, the belief that early man was nothing but a particularly ancient *Homo sapiens* was still widely accepted, a view that was supported by such incidents as the discovery, in the gravel of the Somme (1863), of the perfectly modern-looking[5] lower jaw of Moulin-Quignon and (in 1868) of the more important find of Cro-Magnon man (a typical "white man") in the Upper Pleistocene deposits of Perigord.

Two major and purely accidental events were in great part responsible for the cracking of this narrow frame, each of them initiating and characterizing a particular and transitional stage in the development of human paleontology: first, the discovery of the Neanderthal man, leading to a "Europeo-Neanderthal" conception of fossil man; and, subsequently, the discovery of the Pithecanthropines, which fostered an "Asiatico-prehominian" theory of the origin of man.

Let us consider these two stages, traversed successively in the course of the last fifty years by the science of man, before we attempt, in the third and last part of this paper, to characterize the main conceptions and tendencies which currently prevail among scientists interested today in the problem of fossil man.

A. THE "EUROPEO-NEANDERTHAL" PHASE
OF DEVELOPMENT IN THE SCIENTIFIC
CONCEPTION OF FOSSIL MAN

As early as 1856, the first and most famous Neanderthal calvarium was found in the Rhine Valley. But, strangely enough, owing both to the unsatisfactory state of the fossil's preservation and to the unprepared condition of the scientific minds at the time,[6] the true significance of the specimen was not realized or accepted before the much later discoveries of similar relics, first at Spy (Belgium) in 1887 and soon afterward in southwestern France (Le Moustier, La Chapelle-aux-Saints, La Feyrassie, La Quina, etc.), all the French finds dating from the years 1908–11.

Confronted with such a harvest of remarkably preserved and extremely "primitive" human remains, the anthropologists no longer questioned the existence of some *prae-sapiens,* extinct types of man. But, in an eagerness which is not difficult to understand, they now leaped to the explicit or implicit assumption that the Spy Neanderthal man was the single and unique root from which modern man, as a whole, had grown into existence. This was, of course, an oversimplified view, which induced the bulk of the anthropologists of that time (*a*) to locate the main center of early hominization in the much too small continental corner of western Europe, and (*b*) to assume, for the final development of *Homo sapiens,* the impossibly short span of time separating the deposition of the Mousterian and the Aurignacian cultural layers in the Perigord caves.

Clear traces of this junior period in prehistory, when Neanderthal man was *the* fossil man (or, in reverse, when any true fossil man *had to be* a Neanderthal man) can be found in all the classic scientific books written in the 1920's by such eminent paleontologists as Boule, Keith, Osborn, and others. And even at a later date (that

5. That the mandible really belonged to a recently buried modern man was established shortly afterward by John Evans.

6. Cf. the epic discussion between Huxley and Virchow, the latter holding, in opposition to the former, to the theory that the Neanderthal calvarium belonged to a malformed idiot.

is, as late as 1937) I myself can remember the great Hrdlička dismissing *Sinanthropus* as merely one more specimen in the long list of the already known remains of Neanderthal man.

And yet, in the 1920's (that is, at the very time that Boule was writing his *Hommes fossiles*), this oversimplified conception was already difficult to reconcile with such a paleontological reality as the Piltdown man.[7] Obviously, some fossil older than "l'homme de la Chapelle-aux-Saints" and some cradle bigger than the Perigord were needed to explain the origins of man. Why, then, should this "something" else not be represented by the so-called "Prehominians" of Asia?

B. THE "ASIATICO-PREHOMINIAN" PHASE
OF DEVELOPMENT IN THE SCIENTIFIC
CONCEPTION OF FOSSIL MAN

The *Pithecanthropus* calvarium of Java (1894), just like the Neanderthal calvarium of Germany, was too fragmentary a fossil and came too early to be properly understood at the time of its discovery. And it is, indeed, a most significant fact that, as late as 1923, Boule could still have held it to be his definite scientific opinion that the Trinil skull, found by Dubois, was not human but belonged to some large extinct type of gibbon.

However, a few years later, in the Far East came a sequence of important events: first, in North China, the excavation of a whole series of *Sinanthropus* skulls, associated with ashes and a rich, lithic industry; then, in Java (Oppenhoort, 1931, and Von Koenigswald, 1935), the find of the Solo man and of a harvest of well-preserved, decidedly human, remains of Pithecanthropines; while farther to the west, in

pre-Mousterian horizons, discoveries were made of clearly sub-*sapiens* types of man, both in Germany (Steinheim, 1933) and in Palestine (D. Garrod and McCown, 1932).

The "pan-Neanderthal" theory of human origins had to be abandoned, gradually to be replaced by a complex of new theories which had in common two trends or even assumptions: (*a*) that man originated in central Asia and (*b*) that he was born there of some Pithecanthropine ancestor.

As an extreme example of the first tendency I should like to cite the interesting paper[8] published in Peking (as early as 1925) in which Davidson Black, basing his argument on the stimulating views advanced by W. D. Matthew, who favored the idea of a northern Asiatic center of mammal dispersion, as well as on the bold (but very questionable) theories of Dr. A. Grabau concerning the relationship between the origins of man and the Tertiary uplift of the Himalaya,[9] came to the definite conclusion that high central Asia must be regarded as the cradle of mankind.

A good instance of the second trend of thought is the surprising suggestion made by Weidenreich, on several occasions, that the modern Mongoloids are the direct descendants of *Sinanthropus*.

In his exhaustive book on races Von Eickstedt[10] quotes a long series of authors, all of whom, like himself, favor the hypothesis of an Asiatic origin for man: Abel, Deperet, Gregory, Koppers,

---

7. For the most recent discussion of the possible phylogenic relationship between *Homo sapiens* and Neanderthal man, see F. Clark Howell in *American Journal of Physical Anthropology*, IX (1951), 379–415.

8. Davidson Black, "Asia and the Dispersal of Primates," *Bulletin of the Geological Society of China*, IV (1925), 133–83.

9. Man having supposedly originated from a group of higher apes who had been cut off from the southern forests and isolated in Tibet by the folding of the Himalayan geosyncline.

10. E. von Eickstedt, *Rassenkunde und Rassengeschichte der Menschheit* (Stuttgart: F. Enke, 1934), p. 101.

Mendes-Corrêa, Menghin, Obermaier, Osborn, etc.

But here again, after a while, a weakness developed at the heart of the system. In spite of protracted research, conducted over a period of years in Mongolia, western China, and Chinese Turkestan by American (Roy Chapman Andrews), Chinese (Geological Survey), French (Haardt-Citroën), and Swedish (Sven Hedin) expeditions, absolutely no evidence whatsoever was uncovered which suggested in any way that these areas could ever have played a part in the evolution of the higher Primates, or even in the earlier development of man. In the critical test of actual experience, central Asia, far from being a hot spot and a primordial reservoir, was, on the contrary, found to have been a negative pole, a void area, as far as early hominization is concerned.

Under such conditions, nothing was ultimately left to the prehistorians in their quest for "primordial" man but to turn to the still mysterious depths of continental Africa, whence, at precisely this time, strange reports were forcing their way into scientific circles: an ape-man in the Transvaal (Dart's first *Australopithecus*, 1925) and a puzzling association of human implements and Pliocene-looking fauna in Kenya (Leakey). And, essentially, that is where we still stand today.

III. THE PRESENT STATUS OF THE QUESTION OF FOSSIL MAN

It is almost impossible to describe in a satisfactory way the present stage reached by any current of thought, distorted as the picture is bound to be by lack of perspective and by individual preference. If, however, I reduce my personal angle of estimation as far as I am able to do so, I honestly believe that, considered in its most advanced form, the idea of fossil man can be characterized today as being controlled in its development by a small group of outstanding views, which are summarized below.

A. THE RISING IMPORTANCE OF CONTINENTAL AFRICA IN THE BIRTH AND EARLY DEVELOPMENT OF MAN

Since the time when Schlosser, in 1911, described the small mandible of *Propliothecus* collected in the Oligocene fresh-water beds of Fayum (Egypt), Africa has gradually taken first place as a purveyor not only of diamonds but of the higher types of fossil Primates. On the one hand, there are the Miocene *Proconsul*-bearing beds of Tanganyika and the harvest of Australopithecines in the prehuman fissure-deposits of the Transvaal. And, on the other, there is the astonishing wealth of older Paleolithic industries distributed widely over Kenya, the Belgian Congo, Rhodesia, and South Africa. As far as fossil apes and fossil man are concerned, between Nairobi and Capetown the more one searches, the more one finds a striking reversal of the conditions encountered in central Asia.

Under the pressure of so much evidence, it becomes both difficult and unscientific not to accept the idea that the Dark Continent (the last to have been opened to scientific investigation) is precisely the one which, during the Upper Cenozoic period, acted as the main laboratory for the zoölogical development and the earliest establishment of man on this planet.

It is apparently in the depths of Africa (and not on the shores of the Mediterranean Sea or on the Asiatic plateau), therefore, that the primeval center of human expansion and dispersion must have been located, long before this center shifted, in much later times, toward (or even split between) Eurasia and America.

Around this fundamental proposition, taken as an explicit or implicit basis, the whole of our perspectives concerning the biological and historical processes of hominization (and also the plans for further research in the field for fossil man) is actually in the course of being broadened and readjusted.

B. THE INITIAL RADIUS AND COMPLEXITY OF THE HUMAN PHYLUM

Almost from birth, the idea of fossil man has aroused an endless and especially bitter controversy among scientists (not to mention the philosophers). Speaking zoölogically, did man develop from a *single* line of descent? Or is he (as a result of some convergency) a product of the coalescence of *several* different types of phyla?

On the one hand, there are the "monophyletists," by far the more numerous fraction among the paleo-anthropologists, who hold that man, if traced back to some pre-Neanderthal or Pithecanthropoid ancestor, would emerge as some well-defined and restricted branch of the higher Primates.

And, on the other hand, there is the whole gamut of the "polyphyletists." Some of these (like Klaatsch)[11] contend that the so-called "human species" is a mixture of chimpanzee, gorilla, and orang strains. Others (with Wood-Jones and Osborn) suggest a quite independent origin ("Tarsioid") for man, with the result that the higher Primates (Simpson's "Hominoidea") should no longer be regarded as a natural but rather as a composite group.[12] And still others (Rosa, Montandon)[13] propound the almost inconceivable theory of a "hologenesis," according to which no "human cradle" must be expected anywhere, since zoölogical speciation (so they claim) never operates locally but takes place only by means of a slow condensation of a cloud of individuals who appear sporadically (and simultaneously) over the whole surface of the earth.

Today we are beginning to understand that between these two conflicting theories of, on the one hand, a narrow, *linear* monophyletism and, on the other hand, a confusing polyphyletism *through convergency* there is room for a third and much more satisfactory hypothesis, well supported experimentally by modern genetics, for a speciation which acts simultaneously on a large population of closely related individuals spread over a limited but sufficiently broad "surface of evolution."[14] For if (and as soon as) such a wide and complex cross-section is assumed to exist at the base of any major animal phylum, and more especially at the base of the human stem, then it becomes quite easy to understand the "bushy" structure, more and more in evidence, in the composition of humanity as observed in its fossil stages.

In our new conception of "natural" zoölogical groups and of broad "monophyletic" structures, in which an ever larger place is given to marginal and *divergent* types at the expense of truly ancestral forms: (*a*) the evolutive roots of Hominidae fit perfectly into a Tertiary cluster of "Pongidoid" Primates; (*b*)

11. Cf., in a less crude way: M. Sera, "I Caratteri della facie e il polifiletismo dei Primati," *Giornale per la morfologia dell'uomo e dei primati*, II (1918); G. Sergi, *Le Origini umane* (Torino: Fratelli Bocca, 1913); Ruggieri V. Giuffrida, *Su l'origine dell'uomo* (Bologna: Nicola Zanichelli, 1921); A. Mendes-Corrêa, *Homo* (Coimbra: "Atlantida," 1926).

12. The theory still finds some supporters. Cf. W. C. Osman Hill, "Man's Relation to the Apes," *Man*, 1950, p. 257. See also *Yearbook of Physical Anthropology* (New York: Wenner-Gren Foundation for Anthropological Research, 1951).

13. D. Rosa, *Ologenesi* (Firenze: A. Bemporad e Figlio, 1918); G. Montandon, *L'Ologénèse humaine* (Paris: F. Alcan, 1928).

14. The idea (formulated under the hypothesis of a "zone of hominization" extending, supposedly, subtropically between the forest and the grassland) was already clearly expressed by E. von Eickstedt in 1925 ("Gedanken über Entwicklung und Gliederung der Menschheit," *Mitteilungen der Anthropologischen Gesellschaft in Wien*, IV, 231–54).

within the Hominidae themselves, such aberrant types as the Pithecanthropines or the Neanderthal man, if compared with the modern living types of man, deserve, most accurately, the name of "Para-hominians" (rather than of Pre-hominians); and (c), as a consequence of this clarification, we are in a much better position to appreciate and to handle the major biological problem posed to anthropology by the unquestionable dominance, the subtle complexity, and the progressive unification of *Homo sapiens*.

C. THE PHYLOGENETIC MAKEUP OF *Homo sapiens*

The first, but oversimplified, idea of the early human paleontologists, as I mentioned above, was to connect *Homo sapiens* genetically, and in a direct line, with each newly discovered fossil man, either with the Neanderthal man or with *Pithecanthropus* and *Sinanthropus*.

Today, as a result of a franker recognition and a better understanding of such pre-Neanderthal, "sapientoid" forms as the men of Palestine, the Swanscombe man, the Steinheim man, and the Piltdown man, we are beginning to realize (1) that the formation and rise of *Homo sapiens* has apparently been a long and complicated process, requiring for its achievement (a) a complex core of particularly progressive human subforms and (b) considerable amounts of both land and time to allow those adaptive elements to react on each other in a biologically constructive manner; and (2) that the process of "sapientization," which the most central portion of the primordial human stock had to undergo in order to become fully hominized, is itself controlled by two main types of antagonistic morphogenetic forces: (a) the divergent forces of speciation,[15] which work continu-

ously to produce human subspecific types, and (b) the convergent forces of aggregation ("totalization"), which (through interbreeding and socialization) continually compel the newborn types of man into a most remarkable and, so far badly understood, single superarrangement of a *biological nature* —man as a planetary unit.

Here again, judging by the impressive and constantly increasing mass of old Paleolithic industries which is being continuously unearthed in central and South Africa, it appears very possible that the Dark Continent[16] will be recognized "tomorrow" as the main laboratory in which man, after having been first formed as *Homo,* finally succeeded in reaching the level of *Homo sapiens* just before the dawn of the Upper Paleolithic times.

But we can come to no definite conclusion along this line until we first answer the puzzling and still unsolved question which from the outset presented itself to the prehistorians of the Somme Valley: "What kind of man (or, more probably, what kinds of *men*) is to be held responsible for the hand-ax industries that are so characteristic of the oldest and most central culture deposits of the ancient world?"

D. THE NEED AND THE OPPORTUNITIES FOR BETTER-PLANNED EXCAVATIONS

We cannot hope to have a better understanding of fossil man until we know him by better-preserved and more numerous specimens. And we cannot hope to have such specimens until we have more numerous and more efficiently conducted excavations.

In the early days of prehistory, finds of fossil human remains (with the exception of those dug out in Upper Pleistocene open caves) were, perforce, a matter of luck and random research.

15. Or of "lyse"—to use the term created by Dr. C. Blanc, *Sviluppo per lisi delle forme distinte* ("Quaderni di sintesi," No. 2 [Rome: "Partenia," 1946]).

16. That is to say, the same continent which, in much later times, was to act as a blind corner or a "refuge" for human migrations.

Today we know better. And it is therefore surprising that in the case of paleo-anthropology (just as in so many other branches of science) so much effort should still be dispersed among secondary objectives, while so many first-class sites are as yet insufficiently surveyed.

In short, after a century of research, the essence of what experience has taught us concerning the hunt for fossil human bones can be reduced to the following points: (a) As far as that most difficult of quests is concerned, the hunt for a "precultural man" (if he existed at all), apparently the only promising fields are the Villafranchian lake or cave deposits of the Old World, south of the Himalayan-Alpine ranges. (b) In the easier case of the *old Paleolithic* "cultural man"[17] there is one main, simple, and practical rule for prospecting and excavating: "Still remaining, for the most part,[18] south of the Himalayan-Alpine divide, consider only those deposits, as suitable for survey or research, *in which some animal bones occur in association with human implements.*"[19]

This second directive may, at first glance, seem absurdly "naïve." And yet, aside from a few exceptional places, like northeastern China or Kenya, where fossiliferous Lower Pleistocene soils or lake deposits cover really big areas, it is surprising to observe, if we apply this rule, how little there is left to paleo-anthropological research, even in some of the largest and most promising countries of the world. In India, for instance, where old hand-axes occur "en masse" all the way from the Indus Valley to Madras, I have convinced myself that (with the possible exception of some as yet unexplored caves) the *only area,* so far spotted as being promising for the discovery of fossil man's skeletal remains, is the Narbada basin (in central India). Outside the Narbada lake deposits, no animal bones have ever been found (and consequently no human bones can be expected) in association with stone implements, either because they have been crushed by the gravel or because they have dissolved in the porous loess of the north or in the corrosive laterites of the south.

An urgent and relatively easy task, therefore, and one which I should like to propose to the anthropological organizations of the world, is the making of a *world-map* which would show: (a) in what parts of the world we might (or might not) expect to find traces of either precultural or cultural man (early Paleolithic man, or Middle Paleolithic man, or Upper Paleolithic man);[20] (b) at what localities, in each of these zones, the "hot spots" (fossiliferous fissures and fresh-water sediments) in which there is a reasonable expectancy of discovering human fossil bones are located.

A basic plan of this kind (by concentrating the work of temporary excavation and permanent collecting on the most strategic sites) would, I believe, immeasurably increase the efficiency of paleo-anthropological research.

17. And if one excepts, of course, the case of wild and unpredictable chance.

18. The western expansion of older Paleolithic man as far north as southern England and the eastern marginal advance of the Pithecanthropines as far as Peking may be regarded as local exceptions to this rule.

19. A fact which simply proves that the sediments were not physically or chemically destructive to the bones.

20. According to the present stage of our knowledge, it would seem that man's expansion has proceeded in three major laps: (a) Birth and early development—confined to Africa and southern Asia—culminating in the birth of *Homo sapiens.* (b) Expansion of *Homo sapiens* (Middle and Upper Paleolithic) —the slow conquest of northern Eurasia—first appearance in America? (c) The final expansion and advanced socialization of *Homo sapiens* (Meso- and Neolithic)—the appearance of new centers of hominization outside continental Africa.

E. FOSSIL MAN AND FUTURE MAN

On the whole, during the course of a century, our knowledge of early man has greatly improved and accelerated. Not only has the idea of the existence of fossil man been so universally accepted that it approaches the "banal," but we have now reached a point from which the main phases of man's descent (or ascent) from his most ancient forerunners can be outlined with safety.

In many of its modalities, of course, the process of man's formation still remains scientifically obscure (through lack of fossil evidence). And yet, even if we cannot pretend to have actually reached a complete solution of that question which Darwin propounded so vividly in 1872 in his *Descent of Man,* the problem has been circumscribed and may be regarded as virtually settled, with the result that the subject of the origin of man is bound (and, as a matter of fact, has already begun)

gradually to lose for our minds that prime fascination which it held for our predecessors in its early days.[21]

One century more, perhaps. Then, in accordance with the fate which is common to all types of purely descriptive knowledge (like geography or Linnean systematics), paleo-anthropology, as such, will most probably have become a stabilized branch of science. But then, as compensation, it will also, probably, have become evident to our "descendants" that, by supplying modern society with a historical basis for its belief in some ultra-humanized form of life (and also with a set of biological patterns for its achievement), the study of fossil man, as it was accomplished in the nineteenth and twentieth centuries, was, in retrospect, the condition *sine qua non* for a scientific conception (and a scientific development) of future man.

21. For the modern mind, the problem of origins has been superseded by the question of patterns and processes.

Paleopathology

By ERWIN H. ACKERKNECHT

PALEOPATHOLOGY DEALS with the pathology of prehistoric animals and of man in prehistoric and nonliterate societies. The only documents at its disposal for reconstructing the pathological picture are bones, and sometimes works of art and mummies. The methods of paleopathology have been also occasionally applied with success to "historical" periods where insufficient written documents exist.

The first observations on a pathological fossil bone were published by Esper in 1774 ("sarcoma"—actually healed fracture—in the cave bear, that Job of Paleopathology). Slowly material accumulated first on animals, then on man. These studies gained great impetus in the second half of the nineteenth century, the period of Broca and Virchow. The field became a special discipline during the first thirty years of the twentieth century through the accomplishments of Sir Armand Ruffer (who introduced the name "paleopathology"), Grafton Elliot Smith, Wood Jones, H. U. Williams, Roy L. Moodie, L. Pales, and others. The latter two published treatises on paleopathology (1923 and 1930) with extensive bibliographies. The bibliography after 1930 is given by H. E. Sigerist in Appendix IV of the first volume of his *History of Medicine* (New York, 1951). This period is characterized by the successful use of such technological aids as the X-ray machine and the microscope.

The last twenty years have brought important new detailed knowledge on tumors, prehistoric tuberculosis, etc., although the work has, regrettably enough, not been carried on with the same intensity as before. The main progress during this period lies in the increasing realization that paleopathology gives more than important medical data. *The pathology of a society reflects its general conditions and growth and offers, therefore, valuable clues to an understanding of the total society.* Pioneer work in this direction has been done by Todd, Hooton, Vallois, Ad. Schultz, L. Angel, and others. We have witnessed the first steps from a paleopathology of individuals to a paleopathology of groups and societies. It is to be hoped that, when this point of view is fully assimilated, increased activity in the field will result. In the following survey of the results of this young science, emphasis will be laid on human material. Animal material will be mentioned only occasionally.

THE BONE RECORD

TRAUMATISM

The first healed fractures of animals as evidenced by callus are found in Permian reptiles. A healed fracture was also found in the Neanderthal man. The evidence of healed fractures becomes very extensive in the European Neolithic and in early Egypt. That well-healed fractures alone are no proof for fracture treatment was already maintained by Baudouin and was definitely

shown by Ad. Schultz's work on gibbons.

Head injuries are found in *Sinanthropus,* Neanderthal men, Cro-Magnon men, the European Neolithic, and
the American pre-Columbian, especially in Peru. The latter prevalence might
be due to the use of special weapons
like maces. A certain number of the
Neolithic and old Peruvian trephinings
were apparently provoked by skull fractures. Whether this was the sole reason
for trephining is doubtful. Trephining
itself is part of paleomedicine, not paleopathology, and therefore is not discussed further here.

Numerous arrowheads have been
found in the European Neolithic and in
pre-Columbian America, imbedded especially in vertebrae and extremities.

The famous exostosis of Dubois's
Pithecanthropus might be of traumatic
origin.

MALFORMATION

Evidence of dwarfism, achondroplas-
tic and cretinistic, has been found in
Egypt, in skeletons and statues. Also an
anencephalic mummy has been described. The congenital perforated
sternum has been observed in material
stemming from Neolithic Europe and
from Peru. In the same places evidence
of spina bifida was discovered. Other
congenital anomalies of the vertebral
column have been reported from Peru.
Congenital hip luxation was diagnosed
in skeletons from Neolithic Europe,
pre-Columbian North America, and
Peru.

Congenital clubfoot (talipes equino-
varus) has been found repeatedly in
Egyptian mummies and works of art.
G. E. Smith regarded the clubfoot of
King Siptah (Nineteenth Dynasty,
around 1225 B.C.) as a congenital clubfoot. Slomann interpreted it rather as
an aftereffect of *poliomyelitis.* The
same interpretation was given by J. K.
Mitchell to the shortened femur of a

mummy dated about 3700 B.C.; the deformation on the stele of the priest
Ruma (Copenhagen) offers itself to the
same interpretation. Rolleston diagnosed a Neolithic skeleton from Ciss-
bury as postpoliomyelitic.

Hydrocephalus has been reported
from Roman Egypt as well as copper-
age Turkey, Peru, and ninth-century
Germany.

INFLAMMATION (NONSPECIFIC)

If we are to believe the bone record,
bacterial infection was a rather early
event, and the multicellular organism
reacted to this as to other irritations
by inflammation that is a combination
of necrosis and formation of new tissue.

Periostitis ossificans was first described in Permian reptiles, later in early mammals (especially the cave bear),
and eventually in Neolithic man. Osteitis is particularly often represented
in the form of *sinusitis* (pre-Columbian
North American, Peru, Neolithic
France) and mastoiditis (pre-Columbian North American, Peru, Egypt).

The first known cases of osteomyelitis in Permian reptiles were apparently sequels to infected fractures; osteomyelitis again was very prevalent in
cave bears. It is found in European
Neolithic and ancient Peruvian bones.

Myositis ossificans was found to be
common in fossil animals but rare in
human remains.

SPECIFIC INFLAMMATION (SYPHILIS,
TUBERCULOSIS)

The pre-Columbian existence of syphilis in either hemisphere has been debated heatedly for about four hundred
years. It was hoped that paleopathology
would eventually decide the question.
Starting with Parrot in France in 1877
and with Joseph Jones in North America in 1876, numerous prehistoric bone
lesions have been described as syphilitic. Many of these interpretations have

been discarded. New suspect specimens have appeared.

There are always two great difficulties to overcome in making a definite diagnosis of pre-Columbian syphilis in a bone: (*a*) Is the bone actually pre-Columbian? (*b*) Were the bone changes actually produced by the *Spirocheta pallida* or by some other infectious agent?

The latter question seems not answerable unless a positive serological reaction or other proof of specificity can be obtained. Such proof has not been produced so far. It should always be remembered by those deciding the case on mere morphology that Virchow was able to demonstrate in the tibia of a cave bear the same changes that are usually attributed to syphilis in human bones.

H. U. Williams, who surveyed the question last in 1932, came to the conclusion that certain bones from Pecos, Paracas, Tennessee Mounds, etc., are beyond any doubt both pre-Columbian and syphilitic. These bones are morphologically strongly suggestive of syphilis. But hardly more so than, e.g., the Neolithic material from Petit Morin in the Museum of St. Germain, from Iran (Krogman), from eleventh-century Russia, from Japan (Adachi), which Williams, with the characteristic fervor of an "American-origin" partisan, disregarded. The safest conclusion seems still to give to none of these inflammatory bone changes the definite label of syphilis.

Some of these bones have meanwhile been claimed as specimens of Paget's disease (osteitis deformans).

The problem is subjectively and objectively somewhat simpler in the case of *tuberculosis*. There is at least one tuberculous affection of the bone, the so-called "Pott's disease," in the vertebral column which it is hard to mistake for any other type of infection. On the basis of numerous cases of Pott's disease

the antiquity of tuberculosis seems now established in both hemispheres. Cases of Pott's disease have been described from predynastic Egypt (3000 B.C.), and from the end of the third millennium in Nubia. A particularly convincing case was described by Smith and Ruffer in the mummy of a priest of Ammon (about 1000 B.C.), where the characteristic psoas abscess also was found. The finding of clay sculptures, picturing the typical hunchback in Pott's disease, reinforce these diagnoses. Tuberculous changes in the hip joints of children (dated 2700 and 1900 B.C.) have also been reported from Egypt.

Only one (controversial) case of Pott's disease has been described from the European Neolithic. Pales feels confident as to the tuberculous nature of a Neolithic hip and an ankylosed foot.

In North America not completely convincing pre-Columbian specimens of Pott's disease have been described by Whitney, Means, and Hrdlička. The findings of Hooton (Pecos) and especially of W. A. Ritchie (New York State) leave little doubt concerning the pre-Columbian existence of tuberculosis in North America. The same can be said for South America after the work of Requena and Garcia Frias. Hunchbacked clay figurines again reinforce the diagnosis in the Western Hemisphere.

A parasitism of a much cruder nature may be mentioned at this point. The hair of Egyptian as well as Peruvian mummies is frequently decorated with the eggs of lice.

OSTEOARTHRITIS AND SPONDYLITIS

Spondylitis is here treated together with osteoarthritis, as it is actually the osteoarthritis of the vertebral column. Osteoarthritis is not subdivided in the following into its rheumatoid and osteoarthritic forms, as this subdivision is at present primarily of clinical interest. Suffice it to say that the material reported below shows both forms of chronic arthritis. If, however, it could be shown that, as suggested by T. D. Stewart, the rheumatoid form is less prevalent in some periods and regions, this would throw an important light on the whole rheumatism problem.

Next to traumatism, arthritis is the oldest and most widespread pathological lesion reported in paleopathology. In the animal kingdom it starts with the dinosaurs of the Comanchian and is continuously found up to the present. In the hominids it has been observed everywhere since Neanderthal man. Egyptian material showing it has existed since 4000 B.C.

Spondylitis, arthritis of the vertebral column, which often transforms the finely structured vertebral column into one solid bony mass, is one of the most frequent and most extensive arthritic lesions. Spondylosis is already present in dinosaurs (*Diplodocus*) of the Secondary. The man of La Chapelle-aux-Saints, a Neanderthal, shows spondylitis of the cervicodorsal and the lumbar parts of the vertebral column. Cro-Magnon men suffered from it. Spondylitis is very frequently seen in European Neolithic, the early Egyptian, and the pre-Columbian American. An interesting feature of spondylitis is the changing seat of the lesion along the vertebral column in animals and men. Different subdivisions of the vertebral column are involved. In early man and primitives, lumbar spondylitis is frequent, while dorsal and cervical are rare (the ancient Egyptians are an exception, with frequent dorsal involvement). In modern man cervical involvement is often found. As similar differences exist between the wild horse and the riding horse (the former shows more dorsal, the latter more lumbar, involvement) or between different species of vertebrates, the conclusions seem legitimate that, *on the one hand, these localizations have something to do with areas of* *stress and strain and that, on the other hand, conclusions can be drawn from pathological areas as to living conditions and posture of the material under examination.*

Chronic arthritis of the hip joint has so far been observed only in man, not in animals. Here again it begins with the Neanderthalian Homme de la Chapelle, is found in the European Neolithic, frequently in ancient Egypt, and, for unknown reasons, even more frequently in ancient Peru. Pales has suggested that subluxations of the joints form the basis for many of these cases.

Temporo-maxillary arthritis was found in the Neanderthal man of Krapina, but not in other European skeletons. It is rare today in Western countries. It is, on the other hand, fairly frequent among pre-Columbian North and South Americans, and among present-day West Africans and Melanesians, especially in the New Hebrides and in New Caledonia. Pales explains the puzzling fact by the combined action of predisposing racial anatomical structure and particularly coarse food.

Numerous other joints—for instance, of the phalanges—have been found to be affected, e.g., in mosasaurs, cave bears, Neanderthal man, upper Paleolithic men like Cro-Magnon, Neolithic Europeans, ancient Egyptians, Peruvians, and other pre-Columbian Amerindians. The Patagonians show arthritis only in the joints of the upper extremities. Here we again encounter the problem of selective localization, probably connected with zones of particular functional stress.

The universality of arthritis in bones at all periods, climates, and places does not confirm climatic theories of the disease (moist or cold climate). The existence of osteoarthritis in dinosaurs, cave bears, etc., is not in favor of alcohol or tobacco as causative factors.

RICKETS AND SYMMETRICAL OSTEOPOROSIS

Rickets, an avitaminosis and a bone disease extremely prevalent during the last three hundred years, has been found in a giant Pleistocene wolf and in a domesticated Egyptian ape, but, in general, not in early man. No rickets in the tens of thousands of Egyptian skeletons examined, none in the extensive pre-Columbian material (this is consistent with findings in primitives). Only from the Scandinavian Neolithic and from Indochina (?) has evidence of rickets been reported. Two cases of osteomalacia, a disease often confounded with rickets, have been seen in Peru.

On the other hand, abundant proof of a bone disease that is practically nonexistent among present-day whites and that might be an avitaminosis—symmetrical osteoporosis — has been found in ancient Egypt (Nubia) and ancient Peru. Pecos also offers several examples, and it is supposed to have occurred often among the ancient Maya. Like rickets, symmetrical osteoporosis, which produces the so-called "cribra parietalia" and "cribra orbitalia" —lesions called syphilitic by older authors—is primarily a disease of childhood. Several anemias of childhood and scurvy produce similar pictures. The disease is very rare among Neolithic Europeans and North American pre-Columbians but is common in many present-day non-European populations (African Negroes, Malays, Chinese, Japanese, etc.). Besides avitaminosis, mechanical causes (like skull deformation) have been suggested.

TUMORS

Bone tumors in prehistoric men and animals, especially malignant ones, are surprisingly rare, as compared to findings in present-day men and animals. The oldest osteomas are found in mosasaurs. They occur in the European Neolithic and rather frequently in ancient Peru, especially as osteomata of the auditory duct. To differentiate osteomata—true tumors—from exostoses—mere reactional growth—is not always simple. Other benign tumors—hemiangiomata—have been described in dinosaurs.

Osteosarcomata have been found in the cave bear and perhaps the Pleistocene horse. Human osteosarcomata have been described by Smith and Dawson from the Fifth Dynasty (*ca.* 2750 B.C.) in Egypt. Recently, sarcomatous meningiomata have been described in Egyptian skulls of the First Dynasty (3400 B.C.). Osteosarcomata occur also in ancient Peruvian skulls. Moodie has interpreted some of these Peruvian cranial tumors as residuals of meningiomata.

Bone defects, especially of the skull basis and the sacrum, in Neolithic and ancient Peruvian materials might have been caused by neighboring cancers of the soft parts or their metastases. Such erosions might, of course, also be produced occasionally by aneurysm.

Multiple myeloma has been reported from Neolithic France and pre-Columbian North America.

DENTAL PATHOLOGY

Pyorrhea appears in the animal series with the mosasaurs, among hominids with the Neanderthals. It is found in ancient Europe, Egypt, Peru, Hawaii, etc. Abscess resulting from pyorrhea is described first in an oligocene rhinoceros. In man it starts with the Neanderthal man. Caries, though seen in mosasaur and cave bear, seems to have appeared later on a large scale in man. First clear evidence for it dates from the Neolithic, especially in Scandinavia. In ancient Egypt it struck supposedly only the wealthy. A number of dental malformations are also on record.

SOFT PARTS

Only a small percentage of diseases leave their marks on the bones. In mummies, fortunately, the soft parts are preserved to a certain extent. Mummification can be spontaneous in very dry climates like that of Arizona. Artificial mummification, supported by a dry climate, was practiced on a large scale in ancient Egypt and Peru. Study of mummies has greatly extended our knowledge of prehistoric disease conditions.

One of the most striking findings in Egyptian mummies (by direct inspection and by X-ray) was that of *arteriosclerosis*. It was first described in the aorta of Merneptah (1225–1215), the Pharaoh of the Exodus. Arteriosclerosis has also been demonstrated in Peruvian mummies.

The *lungs* of mummies have shown the following conditions: silicosis (Basketmaker), anthracosis (Egypt, Basketmaker), pneumonia (Egypt, Basketmaker; one of the Egyptian pneumonias contained bacilli resembling plague bacilli), pleurisy (Egypt).

Kidneys of mummies have presented congenital atrophy (Egypt), multiple abscesses (Egypt), stones (Egypt, Basketmaker). In a mummy of the Twentieth Dynasty (1250–1000) the eggs of *Bilharzia* have been demonstrated. Schistosomiasis, caused by *Bilharzia*, which is still one of the main Egyptian health problems, already existed, apparently, 2000 years ago. Vesicovaginal fistula has been observed in female Egyptian mummies, together with other evidence of difficult birth.

Egyptian mummies have, furthermore, contained gallstones, liver cirrhosis, and chronic appendicitis. Skin changes in one case have strongly suggested smallpox, in another one leprosy. Large spleens have been thought of as possible signs of malaria. Prolapsus of rectum and of female genitalia has been seen.

Ruffer, who did the largest amount of microscopic work in paleopathology and demonstrated a large number of structures, could not find traces of any blood corpuscles. This has unfortunately brought about a somewhat defeatist attitude in the search for the latter, in spite of the fact that G. E. Wilson (1927, Basketmaker) and H. U. Williams (1927, Peruvian mummies) were able to demonstrate red blood corpuscles. Krumbhaar (1936) even found not only erythrocytes but monocytes and polymorphonuclear leukocytes in a pre-Columbian tibia from Peru. Great progress in what we might call "paleophysiology" was achieved when Canela (1936) developed a technique to type blood groups from skeletal material. Wyman and Boyd (1937) followed with important work on blood-grouping in mummies.

ART OBJECTS

Art objects from both hemispheres have already been referred to above in the cases of poliomyelitis, Pott's disease, and dwarfism. In the case of the paleolithic sculptures of obese women it is not clear whether we are dealing with actual representations of the artist's wishful thinking or whether such conditions were spontaneous and pathological or artificially produced. Closer scrutiny of the greatly increased volume of paleolithic art might still yield important discoveries.

Peruvian pottery is particularly rich in pathological representations. The outstanding findings are those of verruga Peruviana (Carrion's disease), uta (leishmaniasis), and sand-flea lesions on the soles of feet.

INTEGRATION

The last twenty years have produced specialized findings of great interest as to the prehistory of, e.g., tuberculosis, tumors, blood corpuscles, etc. Much remains to be done in this field. Important biological hypotheses on the age of infectious diseases like those of the late Charles Nicolle remain still to be integrated with the work of paleopathologists. Certain medical conclusions as to the great age of disease and of certain diseases (tuberculosis, poliomyelitis), the legendary character of ideas of the "healthy wild animal" and the "healthy savage," and the identity of basic disease mechanisms throughout time can be safely made today.

Yet, as mentioned above, another task, even more important than its purely medical implications, faces paleopathology today—the task of integrating its data with other types of information, e.g., from archeology or paleoanthropology, in such a way that it realizes its potentialities for an illumination of human society and its dynamics. On the other hand, all those co-operating in such a synthesis will have to pay more attention to the data of paleopathology than has been done in the past.

Pioneer work in integrating the data of paleopathology was undertaken by Todd (1929), when he reconstructed the duration of life in medieval and in primitive communities from bone material. Vallois did the same for early man (1932).

The most important effort in this direction was made by Hooton in his splendid monograph on Pecos in 1930, when, on the basis of the bone record, he reconstructed the life-history of the settlement, utilizing the archeological findings and his exhaustive study of Pecos paleopathology. Hooton found arthritis, traumatism, sinusitis, mastoiditis, osteomyelitis (syphilis?), osteoporosis, Pott's disease, cancer, etc. That he found so much is probably due less to a particularly high morbidity in Pecos than to

his sustained interest in the problem. Hooton set a shining example, unfortunately isolated so far. If a few more sites had been handled with the same thoroughness, we would probably have achieved far greater progress in our field. Bone material should always be studied beyond the traditional examination for its racial nature and *should receive at least the type of attention that is given to material in legal cases.* Physical anthropology has contributed valuable techniques to legal medicine. It could, in turn, profit from adoption of some techniques of legal medicine and other medical technology.

It is no accident that one of the most significant and brilliant recent contributions in integration has come from a pupil of Hooton, J. L. Angel, in his work on the anthropology of the early Greeks. Angel found the growth of Greek culture between 800 and 500 B.C. connected with such phenomena as an increase in body size, life-span, and population volume and a decrease in arthritis, dental pathology, osteoporosis, and infant mortality. He noticed again a decrease in health after 400 B.C. The fact that the one or the other conclusion of Angel might be based on too small a sample does not detract from the value and interest of his studies as a whole. Sigerist has recently integrated in a similar way cultural and paleopathological data on Egypt in the first volume of his *History of Medicine.*

Another important recent contribution has been the work of Ad. Schultz on Primate pathology. We have already mentioned his work on fractures in gibbons. When, besides the lesions we are familiar with in early man and in mummies, he found a high degree of infestation with plasmodia, filaria, and trypanosoma, the conclusion seems legitimate, in view of biological relationships, that man's ancestors were affected in a similar way.

Race

By HENRI V. VALLOIS

THE IDEA of "race" originated prior to any scientific definition. The first classifiers acknowledged the existence, among the human species, of distinct groups; but they did not concern themselves with either the nature or the respective positions of such groups. The only problem which occasionally troubled them was that of the plurality of types, a plurality that seemed to contradict the biblical tradition.

Among the naturalists whose works heralded physical anthropology "properly speaking," the discernment of races remained a preconceived one in the sense that it still rested upon conspicuous differences. During a rather long period the identification of new types was not based upon real research but upon the accounts of explorers.

However, yielding now to scientific problems, now to religious scruples, naturalists were gradually induced not only to enumerate "categories" but also to define their nature. This problem was long thought over by anthropologists of the last century; it is still being discussed, and an answer has not yet been unanimously agreed upon.

On the other hand, in reference to the taxonomic status of human races, some evolution of ideas has taken place. Contrary to the opinion formerly held by some authors, anthropologists now more or less agree that all living human populations belong to one and the same species. But dissension has remained as far as the value of subdivisions is concerned, not so much regarding the racial groups or "great races," such as the White or the Black, whose distinctiveness gives rise to little controversy, but as regarding the races properly speaking. The delimitation of these narrower units, existing amid the former, has given rise to many theoretical and practical difficulties. Among the latter, one of the chief difficulties has originated from the long-favored notion of "pure races."

In the last century the idea prevailed that most present-day populations, if not all, were racially mixed. It determined among anthropologists two different attitudes, which have, nevertheless, sometimes coexisted rather contradictorily in the minds of the same authors. On the one hand, these actual populations were thought to be the result of the mixture of primitive pure races, races that anthropological analysis would succeed in separating. On the other hand, the mixture was admitted to be likely to produce new races. Schematically, it should be possible to distinguish a certain number of categories on a theoretical level: first, more or less pure races; then, different series of mixed populations. According to some authors, such mixed populations had the rank of race. For others they were nothing but "ethnic groups" or "peoples" or "tribes," whose racial ingredients the anthropologist was to identify.

46

Another problem: it was contended for a long time that the "environment" directly transformed living beings. Man should not escape the common law. Therefore, the old naturalists, followed by the anthropologists, often declared that the differentiation of races is due to surroundings, or, in the words of certain others, to "climate." But other anthropologists opposed direct environmental origin for the racial characteristics they considered, on the contrary, as more or less fixed. Once more, what, for some, distinguished races and explained their formation had, for others, neither discriminative nor classificatory value.

Moreover, the situation became further complicated because of the fact that the supporters of the different doctrines had no very fixed ideas about the real nature of racial differences. The old authors often ascribed somatic characters, whose hereditary foundation is now unquestioned, to the immediate influence of external causes. Lawrence attributed the flattening of the nose in black races to the way the women carried their children. Now, as he had adopted a definite position against the inheritance of acquired characteristics, platyrrhiny in his opinion could not be a racial characteristic. Inversely, Buffon seems to have regarded as racial characteristics artificial deformations of whose real origin he was definitely aware!

In short, there prevailed a confused situation, whose many contradictions are not difficult to point out in a retrospective review. On the other hand, it is not easy to restore the historical sequence of notions and ideas, unless one chooses conventionally a certain number of themes. From this point of view, to clear the ground, it is convenient to study different special problems and to retrace rapidly their evolution in time.

RACE AS A MODIFICATION OF SPECIES DUE TO EXTERNAL CAUSES

The concept of race as a modification of species due to environment is one of the oldest, but with time it has undergone a profound transformation. In its primitive form it implied the rapid, or even immediate, action of the external factors, so that race appeared as a contingent or transitory phenomenon.

The most simple form of this doctrine is that which postulates the modifying action of mechanical causes. Vesalius attributed the different forms of the cranium to different ways of cradling infants. This idea reappeared from time to time in the literature (Walcher, 1905; Basler, 1927; Ewing, 1950) without any distinction being generally established between possible deformations and more or less constant racial characteristics. J. L. Myres wrote still more recently (1923) that the Mongoloid facial traits are partly attributable to the fact that children were suckled by mares.

Buffon (1749) seems to have admitted the role of mechanical causes, but he attached decisive importance to nutrition and to climate. He was convinced that, in one and the same environment, after some generations, men "would look alike even if they had come from very distant and different countries and if, primitively, they had been very dissimilar."

The same concept, but limited to a determined region of the body, has been found up to the present time. One knows the ideas of Thomson and Buxton (1923) and Davies (1932) on the action of climate upon the shape of the nose. Semenov (1951) and Sergi (1950) in the same way explained the distinctive characteristics of the Mongol and Berber eyes as a defense reaction of the organism against light and the mechanical action of wind.

Originally, this mechanistic point of view reflected the embarrassment of scientists who could not see their way to explaining the existence of a number of different races. Further, it had to be admitted that this plurality of types had been realized in the short space of time, about 6,000 years, between ourselves and the date attributed to the biblical Creation. This raised formidable problems with regard to religion. More than once the tendency to treat racial characteristics as "accidents" or as theoretically transitory fluctuations followed from scruples of this nature. In the past these have been principally theological; in the present, moral.

One must acknowledge, in any case, that the modern concept of the action of external causes on the modification of human types differs profoundly from the former. The naturalists of the last century stuck, above all, to the obvious subdivisions of the human species: varieties or great races. One does not seem to find, in recent anthropological literature, a doctrine that the differences between human varieties are contingent upon and brought about by the rapid action of the environment.

On the contrary, there are, in this modern literature, well-known facts proving the rapid modification of characteristics used to define races properly speaking, that is to say, categories inferior to the great subdivisions. As a matter of fact, when one establishes the increase in stature of a Mongoloid group transplanted into a new geographical setting, compared to the stature of previous generations remaining in the original country, one does not mean that the emigrants have ceased to belong to the Mongoloid family. Shapiro, who made this remarkable discovery (1939), emphasized that, in his

opinion, the change could not exceed a certain limit.

Thus restricted, the instability of racial groups is rather generally admitted in recent literature, but it has neither the same sense as it had for former naturalists nor the same sense for all modern authors. For some of these, the more or less rapid modifications explained by environmental causes appear as a phenomenon of secondary importance, although very upsetting for the classifier. Others, having emphasized the extraneous modifications, would rather keep to great subdivisions than to races in the strict sense of the word. Boas had adopted such an attitude. Sarasin thought that usual racial characteristics are of little use when one tries to establish the relationship of groups because of the very fact that these characteristics, in his opinion, are unstable.

It follows that, after having been admitted as a sufficient explanation of racial differences, the variability of the anatomical characteristics finally convinced many anthropologists of the low or nonexistent value of the usual racial descriptions as regards the discrimination of types. Anyway, other arguments followed the simple consideration of instability. Since the beginning of this century, it has more than once been emphasized that characteristics varying under the influence of environment concern the phenotype only: they do not allow the passage from the transitory to the permanent which, by definition, constitutes the very substance of race. With diverse slight alterations and some complementary arguments, this point of view figures often in modern literature.

But all anthropologists do not react in the same way to this problem. Some, as we have said, would rather keep to great su^bdivisions, such as Blacks and

Whites, which seem to escape controversies. Others try to separate "good" racial characteristics from "bad" ones. Hooton, for some time, wanted to avoid adaptive characteristics (1926). Afterward, he renounced this distinction, which, no doubt, raises other difficult problems. Without introducing such considerations, many anthropologists keep to empirical data; they think, for example, that stature is a bad characteristic, since various observations show that it changes to a considerable extent at very short intervals. Finally, some investigators have shown themselves more exacting and have advocated the exclusive use of characteristics whose genetic foundation is known.

These discussions show that physical anthropology faces an important problem, the co-ordinated and methodical study of which has scarcely been outlined: the problem of the more or less rapid modifications that mankind undergoes at the present time. In this regard the best-known fact is the increase of stature, a phenomenon whose significance is not absolutely clear. Shapiro has collected data (1939) showing that, at least in one particular instance, the real increase of final stature is to all appearances the case. On the other hand, the data of army anthropometry, which attest the universality of this phenomenon, are more delicate to handle. Morant has recently published (1949) a very thorough study wherein he shows that in the English population only the rhythm of growth has changed, the final stature not having undergone an appreciable change. Kil, a short time before (1939), came to a similar conclusion touching the Norwegian population. If this conclusion could be generalized, one should conclude that stature is not such a "bad" characteristic as one thought. Likewise, many statistics have stressed the existence of a gradual increase of the ce-

phalic index in Europe for the last nine or ten centuries, an increase which is now followed in some groups by a diminution (Pittard, 1935; Schlaginhaufen, 1946). One has thus been able to speak (Czekanowski, 1935) of a periodic oscillation of the index. Very recently, Büchi (1950) has shown the existence of "secular" variations in numerous measurements of head and body. But some of these phenomena admit of other explanations, and the controversies they raise are not yet all settled. In any case, all these examples show the uncertainties still besetting the rapid changes of racial characteristics and the pressing necessity of entering upon their exhaustive study.

INSTABILITY OF CHARACTERISTICS DUE TO CROSS-BREEDING; MIXED RACES, INTERMEDIATE TYPES, UNCLASSIFIABLE GROUPS

Among naturalists and anthropologists of the beginning of the last century, human hybridization sometimes appears as a factor of racial differentiation. Nevertheless, this idea has not been indorsed by every author. Broca was one of the first to stress the heterogeneous nature of European populations. Topinard wrote: "We are all half-breeds." For these authors, however, as for many others, mixed populations are not races but complex groups. The anthropologist must submit these to an arduous analysis in order to distinguish their racial components.

During the first decades of this century, a similar concept endeavored to find support in genetics, but this science was very inadequate at the time. Some authors believed that at least some racial characteristics are transmitted in conformity with a very simple Mendelian law and that, in a hybrid population, their segregation should be easy to prove—hence the idea of searching in an ethnic mixture for the elements which have had a share in its formation (Czekanowski, 1928; Davenport, 1929; and others).

Another tendency postulated the appearance, after cross-breeding, of types as characteristic as "pure" races. Meanwhile, the possibility of tracing back their stocks was not excluded: especially in old literature one finds many indications regarding mixed types, the result of a certain race having been crossed with another. But these types are considered stable, more or less homogeneous, and entitled to a taxonomic rank.

Quatrefages was one of the first anthropologists to admit explicitly that cross-breeding begets new races. The exact origin of this notion would be difficult to trace back, and, nearer to our own time, it has found considerable approval. As an example, besides "protomorphic races," which recall primitive mankind, and "archimorphic races," which separated in the process of evolution, Stratz (1903), going back to an already old expression used by Fritsch (1891), distinguished "metamorphic races," born of the mixture of the former. Czekanowski had admitted the existence of hybrid races due to the mixture of primary races; Haddon (1924) expressed the same point of view, his "secondary races" being but the product of two or many primary races, this product then becoming stabilized through geographic isolation.

Contrary to what took place as the century began, the same idea became largely credited in the new anthropological literature inspired by Mendelism. Thus the Negro-American population, notoriously mixed, appears to several recent American authors as a new race, or at least as a race in the making (particularly Coon, Garn, and Birdsell, 1950). Generally speaking, the idea that cross-breeding could produce fixed

types, liable to the taxonomic rank of race, is very often admitted nowadays.

Thus the question seems settled on the theoretical plane, but, when it comes to determining the "nature" of some concrete populations, one sees the difficulties reappear. Disagreement may happen regarding those "races" which everyone considers "intermediate." Traditionally, these were classified as "mixed" groups (Biasutti and Giuffrida-Ruggeri's "metamorphic" groups). But in particular cases another point of view has been put forward. The notion of "synthetic types," familiar to paleontologists, has been used to find a place for "intermediate" populations, whose hybrid origin is not obvious. Boule and Vallois (1932) have considered some Ethiopian populations as an undifferentiated form rather than a simple mixture of Whites and Blacks. Fleure (1937) thinks that in the British population there can be found a type prior to the differentiation of tall blond dolichocephals and small brown dolichocephals. Haddon had admitted, on his side, that intermediate types could be undifferentiated types. The elements liable to interpretation vary from one case to another, and, for the time being, genetics affords no help in choosing between these points of view.

After having spoken of races born of cross-breeding and intermediate types, one must recall that most anthropologists, if not all, admit the existence of still other groups which are difficult or impossible to classify. The opinion has sometimes been held that it is wrong to try to fix each group in a precise place in a rigid system of classification. If one reviews the literature, one finds that certain authors have had this ambition but that their attitude has not been shared by most others. Even in the very old classifications, some groups are omitted, not through ignorance, but through caution. Cuvier, for instance, left out of his tripartite plan in an indeterminate position the Amerindians and some other branches of mankind. Perhaps he was only obeying religious scruples. But this factor surely did not intervene with other naturalists and anthropologists. This aspect of the question will be more clearly exposed in the part dealing with classifications. For the time being, it is enough to say that the idea has now largely spread that one cannot strictly classify every human group. In this respect the principal difference is probably the following: for some, there is no chance of reaching a more exhaustive classification; for others, one must distinguish between well-studied populations and those which are, as yet, little known. In this last case the obstacle would be of an accidental nature, even if truly impossible to remove. In any case the idea that every population is practically classifiable in a complete and coherent system is not generally admitted nowadays.

RACE AS A COMBINATION OF CHARACTERISTICS IN INDIVIDUALS

We may now, by successive stages, define more closely the very notion of race. The latter may be understood, first of all, as a combination of characteristics discernible in individuals. Even when not explicitly formulated, this concept seems to have presented itself to the minds of the first naturalists. It held for many anthropologists and was expressed by some, in that in the course of their researches they classified individuals on the basis of random characters rather than working on groups (for example, Von Eickstedt, 1936; Schlaginhaufen, 1946).

The same concept seems to have influenced various definitions of race. Quatrefages (1859): "the totality of similar individuals"; Saller (1931): "a combination of hereditary characteristics of a certain variability . . . through which members of one race distinguish themselves from another race"; Martin (1928): "individuals belonging to one race have a certain number of characteristics in common, the combination of which distinguishes them from other groups."

The same idea figures in the first definition of "race" given in 1936 by the Royal Anthropological Institute: the hereditary characteristics which distinguish a race "are held to be such as usually apply to the generality of the individuals studied and not to be pathological characters." But the second definition, following the first, reflects another point of view and considers race as "a biological group or stock possessing in common an undetermined number of associated genetical characteristics by which it can be distinguished from other groups."

This question is linked up with that of the anthropometric "average" man, whose abstract nature seems to have been generally acknowledged. Anyhow, the idea that race is a combination of characteristics repeating itself in each individual case has not been separated from the concept of race as a group, defined by characteristics which do not necessarily combine in the same way in each individual. The difference appears if one compares, for instance, the above-quoted definitions with Broca's or Topinard's, which positively stated that types have no "real existence," or Haddon's point of view, declaring that racial types "exist only in our minds."

RACE AS AN ABSTRACT NOTION

This brings us to a very different idea which has spread more and more, whether linked or not with complementary notions, since the middle of the last century. Broca wrote that "in the experimental sciences, the concept of groups precedes the exact knowledge of every component element." Thus he thought that the physical anthropologist must not try to acknowledge directly every component of one population. The identification of the community is a difficult task, implying long study.

This work must be done in successive stages, and, before acknowledging races, the scientist must describe ethnic types. Topinard (1892) took up this distinction and developed it. The type of a population expresses its more frequent and pronounced characteristics; it is, above all, a "statistical" notion. The type of a race is defined in the same way, with the reservation above, however, that hereditary characteristics are here involved—characteristics which are not attributable to the continuous influence of environment. The determination of races present in a population is a "very laborious operation," for race is not "immediately apparent."

Broca had said that human types "are abstract, ideal concepts." Topinard specifies that race "exists only in a diffused state," for the anthropologist finds himself everywhere in the presence of peoples, not of races. The latter are not "obvious," for the typical individual is rare. "Only chance can give the average cranium or the typical cranium." Broca, after having defined types as abstractions, warned his readers against the tendency of personifying the latter. Topinard illustrates the same thesis with concrete examples but, at the same time, is bent on showing that type, although of an abstract conceptual nature, is a sort of statistical reality.

This way of looking at things had an indisputable effect on later anthropological literature. One finds traces of it in Collignon (1892) and Chantre (1887) and, later, in Deniker (1900), who expressed himself as follows: populations are formed

by the union of individuals belonging usually to two, three, or a greater number of somatological units. These units are theoretical types formed of an aggregation of physical characters combined in a certain way. The separate existence of these units may be established by a minute analysis of the physical characters taken haphazardly in any given ethnic group. Here then are entities, theoretical conceptions exactly like species in zoology; only instead of having within our reach the types of these species as in zoological collections, we are obliged to rest content with approximations thereto, for it is a very rare occurrence to meet with an individual representing the type of the somatological unit to which he belongs.

Among Anglo-American authors who professed similar ideas, one may mention Beddoe (1892–93) and especially Ripley (1899), who expressed himself as follows: "It is not essential to our position, that we should actually be able to isolate any considerable number, nor even a single one, of our perfect racial types in the life." Then he mentions and stresses the following quotation from Topinard:

Race in the present state of things is an abstract conception, a notion of continuity in discontinuity, of unity in diversity. It is the rehabilitation of a real but directly unattainable thing. . . . At the present time rarely, if indeed ever, we discover a single individual corresponding to our racial type in every detail. It exists for us nevertheless.

The idea of "race," an abstract notion, reappears with certain modifications in the works of most Russian physical anthropologists, for example, Vorobieff, as well as in that of Mendes Corrêa (1927), Hooton (1926), and many others. One may say, without risk of committing a grave error, that it is almost a common notion at the present time. Nevertheless, it has not completely supplanted the idea that race manifests itself in the combination of traits in the individual. Sometimes both attitudes coexist in one and the same author. The classifying of individuals by racial categories still exists: Czekanowski even stressed the determination of the systematic status of individuals; he thinks that the consideration of Mendelian laws may make this task easier (1920, 1928).

Developed in the course of the last century, the idea of race as an "abstract notion" precedes, historically speaking, the ideas of the biometrical anthropologists. Apart from a few exceptions, the ideas of the latter were anticipated only from afar. What stands out is the idea that race, at least in the first approximation, is concerned not with individuals but with groups or populations.

BIOMETRICAL ANTHROPOLOGY; THE "STATISTICAL RACE"

Among the physical anthropologists who considered race as an abstract notion, Topinard was probably alone in stressing the fact that racial types are essentially defined by a set of characteristics, such as maximum frequencies, modes, and means. The use of these parameasures became known in anthropology during the last century, but without giving rise to a methodological or doctrinal pronouncement (except for Topinard and, before him, for the Irishman, Grattan, whose article, published in 1858, passed unnoticed).

The essential difference between this tendency and that of the biometrical school consists in the fact that the latter, following Galton's works and Pearson's, use more refined statistical tools and more complex notions than those of mode, means, and dispersion. It consists also in the fact that biometricians were concerned with what Broca or Deniker would have considered types or ethnic groups rather than races. In their studies on European samples, they did not look for racial components, perhaps because, following Pearson, they admitted that the elements amalgamated in these mixtures were nearly impossible to detect. Pearson, indeed, recalled the fact that "we talk as if it was our population which was mixed, and not our germplasm" (1920).

However, the work of the biometrical school—or of the biometrical method—also dealt with widely separated populations or populations belonging to distinct ethnical agglomerations for instance, various tribes of a region; in this case they contributed to the establishment of distinction, sometimes identities, without the admittedly different groups being necessarily racially defined. In opposition to anthropologists who tried to isolate the racial components of populations, biometricians preferred to compare groups which, prior to research, had already been separated according to geographic, ethnographic, or social criteria.

On this level, several attempts have been made to make statistics an instrument of human taxonomy. Pearson (1926) had established the coefficient of racial likeness. Morant and others used it in the comparative study of crania or populations. But the use of this coefficient has not become generalized, and it has been violently criticized on purely mathematical grounds (Fisher, 1936). Czekanowski and his school have also used a statistical process which sometimes causes them to be placed among the representatives of biometry. This method is indeed independent, it does not seem to be comparable to that of Pearson's school, and it has also been criticized for mathematical reasons (Stolyhwo, 1926; Schwidetzki, 1936).

At the present time, two other much more complicated procedures seem highly favored as statistico-taxonomic methods: the discriminant function proposed by Fisher (1940) and the "generalized distance statistic," due to the works of Mahalanobis, Majumdar, and Rao (1941). Stevens (1945) has highly recommended the use of the former in anthropology, but practically speaking, it has hardly begun to spread. As to the "generalized distance," it was used first by the authors of the method, then more recently by Trevor (1947) in his study of certain African populations.

Perfected by distinguished mathematicians, these methods have not been criticized as regards their intrinsic value. But they are too difficult to become widely used. Competent judges have sometimes expressed the opinion that one must have serious reasons to undertake the long and intricate calculations they require. In so far as these two methods are used, they permit one to locate, one with regard to another, several populations simultaneously defined by several characteristics. Besides this, they also enable one to attribute, to one group rather than to another, individuals isolated according to the considered characteristics. The practical difficulties grow with the number of populations and characteristics.

GEOGRAPHICAL OR TERRITORIAL ASPECT OF RACE

We have just seen that the notion of race varies considerably according to epochs, schools, and authors. It is thus interesting to establish that, in the conclusions regarding the identity and number of races, there is often much less disagreement than one could have foretold from the doctrinal or methodological premises. It is probable that some divergences are smoothed out because many physical anthropologists, whether they choose to do so or not, make use of the geographical factor.

On the one hand, it is often admitted that race is "independent" of territory, that its area of dispersion may be discontinuous, and that several races border on the same region. On the other hand, an idea common to authors with different viewpoints consists in the race not being defined by the combination of characteristics one may find in individuals taken one by one, but by a combination of characteristics to be found in a determined geographical setting.

This last idea is implicit in the doctrines of those who, like Agassiz (1853), made the zones occupied by human races correspond to the great subdivisions of animal geography. Although inclosed in a very different context, the same notion is implied in the doctrines which make of race an abstract concept, and sometimes, too, in those of biometricians. Though admitting that a population—at least a European population—is a mixture of races, Broca established maps showing the territorial variations of somatic characteristics and used them to delimit the distribution of racial types. This process has been largely used in anthropology, especially by Ripley, Deniker, Lundborg, and many others. Ehrenreich (1897), Schlaginhaufen (1914), Tchepourkovski (1917), and more recently Bounak (1938) have particularly stressed the importance of the geographical criterion in anthropology. It is probable that the taking into consideration of this principle explains the agreement between classifications which do not make use of exactly the same criteria.

THE CRITERIA OF RACIAL DISTINCTION

Although the choice of different criteria does not in practice involve serious disagreements, it nonetheless creates a serious problem. We have seen, regarding the instability of some somatic descriptions, that anthropologists have sometimes been led to sort out and to choose the "good" racial characteristics, that is to say, those which do not seem to change readily or those which seem, through their nature, to escape natural selection. But the question presents still another aspect.

A type is defined only by a combination of characteristics. Topinard recalled that, if one takes into account only one trait, the type vanishes. How many characteristics must one retain? It is clear that this question has not found a unanimous answer. One can only say that, on the whole, two neighboring tendencies are visible: one prefers to restrict the number of items used in classification, though without limiting the number of studied characteristics. One of the arguments that can be put forward in favor of this restriction is well known: as soon as one multiplies the number of characteristics, that of the classifiable individuals drops sharply. The other tendency, which does not bother with the classification of individuals or at least stresses the study of populations, tends to take a greater number of characteristics into consideration. This second tendency seems to take stock of different considerations: a greater number of racial characteristics will lead to a more complete, more precise, and more "natural" classification. On the contrary, a limited set of traits would risk leaving to one side significant and, from this point of view, important statistical differences.

One cannot say that, during the last decades, the second tendency has taken precedence over the first one. Rather, the two have been combined, and alongside classifications taking into account a limited number of characteristics, more or less sanctioned by custom, one may now find some which also, for instance, take into account the general body configuration. Hooton's (1931–47) represents one of the most conclusive cases.

Thus, by taking into account the general structure of the body, one meanwhile takes the risk of running up against an obstacle. The racial problem is here, in fact, added to that of constitutional types. This superimposition has given rise to the most disparate solutions. For some, constitutions, reduced to morphology only, exist in every race. For others, in two racially distinct populations, one finds different, though perhaps analogous, constitutional types. Yet others envisage constitutional types as mixed with races, notably in European populations, where one has tried to identify leptosomes and Nordics, athletics and Dinarics, pycnics and Alpines.

This last idea seems to have been abandoned. Biometrical research has shown that, in groups definitely distinct from the racial point of view, the same "bipolar deformation" of the mean population type is noticeable, though with some differences, which have been attributed to race (De Sousa, 1934; Schreider, 1951). This suggested the idea that differences in constitutional variations could offer a new criterion of racial distinction (Bean, 1926). But this suggestion has prompted little research.

Another point of view has been put forth regarding the connections between constitution and race. Bounak (1927) has advanced the hypothesis that constitutional types might represent outlines of new races. Weidenreich (1927) professed a similar opinion, when he considered the territorial predominance of some morphological types as otherwise unexplainable. A more moderate hypothesis considers some constitutional characteristics as liable to appear in the formation of races, in so far as these characteristics stand on a genetic basis. But to what extent do they possess such a basis? For lack of direct proofs, constitutionalists so far must be content with favorable presumptive evidence. But these presumptions are few, fewer still than those related to all the racial characteristics whose exact genetic nature is not yet known.

We now come to another aspect of the problem raised by the characteristics used in racial classifications. The idea that race is hereditary is generally admitted. It was certainly familiar to the first naturalists, although they admitted at the same time the rapidly modifying influence of environment and considered racial differences as more or less contingent. All the more reason that this idea of heredity should dominate the recent conceptions of race.

Hrdlička (1941) defined race as "a persistent strain, within any species, or broadly blood-connected individuals carrying steadily, i.e., hereditarily, more or less of well defined physical characteristics which distinguish them fairly from all other strains or races."

Hooton (1931) brings into his definition the idea of "common origin." Boas (1938) uses the same expression and specifies, besides, that race is a "stable type." It would be easy to quote other examples, showing that for anthropologists there is no race without heredity. However, since the earliest stage of its history, physical anthropology has come up, not only against the difficult problem of cross-breedings, but also against that of the modifications due to the continued influence of environment. And one must be careful to emphasize that, in this respect, there was no absolute divergence between partisans and opponents of the theory of acquired characteristics. The first were alone in contending that modifications due to the environment are recorded in the hereditary stock. But both easily acknowledged that certain changes due to external causes are not transmitted to the lineage. The difficulty consisted, therefore, in defining the boundaries of heredity.

Has the situation changed since? Physical anthropology has relied on genetics almost since its origin, and much more so than many branches of zoölogy. Unfortunately, however, genetics has drawn little of its data from man, and, as a result, the anthropologist has been handicapped in making practical use of its findings. Even now, in spite of certain sensational claims, its helpful nature lies almost solely in the study of blood groups. One has thus witnessed the appearance of various conceptions of "serological races" or "physiological races" which have developed progressively from the initial identification of one blood group with a race toward a more elaborated systematics of gene frequencies. These ideas may have satisfied certain anthropologists, but one may say without particular risk that the majority does not seem inclined to accept them as final. One does not feel that they have the right to neglect, for the benefit of serological characteristics alone, the whole body of traits which distinguish the human organism.

It seems that the present situation may be summed up as follows. According to one tendency, it is necessary to base the distinction of human varieties on characteristics whose genetic nature is securely known: therefore, in practice and until we know more, essentially on blood groups. According to the other tendency, physical anthropology must pursue the study of the phenotype. But this second point of view has itself evolved, since several recent anthropologists consider the phenotype as being principally the product of environment: thus implicitly and in spite of genetic premises, their conception of race does not differ practically from that of former naturalists. Buffon and many authors of the last century, whether followers of Lamarck or not, would have indorsed a doctrine explaining a certain number of racial differences environmentally, for instance, through diet (Coon, Garn, and Birdsell, 1950).

It is probable that, being more demanding than their predecessors, the modern neo-Lamarckists would undoubtedly in such a case ask for experimental proofs. In any case, most modern anthropologists interpret the phenotype in a very different manner: though acknowledging its elasticity, they suppose that it reflects, above all, its genotypic background. This justifies the idea of heredity which they maintain in their definitions of race.

For the first tendency, the research upon "good" and "bad" phenotypical characteristics should not be of too great interest. With the second tendency, it keeps all its importance, if by "good" characteristics one understands those which appear as relatively stable. The first tendency may be concerned with the phenotype "as a whole"; the second, hoping that the geneticists will not acknowledge themselves beaten, sometimes tries to establish more or less temporary distinctions and to discern characteristics whose hereditary nature has some chances of being confirmed, even if one cannot make them enter into a precise Mendelian scheme.

THE PROBLEM OF MENTAL CHARACTERISTICS

Yet another aspect worthy of separate consideration is that of the mental characteristics of human races. This question has often been examined in the light of ideas foreign to science. During the last century, some authors kept themselves to physical characteristics only because they felt some repugnance in referring to the "soul" in a matter wherein zoölogy was principally concerned. Very recently, on the contrary, doctrines of political inspiration have proclaimed the intimate liaison between mental characteristics and the variations considered as racial.

If modern anthropologists often take into account physical characteristics only, it is for very different reasons. Some are convinced that mental differences are trivial, except those attributable to the type of culture or to the level of education. Others think that, for lack of precise knowledge, the problem is still too abstruse and the mental characteristics of races too difficult to determine for one to take them into account. Thus, practically, most modern anthropologists consider only the physical differences.

A different attitude is present, however, in a certain number of modern works. Here are some examples. Boas (1931) defined race as "a group of people that have certain bodily and perhaps also mental characteristics in common." Consequently, he adopted a circumspect attitude. Fischer (1933) is more categorical: "Race is a group of men characterized by the common hereditary possession of a physical and mental type distinguishing it from other groups." Czekanowski (1936) attributes to every race a certain number of mental traits: the Nordic race would be full of initiative, disciplined, with a high sense of duty; the Lapponoid race would be intelligent but undisciplined; and so on. Such repertories of mental qualities rarely figure today in the classifications. Czekanowski, besides, endeavored, above all, to acknowledge race according to somatic characteristics. The few anthropologists who take mental characteristics into account seem to add them only when their list of races is established.

One must finally report that the question of mental or cultural characteristics sometimes appears in physical anthropology in a slightly different form and without having repercussions, at least for the time being, on classifications. The notion of "Isolate" seems to act in this way. If the isolation may indeed be geographical, it may also be cultural or social—hence a possible co-incidence between physical and mental characteristics. The question is thus raised as to whether it is really a coincidence or a genetically based correlation. Ashley Montagu (1945), for instance, defines race (which he names "ethnic group") as "one of a number of populations comprising the simple species *Homo sapiens* which individually maintain their differences, physical and cultural, by means of isolating mechanisms, such as geographical and social barriers." For certain authors, physical differences determined by cultural isolation, should the occasion arise, may by inverse action lead to hereditary mental differences. Darlington and Mather (1950) go as far as to postulate an accentuation of these differences; they point out "the increasing contrast of genetic capacity for culture between different genetic groups."

The motivation is new, but certain implications of the idea of both biological and social isolation recall a doctrine which formerly met with some success: that connected, among others, with Vacher de Lapouge, which makes races and social classes (1909) "coincide." This doctrine was given up by anthropologists, and we owe its new growth principally to a few geneticists. The problem of cultural differences has been practically left out of the field of anthropology for a long time; in this way, it has some chances of being reinstated. But it is hardly probable that mental and cultural characteristics will ever be used in classifications.

GENERAL RULES OF CLASSIFICATION

After having thus cleared the way, let us investigate the nature of anthropological classifications. Theoretically, a classification may be founded on two distinct criteria: that of likeness (John Ray was probably the first to follow this principle) and that of kinship (Tournefort). The first classifications of human races, essentially intuitive, were based simultaneously on the idea of likeness and common ancestry, even if these principles were not explicitly formulated. It was only at a later stage, after physical anthropology was born, that the problem was realized to be complex.

Blumenbach was perfectly aware of the relative value of classifications, and he acknowledged that his was arbitrary: the distinction of races, such as he proposed it, was, above all, to be a help to scientists. The idea that the number of races could be nearly unlimited had become familiar to anthropologists from the beginning of the nineteenth century. Hence classification was, above all, for them a means of putting in order a sum of chaotic facts: the number of subdivisions included was largely a question of opportunity or convenience. Naturalists had already proclaimed that classifications had been devised "for the convenience of scientists."

The oldest classifications were the least artificial in reflecting mainly obvious differences, related to the principal varieties or "great races" of recent authors. But the inadequacy of such a scheme whose subdivisions were too large was soon recognized. However, people were not long in acknowledging that a more precise classification was very difficult to accomplish. Moreover, for a long time there was no reliable information regarding many populations. Being doubtful, certain authors preferred to keep to large categories. Others, on the contrary, multiplied races. Because of this, they were more than once reproached for having introduced linguistic or ethnographic groups into classifications which should have taken only somatic characteristics into account.

Toward the end of the last century, however, a considerable effort was made to eliminate in anthropological classification all that was not morphological. Deniker (1889) even tried to establish a "natural" classification, comparable to that of botanists. He systematized several combinations of somatic characteristics and thus defined a large number of races. Others have followed similar methods, but with a more or less different choice of characteristics, so that two classifications inspired by the same "natural" method are not necessarily superimposable. Nor are they necessarily conflicting. A certain number of differences is due only to the number of subdivisions, which vary from one author to another. When the larger categories of one classification agree with categories which another considers as secondary divisions, one may admit that there is no real contradiction. Nor is the disagreement very serious if a group whose existence is acknowledged by two different classifiers is not attached by them to the same category of superior rank (as, for example, the case of Bushmen, Polynesians, etc.). The following case is strange and may seem surprising: one and the same race has been annexed to the blond group by one author, to the brown group by another. Properly speaking, the population which allowed us to acknowledge this "race" numbers, above all, "brunette"-haired individuals.

One must therefore distinguish two distinct aspects in anthropological classifications: that of the identification of types and that of their hierarchical ranking. Regarding the identification, the following factors promote agreement, even if the classifications do not exactly depend on the same criteria: (a) The existence of a certain number of categories separated by manifest differences, upon which everyone agrees; on close inspection it is not only the great races one quotes generally in this connection—Yellows, Blacks, Whites, Australoids—but also some other groups, such as the Pygmy races, the Bushman race, the Ainu race. (b) The existence, among the great races, of a certain number of types showing a distinctive peculiarity sharp enough to be easily separated within the limits of the White Europeans. Such, for instance, is the case of the fair, blue-eyed element, which is not necessarily dolichocephalic, and even of the brown elements, which are generally distributed among several races; but, as regards the latter, disagreement is greater among the classifiers, sharper distinctions being difficult. In the same way, among the Black great race, the distinction of types, such as the Nilotic race, does not seem to give rise to a discussion. (c) A third and last factor is that, as has already been mentioned, all the authors take into account the geographical distribution of the various human groups, even if they do not accept it as a classifying criterion. Bounak (1938) has emphasized that the territorial distribution of the characteristics and of their combinations was neither fortuitous nor completely confused. There is here an element of unification.

One must not conclude from the foregoing, however, that racial classifications are "accidental" and that the basis of all the recent classifications is one and the same. Certain coincidences seem purely fortuitous. Dixon, for instance (1923), based his classification upon three arbitrarily chosen characteristics, more precisely upon three indices, and upon their numerical value. He thus determined a fair number of possible combinations, and it happens that, among the latter, some agree with races known from another source. In this case agreement seems to be due to pure chance. On the contrary, the agreement between Ripley's and Deniker's classifications, as regards the European races, reflects a definite situation, both somatic and geographic. Their differences seem essentially due to the fact that Ripley was satisfied with three principal races, whereas Deniker tried to establish more subtle distinctions.

Finally, one must consider another fact: time affects classifications, and the latest sometimes complement the oldest, without really taking their place. Thus, for Amerindians, Imbelloni's (1938) classification probably may be taken as a development of Eickstedt's (1934).

Although it is fairly easy to acknowledge the agreement between the various classifications regarding the identity or existence of some races, it is with regard to their ranking or reciprocal position that one more easily notices divergences. Must one attribute the Asiatic Negroes to the Black group? Is it correct to unite in one and the same race the various Pygmy types scattered over the world? Are we even right in considering as belonging to the same race human agglomerations which show the same combination of features, though they are separated geographically?

This last question raises the problem in its more general form, and the answer is generally in the affirmative: Two populations showing one combination of characteristics are commonly classified under one racial heading; this is the fundamental principle of racial maps. But this answer again involves the definition or concept of "race," for it is a long time since similarity has been declared not to be proof, but only presumptive evidence, of kinship.

As far back as 1857, Aitken Meigs, after having stressed the gradations linking cranial forms, had expressed the opinion that differences between these did not always imply a diversity of origin and that, inversely, great similarity did not warrant an especially close kinship. The anthropologists of the nineteenth century either invoked the possibility of convergence or recalled that different racial cross-breedings could produce similar types. At the present time, geneticists take over the same concept and recall that one and the same phenotype may suit different genotypes. Here, then, one values the distinction between the classification according to likeness (John Ray) and the classification according to kinship (Tournefort). For some people the fact of race, such as we know it, is nothing but the establishment of a similarity. For others, one must distinguish the particular situations; where similar but geographically separated populations are concerned, one has no right to conclude in favor of their close kinship unless one possesses arguments other than their similarity—archeological, ethnographic, or even historical or linguistic proofs.

In spite of all these reservations, the notion of kinship still remains dominant in the minds of classifiers. Waitz, in one of the best anthropological summaries of the question (1858), declared that, in nearly every classification of mankind, the idea of a common descent of the elements grouped in one and the same race was at least tacitly admitted. The situation does not seem to have changed much since, and the best proof is furnished by the fact that the authors of classifications often publish them with the addition of genealogical trees.

TAXONOMIC POSITION OF RACES

If one admits (Cuénot, 1936, for instance) that the species may be defined by three pairs of criteria: morphology and physiology (M), ecology and distribution (E), internal fecundity and external sterility (S), it appears that the immense majority of men constitutes a group to which the MES triad fully applies. Therefore, they correspond to one and the same species, *Homo sapiens;* and, from the point of view of a general classification, this is a "collective species" (polytypic species, Linnean species).

Being subdivisions of *Homo sapiens,* races are categories inferior to the species. They are, on the other hand, superior to the "elementary species" (biotypes, jordanons) of the geneticists. Obviously, in no human race are the hereditary potentialities homogeneous for all individuals.

Races thus occupy an intermediary place between the collective species and the elementary species. But on such a scale, zoölogists and botanists commonly distinguish two kinds of subdivisions (for certain authors, such as Mayr, 1942, this separation is, for the greater part, artificial): those defined by a precise geographical localization, the *geotypes,* and those defined by life in a given ecological environment, the *ecotypes.* From this point of view, it appears that human races are, above all, geographical units, geotypes. In Europe an extraordinary racial mixture had for centuries created an intermingling which is the despair of physical anthropologists. Even there, one still succeeds, more or less, in placing each race in a limited geographical area. With primitive races (Bushman, African Pygmies, etc.) the localization becomes much more precise, and we have seen that, for some authors, it even becomes the basis of the concept of race. The attribution of a human race to a precise ecological environment is, on the contrary, much more difficult to prove, and most arguments put forward fail in the light of critical investigation. Through selection, certain characteristics undoubtedly have a tendency to be better preserved in certain environments, but one may not say that these environments have really created racial types with all their characteristics. Perhaps the case of various Pyg-

mies is an exception, although one may not positively state that forest is not for them a zone of secondary refuge.

The subdivisions of species do not all have the same value. In the collective species, zoölogists and botanists generally distinguish two degrees: categories of first rank or *subspecies:* they generally have the value of geographic units, of geotypes; and categories of second rank or *varieties,* which also may be geotypes but are often ecotypes, above all, among plants.

For human races, there is also **a** hierarchy, and people generally agree in recognizing two categories: the *primary races* or *great races* or *racial groups* (*Rassenkreise*) and the *secondary races* or *second-rank races* (races *sensu stricto* of various authors).

Great races correspond to the fundamental divisions of mankind in our time. Their geographical localization is very marked. They have the value of real subspecies. One may therefore apply to them the trinominal classification: *H. sapiens albus, H. sapiens niger,* and so on.

Various authors (for instance, G. Sergi, 1911; R. Gates, 1948) have likened these categories to species. It is certain that the morphological and probably physiological differences between them may be large. But if one takes into account their unquestionable interfecundity, expressed not only by the production of fruitful hybrids but by that of entire transitional groups, such a notion cannot be defended. The community of structure of all living men, the existence in all of an identical physical background, in spite of a probable diversity in the mental and affective reactions, further add to the former argument. The subspecies of *H. sapiens* are undoubtedly—like every subspecies —new species in the making. They could have reached the superior category, had the isolation which accompanied their birth persisted. Actually, they cannot be considered as having

reached this stage. One may even presume, under existing conditions, that
they are going to follow an inverse
path.

Secondary races are comparable to
the "varieties" of botanists and zoölogists, but with this difference, that, as
primary races, they are geographical
units. They have also been considered
by various authors as species, and Giuffrida-Ruggeri (1913) has even pronounced the name of "elementary species." It is only too obvious that such a
term cannot be applied to them.

Among the races *sensu stricto*, the existence of third-ranking categories, the
local types, sometimes also called *subraces (Gautypen)*, may often be revealed by detailed analysis. The hypothesis has been put forward that these
types of third rank would be ecotypes.
They are modifications of racial types
in a set environment—seaside regions,
mountainous regions, desert regions—
modifications which one may equate
with those of mammals living in the
same environment. One should then
distinguish among second-ranking races
geographical subgroups which one
could call "subraces," and ecological
subgroups, which could be the real local types. But the exact nature of these
local types has not been thoroughly
studied. One does not know, in particular, to what extent their characteristics
are hereditary.

MISCELLANEOUS

Before finishing this rapid review,
one must point out some facts which
have not appeared in the previous paragraphs. When anthropology stresses
that race is distinguished essentially by
physical characteristics, it is sometimes
meant that not only anatomy (morphology included) but also physiology is
thereby concerned. Actually, physiological anthropology is far behind anatomy,
and this not only because of technical
difficulties but because functional characteristics are often very unstable, so

that differences, if existing, may be established only with great difficulty. No
classification as yet takes into account
the physiological characteristics; anyhow, such an attempt would be impossible before a sufficient number of comparable data has been collected. (These
remarks do not apply to blood groups.)

This does not prevent knowledge of
certain differences which are not being
used in a general classification. Other
important facts have been pointed out
regarding pathology: the differences in
susceptibility of Blacks and Whites toward certain illnesses is currently admitted. In several cases the hereditary
(racial) nature of these differences has
been questioned or doubted; but in
other cases, regarding, for instance,
skin diseases, it does not seem to raise
serious objections. Other cases could be
quoted, bearing on racially distinct
populations: for instance, the very un-
even susceptibility to influenza of certain Pacific Islanders compared to that
of Chinese workers who have immigrated to their islands (Ednet, Donnelley, Isaacs, and Ingram, 1950).

The racial variations of morbidity
have been pointed out for more than a
century. Their real scientific study has
recently begun. This study, together
with its practical importance, must be
pointed out without our being able to
strike a balance at the present time.

In conclusion, it is advisable to mention that research on subjects of the
three main racial groups (Whites, Yellows, and Blacks) agrees on the existence, in each, of twenty-four pairs of
chromosomes. The divergences between authors concern the interpretation of male sexual chromosomes, some
agreeing on the XO formula, others on
the XY, but the partisans of both interpretations use subjects of the same
race. Chromosomic racial differences,
therefore, do not seem to exist, and
there is no reason to speak about cyto-
logical races in man.

BIBLIOGRAPHY

AITKEN MEIGS, J. 1857. "On the Cranial Characteristics of the Races of Man." In NOTT, K. C., and GLIDDON, G. R., *The Indigenous Races of the Earth*. Philadelphia.

BEAN, R. B. 1926. "Human Types," *Quarterly Review of Biology*, I, 360–92.

BEDDOE, J. 1892–93. *The Anthropological History of Europe*. London: Paisley.

BIASUTTI, R. 1912. "Studi sulla distribuzione dei caratteri e dei tipi antropologici," *Memorie geografiche*, supplément no. 18 à la *Rivista geografica italiana*. Firenze.

BOAS, F. 1931. "Race and Progress," *Science*, N.S., LXXIV, 1–18.

BOULE, M., and VALLOIS, H. V. 1932. "L'Homme fossile d'Asselar," *Archives de l'Institut de Paléontologie humaine*, Mém. 9. Paris: Masson.

BROCA, P. 1866. "Anthropologie." In *Dictionnaire encyclopédique des sciences médicales*, V, 276. Paris.

BUFFON, G. LECLERC, COMTE DE. 1749. "Histoire générale et particulière avec la description du Cabinet du Roi," *L'Homme*. Paris.

BUNAK, V.; GREMIATZKI, M.; *et al.* 1948. "Nauka o racatik i racism." *Nauchnogo Issledovatelskogo Institut antropologii moskovskogo Gosudarstvennogo Universiteta, Trudi*, Vol. IV. Moscow and Leningrad: Academy of Sciences.

COLLIGNON, R. 1892. "Considérations générales sur l'association respective des caractères anthropologiques," *L'Anthropologie*, III, 43–54.

COON, C. S.; GARN, S. M.; and BIRDSELL, J. B. 1950. *Races: A Study of the Problems of Race Formation in Man*. Springfield, Ill.: Charles C Thomas.

COUNT, E. W. 1950. *This Is Race*. New York: Schuman.

CZEKANOWSKI, J. 1913. "Zarys metod statystycznych w sastosovaniu de antropologji," *Prace Towarzystwega Naukowego Warsawskiego*, No. 5. Varsovie.

———. 1928. "Das Typenfrequenzgesetz," *Anthropologischer Anzeiger*, V, 335–59.

———. 1935. "Les buts et les méthodes de l'École Anthropologique Polonaise; I," *L'Anthropologie*, VL, 573–90.

DAHLBERG, G. 1942. "An Analysis of the Conception of Race and a New Method of Distinguishing Races," *Human Biology*, XIV, 372–85.

DAVENPORT, C. B. 1929. "Race-crossing in Jamaica," *Carnegie Institution of Washington*, Pub. No. 395.

DENIKER, J. 1889. "Essai d'une classification des races humaines basée uniquement sur les caractères physiques," *Bulletins de la Société d'Anthropologie de Paris*, XII (ser. 3), 320–36.

EDNET, M.; DONNELLEY, M.; ISAACS, A.; and INGRAM, M. W. 1950. "Influenza in an Isolated Community," *The Lancet*, CCLVIII, No. 6. London.

EICKSTEDT, E. VON. 1938–44. *Rassenkunde und Rassengeschichte der Menschheit*. 2d ed. Stuttgart: Enke.

EWING, J. F. 1950. "Hyperbrachycephaly as Influenced by Cultural Conditioning," *Papers of the Peabody Museum of American Archaeology and Ethnology*, Vol. XXIII, No. 2. Cambridge: Harvard University.

FISCHER, E. 1933. "Rasse und Rassenbildung." In *Handwörterbuch der Naturwissenschaften*. 2d ed. Pp. 198–214. Jena: G. Fischer.

FISCHER, R. A. 1936. "The Use of Multiple Measurements in Taxinomic Problems," *Annals of Eugenics*, VII, 179–88. London.

GATES, R. RUGGLES. 1948. *Human Ancestry from a Genetical Point of View*. Cambridge: University Press.

GIUFFRIDA-RUGGERI, V. 1913. "L'Uomo attuale; una specie collettiva," *Società Dante Alighieri*. Milano.

HADDON, A. C. 1924. *The Races of Man and Their Distribution*. 2d ed. Cambridge: Milner & Co.

HOOTON, E. A. 1926. "Methods of Racial Analysis," *Science*, LXIII, 75–81.

HRDLIČKA, A. 1941. "The Races of Man." In *Scientific Aspects of the Race Problem*, pp. 161–87. New York: Longmans, Green & Co.

LUNDBORG, H. 1931. "Die Rassenmischung beim Menschen," *Bibliographia genetica*, Vol. VIII.

MAHALONOBIS, P. G.; MAJUMDAR, D. N.; and RAO, G. R. 1949. "Anthropometric

Survey of the United Provinces, 1941: A Statistical Study," *Sankhya*, IX, 89–324.

MARTIN, R. 1928. *Lehrbuch der Anthropologie*. 2d ed. Vol. I. Jena: Fischer.

MAYR, E. 1942. *Systematics and the Origin of Species*. New York: Columbia University Press.

MORANT, G. M. 1949. "Changes in the Size of British People in the Past Hundred Years," *Homenaje a don Luis de Hoyos Sainz*, I, 235–41. Madrid.

NEUVILLE, H. 1933. "L'espèce, la race et le métissage en anthropologie," *Archives de l'Institut de Paléontologie Humaine*, Mém. 11. Paris: Masson.

PEARSON, K. 1920. "The Problems of Anthropology," *Scientific Monthly*, XI, 451–58.

QUATREFAGES, A. DE. 1889. *Introduction a l'étude des races humaines*. Paris: Schleicher.

Race and Culture. 1936. London: The Royal Anthropological Institute, Le Play House Press.

SALLER, K. 1931. "Die Rassenfrage," *Der Erdball*, V, No. 9, 331–37.

SCHLAGINHAUFEN, O. 1946. *Anthropologia Helvetica; I, Die Anthropologie des Eidgenossenschaft*. I. Zürich: O. Füssli.

SCHREIDER, E. 1941–46. "Caractéristiques respiratoires et variations constitutionnelles chez les Annamites," *L'Anthropologie*, L, 491–504.

SCHWIDETZKY, I. 1936. "Das Geltungsbereich des sogenannten Typenfrequenz-gesetzes," *Zeitschrift für Rassenkunde*, III, 156–61.

SHAPIRO, H. 1939. *Migration and Environment*. New York: Oxford University Press.

STEVENS, W. L. 1945. "Analise discriminante: questoes de método," *Rivista da Faculdade de Ciencias da Universidade de Coimbra*, XIII, No. 1.

STOLYHWO, K. 1926. "Sur la méthode de la diagnose différentielle et sur son application dans l'anthropologie," *Anthropologie*, IV, 220–26. Prague.

STRATZ, C. H. 1904. "Das Problem der Rasseneinteilung der Menschheit," *Archiv für Anthropologie*, I (N.F.), 189–200.

TOPINARD, P. 1879. "De la notion de race en anthroplogie," *Revue d'Anthropologie*, II (ser. 2), 589–660.

TREVOR, J. C. 1947. "The Physical Characters of the Sandawe," *Journal of the Royal Anthropological Institute*, LXXVII, 61–80.

VACHER DE LAPOUGE, G. 1909. *Race et milieu social: essais d'anthroposociologie*. Paris: M. Rivière.

VALLOIS, H. V. 1951. *Les races humaines*. 3d ed. Paris: Presses Universitaires de France.

WALCHER, G. 1905. "Über die Entstehung von Brachy- und Dolichocephalie durch willkürliche Beeinflussung des kindlichen Schädels," *Zentralblatt für Gynäkologie*, XXIX, 193–96.

WEIDENREICH, F. 1927. *Rasse und Körperbau*. Berlin: Springer.

The Contributions of Genetics to Anthropology

By WILLIAM C. BOYD

ONE PURPOSE of physical anthropology, according to Morant,* has been "to unravel the course of human evolution, and it may be taken for granted to-day that the proper study of the natural history of man is concerned essentially with the mode and the path of his descent." While it is doubtful whether all physical anthropologists restrict their studies solely to data bearing on the course of human evolution, nevertheless Morant is probably right in implying that such information seems of high importance to most workers in the field.

Another problem, closely connected with the first, has been to classify men into physical races. Various systems of classification have been used, which have changed with the advance of the science; at the present time, one of the most valuable tools of classification is our growing knowledge of human genetics.

In studying human races, we must consider not only the present-day frequencies of human physical characteristics but also the probable mechanisms by which evolution brought them about. The main agencies causing evolution

* It was the original plan to have the bibliographies of the inventory papers restricted to a selected list of no more than one page in length. This plan was later changed but notice was not given in time for some of the authors to amplify the bibliography and refer to each item specifically in the text.

are, without doubt, mutation and selection. Before evolutionists became acquainted with genetics, other more mystical evolutionary mechanisms had been proposed, and their influence still lingers in some of the anthropological thought of today. One of these fossil remnants is the concept of orthogenesis.

Some workers, paleontologists in particular, were impressed by the seemingly unerring way in which an organism marched from an undifferentiated beginning towards a definite goal. They considered that such evolution could not be accounted for by the Darwinian concepts of variation and selection but must have been directed from the beginning towards its ultimate destiny by some sort of force. The term "orthogenesis" was proposed for this mechanism by Haacke, and the idea was popularized by Eimer and others.

The concept of orthogenesis usually seems to involve two suppositions. The first of these asserts that there is to be found in nature a tendency towards evolution in straight or continuing lines, as shown by paleontological material. The second is the assumption of the existence of some sort of mystic, vitalistic force or principle which not only determines the tendency of organisms to evolve but also directs their evolution along certain apparently predetermined lines. Modern believers in orthogenesis sometimes disclaim any belief in the second part of the doctrine, but an examination of their writings generally reveals a tendency to rely either on this or on some similar concept of an inherent tendency towards perfection.

Now, there is no doubt that some rectilinearity can often be observed in evolution. According to Simpson, the best part of the paleontological record is made up of lines that evolve more or less in one direction over long periods of time. Nevertheless, rectilinear evolution is far from universal. The example most often quoted is the evolution of the horse, involving a gradual increase in size, reduction in number of toes, increase in height and complication of teeth, as if evolution proceeded unhesitatingly in a straight line from *Eohippus* to the modern horse. But this is totally at variance with the facts. All sorts of horses evolved during the Miocene and Pliocene, differing radically in regard to teeth, toes, and so on. One Miocene line developed exceptionally high teeth; however, this was not a continuation of an old "orthogenetic" trend but a new tendency.

A study of genetics shows that orthogenesis is quite unnecessary to explain the degree of rectilinearity actually observed in evolution. It is true that we now think of evolution as resulting from the action of selection on genetic mutations. But this does not mean that there are no limits to what this mechanism can accomplish. The genes of any animal which survives and competes successfully with its fellows in the struggle for existence must be reasonably harmonious with one another, for anything else is not compatible with the continued existence and reproduction of the animal. Each creature is like its ancestors in all but a few respects. The differences which have arisen must necessarily coexist in harmony with the more extensive, more complex, elements which are not different. Each character

is dependent on the interaction of many genes, so that it will be easier to continue a line of evolutionary change for which many of the modifiers are already present than to start off on an entirely new line. Species are not constructed *de novo*, but on the basis of genotypes already existing. In most cases no sort of modification which is within the capabilities of the existing genes and possible mutations would be definitely advantageous, and in many other cases only one particular modification would be an advantage. Thus the unidirectional trend of much evolution becomes clear from a genetic point of view.

Another feature of genetic knowledge which helps to account for directional evolution is the observation that mutation seldom occurs entirely at random at a gene locus. Usually, certain mutations are more frequent than others, and evolution in a direction utilizing these mutations would thus be easier. Examples are known from many studies on *Drosophila*.

One argument formerly brought up by the orthogeneticists against the postulated predominant role of mutation and selection in evolution depended on the very slight nature of the early stages of certain evolutionary trends. For example, the horns of the titanotheres arose gradually from mere thickenings of the skull bones, and developed into large, fully developed weapons. It was asserted that the incipient stages of this bone thickening could not have been of any advantage or use to the animals possessing them; the structure, it was said, started first, and its usefulness came later. Simpson thinks it quite likely that even the initial stages were, in fact, useful. The titanotheres had already become stocky, lumbering creatures with stout heads, very likely addicted to butting one another and their enemies, as they had no other means of fighting. Thickening of the bones of the butting region, no matter how slight, would constitute a definite advantage. One of the lessons of the modern work on variation and survival is that slight modifications actually have differential effects on mortality, and the mathematical work of Fisher and others has demonstrated how profound may be the effect of very slight selection pressures. *Evolution is best understood by thinking of it as always adaptive.* Modern genetics has shown clearly how, as small differences due to single genes accumulate in the course of evolution, the small differences gradually become major differences. When enough gene differences and/or chromosome alterations have accumulated, we have a new species.

If evolution, essentially, is nothing but a change in gene frequencies, by what processes of genetic change were certain variations brought about? Over long periods of time, varieties of animals which were originally similar or identical may become extremely different from one another. The number of genes eventually involved is doubtless large, and separate species may ultimately result. Nevertheless, as far as we know at present, leaving aside chromosomal rearrangements, with which we shall not deal in the present discussion, all inherited modification is the result of (*a*) the production of new genes, (*b*) the loss of genes, and (*c*) the accumulation of changes in gene frequencies. Let us consider the frequency of any gene (say the blood-group B gene in human populations), and ask ourselves what evolutionary agencies might possibly operate to alter the frequency of this gene. Whatever mechanisms we find in operation are, so far as we know, the same ones which have operated in the past to alter the frequencies of human genes and are going to alter such frequencies in the future.

SELECTION

If a certain dominant human gene had a selective advantage over its recessive allele of only one part in 1,000 (or 0.1 per cent), its frequency in the population in question would be increased from 5 to 50 per cent in somewhat less than 3,000 generations, a period of about 60,000–70,000 years. With the possible exception of the Rh blood factors, there is no evidence concerning physical characteristics which is exact enough to enable us to estimate whether any of them have a selective advantage as great as, or perhaps greater than, this. It is extremely likely that some or most of them do. In particular, the general relation between pigmentation and warm sunny climates suggests a selective advantage for pigmentation genes in such environments. The frequency of blonds among the Scandinavians might suggest that in regions with deficient sunlight the reverse would also be true. The rather highly pigmented Eskimo seem to constitute an exception, but it is the opinion of some scholars that they have not inhabited their present cold environment for nearly as long as 70,000 years. Also, the frequency of recessive genes —and most genes for light pigmentation seem to be recessive—increases much more slowly than that of dominants, especially when they are rather scarce in the population to begin with.

Even dominants increase rather slowly at first, and a population starting with 0.18 per cent of a new advantageous dominant gene with a selective advantage of 0.1 per cent would require 3,500 generations to build the frequency of the new gene up to 5.62 per cent. If we start with 0.27 per cent of an advantageous recessive gene, it would require 16,000 generations, or about 400,000 years, to increase it to 4.54 per cent. Perhaps the Eskimo started with too low a frequency of recessive genes for pigment, and mutations to genes for low pigmentation have rarely occurred in this stock. In Table 1 are shown the probabilities that a recessive gene will become fixed in the population (that is, will completely replace the alternative gene or genes at the same chromosome locus) in various population sizes, in three different cases—a selective advantage of

TABLE 1*

CHANCES OF "FIXATION" OF A RECESSIVE GENE, ASSUMING ONE SUCH GENE IN POPULATIONS OF VARIOUS SIZES

Population Size	Advantage of $yy = 0.01$	No Advantage ("Neutral" Gene)	Disadvantage of $yy = 0.01$ (or Advantage = -0.01)
10.........	0.05	0.05	0.05
50.........	0.013	0.010	0.007
200.........	0.0057	0.0025	0.0003
800.........	0.0027	0.0006	0.0000

* The symbol y represents the recessive gene, and yy the homozygous recessive type. Table is taken from J. Wright, *Heredity*, XXXIII (1942), 333-34.

ferent cases—a selective advantage of the double recessive of 0.01, a selective disadvantage of 0.01, and neutrality (that is, the case in which the gene is neither harmful nor beneficial).

Even with a relatively high selective advantage, such as 1 per cent, when the frequency of the gene being acted on is very small or very large (near zero or near 100 per cent), evolution due to selection is extremely slow. But evolutionary change due to selection may be fairly rapid if the advantageous gene is moderately frequent (see Table 2).

These facts have a bearing on the proposals of eugenists, but the important thing to notice is the considerable evidence that, in nature, natural selection can operate rather rapidly, in terms of the lengths of time which have elapsed, if an adequate supply of new

genes, more suitable to changing environments, is available.

In many cases we have actually been able to observe the process of evolution in lower forms, probably by selection, a privilege which was denied Darwin and other pioneers in this field. One of the best-known examples is the increase in the incidence of melanism in certain moths. There seems to be no doubt that melanism among many species has become much more common in

TABLE 2

TIME REQUIRED FOR A GIVEN CHANGE IN THE PER CENT FREQUENCY OF A GENE HAVING A SELECTIVE ADVANTAGE OF 0.01 (I.E., 1 PER CENT) (MODIFIED FROM PÄTAU)*

DOMINANT GENE		RECESSIVE GENE	
Change in Frequency	No. of Generations	Change in Frequency	No. of Generations
0.01– 0.1...	230	0.01– 0.1...	900,230
0.1 – 1.0...	231	0.1 – 1.0...	90,231
1.0 –50.0...	559	1.0 – 3.0...	6,779
50.0 –97.0...	3,481	3.0 –50.0...	3,481
97.0 –99.0...	6,779	50.0 –99.0...	559
99.0 –99.9...	90,231	99.0 –99.9...	231
99.9 –99.99..	900,230	99.9 –99.99..	230

* Little, Brown & Company has kindly given permission to take this and certain of the following tables, in addition to a certain amount of the textual content of this paper, from W. C. Boyd, *Genetics and the Races of Man* (Boston, 1950).

the last century, and that this change has been in some way connected with the progressive industrialization of the areas where these dark-colored moths are found, for the melanotics occur predominantly in and near large cities and in industrial areas. In some cases the entire population of an area has become melanotic. The history of this process has been described by Harrison, and the phenomenon on the Continent of Europe has been described by Hasebroek. A summary of the genetic findings has been given by Ford.

A probable example of the effect of

selection in man is the gradual brachy-cephalization of central Europe, especially among the Slavs (see Table 3).

It has been mentioned by Schwidetsky that well-documented series of skulls from Bohemia and from Russia show that this change progressed from century to century, so that the average cranial index of 73–75 rose as high as 83 by the nineteenth century. Myslivec

TABLE 3

CHANGE IN CRANIAL INDEX OF "NORDIC" AND EAST EUROPEAN TYPES

DATE	CRANIAL INDEX	
	"Nordic"	East European
1200 B.C.	69.2	76.1
A.D. 300..........	69.6	77.1
A.D. 1200	73.5	78.6
A.D. 1935	ca. 81.0	ca. 86.0

suggests that a possible explanation of this phenomenon may be the dominance of the brachycephalic form of head over the dolichocephalic form. This explanation is probably an unconscious expression of the supposed phenomenon of "genophagy."[1] In view of the rapidity with which gene equilibrium is obtained in the absence of selection and mutation, we may doubt that this is really the explanation, for the brachycephalic genes would already have been in equilibrium with the dolichocephalic genes in the early populations. For example, the blood-group gene B was probably introduced into Europe from Asia in historical times. Gene B is dominant over gene O, but there is no evidence that the group O gene is tending to be swamped by B in western Europe (or anywhere

1. Some earlier writers thought that a dominant gene automatically became more and more frequent in a population simply because it was dominant. Since it would thus "eat up" the recessive gene, Laughlin christened this imaginary phenomenon "genophagy."

else). The most probable cause of recent brachycephalization would therefore seem to be the action of natural selection, which leads us to suppose that the brachycephalic individual has some advantage in the struggle for existence over the dolichocephalic individual. What this advantage is, we do not know. Weidenreich suggests that the head of the brachycephalic is balanced better on the vertebral column.

It has been objected that in cases such as this, where we seem to find a secular change in the morphology of a population, the real process has been one of gradual replacement of a long-headed population (for instance) by a roundheaded one. This is always a possibility because man interbreeds so extensively when given a chance and because we cannot obtain data on any population certainly known to have been isolated absolutely over a long period of time. But the way lower forms (e.g., horses) have undergone morphological change during the course of evolution leaves little doubt that such changes do occur, given sufficient time. It does not seem too much to suppose that similar evolutionary forces may act in similar ways in man.

Twenty years ago it was customary to state that valid racial classifications must be based on nonadaptive characters, that is, characters which do not have any great selective value in evolution. One author stated: "If race implies the possession of certain variations as a result of the same ancestry, significant racial criteria should be based principally upon non-adaptive bodily characters." Another wrote: "If a character has selective value, it will be subject to increase or decrease in frequency in the population by the action of selection, and the rate of selection may be surprisingly great. ... Such characters can be useful only for determining recent prehistory." This second author was myself.

It was largely the work of the geneticists which rescued us from this untenable position. Dobzhansky, after quoting the opinion of one contemporary that "the great majority of racial features are obviously not adaptational," said: "This amounts to rejection of the simplest hypothesis which can account for the origin of racial differentiation, namely that it is brought about, at least in part, by natural selection of genotypes possessing adaptive values higher than other genotypes in the environments in which the species normally lives."

Professor Hooton, after quoting a statement that nonadaptive characters are to be preferred, states that "this insistence upon the use of 'non-adaptive' characters in human taxonomy now seems to me impractical and erroneous." He points out that natural selection is one of the most potent forces in human differentiation and that the mutations most likely to be perpetuated are those with survival value.

It is apparent now that we were mistaken when we looked for racial characteristics which were completely unaffected by natural selection and when we thought that racial characteristics which were completely nonadaptive could be handed down from generation to generation to mark common descent. Like other taxonomists, we must base our categories on characters which are indeed acted on by selective agencies.

Therefore, although I once believed, because the blood groups had no apparent selective advantage, that they were more useful than other physical characters in racial classification, it now seems to me unlikely that they can be absolutely "neutral" selectively and that it is likely that they are no more useful (but, of course, no less) than other human genes. At the moment they have the temporary advantage that we know the mechanism of their inheritance, which we do not know for most other normal human characteristics.

MIXTURE

If two populations mix, the new gene frequencies will depend on the original gene frequencies and the numbers of the two parent-populations. If the numbers of individuals of breeding age in the two populations are to each other as c is to d, and the gene frequencies are q_c and q_d, the new gene frequency in the mixed population will be

$$\frac{c\,q_c + d\,q_d}{c + d}.$$

MUTATION

Mutations are the raw material of evolution. They may be increased in frequency by selection. In the absence of selection, a mutation occurring in a sizable population does not increase in frequency, and it is incorrect to assume that such a mutated gene would spread. As an example, let us consider a hypothetical mutation from the blood-group gene O to the gene B (similar arguments apply to immigration of a group B individual into a population all of group O).

Since we have no evidence of a selective advantage for B in any environment we know about, we may state that if one group B individual, heterozygous for the blood-group B gene, enters a population of 999 individuals, none of whom belongs to blood group B or AB, there is no reason to suppose that at the end of 10 or 10,000 or 10,000,000 years the *proportion* of group B in the population descended from this mixture would be any greater than it was originally, namely, 0.1 per cent. It is easy to show mathematically that a new gene without selective advantage, once it appeared in a population (whether it was brought there by migration or arose *de novo* as the result of mutation), would not in the course of time spread through the population, becoming more and more frequent, even if it were a dominant.

In the fourth generation the number of descendants of any individual will, in the average case, be greater than the number in the first generation (his immediate children). If an individual rears four children, he may reasonably expect to have considerably more than four great-great-grandchildren. This will be especially true if the population as a whole is on the increase. Even in a strictly static population (one not increasing or decreasing in size) each mating yields, *on the average*, two children who reach the mating age, four grandchildren, eight great-grandchildren, etc. There is a *chance* that any of these descendants of a newly introduced or mutated B individual will inherit the factor B. So one can visualize, in a lazy sort of way, how the B factor might spread throughout the whole population, like the mycelium of a mold spreading through bread. But this lazy picture is wrong. If we analyze the process more carefully, we see that our B individual will probably have, in a static population, just two children who grow to maturity and have offspring of their own. The probability that one of these will have the gene B is ½, the probability that both will have gene B is ½ × ½ = ¼. If only one has it, the chances that his offspring belong to blood group B are computed in the same way. The probability that the four grandchildren of the original group B are also group B is 1/16 × 1/16 = 1/256. The further down the generations we go, the less likely it becomes that all the descendants of our group B individual will also be group B, until, in the end, the chances against it are overwhelming. Further analysis shows that the *proportional* representation of B in the gene population is therefore likely to stay the same as in the beginning, if no other effects operate.

After gene B has been introduced, there seem to be three factors which might affect the total number of B genes in the population: (*a*) increase in the total size of the population, (*b*) random genetic variation (the Sewall Wright effect), and (*c*) the action of selection, if gene B has any selective value.

A factor which can modify the proportions of different *phenotypes* in man (and other organisms) is inbreeding. In its correct sense, inbreeding means mating between close relatives. Unless this occurs, a population, though it may be cut off from all contact with the outside world, is not inbred; it is merely reproductively isolated.

Inbreeding modifies the proportion of genotypes and phenotypes because close relatives are more likely to be of the same genotype than are unrelated members of the population, and thus inbreeding will mean that matings of dominant with dominant, of recessive with recessive, and of heterozygote with heterozygote, will be relatively more frequent than the other matings (dominant with recessives, etc.).

The result of such matings is that the heterozygotes will continue to produce both dominants and recessives among their offspring, but only half of their offspring are heterozygotes, the remainder being equally divided (on the average) between dominants and recessives. Dominant × dominant matings produce only dominants, and recessive × recessive matings produce only recessives. The range of variability of the population is therefore continually reduced, and the proportion of homozygotes is increased at the expense of the heterozygotes.

A fourth evolutionary mechanism is the Sewall Wright effect, or *random genetic drift*, which depends for its operation on the isolation of one small population from other populations with which it might interbreed. The recognition of the great importance of the mechanism of *random drift* in evolution has been largely due to the mathematical work of Wright.

If we choose a very small group consisting, let us say, of four women and four men, from a larger population which has about the usual European distribution of blood groups, and isolate them on a desert island, it might easily happen by chance that no individual of group B (which usually accounts for only 10-15 per cent of an average European population) would be represented in this particular mating group. Even if one B individual were by chance included, he or she would most likely be a heterozygote, that is of the genotype BO,[2] and any child of his would have a 50-50 chance of not belonging to blood group B (in other words of being A or O). Even if he had a fair number of children, therefore, he might fail to produce any child of group B, and gene B would not be represented in the new generation. The chance of no B in one child is $\frac{1}{2}$, of no B in four children $(\frac{1}{2})^4 =$ 1/16, an event not too unlikely to occur occasionally. Given this situation, as soon as this hypothetical original group B individual died or passed the age of reproduction, the B gene would thus be irretrievably lost to the tribe, unless it were introduced again by mutation. And, of course, the group B individual might be killed before he reached the mating age, or might be sterile, or for some other reason might fail to leave any offspring.

GENETIC DEFINITION OF RACE

In differentiating one group of people from another, the anthropologist

2. In the population of the United States, over 90 per cent of all group B individuals are heterozygous for this gene.

has had to face the difficult problem of deciding just what physical characters are "significant" in their variations. All the existing human types are interfertile and constitute a single Linnaean species. Within this species there are various groups which differ from one another to a greater or less degree, and some of these we may, if we choose, define as "races."

Our increasing knowledge of human genetics is making it possible to define races by selecting characters whose variations in frequency in different populations are significant because they are known to be the expression of individual human genes.

A classification of men on the basis of gene frequencies has a number of advantages. (1) It is objective. Gene frequencies are determined by straightforward counting, or relatively simple computation from quantitative observations of clear-cut, all-or-none characters. The subjective element which complicates attempts to compare the skin colors of two peoples, for example, does not appear. (2) It is quantitative. The degree of similarity between two populations is not a matter of guesswork, but can be compared by calculating from the frequencies of the genes considered. (3) It makes it possible to predict the composition of a population resulting from mixture in any assigned proportions of two populations of known gene frequencies. (4) It encourages clearer thinking about human taxonomy and human evolution. Emotional bias is less likely to operate than in the case of physical appearance such as stature or skin color. There are no prejudices against genes. (5) It permits a sharp separation of the effects of heredity and environment. In the case of a character like stature, it is difficult to say whether genes or food and climate have contributed more to making two populations alike. In the case of blood groups no such problem arises.

We do not mean to assert that the geneticist can classify mankind with no regard to his recent geographical distribution, and cultural factors such as language, since it is obvious that race, as we understand the term, involves common descent. An anthropologist who studied the inhabitants of the British Isles and disregarded the linguistic and cultural distinction between the English and the Welsh would indeed be foolish. Our procedure will be one of generalization and abstraction. The value of the abstractions will be shown when we apply them to new examples. Thus any combination of gene frequencies which we abstract as characteristic of Africans must not reveal little islands of "Negroes" in northern Europe or pre-Columbian America.

In order to use genetic methods in physical anthropological classification, we must understand two points: (*a*) inheritance is particulate in character, and (*b*) the units of heredity soon reach an equilibrium distribution in a population.

The evidence for point *a* was found by Mendel in his pioneer experiments. It has been confirmed by hundreds of geneticists since. It means that hereditary characters do not blend in offspring. Instead, each gene from a parent remains unaffected, ready to appear in future generations, unchanged by its temporary association with a different gene. A gene for blue eyes may be submerged for generations by dominant genes for dark eyes, but, when it again is combined with another recessive gene, it produces eyes as light and blue as it ever did. The particles of heredity, the genes, do not change by association. If they do change, it is by mutation.

Point *b* means that, in any large population mating at random, the various gene frequencies no longer change—except perhaps slowly by selection or mutation—and consequently the physical types (phenotypes) are also constant. The frequency of blue eyes does not decrease, in spite of the fact that blue eyes are recessive. This is the state known to geneticists as "gene equilibrium." Mathematical proof shows that it prevails in a population after one generation of random mating.

One of the clearest expositions of the elementary mathematics underlying the principle of gene equilibrium has been given by Dobzhansky. He says: Suppose that two varieties of a sexually reproducing organism are brought into contact and allowed to interbreed at random. Let us suppose that one variety is homozygous for the dominant gene Y, while the other variety is homozygous for the recessive gene y. If the two varieties are originally present in equal numbers, one half of the original population will consist of YY and the other half of yy individuals. As a result of the mating between these two varieties, we can easily show by writing down the matings and their outcomes that the next generation will consist of 25 per cent of individuals homozygous for Y, 25 per cent homozygous for y, and 50 per cent which are hybrids, or heterozygotes, Yy. In other words, we have again the familiar Mendelian ratio: $YY, 2Yy, yy$.

FALLACY OF TYPES

Starting from the concept of genetically determined characters in a population in genetic equilibrium, we may cast about for a sensible method of race classification. One fallacy may be disposed of here. This is the fallacy of the "type."

Boas pointed out in one of his last papers that, although the logical way to express differences between different human groups was to determine the frequency with which various forms occurred in each group, some anthropologists tend to be impressed by the forms which appear most commonly, and tend to combine these frequent forms in their minds into one imaginary individual which they call "The Type." Sargeant established the ideal type of the Harvard student by having a sculptor make a figure of a youth whose body measurements corresponded to the average of the measurements obtained on a large number of Harvard students from about the year 1892. A knowledge of genetics shows that the type concept has no basis in reality.

Suppose we are liberal, and say that a man is like the ideal in respect to any given measurement if he does not deviate more than do 50 per cent of the total examined; we should nevertheless find, as Boas points out, that the number of measurements is such and the number of their combinations is so great that Sargeant would have found, on the average, among 1,024 individuals taken at random at Harvard, just one who corresponded to his ideal type. Human populations as they actually exist do not produce ideal types. Instead, we must deal with the variations in frequencies of many different genes in different populations.

DEFINITION OF RACE

It would be incorrect and meaningless to define a race as "a group of individuals with identical genetic constitutions," since, as pointed out by Dobzhansky and Epling, groups of identical individuals are simply never found. There is a great deal of genetic variation even within the confines of a race. If we should frame a definition of race along these lines, every single individual would have to belong to a separate race, of which he was the only member, except in the case of identical twins, who might belong to the same race. Dobzhansky and Epling also point out that it would be equally fallacious to define a race as a group of individuals having some single gene in common or some chromosome structure in common. Since so many variable genes and chromosome structures exist, and since these different genes and chromosome structures can form a large variety of combinations, we should be certain to find individuals classified as belonging to one race in so far as some gene, say F, was concerned, but who would belong to a different race in regard to the gene G, and a still different race in regard to the gene H. A race is not an individual, and it is not a single genotype, but it is a group of individuals more or less from the same geographical area (a population), usually with a number of identical genes, but in which many different types may occur.

Dobzhansky and Epling propose to define races as (different) populations which are characterized by different frequencies of variable genes and/or chromosome structures. Dahlberg has proposed a definition of race which amounts to much the same thing. He says: "A race is an isolate or a collection of isolates." By an "isolate" is implied a group of individuals isolated geographically or socially or in some other way who consequently do not freely exchange genes with surrounding peoples. But, within the isolate, mating occurs more or less at random. In the ideal case, one would take account of all the variable genes and chromosome structures in order to describe a given race. At present, we are unable to do this, even in the lower forms such as *Drosophila*, where the genetics are much more thoroughly understood than they are with man. Because our knowledge is incomplete, we have to base our classifications on certain genetic differences that we do know about.

First, we have to decide how much difference there must be in the distribution of the known variable genes and chromosome structures between two populations, before we decide to call them two different races. According to Charles and Goodwin, in some cases the number of genes differentiating two different *species* may be of the order of 40. Statistically significant differences may occur between populations of *Drosophila* in localities only a dozen miles apart, and we could, if we liked, say that these populations are racially distinct. If the concept of race is to be taxonomically useful, however, we should not use the term quite so freely, for otherwise we shall have too many races within each species, and the term will lose much of its value for purposes of classification.

Dobzhansky and Epling show that in *Drosophila*, where far more is known about the genetic structure than in man, it would be useless to delineate a race from the possession of any one gene, or any one particular arrangement of genes in any one particular chromosome. Since genes vary independently, individuals identical in respect to one chromosome would frequently be found to differ profoundly in respect to the arrangement of genes in some other chromosome.

Although the genotype of an individual is derived from the population from which it sprang, it is not absolutely predetermined by the genetic composition of this population (except, of course, in respect to genes for which the population is homozygous). And the extent to which the individual can vary depends, in turn, on the degree of genetic variability which is present in the species in question.

If we make a thorough study of man, genetically and morphologically, we must not expect that the various data collected will all be mutually "consistent." In fact, we must be prepared to find that populations in Greenland and in Australia agree quite well in regard to blood-grouping frequencies (A, B, O, at least) (Table 4), while they markedly disagree in regard to the M and N blood types, in regard to skin color, hair form, and other characteristics. Contemporary physical anthropologists accept this as a necessary and not illogical situation.

As data on the physical characteristics of the human race have accumulated, it has become clear that they usually vary independently of one another, and that whatever races we choose to distinguish will be almost entirely arbitrary, and their distribution will depend on the particular characteristics on which we choose to base them. Dahlberg reminds us that the finding of one "racial" difference does not mean we can forthwith assume that many other differences must exist. The observed difference may be the chief or even the only difference. The only instances in which we may expect a "dividend" of additional similarities will be those in which we are studying populations which have long been isolated genetically and thus have had time to undergo considerable differentiation. The situation is entirely different from the case of the chemical elements, where, when we find one test which clearly differentiates sodium and arsenic, for example, we can safely infer the existence of many other important differences.

We may define a human race as a population which differs significantly from other human populations in regard to the frequency of one or more of the genes it possesses. It is an arbitrary matter which, and how many, gene loci we choose to consider as a significant "constellation"; but it seems better, on the one hand, not to designate a multiplicity of races which differ only in regard to a single pair or a single set of allelic genes and, on the other, not to insist that the races we define must differ from one another with respect to all their genes. To define human races on the basis of genetics, we

TABLE 4*

FREQUENCIES OF BLOOD GROUPS O, A, B, AND AB IN TYPICAL POPULATIONS

POPULATION	PLACE	NUMBER TESTED	O	A	B	AB	p	q	r
			Low A, Virtually No B						
Am. Indians (Utes)	Montana	138	97.4	2.6	0	0	0.013	0.0	0.987
Am. Indians (Toba)	Argentina	194	98.5	1.5	0	0	0.007	0	0.993
Am. Indians (Sioux)	S. Dakota	100	91.0	7.0	2.0	0	0.035	0.010	0.955
Am. Indians (Kwakiutl)	B. Columbia	123	85.4	12.2	2.4	0	0.063	0.013	0.926
			Moderate A, Virtually No B						
Am. Indians (Navaho)	N. Mexico	359	77.7	22.5	0	0	0.125	0	0.875
Am. Indians (Pueblo)	Jemez, etc., N.M.	310	78.4	20.0	1.6	0	0.105	0.007	0.885
			High A, Little B						
Am. Indians (Bloods)	Montana	69	17.4	81.2	0	1.4	0.583	0	0.417
Am. Indians (Blackfeet)	Montana	115	23.5	76.5	0	0	0.515	0	0.485
Australian aborigines	South Australia	54	42.6	57.4	0	0	0.346	0	0.654
Australian aborigines	West Australia	243	48.1	51.9	0	0	0.306	0	0.694
Basques	San Sebastián	91	57.2	41.7	1.1	0	0.239	0.008	0.756
Am. Indians (Shoshone)	Wyoming	60	51.6	45.0	1.6	1.6	0.264	0.011	0.718
Polynesians	Hawaii	413	36.5	60.8	2.2	0.5	0.382	0.018	0.604
Eskimo	Cape Farewell	484	41.1	53.8	3.5	1.4	0.333	0.027	0.642
Australian aborigines	Queensland	447	58.6	37.8	3.6	0	0.216	0.023	0.766
Am. Indians (Flatheads)	Montana	258	51.5	42.2	4.7	1.6	0.250	0.032	0.718
			Fairly High A, and Some B						
W. Georgians	Tiflis	707	59.1	34.4	6.1	0.4	0.198	0.038	0.769
English	London	422	47.9	42.4	8.3	1.4	0.250	0.050	0.692
Belgians	Liége	3,500	46.7	41.9	8.3	3.1	0.257	0.058	0.684
Spanish	Spain	1,172	41.5	46.5	9.2	2.2	0.294	0.068	0.645
Swedes	Stockholm	633	37.9	46.1	9.5	6.5	0.301	0.073	0.616
Icelanders	Iceland	800	55.7	32.1	9.6	2.6	0.190	0.062	0.747
Danes	Copenhagen	1,261	40.7	45.3	10.5	3.5	0.290	0.078	0.638
French	Paris	1,265	39.8	42.3	11.8	6.1	0.276	0.088	0.632
Armenians	fr. Turkey	330	27.3	53.9	12.7	6.1	0.379	0.110	0.523
Irish	Dublin	399	55.2	31.1	12.1	1.7	0.186	0.076	0.744
Lapps	Finland	94	33.0	52.1	12.8	2.1	0.323	0.078	0.574
Melanesians	New Guinea	500	37.6	44.4	13.2	4.8	0.293	0.099	0.613
Micronesians	Saipan	293	50.5	33.8	14.0	1.7	0.207	0.093	0.711
Greeks	Athens	1,200	42.0	39.6	14.2	3.7	0.254	0.102	0.648
Germans	Berlin	39,174	36.5	42.5	14.5	6.5	0.285	0.110	0.604
Turks	Istamboul	500	33.8	42.6	14.8	8.8	0.293	0.116	0.581

* "N." signifies north; "S.," "W.," and "E." south, west, and east, respectively; "fr." signifies from; "n." signifies near. In this table the frequencies of the blood groups O, A, B, and AB are given in per cents, but the gene frequencies are given as straight frequencies, following common practice. The symbol *p* represents the frequency of the gene *A*; *q* the frequency of the gene *B*; and *r* the frequency of the gene *O*.

Apropos of this and succeeding tables in this chapter, we may remark again that no one characteristic is enough to differentiate races satisfactorily.

TABLE 4—*Continued*

POPULATION	PLACE	NUMBER TESTED	O	A	B	AB	*p*	*q*	*r*
			High A and High B						
E. Georgians.......	Tiflis	1,274	36.8	42.3	15.0	5.9	0.283	0.113	0.607
Bulgarians........	Sofia	6,060	32.1	44.4	15.4	8.1	0.308	0.123	0.567
Hungarians........	Budapest	624	36.1	41.8	15.9	6.2	0.282	0.120	0.601
Welsh.............	N. towns	192	47.9	32.8	16.2	3.1	0.206	0.108	0.692
Italians...........	Sicily	540	45.9	33.4	17.3	3.4	0.213	0.118	0.678
Siamese...........	Bangkok	213	37.1	17.8	35.2	9.9	0.148	0.257	0.595
Syrians...........	Meshghara	300	39.3	39.0	17.1	4.6	0.258	0.124	0.628
Finns.............	Häme	972	34.0	42.4	17.1	6.5	0.285	0.126	0.583
"Berbers".........	Algiers	300	39.0	37.6	18.6	4.6	0.251	0.134	0.625
Germans..........	Danzig	1,888	33.1	41.6	18.0	7.3	0.288	0.139	0.575
Ukrainians........	Kharkov	310	36.4	38.4	21.6	3.6	0.261	0.158	0.604
Japanese..........	Tokyo	29,799	30.1	38.4	21.9	9.7	0.279	0.172	0.549
Japanese..........	Kyoto	6,205	29.2	38.0	22.2	10.6	0.279	0.177	0.541
Estonians.........	Estonia	1,844	32.3	36.6	22.4	8.7	0.261	0.170	0.589
Madagascans.......	Madagascar	266	45.5	27.5	22.5	4.5	0.180	0.151	0.674
Russians..........	n. Moscow	489	31.9	34.4	24.9	8.8	0.250	0.189	0.565
Abyssinians.......	Abyssinia	400	42.8	26.5	25.3	5.0	0.178	0.172	0.654
Egyptians.........	Cairo	502	27.3	38.5	25.5	8.8	0.288	0.203	0.523
Bogobos..........	Philippines	302	53.6	16.9	26.5	3.0	0.107	0.163	0.732
Chinese...........	Huang-Ho R.	2,127	34.2	30.8	27.7	7.3	0.220	0.201	0.587
'Iraqis............	Baghdad	386	33.7	31.4	28.2	6.7	0.226	0.208	0.581
Tatars...........	Kazan	500	27.8	30.0	28.8	13.4	0.233	0.225	0.527
Pygmies..........	Belgian Congo	1,032	30.6	30.3	29.1	10.0	0.227	0.219	0.554
Arabs, Bedouin..... (Rwala)	Syrian Desert	208	43.3	22.1	30.3	4.3	0.151	0.200	0.658
Egyptians.........	Assiut	419	24.6	34.4	31.0	10.0	0.272	0.250	0.459
Kirghiz...........	U.S.S.R.	500	31.6	27.4	32.2	8.8	0.206	0.236	0.563
Asiatic Indians......	Goa	400	29.2	26.8	34.0	10.0	0.208	0.254	0.540
Chinese...........	Peking	1,000	30.7	25.1	34.2	10.0	0.193	0.250	0.554
Javanese..........	Ampelgading	450	30.4	24.7	37.3	7.6	0.190	0.271	0.552
Buriats...........	N. Irkutsk	1,320	32.4	20.2	39.2	8.2	0.156	0.277	0.570
Asiatic Indians......	Bengal	160	32.5	20.0	39.4	8.1	0.154	0.278	0.571

should know which genes act to determine physical characters, and which genetically determined characters are most useful as a basis for a physical classification. The inherited characters may be divided into three categories: characters which are fairly common and variable, believed to be inherited, although the mechanism has not yet been worked out; rare pathological conditions whose mechanism of inheritance is known; and normal physiological characters inherited by genetic mechanism which is known exactly.

BLOOD GROUPS

Pathological characters are of little use in classification because of their rarity, and the common characters of uncertain hereditary mechanism are not so useful as characters inherited in a known manner. The ten blood-group systems are the only examples of the third class of characters known at present. In order of discovery, they are: the ABO blood groups, the MNS blood groups, the P blood groups, the secreting factor, the Lewis blood groups, the Rh blood groups, the Lutheran blood groups, the Kell blood groups, the Duffy blood groups, and the Kidd blood groups.

The mechanism of inheritance of the ABO blood groups and the MN blood groups is too well known to require retelling. The anti-S serum, which made a subdivision of the MN groups possible, was first reported from Australia by Walsh and Montgomery. A reasonable interpretation of the data is that there are four alleles at the locus of these genes, namely, Ms, MS, Ns, and NS. If, however, an anti-s serum is found, which Race expects, the interpretation that S and s are a separate pair of alleles, linked to the MN locus, will become more probable.

TABLE 5

FREQUENCY OF S-SUBDIVISIONS OF THE M,N FREQUENCIES IN VARIOUS POPULATIONS

POPULATION	FREQUENCY OF GENE			
	Ms	*MS*	*Ns*	*NS*
Australian aborigines......	0.256	0	0.744	0
New Guinea...	0.04	0.01	0.75	0.28
Maori........	0.500	0.014	0.438	0.048
English.......	0.285	0.255	0.386	0.074

The recently discovered anti-S sera enable the former M,N groups to be subdivided. The S,s gene pair might be another pair of alleles linked to the M,N locus, but it is also possible that the new serum simply enables, instead of the M,N pair, four alleles, *Ms, MS, Ns, NS*, to be distinguished. This greatly increases the anthropological usefulness of this system. It is particularly interesting to note that, although the older M,N results did not particularly distinguish the aborigines of New Guinea from those of Australia (thus not seeming to support the marked differences in frequencies of B), the use of the anti-S serum does. The bloods from Australia never reacted with anti-S, while there is an appreciable amount of S-positive blood in New Guinea (see Table 5).

The distribution of ABO blood groups in various populations is shown in Table 4.

The distribution of the blood groups is shown in Table 6.

The P blood groups were discovered by Landsteiner and Levine, the same year in which they found M and N. The antigen P is inherited as a dominant. Gradations in strength of P are observed, as with other blood-group antigens; it may be that multiple alleles are involved.

The ability to secrete blood-group substances A, B, and H(Q) into the saliva and other body fluids in water-soluble form was shown by Schiff and Sasaki to be inherited as a Mendelian pair, S (secretor) being dominant over s.

The Lewis blood groups were discovered by Mourant, who found a "new" antibody in two samples of serum. Andresen independently discovered an antiserum, which he fortunately called "anti-L," since it proved identical with the anti-Lewis. He observed that the proportion of L-positive infants in his population was higher than the proportion of L-positive adults. He proposed the hypothesis, since confirmed, that L was recessive in adults and dominant in children.

The way in which the frequency of Le^a positive reactions falls off during childhood is shown in Table 7. This was the first example of a recessive agglutinogen in man.

The Lewis blood groups were found to be intimately associated with the secreting factor. All adult individuals reacting with anti-Le^a, and therefore, by hypothesis, Le^a/Le^a genetically, were nonsecretors of A, B, and H. Most Le^a negative persons are secretors, but about 1 per cent secrete neither A, B, H, Le^a, nor Le^b. It is thought that they probably secrete an antigen Le^c, not otherwise yet identified. Thus the genes Le^a, Le^b, Le^c, and S,s would form two series of alleles contiguous to each other.

The Rh blood groups were discovered by Landsteiner and Wiener, although others had probably observed

TABLE 6*

FREQUENCIES OF M,N BLOOD TYPES AND *M* AND *N* GENES
IN VARIOUS POPULATIONS

POPULATION	PLACE	NUMBER TESTED	M	MN	N	*m*	*n*
		Populations with Low N and Therefore High M					
Eskimo...............	E. Greenland	569	83.5	15.6	0.9	0.913	0.087
Am. Indians............ (Navaho)	New Mexico	361	84.5	14.4	1.1	0.917	0.083
Aleuts................	Aleutian Islands	132	67.5	29.4	3.2	0.822	0.179
Am. Indians............ (Utes)	Utah	104	58.7	34.6	6.7	0.600	0.240
Arabs, Bedouin......... (Rwala)	n. Damascus	208	57.5	36.7	5.8	0.758	0.241
Am. Indians............ (Pueblo)	New Mexico	140	59.3	32.8	7.9	0.757	0.243
Am. Indians............ (Blackfeet)	Montana	95	54.7	40.0	5.3	0.747	0.253
Arabs (Bedouin)........	n. Damascus	80	51.3	40.0	8.7	0.713	0.287
		Populations with Low M (High N)					
Australian aborigines....	N.S. Wales	28	0	32.1	67.9	0.160	0.840
Australian aborigines....	Queensland	372	2.4	30.4	67.2	0.176	0.824
Papuans...............	Papua	200	7.0	24.0	69.0	0.190	0.810
Fijians................	Fiji	200	11.0	44.5	44.5	0.332	0.667
Ainu..................	Shizunai	504	17.9	50.2	31.9	0.430	0.570
		Populations with "Normal" M and N Frequencies					
Negroes...............	N.Y.C.	730	....	....	28.1	....	*ca.* 0.530
Basques...............	Spain	91	23.1	51.6	25.3	0.489	0.511
Spanish (m)...........	Spain	134	26.9	55.2	17.9	0.545	0.455
Syrians...............	Boarij	131	24.4	52.7	22.9	0.508	0.492
Filipinos..............	Leyte, Samar, etc.	382	25.9	50.3	23.8	0.510	0.490
Egyptians.............	Cairo	502	27.8	48.9	23.3	0.522	0.477
English...............	London	422	28.7	47.4	23.9	0.524	0.476
Lapps.................	Inari, Finland	56	28.6	48.2	23.2	0.527	0.473
Poles.................	Poland	600	28.2	49.0	22.8	0.527	0.473
Egyptians.............	Assiut	419	26.2	53.1	20.7	0.527	0.472
Indonesians...........	Java, etc.	296	30.4	45.6	24.0	0.532	0.468
Irish.................	Dublin	399	30.0	46.7	23.3	0.533	0.466
Danes................	Copenhagen	2,023	29.1	49.5	21.4	0.538	0.461
Belgians..............	Liége	3,100	28.9	50.3	20.8	0.540	0.460
Germans..............	Berlin	8,144	29.7	50.7	19.6	0.550	0.449
Japanese..............	Kyoto	430	32.0	46.1	21.9	0.551	0.449
Russians..............	Leningrad	701	32.0	46.7	21.3	0.553	0.446
Yugoslavs.............	Moravska	256	30.5	50.0	19.5	0.555	0.445
Germans..............	Danzig	2,018	30.6	50.4	19.0	0.558	0.442
French...............	Paris	400	33.0	45.8	21.2	0.559	0.441
Italians..............	Sicily	300	32.0	48.0	20.0	0.560	0.440
Japanese..............	Tokyo	1,100	32.4	47.2	20.4	0.560	0.440
Syrians...............	Meshghara	306	30.7	52.0	17.3	0.567	0.433
Armenians.............	fr. Turkey	339	34.2	45.4	20.4	0.569	0.431
Hungarians............	Budapest	624	33.5	47.9	18.6	0.574	0.425
Chinese..............	Hong Kong	1,029	33.2	48.6	18.2	0.575	0.425
Ukrainians............	Kharkov	310	36.1	44.3	19.6	0.583	0.417

* "(m)" signifies mixed; "N." signifies north, "E." signifies east, "W." signifies west; "n." signifies near; "*ca.*" signifies approximately; "fr." signifies from. M, MN, and N stand for the percentages of the M, MN, and N blood types; *m* stands for the frequency of the gene for M; *n* for the frequency of the gene for N.

TABLE 6—*Continued*

POPULATION	PLACE	NUMBER TESTED	M	MN	N	m	n
Populations with "Normal" M and N Frequencies—*Continued*							
Welsh................	N. towns	192	30.7	55.3	14.0	0.583	0.416
Scots.................	Glasgow	456	35.0	47.9	17.1	0.589	0.410
Swedes...............	Sweden	1,200	36.1	47.0	16.9	0.596	0.404
Estonians............	Estonia	310	34.8	49.7	15.5	0.596	0.403
'Iraqis...............	Baghdad	387	37.0	47.0	16.0	0.605	0.395
Finns................	Uusimaa	1,050	37.1	47.2	15.7	0.607	0.393
Arabs, Bedouin........ (Jabour)	n. Mosul	206	36.9	49.5	13.6	0.616	0.383
Russians.............	n. Moscow	489	39.9	44.0	16.1	0.619	0.381
E. Caucasians.........	Tiflis	134	38.8	47.8	13.4	0.627	0.373
W. Caucasians........	Tiflis	245	40.0	46.5	13.5	0.632	0.367
Finns................	Karjala	398	45.7	43.2	11.1	0.673	0.327

TABLE 7

DECREASE WITH AGE IN LEWIS POSITIVES

TYPE	CHILDREN								ADULTS	
	0–3 Months		4–6 Months		7–9 Months		10–12 Months			
	No.	Per Cent	No.	Per Cent	No.	Per Cent	No.	Per Cent	No.	Per Cent
Le(a+).........	78	79	74	73	18	36	19	29	166	21
Le(a−).........	21	21	28	27	32	64	46	71	618	79

agglutination due to this system, as they had in the case of other as yet unnamed systems. According to Fisher's (cited by Race) hypothesis, three closely linked adjacent loci, C, D, and E, are involved. According to Wiener's hypothesis, a series of allelomorphic genes, r, R', R'', R_1, R_2, R_o, r^y, R^z are involved. The two theories lead to identical genetic predictions. Other Rh antigens have been found from time to time, so that the following genes are available for the C, D, and E loci, respectively: C, c, C^w, c^v, C^u; D, d, D^u; E, e, E^u. The various antisera are sometimes available pure, more often as mixtures.

The known data regarding the Rh types in various populations are shown in Table 8. No particular dominance relations are observed among these genes. They usually act more strongly when present in double dose.

The antibody which defines the Lutheran blood groups was found by Callender and Race in the serum of a patient who had been transfused many times. The dominant gene responsible for positive reactions was designated as Lu^a and the still hypothetical recessive gene as Lu^b. About 8 per cent of English subjects are positive for Lu^a.

Coombs, Mourant, and Race described a blood-group antibody which was not connected with any of the known antigens. This antibody, which was of the incomplete or "blocking" type, was found in the serum of a mother whose child was thought to be suffering from hemolytic disease. Various other workers later found similar antibodies. About 10 per cent of Bostonians and Londoners react positively with this serum.

The antigen identified by this antibody was called "Kell" and symbolized by K. The allele was symbolized as k. In 1949 Levine found an antibody which reacted with the predicted k antigen, making it possible to separate the heterozygotes Kk from the homozygotes KK.

Cutbush, Mollison, and Parkin reported another blood-group system, called "Duffy" from the name of the patient, who was suffering from hemophilia and who had had several blood transfusions over the preceding twenty years. The gene giving rise to the antigen recognizable by this serum was

TABLE 8

Rh BLOOD TYPES IN VARIOUS POPULATIONS

POPULATION	NO. OF PERSONS TESTED	FREQUENCIES OF Rh TYPES (PER CENT)								
		rh cde	Rh₁ CDe	Rh₂ cDE	Rh₁Rh₂ CDe/cDE	Rh₀ cDe	rh' Cde	rh'' cdE	rh'rh'' Cde/cdE	Rh₁Rh₂ CDe/CDE
Basques	167	28.8	55.1	7.8	6.0	0.6	1.8	......	......	......
"Whites" (France)	501	17.0	51.7	13.6	13.0	3.6	0.4	0.8	0	0
Czechs (Prague)	181	16.0	50.3	11.6	11.6	1.1	0.6	0.6	0	0.6
"Whites" (Hollanders)	200	15.4	51.5	12.3	17.7	1.5	1.5	0	0	0
"Whites" (England)	1,038	15.3	54.8	14.7	11.6	2.3	0.6	0.7	0	......
S. Paulo (Brazil)	138	15.2	55.2	10.1	11.6	5.8	1.4	0.7	......	
"Whites" (Australia)	350	14.9	54.0	12.6	16.6	0.6	0.9	0.6	0	0
"Whites" (England)	927	14.8	54.9	12.2	13.6	2.5	0.7	1.3	......	0.1
"Whites" (U.S.A.)	7,317	14.7	53.5	15.0	12.9	2.2	1.1	0.6	0.01	......
Spanish (Barcelona)	223	13.0	63.2	13.0	9.4	0.5	0	0.5	0	0.5
"Whites" (U.S.A.)	766	12.5	54.7	14.9	13.9	2.2	0.9	0.5	0	0.1
"Arabs" (Baghdad)	300	10.3	50.3	13.7	15.7	8.3	1.0	0.7	0	0
Porto Ricans	179	10.1	39.1	19.6	14.0	15.1	1.7	0.5	0	......
Negroes (U.S.A.)	223	8.1	20.2	22.4	5.4	41.2	2.7	0	0	......
Negroes (U.S.A.)	135	7.4	23.7	16.3	4.4	45.9	1.5	0.7	0	0
Asiatic Indians (Moslems)	156	7.1	70.5	5.1	12.8	1.9	2.6	0	0	......
S. African Bantu	300	5.3	27.0	0	2.3	64.3	1.0	0	0	......
Chinese	132	1.5	60.6	3.0	34.1	0.9	0	0	0	......
Japanese	150	1.3	37.4	13.3	47.3	0	0	0	0	0.7
Japanese	180	0.6	51.7	8.3	39.4	0	0	0	0	
Am. Indians (Mexico, Tuxpan)	95	0	48.1	9.5	38.1	1.1	0	0	0	3.1
Am. Indians (Ramah, N.M.)	105	0	40.0	17.1	36.2	2.9	0.9	0	0	2.9
Am. Indians (Ramah, N.M.)	305	0	28.5	20.0	41.0	0.7	3.0	0	0.7	6.2
Am. Indians (Utah)	104	0	33.7	28.8	37.5	0	0	0	0	......
Am. Indians (Brazil)	238	0	22.7	19.3	53.2	......				4.8
Indonesians	200	0	74	2.5	22.5	0.5	0	0	0.5	0
Filipinos	100	0	87.0	2.0	11.0	0	0	0	0	......
Australian aborigines	100	0	53.0	21.0	15.0	4.0	1.0	0	0	6.0
Australian aborigines	234	0	58.2	8.5	30.4	1.3	1.7	0	0	......
Papuans	100	0	93.0	0	4.0	0	0	0	0	3.0
Maoris	32	0	25.0	31.0	41.0	3.0	0	0	0	......
Admiralty Islanders	112	0	92.9	0.9	6.2	0	0	0	0	......
Fijians	110	0	89.1	1.8	9.1	0	0	0	0	......
New Caledonians (N and NW)	243	0	77.4	2.1	20.5	0	0	0	0	......
Loyalty Islanders	103	0	77.7	2.9	19.4	0	0	0	0	......
Siamese (Bangkok)	213	0	74.7	3.3	21.1	0.5	0	0	0	3.3

designated as Fy^a and the hypothetical allelic gene as Fy^b. An agglutinin for Fy^b was found in 1951 by Ikin, Mourant, Pettenkofer, and Blumenthal in the blood of a lady in Berlin after the birth of her second child. The child appeared normal, and the antibody, which had a titer of 16,000, was discovered in the course of routine examination of the sera of all the mothers in the hospital.

About 65 per cent of the English are positive to anti-Fy^a, a frequency which makes this a very useful character for legal medicine and suggests that it will be useful in anthropology.

Race, Diamond, *et al.* reported the mode of inheritance of a new blood-group factor discovered by Diamond, called "Kidd." The gene symbol, from the name of the patient's son, is Jk^a, and the hypothetical alternative gene Jk^b. About 70 per cent of Bostonians and Londoners are positive to anti-Jk^a.

Other rare or incompletely studied blood-group factors have been reported. None have any anthropological usefulness as yet.

Another normal characteristic—the ability to taste phenyl-thio-urea (PTC) —is doubtless inherited, but the exact mechanism is not yet clear (Harris). Its anthropological usefulness is therefore less than that of the blood groups.

As characters for use in anthropological classification, the blood groups offer several advantages: (*a*) They are inherited in a known way according to Mendelian principles. (*b*) They are not altered by differences in climate, food, illness, or medical treatment. (*c*) Their frequency in a population is stable, in so far as our observations extend. (*d*) They probably arose very early in the course of man's evolution. (*e*) There is a considerable correlation between geography and the distribution of the blood groups. (*f*) The blood groups are sharply distinguishable "all-or-none" characters which do not grade into one another.

The present author has suggested the following tentative racial classification based on gene frequencies.

1. Early European group (hypothetical). Possessing the highest incidence (over 30 per cent) of the Rh negative type (gene frequency of *rh* 0.6) and probably no group B. A relatively high incidence of the gene Rh_1 and A_2. Gene N possibly somewhat higher than in present-day Europeans. Represented today by their modern descendants, the Basques.

2. European (Caucasoid) group. Possessing the next highest incidence of *rh* (the Rh negative gene) and relatively high incidence of the genes Rh_1 and A_2, with moderate frequencies of other blood-group genes. "Normal" frequencies of M and N, i.e., M $= ca.$ 30 per cent, MN $= ca.$ 49 per cent, N $= ca.$ 21 per cent. (The italicized symbols stand for the genes, as opposed to the groups.)

3. African (Negroid) group. Possessing a tremendously high incidence of the gene Rh^o, a moderate frequency of *rh*, relatively high incidence of genes A_2 and the rare intermediate A (A_1, A_2, etc.) and Rh genes, rather high incidence of gene B. Probably normal M and N.

4. Asiatic (Mongoloid) group. Possessing high frequencies of genes A_1 and B, and the highest known incidence of the rare gene Rh^z, but little, if any, of the genes A_2 and *rh* (the Rh negative gene). Normal M and N. (It is possible that the inhabitants of India will prove to belong to an Asiatic sub-race, or even a separate race, serologically, but information is still sadly lacking.)

5. American Indian group. Possessing varying (sometimes high, sometimes zero) incidence of gene A_1, no A_2, and probably no B or *rh*; high incidence of gene N. Possessing Rh^z.

6. Australoid group. Possessing high incidence of gene A_1, no A_2, no rh, high incidence of gene N (and consequently a low incidence of gene M). Possessing Rh^z.

Table 9 shows the world's distribution of these races.

It is encouraging that this classification corresponds well, on the whole, with the facts of geography. It is, however, hardly more than a suggestion of what will eventually be possible when more human genes are investigated and our knowledge of human gene frequencies is extended.

TABLE 9

APPROXIMATE GENE FREQUENCIES IN SIX GENETICALLY DEFINED RACES

Gene	1 Early European	2 European (Caucasian)	3 African (Negroid)	4 Asiatic (Mongoloid)	5 American	6 Australian
$A(p)(A_2+A_1)$....	ca. 0.25	0.2–0.3	0.1–0.2	0.15–0.4	0–0.6	0.1–0.6
Ratio, A_2/A_1*..	>0.5?	0.1–0.3	ca. 0.4	0	0	0
$B(q)$............	<0.01?	0.05–0.20	0.05–0.25	0.1–0.3	0	0
$N(n)$...........	>0.5?	0.3–0.5	ca. 0.5	0.4–0.5	0.1–0.2	0.8–1.0
Rh neg. (r).....	>0.5?	0.4	ca. 0.25	0	0	0
Rh° $(R°)$.......	<0.1?	ca. 0.1	ca. 0.6	ca. 0.1	ca. 0.01	ca. 0.01
PTC†..........	ca. 0.5	0.55–0.7	ca. 0.45	0	0	0
Nonsecreting‡...	?	ca. 0.5	> 0.6	0?	0	?
Other genes§....	?	r'	A 1,2	R^z	R^z	R^z

* For convenience in calculation, the ratio of the two subgroups, A_2 and A_1, and not the ratio of the gene frequencies, p_2/p is given.

† The recessive gene for not tasting phenyl-thio-carbamide.

‡ The recessive gene for not secreting water-soluble blood-group substances into the gastric juice, saliva, etc.

§ Other genes the frequency of which seems to be higher in this population than in other races.

BIBLIOGRAPHY

BOYD, W. C. 1950. *Genetics and the Races of Man.* Boston: Little, Brown & Co.

DOBZHANSKY, T. 1941. *Genetics and the Origin of Species.* New York: Columbia University Press.

EAST, E. M., and JONES, D. F. 1919. *Inbreeding and Outbreeding.* Philadelphia: J. B. Lippincott Co.

FISHER, R. A. 1930. *The Genetical Theory of Natural Selection.* Oxford: Clarendon Press.

GLASS, B. 1943. *Genes and the Man.* New York: New York Bureau of Publications, Teachers College, Columbia University.

HOGBEN, L. 1931. *Genetic Principles in Medicine and Social Science.* London: Williams & Norgate, Ltd.

MAYR, E. 1942. *Systematics and the Origin of Species.* New York: Columbia University Press.

RACE, R. R., and SANGER, R. 1950. *Blood Groups in Man.* Oxford: Blackwell Scientific Publications.

SIMPSON, G. G. 1944. *Tempo and Mode in Evolution.* New York: Columbia University Press.

———. 1949. *The Meaning of Evolution.* New Haven: Yale University Press.

STERN, C. 1949. *Principles of Human Genetics.* San Francisco: W. H. Freeman & Co.

The Strategy of Culture History

By IRVING ROUSE

PIONEER RESEARCH in a science like anthropology is perhaps inevitably haphazard. Subsequently, as problems are defined and techniques developed, a more rational approach becomes possible. The investigator learns to define the objectives of his research and to select the techniques which best enable him to attain those objectives. We in anthropology appear to have reached this stage of research planning with respect to the study of culture history, and therefore a review of the objectives of culture-historical research would seem to be in order.

In the Americas, at least, archeologists are coming to recognize that their studies of culture history must take into consideration the pertinent ethnological data, and vice versa. Some have argued that archeology deserves to be regarded as the central discipline for culture-historical research, since it deals with a much longer time perspective than ethnology and has developed sounder techniques for establishing chronology. However, its descriptive data are so fragmentary that it must yield to ethnology with respect to matters of content, particularly of nonmaterial culture. A co-operative approach, utilizing the special advantages of both archeology and ethnology, should yield the best results.

Linguistics and physical anthropology might also have been brought into the discussion. However, these two disciplines require somewhat different approaches—linguistics, because it concentrates upon one aspect of culture, and physical anthropology, because its subject matter is primarily noncultural. Only the archeologist and the ethnologist purport to study culture as a whole, and it is for this reason that their objectives can conveniently be discussed together.

NATURE OF OBJECTIVES

The term "objective" is used in this article to refer to the end-product of any particular segment in the procedure of culture-historical research. For example, if one makes an archeological survey of a region, locates a series of sites, and plots them on a map, then that map is the objective of the research. It is entirely possible, of course, that the research will not end with the production of the map; that, for example, the map will be used as the basis for selecting sites to excavate. Such a use, however, is considered a separate segment in the procedure, having a different objective than the original, purely geographic one.

For the sake of clarity, we assume a one-to-one relationship between any given segment of a procedure and its result or objective. This means that no segment can have more than one objective or vice versa. Classification, for example, cannot be considered an objective, because there are several different ways of producing a classification of such cultural phenomena as sites or communities: by grouping them according to areas, periods, cultural characteristics, tribal organization, or genetic relationships. We regard the end-result of each of these procedures as a separate objective.

While one may define the goal of any particular research project in terms of its objectives, they cannot be considered the ultimate aim of the research. One accomplishes a series of objectives, in order eventually to build up a picture of the nature and history of the culture under study. It is this picture, or synthesis of the objectives, which is the ultimate goal of the research.

CHOICE OF OBJECTIVES

The quality of a synthesis depends in part upon what objectives are included. It is therefore important for the investigator to make a good choice of objectives before he begins his research. Two alternative approaches to this problem have been proposed. One is to devise a rigid, all-inclusive program of research, in which one objective follows logically upon the previous one until the ultimate, most important objective is reached. The other alternative is to consider each objective independently, bearing in mind that some objectives must necessarily precede others—that pottery, for example, must be classified before a ceramic sequence can be set up—but nevertheless treating each objective as if it were of equal importance for building up the culture-historical picture. Taylor (1948, p. 153) has recently applied the first alternative to archeology, and his "conjunctive approach" could easily be expanded to include ethnological studies of culture history. By contrast, Clark (1947) seems to favor the other alternative. His is the one adopted here. It is felt that a rigid, all-inclusive program of the first type would require too much time and money to be practicable under normal circumstances. Moreover, such a program involves questions of value—of the importance of one objective relative to the others—on which it would be difficult, if not impossible, to reach agreement. Finally, the second alternative seems to be more in accord with present and past practices in anthropology.

In teaching a survey course on world archeology, the writer has been impressed with the fact that the archeology of each part of the world is characterized by a different series of objectives and that the techniques used to reach these objectives vary similarly from area to area. In large part this is probably due to differences in the nature of the archeological material available in the various areas. One quickly develops an interest in chronology, for example, when one excavates in the tells of the Near East, with their elaborate stratigraphy (Clark, 1947, pp. 103–5). On the other hand, chronology assumes less importance in an area like Polynesia, where the sites are shallow, refuse is sparse, and there seems to have been relatively little change in culture through time (Emory, 1943, p. 9).

Once a certain type of approach becomes established in an area, subsequent archeologists tend to adopt it more or less automatically. It then becomes traditional, and there is resistance to the introduction of new objectives and techniques.

A third factor causing variations in objectives and techniques is the interests of the people doing the research. Regions like Middle America, for example, have attracted people interested in the history of art because the remains are aesthetically pleasing. Such people often do not pay so much attention to the ordinary implements found in the sites as do, for example, Eskimo archeologists, who are largely recruited from the ranks of ethnologists and therefore often use ethnological techniques of culture-historical study (cf. Morley, 1946; Birket-Smith, 1947).

Finally, archeologists are subject to the pressures of popular interest and of government policy in planning their research. The popular interest in the "Mound Builders" of midwestern United States, for example, is probably responsible for the fact that many more mounds than habitation sites have been dug in that area, if only because it has been easier to raise the money to excavate mounds (Shetrone, 1941). In Europe and Asia, where governments take more interest in archeology, research has often been planned in terms of consideration of national pride or, in the case of the dictatorships, with the purpose of demonstrating official dogma, as Clark (1947, pp. 189–214) has pointed out.

It is probable that all these factors operate to some extent in the field of ethnology as well as archeology. The writer doubts that they can ever be completely eliminated in either field. Nevertheless, one may hope that surveys like the present one will stimulate some workers to introduce into their respective areas objectives which have not yet been applied there but which appear compatible with the nature of the local data and the interests of the anthropologists concerned.

DESCRIPTIVE OBJECTIVES

It is not proposed to enter intensively into a discussion of the objectives of compiling data, since many of these are more pertinent to studies of process and to applied anthropology. Besides, the subject has received little attention in the literature, so far as the writer is aware. We shall therefore only be able to illustrate the variety of kinds of collections, records, and inferences which have been produced during the course of culture-historical research.

COLLECTIONS

Collections of artifacts are more important to the archeologist than to the ethnologist, both because more specimens can usually be obtained in sites than in modern communities (although not always in so great a variety) and because few other data are available to the archeologist. It is therefore better to discuss the kinds of collections in terms of archeology rather than of ethnology. The following five examples will give some idea of the range of variation.

1. American archeologists have developed to a high degree the technique of collecting potsherds from the surfaces of sites, in order to provide a basis for seriating the sites in chronological order. The collections obtained in this fashion not only are limited to pottery but also are made large enough to comprise a considerably larger number of sherds than would be necessary simply to illustrate the ceramic types. This is because the chronology, or subsequent objective, is not based upon the nature of the typology but rather upon the relative frequency, or popularity, of a given type at any point in time and space (see Phillips, Ford, and Griffin, 1951, pp. 219–36, for an illustration of the method and a discussion of the principles involved).

2. A sharply different form of collection is that obtained by excavating stratigraphically in Paleolithic and Paleo-Indian sites, e.g., at Mount Carmel in Palestine (Garrod and Bate, 1937). Such collections are not limited to any particular variety of artifact, such as pottery, but include all the types found. They are segregated by layers of refuse and subdivisions thereof, in order that the succession of occupations may be determined. The number of specimens is relatively large, since it is customary to excavate large areas.

3. United States archeologists have developed the technique of excavating

by arbitrary 10-inch or 25-cm. levels rather than by layers of refuse, in order to obtain better indications of chronology under the conditions of short-term occupancy which prevail in this country (e.g., Phillips, Ford, and Griffin, 1951, pp. 239–306). Again, all types of artifacts found are collected, but the emphasis is upon pottery. Since the area excavated is generally small, the collections are limited in size. They often lack the rarer types of artifacts but are adequate for ceramic seriation of the kind discussed in paragraph 1 above.

4. Another way of limiting one's collection is in terms of the function of the artifacts. Prehistoric archeologists working in Egypt and on the coast of Peru, for example, have often concentrated upon grave objects, either because of the aesthetic quality of these artifacts or because they lend themselves to seriation. On the north coast of Peru, where Mochica pottery portrays scenes from the life of the people, collections from graves have the further advantage that they permit one to reconstruct the life of the people in some detail (Larco Hoyle, 1945).

5. If one chooses to excavate ruins rather than refuse or graves, it is the practice to segregate the collections obtained by construction units, e.g., according to rooms in the pueblos of the American Southwest. Again all types of artifacts are collected and usually in large numbers, since the excavations tend to be extensive. Collections obtained in this manner are used to determine the sequence of construction of rooms, i.e., the growth pattern of the pueblo under investigation, or to work out the way of life of the inhabitants (Taylor, 1948, pp. 175–80).

The foregoing examples illustrate some of the ways in which archeological collections vary in composition, depending upon how they have been obtained and the uses to which they are to be put. It will be noted that the different types of collection lead to different means of establishing chronology or, in paragraphs 4 and 5, of obtaining art objects or reconstructing the life of the people. By carefully selecting from among alternatives like these, both archeologists and ethnologists should be able to increase the efficiency of their research, i.e., to collect the types of artifacts which are best suited to their subsequent objectives.

RECORDS

For the archeologist, the process of recording data consists of taking down information about the details of the environment which are pertinent to his study and about the strata and structures which he encounters and cannot remove to the laboratory. This is ordinarily not a lengthy process, unless one is excavating elaborate ruins or is fortunate enough to be dealing with a civilization, like that of the Maya, which produced carvings and inscriptions (e.g., Morley, 1946). By contrast, most of the ethnologist's information is obtained in the form of records, and therefore it will be advisable to discuss this kind of objective in terms of ethnology rather than of archeology. Again, five examples are given to illustrate the range of variation.

1. Some ethnologists have chosen to collect information concerning a single aspect of culture from a series of tribes, much as the archeologist does when he makes a ceramic survey. An outstanding example is the American Museum of Natural History's program for the study of the Plains Indian sun dance, in which various researchers recorded data on the sun dance among a large number of Plains tribes and Leslie Spier used their data to reconstruct the development and diffusion of the dance (Wissler, 1915–21).

2. Another type of approach has been to collect data from a number of tribes

by means of a questionnaire which covers as many aspects of culture as possible. This is the approach of the Culture Element Distribution Survey of the University of California, which was designed to provide series of trait lists for use in determining the degree of similarity and differences in the cultures of the tribes studied (Kroeber, 1939*b*).

3. The more familiar ethnographic record, which consists of intensive information concerning a single tribe at a given point in its history, should also be mentioned. Malinowski's studies of Trobriand culture is an example (e.g., Malinowski, 1922). These correspond to archeological collections and records made by excavating extensively in a single site or series of related sites.

4. While most ethnological descriptions of culture are restricted to a single period of time, as in paragraph 3, there have also been attempts to record the nature of the culture during successive periods by combined use of historical documents, recollections of informants, and participant observation. This was Malinowski's objective in the study of Oaxaca markets which he was making at the time of his death. His results may be compared with those obtained in archeology by excavation of a stratified site, again with the proviso that they are expressed primarily in terms of records rather than of collections.

5. In all the foregoing examples, the emphasis is upon the customs of a tribe or community as such. The records obtained tell us little, if anything, about the number of people who conform to any particular custom or about the social groups to which these individuals belong. A few recent studies have been directed toward obtaining this kind of data (e.g., Roberts, 1951), which corresponds to that obtained in archeological investigations into the popularity of ceramic types.

The foregoing examples indicate that ethnological records vary in much the same way as do archeological collections and that, in both cases, different kinds of data lend themselves to different methods of interpretation. In other words, the same considerations are involved in the taking of records as in the collection of artifacts.

INFERENCES

Archeologists are accustomed to make inferences concerning nonmaterial culture in an attempt to compensate for their lack of records, basing these partially upon their collections, partially upon conditions in the sites, and partially upon whatever ethnological or historical information may be applicable. Ethnologists do not ordinarily need to have recourse to such inferences, except when the people studied are secretive or have become acculturated and it is desired to reconstruct the aboriginal form of culture. Three examples from archeology will illustrate this kind of objective.

1. Larco Hoyle's reconstruction of Mochica culture in Peru on the basis of scenes portrayed on grave pottery has already been mentioned. This is in the form of a standard ethnographic description. Indeed, some such descriptions have been termed "prehistoric ethnology" (Smith, 1910).

2. Clark (1952) has just published an unusually rich account of economic life in Europe from Mesolithic to Iron times, which is based upon inferences from a wide variety of sources. Although larger in scope than the Plains Indian sun-dance study mentioned above, this would seem to be comparable, to the extent that it is concerned with a restricted aspect of culture but applies to a large number of groups of people.

3. It is common practice among archeologists working in the midwestern and southeastern United States to compile lists of the traits which character-

ize their cultures. While these lists are often based almost entirely on the collections excavated, there is a growing tendency to include inferences concerning nonmaterial culture. For example, the trait list presented for the University of Chicago's excavation at Kincaid in southern Illinois is organized according to the activities of the occupants of the site (Cole *et al.*, 1951, pp. 360–65). There is a close similarity here to the trait lists of the University of California's Culture Element Distribution Survey, which has been described above. As is noted below, both kinds of trait list are designed to be used for the further objective of determining the degree of relationship among the tribes or cultures studied.

CLASSIFICATORY OBJECTIVES

While most cultural information is presented in the form of a simple description, there also exists the possibility of presentation in terms of a classification. This is a common practice in archeology when large numbers of specimens have been collected and it is not feasible to describe each one of them individually. Instead, the investigator groups them into classes and presents the characteristics of the classes.

In this section we will consider only those kinds of classification which are purely factual, i.e., in which the specimens or other materials are grouped solely in terms of their own attributes. Classifications which involve factors of space, time, or genetic relationship will be considered subsequently under separate headings. Since classification is primarily an archeological procedure, our examples will be taken mainly from that field.

It will be convenient to distinguish between two products of classification: the *class*, or series of objects which are grouped together, and the *type*, or series of attributes which are shared by such a group of artifacts and which dis-

tinguish them as a class (Rouse, 1952, pp. 324–30). If one's principal objective in classifying is to produce a description of artifacts, as assumed at the beginning of this section, one is likely to concentrate on the class and to present its characteristics in some detail. If, on the other hand, one is primarily interested in defining units of culture for use in distribution studies or for some other interpretative purpose, then one will probably emphasize the type at the expense of the class.

Some classifiers (e.g., Phillips, Ford, and Griffin, 1951, pp. 61–64) have attempted to strike a compromise between description of the class and definition of the type. However, the attributes which are significant for the first purpose do not necessarily correspond to those which are pertinent to the second, since the first is an empirical approach and the second involves questions of cultural significance (Taylor, 1948, pp. 113–51). Moreover, a thorough description of a class will probably involve many more attributes than will a definition of the type. In the Midwestern Taxonomic System, which is discussed below, for example, only a few of the traits listed for the class are considered "diagnostic" of the type. For these reasons, it will probably be best to regard description of the class and definition of the type as separate objectives.

With this general background, we may turn to a discussion of specific kinds of classificatory objectives. We shall first consider those in which the primary aim is to form classes of artifacts and then those which emphasize types.

CLASSES OF ARTIFACTS

A standard procedure when the objective is to form classes consists of (1) grouping the artifacts according to their material and (2) subdividing the groups in terms of techniques of manufacture, shape, decoration, and function. The result is a hierarchical series of classes, subclasses, and sometimes sub-subclasses, each of the last consisting of all artifacts which are essentially similar in material, technique, and decoration or whatever other criteria may have been used. The archeologist describes these classes by presenting the distinguishing characteristics of their constituent artifact and illustrating representative examples (Osgood, 1942, pp. 22–25).

An alternative procedure, which has recently become widespread in Paleolithic archeology, is to base the classification almost entirely upon techniques of manufacture, i.e., to group the artifacts in terms of the manner in which they were made (Oakley, 1949, pp. 23–33, 40–68). The procedure is well suited to Paleolithic implements for two reasons: first, because these implements are largely made of flint, which retains the scars of manufacture, and, second, because the Paleolithic artisans themselves seem to have been relatively little concerned with the other criteria which might be used for classification, such as shape and decoration.

In the United States there has recently been some tendency to emphasize function as a criterion for classifying nonceramic artifacts (e.g., Taylor, 1948, pp. 170–71). In this procedure, for example, a series of stone implements is sorted into groups of hoes and axes because they appear to be suited to those respective purposes and there is reason to believe that hoes and axes were useful in the culture—an approach which is reminiscent of the ethnological practice of identifying artifacts by inquiring about their use. Classifications of both the technological and the functional kinds are generally nonhierarchical; i.e., each class is considered an independent entity.

TYPES OF ARTIFACTS

American archeologists have been particularly concerned with establishing types of pottery and, more recently, of projectile points for use in seriating sites and in studying stratigraphy, as noted above. They customarily use a binomial nomenclature, with the first term referring to a representative site and the second to one of the attributes diagnostic of the type. Often they group the various types into larger units, called "series" or "wares," although this is not a necessary part of the procedure (see Phillips, Ford, and Griffin, 1951, pp. 61–69, for a more detailed discussion).

Ceramic typology is sometimes applied to complete vessels, but more often to potsherds. Several archeologists (e.g., Krieger, in Newell and Krieger, 1949, pp. 71–80) have questioned the validity of the latter procedure, pointing out that it sometimes results in assigning sherds from the same vessel to different classes and, therefore, in treating them as examples of different types.

TYPES OF PARTS OF ARTIFACTS

Another possibility in studying ceramic typology or in typing any other kind of artifact or structure is to classify in terms of constituent parts of the vessels. In such cases the objective is to establish types of temper, of rim profile, or of design, to give several examples. The writer has applied the rather inappropriate term "mode" to this kind of type in order to distinguish it from types of whole artifacts, whether complete or fragmentary. In this usage a mode may be defined as a series of attributes which are shared by the corresponding parts of a series of artifacts and which distinguish them as a class (Rouse, 1952, pp. 325–26).

Classification to form modes rather than types is advantageous when one is dealing with potsherds, since it side-steps the question of whether to classify them in terms of whole or fragmentary specimens. It has also been applied to objects of art, where there is likewise reason to believe that individual elements of shape and decoration have had different histories and therefore can profitably be studied as separate entities. Proskouriakoff (1950), for example, has applied this approach to Maya sculpture; she establishes a series of types of designs by classifying separately the individual figures sculptured on Maya stelae, without attempting to make an over-all classification of the stelae as such.

TYPES OF CULTURE

Another kind of type is obtained by classifying sites instead of artifacts, structures, or parts thereof. In so doing, one must be careful to deal only with culturally homogeneous sites or else to divide the sites into culturally homogeneous parts, i.e., into units of occupation characterized by different cultural material. One groups the sites and occupation units into classes on the basis of the similarities and differences in their cultural material, notes the elements of culture which are shared by each class, and uses these elements to define the type of culture represented by the class.

This approach has reached its greatest elaboration in the Midwestern Taxonomic System, which, as the name implies, was originally developed by archeologists working in the central part of the United States. In this system the term "component" is applied to the sites and occupation units which are classified, and the term "focus" to the types of culture formed by classifying components. The system also provides for the foci to be grouped into an ascending series of larger units, called "aspects," "phases," and "patterns," much as the

ceramic types discussed above are grouped into wares or series. The procedure is to list the traits of each component as fully as possible, to classify the components in terms of these traits, and to define the resultant foci, aspects, phases, and patterns by noting the traits which are diagnostic of each (McKern, 1939).

Because of the hierarchical arrangement of aspects, phases, and patterns, some commentators have assumed that the Midwestern System is a genetic classification. However, the originators of the system were careful to point out that the only fundamental parts of the classification are the components and foci. They have always regarded the aspects, phases, and patterns merely as arbitrary groupings, designed to provide a means of arranging the foci until a chronology could be developed to take their place. Now that such a chronology is available, there is a tendency to disregard the larger units or, in the case of the Woodland and Mississippi patterns, to reformulate them as time periods (e.g., Phillips, Ford, and Griffin, 1951, pp. 445–51).

Although concerned with archeology rather than with ethnology, the Midwestern Taxonomic System bears a close resemblance to the Culture Element Distribution Survey of the University of California, in its emphasis upon traits and in its use of those traits as a means of expressing similarities and differences in culture. The components of the Midwestern system correspond to the communities studied in the Cultural Element Survey, and, theoretically at least, the foci, aspects, etc., are comparable to the tribes and groupings of tribes with which the Culture Element Survey is concerned. Indeed, as is noted below, one objective which the originators of the Midwestern System had in mind was to try to trace the history of the modern Indian tribes back into the past in terms of the foci and aspects, viewed as prehistoric tribal units (Griffin, 1943, pp. 327–41).

In conclusion, we will note two variations on the kind of cultural units produced by the Midwestern Taxonomic System. Instead of classifying the components in terms of traits, one may do so in terms of types or modes, i.e., in terms of prior classification of the artifacts or parts thereof. An example of classification according to types is the "industries" of French and British prehistorians (e.g., Breuil, 1949, p. 96), and of classification according to modes, the "styles" established by the writer in the West Indies (Rouse, 1952, p. 327). In the former case the scarcity of material other than stone implements has prevented a more detailed classification in terms of culture traits. In the latter the writer has set up both styles and cultures, the styles defined in terms of ceramic modes and the cultures in terms of traits, as in the case of the Midwestern System.

GEOGRAPHICAL OBJECTIVES

One of the simplest things which either the archeologist or the ethnologist can do—although it is sometimes overlooked by amateurs—is to determine the geographical provenience of one's data —whether the latter consist of sites, specimens, records, inferences, and/or one or more of the variety of classes and types which has just been discussed. This is, of course, an objective of most archeological and ethnological surveys. It can be accomplished in a number of different ways, as the following paragraphs will illustrate.

MAPS AND AERIAL PHOTOGRAPHS

The data may be plotted on maps or aerial photographs. By so doing, for example, one can pinpoint the positions of sites or settlements with relatively great accuracy and also determine their relationships to the features of the landscape. British archeology leads the way in both respects, with its Ordnance Survey, which has produced a series of excellent maps showing the positions of the principal sites as well as modern settlements, and with its pioneer work in aerial photography (Atkinson, 1946, pp. 21–31).

Both archeologists and ethnologists have used maps of sites or settlements to study the distribution of population, though this is feasible in archeology only when a chronology is available. For example, the writer recently plotted the distribution of sites by period for the Indian River area of the state of Florida and was thereby able to show that, whereas the center of population had been inland on the St. Johns River during the earlier periods, it later shifted to the coast (Rouse, 1951*b*, pp. 237–57).

Maps, of course, may also be used to plot the distribution of specimens or of various kinds of culture traits. This is perhaps best illustrated by the work of Swedish anthropologists. In discussing the techniques of South American ceramics, for example, Linné (1925) presents a series of maps which show the occurrences of the techniques in both archeological sites and ethnological communities.

Several American archeologists have studied the distribution of ceramic types in terms of frequencies, or relative popularity, rather than simply by presence or absence. For example, Ford (in Phillips, Ford, and Griffin, 1951, pp. 223–24) has published a series of maps bearing isobar-like lines—Ford refrains from calling these "iso-ceramic lines"— which show the frequencies of occurrence of ceramic types in the lower Mississippi Valley. This kind of approach has not been attempted in ethnology, so far as the writer is aware, but it might well prove fruitful there too.

NATURAL AND CULTURAL AREAS

As an alternative to locating one's data on a map or aerial photograph, one may decide to refer them to natural or cultural areas. In either case the effect is to produce a classification of sites, settlements, or units of culture which is based primarily on geographical factors rather than on cultural criteria, as in the examples previously discussed.

Natural areas are those which have been defined in terms of details of the environment. Such areas figure quite widely in both archeological and ethnological literature (e.g., Fox, 1947; Kroeber, 1939*a*). One reason is that they have the advantage of remaining relatively constant through time, so that they provide an efficient basis for classifying cultural material of different ages —an important consideration in the field of archeology. They are also useful in examining the relationships between environment and culture, as in the two examples cited.

Culture areas are defined in terms of the distribution of cultural material. Such areas have sometimes been used as a means of establishing a chronology —an approach termed the "age-area concept"—but we shall here consider only their uses as descriptive and classificatory devices, since chronology is discussed in another section. From these points of view, one's objective in establishing culture areas may be simply to delimit the distribution of culture, or else, once such areas have been established, one may use them as a device for classifying cultural material, as in the case of natural areas.

On the whole, the concept of culture areas seems to be more applicable to ethnology than to archeology, for the reason that culture areas are not so likely as natural areas to remain constant through time and therefore cannot be so easily projected back from ethnology into prehistory. For example,

Strong (1933) has shown that the Plains Indian culture area of the western United States, as established ethnologically, does not apply to the archeology, since settled agricultural Indians lived much farther out on the plains in prehistoric than in historic times. Similarly, several attempts to establish archeological culture areas in the midwestern and southeastern United States (e.g., Shetrone, 1941) have failed, apparently because peoples and cultures shifted frequently from one part of that region to another before the arrival of Europeans. Indeed, it was this failure of the attempts to establish culture areas which led to the development of the Midwestern Taxonomic System. The originators of the system decided that, since geography had proved to be a poor criterion for classification, they would try a scheme which did not involve the factor of space (McKern, 1939, pp. 302-3).

On the other hand, Bennett (1948) has recently come to the conclusion that there is a central Andean culture area in South America—he calls it an "area co-tradition"—which has retained its identity throughout the neo-Indian period. He suggests that it may be possible to define similar area co-traditions in other parts of the New World, including the southeastern United States, where, as noted above, experience has proved otherwise. It may be suggested that the concept of area co-tradition—although not necessarily the co-tradition defined without reference to area—will work best in a region where the natives had a settled mode of life, as they did in the central Andes.

In places where area co-traditions cannot be set up, it is still possible to establish archeological culture areas by limiting them to restricted periods of time. The writer has been able to proceed in this manner in the Greater Antilles, for example. There we had to distinguish two series of culture areas, one organized around the islands themselves and the other around the passages between the islands, the former referring to Period I in our chronology and the latter to Period III (Rouse, 1951a).

CULTURE CENTERS

Instead of establishing culture areas having definite geographic bounds, one may choose to set up a series of culture centers (Wissler, 1923, pp. 61–63, 203–5). One's data can then be referred to the center which it most closely resembles, if it seems desirable to do so. This is particularly useful in a region like the American Southwest, where several tribes with different cultures live side by side and it is therefore impossible to define a single, culturally homogeneous area.

POLITICAL AND CARTOGRAPHIC AREAS

Tribal territories, modern political divisions, or cartographic units may also be used as devices for classifying cultural material. The first is standard ethnological practice (e.g., Kroeber, 1939a, pp. 8–12), while the other two have been used as substitutes in archeological research. For example, the Gladwins (1930) have calculated the frequencies of culture phases in the southwestern United States by map quadrangles and have plotted these in the form of pie diagrams, in order to present graphically the range of distribution of each phase.

CHRONOLOGICAL OBJECTIVES

In the foregoing discussion of geographical objectives, we have had occasion to refer several times to the necessity for also taking chronology into consideration. The reason for this is that space and time are complementary. If space may be considered two-dimensional (as expressed in the co-ordinates of a map), then time represents the third dimension (perpendicular to the

map). Archeologists, of course, implicitly recognize this when they prepare charts of culture sequence in which the dimensions of space are portrayed horizontally and the dimension of time vertically (e.g., Heizer, 1949, p. 59). In other words, space and time perspectives are but two aspects of the same problem.

It follows from this that the objectives of chronological research should correspond to those already discussed in connection with geography. There is one practical difference, however. Whereas geographical provenience can be accurately measured, one cannot always determine the exact age of cultural material, particularly in archeology, where records are lacking. For this reason, archeologists are accustomed to distinguish between *absolute time,* which is accurately measured, and *relative time,* in which the age of one's material can only be determined relative to other material or in terms of a system of chronology which expresses sequence rather than duration of time.

As in the case of geographical research, the material dated varies from sites, communities, artifacts, records, and inferences to types, modes, industries, styles, or whatever other unit of culture is pertinent to one's study. It is even advisable in some cases to determine the age of culture areas, as noted above. We have attempted in the following discussion to choose examples which illustrate the dating of as many of these kinds of material as possible.

SEQUENCES

The simplest method of dating is to arrange one's material in chronological order without reference to a separate time scale or series of periods. This is the procedure used in the University of Chicago studies of Illinois archeology, where the objective seems to be merely to determine the succession of cultural foci (Cole *et al.*, 1951, pp. 226–31). Sequences of occupations in stratified sites are also commonly presented in this fashion (e.g., Garrod and Bate, 1937). The procedure appears to be most useful in pioneer studies and in those which are restricted to a small area. It is generally replaced by one or more of the following approaches when the situation becomes complex, since it is not the most efficient way of distinguishing overlaps of cultural material in time or differences in sequence among a large number of areas.

TIME SCALES

We have seen that the most common means of expressing geographical perspective is to locate one's material on maps. The comparable procedure in the dimension of time is to establish a time scale and to determine the chronological position of one's material with reference to this scale. By the term "time scale" is meant a continuous measure of time, resembling a rule. It may be either absolute or relative; in the former case, the divisions of the scale represent fixed intervals of time, while in the latter they are variable and hence do not indicate duration.

The most practical absolute time scale is our Christian calendar. Ethnologists are able to use this at will, except when projecting their data back into prehistoric time, but it is seldom available to archeologists, unless they are fortunate enough to encounter written records which contain dates, either in our own calendar or in a native calendar which can be correlated with ours. The date-bearing stelae of classic Maya sites, for example, provide a means of determining the age of those sites and of their periods of occupation, but it is first necessary to correlate the Maya calendar with our own (Morley, 1946, pp. 459–62).

In the absence of a calendar, archeologists are able to fall back upon a series of techniques, such as radiocarbon dating, dendrochronology, varve analysis, synchronization of one's material with the written history of another area, and calculations based upon the rate of accumulation of refuse, to produce absolute dates expressed in terms of the Christian calendar (Clark, 1947, pp. 136–50). These, however, are only approximations and vary greatly in accuracy. As Johnson has pointed out (in Libby, 1952, p. 101), even dates based upon radiocarbon analysis are best used only in conjunction with one or more of the types of relative chronology discussed below.

Some archeologists who lack any form of absolute dating have substituted relative time scales of their own making. Sir Flinders Petrie's system of sequence dating is perhaps the best example; this scholar set up an arbitrary series of dates, numbered from 1 to 80 (although the first thirty numbers have never been used) and assigned his grave lots to these dates (Petrie, 1899). Recently, Ford has developed a number of comparable time scales for use in seriating surface collections; he presents these graphically, marking off the principal division points with letters rather than numbers (e.g., Phillips, Ford, and Griffin, 1951, Figs. 17–21). Such artificial time scales may lead to problems of correlation with the Christian calendar, as in dealing with native calendars (Childe, 1934, pp. 12–13).

In discussing geographical objectives, we noted that maps have been used to trace the distribution of elements of culture in terms not only of simple occurrence but also of relative frequency or popularity. This is likewise true of time scales. Petrie (1899), for example, only attempted to point out the dates when traits occurred, whereas Ford (Phillips, Ford, and Griffin, 1951) employs his time scales as measures against which to plot the changing frequencies of ceramic types.

PERIODS

We have seen that a time scale is the temporal unit which corresponds to a map in the dimensions of space. There is a similar correspondence between a period in time and an area in space. Like an area, a period delimits the boundaries of cultural distribution and can also be considered a device for classifying cultural material, although with reference to time rather than to space.

In a recent publication (Rouse, 1951*b*, p. 235), the writer was able to distinguish three kinds of periods, which will here be called "historic," "natural," and "cultural." It is not often that enough data are available to work with all three of these, and, when there are, it may be more practicable to fuse them into a single series of periods. Nevertheless, we shall discuss them separately.

"Historic" periods are those which have been defined in terms of written records. They can usually be dated and are therefore absolute, corresponding in this respect to the absolute time scales discussed above. As an example, we may cite the earliest Chinese dynasties, which, although named and dated by means of the traditional records, are also known through archeological excavation (Creel, 1937, pp. xvi–xxii).

"Natural" periods, like natural areas, are based upon variations in the nature of the environment. They are relative rather than absolute, unless it has been possible to date them by one of the methods of measuring time mentioned above. The criteria used in setting them up vary from sea-level changes, river-terrace sequences, and studies of the meander patterns of rivers to changes in the nature of the soil, in the climate, and in flora and fauna (Clark, 1947, pp. 121–31). When more than one of these criteria are available, it may be necessary to set up a separate series of periods for each (Movius, 1942, Table 1).

Just as natural areas tend to remain relatively constant through time, so natural periods can often be traced with some regularity through space and therefore provide a relatively convenient means of synchronizing cultural material over a large area. They have also proved useful in studies of the relationship between culture and the environment, particularly when considered in connection with natural areas (e.g., Movius, 1942, pp. 257–62).

Natural periods figure most prominently in research on Pleistocene archeology because of the marked changes in environment which took place at that time (Zeuner, 1950). They also play an important role in studies of post-Pleistocene environmentally marginal regions, such as northern Europe, which is on the border line between a temperate and an arctic climate (Movius, 1942), and Florida, which is poorly drained and therefore easily flooded (Rouse, 1951*b*). Regions like these offer the best opportunity for establishing natural periods, because they are relatively sensitive to changes in the environment.

"Cultural" periods, like cultural areas, are defined in terms of the distribution of culture. If established by use of a calendar or one of the substitute techniques mentioned above, they will represent absolute time. More commonly, however, the periods are based upon seriation, stratigraphy, synchronization, correlation with natural periods, the age-area concept, or some other technique for establishing relative chronology. The criteria used vary greatly, depending upon what kinds of data are available. Paleolithic and Paleo-Indian periods, for example, are defined almost entirely in terms of chipped-stone artifacts (Haury, 1950, pp. 170–75). Neolithic and later periods in the Old World are usually based upon a variety of traits (e.g., Frankfort, 1951, pp. 32–48), while in this country many archeologists define their periods solely in terms of ceramics (e.g., Rouse, 1951*b*, pp. 69–70).

Archeologists have found by experience that cultural periods have a relatively restricted distribution in space. It is therefore common practice to establish a separate set of periods for each area studied. As already noted, these are often presented in the form of charts, with the areas shown across the tops and the periods beneath them (Goggin, 1952, Fig. 2).

Historical, natural, and cultural areas are sometimes considered the endpoints of chronological research, as in the example just given. Alternatively, they may be used as the basis for tracing chronological distributions. Hawkes (1940, Tables I–II), for example, presents a pair of charts on which the temporal distribution of the various Paleolithic and Mesolithic cultures in western Europe is shown relative to the natural periods (glacial and climatic) in that area. He also presents maps which complement the charts by portraying the geographical distributions of the cultures. The writer (Rouse, 1939, Chart 6) has charted the frequency distributions of a series of ceramic modes relative to the cultural periods established for northern Haiti. As a final example, we may note that the current charts of California prehistory show culture periods (called "horizons") down the left side and, contrary to the previous examples, culture areas across the top, with cultures (called "facies") in the bodies of the charts (Heizer, 1949, p. 59).

CULTURE CLIMAXES

The concept of "culture center," which was discussed above in the geographical section, has its temporal counterpart in the concept of "climax." Kroeber (1939*a*, pp. 222–28) defines such a climax as the point at which the culture of a given area reaches its greatest intensity. He notes, for example, that classic Greek civilization culminated in such a climax between 500 and 200 B.C., after which a decline set in. Similarly, Phillips, Ford, and Griffin (1951, p. 453) distinguish two climaxes in the prehistory of the eastern United States, one during the burial mound period about A.D. 500–700 and the other in temple mound times about A.D. 1500–1600.

HORIZONS AND TRADITIONS

While cultural periods and climaxes have a relatively restricted geographical distribution, it often happens that one or more of their traits extend from area to area through a series of contemporaneous periods. Kroeber (1944, pp. 108–11) has applied the term "horizon style" to this phenomenon, as it occurs in Peruvian archeology, where the traits involved are largely ceramic and consist of both techniques of decoration and attributes of design. Such horizon styles are very useful in establishing chronology, because they provide a starting point for seriation, as well as a basis for synchronizing periods over a large region.

It is not uncommon for one or more culture traits to survive from period to period within a single geographic area. Willey (1945) has applied the term "tradition" to this phenomenon, again in connection with Peruvian archeology. He regards a tradition as the counterpart of a horizon style and applies both concepts to the study of ceramic distributions.

STAGES

A final approach to chronology consists of setting up a series of stages reflecting the development of culture instead of simply distribution, as in the case of the periods and horizons just

discussed. Morgan and the other evolutionary ethnologists of the last century used this approach, and it is also
exemplified by the Stone-Bronze-Iron
classification of European prehistory,
which originated in the same intellectual climate (Lowie, 1937, pp. 19-29).

While these early evolutionary
schemes are still useful as an expression
of the degree of cultural development,
they have largely been abandoned as a
means of presenting chronology because they do not conform to the facts
of cultural distribution as now known
(Childe, 1951, pp. 161–79). The Stone-
Bronze-Iron classification, for example,
is homotaxical; i.e., its three stages, as
well as their subdivisions, have occurred
at different times in different places
(Daniel, 1943, pp. 39–43). For this
reason, they are rarely employed any
more as temporal units in the Western
world, although Soviet archeologists
still follow this usage (Golomshtok,
1938, p. 445).

On the other hand, the evolutionary
approach to chronology has recently
been revived in the New World in the
form of "developmental classifications."
Strong (in Bennett, 1948, p. 98), for
example, has set up a series of "cultural
epochs," or stages of cultural development, in Virú Valley, Peru, which he
believes are applicable to the rest of
the central Andes and to Mesoamerica,
if not to other parts of the world. His
formulation would seem to have two
advantages over previous studies of the
same kind: (1) in so far as possible, it
is based upon observed distributions
rather than on conjecture, and (2) for
the most part it is defined in terms of
degree of development rather than of
specific cultural content. It therefore
provides a means of expressing the
broad sweep of chronology over a
whole series of areas without bringing
in the differences in detail from area
to area.

HISTORIC OBJECTIVES

The foregoing objectives all have a
factual orientation, in that they are
concerned solely with the nature and
distribution of culture. There remains
the problem of determining how one's
cultural material happened to take on
its peculiar characteristics and to occur
when and where it did. This is a historical problem and is usually solved by
invoking one or more of the following
processes of culture history.

It is not within the scope of this
paper to discuss the validity of the
processes, since to do so would involve
questions of theory which are considered in another part of the program.
We shall merely consider a representative series of processes as examples of
the manner in which archeologists have
attempted to explain the character and
distribution of cultural material in historical terms.

DIFFUSION AND PERSISTENCE

If geographical study has shown that
a type, industry, or other kind of cultural unit has a widespread and continuous distribution in space, it is customary to conclude that the unit has
diffused from one point in its distribution to the others—usually from the
point where it occurs earliest or in
greatest complexity (e.g., Childe, 1950,
pp. 9–10). Similarly, if the cultural
unit has a continuous distribution
through time, it may be said to have
persisted from the date of its earliest to
the date of its latest occurrence (Rouse,
1939, pp. 14–15).

INDEPENDENT INVENTION

If, on the other hand, the material
under study has a discontinuous distribution in either space or time, one may
invoke the theory of independent invention or parallel development. Opinion differs as to how great the discontinuity should be before one does

this or, indeed, whether independent invention ever takes place at all (Lowie, 1937, p. 158).

MIGRATION AND OTHER MECHANISMS OF SPREAD

After reaching the conclusion that diffusion has taken place, one may proceed to theorize about the manner in which it happened. If a diffused unit is complex, as in the case of a *Kulturkreis,* its spread may be attributed to migration (Schmidt, 1939). If, on the other hand, the unit is relatively simple, anthropologists are more likely to assume that the peoples involved have borrowed the idea from one another (Linton, 1936, pp. 324–46). Alternatively, specimens which appear to be intrusive into a site or community and which occur in such small numbers as to suggest that they have been carried there are best regarded as the result of trade (e.g., Cole *et al.,* 1951, pp. 148–54).

PARTICIPATION IN CULTURE

We have seen that some archeologists trace the geographical and/or temporal distributions of traits in terms of relative frequencies of occurrence. The purpose of so doing is to obtain a measure of the popularity of the traits. It is assumed that these traits are alternatives, to use a term of Linton's (1936, pp. 271–87), and that the individuals participating in the culture have been able to choose from among them. Observations of our own culture have shown that such choices tend to follow the dictates of popularity, and it is believed that this is also true of prehistoric cultures (Phillips, Ford, and Griffin, 1951, pp. 219–23).

The theory of participation in culture is also invoked to explain occurrences of atypical material, such as residues of artifacts left after classification. These residues may be attributed to the individual peculiarities of the artisans (Linton, 1936), unless they prove to be trade objects.

ACCULTURATION

Another way of explaining the nature and distribution of one's cultural material is in terms of contacts between two or more groups of people having different cultures. In ethnology this approach is used mainly in studies of what happens when our civilization comes into contact with "primitive" cultures (Linton, 1940). Archeologists and students of history, on the other hand, deal more often with the mutual interplay of cultures on a more equal basis. Ortiz (1947, pp. 97–103) has suggested substituting the term "transculturation" in such cases, in order to avoid any implication that one of the participating groups is superior to the rest.

ECOLOGICAL ADAPTATION

Both ethnologists and archeologists have frequently had recourse to biological and ecological factors in explaining the facts of culture history. This is well illustrated for ethnology by Kroeber's study of the interrelationships between cultural and natural areas in North America and for archeology by Clark's analysis of the manner in which the economies of prehistoric Europe were adapted to their corresponding biological and physical environments (Kroeber, 1939a; Clark, 1952, pp. 7–21). As both Kroeber and Clark point out, the distribution of cultures and elements of culture sometimes coincides nicely with that of particular biotas and habitats.

PHYLOGENY

A number of archeologists working in the southwestern United States have attempted to explain the particular geographic and temporal distributions of cultures in that area by invoking the biological theory of phylogeny. They have postulated the existence at an early date of a small number of Indian groups, each with its own "basic" culture, and have assumed that these groups, as well as their cultures, gradually split up by a process of fission into the present variety of tribes and cultures. Gladwin and Gladwin (1934) present this reconstruction graphically in the form of a series of diagrams, in which the basic cultures appear at the bottom and lines branch out from them to indicate the presumed lines of descent. Time periods are shown along the sides of the diagrams, but the factor of space is ignored. This type of approach, which amounts to a genetic classification of Southwestern cultures, has been criticized for its failure to take into consideration such historical processes as diffusion and transculturation (Brew, 1946, pp. 44–66).

PARALLEL DEVELOPMENT

An alternate and less rigid genetic approach consists of attributing two or more sequences of types or cultures, such as the traditions discussed above, to parallel development from a single ancestor. The assumption here is that the traits shared by such traditions are the result of common cultural heritage (as in Sapir, 1916, p. 43), but it does not follow that the traditions themselves have to be arranged phylogenetically. Instead, the investigator determines the extension of each tradition in space and time by plotting the distributions of its constituent types or cultures (Goggin, 1952, Fig. 3).

One way of getting at traditions is to start with historic tribes and to work back from them to the prehistoric cultural units which seem to be ancestral. This is known in American archeology as the "direct historical approach" (Strong, 1933, pp. 275–76).

EVOLUTION

The emergence of developmental classifications in American archeology

has already been noted. As Steward (1949) has pointed out, these classifications require the assumption that some elements of culture are more basic than others, with the result that, given the same environmental setting, their appearance in a culture will touch off a series of related changes, which may lift the culture from one stage in the classification to another. Steward has attempted to validate this assumption by comparing the sequences of cultural development in the various arid and semiarid centers of ancient civilization. Regardless of the success of this particular study, it points up the possibility of interpreting the facts of cultural distribution in terms of evolutionary process.

OTHER PROCESSES

Since cultural processes are discussed more fully in another part of this program, it is not considered necessary to give a complete inventory here. We may note in passing, however, that one may also interpret cultural distributions in terms of human physiology or psychology, of art appreciation, or of differences in the physical capabilities of various forms of early man. In any particular instance it is probably best to consider all possible explanations for the facts of culture history (cf. the geological principle of multiple working hypotheses; Chamberlin, 1944).

CONCLUSIONS

An attempt has been made to survey some of the more important objectives of culture-historical research in archeology and ethnology. In conclusion, we would suggest that careful choice among these objectives will improve the efficiency of one's study or program of studies. It is advisable, for example, to avoid duplicating objectives already accomplished as the result of previous research and to select only those objectives which are best suited to the nature of the available data and most compatible with one another, in the sense that they form a logically consistent series, leading to the solution of specific problems. In many cases the success or failure of one's research may depend to a considerable extent upon one's choice of objectives.

REFERENCES

ATKINSON, R. J. C. 1946. *Field Archeology*. London: Methuen & Co., Ltd.

BENNETT, W. C. (ed.). 1948. *A Reappraisal of Peruvian Archaeology*. ("Memoirs of the Society for American Archaeology," No. 4.) Menasha, Wisconsin.

BIRKET-SMITH, K. "Recent Achievements in Eskimo Research," *Journal of the Royal Anthropological Institute*, LXXVII, 145–57. London.

BREUIL, H. 1949. *Beyond the Bounds of History: Scenes from the Old Stone Age*. London: P. R. Gawthorn.

BREW, J. O. 1946. *Archaeology of Alkali Ridge, Southeastern Utah*. . . . ("Papers of the Peabody Museum of American Archaeology and Ethnology, Harvard University," Vol. XXI.) Cambridge.

CHAMBERLIN, T. D. 1944. "The Method of Multiple Working Hypotheses," *Scientific Monthly*, LIX, 357–62.

CHILDE, V. GORDON. 1934. *New Light on the Most Ancient East*. New York: D. Appleton–Century Co.

——. 1950. *Prehistoric Migrations in Europe*. Oslo: Instituttet for Sammenlignende Kulturforskning.

——. 1951. *Social Evolution*. New York: Henry Schuman, Inc.

CLARK, G. 1947. *Archaeology and Society*. 2d ed. London: Methuen & Co., Ltd.

CLARK, J. G. D. 1952. *Prehistoric Europe: The Economic Basis*. London: Methuen & Co., Ltd.

COLE, F. C., *et al.* 1951. *Kincaid: A Prehistoric Illinois Metropolis*. Chicago: University of Chicago Press.

CREEL, H. G. 1937. *Studies in Early Chinese Culture*. Baltimore: Waverly Press, Inc.

DANIEL, G. E. 1943. *The Three Ages: An Essay on Archaeological Method*. Cambridge, England: At the University Press.

EMORY, K. P. 1943. *Polynesian Stone Remains*, pp. 9–21. ("Papers of the Peabody Museum of American Archaeology and Ethnology, Harvard University," Vol. XX.) Cambridge.

FOX, SIR C. 1947. *The Personality of Britain*. 4th ed. Cardiff: National Museum of Wales.

FRANKFORT, H. 1951. *The Birth of Civilization in the Near East*. London: Williams & Norgate.

CARROD, D. A. E., and BATE, D. M. A. 1937. *The Stone Age of Mount Carmel: Excavations at the Wady El-Mughara*. Vol. I. Oxford: Clarendon Press.

GLADWIN, W. and H. S. 1930. *The Western Range of the Red-on-Buff Culture*. ("Gila Pueblo Medallion Papers," No. 5.) Globe, Ariz.: Gila Pueblo.

——. 1934. *A Method for the Designation of Cultures and Their Variations*. ("Gila Pueblo Medallion Papers," No. 15.) Globe, Ariz.: Gila Pueblo.

GOGGIN, J. M. 1952. *Space and Time Perspective in Northern St. Johns Archeology, Florida*. ("Yale University Publications in Anthropology," No. 47.) New Haven.

GOLOMSHTOK, E. A. 1938. "The Old Stone Age in European Russia," *Transactions of the American Philosophical Society*, n.s., XXIX, 191–468. Philadelphia.

GRIFFIN, J. B. 1943. *The Fort Ancient Aspect: Its Cultural and Chronological Position in Mississippi Valley Archaeology*. Ann Arbor: University of Michigan Press.

HAURY, E. W. 1950. *The Stratigraphy and Archaeology of Ventana Cave, Arizona*. Albuquerque, N.M.: University of New Mexico Press.

HAWKES, C. F. C. 1940. *The Prehistoric Foundations of Europe: To the Mycenean Age*. London: Methuen & Co., Ltd.

HEIZER, R. F. (ed.). 1949. *A Manual of Archaeological Field Methods*. Millbrae, Calif.: National Press.

KROEBER, A. L. 1939a. *Cultural and Natural Areas of Native North America*. ("University of California Publications in American Archaeology and Ethnology," Vol. XXXVIII.) Berkeley.

——. 1939b. "Culture Element Distributions. XI. Tribes Surveyed," *Anthropological Records*, Vol. I, No. 7. Berkeley.

——. 1944. *Peruvian Archeology in 1942.* ("Viking Fund Publications in Anthropology," No. 4.) New York.

LARCO HOYLE, R. 1945. *Los Mochicas.* Trujillo, Peru: Museo R. Larco Herrera.

LIBBY, W. F. 1952. *Radiocarbon Dating.* Chicago: University of Chicago Press.

LINNÉ, S. 1925. "The Technique of South American Ceramics," *Göt Kungl. Vetenskaps-och Vitterhets—Samhälles Handlingar*, Vol. XXIX, No. 5, Göteborg.

LINTON, R. 1936. *The Study of Man.* New York: D. Appleton–Century Co.

——. (ed.). 1940. *Acculturation in Seven American Indian Tribes.* New York: D. Appleton–Century Co.

LOWIE, R. H. 1937. *The History of Ethnological Theory.* New York: Farrar & Rinehart, Inc.

McKERN, W. C. 1939. "The Midwestern Taxonomic Method as an Aid to Archaeological Culture Study," *American Anthropologist*, IV, 301–13.

MALINOWSKI, B. 1922. *Argonauts of the Western Pacific.* London: George Routledge & Sons, Ltd.

MORLEY, S. G. 1946. *The Ancient Maya.* Stanford: Stanford University Press.

MOVIUS, H. L., JR. 1942. *The Irish Stone Age: Its Chronology, Development, and Relationships.* Cambridge: At the University Press.

NEWELL, H. P., and KRIEGER, A. D. 1949. *The George C. Davis Site, Cherokee County, Texas.* ("Memoirs of the Society for American Archaeology," No. 5.) Menasha, Wis.

OAKLEY, K. P. 1949. *Man the Tool-Maker.* London: British Museum.

ORTIZ, F. 1947. *Cuban Counterpoint: Tobacco and Sugar.* New York: A. A. Knopf.

OSGOOD, C. 1942. *The Ciboney Culture of Cayo Redondo, Cuba.* ("Yale University Publications in Anthropology," No. 25.) New Haven.

PETRIE, W. M. F. 1899. "Sequence in Prehistoric Remains," *Journal of the Royal Anthropological Institute*, XXIX, 295–301. London.

PHILLIPS, R.; FORD, J. A.; and GRIFFIN, J. B. 1951. *Archaeological Survey in the Lower Mississippi Alluvial Valley, 1940–1947.* ("Papers of the Peabody Museum of American Archaeology and Ethnology, Harvard University," Vol. XXV.) Cambridge.

PROSKOURIAKOFF, T. 1950. *A Study of Classic Maya Sculpture.* ("Carnegie Institution of Washington Publications," No. 593.) Washington, D.C.

ROBERTS, J. M. 1951. *Three Navaho Households: A Comparative Study in Small Group Culture.* ("Papers of the Peabody Museum of American Archaeology and Ethnology, Harvard University," Vol. XL, No. 3.) Cambridge.

ROUSE, I. 1939. *Prehistory in Haiti: A Study in Method.* ("Yale University Publications in Anthropology," No. 21.) New Haven.

——. 1951a. "Areas and Periods of Culture in the Greater Antilles," *Southwestern Journal of Anthropology*, VII, 248–65.

——. 1951b. *A Survey of Indian River Archeology, Florida.* ("Yale University Publications in Anthropology," No. 44.) New Haven.

——. 1952. *Porto Rican Prehistory.* ("Scientific Survey of Porto Rico and the Virgin Islands," Vol. XVIII, Part III.) New York: New York Academy of Sciences.

SAPIR, E. 1916. *Time Perspective in Aboriginal American Culture: A Study in Method.* (Canadian Department of Mines, Geological Survey, Mem. 90; "Anthropological Series," No. 13.) Ottawa.

SCHMIDT, W. 1939. *The Culture Historical Method of Ethnology.* New York: Fortuny's.

SMITH, H. I. 1910. *The Prehistoric Ethnology of a Kentucky Site.* ("Anthropological Papers of the American Museum of Natural History," Vol. VI, No. 1.) New York.

SHETRONE, H. C. 1941. *The Mound-Builders.* New York: D. Appleton–Century Co.

STEWARD, J. H. 1949. "Cultural Causality and Law: A Trial Formulation of the Development of Early Civilizations," *American Anthropologist*, n.s., LI, 1–27.

STRONG, W. D. 1933. "Plains Culture in the Light of Archeology," *American Anthropologist*, n.s., XXXV, 271–87.

TAYLOR, W. W. 1948. *A Study of Archeology*. ("Memoirs of the American Anthropological Association," No. 69.) Menasha, Wis.

WILLEY, G. R. 1945. "Horizon Styles and Pottery Traditions in Peruvian Archaeology," *American Antiquity*, XI, 49–56.

WISSLER, C. (ed.). 1915–21. *Sun Dance of the Plains Indian*. ("Anthropological Papers of the American Museum of Natural History," Vol. XVI, Nos. 1–7.) New York.

———. 1923. *Man and Culture*. New York: Thomas Y. Crowell Co.

ZEUNER, F. E. 1950. *Dating the Past: An Introduction to Geochronology*. 2d ed. London: Methuen & Co., Ltd.

Archeological Theories and Interpretation: Old World

By J. GRAHAME D. CLARK

ANTIQUARIAN STUDIES first developed in the Old World during the sixteenth century as an aspect of the rise of national feeling which followed the break-up of medieval Christendom. In so far as the early antiquaries interpreted the past, they did so in terms of their own particular group; their interests were mainly literary, and their chief aim was to extend the history of their native lands. Archeology proper, based on the study of material things, first began to develop rapidly during the latter part of the eighteenth century, and it was not until 1836 that sufficient material had been assembled to prompt a logical system of classification.

In C. J. Thomsen's three-period system (1836, 1838–43; see also Daniel, 1943, 1950), originally devised as an aid to the explanation of the collections in the Danish National Museum at Copenhagen, we can detect for the first time the influence of a theory of more than parochial application. Although Lamarck failed to devise a convincing explanation of biological evolution, his transformist ideas influenced profoundly the climate of thought and opinion. Thomsen's classification of archeological material into the three ages of Stone, Bronze, and Iron carried conviction because it was based on the concept of a progressive evolution from rude and simple to more efficient and complex.

The announcement of Darwin's theory of natural selection in 1858[1] gave an immediate and lasting impetus to prehistoric studies. Until a convincing theory of evolution had been given to the world, the study of man was not appreciated by more than a few individuals. One may illustrate this in two ways. For one thing, it is evident that the propounders of the three-period system had no conception of the antiquity of man. For instance, in his book on *The Primeval Antiquities of Denmark*, J. J. A. Worsaae assigned an antiquity (not even a duration) of "at least three thousand years" to the Danish Stone Age,[2] a chronology fully consistent

1. The "theory of natural selection" was first made public at a meeting of the Linnaean Society on July 1, 1858, when Lyell communicated parallel papers by Darwin and Wallace. Darwin did not publish *The Origin of Species* until the following year.

2. On p. 8 of the English translation (Worsaae [1849]), Worsaae argued that "the stone-period must be of extraordinary antiquity. If the Celts possessed settled abodes in the west of Europe, more than two thousand years ago, how much more ancient must be the population which preceded the arrival of the Celts. A great number of years must pass away before a people, like the Celts, could spread themselves over the west of Europe, and render the land productive; it is therefore no exaggeration if we attribute to the stone-period an antiquity of, at least, three thousand years."

with that of Archbishop Ussher. On the other hand, the work of those who were, in fact, exploring traces of Paleolithic man was either ignored or explained away. To Dean Buckland, first Reader in Geology at Oxford University and the leading authority on cave exploration of his day, Pleistocene fauna was so much evidence for the biblical Flood, and the Red Lady of Paviland, now recognized as of Upper Paleolithic age, an inserted burial of the Roman period (1823). McEnery's pioneer excavations at Kent's Hole during 1826–41, where he systematically recovered worked flints in association with Pleistocene fauna, were so little regarded that his notebooks were even mislaid after his death (see Garrod, 1926, p. 27). In France it was the same story: Boucher de Perthe's discoveries in the Somme gravels, like those of Tournal in the Grotte de Bize, were ignored by men of science.

Darwin's announcement of the theory of natural selection brought a rapid change of attitude. McEnery's notes were found, and extracts from his *Cavern Researches* were published (1859). That same year a deputation of eminent scientists left England for the Somme Valley and solemnly attested the discoveries of Boucher.[3] The antiquity of man indeed had ceased to be an anomaly and had become a philosophical necessity. There followed an epoch of intensive archeological activity. Systematic investigation of the Dordogne caves was begun by Lartet and Christy in 1863 (1865–75), and two years later Lubbock gave formal recognition to the separate status of the earlier Stone Age by coining the terms "Paleolithic" and "Neolithic" (1865). By 1881 G. de Mortillet had established the main outlines of the classic Paleolithic sequence of France (1881),

3. See *Phil. Trans. Royal Society*, Part II (1860), pp. 277–317; *Archaeologia*, XXXVIII (1860), 1–28.

a sequence which, so far as its later phases were concerned, was completed by Breuil in the early years of the twentieth century (1912). Within two generations the prehistorians had succeeded, at least in France, in spanning the great gulf of time opened up by acceptance of the idea of human evolution. Yet they were not able to answer nearly quickly enough the questions which called insistently for answers.

While archeologists sweated at their digging, distinguished ethnologists sat cosily at their desks, defining the stages through which in inferior times the human race had passed. The idea that human culture, like the animal world, had evolved gradually from simple beginnings was, as we have seen, already current before Darwin won acceptance for his theory of biological evolution. Moreover, the Swedish zoölogist, Sven Nilsson (1838–43), had already sought in 1838 to deduce from comparative ethnology the stages through which humanity had passed in the course of its history.

It was not for nothing that Nilsson's book was translated into English in 1866 by Sir John Lubbock himself (1866). The concept of evolutionary stages deducible from a knowledge of existing cultures was exactly what the anthropologists of the Darwinian era needed. Of Nilsson's many followers I shall mention only Lewis H. Morgan, who characteristically entitled his chief book *Ancient Society* (1877), even though its conclusions were mainly based on a study of contemporary societies. Rejecting Nilsson's phase of herding and nomadism, Morgan accepted in substance his first, third, and fourth stages, which he dubbed, respectively, "savagery," "barbarism," and "civilization." By further subdividing the first two of these, he characterized seven phases of development through which he supposed mankind to have passed. I say "supposed" advisedly, because, of course, these stages were hypothetical. As Dr. Glyn Daniel has recently expressed it (1950, p. 188), his whole scheme, like that of Nilsson, "was based primarily not on archaeological evidence but on the comparative study of modern primitive peoples, the arrangement of these existing economies and societies into an evolutionary sequence, and the projection of this hypothetical sequence into the prehistoric past." Now it would be ridiculous at this time of day to apportion praise or blame to Morgan, Tylor, and the rest: the mid-Victorian anthropologists were confronted by an immense void, for many of them suddenly apprehended, and they merely did what any other scientists would have done under similar circumstances—they plugged the gap with hypotheses. All I am concerned to emphasize at the moment is the fact that their stages were hypothetical; that they were stopgaps against the time when archeological research should have established on a basis of historical fact the actual course of prehistory.

One may legitimately insist, though, that hypothetical prehistory, useful as it may have been seventy or eighty years ago, has long ceased to be respectable. It is not for me to estimate the contribution to ethnology of the culture-historical school of Graebner and Schmidt. What most prehistorians would reject out of hand, though, is any attempt to use the theories of this or any other school (Marxist included) in place of excavation as a means of finding out about the prehistoric past. In this connection I would cite specifically Oswald Menghin's grandiose *Weltgeschichte der Steinzeit* (1931; Clark, 1931). In his opening presidential address to the newly formed Prehistoric Society, Professor Childe (1935, p. 14) pointed out that (*a*) Menghin's "culture cycles" have not been arrived at as a result of wrestling with the archeological data but are, in fact, no more than

"categories borrowed from ethnography into which the archaeological evidence has been fitted"; (*b*) his "culture cycles" do not even exist today—they are "abstractions obtained by isolating traits common to several peoples and areas"; and (*c*) as a result, his "culture traits" are considered without reference to geographical environment. As Childe puts it: "Menghin insists so strongly on an axe as an expression of a historical tradition that the reader may forget that it is an implement for felling trees."

One need hardly feel surprised that, when Menghin's text is examined in close relation to the archeological material, it is seen to abound in contradictions and even in absurdities. To take only one example, Menghin seized upon an assemblage of objects from Kunda in northern Esthonia as a vehicle for the continuation during the postglacial period of his hypothetical "bone culture," without stopping to consider what, in point of fact, these bone and antler objects really signified. In effect, it was a travesty to accept these pieces, all of them from the bed of an old lake and fairly evidently the losses of fishermen, as constituting a veritable culture. Two years after Menghin's book appeared, the Esthonian archeologist Indreko (1948, see esp. pp. 107 ff.) excavated a settlement on the shore of the Kunda lake. There he recovered the true culture of these fishermen, and it comprised, in addition to objects of antler and bone, a broad range of scrapers, knives, and adzes made from flint, quartz, and greenstone. The "bone culture" of Kunda proved to be quite imaginary. As Childe (1935, p. 3) so appositely said in his presidential address, a culture in the archeological sense of the term "is not an *a priori* category elaborated in the studies of philosophers and then imposed from outside upon working archaeologists. Cultures are observed facts."

The attitude revealed in Menghin's

book was indeed anachronistic. This applies with possibly even greater force to the Marxist school of prehistory, shackled as this is to a dogma announced to the world (Marx, 1904, Preface) in the same year as Darwin published his *The Origin of Species*. The mutual attraction of Marxism and prehistory is not hard to understand. To the prehistorian, Marxism might seem to offer an escape from the limitations of archeological evidence: once accept the dogma that the means of production determine the whole structure of society, and the way is open to reconstructing former states of society on the basis of the economic data commonly afforded by archeological research. On the other hand, Marxists find in archeology a means of recovering what they hold to be tangible evidence for the validity of the dogma of the materialist interpretation of history; the very limitations of archeology are, from this point of view, a positive advantage. By a curious inversion Efimenko and other leading Soviet prehistorians of the 1930's actually rejected the classification of prehistoric cultures in terms of material forms in favor of one based on stages in social development, such as preclan, clan, and class societies (for summary with references, see Childe, 1951, pp. 27–29). The short answer to this has recently been given by Childe in his *Social Evolution*, where he points out that "the Russian scheme of classification assumes in advance precisely what archaeological facts have to prove" (1951, p. 29). In reality, it is exceedingly difficult to reach any certain conclusions by archeological means about nonmaterial aspects of life. What is quite sure is that Marxist dogma is no more valid as a substitute for archeological research than were the speculations of Victorian ethnologists. Both are equally out of date.

To return to archeology, it should be emphasized that the period between *The Origin of Species* and the outbreak of the first World War was one of intense activity. The suggestion sometimes made that the prehistorians of this period were blinded by the biological theory of evolution is to betray a lack of historical understanding. The theorisers of the time were the ethnologists, who, until the turn of the century, hardly stirred from their armchairs. When prehistorians did indulge in theory, by no means all of them came out on the side of the evolutionists. In the discussions which raged about the origins of Mycenaean civilization toward the close of the nineteenth century (Daniel, 1950, p. 180), some looked to the north, others to the east; nobody sought an explanation in independent evolution. One of the leading protagonists of the notion that the later prehistoric cultures of Europe were no more than pale reflections of oriental civilizations was Oscar Montelius, the arch-systematizer in terms of periods of the Neolithic and Bronze ages of northern Europe; not only was he fully aware of the historic role of diffusion, but the absolute chronology of his periods was based precisely on contacts between prehistoric and civilized peoples. Prehistorians at this time were preoccupied with establishing time sequences, for the very practical reason that, without some such chronological framework, it was impossible to organize their material or to learn anything of the course of prehistory.

What in reality limited their work was not theoretical obtuseness but historical circumstances. They were pioneers, and they were carrying out their experiments in a restricted part of Europe; the main outlines of Paleolithic archeology were first worked out, for instance, in France, where the sequence happened to be particularly well marked. The first textbooks of prehistory in reality mirrored local results;

yet for long these were the only ones available, and it is not to be wondered at that they should be accepted by students as though of general application.

The great expansion of the area of prehistoric research in the Old World, so largely inspired by the Abbé Henri Breuil during the years immediately after the first World War, soon showed the situation in its true light. As results began to come in from different parts of Africa and Asia and even from central and eastern Europe, it became obvious that the new material would not fit the classic sequence. One of the first to appreciate the implications of the new discoveries was Miss Dorothy Garrod (1928, esp. p. 261). In an address delivered in 1928 she pointed out:

The classification of de Mortillet is based on discoveries made in Europe, and more especially in Western Europe. It therefore represents correctly the sequence in time of a certain number of Palaeolithic cultures seen, as it were, in section over a very limited part of the earth's surface. . . .

It is becoming more and more clear that it is not in Europe that we must seek the origins of the various Palaeolithic peoples who successively overran the West. . . . The classification of de Mortillet therefore only records the order of arrival in the West of a series of cultures, each of which has originated and probably passed through the greater part of its existence elsewhere.

In point of fact, the unilinear evolutionary sequence had already begun to break down some years before, even for the Lower Paleolithic period. When, for instance, the Germans began to investigate their Pleistocene deposits for traces of the earliest human cultures, they found that the classical hand-axes of Chelles and St. Acheul were replaced, or at least strongly supplemented, by flint industries based on the production of flakes. In his great book *El Hombre fosil*, published in 1916, Obermaier had already recognized the existence of these two contemporary

traditions in the Lower Paleolithic period of Europe. Again, in publishing the early flake industry from Clacton, England, Hazzledine Warren pointed out that it had "no cultural connection with the Chellian or Acheulian stage. As knowledge of the Palaeolithic period increases we are realising more fully the divergence of races and cultures which were living contemporaneously together."[4] It was, of course, this realization that undermined acceptance of the textbook sequence.

The French Upper Paleolithic sequence was more finely drawn and correspondingly more vulnerable. For instance, the earliest of the first three main stages, the Aurignacian, was itself divided into three; the designation of these as Lower, Middle, and Upper recorded stratigraphic facts observed in the excavation of French caves and rock-shelters, but it encouraged in some minds the idea that they represented stages in the evolution of a single culture. Yet, even in 1928, Miss Garrod (1928, p. 263) was able from her own experience to suggest that the Middle Aurignacian might prove to be a separate culture originating somewhere in the area of Palestine, where it played a dominant role in Upper Paleolithic times. When ten years later she came to make a fresh survey of the Upper Paleolithic world (1938), not only had this suggestion been substantially proved, but research in southern Russia and central Europe had made it evident that the Upper Aurignacian or Gravettian of France was, in reality, no more than a western extension of another quite distinct culture, which originated farther north than the Middle or true Aurignacian and spread in from the east. To illustrate her thesis, Miss Garrod published distribution maps showing the geographical extent of what she had shown to be two distinct cultures rather than stages in the

4. *Proc. Prehist. Soc. East Anglia*, III, 602.

unilinear development in western Europe of a single tradition.

It might be thought that the greater variation, shorter duration, and smaller geographical range of the Neolithic and later prehistoric cultures would have made it easier to recognize them. Yet here again one should remember that the early prehistorians were primarily concerned in establishing the sequence of archeological material in the areas in which they worked; only when this stage had been passed, could one expect appreciation of the significance of cultures as distinct from periods. In this respect the prehistorians were not notably behind the ethnologists of the day. After all, until the Torres Straits Expedition at the turn of the century, ethnology, at least as it was conducted from the Old World, seems to have consisted very largely in hypotheticating history, and it needed still another generation before monographs like Radcliffe-Brown's *Andaman Islanders* (1922) began to give tangible evidence of a more scientific outlook.

Between the two world wars the attention of prehistorians, like that of ethnologists, was focused on the definition and interpretation of cultures. We have seen already how, even in Paleolithic archeology, the aim had shifted from the definition of chronological periods to the tracing of the genesis and spread of cultures in time and space. By a curious irony of history, one of the first impulses in the sphere of later prehistory came from a school of perverted racialists. German antiquaries, perhaps more than those of any other European country, had from the beginning been absorbed in the history of their own land and people, as witnessed, for example, by the number of lovingly annotated editions of the *Germania* which appeared from the fifteenth century onward. By playing on this sentiment and inflaming it with a spurious racialism, Gustaf Kossinna

(1912, 1926, and others) built up a pan-German school of prehistory, the aim of which was not merely to glorify the German-Nordic past but to depreciate that of other peoples. Now, however much we may deplore such an attitude and however irretrievably deflated is the chronology by which alone the cultural priority of the Germans could be maintained, Kossinna performed a real service by his insistence that prehistory was concerned with peoples who lived and struggled; his definition of cultural groups and his use of distribution maps to illustrate their geographical spread were much in advance of their time.

The new approach, free from any taint of racial or nationalist propaganda, is seen at its best in V. Gordon Childe's *Dawn of European Civilization*, first published in 1925. In this pioneer work Childe defined and described the Neolithic and Early Bronze Age cultures of prehistoric Europe and, so far as possible, traced their genesis and history. At the end of his book he printed maps illustrating the geographical extent of the main cultures at each of four chronological stages. In this way he demonstrated for the first time the actual culture history of the different parts of Europe from the introduction of farming down to the fall of Cnossus.

Even in his first edition, Childe had already made sufficiently plain the marginal character of Europe in relation to the originative centers of ancient civilization in the Old World. As it happened, though, he wrote his book at a time when great advances were being made in our knowledge of the prehistoric foundations of the ancient civilizations of the Near East.[5] As knowledge of these became available,

5. Childe was himself one of the first to make available these advances in his books *The Most Ancient East* (1928) and *New Light on the Most Ancient East: The Oriental Prelude to European Prehistory* (1934).

they made clearer than ever the parochial character of 'later European prehistory. In the third edition of the *Dawn* (1939), Childe was very explicit on this matter:

Our knowledge of the archaeology of Europe and of the Ancient East has enormously strengthened the Orientalists' position. Indeed we can now survey continuously interconnected provinces throughout which cultures are seen to be zoned in regularly descending grades round the centres of urban civilization in the Ancient East. Such zoning is the best possible proof of the Orientalists' postulate of diffusion.

Proceeding outward from the territory of civilized societies to those still occupied by savages, the situation visualized by Childe for his fourth period was somewhat as follows (1939, p. 326):[6] (*a*) "fully literate city-dwellers" in peninsular as well as insular Greece; (*b*) "illiterate townsmen" in Macedonia and Sicily; (*c*) "sedentary villagers with at least a specialised bronze industry and regular commerce to support it" in the Middle Danube Basin, southeastern Spain, and perhaps in the Kuban; (*d*) "less stable . . . less highly differentiated" communities from England across south and central Germany and Switzerland to south Russia; (*e*) self-sufficing Neolithic communities in southern Scandinavia, northern Germany, and Orkney; and (*f*) Arctic hunter-fishers in the forests and on the coasts of the far north. In other words, he viewed the later prehistory of Europe in terms not so much of evolutionary stages as of zones of diffusion and devolution.

During the years immediately before the outbreak of the second World War, therefore, it was possible to view Old World prehistory for the first time as something more than a mere succession of periods. On the one hand, prehistorians could take a bird's-eye view of

6. Childe indicated the major zones on the four end-maps.

the Old Stone Age and form some notion of its main lines of development, not as a unilinear growth, but as the product of a complex history. On the other, they could trace the opening-up of a new and much wider perspective, first in the ancient East and then over progressively wider territories.

It was evident, in the first place, that almost the whole of human history had been passed under conditions approximating that of the state of savagery deduced by Morgan and Tylor from comparative ethnography.[7] Throughout Paleolithic and Mesolithic times, subsistence was based solely on such activities as hunting, fishing, fowling, and gathering. So far as one could tell from the archeological evidence, also, social groups were small, there was a good deal of seasonal movement, and there was little scope for subdivision of labor or rapid technical advance.

Second, it was clear that, over very extensive territories, societies on this level were replaced by others which were based on farming and which corresponded with the hypothetical level of barbarism. Beyond any doubt, it was the adoption of farming which provided a way of escape from the narrow world of savagery and in due course formed a basis for the attainment of literate civilization. The significance of farming, recognized already by Nilsson, led Childe (notably, 1936, 1942) to hail its emergence as constituting a "Neolithic revolution," a phrase, however, which has not everywhere met with full acceptance (see Frankfort, 1951, p. 38, n. 3). The truth is that not nearly

7. E. B. Tylor and John Lubbock (1865) had compared Paleolithic implements from Europe with those of modern savages as early as 1865. A more elaborate treatment of this theme was given by W. J. Sollas in lectures on "Ancient Hunters and Their Modern Representatives" given to the Royal Institution in 1906 (1909). The same concept underlay Sollas' popular but influential volume, *Ancient Hunters* (1924).

enough has been discovered yet about the exact circumstances under which farming first developed. The excavation of successive levels in the tells has revealed in some detail the elaboration of culture made possible by the adoption of farming but relatively little about primitive Neolithic cultures. Discriminating excavations like those conducted by Braidwood and McCown in strategic parts of Mesopotamia and Iran, backed up by systematic application of Carbon 14 tests, promise results (see Frankfort, 1951, pp. 55 and 56, n. 1); but the fact remains that we are still ignorant about the history of this crucial development. So far as the spread of Neolithic economy to Europe is concerned, there is no doubt that the manner as well as the implications could commonly be described as revolutionary,[8] though on the outer margins the change was often more gradual and much less sweeping, so that it is sometimes difficult to distinguish between food-gatherers and farmers.[9]

Writers have differed over the traits by which they diagnose the appearance of civilization, but from Nilsson onward all have agreed upon the significance of writing. It is not merely that writing inaugurates recorded history; in Childe's phrase it is "a significant, as well as a convenient, mark of civilization" (see Childe, 1950). Economic and social elaboration may, it would seem, proceed up to a certain point, but for anything beyond this the adoption of some conventional method of record and transmission is necessary. Thanks to the circumstance that the ancient Meso-

potamians wrote on clay, it has been possible to trace fairly certainly the context in which writing appeared in different sequences. Among the chief concomitants of literacy, Childe notes the existence of specialists playing no direct part in the production of food; the maintenance of regular trade in raw materials, notably in metals; and the adoption of urban life. Childe, indeed, sought to characterize the transition as an "urban revolution," though what the archeological records appear to most observers to show is rather a very gradual elaboration of economic life, with writing appearing at a certain critical point (e.g., Frankfort, 1951, pp. 55 and 56, n. 1).

In its broadest terms, therefore, the concept of stages in the evolution of culture may be held to have been justified by the results of excavation in the Old World. Yet the value of this can easily be overrated. Outside the main originative centers, in territories like Europe and northwest Africa, diffusion and devolution have played an immeasurably greater part than evolution in the building of cultures. Moreover, useful though it may be to recognize the limitations imposed by basic economic factors, diversity of cultural expression remains the most striking fact of prehistory, as it is of ethnography. The object of prehistory is not only to portray a foreshortened picture of human progress but to comprehend the life and character of all the manifold and historically unique societies of prehistoric times.

Although much research will still need to be directed to the refinement of chronological systems and to the sharper definition of the cultural groupings of antiquity, contemporary prehistorians are now freer than before, particularly in the more completely explored regions, to devote their energies to interpreting archeological data in

8. It has been shown beyond any doubt that in a country like Denmark the earliest Neolithic farmers were intrusive, e.g., by C. J. Becker (1947).

9. The symbiosis of fishing and farming economies which still exists on the northwest coast of Norway can be traced back to the Stone Age; see Clark (1952*b*, pp. 51 ff. and 62 ff.).

terms of living societies. The classification of material objects may be essential, but only as a preliminary to the realistic appraisal of societies that were once alive. The whole problem is how to make them live, and it is to this that the energies of contemporary prehistorians are increasingly being directed.

Ecologists have shown that, to understand living things, one has to study them in relation to the other elements in the biome and to the soil and climate of the common habitat (Tansley, 1946). Every organism or community of organisms must needs establish relations with all the other elements of the ecosystem to which it belongs and can be fully understood only in its ecological context. This point of view is fully consistent with, and indeed provides a biological basis for, the historical interpretation of cultural development (Clark, 1952*b*, chap. i). If each culture be viewed as the product of an equation between social inheritance and the various elements in the biome and habitat of the parent-ecosystem, it is hardly to be wondered at in the face of so many variables that the outcome is in every case unique. Ecologically viewed, the diversity of human culture is not an anomaly but almost a necessity of nature.

The ecological approach has been brilliantly exemplified by modern ethnologists, notably by Evans-Pritchard in his study of the Nuer (1940). The situation is much more complicated for prehistorians, though, since no single element in the ecosystem remains constant over any length of time.[10] Yet it is precisely the dynamic character of the relations between human societies and the ecosystems to which they belong that makes them important. During the Old Stone Age, when men

10. These fluctuations, indeed, form the basis of geochronology; see F. E. Zeuner (1950).

were sparsely distributed, were poorly equipped with tools, and lived exclusively by food-gathering, human societies made but a small impression on their environment. As a matter of fact, pollen analysts have succeeded in detecting indications of hunter-fisher groups during postglacial times in parts of northwestern Europe, but these are of a very minor character, involving, for example, a sudden rise and fall in the Chenopodiaceae (Iversen, 1941, p. 39). On the other hand, though the cultural endowment of the men of the Old Stone Age remained stationary or at least progressed very slowly over immense periods of time, the Pleistocene period was marked by great and often repeated fluctuations of climate, vegetation, and fauna (see n. 10). It is becoming ever clearer that understanding of the distribution and migrations of the various Paleolithic cultures revealed by modern prehistoric archeology can be brought about only by correlating more closely cultural with ecological changes over which early man himself exerted no kind of control (e.g., McBurney, 1950).

The spread and intensification of farming, on the other hand, itself precipitated major ecological changes. Recovery of a complete and detailed record of vegetational history for the period in question should reveal not merely the impact of prehistoric farmers but also many vital aspects of their economy. Over large tracts of barbarian Europe, for example, paleo-ecological research has made it possible to trace the spread, first, of a shifting, extensive form of agriculture, accompanied by cutting and burning of forest trees, and then the rise of a more intensive form based on the use of the plow and involving permanent clearance and the creation of fields and meadows. Statistical analysis of the pollen which rained onto ancient bogs and lakes has yielded information about the spread of the new economy—about the transition, if you like, from savagery to barbarism—in temperate Europe, of a kind which could hardly have been obtained by any other means (see Iversen, 1941; Faegri, 1944; Godwin, 1944).

Information about the soils occupied by different groups in prehistoric times has been obtained by systematic plotting of archeological finds on physical base maps. One of the first correlations between culture and soil types was made before the close of the nineteenth century by Penck and Grahmann, who remarked that the Neolithic settlers of central Europe occupied loess formations (see Grahmann, 1898, 1906; Hoops, 1905, pp. 98–99). A great advance was made by Fox in his study of the Cambridge region (1923 and 1948). By plotting a succession of archeological distributions, ranging in age from Neolithic to Anglo-Saxon, on identical maps showing areas of heavier and lighter soils, Fox brought out the dynamic nature of the relationship between economy and land occupation. Changes in the pattern of distribution relative to the geological basis showed that, whereas the earliest farmers of this region confined themselves to the lighter, more easily worked soils, later settlers began to take up the more difficult, but potentially richer, soils needed to support a denser population. A more elaborate survey of a part of northwestern Jutland organized by the National Museum of Denmark between 1942 and 1945 confirmed and amplified Fox's general conclusions and showed beyond any doubt the value of the geographical approach, more especially when taken in conjunction with the results of ecological research (Mathiassen, 1948).

The ecological approach is, of course, by no means limited to the information it can give about such topics as land occupation, forest clearance, and the like. It is vital to the whole question of prehistoric subsistence, whether relating to hunting, agriculture, or herding activities. It is equally essential for a proper assessment of technology, buildings, and means of transportation. There is, indeed, no aspect of economic life that does not gain from being considered from an ecological point of view.

However important the ecological setting may be, it is with the tangible traces of ancient society in the form of objects or structures that the prehistoric archeologist as such is primarily concerned. Prehistorians of the older school paid attention chiefly to the formal, typological characteristics of such material, concentrating on features of value for classification. The modern school is more realistic; it is concerned less with the ideal categories of modern scholars and more with what really happened in prehistoric times. Much more attention is therefore being paid today to the materials from which things were made and to the skills and techniques whereby they were shaped to the needs of society.

To take, first, the case of objects of worked flint and stone, one can point to the very detailed petrological examination of large numbers of ax- and adze-blades carried out in Britain, Germany, and various parts of Scandinavia.[11] By determining the sources of the various stones employed, it has been possible to demonstrate a widespread trade in blades completed up to the stage of polishing. Examination of the actual quarries and places of manufacture has yielded information about the actual extraction and shaping of the material. Particularly outstanding work has been devoted to the technique of the flint-miners of southern England,

11. The most elaborate work to date has been carried out by a subcommittee of the South-Western Group of Museums and Art Galleries in England (see *Proc. Prehist. Soc.,* XVII [1951], 99–158). For a general account see Clark (1952*b,* pp. 245–50).

northern France, and parts of Belgium and Holland (see Clark and Piggott, 1933; Clark, 1952*b*, pp. 174–83). Some prehistorians have sought to throw light on the techniques employed in the production of such objects as hand-axes, laurel-leaf points, blades, and burins, but, successful as such men as Coutier, Knowles (e.g., 1944), and Leakey (e.g., 1934, pp. 47 ff.) have been in producing the forms of prehistoric flint tools, they have not, in fact, done more than demonstrate possible ways in which the various forms could have been produced, and it is noteworthy that different experimenters have arrived at much the same result by different means. The real value of such tests is that they may lead prehistorians to reexamine tools broken in the course of manufacture, as well as the waste products found on prehistoric knapping-places.

So far as bronze objects are concerned, spectrographic as well as chemical analysis has been applied to a wide range of ingots, tools, slags, and natural ores, and the work of men like Desch (1925–38) and Witter (1938) have thrown much light on the source of prehistoric copper. Particularly fine work, also, has been devoted to the actual processes of mining and smelting, notably by Pittioni and Preuschen in the Austrian Alps (Zschocke and Preuschen, 1932; Preuschen and Pittioni, 1937, 1937–38, 1947). As regards the completed products, these were mere lumps of copper-tin alloy of shapes and finish characteristic of the old art-historical school; from a more realistic angle, though, they are the outcome of a highly complex series of processes and activities, which are themselves a main subject matter of prehistory. Perusal of Andreas Oldeberg's *Metallteknik under Forhistorisk Tid* (1942–43), with its formidable bibliography, should alone be sufficient to demonstrate how much work has already been devoted

to such things as ingots, molds, and metal-smiths' tools, as well as to the examination of visible traces of smithing on finished products. Important studies have also been devoted, for example, to the sources of iron and to the methods of ironworking (Childe, 1944, pp. 13 ff.; Clark, 1952*b*, pp. 199–204; Hatt, 1936; Hauge, 1946; Nielsen, 1920–25, pp. 337–440; Stieren, 1935; Weiershausen, 1939), as well as to the sources and methods of production of a wide range of substances of industrial or decorative value.[12]

Pottery, the third prop of traditional archeology and the basis of a veritable pseudo-science, has also been studied, albeit tentatively, for what it can tell of prehistoric life and activities. Attempts have been made to determine to what extent pottery was made from local clays (e.g., Buttler and Haberey, 1936, pp. 106–9), and a good deal of desultory work has been devoted to the actual building of prehistoric fabrics and to their decoration and firing. Realistic study of hand-made wares has already given us an insight into quite distinct aspects of prehistoric life. Extremely important information about the proportions in which cereal crops were grown among various groups of prehistoric people has been gained from systematic counts of impressions of grains incorporated in the walls of different kinds of pottery and burned out in the firing (Hatt, 1937, pp. 20–22; Jessen and Helbaek, 1944). Again, biochemical investigation of residues in the bases of pots and other containers has already thrown some light on food and drink.[13]

Much more detailed attention than before is being given to the more perishable aspects of material culture,

12. E.g., amber and faïence; see Clark (1952*b*, pp. 261 ff.).

13. As an example one may quote beer residues; see J. Gruss (1931); C. Umbreit (1937, pp. 49 and 54); W. Unverzagt (1930).

which, though doubtless less useful for purposes of classification because less persistent, are now valued for the light they can throw on aspects of daily life not normally preserved. Indeed, excavators are now directing their labors to sites capable of yielding organic materials, in which the archeological record is at present deficient but which nevertheless played so important a part in the life of most prehistoric peoples.[14] Among the perishable aspects of material culture to receive attention from archeologists during recent years, a high place must be given to textiles. Attention may be drawn in particular to the meticulous investigations made by Emil Vogt (1937) on carbonized linen textiles from Neolithic deposits in the Swiss lakes and by Margarethe Hald on woolens from the Bronze Age oak-coffin burials and from the Iron Age bog-finds of Denmark (Broholm and Hald, 1940; Hald, 1950). Important work has also been devoted to such materials as wood, bark, basketry, and hides (Clark. 1952b, pp. 207 ff.). The point need not be labored, though, that, once it is accepted that the aim of archeological research is the understanding of prehistoric life, it follows that the maximum range of material culture must be subjected to the closest scrutiny.

In conclusion, it remains to consider how far the archeological material itself can legitimately be interpreted in terms of extant societies (Clark, 1951). The mere fact that we set out to resuscitate prehistoric societies only emphasizes that they are, in fact, dead. Moreover, they have been dead so long that the traces they leave behind them are vestigial. In seeking to interpret fossils in terms of living organisms, pre-

14. For instance, the English Mesolithic site Star Carr was excavated for the express purpose of recovering elements of the British Maglemosian culture previously missing or poorly represented; see Clark (1949, 1950; also 1952a).

historians find themselves somewhat in the same position as paleontologists. Yet there is a highly important difference. As Professor Garrod stressed (1946, pp. 8 ff.), the archeologist is necessarily concerned with factors distinct from, and altogether more complex than, those which control the organisms and processes of external nature; whereas the natural sciences deal with phenomena which conform to natural laws, archeology is concerned with the results of human activities and with a multitude of unique events conditioned by cultural and even personal factors—in a word, with the phenomena of history. The task of reconstructing the life of prehistoric communities is inherently more difficult and hazardous than deducing the behavior of Pleistocene glaciers from observation of existing glaciers obedient to immutable laws.

To the old evolutionists it seemed self-evident that the observations of modern field ethnographers could be applied directly to the interpretation of prehistoric data. Even as late as 1906 General Pitt-Rivers (Myres, 1906, p. 53) could write that "the existing races, in their respective stages of progression, may be taken as the bona fide representatives of the races of antiquity. . . . They thus afford us living illustrations of the social customs . . . which belong to the ancient races from which they remotely sprang." In this we recognize the failure to appreciate the unique historical character of cultures which vitiated the notion of hypothetical prehistory put forward by mid-Victorian anthropologists. We cannot sufficiently remind ourselves that prehistoric man lived in the remote past and can be studied only by prehistorians.

From this dilemma there is no easy way of escape. What is nevertheless sure is that, as Mr. H. G. Wells (1934, p. 31) once reminded us, we have no hope of interpreting Paleolithic or even Bronze Age society in terms of twentieth-century civilization. If we are compelled to resort to the comparative method, we can at least aim at comparing like, as far as possible, with like. The problem is most acute for the prehistoric peoples most widely separated from ourselves in time, cultural attainment, and even in some cases perhaps by biological endowment. Yet even here we can restrict the field of analogy to societies at a common level of subsistence. Further, it seems legitimate to attach greater significance to analogies drawn from societies existing under ecological conditions which approximate those reconstructed for the prehistoric culture under investigation than those adapted to markedly different environments. Even so, as we know from our knowledge of living peoples, great diversity of cultural expression may be found among communities subject to the same economic limitations and occupying similar, if not identical, environments. This suggests that, although the comparative method is likely to give useful clues to general conditions, it can be a dangerous guide to the particular manifestations of culture with which, after all, the archeologist is mainly concerned. When all is said, the main use of ethnographic comparisons for the interpretation of Old Stone Age cultures is to spur the prehistorian to further effort and provide him with clues for purposive archeological research. By emphasizing the vestigial character of existing archeological data—for instance, the flint implements which constitute almost the sole documents for Lower Paleolithic culture—such comparisons are stimulating archeologists to pay more attention to objects made from the organic materials chiefly used by peoples of simple culture (see Clark, 1952*b*, chap. viii; cf. also above, n. 14). Further, by suggesting a variety of pos-

sible functions for artifacts, they are constantly directing the search for circumstantial clues that might not otherwise even suggest themselves. In other words, as was emphasized in an earlier section of this survey, comparative ethnography cannot in any sense of the term be regarded as a substitute for archeology as a means of discovering the prehistoric past of humanity. On the contrary, its main function is precisely to stimulate and give direction to prehistoric research.

Yet knowledge of existing societies can often be applied much more directly to the interpretation of archeological data where this relates to later periods of prehistory. This applies particularly to cases where historical continuity, both of settlement and of tradition, can be proved, as they sometimes can be, for instance, in the Near East, the Mediterranean, and even in the more accessible parts of temperate Europe.[15] Yet one has to remember that this continuity exists mainly, if not entirely, in the economically most depressed stratum of the population, and it is in the highest degree unlikely that the peasants, herdsmen, or fishers concerned will have remained uninfluenced by usages and ideas from the economically dominant urban stratum. Critically approached, however, folk usage can prove an invaluable guide to prehistorians in interpreting archeological data; and in this connection some of the most valuable sources are to be found in the works of historians and other observers writing at a time when urban influence was far less pervasive than it has since become.[16]

15. A very good example is the continuity of mud-and-reed architecture in southern Mesopotamia, which helped Sir Leonard Woolley (1935) to interpret the traces of prehistoric architecture in Sumer.

16. E.g., Greek and Latin authors such as Homer, Herodotus, Caesar, and Tacitus; later historical writings like the *Historia de gentibus septentrionalibus,* published at Rome in 1555

The direct application of a knowledge of folk usage has been demonstrated again and again in the case of enigmatic artifacts recovered in the course of excavation. One may cite as an example (Casson, 1927, pp. 119–20) the circular clay disks found on Minoan sites in Crete and classified by academic archeologists with a splendid inconsequence as "tables either sacred or otherwise, or else as the lids of pithoi." When Stephanos Xanthoudides came to enter them in the inventory of the Candia Museum, he recognized them from direct personal knowledge as the upper disks of potters' wheels, made intentionally heavy so as to give momentum, like those still used on the island for making pithoi. How truly and with what relevance to archeology did Stanley˙ Casson once write[17] of the East Mediterranean that "the economic condition of peasant and small-town life . . . particularly among the islands, hardly differs in simplicity or complexity from what it was either in the Bronze Age or in Classical Greek times." Folk usage is particularly illuminating in relation to basic subsistence. For instance, on the northern margins of temperate Europe one can still observe societies with mixed economies of the kind which, it may be suspected, were commoner in prehistoric times than archeologists have always recognized.

In areas such as Scandinavia and the Baltic states the peasants have been obliged for the last 3,000–4,000 years or so to supplement the inadequate returns from farming by practicing various forms of hunting and catching; here the same rhythm of plowing, sowing, and harvesting, interspersed with hunting and catching the same land and sea mammals, the same fowls and fishes, has persisted since prehistoric times (Brøgger, 1940). Locally, even as with the islanders of Kihnu and Ruhnu in the Gulf of Riga, who specialize in seal-hunting and exchange fats and skins for the grain, iron, and salt of the Esthonian mainland, we find still before us conditions like those which obtained on the margins of farming culture during Neolithic times (Leinbock, 1932). The methods of hunting, trapping, fishing, and fowling, being closely adapted to the life-habits of the animals concerned, have survived with little alteration since prehistoric times.

Again, many of the basic processes of early farming, for which we have only slight clues from antiquity, may, or could until very recently, be seen in actual operation.[18] The implements of tillage, notably the plow, which reflect in their development so much of the history of agriculture, have survived as a rule only in fragments or in representations often difficult to decipher. As Paul Leser (1931) and his many successors (Clark, 1952b, pp. 100–106; Glob, 1951) have emphasized, the indications from prehistoric cultures can be understood only in relation to the wooden plows still used in backward parts of Europe and of the ancient world.

Houses are another aspect of material culture likely to persist with little alteration until some drastic or prolonged change in economic or social conditions destroys the relations estab-

---

and illustrated with a wealth of the most revealing woodcuts; and the descriptions of observant travelers to outlying parts, such as Martin Martin's *Description of the Western Isles of Scotland* (1704; and Stirling, 1934).

17. Stanley Casson once wrote (1938, p. 466): "The economic condition of peasant and small-town life ... particularly among the islands, hardly differs in simplicity or complexity from what it was either in the Bronze Age or in Classical Greek times. The average islander and coast-dweller still lives on the same food, and in similar houses to those of his ancestors."

18. This has been illustrated, for example, in the case of seal-hunting in the Baltic area; see Clark (1946).

lished between human needs and potentialities and such factors as climate,
topography, and materials for building.
Archeological excavation rarely reveals
more than the ground plans of prehistoric buildings, which commonly allow
a variety of plausible reconstructions.
Unless excavators are familiar with
analogous structures in actual use, they
are liable to overlook the details needed
for a right interpretation. It is a matter
of history that Franz Oelmann and his
pupils (Oelmann, 1927, 1929; Buttler,
1936; Bersu, 1940, esp. pp. 90 ff.)
gained their insight into these matters
through their study of peasant dwellings, mainly in central Europe. One
could illustrate, by reference to almost
any aspect of material culture, how
much the prehistorian stands to gain
by seeking to interpret what he finds
in relation to the activities of living societies. The fact remains, though, that
prehistoric research is the only way to
discover what happened in the prehistoric past. Comparative ethnography
can prompt the right questions; only
archeology, in conjunction with the
various natural sciences on which prehistorians freely draw, can give the
right answers.

So far, only a beginning has been
made in unraveling the prehistoric past
of the Old World, and the way ahead
will surely be a long one. Three themes

have emerged from our survey. One is
the fact of material progress, measurable in growth of population, in increasing knowledge of control over
natural forces, and in elaboration of
technology, a progress in which many
prehistorians have recognized the attainment of such stages as savagery, barbarism, and civilization. The second is
the historical uniqueness of each culture, of each communally shared and
regulated mode of life, whether observed by ethnologists or partially reconstituted by prehistorians. If the
study of man has any purpose, this is
surely not to fortify some all-sufficient
and soul-destroying dogma, but rather
to refresh the human spirit by displaying the manifold diversity of man's
achievement in the past as in the present. The third is that prehistory has
meaning for us because prehistoric
peoples once lived and our life is but
a continuation of theirs. As W. G. Collingwood (1944, p. 67) phrased it, "history is concerned not with 'events' but
with 'processes.'" The cultural processes which confront us today as students of man had already begun long
before history was first written down.
As Robert H. Lowie wrote truly (1937,
p. 236): "There is only one natural
unit for the ethnologist—the culture of
all humanity at all periods and in all
places."

REFERENCES

BECKER, C. J. 1947. "Mosefundne Lerkar fra Yngre Stenalder." In *Kongelige nordiske oldskriftselskab Aarbøger, 1947,* pp. 285 ff. Copenhagen.

BERSU, G. 1940. "Excavations at Little Woodbury, Wiltshire," *Proceedings of the Prehistoric Society,* VI, 30–111.

BREUIL, H. 1912. "Les Subdivisions du Paléolithique Supérieur et leur signification," *Comptes rendus du Congrès Internationale d'Anthropologie et d'Archéologie Préhistorique, Geneva, 1912,* pp.

165–238. Rev. ed., separately printed, 1937.

BRØGGER, A. W. 1940. "From the Stone Age to the Motor Age," *Antiquity,* XIV, 163–81.

BROHOLM, H. C., and HALD, M. 1940. *Costumes of the Bronze Age in Denmark.* Copenhagen: Nyt Nordisk Forlag.

BUCKLAND, THE REV. WILLIAM. 1823. *Reliquiae diluvianae; or Observations on the Organic Remains Contained in Caves, Fissures, and Diluvial Gravel, and on Other Geological Phenomena, Attesting the Action of an Universal Deluge.* London.

BUTTLER, W. 1936. "Pits and Pit-Dwellings in Southeast Europe," *Antiquity*, X, 25–36.

BUTTLER, W., and HABEREY, W. 1936. *Die Bandkeramische Ansiedlung bei Köln-Lindenthal.* Berlin: W. de Gruyter.

CASSON, STANLEY (ed.). 1927. *Essays in Aegean Archaeology: Presented to Sir Arthur Evans.* Oxford: Clarendon Press.

——. 1938. "The Modern Pottery Trade in the Aegean," *Antiquity*, XII, 464–73.

CHILDE, V. G. 1928. *The Most Ancient East.* London: Kegan Paul, Trench, Trubner & Co.

——. 1934. *New Light on the Most Ancient East: The Oriental Prelude to European Prehistory.* London: Kegan Paul, Trench, Trubner & Co.

——. 1935. Presidential address to the Prehistoric Society, *Proceedings of the Prehistoric Society*, Vol. I.

——. 1936. *Man Makes Himself.* London: A. Watts & Co.

——. 1939. *Dawn of European Civilization.* 3d ed. London: Kegan Paul, Trench, Trubner & Co.

——. 1942. *What Happened in History.* New York and Hammondsworth: Pelican Books.

——. 1944. "Archaeological Ages as Technological Stages," *Journal of the Royal Anthropological Institute*, LXXIV, 7–24.

——. 1950. "The Urban Revolution," *Town Planning Review*, XX, No. 1, 3–17.

——. 1951. *Social Evolution.* London: A. Watts & Co.

CLARK, J. G. D. 1931. Review of MENGHIN's *Weltgeschichte der Steinzeit, Antiquity*, V, 518–21.

——. 1946. "Seal-hunting in the Stone Age of North-western Europe," *Proceedings of the Prehistoric Society*, XII, 12–48.

——. 1949. "A Preliminary Report on Excavations at Star Carr, Seamer, Scarborough, Yorkshire, 1949," *ibid.*, n.s., XV, 52–69.

——. 1950. *Ibid.*, XVI, 109–29.

——. 1951. "Folk-Culture and the Study of European Prehistory." In *Aspects of Archaeology in Britain and Beyond*

(O. G. S. Crawford volume), pp. 49–65. London.

——. 1952a. "A Stone Age Hunters' Camp," *Scientific American*, CLXXXVI, No. 5, 20–25.

——. 1952b. *Prehistoric Europe.* London: Methuen; New York: Philosophical Library.

CLARK, J. G. D., and PIGGOTT, S. 1933. "The Age of the British Flint Mines," *Antiquity*, VII, 166–83.

COLLINGWOOD, W. G. 1944. *An Autobiography.* Hammondsworth, Middlesex: Penguin Books.

DANIEL, G. E. 1943. *The Three Ages: An Essay in Archaeological Method.* Cambridge: At the University Press.

——. 1950. *A Hundred Years of Archaeology.* London: G. Duckworth & Co.

DESCH, C. H. 1925–38. "Reports on the Metallurgical Examination of Specimens for the Sumerian Committee of the British Association," *Reports of the British Association.*

EVANS-PRITCHARD, E. 1940. *The Nuer.* Oxford: Clarendon Press.

FAEGRI, K. 1944. "Studies on the Pleistocene of Western Norway," *III Bømlo, Bergens Museums Arbok 1943*, pp. 79–81. ("Naturvitens-kapelig," rekke No. 8.) Bergen.

FOX, C. 1923 and 1948. *The Archaeology of the Cambridge Region: A Topographical Study of the Bronze Age, Early Iron Age, Roman and Anglo-Saxon Ages with an Introductory Note on the Neolithic Age.* Cambridge: At the University Press.

FRANKFORT, H. 1951. *The Birth of Civilization in the Near East.* London: Williams & Norgate.

GARROD, D. A. E. 1926. *The Upper Palaeolithic Age in Britain.* Oxford: Clarendon Press.

——. 1928. "Nova et vetera: A Plea for a New Method in Palaeolithic Archaeology," *Proceedings of the Prehistoric Society of East Anglia*, V, 260–67.

——. 1938. "The Upper Palaeolithic in the Light of Recent Discovery," *Proceedings of the Prehistoric Society*, IV, 1–26.

——. 1946. *Environment, Tools, and Man.* Cambridge: At the University Press.

GLOB, P. V. 1951. *Ard og plov i Nordens oltid.* Aarhus.

GODWIN, H. 1944. "Age and Origin of the 'Brechland' Heaths of East Anglia," *Nature*, CLIV, 6 ff.

GRAHMANN, R. 1898. *Das Pflanzenleben der schwäbischen Alb.* 1st ed.

——. 1906. *Geographische Zeitschrift,* XII, 305–25.

GRUSS, J. 1931. "Zwei altgermanische Trinkhörner mit Bier- und Metresten," *Prähistorische Zeitschrift,* XXII, 180–91.

HALD, M. 1950. *Olddanske tekstiler.* Copenhagen: Gyldendalske Boghandel, Nordisk Forlag.

HATT, GUDMUND. 1936. "Nye lagttagelser vedrørende oldtidens jernudvinding i jylland," *Kgl. nordiske oldskriftselskab, Aarbøger for nordisk oldkyndighed og historie,* 1. Halvbind, pp. 19–45. Copenhagen.

——. 1937. *Landbrug i Danmarks oldtid.* Copenhagen.

HAUGE, T. D. 1946. *Blesterbruk og Myrjern.* Oslo.

HOOPS, J. 1905. *Waldbäume und Kulturpflanzen im germanischen Altertum.* Strasbourg.

INDREKO, R. 1948. *Die mittlere Steinzeit in Estland.* Stockholm.

IVERSEN, J. 1941. "Land Occupation in Denmark's Stone Age," *Danmarks geologiske undersøgelser,* II. Raekke, No. 66. Copenhagen.

JESSEN, K., and HELBAEK, H. 1944. *Cereals in Great Britain and Ireland in Prehistoric and Early Historic Times.* ("Der kongelig danske videnskabernes selskab, biologiske skrifter," Vol. III, No. 2.) Copenhagen.

KNOWLES, SIR FRANCIS H. S. 1944. *The Manufacture of a Flint Arrowhead by Quartzite Hammerstone.* ("Occasional Papers on Technology," No. 1.) Oxford: Pitt-Rivers Museum.

KOSSINNA, GUSTAF. 1912. *Die deutsche Vorgeschichte eine hervorragend nationale Wissenschaft.* Leipzig: Kabitzsch.

——. 1926. *Ursprung und Verbreitung der Germanen in vor- und frühgeschichtlicher Zeit.* Leipzig: Kabitzsch.

LARTET, E. A. I. H., and CHRISTY, H. 1865–75. *Reliquiae Aquitanicae.* Edited by T. R. JONES. London.

LEAKEY, L. S. B. 1934. *Adam's Ancestors.* London: Methuen.

LEINBOCK, F. 1932. *Die materielle Kultur der Esten.* Tartu: Akadeemiline Kooperatiiv.

LESER, PAUL. 1931. *Entstehung und Verbreitung des Pfluges.* Münster i.W.: Aschendorff.

LOWIE, ROBERT H. 1937. *A History of Ethnological Theory.* New York: Farrar & Rinehart.

LUBBOCK, SIR JOHN. 1865. *Prehistoric Times.* London: Williams & Norgate.

——. (trans.). 1866. *The Primitive Inhabitants of Scandinavia.* London.

MCBURNEY, C. B. 1950. "The Geographical Study of the Older Palaeolithic Stages in Europe," *Proceedings of the Prehistoric Society,* XVI, 163–83.

MCENERY, J. 1859. *Cavern Researches.* Edited by E. VIVIAN.

MARX, KARL. 1904. Preface to *A Contribution to the Critique of Political Economy.* Chicago: C. H. Kerr Co.

MATHIASSEN, T. 1948. *Studier over Vestjyllands oldtidsbebyggelse.* ("Nationalmuseets skrifter, arkaeologisk-historisk raekke," No. 2.) Copenhagen: Gyldendal.

MENGHIN, OSWALD. 1931. *Weltgeschichte der Steinzeit.* Vienna: A. Schroll & Co.

MORGAN, LEWIS H. 1877. *Ancient Society: or, Researches in the Lines of Human Progress from Savagery through Barbarism to Civilization.* New York: Henry Holt & Co.

MORTILLET, G. DE. 1881. *La Musée préhistorique.* Paris: C. Reinwald.

MYRES, J. L. (ed.). 1906. *The Evolution of Culture and Other Essays.* Oxford: Clarendon Press.

NIELSEN, N. 1920–25. *Mémoires des antiquités du nord.*

NILSSON, SVEN. 1838–43. *Skandinaviens Nordens Urinvånare.* Lund.

OELMANN, F. 1927. *Haus und Hof im Altertum.* Berlin: W. de Gruyter.

——. 1929. "Hausurnen oder Speicherurnen," *Bonner Jahrbücher,* CXXXIV, 1–39.

OLDEBERG, ANDREAS. 1942–43. *Metallteknik under forhistorisk tid.* Lund and Leipzig: Kommissionsverlag O. Harrassowitz.

PREUSCHEN, E., and PITTIONI, R. 1937. "Untersuchungen im Bergbaugebiete

Kelchalpe bei Kitzbühel, Tirol (1931–36)," *Mitteilungen der Prähistorischen Kommission der Akademie der Wissenschaften, in Wien*, III, 1–159.

PREUSCHEN, E., and PITTIONI, R. 1937–38. *Ibid.*

——. 1947. *Ibid.* V, 37–99.

RADCLIFFE-BROWN, A. R. 1922. *Andaman Islanders.* 1st English ed. Cambridge: At the University Press.

SOLLAS, W. J. 1909. "Ancient Hunters and Their Modern Representatives," *Science Progress*, III, 326–53, 500–533, 667–86.

——. 1924. *Ancient Hunters.* 3d ed. 1st ed., 1911. London: Macmillan & Co.

STIEREN, A. 1935. "Vorgeschichtliche Eisenverhüttung in Südwestfalen," *Germania* (Anzeiger der Römisch-germanischen Kommission des deutschen Archäologischen Instituts), XIX, No. 1 (January), 12–20.

TANSLEY, A. G. 1946. *Introduction to Plant Ecology.* London: G. Allen & Unwin.

THOMSEN, C. J. 1836. *Ledetraad til Nordisk oldkyndighed.* Copenhagen.

——. 1838–43. *Skandinaviska Nordens urinvånare.* Copenhagen.

TYLOR, E. B., and LUBBOCK, JOHN. 1865. *Researches into the Early History of Mankind and the Development of Civilization and Prehistoric Times.* London: John Murray.

UMBREIT, C. 1937. *Neue Forschungen zur ostdeutschen Steinzeit und frühen Bronzezeit.* Leipzig: Kabitzsch.

UNVERZAGT, W. 1930. "Römisches Dolium mit Biermaische aus Alzey," *Schumacher Festschrift*, pp. 314–15. Direktion des Römisch-germanischen Zentralmuseums in Mainz, Wilckens.

VOGT, E. 1937. *Geflechte und Gewebe der Steinzeit.* Basel: E. Birkhäuser & Cie.

WEIERSHAUSEN, P. 1939. *Vorgeschichtliche Eisenhütten Deutschlands.* Leipzig: Kabitzsch.

WELLS, H. G. 1934. *The Work, Wealth, and Happiness of Mankind.* London: William Heinemann, Ltd.

WITTER, W. 1938. *Die älteste Erzgewinnung im nordisch-germanischen Lebenskreis*, Vols. I–II. Leipzig: Kabitzsch.

WOOLLEY, SIR LEONARD. 1935. *Development of Sumerian Art.* London: Faber & Faber, Ltd.

WORSAAE, J. J. A. 1849. *The Primeval Antiquities of Denmark.* London: John Henry Parker.

ZEUNER, F. E. 1950. *Dating the Past.* 2d ed. London: Methuen.

ZSCHOCKE, K., and PREUSCHEN, E. 1932. "Das urzeitliche Bergbaugebiet von Mühlbach-Bischofshofen," *Materialien zur Urgeschichte Österreichs*, No. 6. Wien.

Old World Prehistory: Paleolithic

By HALLAM L. MOVIUS, JR.

DURING THE last twenty-five years, our knowledge of the Paleolithic period has been greatly extended beyond the confines of western Europe. This has not resulted in the establishment of as coherent a picture of man's early attempts to develop a material culture as was originally expected. For, when we examine the bewildering array of primitive Stone Age assemblages that are constantly being augmented by fresh discoveries, we can hardly compose them into anything even remotely approaching the ordered general scheme conceived by the early workers. This is certainly not due to the fact that, in reaction against the doctrine of direct typological evolution, we have gone too far in the opposite direction but rather because, once De Mortillet's original scheme was rightly abandoned as provincial and inapplicable outside western Europe, no really adequate alternative approach has been proposed. As a matter of fact, most of the original terms developed by De Mortillet for his "classificatory system" are still in use, and they are now employed in several different senses—chronologic, typologic, technologic, and cultural—sometimes in the same breath. Instead of getting bogged down in questions pertaining to terminology at this point, however, I propose to pass on to a brief consideration of some problems of a more fundamental nature. In this paper an attempt has been made to present a synthesis of the various sequences of Paleolithic cultures within the framework of the larger continental areas. Throughout, the major trends as indicated by the most recent results have been stressed.

EUROPE

Paleolithic research, cradled and developed in Europe during the last century, has made many significant contributions during recent years. Only certain of the more important aspects of the field as a whole can be considered here; the selection has been made partly on the basis of new materials and partly on the basis of new methods that have been and are being developed. In view of the overwhelming mass of data, it is very difficult to present a consecutive account covering the region as a whole, although the major trends can be discerned.

LOWER AND MIDDLE PALEOLITHIC

As is well known, the very simple developmental scheme of Abbevillian (formerly Chellian)-Acheulian-Mousterian for the various Lower and Middle Paleolithic assemblages in western Europe was replaced early in the 1930's as the result of Breuil's investigations in the Somme Valley of northern France (Breuil, with Koslowski, 1931, 1932; Breuil, 1939). According to Breuil's so-called "parallel phyla concept," there was a flake-tool tradition (Clactonian-Levalloisian) which developed in a parallel and more or less independent manner to the core-biface tradition (Abbevillian-Acheulian). This has been widely accepted, certain authors even going so far as to conceive of the flake tools as being introduced by a paleo-anthropic stock of fossil man, and the core-biface complex as attributable to men of neanthropic (or *sapiens*) group. Those who implicitly accept the evidence conceive of "mixed" assemblages when hand-axes and flakes occur together, even suggesting that such mixtures resulted from contacts and migrations of different racial elements. Although the parallel phyla concept is not supported by the field evidence, it is still generally accepted by the majority of workers in the field of Paleolithic archeology.

On purely a priori grounds there is something fundamentally unsound with this hypothesis. As early as 1906, Commont described a large series of flake tools from his classic Acheulian locality at St. Acheul, and in 1908 Déchelette clearly stated that flake implements occurred in intimate and direct association with hand-axes at all the main localities in the Somme region. Later, in 1925, the view was further propounded by Obermaier, who remarked that, although the materials from the Somme gravel pits were collected by the workmen and not obtained during the course of controlled excavation, it was impossible to deny the existence of well-made flake tools side by side with hand-axes. This situation was further defined by Kelley in 1937, and the evidence has made some authorities suspicious of the existence of a clear-cut differentiation between the two traditions.

Now the parallel phyla concept has encountered rather considerable difficulties in those parts of the Old World where Lower Paleolithic hand-ax assemblages and advanced flake industries of Levalloisian type have been recognized. As will be discussed pres-

ently, these two traditions constitute inseparable components of one and the same complex throughout Africa, the Middle East, and India. Nowhere in this vast region has a vertical division between the essentially flake and core techniques been reported. On the basis of this overwhelming mass of unanimous evidence, one is perhaps justified in asking whether the concept of a Levalloisian tradition as an entity separate and distinct from an Acheulian tradition has any real validity in western Europe.

Recent investigations in the demonstrably Second Interglacial gravels of the Amiens region (Somme) indicate that the parallel phyla hypothesis is based on an assumption which is not borne out in the field. For three independent investigators, Breuil, Bordes, and Kelley, have described flakes of characteristic Levalloisian type, together with tortoise cores, in direct and indisputable association with Early-Middle Acheulian materials. Therefore, the Lower Paleolithic of western Europe can no longer be considered aberrant with respect to the Great Hand-Axe Complex as a whole in other parts of the Old World. However, the Clactonian flake industry, mainly restricted to England, can be regarded as a separate and distinct entity that has not been defined as yet outside northwestern Europe.

A typological comparison of the various hand-ax assemblages from widely separated areas will reveal that, with the exception of the material from which they are manufactured, the specimens themselves exhibit a striking degree of uniformity. This applies not only to form but also to the technical processes involved in their manufacture, both of which appear to be alarmingly constant. But this observation does not apply to the accompanying flake tools, including the cores from which the latter were struck, which suggests that it is the technique resorted to in the production of flake implements that is of prime importance. In that this is both a manifestation of tradition, on the one hand, and either diffusion of ideas or possible movements of peoples, on the other, it offers a possible solution to the present dilemma. In any event, the application of detailed typology as a means of studying Lower Paleolithic assemblages is getting us absolutely nowhere, and such elaborate sequences as the seven-fold Acheulian succession in northern France is incomprehensible except for the geological basis on which it has been established.

Recently, Van Riet Lowe has convincingly argued that one of the possible lines of escape from the present stalemate of Lower Paleolithic typology is by paying less attention to the form of the finished tools and attempting to reconstruct the process of their manufacture from the very beginning. Other workers are becoming convinced of the validity of this approach. Indeed, as Watson (1950) has observed, it is likely that a Stone Age community quite readily adopted "the shape of a tool it found in use by alien tribes, once its advantages were manifest, but much less likely that it should have the opportunity of learning, or be prepared, to revolutionize its industrial technique in order to reproduce the precise method of manufacture practiced by the original users of the tool." But the real difficulty with this approach is obvious: one should be familiar with the techniques themselves in order to detect them and assess their significance. In order to acquire the requisite insight into working methods, one should actually be able to reproduce them experimentally. Such technical ability is rare, and there are very few Paleolithic archeologists who can lay claim to it. Nevertheless, it is quite likely that when such an analysis of the Lower

Paleolithic hand-ax assemblages can be made, we may discover the existence of just as complex an interplay of techniques as that which exists between the various Middle and Upper Paleolithic traditions of the Old World.

In general, Paleolithic archeologists have not recognized the fact that early men had at their disposal not just one but several different techniques for flaking stone, as Breuil has rightly insisted. In the majority of instances these are common to a whole group of cultural developments at one and the same time, although in different frequencies. But when the finished tools are examined, the degree of typological uniformity within a given complex is indeed astonishing. Apparently this is due in large measure to the fact that approximately 95 per cent of the collections from open sites (i.e., gravel or sand pits) in western Europe have been made by workmen who save only the best hand-axes, flake tools, and nuclei. It is probable that this has given us a completely false picture of many of the assemblages in question. Nevertheless, even in these highly selected series it is possible to recognize the existence of certain specialized techniques which are limited to only one or possibly two kinds of assemblages and hence provide a fairly reliable and distinctive basis for descriptive purposes. These have been intensively studied by François Bordes (1950, 1951), himself an exceedingly skilful artificer of stone artifacts; and the provisional results of his work indicate that a new approach to problems of the Paleolithic is now being developed. Since this is regarded as of fundamental importance, the results of Bordes's investigations will be considered here in some detail.

The evidence of the occurrence of flakes of Levalloisian type in the Second Interglacial gravels of the Somme Valley, previously discussed, demonstrates that in western Europe, as in Africa, the Middle East, and India, the so-called "prepared" striking-platform/ tortoise-core technique, or faceted platform technique, first appears in the middle of the Acheulian stage of development, continues during the Upper Acheulian, and reaches its final expression in the Mousterian of Levalloisian facies. In western Europe, however, the situation seems to be somewhat more complicated than elsewhere (South and East Africa, for example), owing to the fact that we also have to consider other traditions, such as the Clactonian and the Tayacian, which are only sporadically found elsewhere. As regards the Clactonian, Hazzledine Warren has recently shown that it is by no means comprised exclusively of flakes. Indeed, many of the pieces described as nuclei are nodules of flint alternately worked on one end to a zigzag chopping-tool edge. In reality, the developmental pattern of these various assemblages is extremely complex and can be unscrambled only by an intensive investigation of: (*a*) the flaking techniques employed in the manufacture of the tools, (*b*) the nature of the raw material available for the production of implements, (*c*) the typology of the artifacts, and (*d*) the exact stratigraphic position of each site. The latter problem, of course, belongs in the realm of the natural sciences, and here there is still much basic field work to be done. For our present purposes, however, we can broadly group the localities into the various glacial and interglacial stages, although in many instances it would be very desirable if a more precise relative chronology could be determined.

From a typological point of view, the main criterion for subdividing the Lower and Middle Paleolithic rests on the presence or absence of hand-axes, or *bifaces*, to use a term that does not imply function. Technologically, it is the presence or absence of flakes with faceted striking-platforms and the characteristic Levalloisian preparation of these flakes on the core prior to detachment that are of fundamental importance. But, contrary to generally accepted opinion, these two features are not necessarily related. Therefore, it is necessary to define in a much more precise manner than has previously been attempted exactly what is meant by the "Levalloisian flaking technique," on the one hand, and the discoidal nucleus or "Mousterian flaking technique," on the other. From a historical point of view a Levallois flake is a type of flake first recognized from the gravels at Levallois, a suburb of Paris. Its form has been predetermined on the nucleus by special preparation prior to detachment. For the nucleus an oval-shaped nodule of flint is selected, generally of flattened form, which is roughly flaked along its borders to remove the irregularities. Next the cortex is removed from the upper surface by the detachment of centrally directed flakes, thus forming a surface which recalls the back of a tortoise, the flake scars representing the plates. On one end, perpendicular to the long axis, a striking-platform is prepared by the removal of very small flakes, thereby producing a faceted or scarred surface. A blow delivered by percussion technique (possibly with an intermediate tool) on this surface will yield a flat, oval flake which exhibits on its upper surface the traces of the centrally directed core preparation flakes. These flakes may also be round, triangular, or rectangular, depending on the shape of the nucleus. In the case of the latter, i.e., a rectangular flake, if the length is more than double the width, one has a flake blade, which, if it has been detached from a nucleus that exhibits a series of parallel rather than centrally directed scars, will resemble very closely true blades of the Upper Paleolithic. The

Levalloisian point is a particular type of Levallois flake of elongated triangular form, the shape of which has been predetermined by special preparation of the nucleus.

Now the flakes struck from a certain type of core, known as the "discoidal core" and very typical of Mousterian assemblages, are commonly mistaken for true Levalloisian flakes, as Bordes rightly maintains. The discoidal nucleus also exhibits careful trimming around its edges, as well as the scars of a series of centrally directed flakes. But the objective of the Mousterian knapper was to obtain these centrally directed flakes rather than to prepare the core for the removal of a special type of product. Normally, the discoidal nucleus is more markedly convex (although in certain instances flat or even slightly concave) than the Levalloisian form, and it may be alternately worked on the two faces, giving it a bipyramidal section. In both cases, once the first series of flakes has been removed, the craftsman proceeds by selecting the base of the ridges separating the scars of two previously detached flakes as the striking-platform. According to Bordes, a triangular flake, which resembles a Levalloisian point but with a thick butt and a clumsy appearance, is often produced in this manner. Also in the Mousterian there are flakes with plain, unprepared striking-platforms, frequently inclined toward the lower surface, in which case they are sometimes classed as "Clactonian." But this results from the technique employed—a hammer stone struck on a plain surface—and should not be taken to imply a connection with the true Clactonian assemblages of England. For these pseudo-Clactonian flakes are found in various contexts ranging from the Abbevillian to the Neolithic, including the Upper Paleolithic, and hence the term "Clactonian" should be reserved for the well-known Lower Paleolithic complex in which chopping-tools and choppers constitute the core-tool increment in place of hand-axes. In any case, nothing is yet known to demonstrate a transitional stage between the Clactonian and the typical Mousterian.

After defining the technological processes employed during Middle Paleolithic times in the production of flakes, Bordes applies this to various homogeneous assemblages from different parts of France on a statistical basis. These all come from localities that have produced 100 or more objects that have been selected neither by the workmen nor by collectors for museum display purposes. Of the various indices, four seem to be of fundamental significance, as follows:

1. *Levalloisian index (LI):*

$$\frac{\text{Total no. of Levalloisian flakes, points, and blades} \times 100}{\text{Total no. of flakes and blades of all types}}$$

2. *Index of faceting (IF):*

$$\frac{\text{Total no. of flakes with faceted butts} \times 100}{\text{Total no. of flakes on which the butt is recognizable}}$$

3. *Index of Levalloisian typology (ILty):*

$$\frac{\text{Total no. of Levalloisian flakes, points, and retouched points} \times 100}{\text{Total no. of retouched forms of all types}}$$

4. *Bifacial (hand-ax) index (BI):*

$$\frac{\text{Total no. of bifaces} \times 100}{\text{Total no. of bifacial + unifacial tools}}$$

The preliminary results of Bordes's study, including those recently published in a joint paper with Bourgon (1951), demonstrate the existence of a broad Mousterian Complex, the fundamental characteristics of which can be expressed statistically for the first time. For all practical purposes, this is comprised of the following two main groups that are further broken down into two categories each of two subdivisions:

Until recently it was maintained that the presence or absence of small, triangular, roughly cordiform or lanceolate hand-axes at sites referable to the Mousterian Complex was of chronological significance. But manifestly this is not true. They may be fairly frequent at one site but completely absent at several others, while the associated flake assemblages remain basically the same. Thus it may well be that, in instances where their occurrence is ex-

Group I: Mousterian with bifaces (hand-axes):
1. Levalloisian technique (LI > 25–30)
   A. With faceted butts (IF > 45)
      a) Micoquian of Levalloisian facies (ILty > 30)
      b) Mousterian of Acheulian tradition: Levalloisian facies (ILty < 30)

2. Non-Levalloisian technique (LI < 25–30)
   A. With faceted butts (IF > 45)
      a) Mousterian of Acheulian tradition: non-Levalloisian facies
   B. With unfaceted butts (IF < 45)
      b) Micoquian of non-Levalloisian facies

Group II: Mousterian without or with very few bifaces (hand-axes):

1. Levalloisian technique (LI > 25–30)
   A. With faceted butts (IF > 45)
      a) Mousterian of Levalloisian facies (ILty > 30)
      (= Levalloisian III, IV, VI, and VII of Breuil's scheme)
      b) Typical Mousterian (ILty < 30)

2. Non-Levalloisian technique (LI < 25–30)
   A. With faceted butts (IF > 45)
      a) Proto-Mousterian and Moustero-Tayacian
   B. With unfaceted butts (IF < 45)
      b) Tayacian and Mousterian of La Quina type (= *Charentian*)

tremely sporadic, we are dealing with intermittent or occasional settlement by hand-ax-using groups rather than with a true component of the technological tradition of the region in question. It is likewise possibly attributable to seasonal factors; for, as is well known, the material traits of one and the same group of hunting peoples may differ very profoundly in different places during different seasons. Furthermore, as McBurney (1950) points out, such a group habitually travels over several hundred miles of territory

during the annual cycle of specialized activities connected with hunting, fishing, and collecting. Certainly in southwestern France hand-axes commonly occur at both Mousterian open-air sites, as well as at the cave and rock-shelter stations, and in both cases the associated flake assemblages are invariably characterized by the faceted striking-platform/disk-shaped core technique. In other words, the presence or absence of these tools has no apparent chronological significance, and may be purely a manifestation of specialized activity.

It is also possible that it is due to geographical factors.

Now the application of the geographical approach to Paleolithic problems was first attempted by Charles McBurney two years ago. But a study of this type can be undertaken only when the data are sufficiently numerous and adequate, a situation that has come about in certain sections of Europe only during the postwar period. Since this approach has been demonstrated to be fundamentally sound, especially for the Mesolithic complexes of northwestern Europe, there is no reason to doubt that it will ultimately prove of great value in interpreting Paleolithic problems. McBurney's preliminary work has a direct bearing on the question of hand-axes at Mousterian localities in western and central Europe as a whole. Thus the sites with hand-axes appear to be mainly confined to the maritime lowlands of western Europe, while in the hilly and mountainous districts of the interior an entirely different tradition is encountered. Although the former region lies in the tundra belt immediately south and west of the margins of the last ice sheets, it nonetheless formed a uniform ecological territory, offering a "maritime forest climate without perennially frozen ground." In the upland regions and in the territory between the limits of the northern and Alpine ice sheets, on the other hand, extreme arctic conditions prevailed, with frozen-soil phenomena; this was the true treeless forest tundra. But the available data are not of a sufficiently precise nature to permit a more detailed consideration of the significance of this observation. Nevertheless, it is important, in that it points the direction that will be followed in the future by research on the Paleolithic cultures of the Old World.

One of the facts that emerged in the late 1920's as the result of Breuil's investigations in the Somme Valley is that the Levalloisian technique is characteristic of sites in the north of France, whereas at contemporary localities of the south (Dordogne region in particular) non-Levalloisian workmanship is more common. Bordes (1951) attributes this in large measure to the nature of the raw material. Certainly, it is a self-evident fact that, in dealing with any Stone Age assemblage, this plays a major role. In any case, the large-sized and more or less flat nodules of flint that occur in the chalk country of northern France lend themselves to the Levalloisian method of preparation of the core, thereby facilitating the detachment of a flake of predetermined form. On the other hand, in the south the majority of the nodules of flint are too small to work in this manner. Furthermore, they are often of globular or irregular outline, and there is nothing to be gained by employing the Levalloisian technique. Here we can only state that we agree completely with Bordes in maintaining that the quality and shape in which the raw material occurs have been factors of prime consideration. But, since the non-Levalloisian facies likewise occurs in regions where large-sized nodules of flint exist, it is certainly not the only one involved.

In order to formulate a possible explanation of this situation, it is necessary to consider such additional matters as: (*a*) the enormous length of time involved, which may well represent several tens of millenniums; (*b*) such geographic (i.e., environmental) conditions as those mentioned above; and (*c*) the type of social unit with which we are dealing. In this connection McBurney (1950) has very aptly stated:

It may be an archaeological truism, but it is nevertheless a point of the utmost practical importance, that assemblages of human artifacts require, as evidence, basically different interpretation to samples of organic fossils such as say, shells or pollen. Whereas the latter may be taken to indicate a semi-permanent biological population, the former, from what we know of modern primitive peoples, may well represent communities who ranged sporadically over wide areas outside their main habitat. An Eskimo tribe, for instance, has been described as making an annual trek of over 200 miles across hostile territory to obtain a much-needed raw material.

This concept is borne out by Bordes's conclusion based on considerations of a purely technological nature, namely, that the only significant difference between the materials from the open-air loess sites of northern France and the cave and rock-shelter stations of the south referable to the Mousterian of Levalloisian facies lies in what he has defined as the "Index of Levalloisian Typology" (ILty). In the case of the former, the percentage of Levalloisian flakes which have remained in mint condition or which have been very little retouched does not fall below 40. On the other hand, the average of the ILty for five typical horizons in the Dordogne which have produced Mousterian of Levalloisian facies is less than 10. Although the significance of this fact is not as yet altogether apparent, the various series under consideration cannot be differentiated on any other basis. Indeed, as Bordes suggests, one wonders if the Dordogne localities should not be regarded as the winter camps of the groups who hunted in the loess regions of the north during the summer season. On this basis the discrepancy in Levalloisian flake utilization may well reflect environmental differences of a seasonal nature but produced in both cases by groups which were basically identical. Surely, even if this interpretation cannot be proved until evidence of a much more refined nature is available, it seems a great deal more plausible than the taxonomic approach that was in vogue until recently; for the latter based its conclusions solely on the form and characteristic re-

touch exhibited by a selected series of the finished pieces.

In their recent joint paper Bordes and Bourgon (1951), employing Bordes's statistical approach, have published a detailed treatise based on their analysis of a large series of sites—caves and rock-shelters, as well as loess stations—referable to the newly defined Mousterian Complex. The graphs indicate that, regardless of the technique(s) employed in the production of flakes, the typology of the fundamental categories of implements is surprisingly constant, with the exception of the recently defined Charentian. This can only mean that the basic way of life during the time span under consideration was broadly similar over very wide areas, but the problem of the particular functions of a given type of scraper or point is just as obscure as ever.

Although still in its infancy, the geographical or environmental approach, as advocated by McBurney and others, will doubtless contribute to an understanding of the range of possibilities concerning what tools were used for. But before it can be tested we urgently need new and reliably documented materials from undisturbed sites. In the meantime, by eliminating the Levalloisian in a cultural sense and defining it as one of two basic flaking techniques in use at one and the same time, Bordes has made a fundamental contribution to the methodology of Paleolithic archeology. It certainly helps materially to clarify the situation with respect to the Lower and Middle Paleolithic succession in western Europe. Furthermore, it removes one very grave difficulty in working in this field, namely, the complete lack of anything approaching truly objective criteria in the study of the materials available from the early hunting and gathering levels. Up to now, much of the work has been completely subjective; therefore, the effect of providing a definitive method for assessing the technological increment in any given assemblage will certainly be far-reaching. It will be interesting to follow the more widespread application of this principle in such areas as the Near East, India, North Africa, Egypt, East and South Africa, for example, where problems of the same kind exist. As the method is more broadly applied, it will inevitably be improved, for it is still somewhat cumbersome. Nonetheless, it offers the only recourse yet devised for analyzing a given assemblage in terms of its several components. When combined with chronological and environmental studies, it is reasonably certain that significant results will accrue.

UPPER PALEOLITHIC

Until the middle 1930's the Upper Paleolithic sequence in western Europe seemed fairly straightforward: Aurignacian, Solutrean, and Magdalenian, just as set forth in all the standard textbooks. According to this concept, the "Aurignacian," as originally defined by Breuil (see Breuil, 1937, for references), could be subdivided into Lower, characterized by large curved points with blunted backs and known as "Châtelperron points"; Middle, with the split-base bone point, the busked graver or burin, and various types of steep scrapers; and Upper, of which a straight point with blunted back, apparently evolved from the Châtelperron type and known as the "Gravette point," was typical. This latter stage immediately preceded the Final Aurignacian with its tanged point, known as the "Font Robert type." However, discoveries of the last fifteen or twenty years have shown that, in reality, the Aurignacian succession is very much more complex than was originally suspected.

Formerly the only Upper Paleolithic complex known outside Europe was the Capsian of North Africa, and, since points with blunted backs are characteristic of the Capsian assemblages, the old Lower and Upper Aurignacian could be conveniently derived from this source. The Middle Aurignacian was supposed to have developed *in situ* during an interval when contact with North Africa was temporarily broken. But recent work has shown that (*a*) from a chronological point of view the Capsian is very late in North Africa; (*b*) it is absent in Spain; (*c*) in North Africa it is essentially an inland development, the coastal region everywhere being an Ibero-Maurusian (Oranian) province; and (*d*) many of the forms most characteristic of the Early Capsian (e.g., microburins and lunates) are completely absent in the Early-Upper Paleolithic assemblages of western Europe. On this basis, the claim of Africa as the homeland of the Lower and Upper Aurignacian has been pretty well ruled out.

But the problems of just what constitutes the Aurignacian and where its various components originated still remain obscure. At the only two really adequately excavated Upper Paleolithic localities in the entire Dordogne region—La Ferrassie and Laugerie-Haute—M. Denis Peyrony has found evidence which seems to suggest that the Aurignacian (as conceived in 1912 by Breuil) is an infinitely more complicated series of assemblages than was originally suspected by the creator of the old threefold scheme. In fact, Peyrony recognizes two separate traditions:

Périgordian = Lower (Châtelperronian) and Upper Aurignacian (Gravette/Font Robert) of the old system

Aurignacian = Middle Aurignacian of the Breuil classification

Peyrony's fundamental thesis is that in its later stages the former coexisted with the latter, a situation which can best be shown in the form of a table (Table 1).

At this juncture the writer does not intend to present a critique of Peyrony's scheme. Suffice it to say, however, that his scheme is in part supported by the stratigraphic evidence, although certain of the substages should doubtless be regarded as local variations. This very fundamental and important problem is urgently in need of

when we trace these influences back along the main routes of their supposed diffusion that the situation can be in some measure unscrambled. For here we should find definite geographical regions where relatively pure manifestations of given culture complexes can be recognized.

The argument that the very specialized blade technique—the hallmark of

TABLE 1

BREUIL'S CLASSIFICATION	GARROD'S CLASSIFICATION	PEYRONY'S CLASSIFICATION	
		Périgordian	Aurignacian
Upper Aurignacian	Font Robert stage	*5th phase:* Tanged points; leaf-like points; Noailles burins	*5th phase:* Bone points with simple beveled base
	Gravettian stage	*4th phase:* Gravette points; small-backed blades; female statuettes	*4th phase:* Bone points with biconical section
			3d phase: Bone points with oval section
Middle Aurignacian	Aurignacian	*3d phase:* Truncated or obliquely backed blades; backed blades of misc. types	*2d phase:* Bone points with diamond-shaped section; steep scrapers
		2d phase: Châtelperron points (evolved types); blades with inverse retouch	*1st phase:* Split-base bone points; steep and carinated scrapers
Lower Aurignacian	Châtelperronian	*1st phase:* Châtelperron points (basal Périgordian)	

further investigation; certainly, it is not possible to interpret the data on the basis of the evidence available at present.

As to Upper Paleolithic origins, Professor Garrod believes that, when sections of Europe other than France are considered, it becomes apparent that the French sequence is the result of successive influences superimposed one on the other. According to this view, on the periphery of its distribution the Upper Paleolithic becomes a more or less heterogeneous mass of successive levels which lack meaning. It is only

the Upper Paleolithic—originated outside western Europe is based on two significant facts: (*a*) the lack of a developmental sequence between the Mousterian and the earliest phase of the Upper Paleolithic (indeed, no instance of stratigraphic overlap is known in this entire region) and (*b*) the equally sudden appearance in western Europe at this time of men of developed *sapiens* type. As McBurney (1950) points out, it is considered very unlikely from a biological standpoint that Neanderthal could have evolved into a fully modern form within the time span suggested by the geological evidence, a fact which has convinced most workers that the concept of the rapid immigration into Europe at this time of blade-using modern man should be accepted as a plausible assumption. Nevertheless, it must be frankly admitted at the outset that there is no geological or archeological proof clearly supporting such a postulated earlier occurrence of *Homo sapiens* in association with a blade industry outside the region under consideration.

As to what Garrod has called "Châtelperronian" (= Peyrony's Early Périgordian; Lower Aurignacian of the old scheme), this is claimed to have already had an independent existence in early Upper Pleistocene times in the Near East: Palestine (Mount Carmel Caves) and Syria (Jabrud). Although its precise center is still unknown, it appears in western Europe during the closing stages of the Mousterian as the earliest identifiable blade complex. Possibly it came from central Europe or South Russia, since it is found there at an early date. In any case, nothing has thus far come to light in central Asia to suggest that it originated farther to the east.

The Aurignacian (= Middle Aurignacian of the old system) is also well represented in central Europe, especially in lower Austria and Hungary, as well as through Rumania, the Crimea, and Transcaucasia to the Near East, where it is very widespread and covers a considerably longer time span than in the west. Apparently this manifestation is absent on the South Russian Plain. Although Garrod suggested the Iranian plateau as a possible center where the Aurignacian developed, Coon's recent excavations have certainly contributed nothing to support this hypothesis.

Turning now to Garrod's Gravettian/ Font Robert Complex (= Peyrony's Late Périgordian; Upper Aurignacian of the old scheme), which extends into Spain and Italy, this has a wide distribution in central and eastern Europe and is considered by some authorities to be the classic Upper Paleolithic culture of the South Russian Plain, where true Aurignacian elements seem to be absent. A strong supporting argument for this concept is the fact that in South Russia, central Europe, and the west female statuettes of the Willendorf type are associated with the so-called "Gravettian" complex. Since this stage is absent in the Near East, it is possible that further excavations in the plains region of southern Russia will reveal that the Gravettian was derived from this source. It is also possible, however, that Peyrony is essentially correct in suggesting France for the main center of this development. In any case, on the basis of what we know at present concerning the materials found at stations on the South Russian Plain, this seems to be just as defensible a working hypothesis as any other. Certainly, both Peyrony and Garrod are fully aware that the discoveries of the next generation will, in turn, make further extensive revisions necessary.

In connection with future investigations, it is now generally admitted by Paleolithic archeologists that problems pertaining to the origin and development of the Upper Paleolithic will have to be dealt with on a regional basis. This is certainly a very great step in the right direction. For, in the past, work in this field has been very materially hampered by what may be termed the "index fossil concept"—i.e., approaching central Europe, South Russia, or the Near East (or any other area outside France, for that matter) as if they were some sort of typological appendages of western Europe. In focusing attention on the so-called "pre-Solutrean problem" in central Europe in his recent book, Lothar Zotz, in fact, has advocated this point of view, although the net result is only to complicate further rather than to simplify the problems. For the pre-Solutrean must henceforth be regarded as yet another independent tradition that has to be considered in connection with Early-Upper Paleolithic problems. Zotz notes that bifacial leaf-shaped points, in some instances extremely reminiscent of true Solutrean forms, actually occur sporadically in central Europe in various Late Acheulian, Micoquian, and Mousterian contexts, and he believes that it is from these early developments that the pre-Solutrean is basically derived. The evidence from the most important sites for this development shows that the pre-Solutrean dates from the time of the Würm I/II Interstadial, overlapping and paralleling the Châtelperronian (Early Périgordian). According to Zotz, the pre-Solutrean (also known as the Szeletian or Altmühlian) is a separate cultural manifestation heavily influenced from contemporary Upper Paleolithic sources. In fact, at certain sites it actually underlies Aurignacian horizons. Finally, during Gravettian (Late Périgordian) times, this blossoms out into the true Solutrean of central Europe assigned to the Würm II/III Interstadial on the basis of the evidence from the Czechoslovakian stations of Předmost and Moravany-Dlha.

This evidence certainly opens up a new perspective on Old Stone Age developments in central Europe, made possible only by recognizing and admitting the existence of regional cultural specializations during Middle and Upper Paleolithic times rather than by trying to force the data to fit the strictures of a taxonomic scheme established for an entirely different region over half a century ago. But, at the same time, it makes the problem of where the Solutrean originated even more obscure than ever. Once it was an accepted fact that this complex had reached France

from somewhere to the east, presumably from Hungary. But when the Soviet archeologists failed to find any traces of Solutrean beyond the Dniester, the claim of Hungary began to subside. Then in 1942 Professor Pericot Garcia published the results of his excavations at the Cave of Parpalló near Gandia (south of Valencia in southeastern Spain), where he had discovered a well-developed Solutrean culture with tanged and barbed projectile points, in addition to bifacial leaf-shaped types. The fact that certain of the former were strikingly close to examples known in the Late Aterian of North Africa (Tangier: Mugharet el'Aliya) led many Paleolithic archeologists to suspect that possibly the main focus of the European Solutrean lay in this southwesterly direction. Thus, if Zotz's pre-Solutrean has validity—and there is no reason to suspect otherwise—we now have two centers from which to derive the Solutrean—central Europe and southeastern Spain, where the inspiration apparently came from a Middle Paleolithic derivative known as the Aterian of North Africa. Although in central Europe the pre-Solutrean can also be traced back to Middle Paleolithic sources, this manifestly gets us nowhere with regard to the solution of the problem. In view of the new evidence, however, the development of such a specialized technique as pressure-flaking from complexes on an entirely different technological level from that of the Upper Paleolithic of Europe does not present inherent difficulties of the same magnitude as was true fifteen years ago. Indeed, most workers are quite prepared to accept the Solutrean as due to a diffusion of certain specialized ideas rather than an invasion of new peoples with superior weapons.

By the final stage of the Upper Paleolithic, regional cultural developments can be discerned very clearly. For the Magdalenian, centered in France, is limited in its distribution to western Czechoslovakia, southern Germany, Switzerland, Belgium, and Spain. Elsewhere we have such cultures as the Hamburgian of northwestern Germany, the Creswellian of England, and various evolved Gravettian (in the broad sense) complexes in Italy, parts of central Europe, and South Russia. Because of its truly magnificent naturalistic art, especially that of the Franco-Cantabrian Province, priority here clearly belongs to the Magdalenian, although the discovery of Lascaux some ten years ago has revealed an unexpected richness belonging to an earlier cycle. Now, as is well known, Magdalenian art includes painting in monochrome and polychrome in a wide variety of styles and techniques, engravings on stone, bone, and ivory, and sculptures in both high and low relief. The recent discoveries, especially at Angles-sur-l'Anglin, have emphasized the importance of local centers of artistic development. The real point of issue, however, is whether or not the pictures and drawings were done for purely decorative purposes. It does not seem at all likely that a primitive hunting community, living under the conditions of a rigorous and exacting environment, could have supported a specialized class of professional artists, such as some authorities have suggested. Nevertheless, it is patently clear that certain individuals lived during the Upper Paleolithic who were endowed with a highly developed artistic ability and a true appreciation of aesthetic values. Otherwise, there could not have been such a high development of art. In any case, the whole development clearly owes its existence to the magico-religious idea, especially the custom of hunting magic, as practiced today by living primitive peoples. This is one of the very few problems facing Paleolithic archeologists upon the solution of which ethnological studies would doubtless throw new light.

AFRICA

The Paleolithic of Africa is characterized by a variety of assemblages, some of which are purely local, whereas others are surprisingly similar to, if not identical with, certain of those found in Europe. It is only during recent years that geological investigations on a really adequate basis have been undertaken in this continent, and the results to date indicate that, owing to fluctuations in rainfall, the Pleistocene epoch throughout most of Africa can be subdivided on the basis of a succession of pluvial and interpluvial stages. Perhaps eventually these may be broadly correlated with the successive glacial and interglacial episodes of Europe. The cultural sequences are well established in certain areas, as indicated below, but this does not apply as yet to the continent as a whole.

EGYPT

Even in Paleolithic times Egypt already seems to have been almost as self-sufficient as she was in the dynastic period. Nothing of the rich and complex Upper Paleolithic development of the Near East is found here, but the cause of this cultural isolation from the north and east cannot be explained on the basis of the existing data. The geologic history of the Nile Valley during Late Cenozoic times is well known as the result of the intensive field work done there in the 1920's by Sandford and Arkell for the Oriental Institute of the University of Chicago.

The Abbevillian–Early Acheulian series of the 30-meter terrace calls for no special comment. Some of the very heavily rolled forms may be derived from the 45-meter terrace, although no *in situ* specimens have ever been found there. With the exception of a special form with a triangular section, known as the "Chalossian," these forms are indistinguishable from early Lower Paleolithic materials from western Europe. In association with these early types of hand-axes, very primitive flake tools with plain, high-angled striking-platforms occur. The Late Acheulian of the 15-meter terrace includes pointed hand-axes of Micoquian type, together with developed forms of flake implements; and in the Acheulio-Levalloisian of the 9-meter terrace there are oval or pointed flakes with faceted striking-platforms associated with tortoise-type cores and a few subtriangular hand-axes. In the 3-meter terrace there is a Middle Levalloisian industry in which a reduction in size and an increase in the delicacy of the flakes may be noted. The next series of deposits—the basal aggradational silts—yield an Upper Levalloisian assemblage, including several specialized types of points, as well as a bifacial lanceolate that suggests Aterian examples (Caton-Thompson, 1946a, b). The associated cores show a wide variety of form; in general, they are narrower than in the preceding stage.

Up to this point the main lines of development in the Kharga oasis and the Fayum follow the same basic pattern as outlined above for the Nile Valley. Subsequent to the time of the deposition of the basal aggradational silts, however, this is no longer true, since in each region there was a gradual industrial differentiation. These are: the Sebilian in Upper Egypt and Nubia; the Epi-Levalloisian in Lower Egypt and the Fayum; and the Khargan and the Aterian in the Kharga oasis. All are basically derived from the Late Levalloisian and perpetuate the same technological tradition. Thus Egypt developed along indigenous lines almost completely undisturbed by contemporary developments from outside the area, except for the appearance of the Aterian in the Kharga oasis, as discussed in the section on North Africa. Here only one of these three specialized complexes— the Sebilian—will be briefly considered.

Typical of the Lower Sebilian are flakes of Levallois type of reduced size, often with steeply retouched edges. One characteristic form exhibits a deliberately shortened striking-platform, giving the flake a squat appearance. In the Middle Sebilian backed lunates made on small flakes rather than on microblades, as well as certain subgeometric forms, appear. True Levalloisian flakes now almost completely disappear, although technologically the industry is clearly in the prepared striking-platform/tortoise-core tradition. The Upper Sebilian, which is probably later in time than the last major pluvial episode, approaches the Lower Natufian of Palestine and the Late Capsian of North Africa—both Mesolithic complexes—in many respects. In fact, at Helwan in Upper Egypt a true microlithic industry occurs, which is very like the Natufian of Palestine. But in the Upper Sebilian the occurrence of highly evolved and much reduced flakes and tortoise cores of basic Levalloisian facies serves to link this mesolithic assemblage with the ancient flaking tradition of the Lower and Middle Paleolithic.

EAST AFRICA

Actually, Paleolithic materials have been reported throughout the entire region intervening between Egypt and British East Africa, including the Anglo-Egyptian Sudan, Ethiopia, and Somaliland, the affinities of which have been assessed on a typological basis. But, since almost none of the horizons can be fitted into any of the established Pleistocene chronologies, there is little to be gained by presenting a regional summary of these materials. Now British East Africa—Kenya, Uganda, and Tanganyika—is bisected by the Great Rift Valley, on the walls of which excellent sections of Pleistocene deposits are exposed. The Paleolithic assemblages from sites to the west of this feature show that in prehistoric times this region belonged in equatorial Africa, just as it does at present. Therefore, it will be considered in a subsequent section; here the materials from the definitely savannah country of most of Kenya and Tanganyika will be described.

The earliest-known and most primitive tools from this area, known as the "Kafuan," consist of pebbles with a single edge, flaked on one side only. The Kafuan implements come from definitely Lower Pleistocene deposits and are regarded as one of the oldest archeological manifestations from anywhere in the world. At the classic Middle Pleistocene locality of Olduvai, in northern Tanganyika, a series of beds covering the range of time represented by the Second (Kamasian) Pluvial, the Second Interpluvial, and the Third (Kanjeran) Pluvial are exposed. During the ensuing interpluvial, severe rifting movements occurred, accompanied by erosion and valley-cutting, which mark the close of the Middle Pleistocene in this area. From the basal beds at Olduvai a pebble-tool industry, more evolved than the Kafuan and known as the "Oldowan," has been described by Leakey (1951). These include true chopping tools with edges alternately flaked in two directions, producing a jagged cutting edge. In the immediately overlying beds, pointed chopping tools appear which are regarded as the forerunners of the true bifacial hand-axes that have been reported from the next series of deposits, in association with various types of massive flake tools. At the horizon of the upper-middle part of Bed II at Olduvai, hand-axes of unmistakably Early Acheulian type appear. In Bed III the pointed hand-axes of Middle Acheulian type are associated with cleavers, made on "side-blow" flakes, and proto-Levalloisian flakes. This developmental sequence culminates in the Late Acheulian of Bed IV, where, in addition to finely made pointed hand-axes, there are

rectangular-shaped cleavers and a fully developed Levalloisian flake industry. No other single locality discovered to date can compare with Olduvai in providing a complete and unbroken record of the entire cycle of Lower Paleolithic cultural development.

Contemporary with the widespread geographical changes marking the close of the Middle Pleistocene in East Africa, two distinct types of tool-making traditions are found: (a) the Early Kenya Stillbay, a Levalloisian derivative in which some surviving Acheulian elements are present, and (b) the Kenya Fauresmith, which is basically of Acheulian inspiration and very similar to the Fauresmith of South Africa. In addition to various types of scrapers and points made on Levalloisian-type flakes, the former is characterized by small- to medium-sized bifacially flaked points that resemble minute hand-axes. This complex is very widespread in South Africa, where it shows a number of regional specializations. The Kenya Fauresmith also extends into Ethiopia; carefully shaped round stone balls constitute part of the assemblage. Since these normally occur in groups of twos or threes at the camp sites, they are regarded as bolas weights for use in hunting.

Following the post-Kanjeran interpluvial, the climate once again became markedly humid, and this interval is known as the "Gamblian Pluvial Period," which is of Upper Pleistocene age. The main cultural development known from deposits of this age is the Kenya Stillbay. Its bifacially flaked points often have secondarily retouched edges; and, in the final stages of the development, leaf-shaped forms appear, apparently worked by the technique of pressure-flaking. In the post-Gamblian dry phase, microlithic tools appear for the first time, and the earliest assemblage in which they are found is known as the "Magosian." From a chronological point of view the Magosian must belong to a fairly late horizon, since certain sites of this complex have yielded pottery. In addition to pottery, a true blade technique now appears in East Africa—called the "Kenya Capsian"—which is the immediate forerunner of the Elmenteitan in many of its most distinctive elements. Apparently contemporary with the latter manifestations there occurs a typical microlithic assemblage, the Kenya Wilton; but, since this has a widespread distribution in South Africa, it will be referred to in the next section.

SOUTH AFRICA

The Pleistocene succession in the basin of the Vaal River from near Johannesburg to the confluence with the Orange River has been worked out in great detail. This is also true of the sequences in northern and southern Rhodesia, but within the compass of the present paper, these latter areas connot be considered. The oldest gravels of the Vaal, probably laid down during basal Pleistocene (Early Kageran) times, have not yielded any artifacts as yet, but in the next younger series of deposits pebble tools occur. These artifacts, which are called "pre-Stellenbosch" and which recall both the Kafuan and the Oldowan of East Africa, are found in a series of gravel terraces that range from 300 to 50 feet above the stream. A lower terrace at +50 feet contains Abbevillian types of hand-axes, in many cases made on pebbles, together with primitive flakes. This assemblage is called "Stellenbosch I." Following the interval of heavy rainfall during which these gravels were accumulated, there was a prolonged dry interval, marked by earth movements, for which there is no record of human occupation in South Africa. This is considered to mark the close of the Lower Pleistocene.

A new series of gravels, aggraded at relatively low elevations, are referable to a sequence of geologic episodes probably related to the Kamasian and Kanjeran pluvial periods of the Middle Pleistocene. Three terraces forming distinct levels at +40 feet, +25 feet, and river-bed level carry deposits which not only yield a very rich fauna, but also five stages representing the entire development of the South African Hand-Axe, or Stellenbosch, Complex. Stage I, in which roughly made Abbevillian-like types and primitive flake artifacts predominate, still contains some pebble tools, but these disappear in Stage II. The hand-axes and cleavers of the latter are now more refined and recall Early Acheulian forms of Europe. Together with the developed hand-axes and cleavers made on "side-blow" flakes of Stage III, the Levalloisian, or prepared striking-platform / tortoise-core technique (also called the "faceted platform technique"), has its inception. Also found in groups of twos and threes are faceted polyhedral stones, regarded by some authorities as bolas stones. The cleavers of Stage IV are characteristic, in that they are now made on end-struck flakes with a trapezoidal- rather than a parallelogram-shaped section. This stage corresponds with the Late Acheulian of East Africa, and during it the prepared striking-platform technique continued to develop. The finely made hand-axes of Stage V are comparable to the Micoquian of Europe; these are associated with cleavers that have flared edges and a variety of tools made for special functions on flakes produced by the Levalloisian technique. The climax of the long, uninterrupted Stellenbosch development was brought to a close by a second interval of earth movements and by a dry climate.

The next series of gravels was laid down during an Upper Pleistocene wet phase, probably corresponding to the Gamblian of East Africa. These sediments contain the Fauresmith assemblage, characterized by a marked refinement in the flake tools of Levalloisian facies and the development of small, relatively slender hand-axes and cleavers. In view of the overwhelming proportion of flake artifacts in the Fauresmith, Van Riet Lowe has suggested the possibility that stabbing and throwing spears, as well as hafted tools and weapons of various sorts, now began to replace the earlier hand implements of the Stellenbosch. Following these aggradations, there was an arid interval when semidesert conditions prevailed. The ensuing wet phase, correlated with the Makalian of East Africa, witnessed the development of a series of assemblages referred to as the Middle Stone Age of South Africa. Hand-axes and cleavers no longer occur, the characteristic tools being made on flakes produced by a developed Levalloisian technique (Stillbay, Pietersburg, Mossel Bay, etc.). These include slender unifacial and bifacial spear and lance points, presumably for stabbing or throwing. In the final stages of the Middle Stone Age, known as the "South African Magosian," microlithic elements appear, just as they do in East Africa.

Wind-blown deposits of the post-Makalian dry interval buried the Middle Stone Age sites. A final minor wet phase, presumably paralleled by the Nakuran of East and equatorial Africa, witnessed the introduction of the so-called "Later Stone Age" cultures—Smithfield and Wilton—which are characterized by (a) small tools, including a large number of microliths, (b) the absence of the old Levalloisian technique, (c) parallel rather than convergent flaking, and (d) the widespread use of indurated shale in the manufacture of tools. Smithfield and Wilton are closely related and reveal varying degrees of influence as the result of contact with the culture introduced by the ancestors of the Bantu-speaking peoples. Since both were still extant at the time the first Europeans arrived in South Africa, the area constitutes one of the few places in the Old World where there exists a direct link between archeology and ethnology.

CENTRAL OR EQUATORIAL AFRICA

A very clear demonstration of response in Paleolithic cultural development to environmental conditions can be seen in the case of central or equatorial Africa, as recently pointed out by Goodwin. Here in what Frobenius has called the "Hylaean Area," or the region of the Selva, a special evolution in material culture took place, which is characterized by the occurrence of (a) the bifacial gouge or chisel, (b) the elongated pick—possibly an adze, (c) the tranchet type of ax, and (d) the elongated lance or spearhead. That this very distinctive assemblage, known as the "Sangoan" (formerly Tumbian) culture, was developed in response to environmental conditions has been established on the basis of distribution studies. These show that everywhere it occurs it is included within the 40-inch isohet, or contour of equivalent rainfall, which roughly delimits the tropical forest or equatorial region of central Africa. In addition to an unusually dense vegetation, typical of this area, are widespread deposits of soft alluvium and humus, the present distribution of which suggests very strongly that during the pluvial periods of the past the 50-inch or even the 60-inch isohet expanded to cover the areas adjacent to this zone. Today these are characterized by parklands and open bush country. With this expansion, the Hylaean area likewise expanded, and with it new types of tools developed to cope with the daily exigencies of life under such conditions. But what the latter actually were cannot as yet be determined.

Now the Lower Paleolithic development of the area is essentially a repetition of what has already been outlined for East and South Africa. From a horizon corresponding with the beginning of Middle Stone Age times in the South African sequence, however, the artifactual development of central Africa contrasts very strikingly with the regional assemblages found to the east and south of it. In the latter regions various types of points, flakes, and blade implements predominate in all the so-called "Middle Stone Age" complexes thus far brought to light. Although certain basic tool types overlap to some extent, it is the environmental background of the Sangoan culture that is of prime importance. Possibly when more is known concerning the scope and limitations imposed on human activities by such environmental conditions, we shall be able better to assess the significance of this and interpret the possible function(s) of the various very specialized types of tools. Since the Sangoan is found in deposits laid down after the Kanjeran pluvial, it is of Upper Pleistocene age. Just as in the case of the Fauresmith of South Africa, this development had its origin in the Great Hand-Axe Complex and carries on the same basic tradition. Indeed, the Sangoan is now generally accepted as a direct derivative of the Acheulian complex, which survived in the Hylaean area well down into Upper Pleistocene times. But in the present state of our knowledge it must be accepted as a fact that the radically different ecological conditions in the "retreat area" resulted in an equally radically different cultural development, since we do not even pretend to understand the dynamics involved.

NORTH AFRICA

North Africa's geographic position places it outside the area of direct contact with glacial and periglacial phenomena, which provide the keystone for chronologic studies in Eurasia. But this is in part offset by the existence of circum-Mediterranean marine phenomena linked with world-wide fluctuations of sea-level during Pleistocene and later time. Also there are indications here of arid and pluvial phases corresponding with interglacial and glacial episodes of the north. The only demonstrably Villafranchian (= basal Pleistocene) locality to yield human artifacts is situated at St. Arnaud, near Setif (Algeria). These consist of very crudely worked pebble tools of roughly spherical form and are the oldest implements ever found in the Old World. Lower Paleolithic hand-axes of both Abbevillian and Acheulian type associated with flake tools have been reported in great numbers throughout the entire area, including the Sahara, which was apparently less arid during Middle Pleistocene times than it is at present. The most important Lower Paleolithic sites are in the vicinity of Casablanca, Palikao (southeast of Mascara), Tabelbala, and Gafsa. Although the relative duration of the Lower Paleolithic is unknown in North Africa, the main developmental sequence seems to coincide broadly with that found elsewhere, and in a few isolated instances geological reference points have been established.

The Middle Paleolithic was very widespread, and it persisted in the North African area at least as late as the time of the Würm I/II Interstadial in terms of the Alpine sequence. A wide range of flake-tool assemblages, the most distinctive feature of which is the prominent role played by the prepared striking-platform/tortoise-core technique, is grouped here. Included in this category is the Mousterian, as well as the Aterian, a specialized Mousterian development characterized by tanged points made on flakes and bifacially worked in some instances. In general, the Mousterian seems to follow the Acheulian and to precede the Aterian, and several regional variations of it are claimed. But at two sites in the western part of the area (Morocco and Tangier) a simplified Mousterian follows the Aterian, while at Sidi-Zin, a recently investigated locality in Tunisia, two Acheulian horizons are separated by one yielding characteristically Mousterian tools. Hence contemporaneousness or noncontemporaneousness of similar morphological assemblages has not been demonstrated for the Middle Paleolithic of North Africa, and the various chronological schemes that have been proposed tend to degenerate into purely typological assessments.

The Capsian and Mouillian (formerly known as the "Oranian" or "Ibero-Maurusian"), both blade-tool complexes distinctive of this area, follow the Mousterian/Aterian development. Both date from the end of Upper Paleolithic times, but their main effervescence was during early postglacial (or postpluvial) times. The Capsian distribution is essentially inland and is centered around Gafsa in southern Tunisia and Tebessa in southeastern Algeria, while the Mouillian occurs everywhere along the coast from southern Tunisia to the Atlantic seaboard of Morocco. The Capsian is characterized by backed blades and points, scrapers, burins, and a very wide range of microlithic forms, the latter occurring almost exclusively at the youngest sites. The Mouillian is likewise a microlithic complex, in which the tools, on the whole, are smaller. Both the Capsian and the Mouillian persisted well after the introduction of Neolithic traits into this area.

ASIA

Recent work on the Paleolithic archeology of Asia indicates that during Middle Pleistocene times this vast region was divided into two major culture provinces, each of which has yielded a distinctive sequence. The first of these, which is in the south and east, includes China, Burma, northwestern India, and Java, where the characteristic implement types consist of chop-

pers and chopping tools that are often made on pebbles. None of the well-known Paleolithic complexes of Europe and western Asia seem to be represented. The second major province includes the Near East, Russian Turkestan, and peninsular India, and here a developmental sequence closely paralleling that of Europe, as well as Africa in its early stages, has been reported. Indeed, during Paleolithic times the entire western portion of Asia apparently was mainly inspired by the same technological innovations that motivated contemporary developments in Europe. In fact, many of the same fundamental techniques and types of tools are common to both regions. On this basis, the region encompassed by the Near Eastern lands may be considered in a sense as a southeasterly extension of a very much larger province. Finally, north-central Asia, which apparently was not occupied until toward the close of the Upper Pleistocene, has produced materials the affinities of which can be traced to both of the major provinces. Although the "Western" increment is dominant, the occurrence of pebble tools at sites in this region attests the extremely late survival of the ancient pebble-tool tradition of the Far East.

THE CHOPPER/CHOPPING-TOOL
TRADITION OF SOUTHERN
AND EASTERN ASIA

Uninfluenced by contemporary innovations in Africa, Europe, and western Asia, the archaic and very primitive tradition of making implements of the chopper and chopping-tool varieties either on pebbles or roughly tabular blocks persisted in the Far East as long as the practice of making stone tools survived. In Africa, as previously stated, such pebble-tool developments as the Kafuan, the Oldowan, and the pre-Stellenbosch are widespread and first appear in deposits laid down before the close of the Lower Pleistocene. Although human remains from Java show that man was extant at this time in Asia, no artifactual materials older than the Middle Pleistocene have yet come to light. Now the distinguishing feature of the various regional assemblages found in several sections of southern and eastern Asia is not the presence of a limited range of certain very old and fundamental types of tools; rather it is the absence of the two most distinctive features of the various Lower and Middle Paleolithic assemblages of the west. These are (*a*) the Abbevilleo-Acheulian cycle of hand-ax development and (*b*) the intimately associated prepared striking-platform/tortoise-core, or Levalloisian, technique. In such intermediate regions as northwestern India a certain degree of overlap and fusion of the two basic technological patterns occurs, since bifacial core implements and Levalloisian-type flakes of Western type are found together with numerous pebble tools reminiscent of those from China and Burma. Below is presented a summary of the sequences in the several regions of southern and eastern Asia under discussion.

BURMA

In the terrace gravels of the Irrawaddy Valley of upper Burma a complex known as the "Anyathian" has been recognized, in which hand-axes are absent. Throughout, the Anyathian is characterized by single-edged core implements made of fossil wood and silicified tuff: choppers, chopping tools, and hand-adzes. In addition, there is a series of large crude flake implements with plain high-angle striking-platforms, comparable with those found in other parts of the world at the same general time horizon, but normally associated with early types of hand-axes. For the Early Anyathian is present in three distinct horizons of the gravels exposed on the two highest terraces of the ancestral Irrawaddy, which are of Middle Pleistocene age. The Late Anyathian, a direct development from the earlier assemblages, is characterized by smaller and better-made core and flake artifacts, including such specialized types as true scrapers and points. It is found *in situ* in the fourth Irrawaddy terrace and is Upper Pleistocene in date.

CHINA

Current information concerning early man in China during the Middle Pleistocene is based exclusively on the evidence from the well-known site of Choukoutien, a village at the base of a small limestone hill some 37 miles southwest of Peking. This hill contains an enormously rich series of fissure deposits, three of which were occupied during the interval of time roughly corresponding with the Second Glacial (Mindel), Second Interglacial (Mindel-Riss), and Third Glacial (Riss) stages in terms of the Alpine sequence. These are known as localities 13, 1, and 15. The single artifact from locality 13 is a small pebble tool and is the oldest evidence thus far discovered of human occupation in this part of the world. Associated with the remains of Peking Man (*Sinanthropus*) at the important locality 1 site, a large series of choppers and chopping tools has been described. These are of archaic type and made on river pebbles or other natural pieces of stone; they are associated with a quartz flake industry which includes smaller types of implements, especially scrapers and points. Large hearths occur throughout the deposits, demonstrating that *Sinanthropus* was familiar with the making and use of fire. The third Lower Paleolithic locality, No. 15 of the Choukoutien fissures, has yielded a series of somewhat better-made artifacts than those from locality 1, but nonetheless manufactured by employing the same basic techniques of stone-working which resulted in the production of pebble tools, on the one hand, and quartz flakes, on the other. It is apparent that this complex, known as the "Choukoutienian culture," forms an integral part of the chopper/chopping-tool tradition of eastern Asia.

JAVA

In addition to the famous discoveries of *Pithecanthropus* and other very primitive types of hominids, the former presence of early man on this island is attested by the occurrence of a large number of crude stone artifacts of Lower Paleolithic type from a site just north of Patjitan in south-central Java. Hence this assemblage is known as the "Patjitanian." The main types of implements consist of single-edged choppers, chopping tools, and hand-adzes, manufactured from various silicified rocks, that can scarcely be distinguished from those found in Burma and China. Primitive flakes, with unprepared striking-platforms at a high angle with the long axis of the implement, also occur here. In addition, there is an interesting series of pointed artifacts, including proto-hand-axes and crude hand-axes, the former being unifacial tools (i.e., worked on only one surface), whereas the latter are true bifacial implements. The presence of this hand-ax series in the Patjitanian may be accounted for as either (*a*) the independent development of tools of this type in Java or (*b*) some sort of diffusion or influence from peninsular India, where tools of this type are very common. The absence of hand-axes in Burma and Malaya tends to rule out the latter as a possibility. In defense of the former, all one can say is that a convincing argument can be put forward on typological grounds suggesting that tools of the hand-ax type were independently evolved in Java. But until there is something approaching stratigraphy to go on, it is only possible to speculate. It is a cardinal fact, however, that, to date, noth-

ing has been reported from Java attributable to the Levalloisian prepared striking-platform/tortoise-core technique. This evidence shows that the Patjitanian should be included in the larger culture province of southern and eastern Asia which existed during Middle Pleistocene times.

MALAYA

In the Middle Pleistocene tin-gravels of Perak, northern Malaya, a large series of Lower Paleolithic types of implements made of quartzite was discovered in 1938. These occur at a place called Kota Tampan and therefore are referred to as the "Tampanian" culture; they are almost indistinguishable from those found near Patjitan in Java, briefly discussed above.

INDIA

Certain of the Paleolithic assemblages from this vast region demonstrate that during Paleolithic times it was a marginal area intermediate between the two main provinces of western Asia, on the one hand, and southern and eastern Asia, on the other, from the point of view of the fundamental traditions employed in the manufacture of stone tools. In the Punjab Province of northwestern India assemblages of implements characteristic of both the chopper/chopping-tool and the hand-ax/ Levalloisian flake complexes are found. In this latter area the earliest tools, which are of Second Glacial age (the so-called "Punjab Flake Industry"), consist of large, crude, heavily worn flakes. This development is followed in the Second Interglacial stage by the Early Soan culture, on the basis of the evidence from a series of sites in the Indus and Soan valleys. Pebble tools, including choppers and chopping tools, as well as flake implements, are characteristic. The latter, massive and crude in the early phases of the Soan, develop into forms described as "proto-Levalloisian." In part contemporary with this fundamentally "Eastern" complex is a series of hand-axes of Abbevillian and Acheulian type that recall not only European and African examples but also those of the Madras region of peninsular India. To date, no clearly stratified site has been found in northwestern India to indicate which of the two basic complexes—the Abbevilleo-Acheulian or the Soan—was the earlier in the Punjab. During Upper Pleistocene time the Late Soan is found. Evolved types of pebble tools and a wide range of flake artifacts produced by the prepared striking-platform/tortoise-core technique are typical. In addition, a few parallel-sided flake blades occur in the Late Soan.

Peninsular India is extremely prolific of Paleolithic localities, and invariably the artifactual materials include hand-axes, cleavers, and flake tools that are very reminiscent of assemblages from South and East Africa. But the actual dating and relative chronology of these sites is very little known; indeed, here Pleistocene geology has lagged far behind archeological discovery. As the result of field investigations undertaken during recent years, reports on collection from some eight or nine main areas are available. Admittedly, this is an impressive beginning, but a very great deal more basic work remains to be done. Since the sequence in the Madras region is reasonably well known, a brief summary of the evidence from Vadamadurai and Attirampakkam—the two richest sites—will be presented.

The oldest material comes from Vadamadurai, where the entire sequence is represented. It includes a series of heavily rolled and patinated flakes and Abbevillian-type hand-axes of crude outline and exhibiting deep, irregular flake scars. These are found in a deposit of boulder conglomerate. On typological grounds the next series may be compared with the Early Acheulian; it

also comes from the boulder conglomerate horizon but is far less patinated than the Abbevillian group. The flakes in this series exhibit less cortex on the upper surface and more primary flaking on the core prior to detachment than is true of the older specimens. From detrital laterites overlying the boulder conglomerate a typical Middle Acheulian assemblage has been described. Some of the associated flakes show definite signs of retouch. The next younger materials are found in the nonlaterized deposits carried on three terraces, which were formed during Upper Pleistocene times but cannot be more precisely dated on the basis of the available evidence. Evolved forms of flat-sectioned hand-axes of Upper Acheulian type with more pronounced secondary working of the edges are found in these terraces at both Vadamadurai and Attirampakkam, together with cleavers, tortoise cores, and flakes with faceted butts. The typical cleavers have parallelogrammic cross-sections produced by the so-called "side-blow" technique; these are practically identical with examples from Stellenbosch V of the Vaal Valley in South Africa and from the site of Tashenghrit in North Africa. Hand-axes with an S-twist also merit special mention. The cores exhibit very regular and even working, while the flake tools have faceted striking-platforms with much primary flaking on the upper surface in the best Levalloisian tradition. Among the types of flake implements, there are some side-scrapers and triangular points definitely retouched for use.

More northerly sites, such as those in the Narbada Valley, in Mayurbhanj, and the Gujarat, have yielded hand-axes associated with cleavers and flakes, similar to the Madras localities. And, together with these characteristic Lower Paleolithic forms, there are pebble tools reminiscent of the Soan complex of the Punjab. In other words, the ancient tool-making tradition of the Far East persisted here, just as it did in northwestern India. On this basis it seems likely that old deposits will ultimately be found in this area containing only choppers and chopping tools made on pebbles.

One problem concerning Old Stone Age developments in India that still remains obscure is what happened here during Upper Paleolithic times. From the Krishna Valley, Kurnool District, Madras, and from Khandivili, near Bombay, true blade industries with burins and other characteristically Upper Paleolithic types have been described. But, as yet, all one can say with regard to dating these assemblages is that they appear to be younger than the last pluvial episode and older than the earliest microlithic assemblages, which have a wide distribution in India in association with deposits of sub-Recent age. In many respects the latter situation is very reminiscent of that found in the Near East, Europe, and Africa; in fact, some of the Indian microlithic assemblages are very suggestive of the Wilton. In any case, before any consecutive picture of Paleolithic developments in India can be presented, much intensive work remains to be done. It is therefore encouraging to note that an active research program has been implemented which will inevitably yield substantial results.

THE NEAR EAST

In the western portion of Asia a Paleolithic succession very closely paralleling that of Europe has been reported, but no synthesis of the materials as a whole has ever appeared. The best stratigraphy thus far reported in detail is that revealed at a series of three caves in the Mount Carmel range, south of Haifa in northern Palestine, excavated in the early 1930's under the direction of Dorothy Garrod in the Wadi el-Mugharet, the Valley of the Caves. Three other very fine stratified sites have been dug subsequently—Ksâr 'Akil (near Beirut, Republic of Lebanon), Jabrud (north of Damascus, Syria) and Umm Qatafa (in the Judaean Desert of southern Palestine), but only the Mount Carmel sites can be considered within the compass of the present paper.

The oldest horizon yields a crude flake industry reminiscent of the Tayacian of western Europe. This, in turn, is overlain by an Upper Acheulian assemblage, including typical pear-shaped hand-axes and a large series of flake tools. A small proportion of these flakes exhibits prepared striking-platforms, just as in the case of the Upper Acheulian of the Nile Valley and the Kharga oasis. The next younger horizon is 7.10 meters thick, and it yielded over 44,500 artifacts of developed Acheulian or Micoquian type, hand-axes comprising 16 per cent of the total. The flake tools consist of a wide range of scraper types, and some of them were struck from tortoise cores with characteristically prepared striking-platforms. A surprising discovery in this horizon is the presence of a small number of blade points of the Châtelperron and Audi types of Europe, together with an increment of other types of true blade tools. The associated fauna indicates that a warm, almost tropical, climate with a heavy rainfall prevailed, which gives way to relatively drier conditions in the following level. The latter contains the Lower Levalloiso–Mousterian, in association with which a series of Neanderthaloid burials was discovered by McCown at the Mugharet es-Skhūl, the smallest of the three Mount Carmel caves. On the basis of the available dating evidence, these can be correlated with the Würm I/II Interstadial in terms of Alpine chronology.

Although a few hand-axes exist in the Lower Levalloiso-Mousterian, the industry is definitely in the prepared striking-platform/tortoise-core tradition. In Europe it would be called Mousterian of Levalloisian facies, on the basis of Bordes's terminology. The overlying Upper Levalloiso-Mousterian yields a somewhat more developed assemblage, but the two subdivisions are basically the same, the leading types being side-scrapers and points. This complex, recently reported by Coon from several localities in Iran, is very widespread throughout the Near East, including Anatolia, Iraq, and Arabia. Furthermore, it presents close analogies with contemporary developments in Egypt.

Next in the Mount Carmel sequence, the next level, called "Lower Aurignacian," yields various types of small, delicate blade tools, including points of Châtelperron type. This is overlain by two horizons of fully developed Middle Aurignacian of classic type. Here steep, keeled, and nose scrapers, small spiky points, end-of-blade scrapers, and a variety of burin types predominate. Comparable industries occur at several sites in the Caucasus and from the middle horizon of Siuren I in the Crimea. At the Mugharet el-Wad the true Middle Aurignacian is overlain by Atlitian, which represents a specialized development based on the Middle Aurignacian tradition. Then there is a break in the sequence, the next occupants of the site being the Natufians, who introduced a microlithic technique, including multi-hafted sickle blades, presumably used for harvesting wild grains.

In addition to Palestine, industries very reminiscent of the Middle Aurignacian of Europe are found in Syria, the Lebanon, and Anatolia. But no true blade complex has yet been identified in Iran, although Coon's material from the Hotu Cave on the southern shore of the Caspian Sea apparently dates from terminal Pleistocene times, and presumably the same is true of Garrod's

"extended Gravettian" from Zarzi in eastern Iraq. In any case the Upper Paleolithic materials thus far brought to light in the Near East give one the impression that at this horizon this region should be regarded as a southerly extension of the Eurasiatic blade-using complex rather than as one of the centers where the latter developed. Indeed, no convincing developmental sequence has been found, and the complex as a whole is entirely lacking in Egypt until Mesolithic times.

CENTRAL ASIA

In central Asia significant Paleolithic discoveries have been made in recent years. In Turkmenia surface finds of Acheulian-type hand-axes have been announced from a site 25 miles east of Krasnovodsk, while in Uzbekistan several Mousterian localities have been excavated, the most important of which is Teshik-Tash. This cave is in the Gissar Mountains, near Baisun, approximately 90 miles south of Samarkand. Here a Neanderthal child's burial was discovered associated with five (possibly six) pairs of horns of the Siberian mountain goat. The occurrence of a fully developed Mousterian assemblage, including a few flakes of classic Levalloisian type, in this remote area demonstrates how very widely this complex was distributed during Upper Pleistocene times. No justification whatsoever, on the basis either of the geological or of the paleontological evidence, can be found to support the claim put forward by the Russians that the Teshik-Tash occupation dates from Middle Pleistocene (Mindel-Riss) times.

SIBERIA

Between the Ob Valley, near Tomsk, on the west and the Baikal region on the east (including Transbaikalia and the upper Lena Valley) over 65 localities of Late Glacial and Early Postglacial age have been investigated. Probably the oldest group of these is later than the maximum of the Würm III (Bühl) substage in terms of the Alpine glacial sequence, and hence roughly corresponds in age with the Magdalenian of western Europe. But the age of the youngest group, classed as Mesolithic by the Russian archeologists, is unknown; very likely they belong to the Boreal or even the Early Atlantic interval of the Baltic succession, since associated with them occurs a modern type of fauna. On the other hand, the wooly rhinoceros and the mammoth are present at the oldest stations, together with other cold forms. The former becomes extinct in the next stage, and the reindeer is very abundant. At the third group of localities the mammoth is extinct, while such tundra forms as the arctic fox and the Saiga antelope have now migrated from the region. Finally, only modern forms are found at the youngest sites, as stated above.

The archeological material from the Siberian loess stations is a curious mixture of (*a*) blade tools, together with antler, bone, and ivory artifacts, of classic Upper Paleolithic type; (*b*) points and scrapers made on flakes of "Mousterian" aspect; and (*c*) pebble tools representing a survival of the ancient chopper/chopping-tool tradition of the Far East. At certain sites the *a* and *b*, or archaic, forms may run as high as 65 per cent of the total series, although found in direct association with such specialized types of bone tools as awls and needles, as well as beads and pendants of bone and ivory. Remains of semisubterranean dwellings with sloping sides and centrally located hearths occur here, just as at Upper Paleolithic sites on the South Russian Plain. Another "western" feature is the female statuary in bone; twenty of these objects were found at one site— Mal'ta (about 54 miles from Irkutsk). At Verkholenskaia Gora (near Irkutsk) several large bifacially flaked laurel-leaf points were found, together with a typical assemblage of stone, bone, and antler tools, including barbed bone points, in association with an essentially modern type of fauna. Indeed, the most striking feature of this Siberian Paleolithic is the fact of its relatively late survival. In some localities it actually occurs in the uppermost layers of the loess immediately below a horizon of humus containing Neolithic camp sites.

ORDOS REGION OF NORTHERN CHINA

In the very north of Mongolia a few late Upper Paleolithic stations belonging to the Siberian complex have been reported, but from elsewhere in this vast territory there are only sporadic surface finds doubtfully referable to the Paleolithic on a typological basis. Immediately to the south, however, in the great bend of the Yellow River, several very prolific localities were investigated in the 1920's. These materials are associated with demonstrably Upper Pleistocene deposits. Originally classified as "Moustero-Aurignacian," it is now quite apparent that the Paleolithic of the Ordos has much in common with that of the Yenisei-Baikal region of Siberia; for comparable examples of blade implements are found here in direct association with points and scrapers of Mousterian-like appearance and pebble tools of Choukoutienian tradition. But the actual dating and relative chronology of these sites involve many problems, and a great deal more intensive work of a joint archeological-geological nature is needed before it will be possible to reach final conclusions. Also the problem of terminology will have to be considered sooner or later, for the Ordos and Siberian materials simply do not conform with any Upper Paleolithic assemblages thus far described from other regions of the Old World.

GENERAL CONSIDERATIONS

On the basis of the foregoing, one is perhaps justified in asking how the data pertaining to the nature of the relationships between the various tool-making traditions of the Old World Paleolithic can ever be composed into any sort of a rational scheme. It is obvious that this problem is of basic importance, since it strikes at the shackles of several subjective and completely unwarranted assumptions that have been and are being made by workers in the field of Paleolithic archeology. The most fundamental of these concerns the significance of the various complexes with which we are dealing. Are we, in point of fact, actually studying extinct cultures, for is not our material inevitably reduced to the most imperishable vestiges of the material equipment of the different groups of very primitive hunting peoples which occupied various regions of the globe during Pleistocene times? In the light of this approach, one may indeed wonder if we can ever compose our meager data into a pattern which can be dignified by the term "culture." The time has come, however, to recognize the fallacy in the thinking of the school which seeks some sort of biological interpretation for the bewildering new array of primitive Stone Age assemblages of tools that are being constantly augmented by fresh discoveries. Those who champion this approach attribute changes registered in a particular tool-making tradition at a given point in its development or evolution to contact, or even to the actual merging of two or more divergent evolutionary lines. One could even quote instances in which it has been assumed that two totally distinct tool-making traditions have fused in some sort of a matrimonial alliance. The results of these instances of hybridization are, of course, manifest in the literature by various hyphenated terms, some of which have been mentioned in this paper. Although in many instances an extremely plausible case can be made in defense of the latter practice, it is simply begging the issue, for, causally, the arguments may be simply reduced to typological flimflam. Indeed, identification and definition by the typological approach alone ignore every possible cultural interpretation, and we are left with the curious spectacle of tools interacting among themselves. But, in the final analysis, it must be admitted that, except in very broad terms, we know as yet virtually nothing concerning (*a*) the origin and diffusion of the technological entities with which we are dealing, (*b*) the kind and degree of interplay that occurs when and if two specific tool-making traditions seem to come into contact with each other in a given region, and (*c*) the relationships of the main technological processes employed in the manufacture of stone tools and weapons by early men to one another in time and space. In this connection, it is of significance to note that *all* the fundamental processes used by Paleolithic man in Europe to produce tools are being used today, or have been employed during recent times, by the Australian aborigine, although admittedly the forms of the completed artifacts are quite different.

It is clearly apparent that the principles involved in the diffusion and continuity of a certain tool-making tradition cannot be conceived of in terms of the laws of heredity in the genetic sense of the biologist. For they are not passed on from one generation to another by procreation but by instruction and education. Possibly in some instances the intellectual capacity of a given group of Paleolithic hunters may not have been equal to mastering a certain technological development, but this seems very unlikely. In regions where a specific tool-making tradition of an archaic type persisted, such as in the case of the chopper/chopping-tool tradition of southern and eastern Asia, it is very much more likely that this occurred because of a failure of more advanced techniques to diffuse into the area than because the primitive types of mankind who lived there during Middle Pleistocene times were incapable of understanding the new and improved methods that had been and were being developed elsewhere in the Old World. Broadly speaking, Paleolithic archeology is a study of man's progressive ability to utilize and manufacture tools from raw materials supplied by nature, regardless of what tool-making tradition is dominant. Since there is at present no evidence available to indicate that differences in the material culture and behavior of different racial groups is in any sense of biologic origin, it follows that there is no justification for making an exception to this principle in the case of studies relating to fossil man.

A healthy science is one in which there is continuous re-evaluation of the problem in the light of present evidence and application of this re-evaluation to practice and terminology. As humans we think in terms of the labels we put on things. But if the labeling system does not keep up with thought, it is demonstrably a short time before thought ceases. Paleolithic archeologists are neither the only nor the worst offenders in this respect; however, the shortcomings of such fields as mammalogy need not concern us here. Because we deal with concrete physical entities— the stone artifacts made by men who lived many thousands of years ago— there is always a strong temptation to let the objects fascinate us today, just as they did the nineteenth-century collectors. Putting the label on is only half the game; taking it off again is the other half.

Notwithstanding the fact that their field is a humanistic discipline, Paleolithic archeologists must resort to the natural sciences both for chronological

evidence and for indications of past conditions. For during prehistoric times, just as in the historic range, environmental and geographical factors played a dominant role in conditioning the behavior of various early (or primitive) groups of mankind. Indeed, from the point of view of the development of man's material culture in the archeological sense of the term, these factors, including climate, soil, flora, fauna, natural resources, and topography, should be considered as having provided the stage—scenery, backdrops, lighting, etc. —on which the human drama has been played ever since the emergence of the first primitive hominids from the ancestral primate stock. In a sense, therefore, typology is the joint product of cultural tradition and environment, both of which are constantly changing factors. However, the picture is far more complex, since the rate of change and the degree of interplay between man's cultural achievements and the environment to which he was ever struggling to adapt himself and on which he was dependent for his livelihood have been far from constant. The fact that these variables exist only serves as a further reminder that Paleolithic archeology always is to be regarded as a humanistic discipline.

A survey of the available literature from a historical point of view will demonstrate clearly that the reaction of early man to fundamental changes in stage and setting, which repeatedly occurred during Pleistocene time, has not proceeded at a uniform or even predictable rate. The sum total of the data thus far brought to light bearing on the various Middle and Upper Paleolithic complexes of the Old World makes the basis for this observation abundantly clear. Certain significant facts bearing on this problem have been discussed in this paper; here the question of the possible extent of environmental influence on cultural developments during the earlier periods will be briefly considered. In this regard Dixon's (1928) observation that "the dependence of culture on environment and the closeness of correlation between them is greatest in the lower stages of cultural growth" is directly applicable. Indeed, this is the very essence of the problem: Paleolithic archeology cannot be divorced from its background of the natural sciences without denying it the key to the reconstruction and interpretation, in so far as possible, of human activities of the past. Although few Paleolithic archeologists today would disagree with this concept, it was not appreciated by the early workers in the field, who seem to have felt that their job had been completed as soon as they had produced an orderly classification and description of their material and compared it in a superficial and completely subjective manner with analogous collections from elsewhere in the region. Thus the underlying cause of the dilemma in which the subject finds itself at present is the direct result of the shortcomings of the purely formal taxonomic approach. Indeed, many instances could be cited demonstrating how the data have been abstracted from their real context in order to comply with the preconceptions of those who adhere to this system.

In that Paleolithic archeology is dependent on the natural sciences in several fundamental respects, the dividing line between the two fields cannot be clearly defined. Admittedly, man himself is both a natural and a social being. Along with the higher apes, he has inherited certain physical attributes from a common paleo-anthropoidal ancestral stock, but no one can deny that the degree of divergence between man and apes is tremendous. One of the basic reasons for this has been the capacity of the human organism to invent and develop a material culture—to conceive of and manufacture a varied assortment of tools to assist him in his struggle for survival. The archeological record demonstrates that no other single factor has played a comparably fundamental role in the emergence of man as the only mammal which today has become almost entirely liberated from the limiting factors imposed by environmental and geographical conditions. It is therefore the direct result of his ability to apply common sense and reason to the solution of a given problem and, once having arrived at this solution, to be able to impart the knowledge and experience thus obtained to others of his kind which sets the study of early man in a realm apart from the disciplines governing the natural sciences. But, by forming an alliance with the latter, Paleolithic archeologists can relate their materials not only in time but also to the total environmental picture. Ultimately it may even be possible to postulate within certain limits how the objects from the older horizons could have been employed. Certainly, there is much to be found out regarding what they were not used for, especially on the Lower Paleolithic level of development. In any case, owing to the very generalized nature of these earlier assemblages, direct typological comparison for historical purposes seems to be a completely sterile approach.

In addition to environment, there are other basic factors to be considered, three of which have been interacting throughout the entire span of Paleolithic development: (*a*) the need for a given type of tool, which may have been invented in several places at different times or abandoned if it became useless; (*b*) the inherent properties of the raw material available for implement manufacture; (*c*) the extreme degree of conservatism of early man with regard to the technological traditions that he followed in his daily routine, which, in the final analysis, is the sole basis on which the various assemblages in question can be defined objectively, as Bordes has shown. But it is clear that actual cultural connections cannot be studied in a satisfactory manner until the relative dating can be determined through the medium of techniques far more refined than those now available. Since at present it is extremely difficult to establish the relative age of localities only a few miles apart, it is apparent that we are still far from this goal.

Although certain broad-scale chronological tie-ups have been proposed, we are still a very long way from objectivity in any historical reconstruction of the Paleolithic cultures of the Old World. Indeed, those who have attempted such syntheses during recent years must admit that, regardless of the validity of certain basic concepts, the assumptions on which the entire structure is erected are extremely fragile.

REFERENCES AND SELECTED BIBLIOGRAPHY

ALIMEN, HENRIETTE. 1950. *Atlas de Préhistoire.* Vol. I. Paris: N. Boubée et Cie.

BALOUT, LIONEL. 1948. "Quelques Problèmes nord-africains de Chronologie préhistorique," *Revue Africaine,* XCII, 231–62.

——. 1950. "Le Peuplement préhistorique de l'Algérie," *Documents Algériens, Série Culturelle (Préhistoire),* No. 50.

BORDES, FRANÇOIS. 1950. "Principes d'une Méthode d'Étude des Téchniques de Débitage et de la Typologie du Paléolithique ancien et moyen," *Anthropologie,* LIV, 19–34.

——. 1951. "L'Évolution buissonnante des Industries en Europe occidentale. Considérations théoriques sur le Paléolithique ancien et moyen," *ibid.,* pp. 393–420.

BORDES, FRANÇOIS, and BOURGON, MAURICE. 1951. "Le Complexe Moustérien: Moustériens, Levalloisien et Tayacien," *Anthropologie,* LV, 1–23.

BREUIL, HENRI. 1912. "Les Subdivisions du Paléolithique supérieur et leur Signification," *Compt. rend. du Congrès International d'Anthropologie et d'Archéologie Préhistorique, 14th Session, Geneva.* 2d ed. Lagny: E. Grevin.

——. 1939. "The Pleistocene Succession in the Somme Valley," *Proceedings of the Prehistoric Society,* n.s., V, 33–38.

BREUIL, HENRI, and KOSLOWSKI, L. 1931. "Études de Stratigraphie Paléolithique dans le Nord de la France, la Belgique et l'Angleterre," *Anthropologie,* XLI, 449–88.

——. 1932. *Ibid.,* XLII, 27–47, 291–314.

——. 1934. *Ibid.,* XLIV, 249–90.

BREUIL, HENRI, and LANTIER, R. 1951. *Les Hommes de la Pierre Ancienne (Paléolithique et Mésolithique).* Paris: Payot.

CATON-THOMPSON, GERTRUDE. 1946a. "The Aterian: Its Place and Significance in the Palaeolithic World," *Journal of the Royal Anthropological Institute,* LXXVI, 87–130.

——. 1946b. "The Levalloisian Industries of Egypt," *Proceedings of the Prehistoric Society,* XII, No. 4, 57–120.

——. 1952. *Kharga Oasis in Prehistory.* University of London: Athlone Press.

CLARK, J. G. D. 1952. *Prehistoric Europe: The Economic Basis.* New York: Philosophical Library.

COATES, ADRIAN. 1951. *Prelude to History.* London: Methuen & Co.

DIXON, R. B. 1928. *The Building of Cultures.* New York and London: Charles Scribner's Sons.

FURON, RAYMOND. 1951. *Manuel de Préhistoire Générale.* 3d ed. Paris: Payot.

GARROD, D. A. E. 1938. "The Upper Palaeolithic in the Light of Recent Discovery," *Proceedings of the Prehistoric Society,* IV, No. 1, 1–26.

GARROD, D. A. E., and BATE, D. M. A. 1937. *The Stone Age of Mount Carmel: Excavations at the Wady el-Mughara.* Vol. I. Oxford: Clarendon Press.

GOBERT, E. G. 1950. "Le Gisement Paléolithique de Sidi Zin," *Karthago: Revue d'archéologie africaine,* I, 3–51.

GOBERT, E. G., and VAUFREY, R. 1950. *Le Capsien de l'Abri 402 à Moulaires (Tunisie).* (Direction des Antiquitées et Arts, Tunis, "Notes et Documents," No. 12.)

GOODWIN, A. J. H. 1946. *The Loom of Pre-history: A Commentary and a Select Bibliography of the Prehistory of Southern Africa.* ("South Africa Archaeological Society Handbook Series," No. 2.)

KELLEY, HARPER. 1937. "Acheulian Flake Tools," *Proceedings of the Prehistoric Society,* III, No. 1, 15–28.

KING, W. B. R., and OAKLEY, K. P. 1936. "The Pleistocene Succession in the Lower Parts of the Thames Valley," *Proceedings of the Prehistoric Society,* n.s., II, 52–76.

LEAKEY, L. S. B. 1936. *Stone Age Africa.* London: Oxford University Press.

———. 1951. *Olduvai Gorge: A Report on the Evolution of the Hand-Axe Culture in Beds I–IV.* London and New York: Cambridge University Press.

MCBURNEY, C. M. B. 1950. "The Geographical Study of the Older Palaeolithic Stages in Europe," *Proceedings of the Prehistoric Society,* XVI, 163–83.

MOVIUS, H. L., JR. 1948. "The Lower Palaeolithic Cultures of Southern and Eastern Asia," *Transactions of the American Philosophical Society,* XXXVIII, No. 4, 329–420.

———. 1949. "Old World Palaeolithic Archaeology," *Bulletin of the American Geological Society,* LX, 1443–56.

OAKLEY, K. P. 1950. *Man the Tool-Maker.* 2d ed. London: British Museum of Natural History.

PEYRONY, DENIS. 1933. "Les Industries "Aurignaciennes" dans le Bassin de la Vézère: Aurignacien et Périgordien,"

Bulletin de la Société préhistorique de France, XXX, 543–59.

———. 1936. "Le Périgordien et l'Aurignacien (Nouvelles Observations)," *ibid.,* XXXIII, 616–19.

———. 1946. "Une Mise au Point au Sujet de l'Aurignacien et du Périgordien," *ibid.,* XLIII, 232–37.

———. 1948. "Le Périgordien, l'Aurignacien et le Solutréen en Eurasie d'après les dernières Fouilles," *ibid.,* XLV, 305–28.

SAUTER, MARC R. 1948. *Préhistoire de la Méditerranée.* Paris: Payot. Contains bibliography of important works dealing with southern Europe, North Africa, Egypt, Near Eastern lands, and the Balkans.

VAN RIET LOWE, C. 1945. "The Evolution of the Levallois Technique in South Africa," *Man,* Vol. XLV, Art. 37, pp. 49–59.

———. 1948. "The Older Gravels of the Vaal," *Archaeological Survey of the Union of South Africa,* Ser. VI, pp. 19–30. Pretoria: Department of the Interior.

VAUFREY, RAYMOND. 1933. "Notes sur le Capsien," *Anthropologie,* XLIII, 457–83.

———. 1936. "Stratigraphie capsienne," *Swiatowit,* XVI, 15–34.

WATSON, WILLIAM. 1950. Review of *The Lower Palaeolithic Cultures of Southern and Eastern Asia* by H. L. MOVIUS, JR., *Man,* Vol. L, Art. 244, pp. 151–52.

ZOTZ, LOTHAR F. 1951. *Altsteinzeitkunde Mitteleuropas.* Stuttgart: F. Enke.

Old World Prehistory: Neolithic

By V. GORDON CHILDE

DISTINCTION OF NEW STONE AGE FROM OLD

In the Old World "Stone Age," the following criteria have been proposed to distinguish the Neolithic from the preceding stage: (a) association with a Recent, as against a Pleistocene, fauna; (b) the edging of cutting tools by grinding and polishing instead of mere chipping (hence *âge de la pierre polie*); (c) evidences of the domestication of animals and the cultivation of plants. These three criteria have been found not to coincide. Moreover, stone was still extensively used for knives, missile points, agricultural implements, and even axes in the succeeding "Bronze Age." Hence it is proposed to replace the geological and technological criteria *a* and *b* by an economic one, based on *c* but adjusted to preserve a contrast with the next archeological stage. In the following, Neolithic means "a self-sufficing food-producing economy."

CONCRETE EXAMPLE

This definition may appropriately be clarified and given concrete content by a reference to Denmark, where the concept of a "stone age" was first scientifically elaborated. There relics from peat mosses and coastal shell mounds disclose a vigorous, if sparse, population of hunters, fishers, and collectors, while pollen grains preserved in successive layers of the peat illustrate progressive changes in the composition of the forests from which may be deduced consecutive climatic phases—Boreal, Atlantic, Subboreal, etc. Now at a precise level in several bogs (1) about the end of the Atlantic phase, layers of ashes have been observed, followed by an abrupt decline in the relative frequence of tree pollen and a corresponding rise in the pollen of herbs and grasses. In the sequel tree pollen again increases, but in the exact order—first birch, then hazel, finally mixed oakwood again—that would reflect the natural regeneration of a forest ravaged by fire. But it was no "natural" forest fire. Above the ash layers the bogs show, for the first time, a little cereal pollen and that of *Plantago*, a weed of cultivation. Moreover, from the relevant levels of some bogs and sporadically from certain contemporary shell mounds have been recovered pottery vases, very different in technique and form from those made by the old hunter-fishers, and in these sherds have been observed casts of grains—of barley and of wheat (*Triticum monococcum, T. dicoccum*). A few bones of sheep or goats and of small, and so presumably domesticated, cattle turn up in the same contexts.

So the fires, marked by the ash layers, were lit by farmers carving out for themselves patches of tilth and pasture in the primeval forest. The ashes mark the first colonization of Danish soil by food-producers—the local "Neolithic Revolution." On the other hand, the subsequent regeneration of the forest, wiping out the little clearing, could not have happened, had the colonists possessed substantial flocks and herds to

152

nibble off young trees. It implies rather a simple rural economy like the *jhumming* of the hill tribes in Assam today. By fire, plots are cleared of small trees and scrub. The soil, fertilized by the ashes, is tilled with hoes until exhausted and then abandoned, the whole cycle being repeated elsewhere.

Of course, the new economy thus initiated did not originate in Denmark, since the cereals and animals on which it was based are not native to the zone of temperate forests. The noble grasses from which cereals are sprung probably grew wild in the Mediterranean and subtropical zones, and there, too, wild sheep have existed until the present day. The events in Denmark, just described, are therefore rather distant echoes of a revolution that must have been completed several centuries earlier to the southeast. Nevertheless, we can follow the development of that economy through three periods (termed locally Early, Middle, and Late Neolithic) marked by hundreds of burials richly furnished with weapons and tools of stone, but with none of metal until the beginning of the next archeological period is marked by graves containing daggers and axes and spearheads of bronze.

Still, a couple of gold or bronze trinkets and bone copies of metal pins show that the Danish Late Neolithic over-¹apped in time with the full Early Bronze Age in Bohemia. Four imported copper axes and a copper dagger were found with Danish pottery belonging to the Middle Neolithic phase. Even from Early Neolithic a few scraps or stray objects of copper survive. How, then, shall we fix the exact upper limit of "Neolithic"? How strictly is "self-sufficing" to be understood?

THE UPPER LIMIT OF NEOLITHIC

No known Neolithic community (save for a couple of exceptionally iso-lated insular groups) was, in fact, content to rely exclusively on local materials. Indeed, even in the Old Stone Age, communities in the Dordogne used Mediterranean shells as ornaments, and the troglodytes of Grimaldi on the Riviera used the vertebrae of Atlantic fish. Such an occasional employment of exotic imported materials for ornaments was almost universal in the New Stone Age—amazonite at Shaheinab (Khartoum); Red Sea and Mediterranean shells in the Fayum; *Spondylus* shells throughout the Danubian province right up to the Saale and the Middle Rhine. But ornaments are obviously luxuries which, without impairing the economy at all, could be dispensed with. However, tools, too, were often made of exotic materials; thus obsidian knives were used far from any volcano at Sialk I, Hassuna, all over the Aegean throughout the local Neolithic, in Apulia, etc. Middle Neolithic Danubians on the Meuse sometimes used Niedermendig lava from the Moselle for querns. Such materials might, of course, be won and fetched by periodical expeditions sent out by the consuming group, as is done by contemporary Neolithic tribes in Melanesia and even less advanced Australians.

On the other hand, the Neolithic settlers on Lipari (2) must surely have chosen this otherwise uninviting volcanic islet partly at least to satisfy a demand for obsidian by their equally Neolithic cultural kinsmen in Apulia and Sicily. The axes made from Langdale rock (from Cumberland), found in southern England and Scotland, were hardly quarried by expeditions sent from Wiltshire or the Lothians. Rock for axes or querns might indeed be quarried by parties from farming villages, located a few miles away, but their distribution must mean some kind of intertribal barter. And flint was admittedly mined in Neolithic Europe. Even in chalk, the sinking of shafts and the cutting of galleries have inspired pictures of professional miners, encamped permanently round the shafts. Yet, while professional skill must be admitted, there is no need to postulate full-time specialist miners living by bartering their winnings for food produced by the purchasers. Nor were the obsidian knives, Niedermendig lava querns, Langdale stone axes, or other "imports" mentioned above absolutely indispensable. The Danubian farmers on the Meuse did, in fact, generally grind their grain with grinders of local rock, though doubtless their teeth suffered. Such communities did remain potentially self-sufficient, and flint-miners would not have starved if they could find no market for their products.

The regular use of copper or bronze is taken as marking the end of the Neolithic, because, as soon as anyone had metal weapons, copper was as indispensable for the maintenance of life and independence as U^{236} is today, because full-time specialists were needed to extract and process it and because, unless you lived on a copper lode, you had to import the raw material. For regular supplies you became dependent on technicians outside the local group and must organize your economy to satisfy their demands. Neolithic self-sufficiency is over.

On the other hand, copper objects, as such, no more mark the end of the Neolithic economy than does any other exotic substance. Pins from Dadari and Sialk I, made probably from native copper, mean no more sacrifice of self-sufficiency than do the Red Sea shells and turquoise beads from the same sites. Imported copper objects, as much as imported Mediterranean shells, have been found on European sites that have always, and justly, been regarded as Neolithic. And so, of course, have copper axes and even daggers, as the Middle Neolithic Danish hoard, previously mentioned, shows. But in Denmark, throughout the Middle and Late Neolithic, the local population was unable to secure regular supplies of metal so continued to manufacture and use stone tools and weapons, sometimes in imitation of metal forms, and made do quite successfully therewith. As a whole, that is, Denmark remained Neolithic.

At the same time, the manufacture and use of quite good stone tools did not end with the Neolithic. Copper and bronze were at first extravagantly costly. Their use was at first restricted to weapons, craft tools, and sacred objects (vessels for use in temples or by a divine king); for agricultural operations, rough work, and for the heads of missiles, stone remained in use far into the "Bronze Age." Even metal weapons, like knight's armor in medieval Europe, might remain the prerogative of a privileged minority, though the equipment would still be essential to the independence of the group as a whole. A "regular use of metal," such as should mark the end of the Neolithic, can be attested only by the findings of metal gear buried in graves or by traces of metalworking (slags, crucibles, etc.) in settlements. The one shows that metal supplies were regular enough to equip at least some members of the community with the indispensable armaments, the other that the village could support and supply a full-time professional smith.

CHALCOLITHIC TO BE INCLUDED UNDER NEOLITHIC

To introduce a special term at the point when stray objects of native, or even smelted, copper make their first appearance in any region would seem illogical. Accordingly, "Neolithic" will include in Egypt not only Merimde and Fayum but also the Badarian and Amratian and in Mesopotamia the whole Hassuna-Halaf range. It should include even Ubaid, if Frankfort's (3) view be correct that the clay axes, knives, and sickles were substitutes for, rather than toy imitations of, the metal ones they copy. It will, however, be more convenient to exclude from the present survey cultures which have once enjoyed a full "Bronze Age" economy but, cut off from sources of metal, have reverted to stone tools and weapons. On the other hand, Susa I, Byblos II, the Alcalá–Los Millares horizon in Iberia, the Kuban and Yamno cultures of South Russia, and the Beaker culture all over Europe can quite logically be ignored as being "'Bronze Age" in the above sense.

VERTICAL DIVISIONS OF THE NEOLITHIC

In so far as the use of metal, while still sporadic, marks a step in the direction of the new Bronze Age economy, it may contribute to a typological division of what was often a long period. The only proper chronological division of the Neolithic in any area must, of course, be based on stratigraphy, and, wherever evidence for such a division is available, we shall use the terms "Lower," "Middle," and "Upper" to denote consecutive divisions in a relative sequence. Where, on the contrary, typological criteria, justified, of course, by stratigraphical observations somewhere, are employed, "Early" and "Late" will replace "Lower" and "Upper." I can thus say that the Lower Neolithic of Thessaly is Late Neolithic. But, once more, even the former divisions refer only to relative chronology. In time Early Neolithic of Denmark would still be Bronze Age in Egypt.

A third vertical division with even less chronological implications will be found useful. While cereals and domestic stock can have been introduced into regions where they are not indigenous only by immigrant cultivators and breeders, once introduced, their use may have been adopted by native mesolithic hunter-fishers. Now the first

Early Neolithic cultures in the British Isles, central, and northern Europe seem to owe nothing to the local mesolithic cultures. They may therefore be termed "primary." In the sequel there emerge, side by side with such primary cultures, others which have adopted much of their economy and equipment but yet exhibit traits of the local mesolithic in a greater emphasis on fishing and the chase, in tools and weapons, and even in burial rites. These—Peterborough, Rinyo, etc., in Britain (4); Hinkelstein, Rössen, etc., in central Europe; the "Dwelling Place culture" of Sweden—will be styled "secondary." Of course, what appear locally "primary" might on a wider view turn out to be themselves "secondary." But in the present state of archeological knowledge most cultures go up to a god in the third generation like Homeric kings.

HORIZONTAL DIVISIONS OF THE NEOLITHIC

In the archeological record the Neolithic appears, from the start, split into an embarrassing multitude of cultures, distinguished most easily by the techniques, forms, and ornamentation of pottery and stone vessels, and into not many fewer by differences in house plans, industrial equipment, armaments, burial rites, fashions in dress, ritual paraphernalia, and art styles. For the self-sufficiency of local groups would of itself facilitate divergent specialization. No enumeration, still less description, of all Neolithic cultures can be here attempted. But it may be useful to indicate the main geographical regions, generally at some time forming cultural provinces, from which material for our synthetic account has been drawn: North Africa; the Nile Valley (Sudan, Upper and Lower Egypt); Palestine; Syria as far as drained into the Mediterranean; Mesopotamia, i.e., the rest of Syria and

Assyria as well as Babylonia; Cilicia; Cyprus; Crete; peninsular Greece; southern Italy (Apulia, Sicily); Malta; Iberia; western Europe (the Iberian peninsula, Switzerland, southern and northern France; Brittany; the British Isles); northern Europe (northern Germany, Denmark, southern Sweden); the Danubian löss-lands from the Meuse to the Vistula, from the Bakony to the Harz; the Ukraine; the Balkans (Save-Danube-Morava-Vardar valleys; Thrace and lower Danube); Iran; China (Kansu, Honan). Some regions, such as India or Anatolia, have been excluded for lack of authenticated relevant material. The whole Boreal zone of Eurasiatic coniferous forests and tundra has been omitted on the pretext that such belated food-producing economies as did arise there are not secondary or even tertiary Neolithic but rather secondary Bronze Age reverted. Southeast Asia is omitted on the same grounds and because no information as to the economy is available until the beginning of written history. Metal was certainly used, at least for ornaments, in the "Brahmigiri stone-axe culture" of peninsular India (5). Even the cultures of Honan and Kansu can be admitted only with reservation, since the available literature mentions hardly any genuine closed finds in which the celebrated pottery is reliably associated with other artifacts, still less with food remains.

PRIMARY ECONOMY

PLANTS CULTIVATED

In all the provinces examined, the Neolithic economy was based on the cultivation of cereals combined with stock-breeding, and, wherever adequate data are available, the only cereals cultivated in the Early Neolithic were wheat and barley (6). Of the wheats, *T. monococcum,* though the least likely to be recognized, has been reported from the Early Neolithic of western and northern Europe, of the Danubian löss lands from the Ukraine, Greece, and Mesopotamia (already at Janmo), and rather unexpectedly from the Middle Neolithic of Lower Egypt (el Omari); *T. dicoccum* (emmer) was probably cultivated equally early all over Europe and even in the Early Neolithic of the Fayum, as in the Late Neolithic (Halafian) of northern Mesopotamia. But wheats of the 42-chromosome groups have not yet been identified with certainty in any pure Neolithic context in Hither Asia, though there seems to be a little mixed with emmer in the Middle Neolithic of el Omari in Egypt, not before Middle Neolithic in Denmark, and only doubtfully in the Early Neolithic of the lösslands and Switzerland and the Middle Neolithic of Greece. Barleys are as widespread and early as emmer. Millet (*Panicum miliacum*) was cultivated in the Ukraine, in the Lower Neolithic of Thrace (which does not look Early) and in the Late Neolithic of Macedonia, in Switzerland and in Palestine by the beginning of the local Bronze Age. A single grain of rice has been identified in a sherd from Honan of the local "Neolithic" pottery.

In addition to cereals, peas were probably cultivated in Neolithic Europe, vetch in the Middle Neolithic of Lower Egypt. Orchard husbandry is not well attested, but figs may have been cultivated in Middle Neolithic Greece, olives in southern Spain, apples in Switzerland.

DOMESTIC STOCK

All typically Neolithic sites in the Old World have yielded bones of cattle, sheep and/or goats, and pigs, though the latter seem to be missing from the Middle Neolithic Badarian of Egypt, and sheep from Yang-shao-tsun in Kansu, while only sheep and goats are mentioned in the Yamuqian of Palestine and the Khartoum Neolithic. No economy of proved antiquity was demonstrably based on plant-cultivation uncombined with stock-breeding. No doubt the Natufians of Palestine did reap some kind of grass with specialized reaping knives, and no doubt cereals grew wild around their cave homes. But there is no evidence that it was cereals they reaped, still less that they were cultivated, while only game animals were eaten. So the Natufians must provisionally rank as still "mesolithic."

Nor is there much better evidence for stock-breeding uncombined with cultivation. On the Upper Nile, indeed, at Shaheinab near Khartoum, the food refuse of a group living mainly from hunting, fishing, and collecting included bones of a very small goat and an equally dwarf sheep, while no unambiguous agricultural appliances (sickle teeth or querns) have been reported. Since, however, flint (which, if used for reaping, acquires a characteristic gloss) was not available and the excellent pottery has not yet been exhaustively examined for grain impressions, the negative evidence is exceptionally inconclusive. Apart from this ambiguous Khartoum Neolithic and still less well-dated assemblages in North Africa, all Early Neolithic cultures were based on mixed farming. On the other hand, in the Late Neolithic of the temperate forest zone in Europe the emphasis shifts toward stock-breeding and hunting to such an extent that one might speak of a "separation of pastoral tribes from the mass of the agricultural barbarians," but only with the proviso that, wherever any evidence is available, even the "pastoral tribes" still cultivated cereals.

For the composition of the livestock, food refuse (the only available source) gives unreliable evidence. It is obviously more economical to kill sheep than cows; on the other hand, in temperate Europe many calves had to be killed, owing to lack of winter feed. Still the high proportion of sheep or goats reported from the earliest sites in the Near East and the very low proportion of these animals from corresponding sites in the European forest zone deserve attention.

HUNTING AND GATHERING

Of course, all Neolithic farmers supplemented their diet with produce of the chase, fishing, and collecting. In the Lower Neolithic of the Fayum, indeed, these activities apparently still played a major role in the economy. On the contrary, on the Danubian lösslands and to a lesser degree in northern and western Europe, bones of game and hunting equipment are relatively inconspicuous on Early Neolithic sites; first in Middle and Late Neolithic is a fuller exploitation of the available wide food resources archeologically attested.

RURAL ECONOMY

Two systems of cultivation may be distinguished in advance: (I) dry cultivation, in which the moisture required by the crop is provided by rain, and (II) wet or irrigation cultivation, where rivers, torrents, or springs soak tracts of adjacent land. In a sense intermediate between I and II is the system reported from central Asia, where melting snows on the ranges feed seasonal springs that break out on the lower slopes, forming temporary marshes on which grain may be sown to yield a reliable crop (7).

Under dry cultivation any plot will become exhausted after one or two croppings. The simplest reaction is to start again on a fresh plot. The repetition of this process soon uses up all the land conveniently accessible from a single settlement. Thereupon, the whole settlement is transferred to a new location and the cycle repeated there. This is termed "shifting cultivation" (1) and, though virtually imposed by dry cultivation, (I, 1) is sometimes today practiced by tribes relying on natural irrigation (II, 1). But even under I the exhaustion is not permanent, and restoration of the soil's fertility can be hastened in various ways, depending on climate and natural vegetation. On prairies and park lands (A) recovery can be accelerated by turning livestock onto exhausted plots (I, A, 2) and, still better, by applying farmyard manure or night soil (I, A, 3). This leads to the familiar rotation between fallow and arable (I, A, 2, or I, A, 3). In woodlands (B) the plot, originally cleared by "slash-and-burn" methods, may be allowed to revert to scrub, which after some years is burned down as at the first clearance. The ashes restore the salts removed from the surface humus by the previous crop. A systematic rotation of scrub and arable is the classical form of *Brandwirtschaft* (I, B, 2), as recently practiced east of the Baltic. Under drier conditions a repetition of slash-and-burn is likely to destroy the humus cover so far that the abandoned clearing no longer reverts to bush but is invaded by grass. The farmer can then apply system I, A, 2.

Throughout the Neolithic in the temperate forest zone of Europe, settlements seem to have been so briefly or intermittently occupied that shifting agriculture (I, B, 1) may be plausibly inferred. And in Upper Egypt the smallness of even the Middle Neolithic Badarian cemeteries suggests shifting agriculture, however the crops were watered. But in Lower Egypt even the Lower Neolithic village of Merimde was occupied, apparently continuously, through several archeological phases, while in Hither Asia tell-formation, beginning even in the Lower Neolithic of Jericho, Mersin, Jarmo, and Sialk, implies continuous habitation based presumably on some form of I, A, 2. So, too, in Crete, Greece, and the Balkans

(including the lower Save, the south bank of the middle Danube, and both banks of the lower Danube) most Neolithic settlements take the form of tells, though in Apulia tell-formation has not been observed and shifting agriculture must be assumed for Lower and Middle Neolithic.

METHOD OF CULTIVATION

Since digging-sticks, hoes, and plows can be made entirely of wood, they are not likely to survive in the archeological record. In fact, the earliest actual plows (8) (from upper Italy and Denmark) or representations of plows (from Mesopotamia, Cyprus, and Egypt) belong to the Bronze Age, albeit to its initial phases. Certain heavy stone implements from the Lower Neolithic of Switzerland, Denmark, and the löss-lands have, indeed, been claimed as plow shares on the strength of marks of wear resembling those on wooden plow shares, but this interpretation is even less certain than the treatment of flaked chert and sandstone implements from Neolithic Mesopotamia as hoe blades. On the other hand, undeniable plow furrows have recently been recognized in the soil under Late Neolithic barrows in Denmark and Holland, while the yoking of oxen, presumably to draw plows, is attested in the Upper Neolithic of Switzerland (Vinelz) and in the, probably Middle, Neolithic of the eastern extension of the löss-lands in Poland (9). Hence, while plot cultivation with hoe or digging-stick, appropriate to a I, B, 1 economy, was probably the rule in the temperate forests during the earlier part of the local Neolithic, plow agriculture probably began before the Stone Age ended (at a time when processes considered above combined with climatic factors would have increased the area of grassland). But that was, of course, not before the beginning of the Bronze Age in the Mediterranean area and in Hither Asia and does not help to prove that plow agriculture was Neolithic there.

DWELLINGS

While Neolithic, like Paleolithic, men sheltered or even resided in caves, it is now known that they did not live in holes in the ground ("pit-dwellings") but built quite commodious houses of the most convenient local materials—reeds, pisé, hand-molded bricks, wattle-and-daub, split timbers, or stone (10). On the "Danubian" lösslands the earliest (Lower Neolithic) houses were gabled structures, 6–8 meters wide, but attaining a length of as much as 41 meters, though naturally subdivided like the long houses of the Iroquois or the Kayan. In the same area smaller two-roomed houses, 4.5–6 meters wide and only 6–8 meters long were more normal in the Middle Neolithic and occur also in Switzerland, the Balkans, Greece, the Ukraine, and east of the Baltic. But, in the Late Neolithic, one-roomed huts, only 4–5 meters square, became commoner both in central Europe and in Britain. In Northern Europe a different type of long structure—a row of as many as 26 cabins, each 6 meters long by 3 meters wide, all under one ridgepole—appears from the Early Neolithic.

For the Mediterranean and subtropical zones, where mud was the favorite building material, no generalizations are possible, but even in the Middle Neolithic of Hassuna we have farmhouses composed of several rooms and a courtyard. While circular structures of one kind or another are known from Neolithic Mesopotamia, Cyprus, Thessaly, the Rhineland, etc., their domestic character is in no instance quite beyond question.

FURNITURE

Wooden door frames pivoted on stone sockets in the Neolithic of Hither Asia, on socket holes in the wooden thresholds in temperate Europe. Skara Brae in Orkney shows how Neolithic dwellings, even in the distant Orkney Islands, might be comfortably furnished with fixed beds, wall cupboards, and dresser, and drained by lined channels under the floors, while models of chairs and tables are known from Greece, Thrace, and the Ukraine.

SIZE OF SETTLEMENTS

Even if practicing migratory cultivation, Neolithic farmers lived in regular villages that could be fenced to keep out animals; by Middle Neolithic, these were fortified with ditches and ramparts in western Europe, the lösslands, Greece, Apulia, Palestine, and Cilicia, while around the Alps and in England the houses were built on lake shores or in swamps. If fully explored, such settlements would provide valuable data for estimating the size of the local group and eventually the density of population; but only in temperate Europe have the published excavations been conducted on a large enough scale and with sufficient technical skill to show the number of houses in a single village (see Table 1). Certain areas, though far less reliable, do provide some data for the Near East. In the Lower Neolithic, Jarmo (Kurdistan) (11) covered 3 acres accommodating perhaps 50 houses, while Merimde in Lower Egypt occupied 6 acres. It looks, then, as if Neolithic farming was conducted by groups not exceeding 600 persons.

Long before the attested beginning of "food-production," men had achieved a respectable mastery over nature, and only those techniques will here be mentioned that were developed first or principally after the "Neolithic Revolution."

WOODWORKING TOOLS

"The polished stone celt" was once taken as the hallmark of the New Stone Age but is now known to have been used in the mesolithic of the Baltic and even in the Paleolithic of Russia. It is, however, universal in the Neolithic (save apparently at Sialk in Iran), while the sharpening of flint celts by polishing—attested from the Lower Neolithic in Egypt, Palestine, western and northern Europe—does seem really to be a Neolithic innovation. The edging of flint celts by a transverse blow—the *tranchet technique*—was, however, maintained in northern and western Europe, upper Italy, Palestine, the Kharga

or elbow-shaft (inevitable for adzes) is attested for the Lower Neolithic of Switzerland and the Middle Neolithic of northern Germany. There, mounting with the aid of antler sleeves, known in the mesolithic of western Europe, is attested and also for the löss-lands from the Lower Neolithic; perforated antler sleeves, used in the mesolithic of the Baltic, reappear in the Neolithic of Switzerland, the lower Danubian, the Middle Neolithic of Thessaly, and the Late Neolithic of northern France

TABLE 1

Period	Location	No. of Houses
Lower Neolithic.......	Löss-lands Köln-Lindental* North Barkaert†	20 long houses 54 one-room huts
Middle Neolithic......	North Dümmer‡ Löss-lands, Aichbühl Ukraine, Kolomiščina§	?40 one-room huts 22 two-room huts 41 two- to- three-room huts
Late Neolithic........	Löss-lands, Goldberg Orkney, Skara-Brae	50 one-room huts 6 one-room huts

* Sangmeister, "Zum Charakter der bandkeram. Siedlung," *33 Ber. Römisch-germanisches Kommission* (Berlin, 1943–50).
† *Fra National Museets Arbejdsmark* (Copenhagen, 1949).
‡ *Germanenerbe*, IV (1939), 230–40.
§ T. Passek, *Periodizatsiya Tripol'skikh Poseleniĭ* (Moskva, 1949).

oasis (12), and Egypt; but in the last-named province it is not certainly attested before the Gerzean "Bronze Age" and is certainly absent from the Fayum, which should be Early Neolithic.

AXES AND ADZES

Celts may be used as axes or adzes (13), and it is noteworthy that woodworkers at first displayed a strong preference for adzes in Cyprus, Greece, the Balkans, the Ukraine, all over the löss-lands, and in the Iberian peninsula, and for axes in Egypt, probably in Crete, in western Europe (north of the Pyrenees), and in the north.

SHAFTING

Besides direct mounting on a straight shaft, the mounting of axes on a knee-

and Orkney. In Early Neolithic perforated ax- or adze-heads are virtually confined to the löss-lands but appear later in Greece, the Balkans, and northwestern Europe (see "stone boring").

TEXTILES

The weaving (14) of flax (or some other vegetable fiber) is attested from Lower Neolithic on, wherever evidence can survive—actual linen from Egypt and western Europe, stone or clay spindle-whorls from Hither Asia, Greece, etc. But such whorls were not used by all Neolithic spinners—not, for instance, in the Swiss Lower Neolithic lake dwellings, which have yielded linen fabric—and perhaps served only for spinning wool. How early the latter material was spun and woven by Neolithic societies is otherwise uncertain. As for textile appliances, a horizontal loom is attested for the Amratian (Middle Neolithic) of Egypt, while there is some evidence for warp-weighted vertical looms in Neolithic Europe.

POTTERY

Pottery, an artificial substance, once regarded as distinctive of Neolithic levels, was, in fact, made by pre-Neolithic societies in Denmark and the Sudan and was, on the other hand, absent from the oldest Neolithic of Mesopotamia (Jarmo), Palestine (Jericho), and Cyprus. All Neolithic pottery was made without the aid of a true (fast-spinning) wheel, several methods of freehand building being employed instead. A special kiln has been postulated, but not by all authorities, only for "painted pottery." The earliest pottery of Palestine, Mesopotamia, Iran, Cyprus, Greece, the Ukraine, and possibly Kansu was, in fact, generally fired to give a clear ground surface which might be decorated in darker paints. Such pottery occurs early with other varieties in the Balkans, Dalmatia, and Honan. It appears only in Middle (or Upper) Neolithic strata on the northern Syrian coast, in Cilicia (15) and Apulia, sporadically in Malta and Iberia. Self-colored (black to red) fabrics, on the contrary, characterize the oldest layers in Egypt, northern Syria, Cilicia, Crete, and most of Europe. A coincidence between these two kinds of fabric with arid and moist climatic regimes is obvious, but clearly only partial.

STONE-WORKING

VASES

Vessels more pretentious than mortars were ground out of stone at Jarmo and on Cyprus before vases were molded in clay, and stone vases were also used all over Hither Asia, in Egypt, and in Malta from the beginning of the local Neolithic. A few marble vases in Neolithic horizons in Greece and the Balkans may be merely imports.

BORING AND DRILLING

Stones were perforated for mace-heads, etc., in the mesolithic mainly by percussion supplemented by boring; but throughout the Neolithic some sort of drill was regularly used. In the Lower Neolithic of the Danubian löss-lands and, perhaps first, in the Middle Neolithic of northern Europe, a hollow drill was certainly employed.

BEADS

From early Neolithic times on in Egypt and the Near East, and in China at some stage (if Chou-chia-chai be Neolithic at all), relatively hard stones were pierced by ingenious drills with string-holes, a centimeter or so long, to form beads. Rather softer stones, like callaïs, Kimmeridge shale, and jet, were likewise drilled in the Middle or Upper Neolithic of Atlantic Europe, including the British Isles, but only amber and shell in northern and central Europe. But the Lower Neolithic Danubians' drill (16) for piercing long beads of shell was essentially the same as the oriental lapidaries' instrument.

WEAPONS

PROJECTILES

The bow as well as the spear-thrower having been widely used even in the Paleolithic, it is not surprising that flint arrowheads are common in the Lower Neolithic of Palestine, Egypt, North Africa, western and northern Europe, as well as in all the secondary Neolithic cultures of Europe. (Stone or bone arrowheads occur in China at Yang-shao-tsun and Chou-chia-chai, but apparently not with the painted Pan-shan pottery.) They are surprisingly absent from the Lower Neolithic of the central European löss-lands, the Balkans, Greece, Mesopotamia, and Iran (13). On the other hand, clay sling-bullets do occur throughout the Neolithic of Mesopotamia, Iran, Greece, and the Balkans and appear with painted pottery in the Middle Neolithic of Syria and Cyprus, in Apulia, and even in China.

MACE-HEADS

Clubs were weighted with pear-shaped or globular stone heads in the Early Neolithic of Lower Egypt, Crete, Mesopotamia, and Iran and in the Middle Neolithic of the löss-lands, western and northern Europe. A flat or disk-shaped type was, however, preferred in the Sudan, in Upper Egypt, in the Lower Neolithic of the löss-lands and in the Middle northern Neolithic, and competed with the piriform in the Late Neolithic (Ghassulian) of Palestine.

Battle-axes of stone, imitating copper versions of perforated antler weapons of mesolithic origin, were popular in northern Europe throughout the Neolithic, but appear on the löss-lands, in northwestern Europe, and in the Balkans mainly in the Late Neolithic. In Greece, Italy, Asia Minor, and Mesopotamia they seem to be "Bronze Age," though in Sumer clay models appear as early as the Ubaid horizon.

BURIAL RITES

Inhumation in a flexed or contracted attitude was almost universal in Neolithic cultures. Extended burial was, however, regularly practiced in northern Europe from the Lower Neolithic, occasionally in northwestern Europe, among some secondary Neolithic groups on the löss-lands, in the Ubaid culture of Mesopotamia, and at Chou-chia-chai in China. Cremation occurs sporadically in the earlier Secondary Neolithic of the löss-lands, in the Mid-

dle and Secondary Neolithic of the British Isles (17) and Brittany, and more widely in Late Neolithic Europe north of the Alps.

Collective burial in natural caves or in built or rock-cut chamber tombs, though practiced by the mesolithic Natufians in Palestine and normally all round the eastern Mediterranean throughout the Bronze Age, is not certainly attested there during the local Neolithic save in some sepulchral caves in Crete (18). It was, however, a general Neolithic—but not certainly "Early"—practice in Sardinia, Malta, and most of western Europe. In northern Europe the earliest dolmens built in the Lower Neolithic were probably not collective tombs (19); but by the Middle Neolithic collective burial in megalithic tombs was general. In Spain and Portugal, as in southern France, the best-known "megalithic tombs" must certainly be classed as Bronze Age, but, despite doubts expressed by Childe and Forde, some such tombs in Portugal and Almeria (20) do seem to illustrate a genuinely Neolithic economy.

The erection of a barrow to mark a single grave hardly began in northwestern Europe and the northern parts of the löss-lands before the Late Neolithic, and most such barrows are actually Bronze Age. But ring ditches, inclosing small cemeteries, have been traced back to the Middle Neolithic in the British Isles (17).

TREPANATION

Three trephined skulls come from Lower Neolithic graves on the löss-lands and two from Denmark (21). In the Late Neolithic the operation was performed with extravagant prodigality in France and surprisingly often in northern Europe and the northwestern part of the löss-lands. While the early Neolithic operations may well have been undertaken for curative purposes, the later cases must be regarded as magical.

FIGURINES

One of the most distinctive and widespread traits of the Neolithic was the manufacture in mud, baked clay, stone, chalk, bone, or ivory of female figurines. While the attitudes and styles vary considerably and their functions were not everywhere necessarily the same, some such figures do occur in the Lower Neolithic of Egypt, Palestine, Syria, Mesopotamia, Iran, Cyprus, Cilicia, Crete, Greece, the western Balkans, the Ukraine, Spain, and, albeit rarely, Britain and France. On the central European löss-lands and in Thrace such figures are exceptional in the Lower Neolithic but very abundant in the Middle ranges. In northern Europe they seem unknown, and also, curiously enough, in southern Italy. In the Late Neolithic, female figurines went out of favor in most of temperate Europe, though they were still made in the Balkans and the Near East.

Male figures, on the other hand, are comparatively rare and mostly Late Neolithic. Phalli occur in Lower Neolithic England and Middle Neolithic Thrace. Models of cattle and other beasts, probably domesticated, and sometimes even of houses, chairs, and tables are often associated with female figurines, save in Egypt and Spain.

AMULETS AND "SEALS"

As magico-religious must rank also beads of stone or ivory carved in the forms of birds, animals, etc., which were early popular in Hither Asia, Egypt, Malta, and Iberia. Ax amulets appear in Neolithic contexts in Crete, Lower Egypt, Malta, northern France, and Brittany, but elsewhere seem rather to be "Bronze Age." On the other hand, button-shaped or other beads, bearing an engraved design and therefore capable of being used as seals, appear

already in the Late Neolithic Halafian culture of Mesopotamia and enjoyed a wide vogue in the immediately succeeding Bronze Age horizons of Iran, Syria, Crete, and Asia Minor. A few in stone go back to the Lower Neolithic in peninsular Greece, while clay copies were current in the Lower Neolithic of the western Balkans and the Ukraine and in the Middle Neolithic of the Danubian löss-lands and Thrace; debased versions reached Apulia and Liguria.

TEMPLES

In the Neolithic levels of Jericho in Palestine and of Eridu and Gawra in Mesopotamia, excavation has exposed buildings which by their position on the site of, and by their resemblance to, historical temples must rank as the dwellings of deities. A trinity of mud effigies was, in fact, found in that at Jericho. Some circular buildings in Neolithic Mesopotamia, Cyprus, and Greece may also have been sacred, while the Neolithic Maltese certainly erected elaborate megalithic temples, but nothing compels us to regard these as residences of deities conceived in human form. Still less can any such inference be drawn from offerings of animals, pots, amber beads, stone implements, etc., deposited in bogs in northern Europe (19) from mesolithic times on or from the more dubious "votives" reported from Cretan caves

CHIEFTAINSHIP

Neither domestic architecture nor funerary practices offer any conclusive evidence for the existence of kings in the Near East during the local Neolithic or in temperate Europe until the late Neolithic. Even Nazi excavators looked in vain for a "Führerhaus" in the Lower Neolithic villages of the löss-lands. In the Late Neolithic, however, on the northern part of the löss-lands and in northern Europe, a few barrows covering mortuary houses do look like tombs of chiefs. In western Europe, too, it has been argued that some "megalithic" tombs were built to contain the bones of members of royal lineages only, and it now seems possible that, in Denmark, only chiefs were buried in the Early Neolithic dolmens. Note in all these cases the prominence of pastoralism in the economy. Of course, the negative evidence is quite insufficient to disprove the existence of chiefs but, as far as it goes, may be used as an argument against concentration of economic power.

ART

The art of Neolithic peasants, in contrast to that of Paleolithic hunters and fishers, was notoriously mainly symbolic. Representations of persons, animals, and things are curiously rare. Most widespread are the clay models (noted above), but these can in no case be called lifelike, and it is often hard to be sure what the artist intended to depict. Badarian and Amratian carvings of beasts and birds, the figures painted on Amratian vases, and the undatable engravings and paintings on rock surfaces in the deserts from the Atlantic to the Red Sea and beyond are indeed perfectly recognizable, but are far less lifelike than the Paleolithic cave drawings of France and Cantabria or the tomb paintings of Old Kingdom Egypt or the proto-historic slate palettes and ivories. Frankfort considers the aim to have been naturalistic, only the execution incompetent. But incompetence alone will not explain the representations of the human figure always less lifelike than those of animals. Even the best statuettes are no more like portraits of actual human beings than are Maori ancestor figures or Haida totem poles. Portraits of real men appear abruptly, at the same moment as writing, on the Narmer palette and the marble head from Uruk-Warka.

ORIGIN OF THE NEOLITHIC REVOLUTION

The conclusions of botanists and zoölogists on the probable habitats of ancestral wheats, barleys, and sheep combine with the scanty direct evidence from the excavations at Jericho, Jarmo, Belt Cave (22), and Hassuna to limit the possible cradles of farming. Most Neolithic grains examined bear witness to a long period of cultivation and selection; only from Jarmo do the wheats approximate to wild forms. The Neolithic economy, based upon a combination of cereal cultivation and stockbreeding, most likely took shape somewhere between the Nile and the Jaxartes. Relying, no doubt, on migratory dry cultivation (I, 1) at first, it could in this ecological zone easily develop a tillage-pasture alternation (I, A, 2), since perennial water supplies are rare enough to discourage nomadism. In Hither Asia this stage had been reached at least by the Middle Neolithic of Hassuna. Theoretically, of course, migratory wet cultivation (II, 1) might be just as old. But sedentary farming settlements based on irrigation (II, 2) are not certainly detectable until the Late Neolithic Halafian (Eridu) and Amratian.

THE "URBAN REVOLUTION"

Theoretically, any Neolithic community must have been able to produce a surplus above the minimum required to enable the group to feed itself and its offspring. In fact, the "imports" already found on Early Neolithic sites do imply such a surplus. But it was irrigation cultivation in the Tigris-Euphrates delta (Sumer) and on the Nile that first yielded a reliable social surplus for "trade" or any other purpose. In Sumer the surplus was concentrated, perhaps from the first colonization of the delta, in the granaries and fields of temples that certainly were founded in the Late Neolithic. In Egypt such concentration was demonstrably achieved only when a war chief (who, as such, would concentrate booty in cattle) got himself identified with the personified symbol of group solidarity. In each case the unprecedented accumulation of real wealth created a new world situation—a second economic revolution. It created an effective demand, a reliable market, for metals and all sorts of commodities not obtainable in the river valleys. The satisfying of this demand offered an assured livelihood to full-time specialists and gave opportunities even to distant communities to extract a slice out of the Sumerian or Egyptian accumulation. It has even been suggested that the spread of the Neolithic economy was a by-product of this new effective demand.

The recent discovery of genuinely Neolithic cultures in Egypt and Hither Asia, absolutely prior to the urban revolution and, indeed, to the first indications of the industrial use of metal anywhere, has today deprived of any plausibility the theory that all Neolithic cultures were due to a reversion to the Stone Age, i.e., to a people who had once possessed metal tools, the techniques for their production, and the requisite economic organization, but had for one reason or another lost these. Some such account, indeed, may still hold good for the Pacific and even Southeast Asia; there are some positive grounds for applying it to some of the "Neolithic" colonists of Malta and to those "secondary Neolithic" warrior groups who seem to have played a prominent part in spreading the Neolithic economy among the hunter-fishers of the Boreal zone in Finland, central Russia, and Siberia. Even in Thrace the latest reports imply that the "Neolithic" "Mound Culture" succeeded one of Anatolian Bronze Age type. But in the rest of the Old World the well-known Neolithic cultures resemble so closely the genuinely Neolithic cultures of the Near East that this reversion theory may be dismissed.

Nor is it much more likely that trade to satisfy directly or indirectly the effective demand of the urban civilizations, and to that extent using their accumulated surplus as trading capital, played an effective role in the primary diffusion of the Neolithic economy—i.e., of the cereals, sheep, and techniques on which it was based. Even if the diffusion of megalithic tombs in western and northern Europe be attributed to missionaries who were also traders from the eastern Mediterranean, Early Neolithic farmers had certainly colonized Denmark, probably also Britain and France, before any such missionaries arrived! A strong case can indeed be made for recognizing "influence" from the Bronze Age Orient in Late and even Middle Neolithic cultures in temperate Europe. (Clay objects from the Middle Neolithic Danubian II, for instance, really do look like copies of stone block vases such as were current in the earliest cities of Egypt and Sumer.) But the local Neolithic had begun before such influence is detectable.

THE SPREAD OF THE NEOLITHIC ECONOMY

The first spread of the Neolithic economy was presumably due to actual movements of colonization imposed on Early Neolithic peasants by their migratory rural economy and by their younger children's need for fresh land. For it is a truism in demography that populations quickly respond to such an enlargement of the food supply as the Neolithic revolution offered even in its first stages. Even communities practicing I, 2 or II, 2 must provide for their younger sons and daughters by planting colonies on fresh land. Sooner or later the original bands of migrants or colonists would have been augmented by secondary Neolithic groups, generated by the conversion to food-production of mesolithic hunter-fishers. But the latter would have been likely to modify the original rural economy by altering the balance between stock-breeding and cultivation or otherwise.

The primary spread of Neolithic peasants would have been by land. But, unless we admit independent foci, Cyprus, Crete, Sicily, Malta, and the northern shores of the Mediterranean can have been reached only by sea. In fact, the extensive use of materials like obsidian in Crete, peninsular Greece, Apulia, Sicily, and Malta implies a lot of Neolithic voyaging. There are so many and such close agreements between the Neolithic cultures of Sicily, the Lipari Islands, Apulia, and peninsular Greece that transmarine transmission seems unquestionable. That, too, seems the easiest way of accounting for similar agreements between the Lower Neolithic of Greece and Cyprus and the Middle Neolithic of Cilicia and Syria (Hassuna) (23). Comparable agreements can be observed between the Lower Neolithic in Sicily, Liguria, and the coasts of southern France and eastern Spain (23) and should be explained in the same way.

Were the seed grains and domestic stock conveyed by boatloads of farmers' sons seeking new land across the sea—of course, in the light of information already gathered by fishing expeditions? Or were the voyagers intending merely to camp for a season on the foreign shore in order to obtain by barter from the mesolithic natives obsidian or other commodities for the home market? In the second case the result must be called a "secondary Neolithic" culture, but otherwise the results are essentially the same. Only after the urban revolution, i.e., in the full Bronze Age, would true trading colonies, supplying the reliable civilized market and relying in the last resort on the accumulated social surplus for support, become a significant factor.

A much more formidable obstacle than the sea was presented by the ecological frontier between the Mediterranean and the temperate zones, coinciding largely with the physiographical barrier of the Pyrenees, the Alps, the Balkans, and the Taurus. I, B, 1 and I, A, 1 are different; shifting cultivation is not the same in temperate forests as on grasslands; grazing in woodlands presents problems different from grazing on prairies; houses adapted for mild winters and dry summers are unsuitable where the summers are rainy and the winters snowy. An economy, shaped under the conditions here envisaged would need very drastic adaptation to the temperate European environment. The whole morphology of the Early Neolithic cultures of the löss-lands and western and northern Europe stands in conspicuous contrast to any Greek, Cretan, or Asiatic. (The Neolithic of Honan and Kansu, where the ecological contrast is slight, despite formidable physiographical obstacles, looks, from the very superficial data available, not unlike that familiar in Hither Asia.)

Where, when, and why was the ecological boundary surmounted? The Taurus was never, on the available evidence, crossed by Neolithic peasants; the earliest settlements on the plateau yet known are rightly called "Chalcolithic," since they exhibit an incipient Bronze Age economy. Only one "Neolithic" culture is common to both sides of the Balkan ranges—Childe's Vardar-Morava, Milojčic's Vinča, culture (23) —and it does not initiate either Neolithic series; it is Late (or at least Middle) Neolithic in Thessaly and Macedonia and apparently is preceded by the Starčevo-Körös culture in the middle Danube Basin. In France the impressed cardium-decorated pottery (24), distinctive of the Early Neolithic in southern Italy and all around the western Mediterranean, never penetrates north of the coastal zone. As far as the existing archeological record goes, Mediterranean and temperate cultures are contrasted from the first.

THE NEOLITHIC AS A STAGE

Making due allowance for environmentally controlled divergences, the material classed as "Early Neolithic" from temperate Europe and the Mediterranean at least can legitimately be used to supplement that from Egypt and Hither Asia to document a stage in cultural and economic development intermediate between one characterized by pure food-gathering and one in which the accumulation of a social surplus made possible inter- and intra-communal division of labor and the development of regular trade. Throughout the area here surveyed, the latter developed only out of the Neolithic in Hither Asia directly, in Egypt and the eastern Mediterranean under demonstrable Asiatic influence (seen explicitly in the Gerzean and Early Aegean "Bronze Age" cultures), and elsewhere perhaps always under direct or indirect impulses from literate urban civilizations.

The economic and technological contents of this stage are reasonably definite, their sociological and ideological counterparts less so. It would, for instance, be tempting to treat the widely distributed female figurines as indicative of fertility cults centering round a mother-goddess such as are so widely diffused in the folklore of cereal cultivators. But the very similar Paleolithic figurines, though separated by at least seven millenniums from the earliest Neolithic ones, could just as well be considered indicative of such a cult in the Old Stone Age! And only in Palestine and Mesopotamia did its symbols assume sufficiently human form to need permanent residences during the Neolithic. Again, Neolithic art was highly symbolic, contrasting with the lifelike representations of Paleolithic and civilized art. But the Paleolithic carvings from Arudy and Mezin, like those on Australian *churingas,* are just as symbolic and devoid of recognizable representational content as the patterns on any early Neolithic pot! Social institutions, like clans, chiefs, warfare, and suttee, are not much better or worse attested among Early Neolithic than among older or later societies.

THE NEOLITHIC ACHIEVEMENT

The positive achievement of the Neolithic was the elaboration of a rural economy with an appropriate technology—and presumably ideology —adapted to several environments. The adaptation achieved in the Near East during the Neolithic was good enough to survive without any radical modification until the advent of mechanization; but in the zone of temperate forests a durable adjustment was not perfected until the Iron Age. At the same time, a separation of more pastoral tribes from more sedentary farmers began in Europe certainly, and elsewhere probably, in the course of the Neolithic, though the classical forms of pastoral nomadism, based on the horse or the camel, developed only later.

Neolithic farmers discovered and began the exploitation of most of the best agricultural land—but not, for instance, the rich clay soils of England—many sources of natural raw materials, and the main routes for migration and trade both on land and on sea. They devised satisfactory forms of rural dwellings that have persisted in their respective environments until today, modified but little by subsequent urban developments. Finally, Neolithic farmers must have discovered the secrets of metallurgy, and in Hither Asia, initiated organization for the effective application of them. In Europe, however the technical knowledge was acquired, the distributive machinery, equally essential for a Bronze Age economy, was not perfected without further help from the Near East.

KULTURKREISE

The only direct archeological evidence cited by Menghin (25) for the existence of proto-Neolithic *Schweine-züchter* has been invalidated by subsequent botanical and archeological discoveries. The rare bones of pigs— and other domestic animals—from "mesolithic" shell mounds in Denmark prove to be contemporary with, and are therefore derivable from, those Early Neolithic farmers whose spread across Denmark and Sweden was described in the first pages of this article. Pig bones from "Dwelling Places" in eastern Sweden belong to a much later horizon, contemporary with the Middle Neolithic, and illustrate the start of a secondary (or even tertiary) Neolithic culture, the first steps in swine-breeding by autochthonous hunter-fishers, whether the pigs in question were obtained from neighboring farming groups or tamed, in imitation of their practice, from native wild swine. *Reittierzüchter* could hardly be expected to figure directly in the archeological record and certainly cannot be identified in the Neolithic section. For the rest, the present paper deals with facts and not inferences.

BIBLIOGRAPHICAL NOTES

All statements referring to the Near East and Europe are documented in *New Light on the Most Ancient East* (London, 1952) and *The Dawn of European Civilization* (London, 1950), both by V. G. CHILDE. For China have been used "The Prehistory of the Chinese" (*Bulletin of the Museum of Far Eastern Antiquities*, Vol. XV [Stockholm, 1943]), "Chou-chia chai, Kansu" (*ibid.*, Vol. XVII [1945]), and "Prehistoric Sites in Honan" (*ibid.*, Vol. XIX [1947]), all by J. G. ANDERSSON.

1. IVERSEN. "Landnam i Danmarks Stenalder," *Dansk Geol. Undersøgelser*, II Raekke, No. 66 (Copenhagen, 1942).
2. Dr. L. Bernabó Brea has discovered stratified neolithic and later settlements here, but has not yet published on them.
3. FRANKFORT, H. *The Birth of Civilization in the Near East*, London, p. 46, 1951.
4. PIGGOTT, S. *Neolithic Britain*. Oxford, 1952.
5. *Ancient India*, IV (New Delhi, 1948), 202.
6. BERTSCH, K. and F., *Geschichte unserer Kulturpflanzen*, Stuttgart, 1947. JESSEN and HELBAEK, *Biologisk Skrifter*, Vol. III, No. 2, of "Det kog. danske Videnskabs Selskab." Copenhagen, 1942. HATT, G., *Landbrug i Danmarks Forntid*. Copenhagen, 1937. SCHIEMANN, E., *Weizen, Röggen und Gerste*. Jena, 1948. TACKHOLM, V., *Flora of Egypt*, Vol. I. Cairo, 1941.
7. FIELD, H., and PRICE, K. "Early Agri-

culture in Middle Asia," *Southwestern Journal of Anthropology*, VI (1950), 24.
8. GLOB, P. V., *Ard og Plov*. Aarhus, 1952.
9. NOSEK, S. "Slady kultów religijych wschodniej," *Z Otchłany Wieków*, Vol. XVIII. Warsaw, 1949.
10. CHILDE, V. G. "Neolithic House Types in Temperate Europe," *PPS*, Vol. XV. Cambridge, 1949.
11. *Sumer*, VII, 100. Baghdad, 1951.
12. CATON-THOMPSON, G. *Kharga*. In press.
13. CHILDE, V. G. "Axe and Adze," *JSGU*, Vol. XL. Frauenfeld, 1950.
14. VOGT, E. *Geflechte und Gewebe der Steinzeit*. Basel, 1937.
15. GARSTANG, J. *Mersin*. In press.
16. GLORY, in *Bulletin de la Société préhistorique de France*, XL, 36–40. Paris, 1943.
17. ATKINSON, R. *Excavations at Dorchester, Oxon*. Oxford, 1951.
18. MATZ, F. *Forschungen auf Kreta, 1942*. Berlin, 1951.

19. BECKER, C. J. "Mosefundene Lerkar fra Stenalder," *Aarbøger*. Copenhagen, 1947.
20. LEISNER, G. and V. *Die Megalithgräber der iberischen Halbinsel.* Berlin, 1943.
21. PIGGOTT, S. "A Trepanned Skull of the Beaker Period," *PPS*, VI, 112–31. Cambridge, 1940. MACWHITE, E., in *Quadernos de historia primitiva*, I, 61–69. Madrid, 1946.

22. COON, C. S. *Cave Explorations in Iran, 1949.* Philadelphia, 1951.
23. MILOJČIC, V. *Chronologie der jüngeren Steinzeit Mittel- und Südosteuropas.* Berlin, 1949.
24. BERNABÓ BREA, L. "Le Culture preistoriche della Francia Meridionale," *Rivista di studi Liguri*, XV, 21–45. Bordighera, 1951.
25. MENGHIN, O. *Weltgeschichte der Steinzeit.* Vienna, 1931.

Archeological Theories and Interpretation: New World

By GORDON R. WILLEY

INTRODUCTORY

THIS PAPER is a consideration of some of the principal archeological theories now current in the interpretation of the prehistoric scene in the New World. These theories are intimately involved with both the methods and the results of American archeology. For, as problems are conceived in theory, the attack upon problems is similarly conceived, and methods are selected or forged for this purpose. Likewise, as theory sets up the problem frame of reference, results are inevitably conditioned. For these reasons, in examining American-ist archeological theories, we will turn, first, to methodological structure to see how theory is interwoven with this structure; and, second, we will analyze some of the resultant constructs of American data, relating these to theory. In so doing, there will be overlap with colleagues who are treating, respectively, method and result; nevertheless, theory is the central theme of this presentation.

METHODOLOGICAL STRUCTURE

Archeology is concerned with history both in the broader sense of context and process, as these may be traced through the past, and in the narrower sense of space and time systematization of data. Taylor (1948) has made the useful distinction between the former,

which he refers to as "historiography," and the latter, which he has termed "chronicle." These are, in effect, the two major objectives of modern archeology: (1) processual understanding and (2) skeletal chronology and distribution. Although this concept of the duality of these objectives (history as a chronicle versus history as process) is valid from an analytical standpoint, operationally the archeologist must have both objectives in mind. Even the barest sort of chronological-distributional study of artifact forms is necessarily linked with implicit theory involving cultural process. Similarly, antiquarian or purely "phenomenological" interest in artifacts is not entirely bereft of its functional or processual side, for the mere fact that the object is recognized as something made by man is tied to assumptions about past human conduct.

The objectives of archeology, defined in this way, are approached by the study and manipulation of three basic factors: form, space, and time. The forms are the phenomena themselves, the prehistoric creations or manufactures. These may be dealt with in their individual uniqueness or in their similarity, the latter being the typological approach to the data of form. Space and time are the dimensions of the inquiry. Either or both may be co-ordinated with form to give the historical skeleton or chronicle of the particular datum or data under investigation. Forms may, by themselves, be relevant to function or process (as implied by shape and other inherent qualities), or, taken together with space and time coordinates, they may suggest cultural processes such as diffusion or independent development.

The basic factors of form, space, and time are not dealt with in the abstract but within either or both of two systems of contextual reference: the natural and the cultural. The natural context refers to environmental conditions as these may be revealed in landscape and climate or in the past geological records of these conditions. Such contexts have a bearing both on functional interpretation (cultural-environmental adjustments or failures to adjust) and space-time systematics (geological dating, tree-ring dating, etc.). The cultural context derives from our acceptance of artifactual remains as products of man's culture. It is the context that allows for the historical tracing of prehistoric-to-ethnohistoric developments and for the functional interpretation of dead remains in the light of the living or documented situation. It has as its deepest basis the commonalty of all mankind as creators and bearers of culture, but it may also be viewed in limited frames of reference for specific problems.

Archeological studies or approaches to the prehistoric data follow along two fundamental lines. These are the lines set by the major objectives: history (as limited chronicle) and process. As noted, it is virtually impossible to follow one line to the complete exclusion of the other, but there are definite tendencies of emphasis. For example, Americanist studies over the last thirty years have been largely preoccupied with historical rather than processual objectives, and archeological problems have been framed in accordance with this emphasis. But, whatever the tendency,

it is quite clear that there are in both the historical and the processual approaches differing and advancing levels of interpretative complexity. These stages of complexity in interpretation grow out of the varying concordances and correlations of the basic factors of form, space, and time and the contextual systems of natural and cultural reference. Utilization of the basic factors along complementary historical and processual lines may be charted as shown in Table 1.

On the first level of complexity under the historical category, we have two operations: (1) the identification of specific forms or descriptive typology and (2) the identification of cultural assemblages through descriptive typology and association. Paralleling this, in the processual category, we have: (1) functional or use identification of specific forms and (2) functional interpretation of cultural assemblages of forms or features. On this first level the factors of time and space do not enter directly into the interpretations either in the historical or in the processual categories. The initial historical operation—the identification of specific forms and their classification under a purely descriptive typology—could be, in itself, a consideration of phenomena for the sake of phenomena alone. This is rarely the case, and "phenomenology" is not generally regarded as archeology. Usually, the initial identifying or typological step is geared to a space-time problem of the second level, and this problem motivation is reflected in the organization of the particular typology. Archeological typology in the United States has reflected this trend in recent years, especially as it concerns ceramics. There has been a growing conviction that pottery types as descriptive categories are valueless unless the categories or types also serve as exponents of spatial and temporal differentiation in the study of cultural materials (see Ford, 1949, p.

40; Drucker, 1943, p. 35; Krieger, 1944; Willey, 1949, p. 5). This view seems justifiable as long as the problem is essentially one of space and time correlations. It is, of course, conceivable that a quite different typological breakdown of the same material could be set up for the study of problems of use or function of pottery. In either case, how-

neither space nor time correlates are overtly expressed in this system of archeological culture classification; yet the concept of the assemblage is implicitly grounded in the historical validity of the artifact-feature complex as a *unit*. Such a unity, by the very nature of its internal associations, bespeaks spatial-temporal correlates. The *com-*

TABLE 1

PROBLEM OBJECTIVES	LEVELS OF INTERPRETATIVE COMPLEXITY		
	First	Second	Third
Historical (Descriptive identification and space-time arrangements of data)	1. Identification of specific forms or descriptive typology 2. Identification of cultural assemblages through descriptive typology	1. Culture continuity and change with reference to specific areas 2. Culture continuity and change with reference to the specific chronology of an archeological site or zone	1. Culture continuity and change in both space and time dimensions
Processual (Functional or use identification and interpretations of data)	1. Functional or use interpretation of specific forms 2. Functional interpretation of cultural assemblages of forms or features	1. Functional interpretations of cultural forms or assemblages with reference to specific areas 2. Functional interpretation of cultural forms or assemblages with reference to the specific chronology of an ·archeological site or zone	1. Functional interpretation of cultural forms or assemblages with reference to both area and chronology (usually on a wide scale)

ever, the problems pitched on the second and third levels of interpretative complexity are the determinants for the typological operation of the first level, and such typology is thereby drawn into line with historical or processual objectives at its instigation.

The identification of cultural assemblages through descriptive typology has been conceived of as a step in archeological analysis and synthesis without reference to space or time factors. This has been the *modus operandi* of the American Midwestern Taxonomic System (McKern, 1939). It is true that

ponent, the classificatory unit of the Midwestern system, is an assemblage with a geographical locus (the site) and has sometimes been defined as a time level (period) represented in the human occupation of a particular geographic site. The *focus*, the first order on the ascending taxonomic scale in the Midwestern system, is an abstraction based upon the close typological similarity of two or more *components*. If typological similarity is any indicator of cultural relatedness (and this is surely axiomatic to archeology), then such relatedness carries with it implications of a common or similar history for the *focus*. The same reasoning applies as foci are classified under *aspects*, as aspects are grouped together into *phases*, and as phases are merged as *patterns*. The degree of trait similarity lessens as one works upward in the Midwestern taxonomic hierarchy, and presumably the closeness of historical ties also lessens; yet historical systematization is still inherent in the classification. That this should be so is not, in itself, a drawback. Perhaps the most serious flaw in the Midwestern system is its historico-genetic rigidity. Certain lines and degrees of relationship are laid down from one classificatory order or level to the next, with the result that the extremely complex interrelationships of cultural descent and diffusion are obscured by the arbitrariness of the system. Eventually, the end-product may become as nearly ahistorical as the original classificatory operations of the system, although in a quite different and unintended way.

As there is covert historical theory in the assemblage concept and in the Midwestern Taxonomic System, so there is comparable hidden functional implication. The unity of the assemblage, if historical unity can be assumed, must lead to the conclusion that we are dealing with the remains of an integrated cultural complex in the case of the *component*. The tool types, weapon forms, and settlement traces reflect ancient patterns of behavior that had been welded, with greater or lesser firmness, into a functioning whole. If the data are sufficient, an interpretation of this kind (i.e., hunting community, sedentary village agriculturists, etc.) is certainly feasible on this level. Such functional interpretation is, of course, possible because of the natural and cultural contextual backgrounds which are available even on this simplest level of interpretative complexity. Site ecology provides one such context, while

ethnological or modern analogies to artifacts and architectural features afford another.

The second and third levels of interpretative complexity are, in their historical objectives, concerned with the spatial and temporal arrangement of cultural forms. As stated, this has been the primary usage of artifact typology in American studies over the last three decades. On the second level we have two operations: area distribution studies of forms and chronological distribution studies of forms. These may be carried on independently of each other. Holmes's (1903) great work on the pottery of the eastern United States is an example of the former. In this study, ceramic types were plotted geographically over a wide area, and a number of regional correlations were established. These Holmes designated as "provinces." They were, in effect, areas, established solely upon the trait of pottery, without reference to time depth. The theoretical basis behind Holmes's reconstruction is that of the culture area (Wissler, 1926; Kroeber, 1931), a concept widely used in American ethnology. Each area was assumed to have a generative center which produced the distinctively regional types. At the margins of each area there were blendings with the types radiating from another center or centers. These blendings were assumed to result from diffusions, counterdiffusions, and mergers of ideas or actual products originating in the centers. The culture-area concept is still considered useful by American archeologists and is widely employed, although with reservations. The obvious weakness derives from the attempt to infer the time dimension from the geographic-distributional picture alone. This is inherent in the idea of the generative center and its outlying margins with a time flow from center to margins. It has been demonstrated that neither geographical center nor point of cultural intensity or elaboration can be assumed to be the originative center of a type. In other words, the age-area construct is by no means infallible. For a space-time reconstruction other methods than the geographic-distribution study are necessary.

These methods are the principal ones by which culture continuity and change through time may be demonstrated: stratigraphy and seriation. Prior to 1912, stratigraphic studies on the American scene adhered rather closely to the geologic principles of stratigraphy. Sharp distinctions in physical strata were correlated with changes in cultural types. Sometimes these strata involved natural soil deposition; or in other cases, such as that of Uhle's (1903) stratigraphy at Pachacamac in Peru, artifact types were correlated with major architectural and structural levels in a site. Between 1912 and 1924, Nelson (1916), Kroeber (1918), Spier (1919), and Kidder (1924) introduced a significant modification. This was the principle of the correlation of artifact change with relative depth. The method was applicable to refuse deposits which had grown by occupational accretion. Marked physical stratification of deposits was not necessary. The technique consisted of removing detritus and artifacts from arbitrary depth levels. In studying artifact change by levels, percentage fluctuations of types were noted from level to level, so that rising or declining percentage frequencies of types were correlated with time. Deriving in large part from the mechanical nature of the operation, "continuous stratigraphy" of this kind had important theoretical repercussions on the nature of culture continuity and change. With the continuous depositional record of a site occupation before his eyes, the archeologist could not help being impressed with the evidence for culture dynamics. A number of concepts were formulated to account

for the vertical record in the earth. Types were seen in the refuse history at their inception, were observed approaching and attaining a maximum frequency, and were then traced upward to their "death" or disappearance. One type was seen to "replace" another in this time story. If the stylistic division between an earlier and a later type was sharp, it was hypothesized that new or foreign elements were introduced into the life of the site at a particular point in its history. On the other hand, if the intrinsic qualities of two types showed strong similarity and if their frequency histories allowed it, gradual evolutionary change from one type into another was postulated. These theories, born in the techniques of stratigraphic chronological measurement, served as the basis of functional interpretations with reference to the history of the site. Extended to studies of culture change and continuity over a wide area, the third level of interpretative complexity, they form much of the theoretical underpinning of complex functional interpretation.

J. A. Ford (1949, pp. 44–57; 1951, pp. 91–100) has been one of the chief exponents of time-change and continuity studies in American archeology in recent years. Ford's interest has been concentrated largely upon the dynamics of cultural forms (pottery types) and upon the development of theory in connection with this. His graphic presentations of ceramic stratigraphy emphasize the quality of continuity. Individual types are seen as describing unimodal curves upon vertical scale graphs. These recapitulate "life-histories" of types, their origins, climaxes, and eventual disappearances. That types do behave in this fashion, although with varying rates of speed, seems amply demonstrated by stratigraphic evidences from innumerable archeological sites. That there is also a tendency upon the part of the archeologist occasionally to "force" certain types to conform to an expected unimodal curve seems probable. There are two complicating factors here. One is primarily mechanical. Refuse deposition at any site, or at any one location upon a site, may not give a continuous history of site occupation and artifact usage. In some instances these time gaps may be minor and irrelevant; in others they may be long and crucial. Occupation, desertion, and reoccupation may give an extremely fragmentary picture and one that makes a puzzling frequency graph unless the graph curve is "smoothed" to harmonize with what is conceived of as the normal occurrence pattern. Ford is cognizant of this difficulty but has relied upon large random sampling in site excavations to obviate it, feeling that the hiatus-reoccupation situation is the rare one rather than the rule.

The other complicating factor rises out of the hypothesis that typological change or variability in a site need not always be correlated with chronological change. Instead, it may have its origins in functional differentiation of artifact types. Brainerd (1951, p. 307) has suggested that the irregularities in some of his graphs of Maya ceramics result from this; and he further postulates that graphic regularity may be fairly safely assumed to be an expression of time change, while marked irregularity may result from the sudden introduction of sacred or ceremonial wares into what had heretofore been kitchen dumps. Neither of these complicating factors is sufficient to invalidate the method of plotting continuous stratigraphy or of interpreting cultural continuity, gradual replacement, and evolutionary change from its results. They do, however, indicate that the method is not infallible and that it cannot be consistently employed without careful examination of refuse deposition and

cautious trial and retrial of typological formulations.

Seriation, as it has been developed in American archeology, refers to a "horizontal stratigraphy" of artifact types and their associations rather than to seriation by a priori stylistic or evolutionistic principles. Kroeber (1918) practiced it in its simplest form in the Zuñi region of the southwestern United States when he gathered and pocketed pottery-sherd collections from the surfaces of a number of ruins. These collections showed typological overlap, so that some sites were, for example, represented by types A and B, others by types B and C, and still others by types C and D. Assuming each collection to be a valid historical assemblage, it was evident that a seriation running from type A through type D was present. If, then, time direction could be introduced into the series by relating type D to the historic period at Zuñi, the seriation was transformed into a chronology by which the various sites from which the collections were made could be dated.

Ford has elaborated upon this principle in seriational studies in the Virú Valley of Peru (Ford, 1949) and in the Mississippi Valley (Phillips, Ford, and Griffin, 1951, pp. 213–36). By computing percentage frequencies of pottery types from site surface collections, he has arranged these frequencies and collections into a series. The seriation, however, does not follow along simple lines of typological overlap but is constructed, instead, to reproduce the unimodal curves of pottery-type life-histories comparable to those plotted from vertical refuse stratification. As is seen, this builds directly upon the theories of growth, climax, and decline for cultural forms. In general, it appears to be substantiated, in that the life-history curves of the seriated types tend to duplicate those of the vertical stratigraphy. There are, however, more complications and more possibilities for error with this method than with that of vertical continuous stratigraphy. In the first place, the surface collection is less likely to be a valid historical assemblage than is the subsurface deposit. Opportunities for mixture are, obviously, much greater. Secondly, it has not yet been satisfactorily determined that the surface pottery collection of any site is fully representative of all the types once used at that site. Deep and compact refuse sites may show no types characteristic of their earlier strata on the surface. This does not necessarily confuse the seriation, as such a surface collection would be accurately seriated in accordance with the later strata of occupation at the site. Reliance upon the date for the chronological placement of other features at the site would, though, be questionable. A third complication is the possibility that the surface collections of some sites do show a representative sample of several periods or span a time range three or four times as great as the surface collections of other sites. As all collections are treated as single assemblages, this relativity in the time compression involved is almost certain to produce some peculiar distortions. As with the stratigraphic method, Ford and other practitioners of percentile seriation are aware of these complications. Again, their reliance upon useful results is based upon a large sample and a feeling that the difficulties will tend to cancel out. The method undoubtedly has validity and is supported by other lines of evidence in many instances. My own feeling is that it can be considered as an instrument for gross sorting but not for precision analysis.

While Ford has been essentially interested in the perfection of space-time measurements, W. W. Taylor, Jr., has sounded a counternote in his long critique, "A Study of Archaeology" (1948).

Taylor's interests are with descriptive integration and process rather than with spatial-temporal systematics. His "conjunctive approach," which is the bringing to bear of as many kinds of evidence as practical considerations permit in site excavation and analysis, is most directly concerned with what I have classed as functional interpretation of the second level of complexity. Taylor has made clear that he does not eschew historic chronicle or more sweeping historical and processual reconstructions as legitimate goals of archeology. His attack is, rather, that space-time studies of a limited or broad-scale nature will proceed more soundly and effectively if we are better informed as to the mechanics of cultural process and that an understanding of process must begin with the fullest possible recovery of individual site information. Inasmuch as archeological site excavation is permanently destructive, Taylor's argument is hard to refute. The archeologist most assuredly has an obligation to his data, and it is incumbent upon him to make the fullest possible record. Yet of what should this record consist? It is impossible to gather all pertinent information because data are pertinent only in reference to a problem. This leads us to the question as to whether there are not some problems that can be framed only with reference to landmarks wider than the individual site. If there are—and there seem to be—do we not need the broader historical contexts in which to place them? And is it not essential for this historical orientation to push ahead of the more intensive analyses, particularly those aimed at functional understanding of a particular prehistoric community? This has, in any event, been the course of development in American archeology. Whether it is the purest accident or whether there is inherent logic in what has happened remains a matter of speculation and debate. There is, in my mind, no doubt but that Taylor's critique has had a salutary influence on American archeology. The old problem incentive of chronology and distributions of "cultures" in terms of a few marker "fossils" (usually potsherds) was not sufficient to attract archeologists who were also anthropologists. Taylor's strictures helped crystallize this feeling of discontent.

From this outline of archeological methodology, with particular reference to the Americas, it can be seen that theories of culture change and continuity are fundamental to archeological studies of either a predominantly historical or predominantly functional orientation. At the outset, it must be recognized that certain assumptions concerning culture change and continuity underlie most systematic typology. It has been stated that typology with archeological objectives reflects problem motivations and that these motivations are usually the need for spatial-temporal measuring instruments. This is grounded in the assumption that culture change is reflected in material manufactures and that this change proceeds in both temporal and spatial dimensions. There have been two ways of looking at this. One envisages culture change as a continuous stream, to be segmented into types as this best suits the archeologist's purposes (Ford, 1949). The other view tends to conceive of types as once existent realities in the prehistoric culture under examination (Rouse, 1939). For the former position, the establishment of types is a purely arbitrary procedure, entirely imposed upon the prehistoric phenomena by the classifier. The second opinion sees the typological task more as the recognition of existent entities. The two outlooks are not fully antagonistic, and both seem to arrive at similar results. The concept of the arbitrary segmentation of the stream of culture

change is predisposed to overlook factors of acceleration or deceleration in the speed of change and to minimize the sort of sudden change that would, presumably, result from the impact of influences lying outside the particular culture continuum. There are potential correctives here, such as relative depths of culture refuse or correlations with absolute dating factors, that would serve to check false assumptions about the rate of culture change or the relative time spans that the archeologist might assign to the life-histories of certain types. Yet these are often lacking or poorly controlled, and the impulse to "overregularize," as a result of this typological conception and the cultural theory behind it, is a definite danger. The weaknesses of the concept of the type as a prehistoric reality are of an opposite nature. Certain styles or patterns in the manufacture of artifacts are, perhaps, overemphasized by the archeologist. While others, which impress his consciousness to a lesser degree, may be slighted as "transitional," with the vague implications that they are, somehow, of minor importance in the tracing-out of culture history. It is not an "either-or" choice. Both conceptions have merit. The course of ancient cultures can be plotted as a dynamic flow, and, at the same time, it can be kept in mind that prehistoric artisans were aiming at modalities which to them seemed fixed and which, undoubtedly, did not change at a set rate of speed.

To summarize further, the treatment of archeological assemblages in any historicogenetic system has a basis in theories of continuity and change. Even if space and time factors are not formally observed, principles of continuity and change are expressed in the degrees of trait likeness or unlikeness which are the mechanics for establishing the genetic lines binding the assemblages together. In the overtly historical systems, such as those in vogue in the southwestern United States (Gladwin, 1934; Colton, 1939), lines of relationship and descent are expressed in these terms.

The processes by which, or through which, cultural continuity and change are maintained or accomplished have not received study and reflective thought commensurate with the way these concepts have been invoked by American archeologists. "Evolution" and "diffusion" have been tag names employed, but these are broad categories rather than specific explanations, and there have been few clear theoretical formulations along these lines. For example, the historicogenetic schemes of culture, or culture assemblage, classification in the southwestern United States have a dendritic structure, with "basic" or "root" cultures of the earlier periods diversifying into the various "stems" and "branches" of the later time periods. Obviously, the archeologists who have constructed these classificatory schemes have, as their realities, the cultural assemblages which are represented near the top of the "tree." The monogenic "root" or "trunk" is lost in dim antiquity. But the implications are that the processes of cultural development, or evolution, have been those of monogenesis with "basic" or "mother"-cultures, presumably simple in form and content, diversifying into complex, specialized offspring. Apparently, there is a rather simplistic evolutionary or genetic analogy at work here. To be sure, there is some universal basis for expressing the development of human culture in this fashion. At least the relatively simple, relatively homogeneous, material evidences of the Lower Paleolithic of the Old World give way to growing complexity and diversification. But the question might be asked whether this is in any way recapitulated in Arizona and New Mexico by sedentary pottery-makers during the first millennium of the Christian Era. Such a course of development is a possibility; nevertheless, in this case it appears that evolutionary theory has been very naïvely applied. Monogenesis of southwestern cultures is a postulate to be tested, not an axiomatic explanation.

Diffusionist theory in American archeology has probably received more analysis, or analytical speculation, than has evolutionist theory. It is at the core of most archeological interpretation. Trade, migration, gradual borrowing, and idea or stimulus diffusion have all been advanced in specific instances, both with and without supporting evidence. As with evolutionary hypotheses, theories of diffusion may be legitimately brought forward to explain various patternings in space-time distributions. Adequate support for either class of theory will, however, be more effectively marshaled when greater functional understanding of the data in question is achieved.

SOME PREVAILING AMERICANIST RECONSTRUCTIONS

AMERICAN CULTURAL ORIGINS

If a single dominant motif for Americanist reconstructions of New World aboriginal cultures had to be selected, I think we could safely say that this motif has been "isolationism." This statement is not necessarily critical. The prevailing theories concerning the origins of the early lithic and the later Neolithic cultures of the Americas may be the correct ones. At present, these theories have not been satisfactorily proved, but opposing theory is equally undemonstrated. It is of interest, however, that American opinion is predominantly on the side of the "separateness" of American beginnings and developments.

On the question of the first peopling of the American continents there has been little dispute on the score that these migrants were Asiatics who entered from eastern Siberia. There has, however, been considerable debate as to when they arrived and as to their stage of culture upon arrival. Up to about 1920, prevalent theory, championed by Holmes and Hrdlička, sponsored a relatively late entry for man into the Americas of no more than 2000–3000 B.C. Such a migration was thought to have taken place on a very late Paleolithic or Mesolithic threshold. Following the discovery of Folsom, Yuma, and related lithic finds in the western plains of North America, the earlier theories were drastically revised to allow some 10,000–25,000 years for man's occupancy of the Americas. Such a revision suggested a Paleolithic correlation with the Old World, but this correlation was largely one of time period rather than the diffusion of a specific industry or tool forms. American chronology rested upon geological and faunal associations rather than typology. It was, of course, generally assumed that the old lithic assemblages of the high plains were of Old World derivation; but, for the most part, interest centered in them as isolated entities of the American setting, and there was little systematic effort to link them to specific Asiatic or European complexes.

In spite of the geological-paleontological datings of 10,000-year-old artifacts in the Americas (and this has been recently supported by carbon 14 dates which are almost that old), there is some rather serious contrary evidence which questions the American chronological estimates and tends to minimize the isolation of the North American high plains and early lithic assemblages. Ironically, this evidence is of a strictly archeological rather than a natural science nature. It has been pointed out by both Ward and Movius (personal communications, 1950–51) that the Folsom and Yuma flint types (with the

exception of the fluted point) are found in northeastern Siberia in Neolithic rather than Paleolithic contexts. This eastern Siberian Neolithic follows the period of loess deposition in northern Asia. By 2500 B.C. cord-marked pottery was a part of the Neolithic complex in this part of the world, but chipped stonework of a definite Neolithic kind antedated the pottery. Just how far back these eastern Siberian Neolithic points and scrapers can be dated is the crux of the argument, but both Ward and Movius are of the opinion that 4000 B.C. would be the outside limit. If this is true, there is a glaring chronological discrepancy between these Siberian complexes and the early American lithic. There are three possible interpretations of this dilemma: (1) the American dating of Folsom-Yuma is too early; (2) the Siberian dating of the pre-ceramic Neolithic is too late; or (3) the American Folsom-Yuma complexes were independently invented and bear no historical relationship to the Siberian Neolithic complexes. I believe that we can rule the third explanation out as an extreme "isolationist" point of view. This leaves us with the other two explanations, and these two interpretations of cultural beginnings in the New World remain to be tested. I conclude by pointing out only that the interpretation preferred by most American archeologists relies essentially upon evidence of a nonarcheological nature and that artifact typology and artifact assemblages of northeastern Siberia, that part of the Old World closest to their problem, have not been given full consideration in this theoretical reconstruction.

Although the problem of remote origins is of great importance, perhaps the question of American Neolithic beginnings has been of more dramatic interest. In any event, it has been one of the most bitterly fought—and rightly so. For upon this question hangs much of anthropological thought bearing upon the processes and courses of human development. The empires of the Inca and of Mexico astounded not only the conquistadors of the sixteenth century but also social philosophers ever since. Could such feats of duplication take place guided only by the parallel structure of men's minds and bodies, or was the cultural germ transplanted across the oceans?

Most American prehistorians have been disposed to believe the former: independent development of the New World high civilizations over and above an Upper Paleolithic–Mesolithic base. A number of European scholars have taken issue with this "isolationist" view. Their counterarguments have usually taken the form of trait comparisons between Peru-Mexico, on the one hand, and the Near East–Asia, on the other. In my judgment a demonstration of specific high-level intellectual achievements held in common by both the Old and the New World has never been satisfactorily made. By this I mean that such systems as Middle American writing, enumeration, and astronomy are not duplicated or closely approximated in the Old World. Nor are there duplications or approximations of complex art styles, presumably reflective of religious and intellectual systems, between the two hemispheres. These lacks do not, of course, disprove contact, but they allow for certain eliminations. The absence of complex art styles or complex intellectual attainments makes it almost certain that trans-Pacific diffusions, if they did take place, were not carried out by the mechanisms of organized conquest or religious proselytization. In fact, it is unlikely that such diffusions in any way involved hieratic elements of either Old or New World societies.

It is below this hieratic level of complexity that you find the majority of Old and New World parallels. The most intriguing of these are technological elements or complexes, such as the *cire perdue* method of casting metals, resist-process painting, and bark cloth, to say nothing of agriculture, irrigation, and pottery-making. I believe that it is here, with element complexes of this kind, that the case for contact between the Old and the New World Neolithic will eventually stand or fall. If so, students of this problem should focus their attention upon the formative periods of Middle American and Andean civilizations, for it is at the beginning of and during these formative periods that such element complexes first appear on the American scene. If present American dating estimates are correct, this takes us back a millennium or a millennium and a half before the Christian Era.

Another category of traits, crucial to the rise of the American Neolithic, are the food plants upon which the agriculture was based. A tracing-out of the history of these may be the single most decisive factor in the Asiatic-American diffusion problem. Considerable work has been done along this line, but, as yet, there is strong disagreement among authorities.

There is also a final category of traits, many of which are often adduced in argument, that consists of myths or certain features of primitive social organization. Many of these seem to be nearly world wide. It is unlikely that they offer a very fruitful line of investigation for this particular problem. It may be that some do represent relatively late diffusions, but others could well hark back to the time of the first peopling of the American continents. Significantly, they are not essential parts of a sedentary agriculture-based civilization and thus do not necessarily mark an introduction of possibly foreign ideas instrumental in producing such a civilization.

PREHISTORIC-HISTORIC CONTINUITIES

A full appreciation of the time dimension has been archeology's greatest contribution to American anthropological studies. To European colleagues this may seem a statement of the obvious, but it must be remembered that American anthropology and ethnology of the early twentieth century was not historically minded in the sense of time-depth perspective. This was particularly true of North America, where the absence of native written histories and the fast-disappearing Indian populations centered attention upon the flat-dimensional "present" or late historic period. One of the most outstanding examples of this was in the Great Plains of the United States. Ethnologists had offered speculative "historical reconstructions" of the Plains Indian past, based upon nineteenth-century records and some knowledge of early European colonial events. The significance of the advent of the horse and its impact upon the native cultures had been correctly appraised in part, but the quality of native Plains culture before that event was largely unknown. The nomadic, or seminomadic, horsemen of the later periods led ethnologists to believe that the earlier inhabitants of the region had also been nomads and that, in consequence, their culture had been a rather simple one. Archeology (Strong, 1935; Wedel, 1936) destroyed this hypothesis by showing clearly that the old Plains life had been intensively horticultural and sedentary. Through a series of successive periods prehistoric cultures were linked to proto-historic, historic, and modern descendants. This type of study, sometimes called the "direct historical approach," has a theoretical basis in cultural continuity. Starting with known, documented habitation sites, certain cultural assemblages were identified and associated with particular tribal groups. Earlier archeological assemblages were then sought which

were not too sharply divergent from the known historic ones, and the procedure was followed backward in time.

In tracing prehistoric-historic continuities in this fashion, a number of useful working assumptions are at hand, although all of these must be used with some reservations. Continuity of a culture within the same area is a reasonable expectation, but there is always the possibility of regional shifts through time. The Plains studies showed both a certain amount of regional stability as well as some shifting. Cultural continuity within the same area is reasonably good evidence for linguistic and ethnic continuity, although it is by no means infallible. Thus Pawnee and Lower Loup archeological assemblages are identified as the remains of Pawnee tribesmen, but the culturally similar Upper Republican assemblages, more remote in time, can be associated with the linguistic and biological ancestors of the Pawnee only on the basis of reasonable probability and not certainty.

The establishment of prehistoric-to-historic continuity is of utmost importance as a springboard for further archeological interpretation, and, along with general chronological and distributional studies, it is one of the primary historical problems for the American archeologist. In general, the most successful continuities of this sort have been determined for those regions where there has been relatively little ethnic shifting in aboriginal or proto-historic times and where there still remain native populations with predominantly native cultures. The Eskimo area of the north, the pueblos of the southwestern United States, certain regions of Mexico, the Maya country of Central America, and the Quechua and Aymara areas of the Andes are prime examples. In all of them a certain amount of cultural continuity with the archeological past has been maintained, and this can be correlated with ethnic and linguistic continuities. A general, but not absolute, assumption which Americanists have followed in these reconstructions is that gradual and unbroken continuity of culture also implies continuity of population and that a sudden change or break in continuity is a reasonable indicator of population change.

TRADITIONS AND CO-TRADITIONS

An appreciation of cultural continuities through time has led to the formalization of the tradition. The tradition, as defined, may apply to limited facets of culture, such as the tradition of white-on-red painting of ceramics in Andean South America (Willey, 1945), or to more inclusive and complex cultural patternings. In essence, it is the recognition of a specific line, or lines, of continuity through time, a formal acceptance of the rugged persistence of cultural ideas. These traditions are the means by which prehistoric-to-historic continuities are strung together and by which the archeologist traces culture growth in general.

The tradition cannot be changeless within its continuity, but its internal modifications must lie, or be defined, within certain bounds. Otherwise, it is useless as a device for plotting or demonstrating continuity. An example of a tradition of extremely limited or monotonous inner variability is the cord-marked or fabric-marked pottery of eastern North America. Some years ago American archeologists attempted to visualize the cord-marked wares as basically definitive of an area or a certain chronological period. Subsequent research failed to demonstrate clear-cut regional or temporal stability. In certain periods cord-marked wares were found from southern Canada to Florida and from the Atlantic to the Plains; on other chronological levels the distribution was more restricted. Similarly, in some parts of the eastern United States cord-marking appeared as the earliest-known surface treatment for pottery; but in other sections it was found to persist until the founding of the European colonies. Minor typological distinctions within the cord- and fabric-marked ware were found to have specific, limited spatial and temporal utility; but, as a whole, cord- and fabric-marking was best conceived of as a tradition which had expanded or contracted geographically as it had persisted chronologically with relatively slight internal modifications. In contrast to this is the white-on-red pottery tradition of Peru, where a number of quite elaborate and radically different pottery styles are linked together over several hundred years of prehistory by their common possession of a red-and-white color scheme.

A number of traditions in American archeological data come to mind as examples. Among these was the deep-seated bias of the peoples of the Hohokam region of the southwestern United States area for red-on-buff pottery as opposed to a black-on-white ceramic heritage for the northern Southwest. The broad-lined incised decoration which binds Venezuelan and West Indian pottery styles together is another such tradition, while the shell-tempering of Mississippian wares is still another kind of tradition persistence in the ceramic craft.

The examples I have used have been simple ones and confined to pottery because it is with the pottery medium that American archeologists exercise the greatest control of the time factor. Obviously, however, the concept can apply to other media and other ranges of complexity. Maya calendrical lore would be an example of a highly complex, tightly unified tradition which lasted well over 1,000 years and in which can be recognized stylistic and technical period subdivisions.

The theory underlying the tradition concept is well expressed in the term itself. For "tradition" implies deep-set and channeled activity or patterned ways in which the vitality of a culture expresses itself in strong preference to other possible ways. The conditions surrounding this rigidity of expression which results in the long-time traditional expression are an interesting problem for future investigation. In dealing with such things as pottery decoration, the archeologist is undoubtedly investigating what is relatively trivial in past human events. The failure of polychrome painting to take hold on the northern coast of Peru in the face of the white-on-red tradition, despite several attempts to introduce it, may eventually be revealed as nothing more mysterious than an absence of suitable mineral pigments in that part of the country. On the other hand, the unraveling of seemingly insignificant threads in an attempt to factor out causality may lead us to a greater understanding of "tradition set" and "tradition persistence" in institutions which loom larger in human affairs.

It has been pointed out that cultural traditions do not always adhere firmly to given geographical areas, and this is often true. There do, however, appear to be general regional-traditional correlations. The examination of such correlations has led to a related concept, that of the area co-tradition (Bennett, 1948). The co-tradition, as the name suggests, is based upon the persistence of a number of combined and closely interrelated traditions within a specified area. It is not necessarily the history of any specified ethnic group but the history of cultural continuity within area confines. It affords the archeologist a working device in place of the culture area, for the latter lacked the time dimension and was unsuited to problems of prehistory. The area co-tradition is, in effect, the culture area with

time depth. Within its spatial and temporal limits it must have several basic consistencies. These are the warp and weft which hold it together in spite of subregional and period-to-period differences. The Peruvian or central Andean co-tradition is a good example. In this highland and coastal area all cultural phases partake of certain minimum traits and trait-complexes—Andean-type agriculture, certain pottery and weaving traditions, and architectural types. These and others are the common denominators of the Peruvian co-tradition and so define it. The Peruvian co-tradition is limited in time from the advent of maize agriculture (about 1000 B.C.) to the collapse of the Inca empire in A.D. 1532.

Comparable area co-traditions have been formulated elsewhere. One of the most recent applications of the concept has been in the southwestern United States (Martin and Rinaldo, 1951). Somewhat earlier, Kirchhoff (1943) defined Mesoamerica as a culture area, and, although he did not use the term "co-tradition," it is evident that his thinking includes time-depth perspective. In the far north an Arctic or Eskimoan tradition is surely indicated. Here Larsen and Rainey have defined a dual traditional emphasis within the larger framework, suggesting a land-hunting versus a sea-mammal–hunting economic dichotomy as this can be applied to the various Eskimo periods or phases. In eastern North America it seems most useful for the present, at least, to conceive of three co-traditions. These are by no means new constructs, for they follow along the old taxonomic divisions of Archaic, Woodland, and Mississippian.

DIFFUSIONS

In recent years systematic American archeology has tended to be confined to distinct natural and cultural regions. These have been areas in which, from the outset, it has been more or less clear that certain traditions, or co-traditions, were dominant. Each such region has served as a sort of problem framework, and the archeologist has had a tendency to "feel at home" within the bounds of his own particular region but to show no great desire to go out of it. As a result, there has been somewhat less interest in problems of interareal diffusion than there had been in an earlier era. To date, these continental and hemisphere-wide problems of prehistoric contact remain largely unsolved. Various hypotheses have been formulated, but most of these have yet to be substantiated.

One of the most brilliant and far-reaching of these theories concerning American-wide diffusions was propounded by Spinden (1917) over 30 years ago. The nexus of this idea was that the seed of American Neolithic life—agriculture, pottery-making, and other sedentary arts—were invented as an integral complex and spread from a single Middle American center to both the northern and the southern continents. This is the New World "Archaic hypothesis." Subsequent investigations have shown Spinden to be incorrect in his selection of certain Mexican assemblages as being fully representative of this earliest "Archaic." The relationships of valley of Mexico "Archaic" with early southern Mexican and Central American cultures are bewilderingly complex, and Spinden's formulation, taken *in toto,* does not resolve all these complexities. Nevertheless, the idea in the abstract still merits attention. Recent concepts of a "New World Formative" cultural level (Steward, 1948; Willey, 1948; Strong, 1948) are restatements of Spinden's original theme. The chief difference is that the center of origin of this "Formative" is not so confidently designated as it was for Spinden's "Archaic." Most archeologists who are now writing on this problem see a possibility of a center, or centers, of origin lying anywhere between central Mexico and southern Peru. Yet, aside from this, the "Formative" concept stands upon the same theoretical ground as did the "Archaic" hypothesis. Although the diffusion processes of neither have been fully set forth by their proponents, both theories imply the spread of a functionally related complex: maize horticulture, a sedentary way of life, developed craft specialization, including ceramics, and fundamental socioreligious beliefs tied up with an agricultural economy. Spinden defined specific ceramic (figurine) styles as being associated with this diffusion, and it has been the evidence for these that has failed to appear. The promulgators of the "Formative" admit the lack of a common style for their postulated early level and point, rather, to what seems to be a common ceramic heritage of monochrome wares, certain vessel forms, and decorative techniques.

This difference in the evidence for diffusion—style versus technical elements—leads us to the consideration of another concept: the horizon style. The horizon style was first defined by Kroeber (1944, p. 108) in connection with Peruvian studies. It is the phenomenon of a widespread art style which is registered in a number of local sequences. In accordance with the appearance of the same style from one locality to another, the various sequences are synchronized. The significance of the idea is in the phenomenon of the style as a unique entity. If this uniqueness is accepted, then contemporaneousness or near-contemporaneousness for the several local regional manifestations of the style can be assumed and the "horizon" quality inferred. Establishment of the uniqueness of the style depends upon three factors: its technical quality, its content or representation, and its configuration. The last, the configurational aspect of style, is the crucial factor.

Two specimens might reveal fine-line carving on stone (technical) and a jaguar motif (content), but the delineation of the jaguar (configuration) might be quite different in the two cases. In such an event the archeologist would be dealing with two distinct styles.

This problem of stylistic uniqueness has a bearing on the "Archaic" hypothesis as well as upon most other questions of wide-scale American diffusions. If stylistic identity or close similarity can be established, it can be reasonably assumed that the separate occurrences mark an approximately contemporaneous horizon. For the American "Archaic" or "Formative" there does not appear to be any such style horizon; hence contemporaneousness of the various New World "Formative" cultures is questionable.

The lack of a diffused style is undoubtedly indicative of significant qualities in the processes of diffusion. Or, conversely, stylistic diffusion must presuppose certain conditions which are not necessary for other types of diffusion. The archeologist is not yet in a position to be able to say what these conditions may have been. Speculatively, it seems likely that the diffusion of a complex art style, such as the Chavín or the Maya, implies the diffusion of a social, religious, or political system. The transference of the ideas involved in the duplication of such a style suggests intimate contact and interchange between the localities and regions concerned. In this regard it is probably worthy of note that most of the great American prehistoric styles, such as the classic Maya, the Chavín, the Olmec, or the Mochica, are confined to a single co-traditional area or a fraction thereof. Reliable occurrences outside the recognized geographical limits of these styles are found in such totally different contexts that there has been little difficulty in recognizing them as trade items. An exception is the Inca

style, which spread into both north and south Andean areas. Here, of course, we have documentary evidence that such a diffusion was backed by imperialistic expansion.

As with the problem of widespread "Archaic" or "Formative" relationships, the specific problems of interareal relationships in the Americas involve diffusion of a nonstylistic kind. The southwestern United States was almost certainly dependent upon the cultures of Mexico, but there are no horizon style linkages and only scant evidences of trade. The contacts here were almost certainly those which permitted the passage of technological ideas (ceramics, irrigation, casting of metals) but did not encourage the transfer of social, religious, or political idea systems and their associated symbols (art styles). A somewhat similar situation obtains between the southeastern United States and Mexico. Here the two areas are separated by several hundred miles of desolate wastelands, but in the Southeast a rich agricultural civilization flourished. Perhaps more than in the Southwest, the Southeast reflects the religious and sociopolitical systems of Middle America. The temple mound–plaza ceremonial centers imply this. There is also a southeastern cult art which suggests parallels to the south; however, this so-called "Southern Cult" (Waring and Holder, 1945) of the Southeast has its distinct style (Krieger, 1945), and, if it was Middle American–inspired, it has undergone serious local transformation.

The same condition prevails between the southwestern and southeastern United States. These areas, separated by the staked plains of Texas and other semidesert regions, probably maintained intermittent contact. There are possibilities that one race of maize was passed between the two and that certain pottery vessel form ideas were exchanged. Stylistically, the pottery assemblages in question are radically distinct, and the contact must have been on the level of a stimulus or idea diffusion (Kroeber, 1940).

In areas to the south of Middle America the story of relationships is still most feebly comprehended. The "Formative" levels of western Honduras bear a general technical similarity to those of Middle America, and there is even one horizon marker, Usulatan ware, which provides a secure linkage to the north. Usulatan is, however, such a simple decorative type that it is more comparable to a technique than to a stylistic configuration. It undoubtedly has some value as a time marker but is difficult to interpret as an indicator of complex diffusion. In Nicaragua and Costa Rica certain decorative elements in Nicoya pottery may be traced back to later Mexican periods and offer evidence of stylistic diffusion. To the south of these countries there is little in the way of stylistic linkage to Middle America. The whole of the lower Central American, Colombian, and Ecuadorian area is chopped into a great number of small stylistic regions. Their cross-relations, one to the other, have not yet been worked out, but it seems unlikely that any major stylistic horizon markers will emerge. The relationships from region to region, again, are those of similar technologies and techniques, including such features as pottery vessel forms, which have a general traditional but not a stylistic bond.

The Peruvian co-tradition area is well cemented by horizon styles. Two of these, the Incaic and the earlier Tiahuanacan, extend southward into Argentina and Chile, where they have horizontal significance. For the earlier periods, however, the Peruvian styles are contained within the co-traditional area; and the rise of farming and pottery-making in the south, if it can be dated as coeval with the Peruvian Formative, is stylistically apart from anything such as Chavín.

Eastward into lowland South America it is possible that there are horizon style phenomena, although these have not yet been plotted in space or time. Nordenskiöld's (1913) excavations in the Mojos of Bolivia revealed ceramics in his later periods which bear a certain style resemblance to lower Amazonian painted types. Also, within the Venezuelan–West Indian broad-lined incised tradition there seem to be stylistic divisions which may mark wide geographical time periods. As yet, between Andes and lowland there is scant stylistic cross-referencing. Vague connections exist between the earlier period ceramics of the Bolivian Mojos and the Bolivian altiplano (Bennett, 1936). East from the Peruvian and Ecuadorian Andes, Tello has claimed Chavín similarities, but these claims pass far beyond recognized limits of stylistic comparisons. Northward, in the Colombian inter-Andean valleys are the most likely prospects for Andean-Orinocan-Amazonian stylistic diffusions. Such styles as the urn burials of the Mosquito region (Bennett, 1946) have lowland parallels.

To sum up, the tracing of specific art styles from one major area, or area co-tradition, to another has not proved possible in the Americas. The almost unquestionable basic relationships that once existed between Middle and South America or Middle America and the areas of the southwestern and southeastern United States will have to be plotted by other types of diffusionist evidence. Stimulus diffusion, the spread of technologies and of specific techniques and technical treatments, will probably be the basis for such studies. Admittedly, this is more tenuous evidence than the comparisons of styles or the identification of specific trade items; but interareal historical reconstruction will not be advanced without continued application to these problems.

DEVELOPMENTAL LEVELS

In recent years the old idea of developmental parallelism has been seriously re-examined by American archeologists and culture historians. This hypothesis has been applied to central Andean archeological data (Bennett, 1948; Larco Hoyle, 1948; Strong, 1948; Willey, 1948; Bennett and Bird, 1949). Middle American data (Armillas, 1948), interarea New World comparisons (Steward, 1947; Willey, 1950; Strong, 1951), and even world-wide comparative evaluations (Steward, 1949). Interpretations have varied somewhat, both in the selections and alignments of data and in the emphasis given to deductions of causality. All, however, have dealt principally with the rise and growth of sedentary agricultural communities, with the subsequent technological developments within these, and with the religious and sociopolitical developments known or implied from the data.

In both Central Andean and Middle American areas these developmental formulations are based upon an initial formational or "Formative" stage, in which the sedentary arts were promulgated and developed toward specialization. This initial formational stage was succeeded by a stage of relative cultural crystallization and rigor in which diverse regional specializations expressed themselves in well-defined styles. As such, this second stage was a flowering of the technical and inventive potential of the first stage and has been called the "Classic" or "Florescent." The third major stage is more difficult to define than the others, as the common-denominator qualities are more difficult to abstract. There is also an interesting shift in criteria for this final stage. Whereas the criteria for the first two recapitulate technological and artistic trends, the third stage is not essentially characterized by these factors. In some regions there is an apparent aesthetic decline, although this is a subjective impression difficult to measure. Certainly, there is no technical falling-off, and in some places, such as the central Andes, there are continued technological advances. The single unifying characteristic of the final stage is, rather, the evidence for widespread social, political and religious disturbances. Classic styles disappear, great classic sites of presumed politicoreligious importance are abandoned, some being destroyed, and large-scale migrations of people take place. It is, of course, possible that the archeologist has been overinfluenced by a knowledge of history or legendary history for this final stage. In both Peru and Mexico it seems to have been encompassed in the terminal 500 years antedating the Spanish, and various native accounts from both areas tell of wars of conquest and general turmoil. These accounts are, to a large extent, supported by archeological evidences of military establishments, fortified strongholds, and the like, all of which seem to be more common to the later Peruvian and Mexican periods. Terms such as "Expansionist" or "Militaristic" have, accordingly, been applied to the third major stage.

There has been a strong tendency to equate these developmental stages not only functionally but chronologically. This has been evidenced both within a co-traditional area, such as the central Andes, and in extending the stages from one major co-traditional area to another. As a tentative device, this sort of developmental chronological chart (see Willey, 1948, 1950; Bennett and Bird, 1949) is permissible where absolute dating factors give no clues as to synchronization. It is not, however, likely that developmental stage lines will ultimately be demonstrated to be chronological horizon lines. Within the central Andean area, for example, it is most unlikely that the qualities or traits which mark the advent of the Classic or Expansionist stages will be found to have occurred simultaneously throughout all coastal and highland regions. The same is true for Middle America, and that there should have been synchronization, or even near-synchronization, between Middle America and Peru in the attainment of these levels or stages is even more dubious. This kind of synchronization, even though it has been projected on a most schematic and trial basis, has given a sort of spurious uniformity to the developmental levels in American high cultures and has aroused skepticism toward the whole construct.

The problem of chronological equations as it pertains to the theory of developmental levels leads us directly back to the matter of diffusion. Are the stage parallelisms which some of us have seen as existent between Middle and South America the result of diffusion or developmental uniformity? I do not believe that the question can be posed this simply, for it seems evident that both forces have been operative. Within either of these co-traditional areas it appears quite certain that diffusion from region to region has taken place but that such diffusions have by no means been uniform outpourings which have spread in evenly distributed waves over the whole area. For example, in Peru, the Mochica ceramic style embraces five or six north-coast valleys. In contrast, the idea of constructing large pyramids of adobe is found throughout the north coast, is well established on the central coast, and at least makes an appearance on the northern boundary of the south coast. On the basis of present knowledge, these two complexes—Mochica art and adobe pyramid mound-building—probably diffused at about the same time; yet their patterns of dispersal are

quite different. Certain forces which permitted, or encouraged, the spread of one inhibited the other. The nature of these forces leads us into an interpretative functional analysis of prehistoric Peruvian societies and their environments, obviously a complex problem. With reference to the developmental and diffusionist question, the point here is that the potentialities of cultural development in any given region are not only conditioned by but also condition diffusion. These potentialities are a complex of natural, social, and cultural endowments. The understanding of their interaction is the ambitious goal of the functional or processual problems which the archeologist sets for himself. But even at our present stage of understanding it appears quite evident that developmental potentialities and the diffusion of ideas are closely interrelated. Certainly, metallurgical techniques, as known in the Andes and in Middle America, have a related history. Their acceptance, rejection, emphasis, or de-emphasis from region to region or major area to area depended upon the varying complex potentialities of peoples, cultures, and natural environment. In a vastly more intricate manner the development, spread, and success or failure of such institutions as kingship or empire were dependent upon what happened when the receiving base was fertilized or stimulated by the transient idea.

As we have discussed above, there is a far-flung distribution of certain elements and technologies which are formational to the American Neolithic-type cultures. The similarity of these elements and technologies and their geographic occurrences make it most likely that they have a common heritage. These diffused elements provided the base for the American agricultural civilizations and, in so doing, set certain wide limits for later cultural growth. These cultural foci of this

"Formative" stage must have had opened before them a number of possible courses for development. The directions which these foci took in their growth were selected from the potentialities which each possessed and from the ideas which each generated and transmitted to others.

FUNCTIONAL RECONSTRUCTIONS

It was specifically indicated in our discussion of methodology that the functional objectives of archeology cannot be divorced from the historical ones. Further, in our review and commentary on reconstructions in American prehistory it has been implicit that a greater functional appreciation of the phenomena involved would lead to clearer understanding of what are generally considered historical relationships. It is thus difficult to select certain archeological interpretations and label them as "functional" or "processual," as opposed to diffusionist or developmental reconstructions. In reviewing such selections the close integration of chronicle and process must be borne in mind.

In making functional interpretations of archeological data there are several lines of evidence or means of approach. Some of these are listed in the methodological Table 1.

There is, first, the use interpretation of an artifact or feature. In some instances this can be done by way of general analogy. A pointed flint with an obvious haft is interpreted as a projectile. Or, in other cases, a metate and mano are explained as corn-grinding instruments by analogy with modern use within certain ethnic areas. Sometimes historic documentation gives the lead, as with the disklike stones in southeastern archeology and early accounts of their use in the "chunkee" game. The limitations of the approach are clear. Many archeological objects or features will probably never be properly explained from a functional standpoint. Beyond the obvious and beyond the specific ethnic or ethnohistoric analogy, there is only the sheerest speculation.

The archeological assemblage can be functionally explained in a manner similar to that applied to the artifact. With the assemblage, of course, the archeologist begins to bridge over into the complexities of the space and time factors. The dimensions of space and time can be correlated with and used to help explain changes in artifacts, features, and assemblages.

A third approach utilizes quantitative factors. The numbers of archeological remains, such as the numbers and sizes of sites, can be used to estimate populations and the disposition of populations. With such an approach a control of the chronological factor is a necessity.

A fourth line of evidence is the correlation of space and time distributions of remains with natural environmental types. In the American field there are numerous examples of this. Rouse's study of culture units centering upon West Indian sea passages rather than islands comes to mind. Such a correlation was strong testimony for sea transport and a marine rather than a land orientation (Rouse, 1951).

A fifth approach combines two or more of those listed and presents a rising complexity of interrelated interpretations. It is on this basis that most archeological interpretation with a strong functional bias has been carried out. Examples of such interpretations are actually more numerous than American archeologists realize. The majority of them are imbedded in "standard" (i.e., historically oriented) monographs on archeology. Others are parts of general cultural-historical reconstructions. Some few have been presented primarily as attempts at functional analysis. A brilliant example of functional explanation of archeological data is offered from the North American Plains. Here the archeologist operated with artifact types and artifact assemblages from pre- and post-Columbian times. With the chronological dimension properly in control, it was obvious that certain profound changes had taken place in Plains Indian culture between the pre- and the post-1540 date line. These changes were seen in material culture, but the implications in changes in house and community types as well as artifacts reflected important sociopolitical changes. Added to this was a fairly rich documentation from the late historic period which filled out the picture of Indian life in this area in the late nineteenth century. From these known referents—artifact and assemblage types, chronology, and ethnic documentation—the archeologists and ethnologists were able to explain much of what took place in culture change as the result of the impact of significant technological innovations brought by the Europeans (i.e., horses and guns) (see Wissler, 1914; Strong, 1933, 1940).

In a similar way, but with less specific ethnic documentation, archeologists in the eastern United States have been able to outline events surrounding the introduction of intensive agriculture into this area. To begin with, there is some documentation for the nature of eastern culture in its final post-Columbian periods. This documentation indicates a rich agricultural ceremonialism in certain southern regions and also shows this ceremonialism to have been associated with a mound-plaza, community-center complex. It is further known that the mound-plaza complex is an integral part of the ceremonial, social, and political life of the agricultural civilizations of Middle America. The similarity of this mound-plaza complex between eastern North America and Middle America suggests a historical relationship, and this relationship is further supported by other archeological evidence linking these two major areas. Because of the great chronological depth and elaboration of the mound-plaza complex in Middle American cultures, it is assumed that this is the parent-area for the idea, at least as far as the eastern United States is concerned. With these facts and hypotheses in mind, it is noted that the mound-plaza complex is not known throughout the full range of eastern chronology but appears for the first time somewhere in middle-to-late sequence. With this appearance there is a number of significant changes in eastern society and culture as revealed by archeology. There is a greater utilization of riverine terrace country, there are more and much larger archeological sites, and, finally, there are more frequent finds of maize remains. These the archeologist relates to a specific new and important change in food economy. All these link back with the assumed correlation of the mound-plaza complex with intensive agriculture. Corollary evidence for such a change is seen in a decrease in hunting fetishes (animal teeth, claws, and representations of these) with the rise of the mound-plaza complex. Parallel changes in eastern culture are reflected in a different burial pattern, new pottery styles, and new house types. The functional interrelationship of these with intensive horticulture, if such existed, is obscure; but, like the mound-plaza complex, they may be part of a historical association. In this particular example the archeologist has first established, by ethnic documentation and comparisons to another area, the firm association of an archeological feature (the mound-plaza) with an agricultural way of life. Then, by placing the introduction of this feature in the chronological sequence of eastern native cultures, he has been able to support his association by correlative evidence of a functional type (i.e., increased population, large centers, etc.).

One of the most interesting Americanist problems in functional interpretation has revolved around prehistoric urbanization. Middle American archeologists have posed the question as to what are the factors leading to or promoting urbanization. In this investigation urbanization has been defined as the permanent concentration of large nonfood-producing populations. A review of Middle American data seems to indicate, at the present state of knowledge, that such true cities or urban areas were best known from the late prehistoric periods and from upland country. The valley of Mexico is offered as a classic example, and Tenochtitlan, the Aztec capital, was most surely such an urbanized city. As opposed to this, the earlier Middle American periods and the lowlands seemingly lack evidence of a comparable urbanization. The functional explanations offered for this dichotomy and the important exceptions to it are that large concentrations of nonfood-producers are possible only with intensive food production by others and with relatively rapid food transport. The valley of Mexico apparently met both these conditions. *Chinampa,* or floating-garden farming, is fabulously productive, and water transportation in the lakes in which the Chinampas were located afforded rapid dispersal of produce. To substantiate this case, the archeologists favoring this interpretation point to the multiroomed, closely packed, compartmented dwelling compounds at Teotihuacan as being indicative of early (*ca.* A.D. 500) beginnings of urbanism in the favorable Mexican uplands. The lowland picture seems to be quite different. In the Maya and Olmec areas impressive ceremonial sites were constructed, but mass dwelling concentrations were, presumably, prohibited by the limitations of tropical forest agriculture and transportation difficulties. Urbanism in the lowlands, in the framework of this general interpretation, is looked upon as a very late and politically forced phenomenon. Mayapan is the type-site for such a development in the Maya region. Here a walled, urban concentration is viewed as the result of Mexican influence and conquest, together with a period of local troubles and fighting, leading to more compact living than the environmental potentialities could sustain. Late-period urbanization on the lowland Veracruz coast is thought to have been made possible at Cempoala by artificial irrigation.

This fascinating hypothesis has not met with general acceptance. Perhaps greatest of all difficulties is the lack of adequate settlement study throughout most of Middle America, particularly in the lowlands. Incoming data may require drastic revisions in, or demand the rejection of, these theories; but it is most significant, I think, that the problem of urbanization and its causes can be raised in New World archeology. That such a problem has been framed as a research theme marks a great advance in Americanist studies.

A somewhat different approach from those cited is one which I attempted with Andean data (Willey, 1948). Here the problem lead was in the detail of the data. The particular phenomena in question were the horizon styles, the Peruvian-wide distributions of certain art forms at certain times, and the complete absence of such horizon styles at other times. What were the causative factors behind these diffusions or absences of diffusions? In my attempt to answer this question I projected the various horizon styles against the backgrounds of what could be reconstructed of Peruvian society at the respective time periods involved. These backgrounds could be developed only in the most general terms, such as "warlike," "absence of warfare," "small populations," "expanding populations," etc. Nevertheless, these backgrounds, taken in conjunction with the content of the styles themselves, afforded a basis for a number of reasonable conjectures. Most of these conclusions may never go beyond the conjectural stage because of the limitations of the data. For example, Chavín art is depicted as a horizon style which spread in an era of relative peace. Such a condition immediately sets bounds for the mechanisms by which the style could have spread. For identifying this period as a peaceful one, we have only the absences of fortifications or fortified sites, of abundant weapons, of warlike representations in art, and a knowledge that

population groups were relatively small and isolated from one another. This is not absolute proof of nonmilitaristic society, but, in the absence of evidence to the contrary and until such evidence is forthcoming, I think it justifiable to reconstruct on such a foundation.

The examples I have used are only a few from American archeology, selected largely because they are the ones which I know best. I can only mention the work that has been done on the reconstruction of southwestern social organization from a combination of archeological and ethnological data (Strong, 1927; Steward, 1937; and Martin and Rinaldo, 1950), on Arctic economy (Larsen and Rainey, 1948), and numerous other examples dotted over the American continents.

REFERENCES

ARMILLAS, PEDRO. 1948. "A Sequence of Cultural Development in Meso-America." In BENNETT, WENDELL C. (ed.), *A Reappraisal of Peruvian Archaeology*, pp. 105–11. ("Memoirs of the Society for American Archaeology," Vol. XIII, No. 4.)

BENNETT, WENDELL C. 1936. *Excavations in Bolivia*. ("Anthropological Papers of the American Museum of Natural History," Vol. XXXV, Part IV.)

———. 1946. "The Archaeology of Colombia." In STEWARD, JULIAN (ed.), *Handbook of South American Indians*, II, 823–50. (Bureau of American Ethnology Bull. 143.) Washington, D.C.

———. 1948. "The Peruvian Co-tradition." In BENNETT, WENDELL C. (ed.), *A Reappraisal of Peruvian Archaeology*, pp. 1–7. ("Memoirs of the Society for American Archaeology," Vol. XIII, No. 4.)

BENNETT, W. C., and BIRD, JUNIUS B. 1949. *Andean Culture History*. ("American Museum of Natural History Handbook Series," No. 15.)

BRAINERD, G. W. 1951. "The Place of Chronological Ordering in Archaeological Analysis," *American Antiquity*, XVI, 301–13.

COLTON, H. S. 1939. *Prehistoric Culture Units and Their Relationships in Northern Arizona*. (Museum of Northern Arizona Bull. 17.)

DRUCKER, P. 1943. *Ceramic Sequences at Tres Zapotes, Veracruz, Mexico*. (Bureau of American Ethnology Bull. 140.) Washington, D.C.

FORD, J. A. 1949. *Cultural Dating of Prehistoric Sites in Virú Valley, Peru*. ("Anthropological Papers of the American Museum of Natural History," Vol. XLIII, Part I.)

———. 1951. *Greenhouse: A Troyville–Coles Creek Period Site in Avoyelles Parish, Louisiana*. ("Anthropological Papers of the American Museum of Natural History," Vol. XLIV, Part I.)

GLADWIN, W. and H. S. 1934. *A Method for the Designation of Cultures and Their Variations*. ("Medallion Papers," No. 15.) Globe, Ariz.

HOLMES, W. H. 1903. *Aboriginal Pottery of the Eastern United States*. (20th Annual Report of the Bureau of American Ethnology.) Washington, D.C.

KIDDER, A. V. 1924. *An Introduction to Southwestern Archaeology*. Andover, Mass.: R. S. Peabody Foundation.

KIRCHHOFF, P. 1943. "Mesoamerica," *Acta Americana,* I, No. 1, 92 ff.

KRIEGER, A. D. 1944. "The Typological Concept," *American Antiquity,* IX, 271–88.

——. 1945. "An Inquiry into Supposed Mexican Influences on a Prehistoric 'Cult' in the Southern United States," *American Anthropology,* XLVII, 483–515.

KROEBER, A. L. 1918. *Zuñi Potsherds.* ("Anthropological Papers of the American Museum of Natural History," Vol. XVIII, Part IV.)

——. 1931. "The Culture Area and Age Area Concepts of Clark Wissler." In RICE, S. (ed.), *Methods in Social Science.* Chicago.

——. 1940. "Stimulus Diffusion," *American Anthropology,* XLII, 1–20.

——. 1944. *Peruvian Archaeology in 1942.* ("Viking Fund Publications in Anthropology," No. 4.)

LARCO HOYLE, RAFAEL. 1948. *Cronología arqueológica del norte del Peru.* Buenos Aires.

LARSEN, HELGE, and RAINEY, F. 1948. *Ipiutak and the Arctic Whale Hunting Culture.* ("Anthropological Papers of the American Museum of Natural History," Vol. XLII.)

MCKERN, W. C. 1939. "The Midwestern Taxonomic Method as an Aid to Archaeological Culture Study," *American Antiquity,* IV, 301–13.

MARTIN, P. S., and RINALDO, J. B. 1950. *Sites of the Reserve Phase, Pine Lawn Valley, Western New Mexico.* ("Fieldiana: Anthropology," Vol. XXXVIII, No. 3.)

——. 1951. "The Southwestern Co-tradition," *Southwestern Journal of Anthropology,* VII, 215–29.

NELSON, N. C. 1916. "Chronology of the Tano Ruins, New Mexico," *American Anthropology,* XVIII, 159–80.

NORDENSKIÖLD, E. VON. 1913. "Urnengräber und Mounds in bolivianischen Flachlände," *Baessler Archiv,* III, 205–55.

PHILLIPS, P.; FORD, J. A.; and GRIFFIN, J. B. 1951. *Archaeological Survey in the Lower Mississippi Alluvial Valley, 1940–47.* ("Papers of the Peabody Museum, Harvard University," Vol. XXV.)

ROUSE, IRVING. 1939. *Prehistory in Haiti: A Study in Method.* ("Yale University Publications in Anthropology," No. 21.)

——. 1951. "Areas and Periods of Culture in the Greater Antilles," *Southwestern Journal of Anthropology,* VII, 248–65.

SPIER, L. 1919. *An Outline for a Chronology of Zuñi Ruins.* ("Anthropological Papers of the American Museum of Natural History," Vol. XVIII, Part III.)

SPINDEN, H. J. 1917. "The Origin and Distribution of Agriculture in America," *Proceedings of the XIXth International Congress of Americanists, Washington, 1915,* pp. 269–76.

STEWARD, J. H. 1937. "Ecological Aspects of Southwestern Society," *Anthropos,* XXXII, 87–104.

——. 1947. "American Culture History in the Light of South America," *Southwestern Journal of Anthropology,* III, 85–107.

——. 1948. "A Functional-Developmental Classification of American High Cultures," *American Antiquity,* XIII, No. 4, 103–4.

——. 1949. "Cultural Causality and Law: A Trial Formulation of the Development of Early Civilizations," *American Anthropology,* LI, 1–27.

STRONG, W. D. 1927. "An Analysis of Southwestern Society," *American Anthropology,* XXIX, 1 ff.

——. 1933. "Plains Culture Area in the Light of Archaeology," *ibid.,* XXXV, 271–87.

——. 1935. *An Introduction to Nebraska Archaeology.* ("Smithsonian Miscellaneous Collections," Vol. XCIII, No. 10.)

——. 1940. *From History to Prehistory in the Northern Great Plains,* pp. 353–94. ("Smithsonian Miscellaneous Collections," Vol. C.)

——. 1948. "Cultural Epochs and Refuse Heap Stratigraphy in Peruvian Archaeology." In BENNETT, WENDELL C. (ed.), *A Reappraisal of Peruvian Archaeology,* pp. 93–102. ("Memoirs of the Society for American Archaeology," Vol. XIII, Part II.)

——. 1951. "Cultural Resemblances in Nuclear America: Parallelism or Diffusion?" In TAX, SOL (ed.), *Selected Papers of the XXIXth International Con-*

gress of Americanists, pp. 271–79. Chicago: University of Chicago Press.

TAYLOR, W. W., JR. 1948. "A Study of Archaeology," *American Anthropologist*, L, No. 3, 223–56.

UHLE, M. 1903. *Pachacamac*. Philadelphia.

WARING, A. J., JR., and HOLDER, P. 1945. "A Prehistoric Ceremonial Complex in the Southeastern United States," *American Anthropology*, XLVII, 1–34.

WEDEL, W. R. 1936. *An Introduction to Pawnee Archaeology*. (Bureau of American Ethnology Bull. 112.) Washington, D.C.

WILLEY, GORDON R. 1945. "Horizon Styles and Pottery Traditions in Peruvian Archaeology," *American Antiquity*, XI, 49–56.

——. 1948. "Functional Analysis of 'Horizon Styles' in Peruvian Archaeology," *ibid.*, XIII, No. 4, 8–15.

——. 1949. *Archaeology of the Florida Gulf Coast*. ("Smithsonian Miscellaneous Collections," Vol. CXIII.)

——. 1950. "Growth Trends in New World Cultures." In *For the Dean: Anniversary Volume for Byron Cummings*. Santa Fe: Southwestern Monuments Assoc.

WISSLER, C. 1914. "Influence of the Horse in the Development of Plains Culture," *American Anthropology*, XVI, 1–25.

——. 1926. *The Relation of Nature to Man in Aboriginal America*. New York and London: Oxford University Press.

New World Culture History: South America

By WENDELL C. BENNETT

THE PURPOSE of this paper is to present a summary and analysis of the anthropological approaches to the broad subject of culture history as exemplified by studies done on South American materials. The review does not pretend to give proper consideration to the status of field research in South America, since, with the exception of archeological studies directed exclusively at establishing chronology, most field work is not primarily concerned with culture history. In like fashion, many other interesting and significant studies have been eliminated or but briefly mentioned, since they are not directly pertinent to the major topic. In general, all studies of culture history involve reconstruction on a large scale, covering the whole continent or perhaps the whole hemisphere. The significance of these reconstructions and the interpretations based on them depend heavily on the reliability of the available data, whether these be from archeology, ethnology, linguistics, or museum collections. Consequently, a brief review of the general status of anthropological research in South America is basic for the discussion of these approaches.

STATUS

The six volumes of the *Handbook of South American Indians*, published as Bulletin 143 of the Bureau of American Ethnology (1946–50), under the editorship of Julian H. Steward, provides an excellent summary of what is now known about South American Indians. The *Handbook* covers archeology, ethnology, linguistics, cultural geography, and physical anthropology and presents the findings from both a regional and a topical point of view. The *Handbook*, with its accompanying Bibliography, is obviously an excellent source book, but it also includes a great many original studies and new interpretations.

The annual *Handbook of Latin American Studies* (originally published by the Harvard University Press, now by the University of Florida Press) covers both current bibliography and recent field work for South America. Consequently, a combination of the *Handbook of South American Indians* and the *Handbook of Latin American Studies* provides an up-to-date review of the status of anthropological research in South America. The over-all bibliography is enormous, and the quantity of field research is impressive. Nonetheless, considering the size of the South American continent and the cultural complexity presented, it is quite obvious that significant research is still in its infancy. Only a fraction of the field workers have been professionally trained scholars, and many of the pub-

195

lished accounts are little more than casual by-products from travelers and local residents.

The paucity of research in the major brances of anthropology can be briefly illustrated. For example, intensive archeological investigations have been largely limited to certain sections of Peru and northwestern Argentina. Elsewhere, archeological information is spotty and excavation intermittent. In linguistics the situation is far worse. South American Indian languages are noted for their diversity, but, in spite of this, there is as yet no modern, scientific grammar for any language and but few grammars of any kind. The review of physical anthropology, in Volume VI of the *Handbook of South American Indians*, is based on forty-three series for undeformed prehistoric skulls; eighty-eight series for contemporary tribes, with the measurements largely limited to stature and cephalic index; and only forty series for blood typing. The ethnology of southern South America, the Chaco, and East Brazil is reasonably well known, but for the rest of the continent there are only a few full-length monographs. Serious study of the numerous contemporary Indians of the Andes has only been initiated in the past decade. The same is true for other studies in the general field of social anthropology, such as community study, culture and personality, and analysis of non-Indian cultures.

Even this brief review of the status of anthropological research in South America shows clearly that much remains to be done. Here is a vast and complex area awaiting new investigation in every branch of anthropology, and it is encouraging to note that, since the war, renewed efforts are being made by scholars from many parts of the world. The studies of culture history are not limited to field research monographs, but one would feel more confident of reconstruction of history if field data were more adequate.

CULTURE HISTORY

The major approaches developed for the study of culture history are by no means identified with the South American field, and, in fact, many of the ones which are reviewed here could be equally well, if not better, illustrated for other parts of the world. However, there has long been a great interest in the culture history of South America and a considerable body of literature on the subject. This reflects, in part, the scattered nature of the sources, which can best be organized in terms of their distributional patterns. It is perhaps also due to the gross geographical isolation of the South American continent, which makes the study of its cultural growth appear to be comparatively simple. Although no one totally discounts the possibility of trans-Pacific influences, the principal migration route into South America is considered to be through the narrow Isthmus of Panama. Consequently, the reconstructions of South American culture history involve only two basic problems, namely, the relationship with North America through this narrow passage and the independent developments within the continent.

For the purposes of this review, the principal approaches used in the study of South American culture history have been arranged into a few major categories. This is in part artificial, since some approaches fall into more than one category. However, it serves to unite the contributions of the various subdivisions of anthropology, rather than having each discussed separately. Furthermore, it is hoped that this arrangement will allow comparison of the approaches used for South American culture history with work done in other parts of the world and will also permit discussion of the comparative merits of the different approaches.

DISTRIBUTIONAL STUDIES

The tracing and plotting of the distribution of culture elements or patterns, in terms of a large area, is a basic technique in the study of culture history. Distributional studies have been particularly favored for South America, since they can be based on many types of sources, including, naturally, the extensive museum collections. The study of distributions is the principal basis for the following culture-history approaches.

1. CULTURE-AREA APPROACH

The regional distributions of culture features is basic to the establishment of culture areas. Most students recognize several cultural-geographic divisions of the South American continent, based on the major environmental zones, and there has been a number of detailed classifications of all tribal cultures into cultural areas. The results range from a simple threefold division (southern hunters, tropical forest agriculturists, sedentary Andean farmers) to the twenty-four culture areas recently proposed by Murdock (1951). The culture-area approach is well known and needs little elaboration here. It is essentially a classificatory device useful in ordering the immense range of ethnographic variations. The resulting classifications vary in terms of the basic criteria utilized. Material culture has frequently been emphasized, since it is so suitable for museum study. Murdock (1951) has established a set of nine basic criteria which he considers to be of the greatest significance. All these are positive, observable features, since he objects to the use of negative criteria, that is, the absence of certain features. The first four volumes of the *Handbook of South American Indians* correspond to four major areas, namely, the marginal tribes, tropical forest tribes, Circum-Caribbean tribes, and the Andean civilizations. This regional arrangement was in part a convenience, although it is defended as a valid classificatory cultural device. In Volume V of the *Handbook,* Julian Steward outlines a new classification of culture areas based on sociopolitical patterns. He insists that this does not correspond at all to one based on culture elements, although the actual rearrangement of allocations of cultures is not great. There have been some attempts to classify archeological materials into culture areas, although without great success. Recently the culture-area approach has been applied to contemporary Brazil and other countries.

Fundamentally, a culture-area classification is horizontal, that is, on one time level, and is not in itself a study of culture history. However, historical interpretations inevitably creep in to explain the formation of culture areas. Likewise, one area, like that of the southern hunters, is likely to be interpreted as representing a cultural manifestation earlier than another—for example, the sedentary Andean farmers. However, while such sequences are tempting, their establishment must depend on other criteria.

2. CO-TRADITION APPROACH

The use of the culture-area classification for the archeological materials of South America would require a well-established relative chronology for the whole continent. In other words, it would be improper to use a horizontal time classification for materials known or suspected to be of different periods. In limited regions like the Central Andes, where chronological sequences are reasonably well established, the culture-area approach can be used for specific time periods. When the archeological cultures of the Central Andes are seen to form culture areas at each successive time period, a new phenomenon is presented, namely, a culture area with time depth. The term "area co-tradition" has been used for this over-all history of an area in which the component cultures have been interrelated over a period of time (Bennett, 1948). The area co-tradition approach assumes cultural continuity within the region and mutual influence of the component cultures both in space and in time. It is felt that the isolation of such cultural time blocks will be useful for comparative purposes. Thus far, only two area co-traditions have been described for South America, namely, for the Central Andes and for northwestern Argentina. Elsewhere, a Mesoamerican co-tradition has been roughly outlined, and Martin and Rinaldo (1951) have described a southwestern United States co-tradition. Thus far, no application has been made of the approach outside the Western Hemisphere.

3. KULTURKREIS APPROACH

The cultural-historical distributional studies, developed originally for Southeast Asia and Oceania, have been extended to the Western Hemisphere and South America. American scholars have generally hesitated to accept interpretation of New World phenomena based on Old World data. However, in spite of their hesitancy, American scholars have made quite similar distributional studies, using their own criteria.

4. AGE-AREA APPROACH

The determination of the age of an element from the extent of its distribution has found frequent application in the South American studies. Some of these have dealt with the whole Western Hemisphere, noting, for example, elements which occur both in southern South America and in northern North America and attributing to them appropriate implications of great antiquity. The pitfalls of interpreting time from distribution of isolated elements have been pointed out many times. Under proper controls, the technique is useful, but the dangers are many. Steward, for example, accepts the merits of age-area interpretation for culture elements and patterns but denies its usefulness for sociopolitical units, since, he argues, these are affected by ecological adaptation to local environments. The same adaptation might well affect all elements.

5. NORDENSKIÖLD APPROACH

The type of distributional study developed by Nordenskiöld and his followers is well known in the South American field. Nordenskiöld (1919) used distributional analysis in order to interpret the culture history of a particular group. For example, he concentrated on two Chaco tribes and made distribution maps of the South American occurrences of the elements of their material culture. In his analysis, he first stripped off those elements which could be attributed to European introduction. He next examined the elements which had an essentially Andean distribution and interpreted these in terms of known Andean sequences. The elements with an Amazonian distribution were then examined. He also noted the characteristic Amazonian traits which were not found in the Chaco. The residue of elements still unaccounted for by the above examination were analyzed as being ancient culture elements, local developments, or from Patagonia to the south. These distributional studies, therefore, did not lead to generalization about the culture history of South America but rather to the analysis of the specific culture history of the two Chaco tribes.

6. COOPER APPROACH

The Cooper distribution studies differ from Nordenskiöld's, in that they are applied to a region rather than to specific tribes and in that time periods are utilized where possible. For example, Cooper (1925) dealt with the whole southern South American area. His analysis covered the material and other cultural elements of every tribe in the region. He examined the evidence for time periods and proposed a modern period; a post-horse period, from accounts following the year 1741; a first contact period, from accounts antedating the year 1670; and an ancient period, based on archeological evidence. Tribe-by-tribe comparisons were made from north to south and east to west for each time period. Those culture traits common to the whole region were generally considered to be ancient. For later periods, historic and archeological drifts were traced. The result is an impressive reconstruction of the culture history of southern South America.

7. LINGUISTIC APPROACH

The known correspondence of language and culture lends considerable support to the reconstruction of culture history on the basis of linguistic relationships and distributions. For the South American field, this approach has thus far had limited significance because of the unbelievable diversity of languages, the unreliability of the data, and the lack of good linguistic classifications. In spite of these handicaps, numerous attempts to interpret the language distribution picture have been made. A common approach is one of establishing the supposed centers of origin of certain of the major linguistic stocks, such as Carib and Arawak, and then tracing the distribution of these languages in migration terms. The cluster of independent language stocks found along the eastern margin of the Andes has frequently led to the hypothesis that this region was a refuge area for earlier peoples. Some detailed studies have been made of the known historic distributions of the Tupi-Guaraní and Quechua languages and their correspondences with political expansion and missionary activity. For the Gê linguistic stock in East Brazil, the close correlation of region, language, and culture has been considered as evidence of long local residence. Some have thought that the great diversity of languages in South America implies great antiquity, although this is based on the unproved assumption that the diversification took place in that continent. Others have thought that South America, because of its geographical position, should preserve languages of the earliest migrants into the Western Hemisphere, but as yet there is no supporting evidence for this thesis. On the contrary, known evidence thus far, for the Chibcha, Arawak, and Carib languages, suggests a south-to-north migration rather than the reverse.

8. PHYSICAL-ANTHROPOLOGICAL APPROACH

The distribution of physical types of man should have historical implications. The summary of physical distributional data in Volume VI of the *Handbook* shows some regional correspondences, but the evidence is too scanty for sound interpretations. The same is true of the studies of blood groups, which suggest several successive migrations of small numbers of persons into South America but without being very specific as yet. There is also a dearth of information on sequences of physical types. In spite of a hundred years of collecting and laboratory research, there is as yet no incontestable evidence of the great antiquity of fossil man in South America, nor are there well-established sequences which can be used for broad historical interpretations.

Most of the distributional studies deal with certain general concepts which need some critical examination. One common and fundamental concept is the influence of environment on distribution. Different scholars illustrate the total range of possibilities from one extreme, which attributes no importance to the environment, to the other, which virtually calls for environmental determinalism. However, the great contrast in the South American environmental zones, from tropics to deserts and from plains to extremely high altitudes, must certainly be considered to some extent in all distributional studies.

In the culture-area classifications, for example, some lump all tropical forest cultures together, largely because the emphasis is placed on the techniques necessary to maintain life in the heavy tropics. On the other hand, Murdock (1951), using his multiple set of positive criteria, subdivides the Amazon region into a dozen culture areas. Few students have failed to be impressed by the striking contrasts between the high-altitude basins of the Andes and the desert Pacific coast of Peru, on the one hand, and the tropical forest plains of Amazonia, on the other. The possibility of distributions from west to east is virtually ignored, not on the basis of known evidence but on the presumption that the contrasting environments would make them illogical. However, one of the most interesting developments in the Central Andean archeological field is the recognition of the close cultural relationships of the highland and coastal areas. In fact, it is now argued that there is closer cultural affiliation between a highland basin and the adjacent Pacific coastal valleys than between two separated highland basins. At the same time, Monge (1948) and his colleagues are studying the biological adaptations which are needed for maintaining life in extremely high altitudes and are implying that these are of a magnitude sufficient to prevent free migration and settlement between coast and highland regions.

It is clear that the environmental factors need more careful consideration in all distribution and migration studies. This is true for the study both of material and of nonmaterial elements and patterns. Steward in Volume V of the *Handbook* argues that his sociopolitical units depend in large part on the population density of a given region, which, in turn, is affected by the success of the subsistence activities in the particular environment. On the other hand, care must be used not to attribute our own reactions to environmental contrast to other people. The Andean mountains present innumerable barriers for modern transportation systems, but for pre-Columbian Indians, who traveled essentially on foot, mountains are of little concern.

Survival and loss of culture elements are two related concepts which are commonly employed in the interpretation of distributions. The comparison of southern South America and northern North America is based on the assumption that elements of an ancient cultural stratum have survived in both these areas (Krickeberg, 1934). For southern Patagonia, stratified archeological deposits show that an essentially similar hunting pattern survived from ancient times up to the historic; but in most parts of the New World survival is an unproved assumption. Likewise, when elements have broken distributions, the concept of loss is frequently invoked as an explanation. Both concepts need more rigorous analysis. As now used, survival and loss are treated as simple factors without any consideration given to the possibility of element substitution, modification, or replacement. Distribution analysis needs refinement in terms of our advanced knowledge of the process of culture change.

Migration and diffusion are generally considered to be the two principal mechanisms of distribution, but there is a definite preference for migration in the South American studies. This is doubtless inspired by the geographical position of the South American continent, with its single land-bridge connection with North America. Since the original population is assumed to have come overland from the north, perforce as migrants, the subsequent movements and distributions are likewise attributed to migration. This, in turn, has fostered the view that mobility is a continuing characteristic of the South American Indians. The *Handbook of South American Indians* illustrates the culture history of South America with maps, on which arrows show significant migrations. In general, people are conceived as moving up and down the Andes, wandering widely on the plains of Patagonia, and utilizing the network of rivers in Amazonia for wide-scale travel. Although it is self-evident that migrations must have taken place in the original populating of the South American continent, the assumption of continuing mobility needs to be examined. A careful review of greater Amazonia does not show wide dispersal of culture types. Instead, the subcultures are well restricted to specific areas. The archeological work on the northern coast of Peru presents convincing evidence of a population continuum over a long period of time. In brief, there is considerable evidence that diffusion is of equal importance with migration as a mechanism of distribution.

The concept of "marginal" is constantly employed in culture-history study based on distributions and is the one which needs the most critical review. The concept of "marginal" is used in numerous different ways. In some cases it is frankly geographic in terms of continental land mass, namely, southern South America as marginal. Again,

cultures are classed as marginal if they are located beyond the limits of native agriculture. In a related sense, marginal cultures are those on the periphery of centers of higher civilization. In a totally different sense, cultures which retain primitive, that is to say, presumably ancient, features are considered to be marginal wherever located, which leads to such terms as "internal marginal" and "submarginal." One of the extreme abuses of the term defines "marginal" in respect to present-day centers. For example, the mouth of the Amazon, today the gateway of water travel to the interior, is likewise considered to have been a focal center in the past, and thus cultures located at the outermost tributaries, along the eastern margin of the Andes, are called "marginal." It is self-evident that such inconsistent applications of the concept of "marginal" lead to equally inconsistent interpretations of the culture history of the continent.

CHRONOLOGICAL STUDIES

The chronological approach to culture history encompasses those studies directed toward the establishment of absolute or relative sequences in specific sites or areas as a basis for extension of these to cover larger regions. Such studies fall rather naturally into two fields, namely, archeology and history.

1. ARCHEOLOGICAL APPROACH

One of the major emphases in the archeological excavations in South America, particularly on the part of the North American and European field workers, has been the establishment of relative chronologies for specific sites and regions. The techniques employed by the archeologists need no particular elaboration here, since they are the standard ones for the field and since they will be discussed in other papers. The principal techniques have been grave isolation (sequence dating), refuse stratigraphy, surface survey, pit sampling, strip matching, and typological analysis. These devices are used first for excavations of specific sites, and the resulting sequences are then matched to set up a relative chronology for larger areas. In spite of the interest and the amount of field work thus far accomplished, there are scarcely a dozen well-established sequences in all South America, and few of these cover any extensive ranges in time. At the present time, it is not possible to set up even a tentative sequence for over-all South America or, for that matter, for any component country as a whole. Furthermore, the techniques directed toward establishing sequences often provide only limited information on the total cultural content of each period. There is, however, no question that this detailed chronological approach is one of the soundest procedures for establishing a reliable culture history of a region.

The Midwestern Taxonomic System developed by McKern (1939) and others for the numerous unstratified archeological sites in central United States is, like the culture area, primarily a classificatory device rather than a chronological one. To be sure, some students impute a genetic interpretation to the hierarchy of categories which the system employs, but this is unwarranted. Basically, the Midwestern Taxonomic System treats all the material from a given site or level as a component or unit. Components are grouped together as foci on the basis of specific similarities. Larger classificatory compartments, called "aspect," "phase," and "pattern," are based on more limited and more abstract diagnostics. The system can be diagrammed as a series of concentric boxes. Once time sequences can be established with other techniques, the various categories can be rearranged to match. Thus far,

only limited application has been made of this system in South America, specifically in Venezuela and in lowland Argentina. It could profitably be applied to all other regions, since it places the emphasis on the total content of a site, which is parallel to treating cultures as wholes.

2. HISTORICAL APPROACH

In spite of the wealth of historical documents for certain parts of South America, relatively little study has been directed toward the history of Indian culture as opposed to the Spanish. That such studies would be of great importance is amply illustrated by Kubler's article in Volume II of the *Handbook*, which traces the Indian cultures through the colonial and republican periods of Peru. His analysis of the factors which effected changes in the Indian culture during the historical period not only contributes to the process of culture change but also reveals basic trends which can be projected backward to the pre-Spanish periods. The Argentine scholars, among others, have been interested in the identification and location of Indian tribes at the time of first European contact as revealed by historical documents, and this, in turn, has led to an interest in identifying certain archeological sites with historic tribes (Canals Frau, 1940). More work of this kind is needed. It is restricted, unfortunately, because those trained to handle archival records are seldom well versed in archeology, and vice versa. An ideal study, for example, could be made of the Inca period in Peru, based both on the historical accounts and on the archeological remains.

Most reconstructions of culture history proceed from the earliest culture periods to the most recent. The historical materials indicate that the reverse would be important, particularly in areas like the Central Andes, where sizable native populations still exist, historical documents are rich, and archeological remains abundant. For example, the town of Copacabana, on the Bolivian shore of Lake Titicaca, is today an important religious center which attracts Indian pilgrims in great numbers every year. There is historical evidence that such pilgrimage centers were prominent in the days of the Inca empire, at Pachacamac, Peru, and elsewhere. Furthermore, in various periods of the archeological past, large ceremonial sites, like Tiahuanaco in Bolivia and Chavín de Huántar in Peru, seem to have been similar pilgrimage centers. A study of the contemporary compared with the historic would shed considerable light on the interpretation of the past.

BOTANICAL STUDIES

In recent years the interest of the botanists in the domesticated plants of the New World has opened up a new and potentially valuable approach to culture history. The principal findings thus far have been reviewed by Sauer in Volume VI of the *Handbook of South American Indians,* which serves as the source of the comments here presented. The approach might well be called "ethnobotanical culture history," since it involves the technical studies of the botanists, the historical accounts of domesticated plants for different parts of the New World, evidence from archeological sites, study of the importance and integration of domesticated plants in different cultures, and ultimately leads to reconstruction of distributions and migrations.

Much work remains to be done before even a tentatively reliable statement of the results of this approach can be formulated, but some suggestions can be assembled from Sauer's review. Five regional centers of plant domestication loom important in New World prehistory: northern South America (Colombia), Central America (Guate-

mala), the Central Andes (the altiplano), the montaña section on the eastern slopes of the Andes, and tropical Brazil. There is some indication that these centers varied in importance at different time periods, namely, that the northern South American and the Central American centers were the earliest and that the others came into prominence somewhat later. The various suggestions concerning diffusion and perhaps migration, based on the botanical evidence, are listed.

1. An early, trans-Pacific connection is suggested for the introduction to the New World of maize, amaranth, bottle gourd, and cotton.

2. An early south-to-north distribution (Pacific west coast of South America to Central America) is suggested for "pure" and pod corn, cotton, jackbean, and tobacco.

3. A later north-to-south distribution (Guatemala to the Andes and elsewhere) is suggested for dent corn, Inca lima beans, flint corn, the common bean, and one variety of squash.

4. An early northern Andes (Colombia) to Central Andes migration is indicated by the oca, ulluco, mashua, diploid potato, and guayaba.

5. Later, the Central Andes becomes a center for the south and north distribution of quinua, lupine, beans, and potatoes, all types adapted to high-altitude cultivation.

6. A line of distribution from the montaña area, east of the Andes, through the tropics of the Americas is suggested by sweet manioc, peanut, pepper, sweet potato, and one variety of squash.

7. An important interrelationship of the montaña, tropical Brazil, Venezuela, and the West Indies is indicated by bitter manioc, arrowroot, cashew, xanthosoma, and tropical tobacco.

8. A reverse trans-Pacific distribution, from the New World to Oceania,

is suggested by the coconut, sweet potato, jackbean, and cotton.

The above list is compiled from numerous statements in Sauer's article, but it is doubtful that even he would agree to all of it, nor would other botanists and archeologists. The list is intended only to illustrate the possibilities for culture history in this research approach, which demands the co-operation of archeologists and botanists. In future work, advantage should be taken of the exceptional conditions for preservation on the coast of Peru and more systematic collections of plant remains should be made. In the study of plant distributions, environmental and cultural factors are of recognized importance. We need more detailed studies of the economic importance of different domesticated plants to the contemporary and historical peoples. Once again we are faced with the problem of determining whether plant distributions took place by migration, by diffusion, or perhaps by natural means.

INTERPRETATIONAL STUDIES

Obviously, interpretations are basic to every study of culture history. The present section is concerned with a number of particular types of interpretations developed in South American studies, together with some of the specific conclusions arrived at for the southern continent.

1. DEVELOPMENTAL CLASSIFICATION

The archeologists who have concentrated their efforts on establishing regional chronologies have also been concerned with the types of culture change which are revealed by these long time sequences and their developmental implications. Although an interest in archeological trends and their interpretations has been common in other parts of the world, the recent focusing of attention on developmental classification

for Andean South America has been largely inspired by the 1946 Viru Valley Project on the northern coast of Peru, in which a number of North American and Peruvian scholars collaborated. The sequence of cultural periods established for Viru Valley was carefully examined in terms of the economic, technological, political, religious, and artistic achievements. As a result, definite changes in emphasis were noted for successive periods. Later studies (Bennett and Bird, 1949) have examined the changes which took place in all the Central Andes in so far as the cultural sequences could be reconstructed; and the same approach has been applied to other parts of the Americas. The generalized developmental picture for Peru shows a long initial period of technological advancement, in which techniques of cultivation and manufacture were slowly brought under control and which culminated in a period of artistic florescence. Following this, new technological advance is limited, and the emphasis is shifted to sociopolitical controls, which reach their maximum in the formation of the Inca political empire. The Mesoamerican sequence shows certain parallels to the Peruvian. This led Steward (1949) to examine sequences in other parts of the world, on the basis of which he has proposed a hypothetical developmental pattern with implications of cultural causality and law.

2. FORMATIVE PERIOD

Comparison of the developmental sequences established for Mesoamerica and the Central Andes has led to renewed efforts to explain the relationships between these two centers of New World high civilization. Both are conceived to rest on a common cultural basis, previously called the "archaic" but in developmental terms now labeled the "Formative period." The argument runs that an agricultural economy, based on plant domestication presumably in South America, spread throughout the entire area of what is now called "Nuclear America." It is still undetermined whether this complex was spread by migration or by diffusion, or, for that matter, whether it could not have developed independently. In any case, two major centers of advanced civilization grew out of this Formative basis, one in Mesoamerica, one in the Central Andes, in large part independently of each other. These major developments have largely obscured the common Formative pattern, although it is revealed by the archeological findings, but in the intermediate region the Formative complex persisted and spread around the Caribbean area.

3. CIRCUM-CARIBBEAN

This concept of a distinctive and interrelated cultural development around the Caribbean region was advanced by Steward in the course of his work as editor of the *Handbook of South American Indians*. The *Handbook* initially divided the continent into three major regions, namely, southern South America, the Andes, and the tropical forest, and devoted a volume to each. As the material on the tropical forest region grew in magnitude, two volumes were required, one for the tropical forest proper and the other for the northern section, which also included Central America and the Antilles. In summarizing the contents of this additional volume, Steward became convinced that it had considerable cultural unity. With his great interest in developmental classification and his attention to the importance of the Formative period, he conceived of a new interpretation of the Circum-Caribbean cultures which he presented in Volume V of the *Handbook*. The idea is advanced that a separate, distinctive culture pattern, based essentially on the Formative period complex but also incorporating elements from Mesoamerica and the Central Andes, spread throughout Central America, Colombia, Venezuela, and the Antilles. The concept is well presented but needs more thorough examination, particularly since much of the botanical, archeological, and historical evidence indicates a rather sharp division between the Brazilian tropical forest, Venezuela, and the Antilles, on the one hand, and Colombia and Central America, on the other.

Both the Formative period and the Circum-Caribbean, like other large-scale reconstructions, are based on the assumption that an early common, undifferentiated cultural basis existed in the whole area. In the case of the Formative period, some of the cultural content is derived from archeological evidence, but even a greater amount is the result of reconstruction through the least-common-denominator principle. That is, the high civilizations of Mesoamerica and the Central Andes are compared, and the factors which they share in common are attributed to the Formative basis. While it may be logical to assume not only that the simple precedes the complex but that it is also less differentiated, it does need confirmation. It is doubtless true that differences become more pronounced as civilizations become more complex, but it does not follow from this that the simpler earlier cultures are thus more uniform and therefore more closely related.

4. CERAMICS AND CULTURE

The emphasis of archeologists on relative chronology has led to a heavy dependence on ceramics and ceramic fragments as the basic material. Actually, many of the sequences which have been established are essentially for ceramics rather than for total cultures. Considerable advance has been made, however, in defining the relationship of ceramic history to culture history and culture change. Although contributions in this field are by no means restricted to South America, the illustrations in this report are so limited.

Junius Bird in his excavations on the northern coast of Peru encountered a well-defined, pre-ceramic, agricultural horizon. In the past the spread of ceramics and agriculture has often been interpreted as coterminous, but it is now clear that, in coastal Peru, an agriculture economy covers a long time period before the introduction of ceramics. Furthermore, South American distribution studies show that, in Patagonia, ceramics were spread well beyond the limits of agriculture.

Comparisons of ceramic styles and techniques of manufacture are constantly used to match the sequences of two or more regions and to link two or more time periods. In the Central Andes, certain ceramic techniques, styles, and even complexes have widespread distributions which seem to have taken place at approximately the same time periods. These are called "ceramic horizons" and are used to relate the sequences of different regions. Since the rate and extent of trait distribution are commonly considered as factors for judging relative age, the concept of using the spread of a ceramic technique or style as a horizon time marker might be questioned. For Peru it is felt that the spread was too rapid for time differences to be a significant handicap in the matching procedure. Furthermore, it is possible to use fixed sequences of horizon styles. There are, for example, five major horizon styles in prehistoric Peru which occur in the same sequence in a number of different subareas. Thus they serve to match these regions, even though an absolute time scale might show slight differences. For some of the subareas of Peru, some ceramc styles or features are found to persist through several cultural periods. These are called "ceramic traditions" and serve to link periods. A sufficient number of such traditions is thought to indicate regional population and culture continuity.

The classification of ceramics into types and styles is commonly used for most studies of chronology. In a stratigraphic excavation the percentage occurrence of each type or style is plotted and the changes noted for successive levels. For surface or unstratified unit collections, the different patterns of the percentage occurrence of types can be matched as a basis for time reconstruction. While the primary purpose of all these procedures is to establish a relative chronology, analysis of the rate of increase or decrease of a ceramic type throughout time furnishes information about the nature and the rate of cultural change.

Many scholars resist the validity of using material culture alone as a measure of over-all cultural development, and they would doubtless be even more alarmed at the use of one aspect of material culture, namely, ceramics, as an index in itself. Consequently, Willey's article on ceramics in Volume V of the *Handbook of South American Indians* is of considerable interest. In this, Willey presents a technological classification of the ceramics of South America, shows the regional distribution of each category, gives some evidence of sequence occurrences, arranges the categories in a developmental sequence, and attempts to relate this to the over-all culture history of the continent. His arguments merit consideration and again raise the question of using material culture as an index. The archeologists are naturally greatly interested in this, since their findings are dominated by material culture.

Most archeologists agree that ceramics are a reasonably sensitive measure of cultural change. Although ceremonial pottery may change with greater rapidity than the common cooking ware, both present regular modifications when seen through a time framework. The question is often raised as to how long a style can persist with relatively little change. An interesting study in this respect has been published by Tschopik (1950). He has traced contemporary Aymara ceramic styles back to the beginning of the colonial Spanish period and demonstrated that there has been but little change in these four hundred years.

5. ARCHEOLOGICAL SCIENCE

Archeologists have created a specialized terminology for the treatment of their materials. Most of the technical terms refer to categories of artifacts, techniques, classifications of types, and chronological problems and consequently have been little used outside the specialty. No one denies the importance of chronology as a basis for the study of culture history, and certainly more such work is still the most dominant need in South America. Nonetheless, chronology is but a means, not an end in itself. Once sequences, relative or absolute, are established, the archeologists are still faced with the major problem of interpreting these in a significant way for science. One approach to this problem considers the archeological remains as the skeleton of a past culture and attempts to clothe its bare bones in descriptive wrappings borrowed from contemporary ethnography. This has been reasonably successful for a period such as Mochica on the northern coast of Peru, since preservation is good and the ceramic modeling and painting are faithfully realistic. For most periods, however, the limitations of this approach are self-evident, and a forced application often distorts the picture.

In recent years some scholars have been experimenting with new descriptive methods devised to fit the available archeological materials. Habitation patterns are being based on the types and arrangements of house sites. Architectural layouts are being treated as wholes. Analysis is being made of the archeological emphasis of a period, whether on large-scale public building, skilled craftsmanship, or elaboration of grave offerings. The shift in emphasis from one period to another is being studied, even though the functional significance of this cannot be immediately determined. The utilization of an isolated valley is being viewed as a whole and throughout a time period from the earliest remains to the present day.

Such a positive approach to archeological analysis has great promise, since its possibilities are limitless. It will allow the past to be compared with the contemporary on equal terms, unhampered by the limitations which an ethnographic reconstruction approach presents. In time a new and significant vocabulary must be developed to meet the new concepts. The recognition that archeology is a science in its own right is a step forward comparable in magnitude to the distinction between the superorganic and the organic.

6. TECHNICAL ANALYSIS

Ceramics, metals, woven cloth, and other materials have been subjected to technical analysis by the specialists. Such technical studies have the advantage of dealing directly with the materials themselves rather than depending on reconstructions. For example, the basic process used in making a given metal artifact can be analyzed by a metallurgist in terms of the component metals, the heat at which they were fabricated, and the sequence of technical steps employed. For spinning and weaving, graded scales of skills and complexities can be set up to compare the achievements of different past cultures. In South America these technical studies have been largely limited to metals and weaving.

7. ART ANALYSIS

The quantities of materials, particularly archeological finds, which can be properly classified as art objects have attracted the attention of students of art. Once again many of the art studies are not restricted to ethnographic reconstructions. Instead, the scholars can glean a great deal of information about the artistic interests of the peoples of a given period by analysis of the principal media employed, the methods of expression, the iconography, the repetition of design, the interest in realism as against stylization, and the like. Furthermore, broad interpretations can be made of the over-all approach of the artist to his subject. In the chapter on art in Volume V of the *Handbook,* Kroeber characterizes the over-all artistic expression in South American prehistory. He points out that the South American artist, in contrast to those of Mesoamerica, was bound to technology. This is reflected in the limited emphasis placed on sculpture, painting, and architecture in contrast to ceramics, textiles, and metallurgy.

PROBLEM IN CULTURE HISTORY

Up to the present, most students of culture history in South America have directed their efforts to the reconstruction of sequences. Some of the approaches and achievements have been discussed in the previous pages. It is noteworthy that few of the writers reveal any sense of problem, outside the strictly chronological. There are some exceptions, to be sure, such as the cultural-process and functional interests of the students of developmental classification. There is no intent in this discussion to deny the validity and importance of historical approaches and the reconstruction of sequences. However, chronology must be recognized as merely a setting for scientific study. The ultimate purpose of historical reconstructions is to allow analysis of the process of cultural change, of the study of the relationship of environment to cultural development, and many others.

The present review of anthropological work in South America has been confined to culture history. It is clear, however, that historical study is but one aspect of the total anthropological activity. Many of the field studies, particularly in ethnology, are concerned with South American cultures as illustrations of problems in human behavior and in social science. For example, Holmberg's (1950) study of the Sirionó Indians of Bolivia was directed toward the thesis that perpetual concern about obtaining enough to eat in a nomadic group of this kind would influence many aspects of the cultural behavior. The current series of community studies, principally in Peru and in Brazil, are in no way bound to the subject of culture history. Some are intended to be a sampling of the contemporary cultures of the country. Others are directed toward measuring the impact of modern technology on some of the more backward people of the area. Unfortunately, space does not permit a proper review of these numerous studies.

It is hoped that in the future the students of culture history will devote more attention to the study of problems. For example, the current studies of the Indian cultures in Peru and Bolivia show clearly that the Indians are a social class or caste within a larger system. In other words, one is studying a culture within a culture rather than an independent group. This is often considered to be a modern situation resulting from the European conquest, but there is every reason to believe that similar situations existed in the past, for example, when the Inca absorbed

New World Culture History: South America 209

their weaker neighbors into a large political system. The possibility of a culture within a culture is seldom considered by archeologists, even when they encounter markedly different materials in the same period. The culture historians should devote more attention to recurring historical phenomena in the history of the Western Hemisphere and the possibility of their identification in the more remote past. Two illustrations suffice. One is the introduction of the horse to the plains of Patagonia and to western United States and the similar cultural results in both regions. The other is the phenomenon of revivalism in the Ghost Dance of the Indians of western United States and in the reaction of the Tupi of Brazil following the Portuguese conquest. Such phenomena are useful for historical interpretations but also direct scholarship toward the analysis of possible causal factors. If culture history is to be a part of social science, cause as well as sequence must be included.

REFERENCES

BENNETT, WENDELL C. 1948. *A Reappraisal of Peruvian Archaeology.* ("Memoirs of the Society for American Archaeology," No. 4.) Menasha, Wis.

BENNETT, W. C., and BIRD, JUNIUS. 1949. *Andean Culture History.* ("American Museum of Natural History Handbook Series," No. 15.) New York.

CANALS FRAU, SALVADOR. 1940. "La Distribución geográfica de los aborígenes del Noroeste Argentino en el siglo XVI," *Anales del Instituto de Etnografía Americana,* I, 217–34.

COOPER, JOHN M. 1925. "Culture Diffusion and Culture Areas in Southern South America," *Proceedings of the International Congress of Americanists,* XXI, 406–21.

HOLMBERG, ALLAN R. 1950. *Nomads of the Long Bow.* ("Publications of the Institute of Social Anthropology," No. 10; Smithsonian Institute.) Washington, D.C.: Government Printing Office.

KRICKEBERG, W. 1922. "Die Völker Südamerikas." In BUSCHAN, G. (ed.), *Illustrierte Völkerkunde,* I, 217–423. Stuttgart: Strecker & Schröder.

——. 1934. "Beiträge zur Frage der alten kulturgeschichtlichen Beziehungen zwischen Nord- und Südamerika," *Zeitschrift für Ethnologie,* LXVI, 287–373.

LINNÉ, S. 1925. *The Technique of South American Ceramics.* ("Göt. Kungl. Vetenskaps- och Vitterhets-Samhället Handlingar," Vol. XXIX, No. 5.) Göteborg.

MCKERN, W. C. 1939. "The Midwestern Taxonomic Method, as an Aid to Archaeological Culture Study," *American Antiquity,* IV, 301–13.

MARTIN, PAUL S., and RINALDO, J. B. 1951. "The Southwestern Co-tradition," *Southwestern Journal of Anthropology,* VII, 215–29.

MONGE, CARLOS. 1948. *Acclimatization in the Andes.* Baltimore: Johns Hopkins Press.

MURDOCK, GEORGE P. 1951. "South American Culture Areas," *Southwestern Journal of Anthropology,* VII, 415–36.

NORDENSKIÖLD, E. 1919. *An Ethno-geographical Analysis of the Material Culture of Two Indian Tribes in the Gran Chaco.* ("Comparative Ethnographical Studies," No. 1.) Göteborg: Elanders Boktrykeri Aktiebolag.

STEWARD, JULIAN H. 1949. "Cultural Causality and Law: A Trial Formulation of the Development of Early Civilizations," *American Anthropologist,* LI, 1–27.

—— (ed.). 1946–50. *Handbook of South American Indians* (Bureau of American Ethnology Bull. 143.) Vol. I: *The Marginal Tribes* (1946); Vol. II: *The Andean Civilizations* (1946); Vol. III: *The Tropical Forest Tribes* (1948); Vol. IV: *The Circum-Caribbean Tribes* (1948); Vol. V: *The Comparative Ethnology of South American Indians* (1949); Vol. VI: *Physical Anthropology, Linguistics, and Cultural Geography of South American Indians* (1950).

TSCHOPIK, HARRY. 1950. "An Andean Ceramic Tradition in Historical Perspective," *American Antiquity,* XV, 196–218.

New World Culture History: Middle America

By ALFONSO CASO

When we speak of "cultural horizons in Mesoamerica," we refer to a particular zone of American culture which extends approximately from the southern part of Tamaulipas on the east to the Sinaloa River in western Mexico. This northern boundary follows the western Sierra Madre Mountains to Lake Chapala, then follows the Lerma River and rises again in the east to reach the San Fernando River in Tamaulipas. The southern boundary begins at about the mouth of the Motagua River, continues south almost to Sensenti, Honduras, then turns east, following the present border of El Salvador and Honduras to the big bend of the Lempa River, and follows this stream to the Pacific Ocean.

On the other side of the Lempa River lived Nahuatl-speaking Pipil groups as far south as Ozulután. The Nahuatato lived on the other side of the Gulf of Fonseca, and the end of the gulf was inhabited by Chorotegan peoples. From the Gulf of Fonseca, the line passed through the Estero Real Valley, reaching Managua and Nicaragua lakes, following along the southwestern side of the latter in a line to the Gulf of Nicoya, whose shores were inhabited by Chorotegan groups (Orotiñas and Nicoyas). The area to the west was occupied by small Mesoamerican groups squeezed in among various peoples down to Panama, where the Ciguas lived around the mouth of the Changuina River and the frontier Island of Tojar.

This delimitation for Mesoamerica is valid only from the sixteenth century. Formerly both northern and southern limits were different, but at the present time insufficient data do not permit an accurate definition of the Mesoamerican frontiers for an earlier date.

Mesoamerica is characterized as a cultural unit not only for the sixteenth century but even much earlier. Through the studies of Mendizábal (1929, n.d.), Wissler (1938), Beals (1932), Sauer (1934, 1935), and Kirchhoff (1943), we have an idea of the cultural elements or traits that can be considered typically Mesoamerican. It would take a long time to enumerate the common elements that make this area a cultural unit and which distinguish it from the Southwest of the United States and the northeastern part of Mexico, on the one hand, and from the Southeast of the United States and the Chibchan, Andean, Amazonian, and so-called "Circum-Caribbean" areas, on the other.

By "cultural horizons in Mesoamerica" we refer to the various periods in Mesoamerican development, each characterized by the presence of one or more very important cultural traits diffused over a wide area. This does not mean that a cultural trait, or traits, was adopted throughout the entire zone at the same time, nor does it necessarily follow that it was taken over by each Mesoamerican group. But undoubtedly the invention or assimilation of these elements must have resulted in a change in the basic pattern. On the other hand, we know far more of the life and culture of Mesoamerican peoples, the closer we approach the time of the Conquest; and the data become scarcer and more vague in proportion as we move backward in time.

The cultural horizons to be discussed here are not time divisions of equal length. On the contrary, the horizons approaching the period of European contact at the time of the Spanish Conquest are shorter. But, as we retreat from this epoch of contact, to which pertain the richer data and the bulk of information, the periods become increasingly longer. For this reason, the dates for the beginning of the historical period and of the Toltec horizon are relatively well established, but the tentative dates of the older periods, being based on today's status of knowledge, are simply those that currently seem most probable to us.

On the other hand, one must take into consideration the fact that the shift from one horizon to another could not possibly have occurred simultaneously throughout all the large area that comprises Mesoamerica. Cultural traits must have diffused more or less rapidly around the immediate area of origin or assimilation; but we can be sure that in the same area, with the exception of cases of conquest, the appearance of these elements and the disappearance of hangovers from former periods must have taken place very gradually.

Having stated these reservations, which one must bear in mind when dealing in general terms with the different horizons, the Mesoamerican area is without a doubt not merely a geo-graphical division but also, as we have seen, a cultural unit. Not only were the diverse cultures that existed in the area related to one another at the time of the Spanish Conquest, but they were themselves the result of still older cultures which also resembled one another or stemmed from a common base. In other words, Mesoamerica not only was a cultural unit at the time of the Conquest but had been so during former epochs. Many traits, some of which are very old, such as writing and the ritual of the calendar, the pyramids and the cult of certain gods, seem to have existed in Mesoamerica even during that horizon which we shall call the "Archaic."

It goes without saying that our knowledge is not sufficient at the present time even to attempt to set up the northern and southern limits of Mesoamerica during each horizon, although, as we have said, we can be sure that such boundaries shifted with time. We also wish to call attention to the fact that the very number of these horizons is, in itself, very arbitrary. By using some other criterion than our own, it would not be difficult to reduce these to half their present number if we were eager to make the system more synthetic, or to double their number by employing more analytical criteria. The presentation of these horizons is no more than a classification, and classifications are not an expression of truth, universally valid, but of criteria that seem useful. With future scientific investigations in the pre-Columbian field —archeological, ethnographic, and historical—it will undoubtedly become necessary one day to rearrange our data.

The following horizons seem significant at the present time. They are listed, beginning with the oldest and ending with the most recent, each accompanied by tentative initial and terminal dates. (1) *Prehistoric horizon.*

This period embraces that span of time from the first settling of the Mesoamerican area to the discovery of agriculture and pottery. 25000 B.C.???–5000 B.C.??? (2) *Primitive horizon.* During this horizon agriculture got under way, being preceded perhaps by horticulture. Another significant achievement was the invention of pottery. Life must have been at least partially sedentary, and people were clustered in small groups, forming tiny farming communities or villages. 5000 B.C.???–1000 B.C.?? (3) *Archaic horizon.* Manifestations of high culture are already evident at this early time. The population must have been concentrated first in large villages and later in cities, which dominated a greater territory. Organized religious cults appear, along with representations of gods, writing, and the calendar system. Pottery, although still simple, is technically very well developed. 1000 B.C.??–200 B.C.?? (4) *Formative horizon.* By now, people are concentrated in large metropolitan centers. Enormous pyramids are constructed, implying an organized priesthood and a fairly sophisticated society. Writing and the calendar ritual take on even greater significance, and the pantheon of gods is richly increased. Pottery, too, becomes more complex, and new forms and techniques of manufacture, color, and decorations appear. Local cultures begin to distinguish themselves. The cult of Tlaloc, the Rain God, appears. 200 B.C.??–A.D. 400? (5) *Classic horizon.* The truly great cultures of Mesoamerica flourish at this time, manifesting characteristic cultures in Teotihuacán, El Tajín, Monte Alban III-A, Tzakol, and what has been called the "Old Empire Maya," and elsewhere. This is a period of intercultural contact and exchange, although local cultures retain their distinct personalities. Perhaps the Quetzalcoatl cult appears at this time. A.D. 400?–A.D. 900? (6) *Toltec*

horizon. The most outstanding characteristic of this period is the appearance of metal and the bow and arrow, new forms of writing, counting and calendrical systems, and new gods. The warrior brotherhoods of the Eagle and Tiger are much in evidence. The influence of Tula is widely felt, and the Mixteca-Puebla culture rises to prominence. We begin to have historical data for this period, transmitted by legend and preserved through manuscripts which can now be interpreted. This is the period of the great historical migrations. A.D. 900??–A.D. 1200? (7) *Historical horizon.* The peoples of this period were probably living much as they had for several centuries when the Spaniards came upon them in the sixteenth century. We have rich and abundant cultural data pertaining to these people. Many old elements were held over, and through the study of these traits, together with those of this period, we can understand how, after the fall of the Toltec empire and the disintegration of the League of Mayapan, new and independent groups gained control. Some of these groups in central Mexico were later concentrated to form the Triple Alliance. A.D. 1200?–A.D. 1521. Let us now pass to a brief discussion of these horizons.

PREHISTORIC HORIZON

Although the story of the settling of Mesoamerica is actually part of a greater problem, that of peopling the continent, we shall limit ourselves here to a discussion of the data that exist concerning the presence of man in Mesoamerica at the end of the Pleistocene and the beginning of the Recent, geologically speaking, and of the evidence for the contemporaneousness of man and extinct fauna. That these data belong to the prehistoric period is unquestionable, since there is no sign of the existence of such fauna along with Mesoamerican peoples.

Only a few years ago, the presence of prehistoric man in Mesoamerica was but a hypothesis, inferred from very scarce and from what seemed to be uncertain data. Recent excavations in the valley of Mexico now leave no room for questioning the fact that man lived here at the same time as the mammoth and actually hunted this beast before the great climatic change which resulted in a hotter and drier climate than we have today and which deposited a thick geological layer known as Caliche III or Barrilaco.

Martínez del Río (1943) and Aveleyra (1950) have studied the older finds in some detail and have made a very careful study of the scientific facts implied, in order to prove concretely that man did exist at this time. Both human remains and artifacts of man's material culture have been taken into consideration.

Listing the discoveries, we find the skeletal remains of the Peñón Man, the Xico lower jaw, and the Tepexpan Man. Prehistoric artifacts include those found by the Comisión Científica de México, those found by Hamy and Engerrand in Campeche, Adan in Mitla, Mülleried in the Petén region and Coahuila, Hughes in Tamaulipas, what De Terra calls artifacts of the San Juan culture at Tepexpan and the Chalco Complex.

However, what really clinches the case for man's existence in the Becerra Formation prior to the Caliche III, or Barrilaco (with an age, according to carbon 14 dating, from 11,000 years ± 500, to 16,000) (1951, p. 8), are the Tepexpan Man (De Terra, Romero, and Stewart, 1949), Arellano's discovery of an articulated mammoth accompanied by an obsidian flake (Arellano, 1946), and especially the recent find, four months ago, in Santa Isabel Iztapan. The latter consists of a young mammoth among whose bones were found six stone implements. All these

discoveries belong to the Upper Becerra Formation (Martínez del Río, 1952).

Elsewhere in Mesoamerica, other evidence points to the existence of prehistoric man. We refer now to McNeish's explorations in Tamaulipas (McNeish, 1950), where he stratigraphically distinguished an eight-layer sequence of six cultures, spanning a period from prehistoric times (end of Pleistocene or beginning of Recent) to A.D. 1785, at which date the Pasitas tribe, of the so-called "Los Angeles culture," was wiped out. The Cañón Diablo Complex, that is, McNeish's stratigraphically deepest layer found on the highest river terrace, was not found in assocation with fossils, but he believes it to be of prehistoric date because of its location on the terrace.

We refer now to the human and animal footprints at Lake Managua. These were pressed into soft clay which has since become stone. These footprints were studied by Richardson, Ruppert, and Williams (Richardson, 1940; Richardson and Ruppert, 1941). Recently the latter (Williams, 1950) has again examined them, arriving at the conclusion that they are at least 2,500 years old, but not necessarily more than 5,000. Nevertheless, the presence of bison tracks in the same strata seems to indicate a truly prehistoric age. If the discovery of the Cañón Diablo Complex in the north and the one at Lake Managua in the south should be proved to belong to a really prehistoric horizon, then the evidence for the presence of prehistoric man in Mesoamerica would be strengthened.

In summary, the Mesoamerican finds show that man was inhabiting this part of the continent toward the end of the Pleistocene (Upper Becerra Formation) and at the beginning of the Recent (Totolzingo). This seems logical and is not unexpected, since in both North and South America human and artifact remains point to man's existence in the two great land masses at that time. It is therefore quite natural that, if man passed through the American isthmus region, the only corridor between North and South America, he would have lived there a while and left behind some trace of his existence.

On this first horizon, man must have had a culture which, in general, resembled the European Paleolithic, as regards the type of life and tools, since the people lived by hunting the large game animals which at that time inhabited the valleys and the river basins of Mesoamerica. In other words, man lived as a nomad who followed the herds of elephants, camels, horses, and bison, making use of the skins for clothing. The *atlatl*, or spear-thrower, must have been in use and probably the javelin. Other tools included hammerstones, knives, beaters, scrapers, and awls. Sometimes they sharpened bones, and they knew how to engrave animal figures on bone as on the specimen found at Tequisquiac.

It is not known whether at this time stones were used for grinding seeds and wild roots or whether they had baskets or used fruit rinds or husks and shells for receptacles. During their brief stopovers they sometimes lived in caves or rock-shelters, especially on river terraces or lake shores. We do not know whether they buried their dead and whether they supplied them with grave goods. Although Romero (De Terra, Romero, and Stewart, 1949) is inclined to think that the Tepexpan Man was actually buried, because of the resemblance of his posture to that of Archaic skeletons, this could be simply a coincidence.

If it could be proved that De Terra's Chalco Complex (De Terra, 1946) really possesses all the artifacts that he attributes to it, among which are manos and metates, it would be one very significant link bridging the gap between this horizon and the one to follow.

PRIMITIVE HORIZON

The Primitive horizon is one which we *presume* existed in Mesoamerica, during which time two very important features made their appearance: agriculture and pottery. The domesticated dog and perhaps the turkey were also known. This period is that era of lithic tools in which chipped stone gives way to polished stone.

In general, it may be said that the cultural traits of this horizon make it comparable to the Neolithic period of the Old World. This comparison is to be taken in a very general way, and we cannot eliminate the possibility that men with a late Paleolithic or early Neolithic European culture might have kept up a steady stream of migrations, reaching America by applying their seafaring knowledge to cross the rugged Bering Straits. The invention of agriculture and pottery on this horizon in Mesoamerica can be postulated; but up until now, with the exception of McNeish's La Perra focus in Tamaulipas, of which we shall presently speak, no evidence of a truly primitive horizon lacking agriculture and pottery has been revealed within the Mesoamerican limits. Of course, the simple fact that we have not found it is no sign that it does not exist. Excavations in the next few years could uncover just such a horizon, yielding cultural remains of a truly primitive people.

This is the horizon of which we know least in Mesoamerica. Remains of an agricultural and pre-agricultural people have already been discovered in North and South America. We know that the Cochise culture of Arizona and New Mexico already had metates and manos, which proves the existence of a people who used this simple device for grinding seeds and fruit, and they may well have been the predecessors of the Mogollon and Hohokam cultures. The Ventana Cave people of Arizona were also food-gatherers and used metates and manos (Haury, 1943). Bird (1948) and Strong (1947) found pre-ceramic cultures in the Chicama and Virú valleys dating from 3000 B.C., which preceded the Guanape I people. Other remains of pre-ceramic cultures have been uncovered on the Chilean coast. It would seem hard to believe that, if these primitive cultures existed in both North and South America, they would not also be found in Meso-america.

The La Perra Focus was found by McNeish (1950) underlying material that correlates with Ekholm's Period II of the Panuco region, and this Period II corresponds to the Ticoman-Cuicuilco culture of the valley of Mexico. But the lack of any apparent continuity be-tween the La Perra artifacts and those belonging to the Pueblo I phase of Mc-Neish led him to postulate a great gap between the two cultures. If the La Perra material is earlier than Zacatenco, as the author believes, then 1000 B.C. seems to be the most recent date we can assign to the end of this period. It is very significant that agriculture was already known to the La Perra people; but, on the other hand, they lacked pottery, which led McNeish to suggest that these people were semisedentary, living mainly on the products of agri-culture and food-gathering, and, least of all, by hunting.

Below the La Perra Focus, McNeish found remains of another culture which he calls "Nogales." The latter is distin-guished from the former by the type of lithic instruments present and by the lack of metates, mortars, and manos. According to McNeish, this Nogales culture is pre-agricultural and pre-ceramic and therefore antedates the La Perra Focus.

The Bat Cave discovery reported by Mangelsdorf and Smith (1949) shows that corn was known in New Mexico in very ancient times. According to a com-munication from H. W. Dick to Dr.

J. O. Brew, who kindly gave me the data, the earliest maize discovery was in a layer just on the upper gravel, whose carbon 14 date is 3981 B.C. The oldest corn found in the cave is a true pod corn, and, according to Antevs' geological evidence, the layer is dat-able at 2000 B.C. Of even greater sig-nificance, which Mangelsdorf and Smith point out, is the fact that the evolution of the corn observed in a study of the stratified remains of the cave represents a lapse of time of ap-proximately 3,000 years. According to Mangelsdorf, hybridization with teo-centli, its introgression, could not have occurred later than 500 B.C. Neverthe-less, he points out, the first and second layers each already yield an ear of corn which shows introgression, al-though these could be intrusive in each case. Mangelsdorf concludes that corn did not originate in New Mexico and therefore must have been imported from some other region, before the evolution began, of course. Now if we accept the fact that corn originated in South America, as several botanists are inclined to believe, or in Chiapas or Guatemala, according to others, con-siderable time would have elapsed be-fore the cultivation of corn could have spread to New Mexico. We can there-fore assume that the Bat Cave dis-covery and the carbon 14 date of the gravel suggest that maize must have been cultivated in Central America at least as early as 3000 B.C. This makes it very improbable, of course, that corn, as a cultivated plant, could have been introduced into the American continent from elsewhere. On the other hand, Mangelsdorf's (Mangelsdorf and Oli-ver, 1951) recent studies deny that maize agriculture existed in Southeast Asia before the discovery of America.

On the basis of our present knowl-edge it would be hard to say which of the plants cultivated in Mesoamerica in the sixteenth century were already being grown during this first agricultural horizon. For the present, it seems best simply to enumerate the most important plants cultivated at that time: corn, bean, *chía* (*Salvia hispanica*), *huauhtli* (*Amaranthus paniculatus*), squash, *chilacayote* (*Cucurbita fixifolia*), sweet potato, yuca or manioc, *jícama* (*Pachyrhizus angulatus*), wild potato, peanut, tomato, *tomate* (*Physalis angulata; coztomatl*), chile pepper, *chayote* (*Sechium edule*), pineapple, avocado, papaya, sweetsop, *chirimoya* (*Annona squamosa; A. reticulata*), soursop, guayaba, *mamey* (*Calocarpum mammosum*), *zapote negro* (*Dyospiros ebenaster*), *zapote blanco* (*Casimiroa edulis*), *zapote amarillo* (*Sargentia gregii*), *chico zapote* (*Achras zapota*), nut, plum, *arrayan* (*Myrtus arrayan*), *tejocote* (*Crataegus mexicana*), *capulin* (*Prunus capuli*), *nanche* (*Byrsonima crassifolia*), cactus, *pitahaya* (*Acanthrocerus pentagonus*), *maguey* (*Agave americana*), *xoconochtli*, *mezquite* (*Prosopis juliflora*), *jinicuil* (*Inga radians*), indigo, *palo de Campeche* (*Hematoxylum campechianum*), tobacco, cotton, rubber, *guayule* (*Parthenium argentatum*), sisal, *zacaton* (*Epicampes macroura*), *ixtle* (*Agave ixtli*), vanilla, coconut, *guamuchil* (*Pithecolobium dulce*), *jocote* (*Spondius lutea*), *achiote* (*Bixa orellana*), *izotl* (*Yucca elephantipes*), *balche* (*Lonchocarpus longistilus*), cacao, *parota* (*Enterolobium cyclocarpum*) (Caso, 1946).

Of course, not every one of these plants listed was grown in all parts of Mesoamerica, not even in the sixteenth century, but they were known at that time throughout the area, owing to trade or tribute, and were taken to all the large economic and political centers. For example, cacao cannot be cultivated in the valley of Mexico, which is at an altitude of more than 7,000 feet, but both as a drink and as a medium of exchange it was a basic element of Aztec economy.

As to whether agriculture was invented in Mesoamerica, in the Amazon Basin, or in Peru, I do not think that at the present time we have sufficient data either to prove its origin in any one of these three regions or to deny independent invention.

As for the origin of pottery, a truly primitive ware has not been found in Mesoamerica. Although baskets covered with clay on the outside have been found in northern Mexico, finds lie outside the boundaries of Mesoamerica (Borbolla, 1946). On the other hand, in the last century and even today in some parts of Chiapas, water has been heated by dropping hot stones into a gourd vessel, called a *huacal*, according to Becerra (1939). It is not unlikely that truly primitive pottery will be found in Mesoamerica in the future, which will help explain the transition which must have taken place between such advanced cultures as the Archaic, and the pre-ceramic and pre-agricultural cultures of the Prehistoric horizon. Actually, we know very little regarding the Primitive horizon. It is inferred as a step that must have existed between the Prehistoric horizon and that of the Archaic, which follows.

ARCHAIC HORIZON

It may seem strange that I have revived this term which is so out of style in Mesoamerican investigations, but, among the names suggested for early cultures, I have not found one that improves on Spinden's choice for the oldest pottery horizon found in the valley of Mexico (Spinden, 1922).

To me, the Archaic horizon should include only the first part of what has recently been called the "Formative horizon." That is, certain cultures, such as Teotihuacán I and Monte Alban II, seem to be truly formative cultures leading to the great classic cultures;

but I do not see enough traits shared by these phases and the earlier ones to warrant the lumping of all these into what we should call "archaic." The Archaic horizon actually possesses elements that are survivals from the Primitive horizon.

I do not believe that large metropolitan centers existed in any part of Mesoamerica at this time. The people, who depended on agriculture for their living and made pottery technically well-developed, even though still simple in decoration, did not yet have the complex religion, rituals, and social structure that are found on the Formative horizon and which, of course, continue into the later Classic cultures.

Characteristic of this horizon is precisely the fact that the people were sedentary, although they must have depended to a certain extent on hunting, fishing, and gathering. Life rotated around agriculture; the nude, hand-modeled female figurines which are believed to have represented the beginning of a fertility and earth cult had already appeared.

Nevertheless, there are no large representations of gods from this horizon, which we find on later levels. There are no representations of the Rain or Wind God, of the Sun, the Moon or Venus, etc. Even Huehueteotl, the Old God of Fire, does not appear until the Formative horizon. The same holds true for Xipe-Totec, "the Flayed God." This would seem to indicate that, on the Archaic level, Mesoamerican people lived in large villages, where the ceremonial aspects of their society were not yet very developed, rather than in large cities, with ceremonial centers and complex and specialized cults.

Undoubtedly this primitive Archaic horizon must have been very much like those cultures which Vaillant uncovered at El Arbolillo and Zacatenco (Vaillant, 1930), but this would not apply to his upper-level cultures, that is the Tico-man phases (Vaillant, 1931). Ticoman would fall into the true Formative horizon, along with Teotihuacán I and the cultures of Monte Negro, Monte Alban I, Monte Alban II, and Chicanel. On the Formative horizon we will find that the characteristic Mesoamerican ceremonial centers had already become of great significance.

According to carbon 14 dating, which agrees with our guess dates based on archeological analysis, the pottery of Monte Negro has an approximate age of 2,600 years ± 170, which would date it around the sixth century B. C. (Johnson, 1951). Consequently, the Archaic horizon must have developed more or less from 1000 B.C. to 200 B.C. Nevertheless, at the end of this horizon, organized cults, writing, and the calendar system began to appear.

Monte Negro and Monte Alban I in the Oaxaca region mark the end of this horizon or the beginning of the next (Caso, 1939).

FORMATIVE HORIZON

People at this time were already living in large cities. Enormous monuments were constructed, such as the Pyramid of the Sun at Teotihuacán, the pyramid decorated with painted insects in Cholula, the Observatory or Building J in Monte Alban, and Temple E-VII-Sub in Uaxactún. The calendar and writing were already well developed. I believe that it was in this period that the predecessors of the Maya culture discovered the principle of position numerals and the zero. A great number of inventions were made during this period. The pantheon of gods was increased; pottery became more complex, with new forms, techniques, colors, and decorations, one example being an al fresco technique of painting vessels. The Tlaloc "Tiger-Serpent" cult appears, and probably the great culture of La Venta flourished, as well as Monte Alban II and perhaps the oldest phase of Tzakol, which was preceded by such very advanced cultures as Miraflores (Kidder, Jennings, and Shook, 1946). This is the period of San José II, Chamá I and II, and also Holmul I. The horizon is truly formative, because we find the first signs of local variation in cultures, which later becomes so well defined on the Classic horizon. The profile of these local cultures becomes more and more individualized. Nevertheless, the Mesoamerican pantheon of gods has not yet developed to its fullest extent; we do not find the great gods in their characteristic representations, and there is no indication that some of them, such as Quetzalcoatl, were worshiped. On the other hand, the Earth Goddess, the Rain God, the Fire God, and Xipe-Totec are portrayed on various objects of these cultures, already showing the regional styles which were beginning to develop.

In the Huasteca region, Periods I and II of Pavón would fall into the Formative horizon, as would the Prisco level and the lowest strata found at Tancol (Ekholm, 1944).

CLASSIC HORIZON

The Classic horizon includes such manifestations as Teotihuacán II–III, Monte Alban III-A, and Yucuñudahui in Oaxaca; in the Maya area the so-called "Old Empire," Tzakol, San José III, and Chamá III. In the Huasteca region the Classic horizon includes Pavón III and IV and the end of the Prisco phase. El Tajín in the Totonac area is also included here. The corresponding manifestations in western Mexico are Chametla I, Huatabampo, Tuxcacuexco, Los Ortices, and the Delicias and Apatzingán phases in Michoacán (Kelly, 1949). The horizon is characterized by marking the peak of Mesoamerican cultures, that period of greatest achievement in which heights were reached not only in pottery-making but also in art, painting, and sculp-

ture. If we compare what was going on at this time in four places that we are well acquainted with—the Maya area, the valley of Oaxaca, the valley of Mexico, and the central part of Veracruz—we see an extraordinary development of local cultures, with a very distinct personality in the art style, pottery, writing, and calendar of each, although at the same time a free cultural exchange was taking place among these thriving centers. For example, Monte Alban received influences from Teotihuacán and El Tajín; Kaminaljuyú shows ceramic features of El Tajín, Teotihuacán, and Monte Alban; and the influence of Tajín at Teotihuacán is undeniable.

Nevertheless, these relationships should not be interpreted as evidence of conquests or migrations but simply as the result of commercial or cultural contact. Each of these centers mentioned not only was a city but also exercised cultural control over a much greater area. All of which seems to point either to empires subjected to political and military heads or to a confederation of cities that shared a common culture.

The Classic horizon is of great significance to us because at this time the characteristic elements of the historic cultures were already present, and probably a considerable portion of Mesoamerican peoples was already permanently located in the habitat where these Classic cultures developed. Thus, while during former horizons we could not yet speak of a Zapotec culture and we do not even know what to call the predecessors of the Zapotec, from Classic times on, in that area of the Oaxaca Valley which yields remains of Monte Alban III-A, the Zapotec culture was undoubtedly already formed, with its basic elements and characteristics. The same holds true for the Petén Maya and the peoples of highland Guatemala. However, it is improbable that, in the legendary data that have come down to us, we have any true historical facts for this period. This is one reason why it is so urgent that the accurate historical data on the Maya stelae should be interpreted. The earliest data from Mixtec codexes, which I believe date from the end of the seventh century, are so confused with the theogony of that nation that they can hardly be considered historical sources (Caso, 1951). But we can be sure that the Maya stelae will reveal the history of that people, once we are able to translate the inscriptions that are just now beginning to be understood, according to a new interpretation of hieroglyphs (Thompson, 1950).

As regards pottery on this horizon, the discovery of the use of the mold is important; in funerary architecture, the cruciform tomb developed; and in the field of religion, certain deities appear, such as the "Butterfly God." Finally, the appearance of Quetzalcoatl, the "Plumed Serpent," is firmly established, in constant association with the Rain God.

TOLTEC HORIZON

Undoubtedly, a very significant change took place in"Mesoamerican culture during the horizon called the "Toltec." Of course, it is at this time, or possibly at the end of the former horizon, that the use of metal was introduced into Mesoamerica. The knowledge of working gold, silver, and copper probably came from the region of Costa Rica and Panama, penetrated the Maya area, Oaxaca, and then arrived in central Mexico to spread later through the northern part of Mesoamerica. At this time the Aztatlan Complex of Sinaloa was flourishing and, on the northeastern side of Mesoamerica, Pavón V and Las Flores. Clay pipes appear on this horizon.

Another characteristic of the Toltec horizon, aside from the new ceramic features of each zone, is the appearance of the bow and arrow, probably introduced into Mesoamerica by the nomads of northern Mexico, along with the *chita,* or carrying net, and less important features, such as certain feather adornments, etc.

Two significant pottery types appear at this time, Plumbate and Fine Orange.

New forms in sculpture include the so-called *chac-mool,* and other innovations include the formation of societies, such as the Eagle and Tiger Warriors, and architectural features, such as the caryatids which supported tables or thrones, rings for ball courts, the representation of the sun with rays, the *tzompantli* (skull rack), etc. (Caso, 1941). Glyph-writing underwent certain modifications of importance; Aztec gods were represented in sculpture, in painting, and in codexes, with the possible exception of the tribal god, Huitzilopochtli. True historical data for this period are provided through the Mixtec codexes and through legendary narrations which have been preserved through other codexes and legends which the Aztecs and Mayas still remembered.

At the end of this period, the pressure exerted by the nomadic people of the north resulted in large-scale migrations, which spread over central Mexico and whose repercussions were felt to the southern limits of Mesoamerica. Probably toward the end of this period, the Mesoamerican people to the north were overrun, which resulted in the recession of the northern boundary of this culture area.

A new form of writing appears in the codexes and inscriptions, and new ceramic forms also appear. These manifestations are known as the Mixteca-Puebla culture.

Tula, the center of a great empire, exerts an influence felt as far as the southern limits of Mesoamerica, and the influence called "mexicana," which is really Toltec, is apparent in Chichén Itzá, Tulúm, and other Maya cities.

The end of the Toltec horizon marks the beginning of what we call the "Historical."

HISTORICAL HORIZON

The Historical horizon began approximately in the twelfth century A. D., and ended with the arrival of the Spanish Conquistadors in 1519.

Pre-Columbian and post-Columbian codexes and chronicles, together with reports left by the missionaries and Spaniards, provide abundant information regarding the life and culture of Mesoamerican peoples at this time. Other information was kept alive by word of mouth and later, when the Latin way of writing had been learned, was written down either in a native Indian language or in Spanish.

The people who had lived through the upheaval which resulted in the fall

of the Toltec empire had settled once more in their own territory, when the Spaniards caught them by surprise. Their cultures were mainly a continuation of those elements which had already existed in Toltec times, with a simple evolution; the calendar, writing, the same way of making numbers, building, pottery-making, and even the same religion were carried over, all of which shows the intimate relationship that existed between this horizon and the former one.

At the time of the arrival of the Spanish Conquistadors, a great seat of power was being created in central Mexico under the Aztecs, while the Maya cities had not yet been able to reorganize themselves after the impact of the fall of Mayapan. The Zapotecs and Mixtecs were fighting each other to gain control of the valley of Oaxaca, and to the south the Maya culture seems to have been set back by the Pipils and Lenca tribes.

REFERENCES

ARELLANO, A. R. V. 1946. "El Elefante fósil de Tepexpan y el hombre primitivo," *Revista mexicana de estudios antropológicos,* VIII, 89–94.

AVELEYRA, LUIS. 1950. *Prehistoria de México.* ("Ediciones mexicanas.") Mexico City.

BEALS, RALPH L. 1932. *The Comparative Ethnology of Northern Mexico before 1750.* ("Ibero Americana," Vol. II.) Berkeley, Calif.

BECERRA, M. E. 1939. "Hervir el agua en guacal," *Revista mexicana de estudios antropológicos,* III, 191–94.

BIRD, J. B. 1948. In BENNETT, WENDELL C. (ed.), *A Reappraisal of Peruvian Archaeology.* ("Memoirs of the Society for American Archaeology," Vol. XIII, No. 4, Part II.)

BORBOLLA, D. F. R. DE LA. 1946. "Arqueología del sur de Durango," *Revista mexicana de estudios antropológicos,* VIII, 111–20.

CASO, A. 1939. "Informe de las exploraciones en Oaxaca, durante la 7a. y la 8a.

temporadas," *XXVII Congreso Internacional de Americanistas,* II, 159.

——. 1941. "El complejo arqueológico de Tula y las grandes culturas indígenas de México," *Revista mexicana de estudios antropológicos,*. V, 85–95.

——. 1946. "Contribución de las culturas indígenas de México, a la cultura mundial," *México en la cultura,* p. 51. Mexico City.

——. 1951. "Explicación del reverso del Codex Vindobonensis," *Memorias del Colegio Nacional,* V, 9. Mexico City.

EKHOLM, GORDON F. 1944. *Excavations at Tampico and Panuco in the Huasteca, Mexico.* ("Anthropological Papers of the American Museum of Natural History," Vol. XXXVIII, Part V.) New York.

HAURY, EMIL W. 1943. "The Stratigraphy of Ventana Cave, Arizona," *American Antiquity,* VIII, No. 3, 218–23.

JOHNSON, FREDERICK. 1951. "Radiocarbon Dating," *American Antiquity,* XVII, No. 1, Part II, 1–19.

KELLY, ISABEL. 1949. *The Archaeology of the Autlán-Tuxcacuesco Area of Jalisco.* ("Ibero Americana," Vol. XXVII.) Berkeley, Calif.

KIDDER, A. V.; JENNINGS, J. D.; and SHOOK, E. M. 1946. *Excavations at Kaminal Juyu, Guatemala.* ("Publications of the Carnegie Institution of Washington," No. 561.) Washington, D.C.

KIRCHHOFF, PAUL. 1943. "Mesoamérica," *Acta Americana,* I, No. 1, 92–107.

McNEISH, R. S. 1950. "A Synopsis of the Archaeological Sequence in the Sierra de Tamaulipas," *Revista mexicana de estudios antropológicos,* XI, 79–96.

MANGELSDORF, P. C., and OLIVER, DOUGLAS L. 1951. *Whence Came Maize to Asia?* ("Botanical Museum Leaflets, Harvard University," Vol. XIV, No. 10.)

MANGELSDORF, P. C., and SMITH, C. E., JR. 1949. *New Archaeological Evidence on Evolution in Maize.* ("Botanical Museum Leaflets, Harvard University," Vol. XIII, No. 8.)

MARTÍNEZ DEL RÍO, PABLO. 1943. *Los Orígenes americanos.* 2d ed. Mexico City.

———. 1952. *El Mamut de Sta. Isabel Iztapa.* ("Cuadernos americanos," Vol. XI, No. 4.)

MENDIZÁBAL, MIGUEL O. DE. n.d. "Géneros de vida y regímenes alimenticios de los grupos indígenas del territorio mexicano," *Obras completas,* II, 31. Mexico City.

———. 1929. "Influencia de la sal en la distribución geográfica de los grupos indígenas de México," *ibid.,* II, 197. Mexico City.

RICHARDSON, F. B. 1940. *Nicaragua,* pp. 300–301. ("Carnegie Institution of Washington Year Book," No. 40.)

RICHARDSON, F. B., and RUPPERT, K. 1941. *Nicaragua,* pp. 269–71. ("Carnegie Institution of Washington Year Book," No. 41.)

SAUER, CARL. 1934. *The Distribution of Aboriginal Tribes and Languages in N.W. Mexico.* ("Ibero Americana," Vol. V.) Berkeley, Calif.

———. 1935. *Aboriginal Population of N.W. Mexico.* ("Ibero Americana," Vol. X.) Berkeley, Calif.

SPINDEN, H. J. 1922. *Ancient Civilizations of Mexico and Central America,* pp. 43–65. 2d ed. New York.

STRONG, WILLIAM D. 1947. "Finding the Tomb of a Warrior-God," *National Geographic,* XCI, 453–82.

TERRA, HELMUT DE. 1946. "New Evidence for the Antiquity of Early Man in Mexico," *Revista mexicana de estudios antropológicos,* VIII, 69–88.

TERRA, HELMUT DE; ROMERO, JAVIER; and STEWART, T. D., 1949. *Tepexpan Man.* ("Viking Fund Publications in Anthropology," No. 11.) New York.

THOMPSON, J. E. 1950. *Maya Hieroglyphic Writing,* Introd. ("Publications of the Carnegie Institution of Washington," No. 589.) Washington, D.C.

VAILLANT, G. C. 1930. *Excavations at Zacatenco.* ("Anthropological Papers of the American Museum of Natural History," Vol. XXXII, Part I.) New York.

———. 1931. *Excavations at Ticomán* ("Anthropological Papers of the American Museum of Natural History," Vol. XXXII, Part II.) New York.

WILLIAMS, HOWEL. 1950. *Nicaragua,* pp. 198–200. ("Carnegie Institution of Washington Year Book," No. 49.)

WISSLER, CLARK. 1938. *The American Indian.* 3d ed. New York: Oxford University Press.

Human Ecology

By MARSTON BATES

THE WORD "oecology" was coined by Ernst Haeckel (1870) in the course of an effort to formulate a logical scheme of zoölogical sciences. His primary division was into the sciences concerned with structure (morphology) and those concerned with function (physiology). His scheme still seems logical, and his definition of ecology agrees closely with what many of us today think ecology ought to be. He wrote that

just as morphology falls into two main divisions of anatomy and development, so physiology may be divided into a study of inner and outer phenomena, or of "Relations-Physiologie" and "Conservations-Physiologie." The first is concerned with the functioning of the organism in itself, the second with its relationships with the outer world. These two disciplines thus have their points of origin in entirely different and widely separated regions of science.

The outer physiology, the study of the relations of animals with the outside world, may in turn be divided into two parts, the ecology and the chorology, of animals. By *ecology*, we understand the study of the economy, of the household, of animal organisms. This includes the relationships of animals with both the inorganic and the organic environments, above all the beneficial and inimical relations with other animals and plants, whether direct or indirect; in a word, all of the intricate interrelations that Darwin referred to as the conditions of the struggle for existence. This ecology (often also called "biology" in the narrowest sense) comprises the largest part of so-called "natural history" in the usual sense of the word.

Haeckel's word "chorology" did not catch on; the concept was too closely similar to that of zoögeography. Ecology, however, has gradually become established as a word and as a science, though there is no universal agreement about its usage or its meaning. This is particularly true in the case of "human ecology." Yet any appraisal of the development of human ecology requires a reasonably explicit statement of what is meant by the term.

A casual survey of usage in recent literature and in university organization shows at least five rather divergent ways in which ecology is being applied as a label for human studies.

1. Human ecology stemming from medicine, stressing the environmental relations of disease and growing from this into related fields of thought. The medical science of epidemiology is very readily transposed into the "ecology of disease"; and the word "ecology" also fits readily into the vocabulary of public health workers, since they are always concerned with the environmental relations of man (Corwin, 1949). Cambridge University, in England, has established a Department of Human Ecology, dedicated to the study of public health and epidemiological problems, and the philosophy of this has been described in the inaugural lecture of the professor (Banks, 1950).

222

2. Human ecology stemming from geography. "Geography" is as protean a word as "ecology," and the two are sometimes used as though they were synonyms. Thus a textbook of geography may have the subtitle "an ecological study of society" (White and Renner, 1948), and definitions of "human geography" and "human ecology" frequently appear to be interchangeable. The question "What is geography?" has been debated at length (e.g., Parkins, 1934), as has the problem of distinguishing between ecology and geography (Barrows, 1923; Thornthwaite, 1940). The special hazards of "environmentalism" in geography have been discussed by Platt (1948).

This geographical usage of "ecology" has a specialized subsidiary, in which "environment" is equated with "climate," so that study of men and environment comes to mean man and climate. This usage is illustrated by the *Journal of Human Ecology* published by the Weather Science Foundation of Crystal Lake, Illinois.

3. Human ecology stemming from sociology. The American sociologists have attempted to give ecology a specific meaning as the study of community structure. This is illustrated in the books by Hawley (1950) and Quinn (1950).

4. Human ecology as a tag to indicate that a particular study has broad relevance to problems of human conduct. This sort of usage is nicely shown by the title of a book by Zipf (1949): *Human Behavior and the Principle of Least Effort: An Introduction to Human Ecology.* The book is largely devoted to language analysis, and, as far as I can discover, the word "ecology" does not occur in the text.

5. Human ecology stemming from anthropology. Here I would classify attempts to use the word in the original sense of Haeckel, only with "man" instead of "animal" as the central focus

of interest. The book by Bews (1935) exemplifies this usage.

Clearly, the term "human ecology" has not yet come to be generally applied to a specific and well-defined field of inquiry, and it seems likely that attempts like those of the sociologists so to limit it will fail because their usage is at variance with the usual interpretation of the word in biology. It seems to me better that the word be left with a general and rather vague meaning. The tendency in both the biological and the social sciences to develop numerous special subsciences with "-ology" labels has many unfortunate consequences. It tends to foster the development of special technical vocabularies for each of the segregated fields and thus to hamper the development of general concepts and the study of broad interrelationships. Specialization is necessary, but it does not seem so necessary to freeze our patterns of specialization into a congeries of formal disciplines with labels like "ecology," "demography," "climatology," and so forth. The extreme result of such splitting can be seen in the medical sciences; but the tendency, I think, has handicapped the biological sciences as compared with the physicochemical sciences, where specialization has less often had formal, Greek-root labeling.

It might be useful to regard ecology as a pervasive point of view rather than as a special subject matter. The ecological point of view—whereby the organism is regarded as a whole unit functioning in its environmental context—would carry over from the biological to the social sciences and might thus be especially helpful in relating the concepts of the one field to those of the other. The establishment of such relations is not easy, and most attempts to transfer concepts have possibly been misleading.

Biologists are likely to be impressed by the fact that man is an animal and to reason that his behavior must thus be explicable in biological terms. But any animal is also an aggregation of chemical elements. Biologists do not argue that, because of this, animal behavior must be completely explicable in known physicochemical terms. They recognize that the factor of life influences the whole nature of scientific study, so that physicochemical propositions must be examined anew in the living context. With the shift from animal to man, an analogous shift has been made because of the complicating factor of culture, and biological propositions must be examined anew in the cultural context.

An important and difficult problem in the scientific study of man is the problem of sorting out the cultural from the biological elements or of finding the biological elements by dissecting away the cultural overlay. The ecological approach might be particularly suitable for this, because, in attempting to analyze the environmental relationships of man, the necessity of finding some method of sorting out and handling the physical, biological, and cultural factors becomes obvious at once. The peculiarity and pervasiveness of the cultural factors are even more emphasized if this study is approached from a background of animal ecology.

Biochemistry is a protean sort of science that has served to bridge the apparent gap between the physical and the biological sciences. Perhaps in a comparable way, ecological anthropology—or human ecology—may furnish the conceptual interconnections between the biological and the social sciences. Human ecology, then, would be the natural history of man, or, in its narrowest sense, the biology of man. This, returning to Haeckel's original definition, means his "outer physiology."

The little book by Elton (1927) provides the easiest introduction to animal ecology. A group of Chicago authors (Allee *et al.*, 1949) have written a comprehensive review of the subject. They found it convenient, in organizing their material, to use four main topical divisions: "The Analysis of the Environment," "Populations," "The Community," and "Ecology and Evolution." These topics may also serve conveniently for summarizing some of the material in which the ecological point of view seems pertinent in human studies.

ANALYSIS OF THE ENVIRONMENT

The concept of "environment" is certainly difficult and may even be misleading; but we have no handy substitute. It seems simple enough to distinguish between the organism and the surrounding environment and to separate forces acting on an organism into those that are internal and inherent and those that are external and environmental. But in actual practice this system breaks down in many ways, because the organism and the environment are constantly interacting so that the environment is modified by the organism and vice versa. I have attempted elsewhere (Bates, 1950) a slight and superficial analysis of this situation from the biological point of view.

In the case of man, the difficulties with the environmental concept are compounded because we have to deal with man as an animal and with man as a bearer of culture. If we look at man as an animal and try to analyze the environmental forces that are acting on the organism, we find that we have to deal with things like climate, soil, vegetation, and such-like factors common to all biological situations; but we also find, always, very important environmental influences that we can only class as "cultural," which modify the physical and biological factors. But man, as we know him, is always a bearer of culture; and, if we study human culture, we find that it, in turn, is modified by the environmental factors of climate and geography. We thus easily get into great difficulties from the necessity of viewing culture, at one moment, as a part of the man and, at another moment, as a part of the environment.

This perhaps helps to explain the difference in materials, emphasis, and conclusions that one is likely to find between textbooks of human geography and textbooks of cultural anthropology. The geographer tends to regard culture as a part of the man and is thus preoccupied in describing and explaining the environmental relationships of the man-culture system. The anthropologist, on the other hand, is likely to be preoccupied with culture as a thing-in-itself, and he thus tends to describe and explain human behavior directly in cultural terms. It may be that the chief virtue in stressing an ecological point of view lies in the consequent necessity of reconciling these apparent differences: of treating culture in one context as a part of the man and in another as a part of the environment.

The difficulties introduced by cultural factors are apparent in the studies of the effect of climate on man. The biologist can study the temperature conditions of the normal habitats of his organisms in nature and can check the effect on them of other temperature conditions in laboratory experiments, thus arriving at a description of the optimum and limiting temperatures for various species or for particular kinds of activity. But with man the variable of culture is always interposed between the climate and the organism—clothing, housing, and custom must always be taken into account.

Human geographers, in their study of climate, have relied largely on measurements of climate derived from standard meteorological stations. Such measurements, because of their standardiza-

tion, are essential for the comparison of conditions in different geographical regions; they serve as a sort of index to differences or similarities. But biologists have come to recognize that very few organisms live under the environmental conditions measured in a Stevenson screen and that, for purposes of ecological study, other sorts of environmental conditions must be measured. In addition to the geographical climate, we must take into consideration the "ecoclimate" (the climate of the habitat) and the "microclimate" (the climate surrounding the individual organism). These concepts have as yet been little used in human studies, but they would surely be useful. The ecoclimate for man would be the climate of the cities, villages, clearings, or forests in which he lives, perhaps extending to the climate of the interior of his houses. The microclimate would be the climate that affected him directly as an organism—the conditions directly surrounding his skin, under his clothes, or inside his bedding.

Studies of this sort are becoming of increasing interest, particularly to the physiologists, and they are often carried out under some such rubric as "environmental physiology." Investigation at this level was greatly stimulated during the second World War by the necessity of determining suitable clothing design for arctic, tropical, and desert conditions. These studies have been summarized in books edited by Adolph (1947) and Newburgh (1949), which, in turn, contain extensive bibliographies. The introductory chapter by Frederick Wulsin in the Newburgh book forms a sort of synthesis of the geographical, physiological, and anthropological points of view toward these problems of climate-culture-man, thus outlining what could well be called the "ecological approach."

We have, on the one hand, the problem of the climatic relations of man as a species and, on the other hand, the problem of possible differences among human races in climatic adaptation. It is easy to assume that, since the races show a pattern of geographical distribution, they represent adaptations to different geographical environments; and, with a certain amount of ingenuity, all sorts of adaptive traits can be described. These, however, often break down under close analysis. The problem is one aspect of the general biological problem of adaptive differences among closely related populations. There is an extensive literature on this subject. The discussion, as long as it stayed at the descriptive stage, was, in general, unrewarding, and we are only beginning to understand adaptive differences in populations as we make progress with laboratory analysis of physiological characters. The diagnostic, structural characters of populations often turn out to be nonadaptive but to be correlated with differences in physiology or behavior that clearly are adaptive.

With man, of course, we again have the complicating factor of culture, since the different human races are often the bearers of different types of culture. We may, indeed, get involved in very parallel sorts of arguments in discussing racial adaptations to climate and cultural adaptations to climate. We have also to distinguish between the inherent adaptive traits of the population and the acclimatization of the individual growing up in a particular environment. Coon, Garn, and Birdsell (1950), for instance, have described races largely in adaptive terms. As an example, they point out that "a Yahgan Indian can go fishing in his canoe in chilly Antarctic waters for hours at a time with no clothing but a single sealskin on his back, and no other heat than a smoldering fire in the clay hearth amidships. An urban New Yorker would probably catch pneumonia were

he to try to follow the Fuegian's example." Sure; but what if the New Yorker had been raised from infancy in the Yahgan environment? The experimental approach to such questions with man is very difficult; but otherwise how are we to distinguish between inherent differences in racial physiology, differences in individual acclimatization, and differences in cultural conditioning?

The experiments are arranged for us in places where different races live in the same climatic environment, with similar or different cultures, and here surely is a rewarding field for ecological or physiological study. A beginning has been made in studies like those by Robinson and others (1941) on Negroes and Whites in the southern United States; such studies have generally failed to show clear physiological differences between the races in things like adaptation to work under heat stress. For literature references I might cite, in addition to Coon, Garn, and Birdsell (1950), Price (1939), and Bates (1952).

The analysis of the human environment should go beyond climate, to include factors like physiography, resources, food supply, and disease. The study of physiography and resources has fallen largely to the geographers, but the ecologist would have to consider them, too. The ecological point of view, with its center of interest on man as a functioning organism, may again give a different perspective on cultural problems. The geographer perhaps tends to stress the ways in which physiography and resources have shaped cultural patterns, while the ecological approach would bring out more strongly the ways in which the meaning of these environmental factors change under different cultural circumstances. The sea that is a barrier to a man of one culture may be a highway for a man of another. We are likely to think of resources in terms of our Western industrial culture; but the term has equal validity, though with different meanings, for peoples of other cultures.

This is nicely brought out in the study of the Nuer by Evans-Pritchard (1940)—a study that might easily be called ecological—in which he develops concepts of "ecologic time" and "ecologic distance." It is also brought out in the studies like those by Kroeber (1939) and Steward (1938) on American Indian cultures.

Food supply (nutrition) and disease have in common the fact that they have generally been studied by physiologists and physicians. Foods have got surprisingly little attention from anthropologists, and physiologists and nutritionists have tended to confine their interest to the food materials of contemporary Western culture. The result is a wide gap in our knowledge of human ecology, which is only gradually being filled by extension from both the anthropological and the nutritional sides. The work of Richards (1932) should be cited in connection with the anthropological side of this problem, and a paper by Laura Thompson (1949) may serve as an example of an ecological approach to a nutritional study. Analytical studies of the food values of the materials used by different peoples are slowly increasing in frequency; a paper by Anderson *et al.* (1946) is a good example of this recent work.

The neglect of the study of disease as an environmental factor influencing human development is understandable, though nonetheless regrettable. It reflects the rarity with which medical and anthropological interests have been combined in a single investigator or in a working team. The disease picture of the world has, of course, altered radically in the last few hundred years through the spread of pathogens in the course of Western expansion and trade.

It will probably always be impossible to form an accurate picture of disease distribution in the pre-Columbian world; yet this disease pattern was surely an important element in determining the pace and direction of human evolution and cultural development. It is worth while, then, to try to garner and evaluate all the clues that we can find.

We can get an idea of the environmental importance of disease from its relation to recorded history. Zinsser (1935) has brought this out in his classic study of typhus and history. Hackett (1937) has reviewed the evidence with regard to the relation between malaria and historical developments in Greece and Italy. It seems to me probable that malaria was brought to America by the Spaniards—and what a different environment tropical America would present for man without malaria! The whole history of European-American cultural contact is understandable only when disease is taken into account—smallpox, malaria, yellow fever, and the rest of the list of contagions that Western man brought suddenly to new areas.

But the chief interest of disease for the ecologist perhaps lies in its effect on the equations of population dynamics, since the behavior of populations is one of his chief study interests.

POPULATIONS

Biology has become more and more preoccupied with the study of populations. This stems in part from the realization, which became general about the turn of the century, that "species" was definable only in population terms —that a "species" was a population with certain characteristics more or less isolated from similar populations by reproductive behavior. The individual organism studied by the biologist was significant largely in so far as it represented a sample from a population.

Evolution, then, became a history not so much of changes in individuals as of changes in populations. Population genetics, population behavior, and the community relations of mixed populations thus became matters of great interest.

The ecologist studying the environmental relations of organisms would have to be concerned as much with populations and with communities of populations as with individuals. The study of the behavior of populations and communities has, in fact, come to be the chief function of ecology, since individual reactions are still most often studied under the rubric "physiology." There has been an attempt in America to split ecology into two sciences: an "autecology," concerned with individual reactions, and a "synecology," concerned with populations and communities. This seems to me an extreme of the deplorable separatist tendency in labeling biological sciences.

The study of human populations has, for the most part, had little relation with this biological interest. Such studies are generally carried out under the label "demography" and are primarily concerned with the collection and analysis of statistical material. Since statistical material is, for the most part, available only for regions under Western domination, demography has largely been concerned with the study of population conditions within Western culture. This, from the point of view of anthropology and human evolution, represents a rather special case. As statistical services are developed in non-Western areas, demographic studies of great interest and significance become possible, like the recent study of India by Kingsley Davis (1951). For the most part, however, the fragmentary records available for non-Western cultures can hardly be dealt with by standard methods. The inadequacy of the material presently available is nicely shown by the scholarly compilation of African materials made by Kuczynski (1948).

For the ecologist, the situation in the modern world is the end-point of a series of historical processes, and he would like to understand not only the factors governing this present situation but also the changes that occurred in the past. Carr-Saunders (1922) has written a review of population history from this evolutionary point of view, and Gordon Childe (1951) has summarized our archeological knowledge in terms of possible population dynamics. Childe has provided a conceptual framework for the study of population history by relating it to three cultural "revolutions"—the Neolithic, which turned on the domestication of plants and animals; the Urban, which involved the organization of cities and the specialization of working functions; and the Industrial, based on the exploitation of power sources, such as steam and electricity.

We can appreciate the effect of the Industrial Revolution on human population growth because it is recent and well-documented. It is analyzed in every textbook of population study. Childe argues, and documents from archeological materials, the existence of similar great changes in population relations with each of the previous revolutions. He is saying, in other words, that we must examine human population dynamics in four quite different environmental contexts: that of food-gathering economy, that of Neolithic economy, that of urban economy, and that of industrial economy.

Most of human evolution, through the million years of the Pleistocene, must have taken place in the context of a food-gathering economy. Our understanding of this evolutionary process, then, is going to depend on our understanding of the social, biological, and environmental relationships that prevailed under such an economy. The factors governing natality, mortality, and population density would be quite different from those operating in a post-Neolithic economy and should be a matter of keen concern to every student of human evolution. But our relevant information seems to be very scanty. Krzywicki (1934) has attempted to summarize what is known about the vital statistics of "primitive" peoples, but he found little that is clear or definite. The anthropologists who have studied contemporary food-gathering people have generally been little interested in these problems of quantitative relationships.

Children, in such an economy, are a handicap longer than they are in an agricultural economy. Lactation is prolonged, and a mother cannot handle more than one infant at a time. There seems to be considerable evidence that infanticide has been general among food-gathering peoples available for study, so that children are spaced several years apart. Taboos on intercourse may also have existed, though these seem more characteristic of agricultural peoples. One wonders how far back in time infanticide extends; and whether possibly in Pleistocene man the spacing of infants may have been governed by the suppression of ovulation during lactation—a matter that has been insufficiently studied in contemporary man. Factors governing death must also have had special characteristics during the Pleistocene. I cannot see how, with sparse populations organized into small bands wandering over limited territories, contagious diseases can have had the importance that they have assumed under other population conditions. Disease may well have been caused chiefly by pathogens with life-histories insuring maintenance and dispersal—as in the case of malaria, yellow fever, and the various helminths. Perhaps the contagions developed with the closer man-to-man association of post-Neolithic economies.

Such questions are the sort that arise when one takes an ecological view of human populations. They are difficult questions but not hopeless ones, and many students have undertaken imaginative attacks on the problems they pose. The studies of Weidenreich (1939) suggest that possibly the chief cause of death for Pleistocene man was man. Vallois (1937) has shown how one can get clues to the average life-span of fossil man. Such studies, always difficult, become somewhat easier as one moves forward in time, and all sorts of studies become possible with archeological materials. It is perhaps unjust to cite random examples without carefully surveying the literature, but I might cite the studies of Angel (1947) on Greek skeletons and of Cook (1949) on the population of central Mexico. The study by Russell (1948) of British medieval populations shows what can be accomplished by careful detective work among the records of more recent times.

THE COMMUNITY

No organism lives in isolation, nor is the behavior of any organism understandable without reference to other organisms. The oak tree, the cricket, the nitrifying bacterium, the mushroom of the fairy ring—all are involved with one another in complicated patterns of food and energy relations, of protection and support, of competition and co-operation. But these relationships are not diffused at random through the biosphere. Closely associated organisms tend to form systems of relationships among themselves, forming patterns that are relatively complete and independent of other similar aggregations. Such associations, which go to make up a particular kind of forest, a pond, a bog, a coral reef, or tidal flat, are called "biotic communities."

The study of such communities is a major preoccupation of biological ecology. I cannot see, however, how this study can carry over directly to the human field. The human community is a very different thing from the biotic community and must be studied by very special methods. It is an accident of language convenience that we use the same word for both concepts. A biotic community is perhaps more properly called a "biocenosis" or "biome," and with such labeling the semantic confusion disappears. We may be able to call both Miami and the sawgrass swamps of the Everglades "communities," but we cannot call them both "biocenoses."

Post-Neolithic man has come to form a biological community system of his own, with his domesticated plants and animals, his parasites and hangers-on, like weeds and rats and cockroaches; and the relationships among these organisms make an interesting and important field for study. But it is biological ecology as much as human ecology. When we move on into the field of social relations within the human community, to the study of Miami or of a Seminole village, we have moved into a field where biological factors are so completely swamped by cultural factors that we had better frankly admit that we have moved into a whole new area of science, where even analogies may be dangerous. Yet man as a bearer of culture has developed from man as an animal, and his biological inheritance is still with him. The ecological point of view may be useful in trying to understand this biological basis of human nature.

Man is definitely a social animal—that is, he customarily lives as a part of aggregations that are larger than the family (parents and immediate offspring). The most simple known human economies are based on groups of several families, and it seems probable that

man has been a social animal for a very long time. The fossil record gives some evidence of this, though necessarily indirect. It seems to me probable that man was a social animal before he became a bearer of culture, since I cannot imagine how the primordial elements of culture could have arisen in a non-social animal.

For the biological roots of human social behavior, then, we must look to the social mammals, and particularly the social primates. I think our psychologists have been too much preoccupied with the behavior of caged animals, and especially of the great apes. It is true that the apes are man's closest living relatives, but this does not mean that man must necessarily, at some time, have passed through a period of apelike behavior. The fossil record increasingly indicates a long evolutionary separation of the human and ape lines, with man perhaps developing from the extinct Australopithecines. The Pongid apes do not seem to be particularly strongly social—though we know extraordinarily little about their behavior in nature, since in the ape's natural habitat he is able to keep out of the way of observing man. The most careful field study of an ape, that by Carpenter (1940) on the gibbon, shows that the animal lives in family, rather than clan or tribal, groups; and there is evidence that the groupings in the other apes are small. Now it may perfectly well be that the Australopithecines were much more strongly social than the present Pongids and thus that man and his immediate ancestors have been social for several million years, while the Pongid line was going about the business of family living.

Whatever the case, since the Pongids present insurmountable difficulties for field study, we are driven to use more amenable primates for studies of field behavior. The finest field study of a social primate yet to be made is that of Carpenter (1934) on the howler monkeys of Panama. It is ironic that this splendid field study covers an animal that is unknown in the laboratory, while the best-known laboratory animals, the Indian rhesus and the American Cebus, have not been studied in their native habitats. It would seem particularly easy, and surely rewarding, to carry out detailed field studies of the rhesus monkeys in India.

There is not space here to consider the relevance to human problems of the various elements of studies of behavior in social mammals: social organization and leadership, the peck-order, sexual relations, co-operative behavior in food-gathering, communications, in-group and out-group relations, and so forth. It may be well, however, to consider one important topic—territory.

The contemporary realization of the importance of territory in vertebrate behavior dates from the publication of a book by Eliot Howard (1920) called *Territory in Bird Life.* A variety of kinds of territory are now recognized, but territorial, or "home-range," behavior of some sort appears to be universal in birds and mammals. General discussion of territorial phenomena can be found in papers by Nice (1941), Errington (1946), and Davis (1949). In the social mammals, such as deer, wolves, and monkeys, the herd or clan has a definite territory over which it ranges and which it defends from intrusion by solitary individuals or members of other herds or clans. Carpenter's howler study contains a particularly good analysis of territorial behavior in those animals.

Since territorialism seems to be a universal phenomenon among mammals, it must have characterized man's mammalian ancestors. It seems, in fact, to project in a recognizable form in contemporary food-gathering cultures (e.g., with the Semang of Malaya, as described by Forde [1934]). Man's "instinctive" (precultural) equipment, then, would include elements leading to group cohesion and territorial restriction. This has considerable implications. For one thing, Errington (1946) has shown how territory availability may be the immediate factor governing limitation of mammalian population—the excess individuals unable to find and occupy territories being those most subject to predation and to the hazards of the physical environment. The population of Pleistocene man may, similarly, have been governed by the territorial requirements of the small tribal groups. The frequency with which the cause of death in Pleistocene man was his fellow-man (Weidenreich, 1939) may well indicate that territorial arrangements were maintained aggressively by these early men.

Sir Arthur Keith (1949) has carried the implications of territory in human evolution to an extreme. He is so impressed with the fixity of tribe-territorial arrangements that he would allow early man no mobility at all. I do not see that his deductions necessarily follow. All mammals, as far as they have been studied, show strong territorial habits; yet populations have spread over the globe, fused, separated, replaced one another, in the most complex fashions. Territory serves as a brake on population movements in normal times, but it by no means precludes such movements. At most, the tribe-territory arrangements of early man would mean that "migrations" would not be the vast movements that we sometimes imagine, like the sweeping of the hordes of Huns across Asia. Migration with food-gathering man would rather be a sort of infiltration process, an accumulation of small territorial readjustments and perhaps, under environmental stress, the complete displacement of the small tribal groups. But such displacements can, in the frame of geologic time, cover the whole planet.

The Neolithic discovery of agriculture and pastoralism would mark the end of the simple pattern of clan and territory. Cultural adaptations enabled men to live in larger aggregations, so that the village, the city, and finally the nation could be built up. With this history one can hope that eventually mankind as a whole will be the social unit, and the planetary surface the tribal territory. But these processes are governed by cultural evolution, and I often suspect that many of our troubles are caused by biological hangovers from our long Pleistocene submission to clan loyalties and territorial defense.

ECOLOGY AND EVOLUTION

Haeckel, in his original definition of ecology, pointed out that it would be concerned with "alle diejenigen verwickelten Wechsel, welche Darwin als die Bedingungen des Kampfes um's Dasein bezeichnet." The phrase "struggle for existence" is rather out of fashion because it clearly carries implications that may be dangerously misleading. We might better say now that ecology is concerned with the external factors that control the survival and abundance of individuals and populations, whether or not this involves "struggling."

This is perhaps half of evolution, the other half (genetics) being concerned with the internal factors of the organism itself, with the mechanisms that lead to the development of new potentialities in the organism (mutation or the origin of variation), and with the mechanisms that govern the inheritance of these potentialities. Neither half makes sense by itself, because the organism is meaningless except in some environmental context; and the environment is meaningless (to the biologist) except in terms of organic processes. The "nature versus nurture" controversy, in other words, turns on meaningless terms.

Yet the internal and external factors, which together result in the living systems that we can observe, require different methods of study, so that the distinction between the ecological and the genetic points of view is fruitful, at least at our present level of understanding—a fruitfulness that depends on the geneticist's having a considerable knowledge of ecological work and vice versa. This condition is coming generally to prevail among biologists, but its development among students of man is hampered by the special difficulties of both human genetics and human ecology. The realization of the need, however, is certainly growing.

The 1950 *Cold Spring Harbor Symposium of Quantitative Biology* (Vol. XV of the series) was devoted to the "Origin and Evolution of Man." This provides an excellent summary of the background knowledge and current interests of physical anthropologists and human geneticists. But in reading the volume, one is impressed by the general lack of emphasis on the ecological aspects of the problem under review. There is only rather incidental discussion of the forces governing survival in human populations and of possible changes in such forces in different geological and geographical circumstances, of human environmental adaptations, and of human population dynamics.

Partly this situation reflects the interests of the particular people writing the chapters of this symposium. A truly balanced and complete coverage of the topics directly pertinent to human evolution would hardly be manageable, and the symposium was quite sensibly directed at the more specific objective of furthering understanding between the geneticists and the physical anthropologists. But it also reflects a relative scarcity of students preoccupied with the ecological aspects of human evolution. Structure is more easily handled than function, and perhaps the structural problems—the fossil lineages, the racial traits, and the genetic mechanisms—must be clarified before we can even define the functional questions. Surely now, however, we have reached the point where the functional, ecological relations can be fruitfully emphasized.

Both the biological and the social sciences are in a stage of development where students are preoccupied with facts and wary of speculation. This, in the present connection, may be something of a handicap. We have a modicum of facts about Pleistocene man and the Pleistocene environment, and more abundant information about contemporary man and his environment. It seems to me that now we need a certain amount of bold speculation, aimed at relating these, to furnish us with hypotheses that will help us in organizing our facts and in guiding our search for new facts. Our hypotheses, however carefully we frame them, are bound to be wrong, but we are, I think, overly afraid of being wrong. The process of science seems to consist in setting up and demolishing conceptual schemes. As Conant (1951) has said: "Science is an interconnected series of concepts and conceptual schemes that have developed as a result of experimentation and observation and are fruitful of further experimentation and observation." Our information about man's relations with his environment seems, at every point, to be meager indeed; but it also seems to be scattered and unrelated. Perhaps more than new information, we need a consolidation and relation of these facts that have been so diversely garnered; and the questions of origins, of evolution, provide a convenient focus for this consolidation process.

I have tried, in this paper, to outline some of the topics that seem particularly appropriate for study from the ecological point of view. But, in closing, I should like to emphasize again that I do not think "ecology" can profitably be developed as a special subject matter, a special discipline within the complex of the social sciences. The subject, man, is divisible only as a matter of arbitrary convenience. We have to specialize in order to be able to handle the materials that we must study; but I think the arbitrary basis of our specialization is more easily kept in mind if we use vernacular labels for our topics—environmental analysis or adaptation, population, community structure, evolution, or what-have-you. Some topics will be more readily studied from an ecological point of view, others from a physiological, morphological, geographical, or some other point of view. But the subject—man, his origins, his present circumstances, and his destiny— forms a single pattern that cannot be broken into pieces that are separately understandable.

REFERENCES

ADOLPH, E. F., and ASSOCIATES. 1947. *Physiology of Man in the Desert.* New York: Interscience Publishers.

ALLEE, W. C.; EMERSON, A. E.; PARK, O.; PARK, T.; and SCHMIDT, K. P. 1949. *Principles of Animal Ecology.* Philadelphia: W. B. Saunders Co.

ANDERSON, R. K.; CALVO, JOSÉ; SERRANO, GLORIA; and PAYNE, G. C. 1946. "A Study of the Nutritional Status and Food Habits of Otomi Indians in the Mezquital Valley of Mexico," *American Journal of Public Health,* XXXVI, 883–903.

ANGEL, J. L. 1947. "The Length of Life in Ancient Greece," *Journal of Gerontology,* II, 18–24.

BANKS, A. L. 1950. *Man and His Environment.* Cambridge: At the University Press.

BARROWS, H. H. 1923. "Geography as Human Ecology," *Annals of the Association of American Geographers,* XIII, 1–14.

BATES, MARSTON. 1950. *The Nature of Natural History*. New York: Charles Scribner's Sons.

———. 1952. *Where Winter Never Comes: A Study of Man and Nature in the Tropics*. New York: Charles Scribner's Sons.

BEWS, J. W. 1935. *Human Ecology*. London: H. Milford.

CARPENTER, C. R. 1934. *A Field Study of the Behavior and Social Relations of Howling Monkeys (Alouatta palliata)*. ("Comparative Psychology Monographs," Vol. X, No. 2.) Baltimore, Md.: Johns Hopkins Press.

———. 1940. *A Field Study in Siam of the Behavior and Social Relations of the Gibbon (Hylobates lar)*. ("Comparative Psychology Monographs," Vol. XVI, No. 5.) Baltimore, Md.: Johns Hopkins Press.

CARR-SAUNDERS, A. M. 1922. *The Population Problem: A Study in Human Evolution*. Oxford: Clarendon Press.

CHILDE, V. G. 1951. *Man Makes Himself*. ("Mentor Books.") New York: New American Library. First published in England in 1936.

CONANT, J. B. 1951. *Science and Common Sense*. New Haven: Yale University Press.

COOK, S. F. 1949. *Soil Erosion and Population in Central Mexico*. ("Ibero-americana," No. 34.) Berkeley: University of California Press.

COON, C. S.; GARN, S. M.; and BIRDSELL, J. B. 1950. *Races: A Study of the Problems of Race Formation in Man*. Springfield, Ill.: Charles C. Thomas.

CORWIN, E. H. L. (ed.). 1949. *Ecology of Health*. (New York Academy of Medicine Centennial, Institute on Public Health, 1947.) New York: Commonwealth Fund.

DAVIS, DAVID. 1949. "An Animal's Home Is Its Castle," *Scientific Monthly*, LXIX, 249–53.

DAVIS, KINGSLEY. 1951. *The Population of India and Pakistan*. Princeton, N.J.: Princeton University Press.

ELTON, CHARLES. 1927. *Animal Ecology*. New York: Macmillan Co.

ERRINGTON, P. L. 1946. "Predation and Vertebrate Populations," *Quarterly Review of Biology*, XXI, 144–77, 221–45.

EVANS-PRITCHARD, E. E. 1940. *The Nuer: A Description of the Modes of Livelihood and Political Institutions of a Nilotic People*. London: Oxford University Press.

FORDE, C. D. 1934. *Habitat, Economy, and Society: A Geographical Introduction to Ethnology*. New York: E. P. Dutton Co.

HACKETT, L. W. 1937. *Malaria in Europe: An Ecological Study*. London: H. Milford.

HAECKEL, ERNST. 1870. "Ueber Entwickelungsgang und Aufgabe der Zoologie," *Jenäische Zeitschrift für Medicin und Naturwissenchaft*, V, 353–70.

HAWLEY, A. H. 1950. *Human Ecology: A Theory of Community Structure*. New York: Ronald Press Co.

HOWARD, H. E. 1920. *Territory in Bird Life*. London: John Murray.

KEITH, SIR ARTHUR. 1949. *A New Theory of Human Evolution*. New York: Philosophical Library.

KROEBER, A. L. 1939. *Cultural and Natural Areas of Native North America*. Berkeley: University of California Press.

KRZYWICKI, LUDWIK. 1934. *Primitive Society and Its Vital Statistics*. London: Macmillan & Co., Ltd.

KUCZYNSKI, R. R. 1948. *Demographic Survey of the British Colonial Empire*, Vol. I: *West Africa*. London and New York: Oxford University Press.

NEWBURGH, L. H. (ed.). 1949. *Physiology of Heat Regulation and the Science of Clothing*. Philadelphia: W. B. Saunders Co.

NICE, MARGARET. 1941. "The Role of Territory in Bird Life," *American Midland Naturalist*, XXVI, 441–87.

PARKINS, A. E. 1934. "The Geography of American Geographers," *Journal of Geography*, XXXIII, 221–30.

PLATT, R. S. 1948. "Environmentalism versus Geography," *American Journal of Sociology*, LIII, 351–58.

PRICE, A. G. 1939. *White Settlers in the Tropics*. ("Special Publications," No. 23.) New York: American Geographical Society.

QUINN, J. A. 1950. *Human Ecology*. New York: Prentice-Hall Book Co., Inc.

RICHARDS, AUDREY I. 1932. *Hunger and Work in a Savage Tribe: A Functional*

Study of Nutrition among the Southern Bantu. London: George Routledge & Sons.

ROBINSON, S.; DILL, D. B.; WILSON, J. W.; and NIELSEN, M. 1941. "Adaptations of White Men and Negroes to Prolonged Work in Humid Heat," *American Journal of Tropical Medicine,* XXI, 261–87.

RUSSELL, J. C. 1948. *British Medieval Population.* Albuquerque: University of New Mexico Press.

STEWARD, J. H. 1938. *Basin-Plateau Aboriginal Sociopolitical Groups.* (Bureau of American Ethnology Bull. 137.) Washington: Government Printing Office.

THOMPSON, LAURA. 1949. "The Relations of Men, Animals, and Plants in an Island Community (Fiji)," *American Anthropologist,* LI, 253–67.

THORNTHWAITE, C. W. 1940. "The Relation of Geography to Human Ecology," *Ecological Monographs,* X, 343–48.

VALLOIS, H. V. 1937. "La Durée de la vie chez l'homme fossile," *Anthropologie,* XLVII, 499–532.

WEIDENREICH, FRANZ. 1939. "The Duration of Life of Fossil Man in China and the Pathological Lesions Found in His Skeleton," *Chinese Medical Journal,* LV, 34–44.

WHITE, C. L., and RENNER, G. T. 1948. *Human Geography: An Ecological Study of Society.* New York: Appleton-Century-Crofts.

ZINSSER, HANS. 1935. *Rats, Lice, and History.* Boston: Little, Brown & Co.

ZIPF, G. K. 1949. *Human Behavior and the Principle of Least Effort: An Introduction to Human Ecology.* Cambridge, Mass.: Addison-Wesley Press.

Historical Linguistics and Unwritten Languages

By JOSEPH H. GREENBERG

I. HISTORICAL LINGUISTICS AND DESCRIPTIVE LINGUISTICS

UNLIKE SOME other aspects of anthropology affected by the functionalist attack on history, the validity and fruitfulness of the historic approach in linguistics has never been seriously questioned. The objections which have been raised to certain assumptions of classical Indo-European comparative linguistics, such as the existence of sound laws without exceptions or the overliteral interpretation of the family-tree metaphor of language relationship, have not involved any fundamental doubt as to the legitimacy and value of historical reconstruction as such; at the most, they have, in the case of the Italian group of neo-linguists,[1] suggested specific alternative reconstructions of certain Proto-Indo-European forms.

The possibility of the application of traditional Indo-European methods to "primitive" (i.e., unwritten) languages has been deprecated by some Indo-Europeanists (Vendryes, 1925). It is

evident that, while in principle the same procedures are appropriate, the absence of direct documentation for earlier historic periods is a distinct methodological handicap. The last decades, however, have seen the successful employment of classical reconstruction methods in a number of areas, including Central Algonkian by L. Bloomfield, Bantu by C. Meinhof, and Malayo-Polynesian by O. Dempwolff. It should be borne in mind that in all these cases we have rather closely related forms of speech, so that the task involved is more comparable to the reconstruction of Proto-Germanic or Proto-Slavic than that of Proto-Indo-European. These attempts do furnish an important demonstration of the universal scope of those mechanisms of linguistic change which were already known to function in the more restricted area of the traditionally studied Indo-European, Finno-Ugric, and Semitic stocks (Hockett, 1948).

Much more serious than skepticism regarding the possibility of linguistic reconstruction in the absence of early written records is the widely held opinion, which will be discussed in a later section of this paper, that remote relationships or even those of the order existing within the Indo-European family cannot be established for primitive languages because of the far-reaching

1. The reconstructions of the neo-linguistic school are not generally accepted by other scholars. For an exposition of neo-linguistic method, see G. Bonfante (1945). For a hostile critique see Robert Hall, Jr. (1946). It should perhaps be added that the approach of L. Hjelmsler in Denmark seems to exclude diachronic problems from language in principle but that this remains hardly more than a theoretic model.

influence which one language can exercise on another even in fundamental traits of grammatical structure. It is even claimed that the genetic question here loses its meaning, in that one language can go back to several distinct origins and cannot therefore be said to belong to one family more than to another (Boas, 1920). It is worth observing that even in these cases the value of historic investigation is not denied as providing evidence of specific contacts, even though, it is held, the genetic question cannot be resolved. Thus Uhlenbeck, who, in his later writing, takes the view of genetic connections just mentioned, has lavished much time and effort on an attempt to show resemblances between the Uralic languages and Eskimo which require a historical explanation, while avoiding commitment as to the nature of the historic relationship involved.

While historic linguistics thus continues as a legitimate and major area of linguistic endeavor, it is undeniable that, with the rise of structural schools in European and American linguistics, the center of interest has shifted in the recent period from the historical problems which dominated linguistic science in the nineteenth century to those of synchronic description. The present preoccupation with descriptive formulations, which appears to be the linguistic analogue of the rise of functionalism, can contribute much that is valuable to diachronic studies. Most obviously, perhaps, any advance in descriptive techniques, by improving the quality of the data which constitute the basis of historical investigation, can furnish material for hypotheses of wider historical connections and likewise increase the precision of reconstruction for those already established. Another factor of great significance is the influence of the fundamental approach to language which all structuralists share, whatever their other di-

vergences, namely, the concept of languages as a system of functional units. In its diachronic aspect this provides us with a view of change as related to a system and at least partially explainable in terms of its internal functioning through time. In the realm of sound patterns, some of these implications have been realized for some time. Thus Trubetskoy, as well as others, has distinguished between those sound changes which affect the sound structure of the language and those which leave it unchanged (Jakobson, 1931). This clearly parallels the synchronic distinction between phonetic and phonemic sound differences. Under the influence of this manner of thinking, sound change in language is more and more considered in terms of the shifts and realignment it produces in the sound structure of language rather than as a haphazard set of isolated changes, as in the traditional handbooks of historical linguistics.[2] The more rigorous formulation of alternations in the phonemic shape of morphemes (morphophonemics) has also borne fruit in Hoenigwald's exposition of the bearing of such data on internal reconstruction, that is, the reconstruction of certain aspects of the former states of a given language without resort to either related languages or historical records (Hoenigswald, 1950). Although historical linguists had in effect used this method without formulation, the emphasis on rigorous formulation of assumptions is, on the whole, beneficial in an area, such as historical reconstruction, in which it has so largely been lacking.

Although there is thus no fundamental opposition between the historical and descriptive approaches to language, the focusing of attention on syn-

2. Examples are the recent studies of Grimm's laws and other changes in Germanic by Twaddel and others, and various studies by Martinet of sound shifts (e.g., 1950).

chronic problems in the recent historic period, combined with the traditional concentration of linguistic forces in the areas of a few major Eurasiatic speech families, has led to comparative neglect of the basic problems of historical research in unwritten languages.

II. THE ESTABLISHMENT OF LINGUISTIC RELATIONSHIP

The fundamental achievement of nineteenth-century science in linguistics, as in certain other areas, notably biology, was to replace the traditional static interpretation of similarities in terms of fortuitous coincidence among species as kinds, all of which were created at the same time and could vary only within fixed and narrow limits, with a dynamic historic interpretation of similarities as reflecting specific historical interrelationships of varying degrees of remoteness. Taxonomy, the science of classification, thus was no longer the attempt to find essential features connecting certain things more closely than others as part of a divine plan but rather based itself on the selection of those criteria which reflected actual historic relationships. In the language of biology, it was the search for homologies rather than mere analogies. In spite of the fruitfulness of the Indo-European hypothesis and the further successes of similar hypotheses in establishing the Finno-Ugric, Semitic, and other families, the assumptions on the bases of which these first victories of linguistics as a science were obtained were never clearly formulated, and the extension of these methods to other areas of the world has suffered from the beginning from a lack of clarity regarding the criteria of genetic relationship, resulting, in almost every major area, in a welter of conflicting classifications and even in widespread doubt as to the feasibility of any interpretation of linguistic similarities in terms of historical connections. Yet assumptions which have been the very foundation on which the edifice of modern linguistics has been reared and which have helped give it a rigorousness of method and precision of result which are admittedly superior to those dealing with any other phase of human cultural behavior should not be lightly abandoned unless, of course, the data actually demand it. In what follows, an attempt is made to formulate the principles in accordance with which similarities in language can be given a historical interpretation. It is hoped that this will furnish the guiding principles on the basis of which problems in the subsequent sections referring to specific areas can receive a reasonable solution.

The fundamental assumption concerning language on the basis of which historical interpretation of linguistic similarities becomes possible seems to have been first explicitly formulated by the great Swiss linguist, Ferdinand de Saussure, in his *Cours de linguistique générale*, although its relevance for historical problems is not there stated. According to De Saussure, language is a system of signs having two aspects, the *signifiant* and the *signifié*, equivalent, in the terminology of Bloomfield and of American linguists, to "form" and "meaning," respectively. Moreover, the relationship between these two aspects of the linguistic sign is essentially arbitrary. Given any particular meaning, there is no inherent necessity for any particular set of sounds to designate it in preference to any other. Although first stated in this manner by De Saussure, this assumption actually underlies the nineteenth-century hypotheses of linguistic relationships and represents essentially the solution accepted by all modern linguists of the controversy descending from the Greeks concerning the naturalness versus the conventionality of language.

Given the arbitrariness of the relationship between form and meaning, resemblances between two languages significantly greater than chance must receive a historical explanation, whether of common origin or of borrowing.

This statement regarding the arbitrariness of the sign does need some qualification, in that there is a slight tendency for certain sounds or sound combinations to be connected more frequently with certain meanings than might be expected on a purely chance basis. Conspicuous instances are the nursery words for "mother" and "father" and onomatopoeias for certain species of animals. This is generally recognized as only a slight derogation from the principle of the arbitrariness of the sign, since the sound can never be predicted from the meaning; and, since such instances are* relatively a minor factor from the point of view of frequency of occurrence, they will add slightly to the percentage of resemblances to be expected beyond those merely the result of chance between any two unrelated languages; but they are not adequate for the explanation of wholesale resemblances between two particular languages, such as French or Italian. Moreover, the few resemblances which rest on this factor can be allowed for by assigning them less weight in judging instances of possible historical connections between languages. This factor making for specific resemblances between languages will hereafter be called, somewhat inappropriately, "symbolism," in accordance with the terminology employed by psychologists.

Given any specific resemblance both in form and in meaning between two languages, there are four possible classes of explanations. Of these four, two —chance and symbolism—do not involve historic relationship, in contrast to the remaining pair—genetic relationship and borrowing. These four sources of similarity have parallels in nonlinguistic

aspects of culture. Genetic relationship corresponds to internal evolution, borrowing to diffusion, chance to convergence through limited possibilities (as in art designs), and symbolism to convergence through similarity of function.

Up to this point resemblances in form between two languages unaccompanied by similarity of meaning and those of meaning not bound to similarity of form have not been considered. I believe that such resemblances must be resolutely excluded as irrelevant for the determination of genetic relationship. They practically always arise through convergence or borrowing. Form without function (e.g., the mere presence of tonal systems or vowel harmony in two languages) or function without form (e.g., the presence of gender morphemes in two languages expressed by different formal means) is often employed as relevant for the determination of relationship, sometimes as the sole criterion, as in Meinhof's definition of Hamitic, or in conjunction with other criteria. The preference for agreements involving meaning without accompanying sound resemblances is sometimes based on metaphysical preconceptions regarding the superiority of form over matter (Kroeber, 1913).

Resemblance in meaning only is frequently the result of convergence through limited possibilities. Important and universal aspects of human experience, such as the category of number or a system of classification based on sex or animation in the noun or one of tense or aspect in the verb, tend to appear independently in the most remote areas of the world and can never be employed as evidence for a historical connection. That the dual number occurs in Yana (California), ancient Greek, and Polynesian is obviously an instance of convergent development. Sometimes semantic similarity without similarity in the formal means of expression is present in contiguous lan-

guages of similar or diverse genetic connection. In these cases we have the
linguistic analogue of Kroeber's concept
of "stimulus diffusion"—indeed, a remarkably clear-cut instance of this process. Languages spoken by people in
constant culture contact forming a culture area tend to share many such semantic traits through the mechanism
of diffusion. This process may be carried to the point where it is possible to
translate almost literally from one language to another. However, since it is
precisely the semantic aspect of language which tends to reflect changes
in the cultural situation and since such
semantic resemblances cover continuous
geographical areas, these resemblances
are clearly secondary, however far-
reaching they may be in extent. Beyond the inherent probabilities, there
is much empirical evidence in areas
from which documented history exists.
Those traits, which various Balkan languages share in common and which are
one of the marks of the Balkans as a
cultural area, are largely semantic, involving a difference in the phonemic
content employed as the mode of expression. Thus Rumanian, Serbian, and
Greek express the future by "to wish"
followed by an infinitive, but in Rumanian we have (1st person sing.)
voiu + V, in Serbian *ću* + V, and in
Greek *tha* + V. These are all known
to be historically relatively recent and
not a result of the more remote Indo-
European genetic connections which all
of them share. Roughly similar arguments hold for resemblances of form
without meaning. There are limited
possibilities for phonemic systems. For
example, such historically unconnected
languages as Hausa in West Africa,
classical Latin, and the Penutian Yokuts
share a five-vowel system with two
significant degrees of length (*a, a•, e, e•,
i, i•, o, o•, u, u•*). Some resemblances
in form without function are the result
of the influence of one language on

another, e.g., the clicks of Zulu which
have been borrowed from the Khoisan
languages. Normally, when related languages have been separated for a fairly
long period, we expect, and find, considerable differences both in their sound
systems and in their semantic aspects
resulting from differential drift and the
diversity of the cultural circumstances
under which their speakers have lived.
Too great similarities in such matters
are suspect.

Since, as has been seen, resemblances
in form without meaning and meaning
without form are normally explainable
by hypotheses other than genetic relationship, their presence does not indicate, nor their absence refute, it.
Hence they may be left out of consideration as irrelevant for this particular problem.

The evidence relevant to the determination of genetic relationship then
becomes the extent and nature of mean-
ing-form resemblances in meaningful
elements, normally the minimal element, the morpheme. Lexical resemblance between languages then refers
to resemblances in root morphemes,
and grammatical resemblances refer
to derivational and inflectional morphemes. The two basic methodological
problems become the exclusion of convergence and symbolism, on the basis
of significantly more than chance resemblance leading to a hypothesis of
some kind of historical connection, and
among these the segregation of those
cases in which borrowing is an adequate explanation of the more-than-
chance resemblances from those instances in which this is inadequate and
genetic relationship must be posited.

The first approach to the problem of
more than chance resemblances is quantitative. We may ask how many resemblances may be expected between any
two languages which are not genetically related and have not borrowed from
each other or from a mutual source.

Several approaches seem possible. One would involve the calculation for each of the two languages of the expected number of chance resemblances on the basis of its phonemic structure and allowed phonemic sequences arranged in terms of what may be called "resemblance classes," based on a resolution as to what phonemes are to be considered similar to others for the purposes of the comparison. To such a procedure there are several objections. It does not eliminate the factor of symbolism, and it does not take into account the relative frequencies of the phonemes in each language. If, for example, in comparing two particular languages, it were agreed that the labials would all be treated as resembling one another and the dentals likewise and if, in both languages, dentals were five times as frequent as labials, the possibility of chance resemblance would be much greater than if they were equal. This objection could, of course, be met in principle by a weighting in terms of frequency, but in actual practice it would be difficult to carry out.

A more desirable procedure would be the following. Let us suppose that we have a list of one thousand morphemes matched for meaning in the two languages. In language A the first morpheme is *kan*, "one." Instead of calculating the abstract probability of a form resembling *kan* sufficiently to be considered similar, let us actually compare *kan* in form with all the thousand items on the other list. Let us likewise compare the meaning "one" with all the meanings on the other list. The chance probability of the existence of a form resembling *kan*, "one," in both form and meaning in list B will then be the product of form resemblances and meaning resemblances divided by 1,000, the total number of items. We should then do this for each morpheme in list A and total the probabilities. As can be seen, this is a very tedious procedure.

Moreover, it will not include resemblances due to symbolism.

A much more practical method, which takes into account both chance and symbolism, is simply to take a number of languages which are admittedly unrelated and ascertain the number of resemblances actually found. The difficulty here is that results will vary with the phonetic structure of the languages. A number of such counts indicates that approximately 4 per cent is the modal value, employing a very generous interpretation of what constitutes similarity. Where, however, the two languages are similar in the phonemic structure of their morphemes, the degree of resemblance can become significantly larger. For example, between Thai and Jur, a Nilotic language, which have very similar phonemic structures, it reaches 7 per cent. It can be safely asserted that a resemblance of 20 per cent in vocabulary always requires a historical explanation and that, unless similarity of phonetic structure leads to the expectation of a high degree of chance similarity, even 8 per cent is well beyond what can be expected without the intervention of historical factors. This factor of the similarity or difference of the phonemic structure of morphemes is so important that in doubtful cases a simplified version of the second test, that of matching lists, should probably be applied. We might compare a particular form in list B with all those in list A from the phonemic point of view only, allowing merely one meaning, that of its partner in list A, presumably the nearest semantic equivalent. We then compare with the expected frequency of resemblances (which is, of course, smaller than by the first method) only those cases of resemblances on the list in which the two forms are matched as nearest semantic equivalents. Thus, if as our first matching pair we had A *nem*, B *kan*, "one," and later in the list A *ken*, B *sa*, "only," the resemblance between A *ken*, "only," and B *kan*, "one," would be disregarded as not occurring in a matching pair.

In actual fact, however, this test can probably be dispensed with, since the mere quantity of resemblances in the form and meaning of morphemes is not the decisive factor in more doubtful cases. There are additional considerations based on the weightings to be accorded to individual items and the further fact that isolated languages are seldom found. The bringing-in of closely related languages on each side introduces new factors of the highest importance, which should lead to a definite decision.

Other things being equal, the evidential value of a resemblance in form and meaning between elements in two languages is proportional to the length of the item. A comparison such as A, *-k*; B, *-k*, "in," is, from this point of view at least, less significant than such a resemblance as A, *pegadu*; B, *fikato*, "nose." More important is the following consideration. The unit of comparison is the morpheme with its variant allomorphs, if these exist. If the two languages agree in these variations, and particularly if the variants are rather different in phonemic content, we have not only the probability that such-and-such a sequence of phonemes will occur in a particular meaning but the additional factor that it will be accompanied by certain variations in certain combinations. Agreement in such arbitrary morphophonemic variations, particularly if suppletive, i.e., involving no phonemic resemblance between the variants, is of a totally different order of probability than the agreement in a nonvarying morpheme or one in which the languages do not exhibit the same variation. Even one instance of this is hardly possible without historical connection of some kind, and, since, moreover, it is hardly likely to be borrowed, it virtually guarantees genetic relation-

ship. We may illustrate from English and German. The morpheme with the main alternant *hæv*, "have," in English resembles the German chief allomorph *ha:b*, "have," both in form and in meaning. In English, *hæv* alternates with *hæ-* before *-z* of the third person singular present (*hæ-z*, "has"). In German, correspondingly, *ha:b* has an alternant *ha-* in a similar environment, before *-t*, indicating third person singular present, to form *ha-t*, "has." Likewise, English *gud*, "good," has the alternant *be-* before *-tər*, "comparative" and *-st*, "superlative." Similarly, German *gu:t*, "good," has the alternant *be-* before *-sər*, "comparative," and *-st*, "superlative." The probability of all this being chance, particularly the latter, which is suppletive, is infinitesimal. Since it is precisely such arbitrary variations, "irregularities" in nontechnical languages, which are subject to analogical pressure, they tend to be erased in one or the other language, even if some instances existed in the parent-languages. Where they exist, however, they are precious indications of a real historical connection.

More generally applicable are considerations arising from the fact that the comparison is only in rare instances between two isolated languages. The problem as to whether the resemblances between two languages are merely the result of chance plus symbolism can then be tested by a number of additional methods. Let us say that, as is frequently the case, one or more other languages or language groups resemble the two languages in question but in the same indecisive way, that is, that this third or fourth language is not conspicuously closer to one than to the other of the two languages with which we have been first concerned. The following fundamental probability consideration applies. The likelihood of finding a resemblance both in form and in meaning simultaneously in three languages is the square of its probability in two languages. In general, the original probability must be raised to the $n-1$-power where a total of n languages is involved, just as the probability of throwing a 6 once on a die is $\frac{1}{6}$, but twice is $(\frac{1}{6})^2$ or 1/36. Similarly, if each of three languages shows a resemblance of 8 per cent to the other, which might in extreme cases be the result of mere chance, the expectation of the three languages all agreeing in some instance of resemblance in form and meaning will be $(8/100)^2$ or 64/10,000. In 1,000 comparisons, agreement among all three languages should occur only 6.4 times, that is, it will occur in 0.0064, or less than 1 per cent, of the comparisons. Hence a number of instances of such threefold agreements is highly significant. If four or more languages which are about equally distant from one another agree in a number of instances, a historical connection must be assumed, and if this agreement involves fundamental vocabulary or morphemes with a grammatical function, genetic explanation is the only tenable explanation.

This may be illustrated from the Afroasiatic (Hamito-Semitic) family of languages consisting of five languages or language groups—Egyptian, Berber, Semitic, Chad (Hausa and others), and Cushite. The forms involved are guaranteed as ancestral in each group by the requirement of earliest attestation, as in the requirement for Egyptian that it occur in the Pyramid Texts, our oldest document, or of appearance in at least two genetic subgroups (as in the case of Chad and Cushite), so that, in effect, we are comparing five languages. Allowing again the very high total of 8 per cent of chance resemblance between any two of the languages, the expected number of occurrences of morphemes similar in form and meaning in all five groups simultaneously becomes $(8/100)^4$ or 2,816/100,000,000. Assuming that about 1,000 forms are

being compared from each language, this leads to the expectation of 2,816/-100,000 of a morpheme. That is, if one compared a series of five unrelated languages at random, employing 1,000 words in each case, the operation would lead to a single successful case in approximately 35 such sets of comparisons. As a matter of fact, eleven morphemes are found in the case of Hamito-Semitic instead of the expected 1/35. There is only an infinitesimal probability that this could be the result of pure chance. In this case, the morphemes involved include such examples as -t, fem. sing. and -ka, second person singular masculine possessive. Genetic relationship, of which there are many other indications, seems the only possible explanation here.

Languages should never be compared in isolation if closer relatives are at hand. For the tendency of those particular forms in a language which resemble another language or group of languages to reappear with considerable frequency in more closely related forms of speech is a valuable index of the existence of a real historical connection. The statistical considerations involved may be illustrated once more from the Hamito-Semitic family. The question whether Hausa is indeed related to Egyptian, Semitic, Berber, and the Chad language has always been treated through isolated comparisons between Hausa and the other groups, while the existence of more than seventy languages of the Chad group which show a close and obvious relation to Hausa has been ignored.

A comparison of basic vocabulary between Hausa and Bedauye, a contemporary language of the Cushite branch of Hamito-Semitic, shows 10 per cent agreement in vocabulary. It is clear that Hausa will have lost certain Proto-Hamito-Semitic words retained by Bedauye, and vice versa. The percentage of retained vocabulary is expressed by a simple mathematical relation, the square root of the proportion of resemblances. The proportion of Hausa vocabulary which is of Proto-Hamito-Semitic origin should therefore be $\sqrt{10/100}$, or approximately 32/100. If we now take another Chad language belonging to a different subgroup than Hausa, namely, Musgu, the percentage of resemblance to Hausa is 20 per cent. Applying the same reasoning, the percentage of Hausa vocabulary retained from the time of separation from Musgu, that is, from the Proto-Chad period, is $\sqrt{20/100}$, or approximately 45/100. If, then, we take forms found in Hausa which resemble Egyptian, Berber, Semitic, or Cushite and because of the existence of a true genetic relationship these forms actually derive from Proto-Hamito-Semitic, they must also be Proto-Chad. Since Hausa has lost its forms since the Proto-Chad period independently of Musgu, which belongs to another subbranch, a true Proto-Hamito-Semitic form in Hausa should reappear by chance in Musgu $32/100 \div 45/100$ of the time, that is, 32/45. On the other hand, if Hausa is not related to the other Hamito-Semitic languages, the apparent resemblances to them are accidental, and these words should reappear in Musgu no more frequently than any other, that is, 20 per cent of the time, 9/45 rather than 32/45. An actual count shows that, of 30 morphemes in Hausa which resemble those of branches other than Chad, 22 occur in Musgu. This is 22/30 or 33/45, remarkably close to the expected 32/45. On the other hand, of 116 forms which show no resemblances to those of other Hamito-Semitic branches, only 14 occur in Musgu.

Beyond the frequency of resemblances and their distribution in other languages of the same group, the form which the resemblances take is likewise of importance. If the resemblances are

actually the result of historical relationship, even cursory reconstruction should show greater resemblance in most cases between the reconstructed forms than between those of two isolated languages. If the resemblances are all convergences, on the whole, reconstruction should increase the difference of the forms. This can be done in a tentative manner as the comparison proceeds and without necessarily involving the full apparatus of formal historical reconstruction, which is often not feasible with poor material or where the relationship is fairly remote and no written records are available. If, for example, we compared present-day Hindustani and English, we would be struck by a number of resemblances in basic vocabulary, including numerals, but the hypothesis of chance convergence would certainly appear as a plausible alternative. Even without going beyond contemporary Germanic languages, on the one hand, and Indo-Iranian languages, on the other, reconstruction would show a strong tendency to convergence of forms as we went backward in time, suggesting a real historical connection. Thus English *tuwþ* resembles Hindustani *dā:t* only slightly. On the Germanic side comparison with High German *tsa:n* already suggests a nasal consonant corresponding to the nasalization of the Hindustani vowel. Conjecture of a possible *°tanþ* or the like as a source of the English and German form is confirmed by the Dutch *tand*. On the other hand, comparison of Hindustani with other Aryan languages of India suggests that the Hindustani nasalized and long vowel results from a former short vowel and nasal consonant, as in Kashmiri and Sindir *dand*. Reconstruction has thus brought the forms closer together.

Last, and very important, a degree of consistency in the sound correspondences is a strong indication of historical connection. Thus, reverting to the

English-Hindustania comparison, the presence of *t* in English *tuw*, "two," *ten*, "ten," and *tuwþ*, "tooth" corresponding to Hindustani *d* in *dō, das,* and *dā:t*, respectively, is a strong indication of real historical relationship.

Assuming that such a relationship has been established, there still remains the problem of whether the resemblances in question can be explained by borrowing. While in particular instances the question of borrowing may be doubtful, I believe it is always possible to tell whether or not a mass of resemblances between two languages is the result of borrowing. The most important consideration is the a priori expectation and historical documentation of the thesis that borrowing in culture words is far more frequent than in fundamental vocabulary and that derivational, inflectional, pronominal morphemes and alternating allomorphs are subject to borrowing least frequently of all.

The oft repeated maxim of the superiority of grammatical over vocabulary evidence for relationship owes what validity it has to this relative impermeability of derivational and inflectional morphemes to borrowing. On the other hand, such elements are shorter, hence more often subject to convergence, and usually few in number, so that in themselves they are sometimes insufficient to lead to a decision. Lexical items are, it is true, more subject to borrowing, but their greater phonemic body and number give them certain compensatory advantages. While it cannot be said, a priori, that any single item might not on occasion be borrowed, fundamental vocabulary seems to be proof against mass borrowing. Swadesh, in a recent discussion of the problem of borrowing versus genetic explanations, presents quantitative evidence for the relative impermeability of fundamental vocabulary in sev-eral instances where the history of the language is known (Swadesh, 1951).

The presence of fundamental vocabulary resemblances well beyond chance expectation, not accompanied by resemblances in cultural vocabulary, is thus a sure indication of genetic relationship. This is a frequent, indeed normal, situation where a relationship is of a fairly remote order. Pronoun, body parts, etc., will agree while terms like "pot," "ax," "maize," will disagree. The assumption of borrowing here runs contrary to common sense and documented historic facts. A people so strongly influenced by another that they borrow terms like "I," "one," "head," "blood," will surely have borrowed cultural terms also. Where the mass of resemblances is the result of borrowing, a definite source will appear. The forms will be too similar in view of the historical remoteness of the assumed relationship. Moreover, if, as is usual, the donor language is not isolated, the fact that the resemblances all point to one particular language in the family, usually a geographically adjacent one, will also be diagnostic. Thus the Romance loan words in English are almost all close to French, in addition to hardly penetrating the basic vocabulary of English. If English were really a Romance language, it would show roughly equal similarities to all the Romance languages. The absence of sound correspondences is not a sufficient criterion, since, where loans are numerous, they often show such correspondence. However, the presence of a special set of correspondences will be an important aid in distinguishing loans in doubtful instances. Thus French loan words in English show regular correspondences, such as Fr. *š* = Eng. *č* or Fr. *ã* = Eng. æn (*šãs:čæns; šãt: čænt; še:z:čejr,* etc.).

Genetic relationship among languages is, in logical terminology, transitive. By a "transitive" relation is meant a relation such that, if it holds between A and B and between. A and C, it must also hold between B and C. If our criteria are correct and languages do have single lines of origin, we should never be led by their application to a situation in which A appears to be related both to B and to C, but B and C themselves cannot be shown to be related. If this were so, A would consist equally of two diverse components, that is, would be a mixed language of elements of B and C. This situation is sometimes said to exist, and even on a mass scale. Africa is perhaps most frequently mentioned in this connection. Thus Boas (1929) writes: ". . . a large number of mixed languages occur in Africa. His [Lepsius'] conclusions are largely corroborated by more recent investigation of the Sudanese languages."

Close investigation shows that, of the hundreds of languages in Africa (800 is the conventional estimate), there is only one language concerning which the problem of genetic affiliation could conceivably lead to two disparate classifications, the Mbugu language of Tanganyika. Even here the answer is clear that, in spite of the borrowing of Bantu prefixes and a large amount of vocabulary, mostly nonfundamental, the language belongs to the Cushite branch of Hamito-Semitic. The pronouns, verb forms, and almost all the fundamental vocabulary are Cushitic. The conventional African classification based on purely formal criteria, such as tone, combined with purely semantic, such as gender, had no connection with historical reality, and the necessarily contradictory results which followed led to the assumption of widespread mixture. If, as was done, we define a Sudanese language as monosyllabic, tonal, and genderless, and a Hamitic language as polysyllabic, toneless, and having sex gender, a polysyllabic, tonal language with sex gender (like Masai) will have to be interpreted as the result of a mixture of Sudanic and Hamitic elements.

The last full-scale treatment of this subject is Meillet's, which was followed by the counterarguments of Schuchardt, Boas, and others and a discussion of these objections by Meillet (1914). The present discussion is in fundamental agreement with Meillet in asserting that the genetic question always has a meaning and is susceptible of an unambiguous answer. Meillet differentiates between concrete grammatical resemblances involving both form and meaning and those involving meaning only without form, but only in passing. Similarly, he mentions rather casually the fact that fundamental vocabulary is not commonly borrowed, but does not exploit this insight. The advantages gained by collateral comparison with additional closely related languages, and the statistical significance of coincidences in three or more languages are not considered. The result is an unnecessarily skeptical attitude toward the possibilities of establishing genetic classification where there are no early written documents or where the grammatical apparatus is slight or nonexistent (e.g., Southeast Asia).

The objections of Schuchardt and Boas are in large part taken into account in the present analysis by the distinction between resemblances based on form and meaning which result from contact with other linguistic systems and those involving form only or meaning only. It would perhaps be desirable to distinguish these by the terms "borrowing" and "influence," respectively. Justice is then done to Boas' insistence that diffusion is prominently operative in linguistic as in other cultural phenomena, by setting no limit to influence, which in the case of Creole language reaches its peak, while maintaining, in accordance with all the available evidence, that there are definite bounds to borrowing, since it tends to cluster in nonfundamental vocabulary and makes only rare and sporadic inroads into basic vocabulary and inflectional and derivational morphemes. What is commonly said about the grammatical effects of one language on another refers almost entirely to influence, not borrowing, in the sense of the terms as employed here.

In other words, the effects of one language upon another are extremely widespread, fundamental, and important. What is maintained here is merely that the results are of a kind that can be distinguished from those caused by genetic relationship. Nor is it asserted that the genetic affiliation of a language is the sole important historic fact concerning it. The effects of borrowing and influence, being more recent chronologically and giving specific insights into the nature of the contacts involved, may frequently be of greater significance to the ethnologist and culture historian than the factor of more remote genetic affiliation.

These two types of historical connections between languages are carefully distinguished by Trubetskoy. A group of languages which have affected one another by influence and borrowing and form a group analogous to a culture area is termed a *Sprachbund,* while a group of genetically linked languages is termed a *Sprachfamilie.* They become genera of the larger species, *Sprachgruppe,* taking in all types of historical connections between languages (Trubetskoy, 1928).

The common habit of confusing these two situations by the use of the term "mixed language," as though a language were a mechanical aggregate of a number of components which enter into it the same way but merely in different proportions that English is, say, 48 per cent Germanic, 43 per cent French, 4 per cent Arabic, and 0.03 per cent Aztec (because of "tomato," "metate," etc.) is a gross oversimplification

and fails to distinguish the different origin and function of the Germanic as opposed to the Romance-Latin and other components in English.

From what has been said, it should be evident that the establishment of genetic relationships among languages is no mere *jeu d'esprit*. It is the indispensable preliminary to a determination of the causes of resemblances between languages by leaving borrowing as the only remaining source where more than chance resemblance does not lead to a hypothesis of relationship. Where such a relationship is present, it provides the basis for separation of autonomous from foreign elements through reconstruction of the ancestral language. Without such reconstruction, an understanding of the process of change in language undergoes a severe limitation to those few areas of the globe in which documented materials concerning the earlier forms of languages exist.

III. SELECTED REGIONAL SKETCHES

A. AFRICA

The attempt to reduce the number of language families in Africa at all costs, leading to overambitious syntheses combined with a disregard of concrete resemblances in form and meaning between elements of language in favor of typological criteria, such as the presence of tone, noun classes, sex gender, monosyllabic roots, etc., has characterized African linguistic classification from the earliest systematic attempts (Lepsius, F. Müller, etc.) onward.

The dominant classification in England and the United States has been a kind of synthesis, varying in details with different writers, based chiefly on the investigations of Westermann on the Sudanic languages and Meinhof on the Hamitic. Clear statements of the basis of this classification can be found in Werner (1915) and in Tucker (1940), as well as elsewhere. According to this view, there are three great indigenous language families in Africa —Sudanic, Bantu, and Hamitic, with Semitic as a separate but late intrusion and Bushman as possibly related to Sudanic. A disputed point has been the status of Hottentot, which most assign to Hamitic with Meinhof but which some classify with Bushman to form a Khoisan family, while others leave it independent or at any rate unclassified. Each of the three main families has its basic characteristics. Thus Sudanic is monosyllabic, tonal, lacks stress, grammatical gender, and all inflection, and places the genitive before the possessed noun. Hamitic, at the opposite extreme, is defined as polysyllabic, possessing Ablaut variation, having grammatical gender and inflection, lacking tone, and placing the genitive after the noun. In addition, it possesses the characteristic of polarity, which can best be illustrated by an example. The Somali language uses the same affirmative for the singular of the masculine and the plural of the feminine, while another element marks simultaneously the singular of the feminine and the plural of the masculine. Meinhof often expressed the opinion that the Bantu languages, which are assigned characteristics almost midway between the Sudanic and Hamitic families, were the result of a mixture of the two or, as he once expressed it, "had a Hamitic father and Sudanic mother" (Meinhof, 1912).

It is admitted that few languages exhibit the traits of one of these families in full purity. Deviations from the ideal pattern are attributed to influences of one family on the other. It is held that such intimate fusions may result that the choice of the fundamental component can in certain cases be made only by an arbitrary decision. Such mixed groups of languages are the Semi-Bantu, formed from Sudanic and Bantu; Nilo-Hamitic, a fusion of Sudanic with Hamitic; and, in the view of many, Hottentot, with a Sudanic-like Bushman element and a Hamitic element.

It is clear that by applying such criteria, which have no reference to the concrete relations between the form and the meaning of specific linguistic signs, Chinese is a Sudanic language and Old French is Hamitic. The latter, indeed, possesses a very striking bit of polarity in the use of -*s* to indicate the nominative singular and plural accusative of the noun as opposed to a zero suffix indicating the accusative singular and nominative plural (e.g., *murs*: *mur = mur*: *murs*). In addition, it possesses gender, Ablaut, and all the other stated characteristics of Hamitic speech. On the other hand, we are led to a crowning absurdity, in that forms of speech that are probably mutually intelligible can be classified as genetically distinct. Thus Meinhof, in classifying the languages of Kordofan, west of the Upper Nile, paid no attention to any other factor than the existence or absence of class prefixes in the noun. Three of these languages—Tegele, Tagoy, and Tumele—are similar, probably to the point of mutual intelligibility. Meinhof (1915–19) states: "A comparison of vocabulary shows that the numerals [*sc.* of Tegele] completely agree with those of Tumele. Moreover they are for the most part identical with the Tagoy numerals. Besides, a number of word stems and some verb forms of Tegele are identical with Tagoy and Tumele. But the grammatical structure of the noun indicates that Tegele is a Sudanic language because noun classification is absent while Tagoy and Tumele have clear noun classes. Apparently there has been a mixture of two diverse elements."

The other classification which has enjoyed currency is that of A. Drexel, adopted with a few modifications by Schmidt and by Kiekers in their respective volumes on the languages of the world. The Drexel classification embodies an attempt to demonstrate *sprachenkreise* in Africa parallel to the *kulturkreise* of the Graebner-Schmidt culture-historical school. This involves such violence to linguistic facts as the separation of the closely knit Mandingo group of languages into two unrelated families and the assumption of special Fulani-Malayo-Polynesian and Kanuri-Sumerian connections. There is no clear statement of the method employed in arriving at such conclusions.

The recent Greenberg (1949–50) classification concentrates on specific criteria which are relevant for actual historical relationship. The large heterogeneous Sudanic group, to which Westermann, in his more recent writings, denied genetic unity is split into a number of major and some minor stocks. The most important of those, Westermann's West Sudanic, shows a genetic relationship to Bantu, as evidenced by a mass of vocabulary resemblances, agreement in noun-class affixes, and phonetic correspondences, including those relating to tone, to which Westermann himself had drawn attention and to which he had even attributed a genetic significance, without, however, modifying his general scheme of language families to take account of it. The Semi-Bantu languages show a special resemblance to the Bantu languages simply because they belong to the same subgroup of languages in the larger family, to which the name "Niger-Congo" is applied. Since these Semi-Bantu languages do not possess common features as against Bantu, the Bantu language must be classified as merely one of over twenty subgroups within that one of the fifteen branches of the vast Niger-Congo family which includes both Bantu and "Semi-Bantu" languages.

Other major independent families formerly classified as Sudanic are Central Saharan, Central Sudanic, and Eastern Sudanic. This latter family includes the so-called "Nilo-Hamitic" languages, along with the closely related Nilotic languages in a single subfamily.

Hottentot is treated along with the central Bushman languages as a single subgroup within the Khoisan languages, the other branches being Northern Bushman and Southern Bushman. The Khoisan languages, in turn, are related to Sandawe and Hatsa in East Africa to form a single Click family. Of Meinhof's various proposed extensions of Hamitic, Fulani is assigned to the westernmost subfamily of Niger-Congo; the "Nilo-Hamitic" languages (Masai, Nandi, etc.) are classed as Eastern Sudanic; and Hottentot belongs to the Click family. Hausa, along with numerous other languages of the Chad family, is put, along with the traditionally Hamitic Berber, Cushite, and Ancient Egyptian and with Semitic, into the Hamito-Semitic family, for which the name "Afroasiatic" is proposed, since there is no linguistic justification for granting Semitic a special status. The term "Hamitic," which has been the basis of much pseudo-historical and pseudo-physical reconstruction in Africa, is thus abandoned as not designating a valid linguistic entity. The Afroasiatic family thus consists of five co-ordinate branches: (1) Berber, (2) Egyptian, (3) Semitic, (4) Cushite, and (5) Chad.

The Greenberg classification assumes a total of sixteen independent families in Africa. There is some possibility of a reduction in this total. The hypotheses of a Kunama–Eastern Sudanic and a Songhai-Niger-Congo relationship, in particular, are worth investigating.

Westermann has indicated his adherence to this new classification in all essentials and is expected to espouse it in a forthcoming article in the journal *Africa*.[3]

There is general agreement on the existence of only two extensive groups of related languages in Oceania—the Malayo-Polynesian and the Australian. The remaining families are the Tasmanian and a whole series of unrelated language families in New Guinea and neighboring islands, to which the cover-name "Papuan" is applied, with the general understanding that there is no proof or even likelihood that these languages form a single stock. Regarding Malayo-Polynesian, there is general consensus concerning which languages are to be included in the family, and the historical work of reconstruction of the ancestral Malayo-Polynesian and other languages will be considered in the following section on "Southeast Asia."

For the other large group, the Australian languages, although the existence of widespread relationships within the continent is asserted by all investigators, there is lack of unanimity regarding the number of families, some maintaining the unity of Australian languages and others denying it.

The linguists of the period before W. Schmidt's important work were acquainted almost exclusively with the languages of the large group which covers all the south and much of the north of the continent and ignored or were unaware of certain languages of the extreme northwestern and north-central parts of Australia which differ considerably from the great mass of Australian languages. These observers, therefore, assumed the unity of all Australian languages and were concerned chiefly with hypotheses of outside connections, with Africa, with India (Dravidian), or, in the case of Trombetti, with an Australian-Papuan-Andama-

3. Personal communication.

nese group. This latter attempt, like all the others, proved abortive in this instance, if for no other reason than that the Papuan member is no linguistic unit of any sort (Ray, 1907).

It was Schmidt (1913, 1914, 1917–18) who laid the foundations of a more careful study of the problem in a series of articles in *Anthropos*, later republished as *Die Gliederung der australischen Sprachen* (1919). Schmidt distinguishes two main families of Australian languages: the southern, which covers approximately the southern two-thirds of the continent, and a northern. He explicitly denies the existence of a genetic relationship between these two groups. Unlike the southern family, which constitutes a true genetic unity, the northern, according to Schmidt, is not a family at all but consists of numerous diverse, unrelated forms of speech. In the light of clear statements to this effect, it is difficult to know what is meant in a historical sense by Schmidt's threefold division of these northern languages into those whose words end in consonants as well as vowels, those whose words end in vowels only, and those whose words end in vowels and liquids but not in other consonants. This last group occupies, according to Schmidt, an intermediate position between the other two, probably through a process of language mixture. This threefold division of the northern languages, as well as the separation into a northern and a southern family, seems strongly motivated by an attempt at correlation with the *kulturkreise* established in this area by the ethnological school of which Schmidt is a leading exponent. Kroeber (1924), in a review of Schmidt's work, criticized this division on the ground of obvious fundamental vocabulary resemblances between the northern and southern languages. He followed this up with a study of the distribution of common vocabulary items, which showed a sublime disregard in their distribution for the fundamental east-west dividing line which Schmidt had drawn across the Australian continent.

In a series of articles in *Oceania* (1939–40, 1941–43), Capell made substantial contributions to our knowledge of the languages of the northwestern and north-central parts of the continent and also revealed the surprising fact that many of these languages had noun-prefix classes resembling those of the Bantu languages in Africa in their general functioning but, one should hasten to add, without specific resemblances to them in form and meaning. Capell asserts the fundamental unity of all Australian languages. He divides them into suffixing languages, roughly equivalent to Schmidt's southern family, and prefixing languages, corresponding to Schmidt's northern division. The criterion employed is existence of verb suffixes or prefixes to form tenses and moods and to indicate pronominal reference. It is admitted that the northern languages are, to some extent, suffixing also. Within the northern group we have, again, a threefold division on principles different from those of Schmidt. Groups with multiple noun classes, two classes, and no classes are distinguished. Capell admits, in effect, that this is not a genetic analysis. It leads, as he himself points out, to an inevitable cul-de-sac similar to that of Meinhof in Africa, cited above. We are confronted with a pair of languages—Nungali and Djämindjung—which are almost identical except that Nungali has noun classes and Djämindjung has none. A similar pair is Maung and Iwaidja. Concerning these latter, Capell observes: "It is safe to say, however, that had Iwaidja multiple classification, it would hardly be more than a dialect of Maung" (Capell, 1939–40, p. 420).

The solution suggested here is a simple one, if one keeps in mind a primary canon of classification, one so obvious that it would hardly seem to need statement, yet is frequently disregarded in practice. Languages should be classified on linguistic evidence alone. Among the irrelevancies to be excluded is the extent of the area in which the language is found and the number of speakers. There is no reason to expect that families of genetically equal rank should necessarily occupy territories approximately equal in extent. Germanic and Tokharian are co-ordinate branches of Indo-European, but a greater contrast in territory and population could hardly be imagined. Germanic covers substantial portions of four continents and numbers hundreds of millions of speakers. Tokharian has no speakers at all, since it is extinct.

The extent of fundamental vocabulary resemblance, including pronouns, among all languages in Australia and the specific similarities in the noun prefixes which connect many north Australian languages provide sufficient evidence of a single Australian family. This family has numerous subgroups, certainly at least forty, of which the large southern subgroup is just one which has spread over most of the continent (including the Murngin languages in northeast Arnhemland and the languages of the western Torres Straits Islands). The ancestral Australian language had noun classes, and the southern subgroup has, like some of the northern languages (the prefixing, classless language of Capell's classification), lost these classes. It still maintains a survival, however, in the distinction of a masculine and a feminine singular pronoun found in certain southern languages in which the af-formatives employed resemble those of the masculine and feminine singular classes among the class languages.

C. SOUTHEAST ASIA

There are sharp differences of opinion regarding linguistic relationships in this area. The following are the outstanding problems: (1) the validity of Schmidt's hypothesis of an Austroasiatic family consisting of Mon-Khmer, Munda, and other languages; (2) the validity of Schmidt's Austric hypothesis connecting Austroasiatic in turn with Malayo-Polynesian; (3) the affiliations of Thai and Annamite, connected by some with Chinese in one subbranch of the Sino-Tibetan family, while others place Thai with Kadai and Indonesian (Benedict) and Annamite with Austroasiatic (Schmidt and others); (4) the linguistic position of the Man (Miao-Yao) and Min-Hsia dialects spoken by aboriginal populations in China.

Accepting certain earlier suggestions and adding some of his own, Schmidt (1906) has proposed that the following groups of languages are related to one another in his Austroasiatic stock: (1) Mon-Khmer, (2) the Palaung-Wa languages of the middle Salween, (3) Semang-Sakai, (4) Khasi, (5) Nicobarese, (6) the Munda group, (7) Annamite-Muong, (8) the Cham group. If we except Cham, which most writers consider Malayo-Polynesian, a conclusion which can hardly be doubted, then all these languages share numerous resemblances in fundamental vocabulary, extending to pronouns. Moreover, excepting Annamite, which has shed all its morphological processes, there are certain important derivational morphemes whose rather uncommon formal nature (infixes), combined with their basic functions in the grammar, absolutely excludes chance and makes borrowing a completely improbable explanation. I do not see how such coincidences as an infixed -*m* in the Mon of Burma and the languages of the geographically remote Nicobar Islands, both with agentive meaning, to mention only one of a number of such instances, can be the result of anything but genetic relationship.

Maspero has sought to demonstrate a close connection between Annamite

and Thai, which he considers to be Sino-Tibetan. This case rests chiefly on the irrelevant argument from form only —the monosyllabism and tonicity of Annamite, in which it resembles Thai and Chinese. The extensive lexical resemblances to Thai, which hardly touch basic vocabulary, must be looked upon as mostly borrowing with some convergence. On the other hand, the mass of fundamental vocabulary points clearly in the direction of the Austroasiatic languages, and I do not see how any hypothesis of borrowing can explain it. If borrowed, the source is not evident, since Annamite now resembles one, now another, of the Austroasiatic languages. It often shows an independent development from a hypothetical reconstruction which can hardly be the result of anything but internal development from the ancestral Austroasiatic form. Thus Annamite *mōt*, "one," makes sense as an independent contraction from *moyat, found in this form only in the distant Mundari language of India. The language geographically nearest to Annamite Khmer has *muy*, presumably < *moy* with loss of final -*at*. Santali, the chief Munda language, has *mit* < *miyat < *moyat. The absence of the modest morphological apparatus of other Austroasiatic languages in Annamite cannot be used as an argument for any other relationship. The ancient maxim *ex nihilo nihil fit* may be appropriately applied in this instance.

Schmidt's further hypothesis of the relationship of Austroasiatic to the Malayo-Polynesian languages is of a far more doubtful nature. Most of the numerous etymologies proposed by Schmidt are either semantically or phonetically improbable or not attested from a sufficient variety of languages in one family or the other. Even with these eliminated, there remains a considerable number of plausible, or at least possible, etymologies, but very few of these are basic. Both language families employ prefixes and infixes, and the latter mechanism is certainly not very common. However, concrete resemblances in form and meaning of these elements which can reasonably be attributed to the parent-language of both groups are very few. Only *pa-*, causative, seems certain. In view of this, the Austric hypothesis cannot be accepted on present evidence. It needs to be reworked, using Dempwolff and Dyen's reconstructed Malayo-Polynesian forms, as well as taking into account the Thai and Kadai languages, which, as we shall see, are related to Malayo-Polynesian.

The traditional theory regarding Thai is that it forms, along with Chinese, the Sinitic branch of Sino-Tibetan. Benedict has proposed the relationship of Thai to the Kadai group, in which he includes certain languages of northern Indo-China, southern continental China, and the Li dialects of the island of Hainan. He has further posited the relationship of this Thai-Kadai family to Malayo-Polynesian (Benedict, 1942). Of the relation of Thai to the Kadai languages, which in the case of the Li dialects is particularly close, there can be no reasonable doubt. At the least, the traditional theory would have to be revised to include the Kadai languages, along with Thai, in Sinitic. I believe, however, that the connection of Thai with Chinese and Sino-Tibetan must be abandoned altogether and that Benedict's thesis is essentially correct. Thai resemblances to Chinese are clearly borrowings. They include the numerals from 3 on and a number of other words which are certainly the result of cultural contact. Thai is otherwise so aberrant that it must be at least another independent branch of Sino-Tibetan. Yet, when resemblances are found, the forms are always like Chinese—altogether too like Chinese, one should add. Applying a test suggested earlier, it is found that those words in Thai which resemble Malayo-Polynesian tend to reappear in the Kadai languages, while those which are like Chinese do so only rarely. The proportion of fundamental vocabulary resemblances between Thai-Kadai and Malayo-Polynesian runs to quite a high number, far beyond chance and hardly explainable by borrowing, in view of the geographical distances involved.

I believe that Benedict's thesis needs restatement in some details of grouping, where, as so often happens, he has been led astray by nonlinguistic considerations, in this case the importance of Thai as a culture language. Thai shows special resemblance to the Li dialects of such far-reaching importance that Benedict's twofold division of Kadai into Laqua-Li and Lati-Kelao must be emended to put Thai along with Li in the first subgroup. In addition, the language of the Mohammedan population of Hainan does not belong, interestingly enough, with the Li dialects of the rest of the island but forms a third subdivision alongside the continental Lati-Kelao. The emended picture is shown in the accompanying diagram.

The Miao-Yao dialects of China have variously been called "Mon-Khmer" (i.e., Austroasiatic), "Sino-Tibetan," or "independent." There seems no good reason to classify them as other than a separate branch of Sino-Tibetan, no

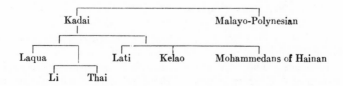

more divergent than, say, the Karen languages of Burma. The evidence cannot be summarized here. The Min-Hsia language has been variously called a "Sino-Tibetan" or "Austroasiatic" language with a Chinese overlay. It likewise seems to be Sino-Tibetan. When the obvious Chinese borrowings are accounted for, the language still appears to show a special affinity to Chinese in fundamentals, so that it should probably be included in the Sinitic subbranch.

The question is here raised concerning the status of the Nehari language of India, classed by Grierson as Munda. It has been strongly influenced by Kurku, a neighboring Munda language; but, when allowance is made for this, the fundamental vocabulary and morphology of the language do not resemble those of any other family in the area. It may therefore be the only language of an independent stock. More material is needed to decide this question.

In summary, the language families of Southeast Asia are probably the following: (1) Sino-Tibetan, (2) Austroasiatic, (3) Kadai-Malayo-Polynesian, (4) Andaman Islands, (5) Nehari(?).

D. AMERICA NORTH OF MEXICO

The present discussion is restricted to a few remarks of somewhat impressionistic character because of my lack of acquaintance with the linguistic data from this area. However, even cursory investigation of the celebrated "disputed" cases, such as Athabaskan-Tlingit-Haida and Algonkin-Wiyot-Yurok, indicate that these relationships are not very distant ones and, indeed, are evident on inspection. Even the much larger Macro-Penutian grouping seems well within the bounds of what can be accepted without more elaborate investigation and marshaling of supporting evidence. The difference between Oregon and California Penu-

tian is comparable to that between any two of the subdivisions of the Eastern Sudanic family in Africa. The status of Algonkin-Mosan and Hokan-Siouan and the position of Zuni (which Sapir himself entered in the Azteco-Tanoan family with a query) strike me as the most doubtful points of Sapir's sixfold classification. The existence of a Gulf group, as set forth recently by Haas, with a membership of Tunican, Natchez, Muskoghean and Timucua appears certain, as does the relationship of the Coahuiltecan languages both to the Gulf group and to the California Hokan in a single complex. Likewise, as Sapir pointed out, Yuki is probably no more than a somewhat divergent California Hokan language. The connection of Siouan-Yuchi and Iroquois-Caddoan with these languages is possible but far from immediately evident. Within Algonkin-Mosan, Salish-Chemakuan-Wakashan seems certain, as does Algonkin-Beothuk-Wiyot-Yurok (Beothuk may well be an Algonkin language). On the other hand, the relation of these two groups to each other and to Kutenai requires further investigation. Within the Azteco-Tanoan group it is clear that Kiowa is close to Tanoan and that Kiowa-Tanoan is related to Uto-Aztecan, as demonstrated by Trager and Whorf. The position of Zuni, as noted above, is very doubtful.

IV. LANGUAGE AND HISTORICAL RECONSTRUCTION

Ethnologists are rightly interested in comparative linguistic work, not so much for its own sake as for the light it sheds on other aspects of culture history. The basis for any discussion of this subject is inevitably the classic treatment of Sapir in his *Time Perspective in Aboriginal American Culture.* In spite of the brevity of this discussion, it is astonishingly complete, and there is little one would want to add to it, in spite of the lapse of time. The single most significant comment that might be made is that it serves as an essentially adequate basis for work in this field but that relatively little has been done toward the actual application of its principles. The problems involved are some of the most difficult in scientific co-operation and not easily solved. On the one hand, linguistic evidence is peculiarly suited to misapplication by ethnologists, who sometimes tend to use it mechanically and without at least an elementary understanding of the linguistic method involved. On the other hand, the linguist is often not greatly interested in problems of culture history, and the recent trend toward concentration in descriptive problems of linguistic structure draws him still further from the ordinary preoccupations of archeologists and historically oriented ethnologists. Perhaps the ultimate solution is an intermediate science, ethnolinguistics, which will treat the very important interstitial problems, both synchronic and historical, which lie between the recognized fields of ethnology and linguistics.

The most important and promising recent development in this area is the possibility of establishing at least an approximate chronology for linguistic events in place of the relative time relations of classical historical linguistics. This method, known as "glottochronology" and developed chiefly by Swadesh and Lees, works on the assumption that rate of change in basic vocabulary is relatively constant. A chronological time scale is provided by comparisons of vocabulary from different time periods of the same languages in areas with recorded history. The results thus far indicate an average of *ca.* 81 per cent retention of basic vocabulary in one millennium. Thus, by comparing two related languages for which no earlier recorded material is available,

the percentage of basic vocabulary differences will allow of an approximation of the date of separation of the two forms of speech.

By combining with this a rigorous application of Sapir's insight regarding the probable center of origin of a linguistic group, on the basis of a center of gravity calculated from the distribution of genetic subgroups, an instrument of historical reconstruction surpassing any previous use of linguistic data for these purposes becomes possible.

The center-of-gravity method may be briefly described as follows: Within each of the genetic subgroups of a linguistic family, the center of distribution is selected. If the subgroup is itself divided into clear dialect areas, the central point of each dialect area is calculated and the position of all is averaged to obtain the probable center of dispersal of the subgroup. The centers of the various subgroups are then averaged to obtain the most probable point of origin for the entire family. A correction in order to minimize the influence of single aberrant groups may be made by calculating a corrected center of gravity from the one reached by the above method. The distance of the center of each subfamily is calculated from the center of gravity of the whole family. Then those subgroups which are most distant are weighted least, by multiplying the center of position of each subgroup by the reciprocal of the ratio of its distance to that of the most distant subgroup, and thus calculating a corrected value. Such results, mechanically arrived at, should, of course, be evaluated in terms of geographical and other collateral knowledge.

V. GOALS, METHODS, AND PROSPECTS

The goals and methods of comparative linguistics, particularly as applied to the field of primitive languages, are clear and generally agreed upon. The aims of this branch of science might be phrased in terms of the establishment of all possible genetic relationships between languages, the detection of all borrowings and the direction they have taken, and the maximal reconstruction of the ancestral languages which have given rise to the present languages. This is of value not only for its own sake and because these results can be employed toward general historical reconstruction but also because it gives us our basic knowledge of historic change in language under diverse circumstances. It is not until considerable data have been amassed in this field and a considerable variety of historical development in different areas has been traced that questions regarding overall change from one morphological or phonological type to another, leading to general laws of linguistic change, can ever be possible.

Problems of method, also, are in the main agreed upon. These resolve themselves into two main types: those pertaining to the determination of relationship and those concerning reconstruction. The latter problems are less controversial, and, in the United States at least, there is general agreement on the employment of what are essentially the procedures of classical Indo-European linguistics. The problems of establishing genetic relationships beyond the most self-evident ones, such as those of Powell in North America, admittedly involve more differences of opinion both in Europe and in America. The abandonment of concrete criteria in favor of meaning without form or form without meaning and the abandonment of the traditional view regarding genetic relationship in some parts of the world in favor of the apparent profundity of analyses in terms of superposed strata have led only to increasing confusion and conflicting analyses, as they inevitably must. Moreover, only on the basis of clearly defined families established through specific form-meaning resemblances can reconstruction be attempted and with it the possibility of the study of historic process in language.

The greatest single obstacle to the rapid future growth of the field does not lie, however, in any conflict regarding aims or methods. It is rather the lack of trained people in sufficient number to provide the descriptive data for a vast number of languages, some of them near extinction. The topheavy concentration of linguistic scientists in the area of a very small number of language families of Eurasia and the extreme paucity of fully trained workers in such large areas as South America and Oceania are a grave handicap to future development of this field, as well as of linguistics as a whole. At the last meeting of the Linguistic Society of America, approximately 90 per cent of the papers presented on specific languages concerned a single language family, Indo-European.

The absence of effective liaison even between anthropological linguists and other branches of anthropology and its nonexistence in the case of other linguists, while an understandable consequence of the contemporary trend toward specialization, are likewise dangerous. Unless these situations are met and to some degree overcome, comparative linguistics must fall far short of the inherent possibilities afforded by the transparency of its material and the sophistication of its method of making a unique and significant contribution to the science of anthropology as a whole.

LITERATURE CITED

BENEDICT, P. 1942. "Thai, Kadai and Indonesian: A New Alignment in Southwestern Asia," *American Anthropologist,* XLIV, 576–601.

BOAS, F. 1920. "The Classification of American Languages," *American Anthropologist,* XXII, 367–76.

——. 1929. "Classification of American Indian Languages," *Language,* V, 1–7.

BONFANTE, G. 1945. "On Reconstruction and Linguistic Method," *Word,* I, 83–94, 132–61.

CAPELL, A. 1939–40. "The Classification of Languages in North and Northwest Australia," *Oceania,* X, 241–72, 404–33.

——. 1941–43. "Language of Arnhem Land, North Australia," *ibid.,* XII, 364–92; XIII, 24–50.

GREENBERG, J. H. 1949–50. "Studies in African Linguistic Classification," *Southwestern Journal of Anthropology,* V, 79–100, 309–17; VI, 47–63, 143–60, 223–37, 388–98.

HALL, ROBERT, JR. 1946. "Bartoli's 'Neolinguistica,' " *Language,* XXII, 273–83.

HOENIGSWALD, H. 1950. "The Principal Step in Comparative Grammar," *Language,* XXVI, 357–64.

HOCKETT, C. 1948. "Implications of Bloomfield's Algonkin Studies," *Language,* XXIV, 117–31.

JAKOBSON, R. 1931. "Principes de phonologie historique," *TCLP,* IV, 247–67.

KROEBER, A. L. 1913. "The Determination of Linguistic Relationship," *Anthropos,* VIII, 389–401.

——. 1924. "Relationship of the Australian Languages," *Journal and Proceedings of the Royal Society of New South Wales,* pp. 101–17.

MARTINET, A. 1950. "Some Problems of Italic Consonantism," *Word,* VI, 26–41.

MEILLET, A. 1914. "Le Problème de la parenté des langues," *Scientia,* XV, No. XXXV, 3.

MEINHOF, CARL. 1912. *Die Sprachen der Hamiten.* Hamburg: L. Friederichsen.

——. 1915–19. "Sprachstudien im ägyptischen Sudan," *Zeitschrift für Kolonialsprachen,* VI, 161–205; VII, 36–133, 212–50, 326–35; VIII, 46–74, 110–39, 170–96, 257–67; IX, 43–64, 89–117, 167–204, 226–55.

RAY, S. 1907. *Linguistics.* ("Reports of the Cambridge Anthropological Expedition to Torres Straits," Vol. III.) Cambridge: At the University Press.

SCHMIDT, W. 1906. *Die Mon-Khmer Völker.* Braunschweig: F. Vieweg & Sohn.

——. 1913. "Dei Gliederung der australischen Sprachen," *Anthropos,* VIII, 526–54.

——. 1914. *Ibid.,* IX, 980–1018.

——. 1917. *Ibid.,* XII, 437–39.

——. 1918. *Ibid.,* XIII, 747–817.

——. 1919. *Die Gliederung der australischen Sprachen.* Vienna: Mechitharisten-Buchdruckerei.

SWADESH, M. 1951. "Diffusional Cumulation and Archaic Residue as Historical Explanation," *Southwestern Journal of Anthropology,* VII, 1–21.

TRUBETSKOY, N. 1928. *Actes du premier Congrès International de Linguistes à La Haye.* Leiden: Sijthoff.

TUCKER, A. N. 1940. *The Eastern Sudanic Languages.* London: Oxford University Press.

VENDRYES, J. 1925. *Language: A Linguistic Introduction to History.* Translated by PAUL RADIN. New York: A. Knopf.

WERNER, A. 1915. *The Language Families of Africa.* London: Society for Promoting Christian Knowledge.

The Relation of Language to Culture

By HARRY HOIJER

CULTURAL ANTHROPOLOGISTS, during the last twenty-five years, have gradually moved from an atomistic definition of culture, describing it as a more or less haphazard collection of traits, to one which emphasizes pattern and configuration. Kluckhohn and Kelly perhaps best express this modern concept of culture when they define it as "all those historically created designs for living, explicit and implicit, rational, irrational, and non-rational, which exist at any given time as potential guides for the behavior of men" (1945, p. 97). Traits, elements, or, better, patterns of culture in this definition are organized or structured into a system or set of systems, which, because it is historically created, is therefore open and subject to constant change.

With this greater understanding of the nature of culture taken as a whole has come a new conception of the interrelationship of language and culture. Language may no longer be conceived as something entirely distinct from other cultural systems but must rather be viewed as part of the whole and functionally related to it. We have, then, a new set of problems, centering about this relationship, which are as yet only imperfectly envisaged and for the most part little examined. It is the purpose of this report to review these problems and to present them for your consideration and discussion.

It may be noted incidentally that this area of research has as yet no generally accepted designation. The terms "ethnolinguistics" and "metalinguistics," often employed, have still a wide variety of meanings, differing almost from one student to the next (see, e.g., Olmsted, 1950). "Ethnolinguistics" is perhaps the more diffuse in meaning: it has been applied to studies (like Sapir's "Time Perspective," 1916) which illustrate the role of linguistic research relative to the history of cultures; to the study of situations like the etiquette of receiving a guest (Voegelin and Harris, 1945, p. 457), where "talk and non-vocal behavior together constitute an ethnolinguistic situation"; to studies (like Mead's, 1939; also Lowie, 1940) of the usefulness of languages as tools of ethnological research; to the studies of Whorf (e.g., 1941c) and others on the relation of habitual behavior and thought to language; and probably to still other and diverse researches. "Metalinguistics," though more restricted (it has been applied, so far, mainly by Trager to the work of Whorf), has the disadvantage of a possible confusion with "metalanguage," a term much used by philosophers interested in semiotics, or the general theory of signs (Carroll et al., 1951, p. 4).

1. As a first step in the presentation that follows, it is necessary to examine the proposition (more or less generally accepted by anthropologists, at least since Tylor's time) that language does not stand separate from culture but is an essential part of it. Voegelin has

recently queried this proposition, finding it "debatable." He adds:

It is obvious that one does not find culture in limbo, since all human communities consist of human animals which talk; but culture can be, and as a matter of fact, is characteristically studied in considerable isolation; so also in even greater isolation, the human animal is studied in physical anthropology, and not *what* the human animal talks about, but rather the *structure* of his talk is studied in linguistics. *What* he talks about is called (by philosophers and semanticists) *meaning;* but for most anthropologists *what* he talks about is *culture* [1949a, p. 36].

Later, in answer to Opler's criticism, Voegelin attempts to justify this view:

If language were merely a part of culture, then linguists should be competent to discuss other parts of culture by virtue of their training in linguistics. We must admit that if a linguist can discuss problems in culture, it is by virtue of his being a student in culture, also, rather than by a transfer from linguistic training; and vice versa.

If language were merely a part of culture, primates should be able to learn parts of human language as they actually do learn parts of human culture when prodded by primatologists. No sub-human animal ever learns any part of human languages,—not even parrots. The fact that *Polly wants a cracker* is not taken by the parrot as part of a language is shown by the refusal of the bird to use part of the utterance as a frame (*Polly wants a ...*) with substitutions in the frame. ... As George Herzog has phrased this, imitative utterances of sub-human animals are limited to one morpheme; to the parrot, then, *Polly wants a cracker* is an unchangeable unit. From this point of view, we can generalize: an inescapable factor of all natural languages is that they are capable of multi-morpheme utterances [1949b, p. 45].

Voegelin's first point, that a specialist in one aspect of culture should thereby be equally competent in all others, raises some interesting queries. Would he also insist that a political scientist (who most certainly is a specialist in

an important aspect of culture) be equally competent as a sociologist, economist, or anthropologist? Is it true that cultural anthropologists are equally competent in social organization, technology, religion, and folklore? Can we not allow, in view of the wide range of the concept of culture (even omitting language), that a scholar be permitted to specialize? Linguistics, to be sure, requires a good many specialized methods and techniques, but so does folklore, and is that any reason for excluding the subject matter of either linguistics or folklore from culture?

The second point, that primates and other subhuman animals may learn something of culture (when "prodded") but nothing of language, opens the important question of the nature of culture. What do primates learn under the training of primatologists, and are these items truly a part of culture? It is, of course, firmly established that primates acquire techniques and learn to solve problems, though only very simple ones, much as men do. But the primate's learning is cumulative only in the sense that he adds new tricks to his repertory; there is no evidence that he abstracts from problems already learned certain general principles that might be combined to solve problems of increasing complexity. In brief, the primate learns only unchangeable units of human behavior by imitation or trial and error, just as the parrot learns single and unrelated (to him) morpheme utterances. The trick learned by the primate, like the utterances of the parrot, is not seen as a frame in which substitutions are possible but only as an act complete in itself and discrete from all others.

A human culture, on the other hand, is no mere repertory of discrete acts. Anthropologists, or at least most of them, have long since abandoned the notion that a culture is simply a collection of traits, of acts and artifacts. A culture is, rather, in the words of

Kluckhohn and Kelly, "a historically derived system of explicit and implicit designs for living, which tends to be shared by all or specially designated members of a group" (1945, p. 98). The emphasis in this definition lies on the phrase "designs for living"; a culture is only manifest in acts and artifacts, it does not consist of acts and artifacts. What the human learns, in the process of enculturation, is an organized (or structured) set of ways of behaving, which he abstracts from and applies to situations of his daily experience as these arise. In the course of time, and especially under the impact of many new situations (for example, during times of rapid acculturation), there emerge, in the human group, new ways of living and modifications of old ways, abstracted, consciously or unconsciously, from the situations and problems faced by members of the group. It is this feature of cumulating abstracted ways of living that so clearly distinguishes man's culture from the pseudo-culture of the primate, for the latter is but a random collection of discrete acts, possessed by individual animals and not shared, except by the accident of imitation, by others in the group and entirely without possibility of development except by the adding of new acts.

Language fits into this conception of culture without difficulty. Just as a culture consists of all ways of behaving that are historically derived, structured, and tending "to be shared by all or specially designated members of a group," so does a language include ways of speaking (a segment of behaving) with precisely the same attributes. A language, like the rest of culture, is acquired by learning, not discrete utterances (acts) of the *Polly wants a cracker* type, but frames in which all meaningful utterances may be fitted. Languages, like other aspects of cultures, are diverse, not alike; each society has its own language as it has its

own techniques, social and political forms, and patterns of economic and religious behavior. A language, like any other aspect of culture, is cumulative and ever changing, the "mountainous and anonymous work of unconscious generations" (Sapir, 1921, p. 235). Finally, it is quite impossible to conceive of either the origin or the development of culture apart from language, for language is that part of culture which, more than any other, enables men not only to make their own experiences and learning continuous but, as well, to participate vicariously in the experiences and learning of others, past and present, who are or have been members of the group. To the extent that a culture as a whole is made up of common understandings, its linguistic aspect is its most vital and necessary part.

2. The argument that language is an essential part of culture does not, of course, make its relationship with other aspects of culture apparent at first sight. It is, indeed, perfectly clear that language plays a unique role in the total network of cultural patterns, since, for one thing, it apparently functions together with most, if not all, other cultural behavior. Language, as Sapir has noted, "does not as a matter of fact stand apart from or run parallel to direct experience but completely interpenetrates with it" (1933, p. 11). It is an important question, therefore, to determine just what such interpenetration with experience signifies for the speakers of a language, and how it may relate to other aspects of their culture.

Most studies of the relation of language to culture, until recently, have emphasized an external and fairly obvious relation between vocabulary and the content of culture. It has been noted, over and over again, that the vocabulary of a people inventories their culture and reflects, with greater or less accuracy, the particular interests and emphases a people may have in such areas of their culture as technology, social organization, religion, and folklore. Peoples who, like the Chiricahua Apache, live by hunting and collecting are found to have detailed lists of animal and plant names and to name the topographic features of their environment with care and precision. Others, like the Australian aborigines, who emphasize kinship as a means of social control, have a large and complicated vocabulary of kin terms. Status systems, among such peoples as the Japanese and Koreans, are similarly reflected in vocabulary and even in certain partially grammatical features of language, such as the pronominal system.

The study of languages and their vocabularies may also be useful to the culture historian. This is evident, externally, simply in the geographical distribution of related languages, for such distribution often yields important clues as to the earlier location of a population and its later migrations. An illustration is found in the distribution of the Athapaskan-speaking Indians of today, where we find some eight or nine main linguistic subdivisions in western Canada and Alaska, while two others are found, respectively, along the Pacific Coast from Washington to northern California and among the Navaho and Apache tribes of the Southwest. The conclusion here is a clear one: there is little doubt, on linguistic grounds alone, that the original location of these peoples is the northern one and that, therefore, the Pacific Coast and southwestern Athapaskan-speaking societies have migrated southward to their present position.

Internal linguistic evidence may also be used, as Sapir has noted, to set cultural elements in chronologic relations with one another:

Language, like culture, is a composite of elements of very different age, some of its features reaching back into the mists of an impenetrable past, others being the product of a development of yesterday. If

we now succeed in putting the changing face of culture into relation with the changing face of language, we shall have obtained a measure, vague or precise according to specific circumstances, of the relative ages of the culture elements. In this way language gives us a sort of stratified matrix to work in for the purposes of unraveling culture sequences [1916, p. 432].

Applications of this method are numerous; we need call attention, as illustration, to only two, Sapir's "Internal Linguistic Evidence of the Northern Origin of the Navaho" (1936) and Herzog's "Culture Change and Language: Shifts in the Pima Vocabulary" (1941).

Vocabulary, then, is quite clearly linked with many features of nonlinguistic culture, synchronically and diachronically, and the study of vocabulary is useful, if not essential, to a complete and well-rounded ethnographic account. But this use of linguistic data or even the clear association between vocabulary and the content of culture proves no more than the fact that language has a cultural setting. The same is true of the reverse situation, that is, that the linguist, if he is successfully to define vocabulary items, must know something of the rest of the culture. However, as Sapir remarked some years ago, "this superficial and extraneous kind of parallelism is of no real interest to the linguist except in so far as the growth or borrowing of new words throws light on the formal trends of the language. The linguistic student should never make the mistake of identifying a language with its dictionary" (1921, p. 234).

A language is, of course, far more than its dictionary, which may, indeed, be regarded more as a product of the language than as a part of it. To understand the true interrelationship of language and other cultural systems, we need to study, not the products of the language, but its patterns, lexical, morphological, and syntactic, and the relation of these, should such relations exist, to other patterns in the culture. It is this study that will be the concern of the sections that follow.

3. The central problem of this report is, then, a thesis suggested by Sapir in many of his writings and later developed in more detail by Whorf and others. In terms of this thesis, peoples speaking different languages may be said to live in different "worlds of reality," in the sense that the languages they speak affect, to a considerable degree, both their sensory perceptions and their habitual modes of thought. Sapir has stated this thesis in the following words:

Language is a guide to "social reality." Though language is not ordinarily thought of as of essential interest to the students of social science, it powerfully conditions all our thinking about social problems and processes. Human beings do not live in the objective world alone, nor alone in the world of social activity as ordinarily understood, but are very much at the mercy of the particular language which has become the medium of expression for their society. It is quite an illusion to imagine that one adjusts to reality essentially without the use of language and that language is merely an incidental means of solving specific problems of communication or reflection. The fact of the matter is that the "real world" is to a large extent unconsciously built up on the language habits of the group. No two languages are ever sufficiently similar to be considered as representing the same social reality. The worlds in which different societies live are distinct worlds, not merely the same world with different labels attached.

The understanding of a simple poem, for instance, involves not merely an understanding of the single words in their average significance, but a full comprehension of the whole life of the community as it is mirrored in the words, or as it is suggested by their overtones. Even comparatively simple acts of perception are very much more at the mercy of the social patterns called words than we might suppose. If one draws some dozen lines, for instance, of different shapes, one perceives them as

divisible into such categories as "straight," "crooked," "curved," "zigzag" because of the classificatory suggestiveness of the linguistic terms themselves. We see and hear and otherwise experience very largely as we do because the language habits of our community predispose certain choices of interpretation [1929, p. 162].

Whorf, in a later study inspired by Sapir's example, analyzes "many hundreds of reports [to an insurance company] of circumstances surrounding the start of fires." He finds in these that "not only a physical situation *qua* physics, but the meaning of that situation to people, was sometimes a factor, through the behavior of the people, in the start of the fire" (1941c, p. 75). These instances, he says, "suffice to show how the cue to a certain line of behavior is often given by the analysis of the linguistic formula in which the situation is spoken of, and by which to some degree it is analyzed, classified, and allotted its place in that world which is 'to a large extent unconsciously built up on the language habits of the group'" (1941c, p. 77).

Comparison of widely divergent languages provides ample illustration of the fact that languages categorize reality in many different ways. Systems of kinship terminology, for example, obviously do not symbolize one system of biological relationships common to all mankind but denote, rather, socially and culturally determined relationships peculiar to a given society. English terms like "father," "mother," "brother," "sister," and "cousin" find no precise parallels in the vocabularies of peoples who do not share our system of kinship. Among the Chiricahua Apache, for instance, there are but two terms for relatives within one's own generation; these terms (*-k'is* and *-làh*) are used to all such relatives whether they are siblings, near cousins, or only remote cousins. *-k'is* is applied to all who are of the same sex as the speaker; *-làh*, to all who are of the opposite sex. Corresponding to these terms are contrasting patterns of behavior, to which, of course, the words themselves are cues. The Chiricahua Apache treats kin addressed as -*k'is* with great affection and familiarity; they are, in this society, the people with whom an individual feels most secure and at ease. In contrast, relatives addressed as -*làh* are treated with excessive formality and circumspection; one must even avoid being together with one's -*làh* except in the presence of others (Opler, 1941).

Similar examples may be given in respect to terms relating to the physical environment. Among the Navaho, for example, we find color terms corresponding roughly to our "white," "red," and "yellow," but none which are equivalent to our "black," "gray," "brown," "blue," and "green." Navaho has two terms corresponding to "black," one denoting the black of the darkness, the other the black of such objects as coal. Our "gray" and "brown" are, however, denoted by a single term in Navaho, and so also are our "blue" and "green." The Navaho, in brief, divide the color spectrum, in so far as their vocabulary is concerned, into segments different from our own.

Another fruitful source of examples is found in personal pronouns, especially those for the second and third persons. It is well known that many European languages have two second person pronouns (as French *tu, vous*) where only one is found in modern English. Navaho has no equivalents for English "he," "she," and "it"; this segmentation, a trace of an old gender system, does not exist in Navaho. But Navaho does divide third person pronouns into four categories: (1) that employed of persons or beings psychologically close to the speaker or of preferred interest, (2) that employed of persons or beings psychologically remote, such as non-Navaho (when contrasted with Navaho) or relatives treated with formality

(as opposed to those treated with familiarity), (3) the indefinite third person, an "it" that refers only to an unspecified actor or goal, and (4) the third person that has reference to a place, condition, or time.

A final, and revealing, illustration may be added from the language of the Chiricahua Apache, the place name *tónòogàh*, for which the English equivalent (not the translation) is "Dripping Springs." Dripping Springs, a noun phrase, names a spot in New Mexico where the water from a spring flows over a rocky bluff and drips into a small pool below; the English name, it is evident, is descriptive of one part of this scene, the movement of the water. The Apache term is, in contrast, a verbal phrase and accentuates quite a different aspect of the scene. The element *tó*, which means "water," precedes the verb *nòogàh*, which means, roughly, "whiteness extends downward." *tónòogàh* as a whole, then, may be translated "water-whiteness extends downward," a reference to the fact that a broad streak of white limestone deposit, laid down by the running water, extends downward on the rock.

While these examples, and many other similar ones, seem clearly to indicate that language habits influence *sensory* perceptions and thought, we must not overestimate this influence. It is simply not true, for example, that the Chiricahua Apache, because he does not in speech distinguish between -*k'is*, is also unable to distinguish his siblings (of the same sex) from other relatives of that class in the same generation. He may, of course, distinguish them, much as we have been able to define in English terms like -*k'is* and -*làh*, that is, by circumlocutions of one sort or another. In the same way, it is perfectly evident that the Navaho, while they denote "brown" and "gray" by one term and "blue" and "green" by another, are quite able to discern the difference between brown and gray, blue and green. Again this may be done, should ambiguity otherwise result, by circumlocution, just as we can quite simply express in English the difference between the two Navaho words for our "black."

The fact of the matter, then, is not that linguistic patterns inescapably limit sensory perceptions and thought, but simply that, together with other cultural patterns, they direct perception and thinking into certain habitual channels. The Eskimo, who distinguishes in speech several varieties of snow surface (and who lacks a general term corresponding to our "snow"), is responding to a whole complex of cultural patterns, which require that he make these distinctions, so vital to his physical welfare and that of the group. It is as if the culture as a whole (including the language) selected from the landscape certain features more important than others and so gave to the landscape an organization or structure peculiar to the group. A language, then, as a cultural system, more or less faithfully reflects the structuring of reality which is peculiar to the group that speaks it. Sapir says:

> To pass from one language to another is psychologically parallel to passing from one geometrical system of reference to another. The environing world which is referred to is the same for either language; the world of points is the same in either frame of reference. But the formal approach to the same item of experience, as to the given point of space, is so different that the resulting feeling of orientation can be the same neither in the two languages nor in the two frames of reference. Entirely distinct, or at least measurably distinct, formal adjustments have to be made and these differences have their psychological correlates [1924, p. 153].

4. The most important of the studies that document the thesis outlined in section 3 is undoubtedly the work of Benjamin L. Whorf, specifically his paper on "The Relation of Habitual Behavior and Thought to Language" (1941c). Whorf's views are also summarized, in briefer and less technical form, in three other articles: "Science and Linguistics" (1940b), "Linguistics as an Exact Science" (1941a), and "Languages and Logic" (1941b). All four papers were reprinted in 1949, under the title *Four Articles on Metalinguistics,* by the Foreign Service Institute, Department of State, Washington, D.C. We shall summarize only the first of the papers listed above.

Whorf begins, as we have already noted, by an analysis of instances in which the meaning of a situation, as well as certain physical realities, appears to have influenced behavior. He notes, however, that such lexical meanings are limited in range and that "one cannot study the behavioral compulsiveness of such materials without suspecting a much more far-reaching compulsion from large-scale patterning of grammatical categories, such as plurality, gender and similar classifications (animate, inanimate, etc.), tenses, voices, and other verb forms, classifications of the type of 'parts of speech,' and the matter of whether a given experience is denoted by a unit morpheme, an inflected word, or a syntactical combination" (1941c, p. 77). These grammatical patterns tend in the same direction as the smaller and more limited lexical patterns. To be brief: the influence of language upon habitual thought and behavior does not "depend so much on *any one system* (e.g., tense, or nouns) within the grammar as upon the ways of analyzing and reporting experience which have become fixed in the language as integrated 'fashions of speaking' and which cut across the typical grammatical classifications, so that such a 'fashion' may include lexical, morphological, syntactic, and otherwise systemically diverse means coordinated in a certain frame of consistency"

(1941c, p. 92). Stemming from the fashions of speaking, or at least indicated by them, are features of the "habitual thought" or "thought world" of a people, by which Whorf means "more than simply language, i.e. than the linguistic patterns themselves." The thought world includes "all the analogical and suggestive value of the [linguistic] patterns . . . and all the give-and-take between language and the culture as a whole, wherein is a vast amount that is not linguistic yet shows the shaping influence of language. In brief, this 'thought world' is the microcosm that each man carries about within himself, by which he measures and understands what he can of the macrocosm" (1941c, p. 84).

The fashions of speaking peculiar to a people, like other aspects of their culture, are indicative of a view of life, a metaphysics of their culture, compounded of unquestioned, and mainly unstated, premises which define the nature of their universe and man's position within it. Kluckhohn and Leighton, in speaking of the Navaho, hold that "the lack of equivalences in Navaho and English is merely the outward expression of inward differences between two peoples in premises, in basic categories, in training in fundamental sensitivities, and in general view of the world" (1948, p. 215). It is this metaphysics, manifest to some degree in all the patterns of a culture, that channelizes the perceptions and thinking of those who participate in the culture and that predisposes them to certain modes of observation and interpretation. The metaphysics, as well, supplies the link between language as a cultural system and all other systems found in the same culture.

It does not follow, of course, that a cultural metaphysics is prohibitive of variation and change; it is not a closed logical system of beliefs and premises but rather a historically derived psychological system open to change. This

may be shown by the history of our own culture. As Sapir puts it:

As our scientific experience grows we must learn to fight the implications of language. "The grass waves in the wind" is shown by its linguistic form to be a member of the same relational class of experiences as "The man works in the house." As an interim solution of the problem of expressing the experience referred to in this sentence, it is clear that language has proved useful, for it has made significant use of certain symbols of conceptual relation, such as agency and location. If we feel the sentence to be poetic and metaphorical, it is largely because other more complex types of experience with their appropriate symbolisms of reference enable us to re-interpret the situation and to say, for instance, "The grass is waved by the wind" or "The wind causes the grass to wave." The point is that no matter how sophisticated our modes of interpretation become, we never really get beyond the projection and continuous transfer of relations suggested by the forms of our speech. After all, to say "Friction causes such and such a result" is not very different from saying "The grass waves in the wind." Language is at one and the same time helping and retarding us in our exploration of experience, and the details of these processes of help and hindrance are deposited in the subtler meanings of different cultures [1916, pp. 10–11].

5. To return to Whorf, he now proceeds to compare Hopi, an American Indian language, with the languages of western Europe. In the course of his study, it soon became evident that the grammar of Hopi bore a relation to Hopi culture, and the grammar of European tongues to our own "Western" or "European" culture. And it appeared that the interrelation brought in those large subsummations of experience by language, such as our own terms "time," "space," "substance," and "matter." Since with respect to the traits compared there is little difference between English, French, German, or other European languages with the *possible* (but doubtful) exception of Balto-Slavic and non-Indo-European, I have

lumped these languages into one group called SAE or "Standard Average European" [1941c, pp. 77–78].

Whorf reports, however, only a portion of the whole investigation, summed up in two questions: "(1) Are our own concepts of 'time,' 'space,' and 'matter' given in substantially the same form by experience to all men, or are they in part conditioned by the structure of particular languages? (2) Are there traceable affinities between (a) cultural and behavioral norms and (b) large-scale linguistic patterns?" (1941c, p. 78).

In the last question Whorf emphasizes that he is not seeking a correlation between language and the rest of culture, in the naïve sense that types of linguistic structure (e.g., "isolating," "synthetic," "inflectional," and the like) may be linked with broad cultural categories based, for example, on technology (e.g., "hunting" versus "agricultural," etc.). In this he follows general anthropological practice, summed up by Sapir in the following words: "All attempts to connect particular types of linguistic morphology with certain correlated stages of cultural development are vain. . . . Both simple and complex types of language of an indefinite number of varieties may be found at any desired level of cultural advance" (1921, p. 234). The relation of language to the rest of culture, as we have already indicated (see sec. 4), lies rather in the fact that all cultural systems (including language) refer back to the unformulated metaphysics that serve as the *raison d'être* of the culture as a whole. It is perhaps this relationship that Sapir envisaged when he said: "If it can be shown that culture has an innate form, a series of contours, quite apart from the subject-matter of any description whatsoever, we have something in culture that may serve as a term of comparison with and possibly as a means of relating it to language" (1921, pp. 233–34).

6. Hopi and SAE, it appears, contrast markedly in a number of large-scale linguistic patterns: (a) plurality and numeration, (b) nouns of physical quantity, (c) phases of cycles, (d) temporal forms of verbs, and (e) duration, intensity, and tendency. We may summarize these contrasts in the following paragraphs:

a) SAE applies the frame *cardinal number plus plural noun* to two objectively different situations: to aggregates, like "ten apples" or "ten men," which may be perceived as such, and to cycles, like "ten days," which may not be objectively perceived but form instead a metaphorical or imagined aggregate. In contrast, Hopi restricts cardinal numbers and plurals to entities that form or can form an objective group; it has no imaginary aggregates. For an expression like "ten days" Hopi uses ordinals with singulars, roughly as in the English expressions "until the eleventh day" or "after the tenth day." The significant contrast between SAE and Hopi lies, then, in that SAE may use the same frame for both aggregates and cycles (though cycles may also be differently expressed), whereas Hopi makes a clear linguistic difference between the two.

b) SAE distinguishes, by linguistic form, two kinds of noun: individual (bounded) nouns, which denote bodies with definite outlines (e.g., "dog," "man," "stick"), and mass (unbounded) nouns, which denote indefinite continua without boundaries or outlines (e.g., "air," "water," and "milk"). Not all the physical quantities denoted by mass nouns are, however, encountered as unbounded extents; we frequently have occasion to individuate them. We do this by means of a binomial frame composed of an individual noun, the relator "of," and the mass noun, as, for example, in "glass of water" or "piece of cheese." In many instances this frame may be interpreted as "container full of something," as in "cup of coffee," "bowl of milk," or "bag of flour," but in others the mass noun is individuated only as a body-type, as in "piece of wood," "lump of coal," or "pane of glass." The influence of the container-contents frame, according to Whorf, carries over to the body-type frame, so that in the latter, the body-type seems to contain something—a "stuff," "matter," or "substance"—that may therefore exist both as a formless item and as manifest in a body-type. This language pattern, then, often requires us "to name a physical thing by a binomial that splits the reference into a formless item plus a form" (1941c, p. 80).

Hopi nouns, in contrast, always have an individual sense, even though the boundaries of some items are vague or indefinite. There is no contrast between individual and mass nouns, hence no reference to container or body-type, and no "analogies on which to build the concept of existence as a duality of formless item and form" (Whorf, 1941c, p. 80).

c) Phases of cycles, the subjective consciousness of becoming later and later, are denoted in SAE by terms like "summer," "morning," "sunset," or "hour" that are linguistically little different from other nouns. They may be subjects ("summer has come"), objects ("he likes the summer"), singulars or plurals ("one summer" versus "many summers"), and numerated or counted as discrete "objects" ("forty summers"), much in the same way as with nouns denoting physical quantities. The experience of time and phasing thereby tends to be objectified in SAE as a sequence of separable units. More than this, the noun "time" itself may be treated as a mass noun, denoting an unbounded extent, and by its use in binomial frames like "moment of time" (linguistically parallel to "glass of water" or "piece of wood") "we are assisted to imagine that 'a summer' actually contains or consists of such-and-

such a quantity of 'time'" (Whorf, 1941c, p. 81).

In Hopi terms, denoted phases of cycles are linguistically distinct from nouns or other form classes; they are a separate form class called "temporals." "There is," says Whorf, "no objectification, as a region, an extent, a quantity, of the subjective duration-feeling. Nothing is suggested about time except the perpetual 'getting later' of it. And so there is no basis here for a formless item answering to our 'time'" (1941c, p. 81).

d) The temporal forms of SAE verbs, by which they are divided into a system of three major tenses—past, present, and future—is, to Whorf, another manifestation of the larger scheme of objectifying time that we have already found in other SAE linguistic patterns. Just as we set time units like hours, days, and years in a row, so do we arrange the past, present, and future on a linear scale, the past behind the present and the future before it. Though time, in reality, is a subjective experience of "getting later" or "changing certain relations in an irreversible manner," we can and do, by virtue of our general tendency to objectify time and our tense system, "construct and contemplate in thought a system of past, present, future, in the objectified configuration of points on a line" (1941c, p. 82). This often leads to certain inconsistencies, notable particularly in the diverse usages of the English present tense, as illustrated by equational statements (e.g., "Man is mortal"), inclusion in a sensuous field (e.g., "I see him"), and customarily valid statements (e.g., "We see with our eyes").

Hopi verbs have no tenses but only validity forms, aspects, and modal clause-linkage forms. There are three validity forms: (1) denoting simply that the speaker is reporting a past or present event, (2) that the speaker expects that an event will take place, and (3) that he makes a customarily valid statement. Aspect forms report differing degrees of duration in respect to the event; and the modal forms, employed only when an utterance includes two verbs or clauses, "denote relations between the clauses, including relations of later to earlier and of simultaneity." There is, therefore, no "more basis for an objectified time in Hopi verbs than in other Hopi patterns" (Whorf, 1941c, p. 82).

e) Duration, intensity, and tendency must, according to Whorf, find expression in all languages, but they need not be expressed in the same ways. In SAE it is characteristic to express them largely by metaphors of spatial extension, that is, by metaphors "of size, number (plurality), position, shape, and motion. We express duration by long, short, great, much, quick, slow, etc.; intensity by large, great, much, heavy, light, high, low, sharp, faint, etc.; tendency by more, increase, grow, turn, get, approach, go, come, rise, fall, stop, smooth, even, rapid, slow, and so on through an almost inexhaustible list of metaphors that we hardly recognize as such since they are virtually the only linguistic media available. The non-metaphorical terms in this field, like early, late, soon, lasting, intense, very, tending, are a mere handful, quite inadequate to the needs." This situation, it is clear, derives from our whole scheme of "imaginatively spatializing qualities and potentials that are quite non-spatial (so far as any spatially-perceptive senses can tell us)"; it rests on the patterns we have described in the preceding (1941c, p. 83).

Hopi, as might be expected, has no such metaphors. "The reason is clear when we know that Hopi has abundant conjugational and lexical means of expressing duration, intensity, and tendency directly as such, and that major grammatical patterns do not, as with us, provide analogies for an imaginary space." Hopi aspects "express duration and tendency of manifestations, while some of the 'voices' express intensity, tendency, and duration of forces or causes producing manifestations. Then a special part of speech, the 'tensors,' a huge class of words, denotes only intensity, tendency, duration, and sequence. . . . A striking feature is their lack of resemblance to terms of real space and movement that to us 'mean the same.' There is not even more than a trace of apparent derivation from space terms" (Whorf, 1941c, pp. 83–84).

7. From the linguistic comparisons summarized in section 6, Whorf infers "certain dominant contrasts" in "habitual thought" in SAE and Hopi, that is, in the "microcosm that each man carries about within himself, by which he measures and understands what he can of the macrocosm."

The SAE microcosm has analyzed reality largely in terms of what it calls "things" (bodies and quasi-bodies) plus modes of extensional but formless existence that it calls "substances" or "matter." It tends to see existence through a binomial formula that expresses any existent as a spatial form plus a spatial formless continuum related to the form as contents is related to the outlines of its container. Non-spatial existents are imaginatively spatialized and charged with similar implications of form and continuum [1941c, p. 84].

The Hopi microcosm, on the other hand,

seems to have analyzed reality largely in terms of *events* (or better "eventing"), referred to in two ways, objective and subjective. Objectively, and only if perceptible physical experience, events are expressed mainly as outlines, colors, movements, and other perceptive reports. Subjectively, for both the physical and non-physical, events are considered the expression of invisible intensity-factors, on which depend their stability and persistence, or their fugitiveness and proclivities. It implies that existents do not "become later and later" all in the same way; but some do so by growing, like plants, some by diffusing and vanishing, some by a process of metamorphoses, some by enduring in one shape till affected by violent forces. In the nature of each existent able to manifest as a definite whole is the power of its own mode of duration; its growth, decline, stability, cyclicity, or creativeness. Everything is thus already "prepared" for the way it now manifests by earlier phases, and what it will be later, partly has been, and partly is in act of being so "prepared." An emphasis and importance rests on this preparing or being prepared aspect of the world that may to the Hopi correspond to that "quality of reality" that "matter" or "stuff" has for us [Whorf, 1941c, p. 84].

The microcosm, here derived largely from an analysis of the linguistic system in a culture, is co-ordinated in many ways, says Whorf, to habitual behavior, that is, to the ways in which people act, rather than talk, about situations. He illustrates this point by describing and analyzing a characteristic feature of Hopi behavior, their emphasis on preparation: "This includes announcing and getting ready for events well beforehand, elaborate precautions to insure persistence of desired conditions, and stress on good will as the preparer of right results" (1941c, p. 85).

Hopi preparing behavior

may be roughly divided into announcing, outer preparing, inner preparing, covert participation, and persistence. Announcing ... is an important function in the hands of a special official, the Crier Chief. Outer preparing ... includes ordinary practising, rehearsing, getting ready, introductory formalities, preparing of special food, etc. (all of these to a degree that seems over-elaborate to us), intensive sustained muscular activity like running, racing, dancing which is thought to increase the intensity of development of events (such as growth of crops), mimetic and other magic, preparation based on esoteric theory involving perhaps occult instruments ... and finally the great cyclic ceremonies and dances, which have the significance of preparing rain and crops [Whorf, 1941c, p. 85].

"Inner preparing is the use of prayer and meditation, and at lesser intensity good wishes and good will, to further desired results" (Whorf, 1941c, p. 85). The Hopi, as fits with their microcosm, lay great stress on the powers of desire and thought, to them "the earliest, and therefore the most important, most critical and crucial, stage of preparing. Moreover, to the Hopi, one's desires and thoughts influence not only his own actions, but all nature" (1941c, pp. 85–86). Unlike ourselves, whose thinking is tied in with concepts of imaginary space, the Hopi supposes that his thinking, say of a corn plant, has actual contact or interaction with it. "The thought should then leave some trace of itself with the plant in the field. If it is a good thought, one about health and growth, it is good for the plant; if a bad thought, the reverse" (1941c, p. 86).

Covert preparation is mental collaboration from people who do not take part in the actual affair, be it a job of work, hunt, race, or ceremony, but direct their thought and good will toward the affair's success ... it is primarily the power of directed thought, and not merely sympathy or encouragement, that is expected of covert participants [Whorf, 1941c, pp. 86–87].

Finally, Hopi preparation, again in consonance with their microcosm, places great emphasis on

persistence and constant insistent repetition. ... To us, for whom time is a motion on a space, unvarying repetition seems to scatter its force along a row of units of that space, and be wasted. To the Hopi, for whom time is not a motion but a "getting later" of everything that has ever been done, unvarying repetition is not wasted but accumulated. It is storing up an invisible change that holds over into later events ... it is as if the return of the day were felt as the return of the same person, a little older but with all the impresses of yesterday, not as "another day," i.e. like an entirely different person. This principle joined with that of thought power and with traits of general Pueblo culture is expressed in the theory of the Hopi ceremonial dance for furthering rain and crops, as well as in its short, piston-like tread, repeated thousands of times, hour after hour [Whorf, 1941c, p. 87].

8. In a similar vein, Whorf now attempts to summarize some of the linguistically conditioned features of our own culture, "certain characteristics adjusted to our binomialism of form plus formless item or 'substance,' to our metaphoricalness, our imaginary space, and our objectified time," all of which, as we have seen, are linguistic (1941c, p. 87). The form-substance dichotomy supports, in Whorf's view, much of Western philosophy, at least that which holds a dualistic view of the universe, and it similarly supports traditional Newtonian physics. Other philosophies (involving, for example, monistic, holistic, and relativistic views of reality) and the physics of relativity, though formulable in our culture, "are badly handicapped for appealing to the 'common sense' of the Western average man. This is not because nature herself refutes them ... but because they must be talked about in what amounts to a new language." Newtonian conceptions of space, time, and matter, on the other hand, find a ready acceptance in our "common sense," for: "They are recepts from culture and language. That is where Newton got them" (1941c, p. 88).

Our habit of objectifying time, since it "puts before imagination something like a ribbon or scroll marked off into equal blank spaces, suggesting that each be filled with an entry" (Whorf, 1941c, p. 88), fits well with our cultural emphasis on historicity; the keeping of records, diaries, and accounts, our habit of producing, for the future, schedules, programs, and budgets; and, as well, the complicated mechanism of our commercial structure, with its emphasis on "time wages, rents, credit, interest, depreciation charges, and insurance premiums. No doubt this vast system once built would continue to run under any sort of linguistic treatment of time; but that it should have been built at all, reaching the magnitude and particular form it has in the western world, is a fact decidedly in consonance with the patterns of the SAE languages" (1941c, p. 89).

9. Whorf adds further details on the linguistically conditioned features of western European culture, but we have perhaps summarized enough to make the contrast with the Hopi clear. Whorf turns next to the historical implications of his hypothesis, a brief attempt to answer the question: "How does such a network of language, culture, and behavior [as the SAE and Hopi] come about historically? Which was first, the language patterns or the cultural norms?" He summarizes the answer as follows:

In the main they have grown up together, constantly influencing each other. But in this partnership the nature of the language is the factor that limits free plasticity and rigidifies channels of development in the more autocratic way. This is because language is a system, not just an assemblage of norms. Large systemic outlines can change to something really new only very slowly, while many other cultural innovations are made with comparative quickness [1941c, p. 91].

It might be added, however, that the dichotomy between linguistic systems and other systems in the culture is by no means so sharp as Whorf suggests. Not all nonlinguistic aspects of a culture are mere "assemblages of norms"; there are some that are also structured, perhaps as rigidly so as language and possibly, therefore, as resistant to change. The important point of difference, as between other cultural systems and language, it seems to me, is not that language is the more rigidly systemic but that the linguistic system so clearly interpenetrates all other systems within the culture. This alone might account for its larger role, if it has that, in the limiting of "free plasticity" and the rigidifying of "channels of development."

It is here, too, that we should raise the question, so often discussed: How does the hypothesis that language connects so intimately with other aspects of culture square with the fact, many times noted, that closely related languages (e.g., Hupa and Navaho) may be associated with cultures quite different in other respects and, vice versa, that cultures otherwise much alike (e.g., those of the Pueblo or Plains Indians) may be linked with languages that are very different? Does not this lack of coincidence between the boundaries of language groups and culture areas suggest that language and culture are distinct variables, not necessarily connected in any basic fashion?

If language and culture have been regarded by some as distinct variables (see, for example, Carroll et al., 1951, p. 37), it is perhaps because (1) they define language too narrowly and (2) they limit culture (especially in establishing culture areas) to its more formal and explicit features, those which are most subject to borrowing and change.

It is quite possible that the features of a language (largely phonemic) by means of which we link it to others in a stock or family are among the least important when we seek to connect it to the rest of culture. The fashions of speaking that Whorf finds so important to habitual behavior and thought are, after all, derived from the lexical, morphological, and syntactic patterns of a language, and these, in turn, are arrangements of phonemic materials. Two or more languages, then, may well have their phonemic materials from the same historical source and yet develop, under the stimulus of diverse microcosms, quite different fashions of speech. In short, the fact that languages belong to a common stock does not prove that they have the same fashions of speaking; such proof, if it is forthcoming at all, must be demonstrated empirically.

The cultures included in the same culture area, on the other hand, tend to resemble one another only in discrete cultural features, those which are easily diffused, and not necessarily in the ways in which these features are combined into fashions of behaving or in the basic premises to which such fashions of behaving may point. The Navaho and Hopi, for example, both within the southwestern area, display many isolated points of similarity, in their common possession of clans, sand paintings, and other features of ritual and in certain weaving and horticultural techniques and products. But the patterning or arrangement of these traits in the two cultures is widely divergent; the patterning of Navaho ritual and family (or clan) organization, for example, is not at all like that of the Hopi. It is not surprising, therefore, that Whorf's (1941c) and my own (1951) accounts of the Hopi and Navaho languages, respectively, reveal wholly distinct linguistic microcosms, or that the Kluckhohn and Leighton description of the Navaho view of life (1948, pp. 216–38) is quite foreign to that given by Whorf for the Hopi.

10. To return to Whorf, he now sums up by providing answers to the questions posed in his paper. In response to the first of these ("Are our own concepts of 'time,' 'space,' and matter' given in substantially the same form by experience to all men, or are they in part conditioned by the structure of particular languages?" [1941c, p. 78]), he replies that concepts of "time" and "matter" appear, as between SAE and Hopi at least, to depend in large part on their separate linguistic structures.

Our own "time" differs markedly from Hopi "duration." It is conceived as like a space of strictly limited dimensions, or sometimes as like a motion upon such a space, and employed as an intellectual tool accordingly. Hopi "duration" seems to be inconceivable in terms of space or motion, being the mode in which life differs from form, and consciousness *in toto* from the spatial elements of consciousness. Certain ideas born of our own time-concept, such as that of absolute simultaneity, would be either very difficult to express or devoid of meaning under the Hopi conception, and would be replaced by operational concepts. Our "matter" is the physical subtype of "substance" or "stuff," which is conceived as the formless extensional item that must be joined with form before there can be real existence. In Hopi there seems to be nothing corresponding to it; there are no formless extensional items; existence may or may not have form, but what it also has, with or without form, is intensity and duration, these being non-extensional and at bottom the same [1941c, p. 92].

The concept of space does not differ so strikingly, and Whorf suggests that

probably the apprehension of space is given in substantially the same form irrespective of language.... But the *concept of space* will vary somewhat with language, because as an intellectual tool [as, e.g., in Newtonian and Euclidean space, etc.] it is so closely linked with the concomitant employment of other intellectual tools, of the order of "time" and "matter," which are linguistically conditioned. We see things with our eyes in the same space forms as the Hopi, but our idea of space has also the property of acting as a surrogate of non-spatial relationships like time, intensity, tendency, and as a void to be filled with imagined formless items, one of which may even be called "space." Space as sensed by the Hopi would not be connected mentally with such surrogates, but would be comparatively "pure," unmixed with extraneous notions [1941c, pp. 92–93].

Whorf answers the second question of his paper ("Are there traceable affinities between [a] cultural and behavioral norms and [b] large-scale linguistic patterns?" [1941c, p. 78]) as follows:

There are connections but not correlations or diagnostic correspondences between cultural norms and linguistic patterns. Although it would be impossible to infer the existence of Crier Chiefs from the lack of tenses in Hopi, or vice versa, there is a relation between a language and the rest of the culture of the society which uses it. There are cases where the "fashions of speaking" are closely integrated with the whole general culture, whether or not this be universally true, and there are connections within this integration, between the kind of linguistic analyses employed and various behavioral reactions and also the shapes taken by various cultural developments. Thus the importance of Crier Chiefs does have a connection, not with tenselessness itself, but with a system of thought in which categories different from our tenses are natural. These connections are to be found not so much by focusing attention on the typical rubrics of linguistic, ethnographic, or sociological description as by examining the culture and the language (always and only when the two have been together historically for a considerable time) as a whole in which the concatenations that run across these departmental lines may be expected to exist, and if they do exist, eventually to be discoverable by study [1941c, p. 93].

11. Another attempt to show how a language may influence "the logical concepts of the people who speak it" is found in the work of Lee on the language of the Wintu Indians of California (see 1938, 1944a, b). We shall summarize two of these in detail: "Conceptual Implications of an Indian Language" and "Linguistic Reflection of Wintu Thought."

Lee begins the first of these papers as follows:

It has been said that a language will delineate and limit the logical concepts of the individual who speaks it. Conversely, a language is an organ for the expression of thought, of concepts and principles of classification. True enough, the thought of the individual must run along its grooves; but these grooves, themselves, are a heritage from individuals who laid them down in an unconscious effort to express their attitude toward the world. Grammar contains in crystallized form the accumulated and accumulating experience, the Weltanschauung of a people.

The study which I propose to present below is an attempt to understand, through a study of grammar, the unformulated philosophy of the Wintu tribe of California [1938, p. 89].

12. A Wintu verb, according to Lee, must employ one of two stems (here denominated as I and II), differentiated as ablaut forms (e.g., *wir-*, I, and *wer-*, II, "to come"). Stems of Type I denote states or events in which the grammatical subject of the verb participates as free agent and in which the speaker (whether or not identical with the grammatical subject) also participates "insofar as he has become cognizant of the activity or state described" (1938, p. 94).

A speaker "can use the stem [of Type I] alone, without suffix, thus stating generally known fact. But if he tries to particularize this, to delimit it as to time or subject, he is forced to quote, in the same breath, that particular experience of his which is the authority for his statement" (1938, p. 90). There are five suffixes for this purpose, as follows: denoting (1) that the speaker knows the state or event from hearsay; (2) that the speaker knows the state or event through having seen it or because there is unquestioned evidence; (3) that the speaker knows the state or event from sensory evidence other than visual (i.e., from the sense of smell, hearing, feeling, etc.); (4) that the speaker infers the state or event from circumstantial sensory evidence (e.g., Coyote, who sees Hummingbird's tracks end suddenly, and that the valley to the south is covered with gay flowers, says inferentially that Hummingbird must have gone south); and (5) that

the speaker infers the state or event from previous knowledge not obtained by hearsay or visual or other sensory evidence (e.g., a man who knows his father-in-law is bedridden and has been alone for a long time says, inferentially, "my father-in-law is hungry").

"The distinctions made by the suffixes so far given correspond to subjective differences in the speaker, not the grammatical subject. Other affixes, added to the stem and preceding any personal or temporal suffixes there may be, indicate differences of attitude on the part of the grammatical subject" (1938, p. 92). There are three of these: (1) indicating intent or purpose, (2) indicative of desire or effort, and (3) denoting "approximation, not quite related experience, whether past, present, or future" (1938, p. 93).

Type II stems denote states or events that exist or take place "irrespective of the agency of the subject" and which the speaker, "in speaking of it ... asserts a truth which is beyond experience" (1938, p. 89). In statements belonging to this category, "attention is concentrated on the event and its ramifications, not on the actor. The verb is not particularized in terms of participation. There are rarely any personal suffixes, and the speaker never refers to himself. He is not an authority. He speaks of the unknown, and when he makes his assertion, he asserts truth which is subject neither to experience, doubt or proof" (1938, p. 95).

Stems of Type II are used to form the passive and medio-passivĕ, to form the imperative, to "pose questions whose answers do not depend on knowledge on the part of speaker or hearer, and to make wishes of the day-dream type. The suffix of ignorance, used variously to express negation, interrogation, or wonder, is attached to this stem" (1938, p. 94). In addition, Type II stems take a suffix which "is used to express, all in one, futurity.

causality, potentiality, probability, necessity; to refer to an inevitable future which might, can and must be, in the face of which the individual is helpless" (1938, p. 95).

These distinctions imply, according to Lee, that "the Wintu has a small sphere wherein he can choose and do, can feel and think and make decisions. Cutting through this and circumscribing it, is the world of natural necessity wherein all things that are potential and probable are also inevitable, wherein existence is unknowable and ineffable. This world the Wintu does not know, but he believes in it without question; such belief he does not tender even to the supernatural, which is within experience and can be referred to by means of -*nte* (I sense)" (1938, p. 102).

13. Lee's second paper, "Linguistic Reflection of Wintu Thought" (1944*b*), offers more evidence, from both language and other aspects of Wintu culture, to the same end. In language she notes that Wintu lacks a plural form of the noun; where plurality is expressed at all in the case of nouns, it is by means of a "root which is completely different from the singular word; *man* is wi• Da but *men* is q'i• s" (1944*b*, p. 181). But Wintu does emphasize a distinction between particular and generic, even though this is optional rather than compulsory, as is the case with our singular-plural distinction. Thus, from a primary form meaning "whiteness," a generic quality, the Wintu derive, by suffixation, a particular, meaning "the white one"; from a word meaning "deer" in the generic sense (e.g., "he hunted deer") a derivative referring to a particular deer (e.g., "he shot a deer"). In two versions of the same tale, told respectively by a man and a woman, "the man refers to a man's weapons and implements in the particular; the woman mentions them all as generic. The use

of the word sɛm ... is illuminating in this connection. As sɛm generic, it means *hand* or *both hands* of one person, the fingers merged in one mass; spread out the hands, and now you have delimited parts of the hand, sɛmum, *fingers*" (1944*b*, p. 182).

Lee sees the distinction between verb stems of Types I and II as parallel to this differentiation between the generic mass nouns (e.g., *sɛm*, "hand") and those which particularize (e.g., *sɛmum*, "fingers"). Verb stems of Type I are used in statements of experience which are particularizations of a given and undivided reality, particularizations in which the speaker's "consciousness, cognition, and sensation act as a limiting and formalizing element upon the formless reality," as appears to be demonstrated by the suffixes we have already illustrated (1944*b*, p. 183). The formless reality, given in the Wintu-conceived universe and accepted by them in faith, may only be expressed by verbs using Type II stems.

"Alone this stem forms a command ... the statement of an obligation imposed from the outside. With the aid of different suffixes, this stem may refer to a timeless state, as when setting given conditions for a certain activity; or to what we call the passive, when the individual does not participate as a free agent. In general, it refers to the not-experienced and not-known" (1944*b*, p. 183).

In brief (and Lee illustrates this point in many other regions of the language), these fashions of speaking suggest that

the Wintu assumes that reality is, irrespective of himself. Reality is unbounded content; in this he finds qualities which are not rigidly distinguished from each other. Toward reality he directs belief and respect. Upon it, as it impinges upon his consciousness, he imposes transitory shape. He individuates and particularizes, impressing himself only within careful limits, performing acts of will with diffidence and circumspection. He leaves the content essentially unaffected; only in respect to form does he pass judgement [1944b, p. 181].

This premise of "an original oneness," upon which the Wintu may impose "transitory shape" and from which he may individuate and particularize, underlies

not only linguistic categories, but his thought and behavior throughout. . . . It explains why kinship terms are classified, not with the substantives, but with the pronouns such as *this;* why the special possives [possessives?] used with them, such as the n D, in n DDa·n: *my father,* are really pronouns of participation, to be used also with aspects of one's identity as, for example, my act, my intention, my future death. To us, in the words of Ralph Linton, "society has as its foundation an aggregate of individuals." For the Wintu, the individual is a delimited part of society; it is society that is basic, not a plurality of individuals [1944b, p. 185].

Similar reflections of "the concept of the immutability of essence and the transiency of form, of the fleeting significance of delimitation," are found in Wintu mythology. The creator, "he who is above," came from matter that was already there; people did not "come into being," they "grow out of the ground," which always existed. "Dawn and daylight, fire and obsidian have always been in existence, hoarded; they are finally stolen, and given a new role." The names of myth characters, such as Coyote, Buzzard, Grizzly-Bear, Grosbeak, and Loon, probably "refer to something undelimited, as we, for example, distinguish between fire and a fire. These characters die and reappear in another myth without explanation. They become eventually the coyotes and grizzly-bears we know, but not through a process of generation. They represent a prototype, a genus, a quality which, however, is not rigidly differentiated from other qualities" (1944b, p. 186).

14. Lee's conclusions, it is evident, closely parallel those of Whorf and offer further illustration and testing of his hypothesis. There is only a little more data of this sort; some, which we lack the space to summarize, may be found in Astrov (1950) and Hoijer (1948, 1951) on the Navaho; Lee (1940) on the Trobriand language; and Whorf (1940a) on the language of the Shawnee. Other items in the bibliography relate mainly to theoretical discussion (see Kroeber, 1941; Nida, 1945; Voegelin and Harris, 1945; Greenberg, 1948; Hockett, 1949; Emeneau, 1950; Olmsted, 1950; Voegelin, 1950; Lévi-Strauss, 1951) either on points covered in this report or on others we have not treated in detail. The bibliography is not meant to be exhaustive; there is doubtless other material, especially in European sources, which has escaped my notice.

15. In conclusion, there is much in the thesis we have outlined that requires testing; the work of Whorf (on Hopi), Lee (on Wintu), and myself (on Navaho) serves only to rough out a hypothesis on the relation of language to culture, not conclusively to demonstrate it. We must, as Whorf has noted (1941c, p. 93), have many more contrastive studies of whole cultures, including linguistic as well as other patterns of culture, directed toward the discovery of diverse systems of thought and the connection of these to fashions of speaking and behaving generally. The reports on the Hopi, Wintu, and Navaho that we have, brief as they are, sufficiently point up the need for further research and suggest that such research may be fruitful.

The material reviewed also suggests that studies of this sort have a value, not only for the narrower disciplines of linguistics and anthropology, but as well for all of science. As Whorf has noted, the analysis and understanding of linguistic microcosms different from our own point "toward possible new types of logic and possible new cosmical pictures" (1941*b*, p. 16), of the greatest importance for an understanding of our own modes of thought and their evolution. "Western culture has made, through language, a provisional analysis of reality and, without correctives, holds resolutely to that analysis as final." But there are other cultures, "which by aeons of independent evolution have arrived at different, but equally logical, provisional analyses," and these may serve as correctives to our own (1941*b*, p. 18).

REFERENCES AND BIBLIOGRAPHY

ASTROV, MARGOT. 1950. "The Concept of Motion as the Psychological Leitmotif of Navaho Life and Literature," *Journal of American Folklore*, LXIII, 45–56.

CARROLL, JOHN B., *et al.* 1951. "Report and Recommendations of the Interdisciplinary Summer Session in Psychology and Linguistics, June 18–August 10, 1951." Ithaca, N.Y.: Cornell University. (Mimeographed.)

EMENEAU, M. B. 1950. "Language and Non-linguistic Patterns," *Language*, XXVI, 199–209.

GREENBERG, JOSEPH. 1948. "Linguistics and Ethnology," *Southwestern Journal of Anthropology*, IV, 140–47.

HERZOG, GEORGE. 1941. "Culture Change and Language: Shifts in the Pima Vocabulary." In SPIER, LESLIE (ed.), *Language, Culture, and Personality*, pp. 66–74. Menasha, Wis.

HOCKETT, CHARLES. 1949. "Biophysics, Linguistics, and the Unity of Science," *American Scientist*, XXXVI, 558–72.

HOIJER, HARRY. 1948. "Linguistic and Cultural Change," *Language*, XXIV, 335–45.

——. 1951. "Cultural Implications of Some Navaho Linguistic Categories," *ibid.*, XXVII, 111–20.

KLUCKHOHN, CLYDE, and KELLY, WILLIAM. 1945. "The Concept of Culture." In LINTON, RALPH (ed.), *The Science of Man in the World Crisis*, pp. 76–106. New York: Columbia University Press.

KLUCKHOHN, CLYDE, and LEIGHTON, DOROTHEA. 1948. *The Navaho.* Cambridge: Harvard University Press.

KROEBER, A. L. 1941. "Some Relations of Linguistics and Ethnology," *Language*, XVII, 287–91.

LEE, D. DEMETRACOPOULOU. 1938. "Conceptual Implications of an Indian Language," *Philosophy of Science*, V, 89–102.

——. 1940. "A Primitive System of Values," *ibid.*, VII, 355–79.

——. 1944*a*. "Categories of the Generic and Particular in Wintu," *American Anthropologist*, XLVI, 362–69.

——. 1944*b*. "Linguistic Reflection of Wintu Thought," *International Journal of American Linguistics*, X, 181–87.

LÉVI-STRAUSS, CLAUDE. 1951. "Language and the Analysis of Social Laws," *American Anthropologist*, LIII, 155–63.

LOWIE, ROBERT H. 1940. "Native Languages as Ethnographic Tools," *American Anthropologist*, XLII, 81–89.

MEAD, MARGARET. 1939. "Native Languages as Fieldwork Tools," *American Anthropologist*, XLI, 189–205.

NIDA, EUGENE A. 1945. "Linguistics and Ethnology in Translation Problems," *Word*, I, No. 2, 1–15.

OLMSTED, DAVID L. 1950. *Ethnolinguistics So Far.* ("Studies in Linguistics, Occasional Papers," No. 2.)

OPLER, MORRIS E. 1941. *An Apache Life-Way: The Economic, Social, and Religious Institutions of the Chiricahua Indians.* Chicago: University of Chicago Press.

SAPIR, EDWARD. 1916. "Time Perspective in Aboriginal American Culture: A Study in Method." In *Selected Writings of Edward Sapir*, pp. 389–462. Berkeley and Los Angeles: University of California Press, 1949.

——. 1921. *Language.* New York: Harcourt, Brace & Co.

——. 1924. "The Grammarian and His Language." In *Selected Writings of Edward Sapir*, pp. 150–59. Berkeley and Los Angeles: University of California Press, 1949.

——. 1929. "The Status of Linguistics as a Science," *ibid.*, pp. 160–66.

——. 1933. "Language," *ibid.*, pp. 7–32.

——. 1936. "Internal Linguistic Evidence Suggestive of the Northern Origin of the Navaho," *ibid.*, pp. 213–24.

VOEGELIN. C. F. 1949a. "Linguistics without Meaning and Culture without Words," *Word*, V, 36–42.

——. 1949b. "Relative Structurability," *ibid.*, pp. 44–45.

——. 1950. "A 'Testing Frame' for Language and Culture," *American Anthropologist*, LII, 432–35.

——. 1951. "Culture, Language, and the Human Organism," *Southwestern Journal of Anthropology*, VII, 357–73.

VOEGELIN, C. F., and HARRIS, ZELLIG. 1945. "Linguistics in Ethnology," *South-western Journal of Anthropology*, I, 455–65.

WHORF, BENJAMIN L. 1940a. "Gestalt Techniques of Stem Composition in Shawnee," *Prehistory Research Series, Indiana Historical Society*, I, No. 9, 393–406.

——. 1940b. "Science and Linguistics." In *Four Articles on Metalinguistics*, pp. 1–5. Washington, D.C.: Foreign Service Institute, Department of State, 1949.

——. 1941a. "Linguistics as an Exact Science," *ibid.*, pp. 7–12.

——. 1941b. "Languages and Logic," *ibid.*, pp. 13–18.

——. 1941c. "The Relation of Habitual Thought and Behavior to Language," *ibid.*, pp. 20–38.

Style

By MEYER SCHAPIRO

I

By STYLE IS meant the constant form—and sometimes the constant elements, qualities, and expression—in the art of an individual or a group. The term is also applied to the whole activity of an individual or society, as in speaking of a "life-style" or the "style of a civilization."

For the archeologist, style is exemplified in a motive or pattern, or in some directly grasped quality of the work of art, which helps him to localize and date the work and to establish connections between groups of works or between cultures. Style here is a symptomatic trait, like the nonaesthetic features of an artifact. It is studied more often as a diagnostic means than for its own sake as an important constituent of culture. For dealing with style, the archeologist has relatively few aesthetic and physiognomic terms.

To the historian of art, style is an essential object of investigation. He studies its inner correspondences, its life-history, and the problems of its formation and change. He, too, uses style as a criterion of the date and place of origin of works, and as a means of tracing relationships between schools of art. But the style is, above all, a system of forms with a quality and a meaningful expression through which the personality of the artist and the broad outlook of a group are visible. It is also a vehicle of expression within the group, communicating and fixing certain values of religious, social, and moral life through the emotional suggestiveness of forms. It is, besides, a common ground against which innovations and the individuality of particular works may be measured. By considering the succession of works in time and space and by matching the variations of style with historical events and with the varying features of other fields of culture, the historian of art attempts, with the help of common-sense psychology and social theory, to account for the changes of style or specific traits. The historical study of individual and group styles also discloses typical stages and processes in the development of forms.

For the synthesizing historian of culture or the philosopher of history, the style is a manifestation of the culture as a whole, the visible sign of its unity. The style reflects or projects the "inner form" of collective thinking and feeling. What is important here is not the style of an individual or of a single art, but forms and qualities shared by all the arts of a culture during a significant span of time. In this sense one speaks of Classical or Medieval or Renaissance Man with respect to common traits discovered in the art styles of these epochs and documented also in religious and philosophical writings.

The critic, like the artist, tends to conceive of style as a value term; style

278

as such is a quality and the critic can say of a painter that he has "style" or of a writer that he is a "stylist." Although "style" in this normative sense, which is applied mainly to individual artists, seems to be outside the scope of historical and ethnological studies of art, it often occurs here, too, and should be considered seriously. It is a measure of accomplishment and therefore is relevant to understanding of both art and culture as a whole. Even a period style, which for most historians is a collective taste evident in both good and poor works, may be regarded by critics as a great positive achievement. So the Greek classic style was, for Winckelmann and Goethe, not simply a convention of form but a culminating conception with valued qualities not possible in other styles and apparent even in Roman copies of lost Greek originals. Some period styles impress us by their deeply pervasive, complete character, their special adequacy to their content; the collective creation of such a style, like the conscious shaping of a norm of language, is a true achievement. Correspondingly, the presence of the same style in a wide range of arts is often considered a sign of the integration of a culture and the intensity of a high creative moment. Arts that lack a particular distinction or nobility of style are often said to be style-less, and the culture is judged to be weak or decadent. A similar view is held by philosophers of culture and history and by some historians of art.

Common to all these approaches are the assumptions that every style is peculiar to a period of a culture and that, in a given culture or epoch of culture, there is only one style or a limited range of styles. Works in the style of one time could not have been produced in another. These postulates are supported by the fact that the connection between a style and a period, inferred from a few examples, is confirmed by objects discovered later. Whenever it is possible to locate a work through nonstylistic evidence, this evidence points to the same time and place as do the formal traits, or to a culturally associated region. The unexpected appearance of the style in another region is explained by migration or trade. The style is therefore used with confidence as an independent clue to the time and place of origin of a work of art. Building upon these assumptions, scholars have constructed a systematic, although not complete, picture of the temporal and spatial distribution of styles throughout large regions of the globe. If works of art are grouped in an order corresponding to their original positions in time and space, their styles will show significant relationships which can be co-ordinated with the relationships of the works of art to still other features of the cultural points in time and space.

II

Styles are not usually defined in a strictly logical way. As with languages, the definition indicates the time and place of a style or its author, or the historical relation to other styles, rather than its peculiar features. The characteristics of styles vary continuously and resist a systematic classification into perfectly distinct groups. It is meaningless to ask exactly when ancient art ends and medieval begins. There are, of course, abrupt breaks and reactions in art, but study shows that here, too, there is often anticipation, blending, and continuity. Precise limits are sometimes fixed by convention for simplicity in dealing with historical problems or in isolating a type. In a stream of development the artificial divisions may even be designated by numbers—Styles I, II, III. But the single name given to the style of a period rarely corresponds to a clear and universally accepted characterization of a type. Yet direct acquaintance with an unanalyzed work of art will often permit us to recognize another object of the same origin, just as we recognize a face to be native or foreign. This fact points to a degree of constancy in art that is the basis of all investigation of style. Through careful description and comparison and through formation of a richer, more refined typology adapted to the continuities in development, it has been possible to reduce the areas of vagueness and to advance our knowledge of styles.

Although there is no established system of analysis and writers will stress one or another aspect according to their viewpoint or problem, in general the description of a style refers to three aspects of art: form elements or motives, form relationships, and qualities (including an all-over quality which we may call the "expression").

This conception of style is not arbitrary but has arisen from the experience of investigation. In correlating works of art with an individual or culture, these three aspects provide the broadest, most stable, and therefore most reliable criteria. They are also the most pertinent to modern theory of art, although not in the same degree for all viewpoints. Technique, subject matter, and material may be characteristic of certain groups of works and will sometimes be included in definitions; but more often these features are not so peculiar to the art of a period as the formal and qualitative ones. It is easy to imagine a decided change in material, technique, or subject matter accompanied by little change in the basic form. Or, where these are constant, we often observe that they are less responsive to new artistic aims. A method of stone-cutting will change less rapidly than the sculptor's or architect's forms. Where a technique does coincide with the extension of a style, it is the formal traces of the technique rather than the operations as such that are important

for description of the style. The materials are significant mainly for the textural quality and color, although they may affect the conception of the forms. For the subject matter, we observe that quite different themes—portraits, still lifes, and landscapes—will appear in the same style.

It must be said, too, that form elements or motives, although very striking and essential for the expression, are not sufficient for characterizing a style. The pointed arch is common to Gothic and Islamic architecture, and the round arch to Roman, Byzantine, Romanesque, and Renaissance buildings. In order to distinguish these styles, one must also look for features of another order and, above all, for different ways of combining the elements.

Although some writers conceive of style as a kind of syntax or compositional pattern, which can be analyzed mathematically, in practice one has been unable to do without the vague language of qualities in describing styles. Certain features of light and color in painting are most conveniently specified in qualitative terms and even as tertiary (intersensory) or physiognomic qualities, like cool and warm, gay and sad. The habitual span of light and dark, the intervals between colors in a particular palette—very important for the structure of a work—are distinct relationships between elements, yet are not comprised in a compositional schema of the whole. The complexity of a work of art is such that the description of forms is often incomplete on essential points, limiting itself to a rough account of a few relationships. It is still simpler, as well as more relevant to aesthetic experience, to distinguish lines as hard and soft than to give measurements of their substance. For precision in characterizing a style, these qualities are graded with respect to intensity by comparing different examples directly or by reference to a standard work. Where quantitative measurements have been made, they tend to confirm the conclusions reached through direct qualitative description. Nevertheless, we have no doubt that, in dealing with qualities, much greater precision can be reached.

Analysis applies aesthetic concepts current in the teaching, practice, and criticism of contemporary art; the development of new viewpoints and problems in the latter directs the attention of students to unnoticed features of older styles. But the study of works of other times also influences modern concepts through discovery of aesthetic variants unknown in our own art. As in criticism, so in historical research, the problem of distinguishing or relating two styles discloses unsuspected, subtle characteristics and suggests new concepts of form. The postulate of continuity in culture—a kind of inertia in the physical sense—leads to a search for common features in successive styles that are ordinarily contrasted as opposite poles of form; the resemblances will sometimes be found not so much in obvious aspects as in fairly hidden ones—the line patterns of Renaissance compositions recall features of the older Gothic style, and in contemporary abstract art one observes form relationships like those of Impressionist painting.

The refinement of style analysis has come about in part through problems in which small differences had to be disengaged and described precisely. Examples are the regional variations within the same culture; the process of historical development from year to year; the growth of individual artists and the discrimination of the works of master and pupil, originals and copies. In these studies the criteria for dating and attribution are often physical or external—matters of small symptomatic detail—but here, too, the general trend of research has been to look for features that can be formulated in both structural and expressive-physiognomic terms. It is assumed by many students that the expression terms are all translatable into form and quality terms, since the expression depends on particular shapes and colors and will be modified by a small change in the latter The forms are correspondingly regarded as vehicles of a particular affect (apart from the subject matter). But the relationship here is not altogether clear. In general, the study of style tends toward an ever stronger correlation of form and expression. Some descriptions are purely morphological, as of natural objects—indeed, ornament has been characterized, like crystals, in the mathematical language of group theory. But terms like "stylized," "archaistic," "naturalistic," "mannerist," "baroque," are specifically human, referring to artistic processes, and imply some expressive effect. It is only by analogy that mathematical figures have been characterized as "classic" and "romantic."

III

The analysis and characterization of the styles of primitive and early historical cultures have been strongly influenced by the standards of recent Western art. Nevertheless, it may be said that the values of modern art have led to a more sympathetic and objective approach to exotic arts than was possible fifty or a hundred years ago.

In the past, a great deal of primitive work, especially representation, was regarded as artless even by sensitive people; what was valued were mainly the ornamentation and the skills of primitive industry. It was believed that primitive arts were childlike attempts to represent nature—attempts distorted by ignorance and by an irrational content of the monstrous and grotesque. True art was admitted only in the high cultures, where knowledge of natural forms was combined with a rational ideal which brought beauty and decorum to the image of man. Greek art and the art of the Italian High Renaissance were the norms for judging all art, although in time the classic phase of Gothic art was accepted. Ruskin, who admired Byzantine works, could write that in Christian Europe alone "pure and precious ancient art exists, for there is none in America, none in Asia, none in Africa." From such a viewpoint careful discrimination of primitive styles or a penetrating study of their structure and expression was hardly possible.

With the change in Western art during the last seventy years, naturalistic representation has lost its superior status. Basic for contemporary practice and for knowledge of past art is the theoretical view that what counts in all art are the elementary aesthetic components, the qualities and relationships of the fabricated lines, spots, colors, and surfaces. These have two characteristics: they are intrinsically expressive, and they tend to constitute a coherent whole. The same tendencies to coherent and expressive structure are found in the arts of all cultures. There is no privileged content or mode of representation (although the greatest works may, for reasons obscure to us, occur only in certain styles). Perfect art is possible in any subject matter or style. A style is like a language, with an internal order and expressiveness, admitting a varied intensity or delicacy of statement. This approach is a relativism that does not exclude absolute judgments of value; it makes these judgments possible within every framework by abandoning a fixed norm of style. Such ideas are accepted by most students of art today, although not applied with uniform conviction.

As a result of this new approach, all the arts of the world, even the drawings of children and psychotics, have become accessible on a common plane of expressive and form-creating activity. Art is now one of the strongest evidences of the basic unity of mankind.

This radical change in attitude depends partly on the development of modern styles, in which the raw material and distinctive units of operation—the plane of the canvas, the trunk of wood, tool marks, brush strokes, connecting forms, schemas, particles and areas of pure color—are as pronounced as the elements of representation. Even before nonrepresentative styles were created, artists had become more deeply conscious of the aesthetic-constructive components of the work apart from denoted meanings.

Much in the new styles recalls primitive art. Modern artists were, in fact, among the first to appreciate the works of natives as true art. The development of Cubism and Abstraction made the form problem exciting and helped to refine the perception of the creative in primitive work. Expressionism, with its high pathos, disposed our eyes to the simpler, more intense modes of expression, and together with Surrealism, which valued, above all, the irrational and instinctive in the imagination, gave a fresh interest to the products of primitive fantasy. But, with all the obvious resemblances, modern paintings and sculptures differ from the primitive in structure and content. What in primitive art belongs to an established world of collective beliefs and symbols arises in modern art as an individual expression, bearing the marks of a free, experimental attitude to forms. Modern artists feel, nevertheless, a spiritual kinship with the primitive, who is now closer to them than in the past because of their ideal of frankness and intensity of expression and their desire for a simpler life, with more effective participation of the artist in collective occasions than modern society allows.

One result of the modern development has been a tendency to slight the content of past art; the most realistic representations are contemplated as pure constructions of lines and colors. The observer is often indifferent to the original meanings of works, although he may enjoy through them a vague sentiment of the poetic and religious. The form and expressiveness of older works are regarded, then, in isolation, and the history of an art is written as an immanent development of forms. Parallel to this trend, other scholars have carried on fruitful research into the meanings, symbols, and iconographic types of Western art, relying on the literature of mythology and religion; through these studies the knowledge of the content of art has been considerably deepened, and analogies to the character of the styles have been discovered in the content. This has strengthened the view that the development of forms is not autonomous but is connected with changing attitudes and interests that appear more or less clearly in the subject matter of the art.

IV

Students observed early that the traits which make up a style have a quality in common. They all seem to be marked by the expression of the whole, or there is a dominant feature to which the elements have been adapted. The parts of a Greek temple have the air of a family of forms. In Baroque art, a taste for movement determines the loosening of boundaries, the instability of masses, and the multiplication of large contrasts. For many writers a style, whether of an individual or a group, is a pervasive, rigorous unity. Investigation of style is often a search for hidden correspondences explained by an organizing principle which determines both the character of the parts and the patterning of the whole.

This approach is supported by the experience of the student in identifying a style from a small random fragment. A bit of carved stone, the profile of a molding, a few drawn lines, or a single letter from a piece of writing often possesses for the observer the quality of the complete work and can be dated precisely; before these fragments, we have the conviction of insight into the original whole. In a similar way, we recognize by its intrusiveness an added or repaired detail in an old work. The feel of the whole is found in the small parts.

I do not know how far experiments in matching parts from works in different styles would confirm this view. We may be dealing, in some of these observations, with a microstructural level in which similarity of parts only points to the homogeneity of a style or a technique, rather than to a complex unity in the aesthetic sense. Although personal, the painter's touch, described by constants of pressure, rhythm, and size of strokes, may have no obvious relation to other unique characteristics of the larger forms. There are styles in which large parts of a work are conceived and executed differently, without destroying the harmony of the whole. In African sculpture an exceedingly naturalistic, smoothly carved head rises from a rough, almost shapeless body. A normative aesthetic might regard this as imperfect work, but it would be hard to justify this view. In Western paintings of the fifteenth century, realistic figures and landscapes are set against a gold background, which in the Middle Ages had a spiritualistic sense. In Islamic art, as in certain African and Oceanic styles, forms of great clarity and simplicity in three dimensions—metal vessels and animals or the domes of buildings—have surfaces spun with rich mazy patterns; in Gothic and Baroque art, on the contrary, a complex surface treatment is associated with a correspondingly complicated silhouette of the whole. In

Romanesque art the proportions of figures are not submitted to a single canon, as in Greek art, but two or three distinct systems of proportioning exist even within the same sculpture, varying with the size of the figure.

Such variation within a style is also known in literature, sometimes in great works, like Shakespeare's plays, where verse and prose of different texture occur together. French readers of Shakespeare, with the model of their own classical drama before them, were disturbed by the elements of comedy in Shakespeare's tragedies. We understand this contrast as a necessity of the content and the poet's conception of man—the different modes of expression pertain to contrasted types of humanity—but a purist classical taste condemned this as inartistic. In modern literature both kinds of style, the rigorous and the free, coexist and express different viewpoints. It is possible to see the opposed parts as contributing elements in a whole that owes its character to the interplay and balance of contrasted qualities. But the notion of style has lost in that case the crystalline uniformity and simple correspondence of part to whole with which we began. The integration may be of a looser, more complex kind, operating with unlike parts.

Another interesting exception to the homogeneous in style is the difference between the marginal and the dominant fields in certain arts. In early Byzantine works, rulers are represented in statuesque, rigid forms, while the smaller accompanying figures, by the same artist, retain the liveliness of an older episodic, naturalistic style. In Romanesque art this difference can be so marked that scholars have mistakenly supposed that certain Spanish works were done partly by a Christian and partly by a Moslem artist. In some instances the forms in the margin or in the background are more advanced in style than the central parts, anticipating a later stage of the art. In medieval work the unframed figures on the borders of illuminated manuscripts or on cornices, capitals, and pedestals are often freer and more naturalistic than the main figures. This is surprising, since we would expect to find the most advanced forms in the dominant content. But in medieval art the sculptor or painter is often bolder where he is less bound to an external requirement; he even seeks out and appropriates the regions of freedom. In a similar way an artist's drawings or sketches are more advanced than the finished paintings and suggest another side of his personality. The execution of the landscape backgrounds behind the religious figures in paintings of the fifteenth century is sometimes amazingly modern and in great contrast to the precise forms of the large figures. Such observations teach us the importance of considering in the description and explanation of a style the unhomogeneous, unstable aspect, the obscure tendencies toward new forms.

If in all periods artists strive to create unified works, the strict ideal of consistency is essentially modern. We often observe in civilized as well as primitive art the combination of works of different style into a single whole. Classical gems were frequently incorporated into medieval reliquaries. Few great medieval buildings are homogeneous, since they are the work of many generations of artists. This is widely recognized by historians, although theoreticians of culture have innocently pointed to the conglomerate cathedral of Chartres as a model of stylistic unity, in contrast to the heterogeneous character or stylelessness of the arts of modern society. In the past it was not felt necessary to restore a damaged work or to complete an unfinished one in the style of the original. Hence the strange juxtapositions of styles within some medieval objects. It should be said, however, that some styles, by virtue of their open, irregular forms, can tolerate the unfinished and heterogeneous better than others.

Just as the single work may possess parts that we would judge to belong to different styles, if we found them in separate contexts, so an individual may produce during the same short period works in what are regarded as two styles. An obvious example is the writing of bilingual authors or the work of the same man in different arts or even in different genres of the same art—monumental and easel painting, dramatic and lyric poetry. A large work by an artist who works mainly in the small, or a small work by a master of large forms, can deceive an expert in styles. Not only will the touch change, but also the expression and method of grouping. An artist is not present in the same degree in everything he does, although some traits may be constant. In the twentieth century, some artists have changed their styles so radically during a few years that it would be difficult, if not impossible, to identify these as works of the same hand, should their authorship be forgotten. In the case of Picasso, two styles—Cubism and a kind of classicizing naturalism—were practiced at the same time. One might discover common characters in small features of the two styles—in qualities of the brushstroke, the span of intensity, or in subtle constancies of the spacing and tones—but these are not the elements through which either style would ordinarily be characterized. Even then, as in a statistical account small and large samples of a population give different results, so in works of different scale of parts by one artist the scale may influence the frequency of the tiniest elements or the form of the small units. The modern experience of stylistic variability and of the unhomogeneous within an art style will per-

haps lead to a more refined conception of style. It is evident, at any rate, that the conception of style as a visibly unified constant rests upon a particular norm of stability of style and shifts from the large to the small forms, as the whole becomes more complex.

What has been said here of the limits of uniformity of structure in the single work and in the works of an individual also applies to the style of a group. The group style, like a language, often contains elements that belong to different historical strata. While research looks for criteria permitting one to distinguish accurately the works of different groups and to correlate a style with other characteristics of a group, there are cultures with two or more collective styles of art at the same moment. This phenomenon is often associated with arts of different function or with different classes of artists. The arts practiced by women are of another style than those of the men; religious art differs from profane, and civic from domestic; and in higher cultures the stratification of social classes often entails a variety of styles, not only with respect to the rural and urban, but within the same urban community. This diversity is clear enough today in the coexistence of an official-academic, a mass-commercial, and a freer avant-garde art. But more striking still is the enormous range of styles within the latter—although a common denominator will undoubtedly be found by future historians.

While some critics judge this heterogeneity to be a sign of an unstable, unintegrated culture, it may be regarded as a necessary and valuable consequence of the individual's freedom of choice and of the world scope of modern culture, which permits a greater interaction of styles than was ever possible before. The present diversity continues and intensifies a diversity already noticed in the preceding stages of our culture, including the Middle Ages and the Renaissance, which are held up as models of close integration. The unity of style that is contrasted with the present diversity is one type of style formation, appropriate to particular aims and conditions; to achieve it today would be impossible without destroying the most cherished values of our culture.

If we pass to the relation of group styles of different visual arts in the same period, we observe that, while the Baroque is remarkably similar in architecture, sculpture, and painting, in other periods, e.g., the Carolingian, the early Romanesque, and the modern, these arts differ in essential respects. In England, the drawing and painting of the tenth and eleventh centuries—a time of great accomplishment, when England was a leader in European art—are characterized by an enthusiastic linear style of energetic, ecstatic movement, while the architecture of the same period is inert, massive and closed, and is organized on other principles. Such variety has been explained as a sign of immaturity; but one can point to similar contrasts between two arts in later times, for example, in Holland in the seventeenth century where Rembrandt and his school were contemporary with classicistic Renaissance buildings.

When we compare the styles of arts of the same period in different media—literature, music, painting—the differences are no less striking. But there are epochs with a far-reaching unity, and these have engaged the attention of students more than the examples of diversity. The concept of the Baroque has been applied to architecture, sculpture, painting, music, poetry, drama, gardening, script, and even philosophy and science. The Baroque style has given its name to the entire culture of the seventeenth century, although it does not exclude contrary tendencies within the same country, as well as a great individuality of national arts. Such styles are the most fascinating to historians and philosophers, who admire in this great spectacle of unity the power of a guiding idea or attitude to impose a common form upon the most varied contexts. The dominant style-giving force is identified by some historians with a world outlook common to the whole society; by others with a particular institution, like the church or the absolute monarchy, which under certain conditions becomes the source of a universal viewpoint and the organizer of all cultural life. This unity is not necessarily organic; it may be likened also, perhaps, to that of a machine with limited freedom of motion; in a complex organism the parts are unlike and the integration is more a matter of functional interdependence than of the repetition of the same pattern in all the organs.

Although so vast a unity of style is an impressive accomplishment and seems to point to a special consciousness of style—the forms of art being felt as a necessary universal language —there are moments of great achievement in a single art with characteristics more or less isolated from those of the other arts. We look in vain in England for a style of painting that corresponds to Elizabethan poetry and drama; just as in Russia in the nineteenth century there was no true parallel in painting to the great movement of literature. In these instances we recognize that the various arts have different roles in the culture and social life of a time and express in their content as well as style different interests and values. The dominant outlook of a time—if it can be isolated—does not affect all the arts in the same degree, nor are all the arts equally capable of expressing the same outlook. Special conditions within an art are often strong enough to determine a deviant expression.

V

The organic conception of style has its counterpart in the search for biological analogies in the growth of forms. One view, patterned on the life-history of the organism, attributes to art a recurrent cycle of childhood, maturity, and old age, which coincides with the rise, maturity, and decline of the culture as a whole. Another view pictures the process as an unfinished evolution from the most primitive to the most advanced forms, in terms of a polarity evident at every step.

In the cyclical process each stage has its characteristic style or series of styles. In an enriched schema, for which the history of Western art is the model, the archaic, classic, baroque, impressionist, and archaistic are types of style that follow in an irreversible course. The classic phase is believed to produce the greatest works; the succeeding ones are a decline. The same series has been observed in the Greek and Roman world and somewhat less clearly in India and the Far East. In other cultures this succession of styles is less evident, although the archaic type is widespread and is sometimes followed by what might be considered a classic phase. It is only by stretching the meaning of the terms that the baroque and impressionist types of style are discovered as tendencies within the simpler developments of primitive arts.

(That the same names, "baroque," "classic," and "impressionist," should be applied both to a unique historical style and to a recurrent type or phase is confusing. We shall distinguish the name of the unique style by a capital, e.g., "Baroque." But this will not do away with the awkwardness of speaking of the late phase of the Baroque style of the seventeenth century as "baroque." A similar difficulty exists also with the word "style," which is used for the common forms of a particular period and the common forms of a phase of development found in many periods.)

The cyclical schema of development does not apply smoothly even to the Western world from which it has been abstracted. The classic phase in the Renaissance is preceded by Gothic, Romanesque, and Carolingian styles, which cannot all be fitted into the same category of the archaic. It is possible, however, to break up the Western development into two cycles—the medieval and the modern—and to interpret the late Gothic of northern Europe, which is contemporary with the Italian Renaissance, as a style of the baroque type. But contemporary with the Baroque of the seventeenth century is a classic style which in the late eighteenth century replaces the Baroque.

It has been observed, too, that the late phase of Greco-Roman art, especially in architecture, is no decadent style marking a period of decline, but something new. The archaistic trend is only secondary beside the original achievement of late imperial and early Christian art. In a similar way, the complex art of the twentieth century, whether regarded as the end of an old culture or the beginning of a new, does not correspond to the categories of either a declining or an archaic art.

Because of these and other discrepancies, the long-term cyclical schema, which also measures the duration of a culture, is little used by historians of art. It is only a very rough approximation to the character of several isolated moments in Western art. Yet certain stages and steps of the cycle seem to be frequent enough to warrant further study as typical processes, apart from the theory of a closed cyclical form of development.

Some historians have therefore narrowed the range of the cycles from the long-term development to the history of one or two period styles. In Romanesque art, which belongs to the first

stage of the longer Western cycle and
shares many features with early Greek
and Chinese arts, several phases have
been noted within a relatively short period that resemble the archaic, the classic, and the baroque of the cyclical
scheme; the same observation has been
made about Gothic art. But in Carolingian art the order is different; the more
baroque and impressionistic phases are
the earlier ones, the classic and archaic
come later. This may be due in part to
the character of the older works that
were copied then; but it shows how
difficult it is to systematize the history
of art through the cyclical model. In
the continuous line of Western art,
many new styles have been created
without breaks or new beginnings oc-
casioned by the exhaustion or death of
a preceding style. In ancient Egypt, on
the other hand, the latency of styles is
hardly confirmed by the slow course
of development; an established style
persists here with only slight changes
in basic structure for several thousand
years, a span of time during which
Greek and Western art run twice
through the whole cycle of stylistic
types.

If the exceptional course of Carolingian art is due to special conditions,
perhaps the supposedly autonomous
process of development also depends
on extra-artistic circumstances. But the
theorists of cyclical development have
not explored the mechanisms and conditions of growth as the biologists have
done. They recognize only a latency
that conditions might accelerate or de-
lay but not produce. To account for
the individuality of the arts of each
cycle, the evident difference between a
Greek, a western European, and a
Chinese style of the same stage, they
generally resort to racial theory, each
cycle being carried by a people with
unique traits.

In contrast to the cyclical organic
pattern of development, a more refined

model has been constructed by Hein-
rich Wölfflin, excluding all value judgment and the vital analogy of birth,
maturity, and decay. In a beautiful
analysis of the art of the High Renaissance and the seventeenth century, he
devised five pairs of polar terms,
through which he defined the opposed
styles of the two periods. These terms
were applied to architecture, sculpture, painting, and the so-called "decorative arts." The linear was contrasted
with the picturesque or painterly (*malerisch*), the parallel surface form with
the diagonal depth form, the closed (or
tectonic) with the open (or a-tectonic),
the composite with the fused, the clear
with the relatively unclear. The first
terms of these pairs characterize the
classic Renaissance stage, the second
belong to the Baroque. Wölfflin believed that the passage from the first
set of qualities to the others was not a
peculiarity of the development in this
one period, but a necessary process
which occurred in most historical
epochs. Adama van Scheltema applied
these categories to the successive stages
of northern European arts from the
prehistoric period to the age of the migrations. Wölfflin's model has been
used in studies of several other periods
as well, and it has served the historians
of literature and music and even of
economic development. He recognized
that the model did not apply uniformly
to German and Italian art; and, to explain the deviations, he investigated
peculiarities of the two national arts,
which he thought were "constants"—
the results of native dispositions that
modified to some degree the innate
normal tendencies of development. The
German constant, more dynamic and
unstable, favored the second set of
qualities, and the Italian, more relaxed
and bounded, favored the first. In this
way, Wölfflin supposed he could explain the precociously *malerisch* and
baroque character of German art in its

classic Renaissance phase and the persistent classicism in the Italian Baroque.

The weaknesses of Wölfflin's system have been apparent to most students of art. Not only is it difficult to fit into his scheme the important style called "Mannerism" which comes between the High Renaissance and the Baroque; but the pre-Classic art of the fifteenth century is for him an immature, unintegrated style because of its inaptness for his terms. Modern art, too, cannot be defined through either set of terms, although some modern styles show features from both sets—there are linear compositions which are open and painterly ones which are closed. It is obvious that the linear and painterly are genuine types of style, of which examples occur, with more or less approximation to Wölfflin's model, in other periods. But the particular unity of each set of terms is not a necessary one (although it is possible to argue that the Classic and Baroque of the Renaissance are "pure" styles in which basic processes of art appear in an ideally complete and legible way). We can imagine and discover in history other combinations of five of these ten terms. Mannerism, which had been ignored as a phenomenon of decadence, is now described as a type of art that appears in other periods. Wölfflin cannot be right, then, in supposing that, given the first type of art—the classic phase—the second will follow. That depends perhaps on special circumstances which have been effective in some epochs, but not in all. Wölfflin, however, regards the development as internally determined; outer conditions can only retard or facilitate the process, they are not among its causes. He denied that his terms have any other than artistic meaning; they describe two typical modes of seeing and are independent of an expressive content; although artists may choose themes more or less in accord with these forms, the latter do not arise as a means of expression. It is remarkable, therefore, that qualities associated with these pure forms should be attributed also to the psychological dispositions of the Italian and German people.

How this process could have been repeated after the seventeenth century in Europe is a mystery, since that required—as in the passage from Neo-Classicism to Romantic painting—a reverse development from the Baroque to the Neo-Classic.

In a later book Wölfflin recanted some of his views, admitting that these pure forms might correspond to a world outlook and that historical circumstances, religion, politics, etc., might influence the development. But he was unable to modify his schemas and interpretations accordingly. In spite of these difficulties, one can only admire Wölfflin for his attempt to rise above the singularities of style to a general construction that simplifies and organizes the field.

To meet the difficulties of Wölfflin's schema, Paul Frankl has conceived a model of development which combines the dual polar structure with a cyclical pattern. He postulates a recurrent movement between two poles of style —a style of Being and a style of Becoming; but within each of these styles are three stages: a preclassic, a classic, and a postclassic; and in the first and third stages he assumes alternative tendencies which correspond to those historical moments, like Mannerism, that would be anomalous in Wölfflin's scheme. What is most original in Frankl's construction—and we cannot begin to indicate its rich nuancing and complex articulation—is that he attempts to deduce this development and its phases (and the many types of style comprehended within his system) from the analysis of elementary forms and the limited number of possible combinations, which he has investigated with great care. His scheme is not designed to describe the actual historical development—a very irregular affair—but to provide a model or ideal plan of the inherent or normal tendencies of development, based on the nature of forms. Numerous factors, social and psychological, constrain or divert the innate tendencies and determine other courses; but the latter are unintelligible, according to Frankl, without reference to his model and his deduction of the formal possibilities.

Frankl's book—a work of over a thousand pages—appeared unfortunately at a moment (1938) when it could not receive the attention it deserved; and since that time it has been practically ignored in the literature, although it is surely the most serious attempt in recent years to create a systematic foundation for the study of art forms. No other writer has analyzed the types of style so thoroughly.

In spite of their insights and ingenuity in constructing models of development, the theoreticians have had relatively little influence on investigation of special problems, perhaps because they have provided no adequate bridge from the model to the unique historical style and its varied developments. The principles by which are explained the broad similarities in development are of a different order from those by which the singular facts are explained. The normal motion and the motion due to supposedly perturbing factors belong to different worlds; the first is inherent in the morphology of styles, the second has a psychological or social origin. It is as if mechanics had two different sets of laws, one for irregular and the other for regular motions; or one for the first and another for the second approximation, in dealing with the same phenomenon. Hence those who are most concerned with a unified approach to the study of art have split

the history of style into two aspects which cannot be derived from each other or from some common principle.

Parallel to the theorists of cyclical development, other scholars have approached the development of styles as a continuous, long-term evolutionary process. Here, too, there are poles and stages and some hints of a universal, though not cyclical, process; but the poles are those of the earliest and latest stages and are deduced from a definition of the artist's goal or the nature of art or from a psychological theory.

The first students to investigate the history of primitive art conceived the latter as a development between two poles, the geometrical and the naturalistic. They were supported by observation of the broad growth of art in the historical cultures from geometric or simple, stylized forms to more natural ones; they were sustained also by the idea that the most naturalistic styles of all belonged to the highest type of culture, the most advanced in scientific knowledge, and the most capable of representing the world in accurate images. The process in art agreed with the analogous development in nature from the simple to the complex and was paralleled by the growth of the child's drawings in our own culture from schematic or geometrical forms to naturalistic ones. The origin of certain geometrical forms in primitive industrial techniques also favored this view.

It is challenging and amusing to consider in the light of these arguments the fact that the Paleolithic cave paintings, the oldest known art, are marvels of representation (whatever the elements of schematic form in those works, they are more naturalistic than the succeeding Neolithic and Bronze Age art) and that in the twentieth century naturalistic forms have given way to "abstraction" and so-called "subjective" styles. But, apart from these paradoxical exceptions, one could observe in historical arts—e.g., in the late classic and early Christian periods—how free naturalistic forms are progressively stylized and reduced to ornament. In the late nineteenth century, ornament was often designed by a method of stylization, a geometrizing of natural motives; and those who knew contemporary art were not slow to discern in the geometrical styles of existing primitives the traces of an older more naturalistic model. Study shows that both processes occur in history; there is little reason to regard either one as more typical or more primitive. The geometrical and the naturalistic forms may arise independently in different contexts and coexist within the same culture. The experience of the art of the last fifty years suggests further that the degree of naturalism in art is not a sure indication of the technological or intellectual level of a culture. This does not mean that style is independent of that level but that other concepts than those of the naturalistic and the geometrical must be applied in considering such relationships. The essential opposition is not of the natural and the geometric but of certain modes of composition of natural and geometric motives. From this point of view, modern "abstract" art in its taste for open, asymmetrical, random, tangled, and incomplete forms is much closer to the compositional principles of realistic or Impressionist painting and sculpture than to any primitive art with geometrical elements. Although the character of the themes, whether "abstract" or naturalistic, is important for the concrete aspect of the work of art, historians do not operate so much with categories of the naturalistic and geometrical as with subtler structural concepts, which apply also to architecture, where the problem of representation seems irrelevant. It is with such concepts that Wölfflin and Frankl have constructed their models. Nevertheless, the representation of

natural forms has been a goal in the arts of many cultures. Whether we regard it as a spontaneous common idea or one that has been diffused from a single prehistoric center, the problem of how to represent the human and animal figure has been attacked independently by various cultures. Their solutions present not only similar features in the devices of rendering but also a remarkable parallelism in the successive stages of the solutions. It is fascinating to compare the changing representation of the eyes or of pleated costume in succeeding styles of Greek, Chinese, and medieval European sculpture. The development of such details from a highly schematic to a naturalistic type in the latter two can hardly be referred to a direct influence of Greek models; for the similarities are not only of geographically far separated styles but of distinct series in time. To account for the Chinese and Romanesque forms as copies of the older Greek, we would have to assume that at each stage in the post-Greek styles the artists had recourse to Greek works of the corresponding stage and in the same order. Indeed, some of the cyclical schemas discussed above are, in essence, descriptions of the stages in the development of representation; and it may be asked whether the formal schemas, like Wölfflin's, are not veiled categories of representation, even though they are applied to architecture as well as to sculpture and painting; for the standards of representation in the latter may conceivably determine a general norm of plasticity and structure for all the visual arts.

This aspect of style—the representation of natural forms—has been studied by the classical archeologist, Emanuel Löwy; his little book on *The Rendering of Nature in Early Greek Art*, published in 1900, is still suggestive for modern research and has a wider application than has been recognized.

Löwy has analyzed the general principles of representation in early arts and explained their stages as progressive steps in a steady change from conceptual representation, based on the memory image, to perspective representation, according to direct perception of objects. Since the structure of the memory image is the same in all cultures, the representations based on this psychological process will exhibit common features: (1) The shape and movement of figures and their parts are limited to a few typical forms; (2) the single forms are schematized in regular linear patterns; (3) representation proceeds from the outline, whether the latter is an independent contour or the silhouette of a uniformly colored area; (4) where colors are used, they are without gradation of light and shadow; (5) the parts of a figure are presented to the observer in their broadest aspect; (6) in compositions the figures, with few exceptions, are shown with a minimum of overlapping of their main parts; the real succession of figures in depth is transformed in the image into a juxtaposition on the same plane; (7) the representation of the three-dimensional space in which an action takes place is more or less absent.

Whatever criticisms may be made of Löwy's notion of a memory image as the source of these peculiarities, his account of archaic representation as a universal type, with a characteristic structure, is exceedingly valuable; it has a general application to children's drawings, to the work of modern untrained adults, and to primitives. This analysis does not touch on the individuality of archaic styles, nor does it help us to understand why some cultures develop beyond them and others, like the Egyptian, retain the archaic features for many centuries. Limited by an evolutionary view and a naturalistic value norm, Löwy ignored the perfection and expressiveness of archaic

works. Neglecting the specific content of the representations, this approach fails to recognize the role of the content and of emotional factors in the proportioning and accentuation of parts. But these limitations do not lessen the importance of Löwy's book in defining so clearly a widespread type of archaic representation and in tracing the stages of its development into a more naturalistic art.

I may point out here that the reverse process of the conversion of naturalistic to archaic forms, as we see it wherever works of an advanced naturalistic style are copied by primitives, colonials, provincials, and the untrained in the high cultures, can also be formulated through Löwy's principles.

I should point out, finally, as the most constructive and imaginative of the historians who have tried to embrace the whole of artistic development as a single continuous process, Alois Riegl, the author of *Stilfragen* and *Die spätrömische Kunstindustrie*.

Riegl was especially concerned with transitions that mark the beginning of a world-historical epoch (the Old Oriental to the Hellenic, the ancient to the medieval). He gave up not only the normative view that judges the later phases of a cycle as a decline but also the conception of closed cycles. In late Roman art, which was considered decadent in his time, he found a necessary creative link between two great stages of an open development. His account of the process is like Wölfflin's, however, though perhaps independent; he formulates as the poles of the long evolution two types of style, the "haptic" (tactile) and the "optic" (or painterly, impressionistic), which coincide broadly with the poles of Wölfflin's shorter cycles. The process of development from the haptic to the optic is observable in each epoch, but only as part of a longer process, of which the great stages are millennial and correspond to whole cultures. The history of art is, for Riegl, an endless necessary movement from representation based on vision of the object and its parts as proximate, tangible, discrete, and self-sufficient, to the representation of the whole perceptual field as a directly given, but more distant, continuum with merging parts, with an increasing role of the spatial voids, and with a more evident reference to the knowing subject as a constituting factor in perception. This artistic process is also described by Riegl in terms of a faculty psychology; will, feeling, and thought are the successive dominants in shaping our relations to the world; it corresponds in philosophy to the change from a predominantly objective to a subjective outlook.

Riegl does not study this process simply as a development of naturalism from an archaic to an impressionistic stage. Each phase has its special formal and expressive problems, and Riegl has written remarkably penetrating pages on the intimate structure of styles, the principles of composition, and the relations of figure to ground. In his systematic account of ancient art and the art of the early Christian period, he has observed common principles in architecture, sculpture, painting, and ornament, sometimes with surprising acuteness. He has also succeeded in showing unexpected relationships between different aspects of a style. In a work on Dutch group portraiture of the sixteenth and seventeenth centuries, a theme that belongs to art and social history, he has carried through a most delicate analysis of the changing relations between the objective and the subjective elements in portraiture and in the correspondingly variable mode of unifying a represented group which is progressively more attentive to the observer.

His motivation of the process and his explanation of its shifts in time and space are vague and often fantastic. Each great phase corresponds to a racial disposition. The history of Western man from the time of the Old Oriental kingdoms to the present day is divided into three great periods, characterized by the successive predominance of will, feeling, and thought, in Oriental, Classical, and Western Man. Each race plays a prescribed role and retires when its part is done, as if participating in a symphony of world history. The apparent deviations from the expected continuities are saved for the system by a theory of purposive regression which prepares a people for its advanced role. The obvious incidence of social and religious factors in art is judged to be simply a parallel manifestation of a corresponding process in these other fields rather than a possible cause. The basic, immanent development from an objective to a subjective standpoint governs the whole of history, so that all contemporary fields have a deep unity with respect to a common determining process.

This brief summary of Riegl's ideas hardly does justice to the positive features of his work, and especially to his conception of art as an active creative process in which new forms arise from the artist's will to solve specifically artistic problems. Even his racial theories and strange views about the historical situation of an art represent a desire to grasp large relationships, although distorted by an inadequate psychology and social theory; this search for a broad view has become rare in the study of art since his time. And still rarer is its combination with the power of detailed research that Riegl possessed to a high degree.

To summarize the results of modern studies with respect to the cyclical and evolutionary theories:

1. From the viewpoint of historians who have tried to reconstruct the precise order of development, without pre-

suppositions about cycles, there is a continuity in the Near East and Europe from the Neolithic period to the present—perhaps best described as a tree with many branches—in which the most advanced forms of each culture are retained, to some extent, in the early forms of succeeding cultures.

2. On the other hand, there are within that continuity at least two long developments—the ancient Greek and the Western European medieval-modern—which include the broad types of style described in various cyclical theories. But these two cycles are not unconnected; artists in the second cycle often copied surviving works of the first, and it is uncertain whether some of the guiding principles in Western art are not derived from the Greeks.

3. Within these two cycles and in several other cultures (Asiatic and American) occur many examples of similar short developments, especially from an archaic linear type of representation to a more "pictorial" style.

4. Wherever there is a progressive naturalistic art, i.e., one which becomes increasingly naturalistic, we find in the process stages corresponding broadly to the line of archaic, classic, baroque, and impressionist in Western art. Although these styles in the West are not adequately described in terms of their method of representation, they embody specific advances in range or method of representation from a first stage of schematized, so-called "conceptual," representation of isolated objects to a later stage of perspective representation in which continuities of space, movement, light and shadow, and atmosphere have become important.

5. In describing the Western development, which is the model of cyclical theories, historians isolate different aspects of art for the definition of the stylistic types. In several theories the development of representation is the main source of the terms; in others

formal traits, which can be found also in architecture, script, and pottery shapes, are isolated; and, in some accounts, qualities of expression and content are the criteria. It is not always clear which formal traits are really independent of representation. It is possible that a way of seeing objects in nature—the perspective vision as distinguished from the archaic conceptual mode—also affects the design of a column or a pot. But the example of Islamic art, in which representation is secondary, suggests that the development of the period styles in architecture and ornament need not depend on a style of representation. As for expression, there exist in the Baroque art of the seventeenth century intimate works of great tragic sensibility, like Rembrandt's, and monumental works of a profuse splendor; either of these traits can be paralleled in other periods in forms of nonbaroque type. But a true counterpart of Rembrandt's light and shadow will not be found in Greek or Chinese painting, although both are said to have baroque phases.

VI

We shall now consider the explanations of style proposed without reference to cycles and polar developments.

In accounting for the genesis of a style, early investigators gave great weight to the technique, materials, and practical functions of an art. Thus wood-carving favors grooved or wedge-cut relief, the column of the tree trunk gives the statue its cylindrical shape, hard stone yields compact and angular forms, weaving begets stepped and symmetrical patterns, the potter's wheel introduces a perfect roundness, coiling is the source of spirals, etc. This was the approach of Semper and his followers in the last century. Boas, among others, identified style, or at least its formal aspect, with motor habits in the handling of tools. In modern art this viewpoint appears in the program of functionalist architecture and design. It is also behind the older explanation of the Gothic style of architecture as a rational system derived from the rib construction of vaults. Modern sculptors who adhere closely to the block, exploiting the texture and grain of the material and showing the marks of the tool, are supporters of this theory of style. It is related to the immense role of the technological in our own society; modern standards of efficient production have become a norm in art.

There is no doubt that these practical conditions account for some peculiarities of style. They are important also in explaining similarities in primitive and folk arts which appear to be independent of diffusion or imitation of styles. But they are of less interest for highly developed arts. Wood may limit the sculptor's forms, but we know a great variety of styles in wood, some of which even conceal the substance. Riegl observed long ago that the same forms occurred within a culture in works of varied technique, materials, and use; it is this common style that the theory in question has failed to explain. The Gothic style is, broadly speaking, the same in buildings; sculptures of wood, ivory, and stone; panel paintings; stained glass; miniatures; metalwork, enamels, and textiles. It may be that in some instances a style created in one art under the influence of the technique, material, and function of particular objects has been generalized by application to all objects, techniques, and materials. Yet the material is not always prior to the style but may be chosen because of an ideal of expression and artistic quality or for symbolism. The hard substances of old Egyptian art, the use of gold and other precious luminous substances in arts of power, the taste for steel, concrete, and glass in modern design, are not external to the artist's first goal but parts of the original conception. The compactness of the sculpture cut from a tree trunk is a quality that is already present in the artist's idea before he begins to carve. For simple compact forms appear in clay figures and in drawings and paintings where the matter does not limit the design. The compactness may be regarded as a necessary trait of an archaic or a "haptic" style in Löwy's or Riegl's sense.

Turning away from material factors, some historians find in the content of the work of art the source of its style. In the arts of representation, a style is often associated with a distinct body of subject matter, drawn from a single sphere of ideas or experience. Thus in Western art of the fourteenth century, when a new iconography of the life of Christ and of Mary was created in which themes of suffering were favored, we observe new patterns of line and color, which possess a more lyrical, pathetic aspect than did the preceding art. In our own time, a taste for the constructive and rational in industry has led to the use of mechanical motives and a style of forms characterized by coolness, precision, objectivity, and power.

The style in these examples is viewed by many writers as the objective vehicle of the subject matter or of its governing idea. Style, then, is the means of communication, a language not only as a system of devices for conveying a precise message by representing or symbolizing objects and actions but also as a qualitative whole which is capable of suggesting the diffuse connotations as well and intensifying the associated or intrinsic affects. By an effort of imagination based on experience of his medium, the artist discovers the elements and formal relationships which will express the values of the content and look right artistically. Of all the attempts made in this direction, the most successful will be repeated and developed as a norm.

The relationship of content and style is more complex than appears in this theory. There are styles in which the correspondence of the expression and the values of the typical subjects is not at all obvious. If the difference between pagan and Christian art is explained broadly by the difference in religious content, there is nevertheless a long period of time—in fact, many centuries —during which Christian subjects are represented in the style of pagan art. As late as 800, the Libri Carolini speak of the difficulty of distinguishing images of Mary and Venus without the labels. This may be due to the fact that a general outlook of late paganism, more fundamental than the religious doctrines, was still shared by Christians or that the new religion, while important, had not yet transformed the basic attitudes and ways of thinking. Or it may be that the function of art within the religious life was too slight, for not all concepts of the religion find their way into art. But even later, when the Christian style had been established, there were developments in art toward a more naturalistic form and toward imitation of elements of ancient pagan style which were incompatible with the chief ideas of the religion.

A style that arises in connection with a particular content often becomes an accepted mode governing all representations of the period. The Gothic style is applied in religious and secular works alike; and, if it is true that no domestic or civil building in that style has the expressiveness of a cathedral interior, yet in painting and sculpture the religious and secular images are hardly different in form. On the other hand, in periods of a style less pervasive than the Gothic, different idioms or dialects of form are used for different fields of content; this was observed in the discussion of the concept of stylistic unity.

It is such observations that have led students to modify the simple equation of style and the expressive values of a subject matter, according to which the style is the vehicle of the main meanings of the work of art. Instead, the meaning of content has been extended, and attention has been fixed on broader attitudes or on general ways of thinking and feeling, which are believed to shape a style. The style is then viewed as a concrete embodiment or projection of emotional dispositions and habits of thought common to the whole culture. The content as a parallel product of the same viewpoint will therefore often exhibit qualities and structures like those of the style.

These world views or ways of thinking and feeling are usually abstracted by the historian from the philosophical systems and metaphysics of a period or from theology and literature and even from science. Themes like the relation of subject and object, spirit and matter, soul and body, man and nature or God, and conceptions of time and space, self and cosmos are typical fields from which are derived the definitions of the world view (or *Denkweise*) of a period or culture. The latter is then documented by illustrations from many fields, but some writers have attempted to derive it from the works of art themselves. One searches in a style for qualities and structures that can be matched with some aspect of thinking or a world view. Sometimes it is based on a priori deduction of possible world views, given the limited number of solutions of metaphysical problems; or a typology of the possible attitudes of the individual to the world and to his own existence is matched with a typology of styles. We have seen how Riegl apportioned the three faculties of will, feeling, and thought among three races and three major styles.

The attempts to derive style from thought are often too vague to yield more than suggestive *aperçus;* the method breeds analogical speculations which do not hold up under detailed critical study. The history of the analogy drawn between the Gothic cathedral and scholastic theology is an example. The common element in these two contemporary creations has been found in their rationalism and in their irrationality, their idealism and their naturalism, their encyclopedic completeness and their striving for infinity, and recently in their dialectical method. Yet one hesitates to reject such analogies in principle, since the cathedral belongs to the same religious sphere as does contemporary theology.

It is when these ways of thinking and feeling or world views have been formulated as the outlook of a religion or dominant institution or class of which the myths and values are illustrated or symbolized in the work of art that the general intellectual content seems a more promising field for explanation of style. But the content of a work of art often belongs to another region of experience than the one in which both the period style and the dominant mode of thinking have been formed; an example is the secular art of a period in which religious ideas and rituals are primary, and, conversely, the religious art of a secularized culture. In such cases we see how important for a style of art is the character of the dominants in culture, especially of institutions. Not the content as such, but the content as part of a dominant set of beliefs, ideas, and interests, supported by institutions and the forms of everyday life, shapes the common style.

Although the attempts to explain styles as an artistic expression of a world view or mode of thought are often a drastic reduction of the concreteness and richness of art, they have been helpful in revealing unsuspected levels of meaning in art. They have established the practice of interpreting

the style itself as an inner content of the art, especially in the nonrepresentational arts. They correspond to the conviction of modern artists that the form elements and structure are a deeply meaningful whole related to metaphysical views.

VII

The theory that the world view or mode of thinking and feeling is the source of long-term constants in style is often formulated as a theory of racial or national character. I have already referred to such concepts in the work of Wölfflin and Riegl. They have been common in European writing on art for over a hundred years and have played a significant role in promoting national consciousness and race feeling; works of art are the chief concrete evidences of the affective world of the ancestors. The persistent teaching that German art is by nature tense and irrational, that its greatness depends on fidelity to the racial character, has helped to produce an acceptance of these traits as a destiny of the people.

The weakness of the racial concept of style is evident from analysis of the history and geography of styles, without reference to biology. The so-called "constant" is less constant than the racially (or nationally) minded historians have assumed. German art includes Classicism and the Biedermeier style, as well as the work of Gruenewald and the modern Expressionists. During the periods of most pronounced Germanic character, the extension of the native style hardly coincides with the boundaries of the preponderant physical type or with the recent national boundaries. This discrepancy holds for the Italian art which is paired with the German as a polar opposite.

Nevertheless, there are striking recurrences in the art of a region or nation which have not been explained. It is astonishing to observe the resemblances between German migrations art and the styles of the Carolingian, Ottonian, and late Gothic periods, then of German rococo architecture, and finally of modern Expressionism. There are great gaps in time between these styles during which the forms can scarcely be described in the traditional German terms. To save the appearance of constancy, German writers have supposed that the intervening phases were dominated by alien influences or were periods of preparation for the ultimate release, or they conceived the deviant qualities as another aspect of German character: the Germans are both irrational and disciplined.

If we restrict ourselves to more modest historical correlations of styles with the dominant personality types of the cultures or groups that have created the styles, we meet several difficulties; some of these have been anticipated in the discussion of the general problem of unity of style.

1. The variation of styles in a culture or group is often considerable within the same period.

2. Until recently, the artists who create the style are generally of another mode of life than those for whom the arts are designed and whose viewpoint, interests, and quality of life are evident in the art. The best examples are the arts of great monarchies, aristocracies, and privileged institutions.

3. What is constant in all the arts of a period (or of several periods) may be less essential for characterizing the style than the variable features; the persistent French quality in the series of styles between 1770 and 1870 is a nuance which is hardly as important for the definition of the period style as the traits that constitute the Rococo, Neo-Classic, Romantic, Realistic, and Impressionist styles.

To explain the changing period styles, historians and critics have felt the need of a theory that relates particular forms to tendencies of character and feeling. Such a theory, concerned with the elements of expression and structure, should tell us what affects and dispositions determine choices of forms. Historians have not waited for experimental psychology to support their physiognomic interpretations of style but, like the thoughtful artists, have resorted to intuitive judgments, relying on direct experience of art. Building up an unsystematic, empirical knowledge of forms, expressions, affects, and qualities, they have tried to control these judgments by constant comparison of works and by reference to contemporary sources of information about the content of the art, assuming that the attitudes which govern the latter must also be projected in the style. The interpretation of Classical style is not founded simply on firsthand experience of Greek buildings and sculptures; it rests also on knowledge of Greek language, literature, religion, mythology, philosophy, and history, which provide an independent picture of the Greek world. But this picture is, in turn, refined and enriched by experience of the visual arts, and our insight is sharpened by knowledge of the very different arts of the neighboring peoples and of the results of attempts to copy the Greek models at later times under other conditions. Today, after the work of nearly two centuries of scholars, a sensitive mind, with relatively little information about Greek culture, can respond directly to the "Greek mind" in those ancient buildings and sculptures.

In physiognomic interpretations of group styles, there is a common assumption that is still problematic: that the psychological explanations of unique features in a modern individual's art can be applied to a whole culture in which the same or similar features are characteristics of a group or period style.

If schizophrenics fill a sheet of paper

with closely crowded elements in repeat patterns, can we explain similar tendencies in the art of a historic or primitive culture by a schizophrenic tendency or dominant schizoid personality type in that culture? We are inclined to doubt such interpretations for two reasons. First, we are not sure that this pattern is uniquely schizoid in modern individuals; it may represent a component of the psychotic personality which also exists in other temperaments as a tendency associated with particular emotional contents or problems. Secondly, this pattern, originating in a single artist of schizoid type, may crystallize as a common convention, accepted by other artists and the public because it satisfies a need and is most adequate to a special problem of decoration or representation, without entailing, however, a notable change in the broad habits and attitudes of the group. This convention may be adopted by artists of varied personality types, who will apply it in distinct ways, filling it with an individual content and expression.

A good instance of this relationship between the psychotic, the normal individual, and the group is the practice of reading object forms in relatively formless spots—as in hallucination and in psychological tests. Leonardo da Vinci proposed this method to artists as a means of invention. It was practiced in China, and later in Western art; today it has become a standard method for artists of different character. In the painter who first introduced the practice and exploited it most fully, it may correspond to a personal disposition; but for many others it is an established technique. What is personally significant is not the practice itself but the kinds of spots chosen and what is seen in them; attention to the latter discloses a great variety of individual reactions.

If art is regarded as a projective technique—and some artists today think of their work in these terms—will interpretation of the work give the same result as a projective test? The tests are so designed as to reduce the number of elements that depend on education, profession, and environment. But the work of art is very much conditioned by these factors. Hence, in discerning the personal expression in a work of art, one must distinguish between those aspects that are conventional and those that are clearly individual. In dealing with the style of a group, however, we consider only such superindividual aspects, abstracting them from the personal variants. How, then, can one apply to the interpretation of the style concepts from individual psychology?

It may be said, of course, that the established norms of a group style are genuine parts of an artist's outlook and response and can be approached as the elements of a modal personality. In the same way the habits and attitudes of scientists that are required by their profession may be an important part of their characters. But do such traits also constitute the typical ones of the culture or the society as a whole? Is an art style that has crystallized as a result of special problems necessarily an expression of the whole group? Or is it only in the special case where the art is open to the common outlook and everyday interests of the entire group that its content and style can be representative of the group?

A common tendency in the physiognomic approach to group style has been to interpret all the elements of representation as expressions. The blank background or negative features like the absence of a horizon and of consistent perspective in paintings are judged to be symptomatic of an attitude to space and time in actual life. The limited space in Greek art is interpreted as a fundamental trait of Greek personality. Yet this blankness of the background, we have seen, is common to many styles; it is found in prehistoric art, in Old Oriental art, in the Far East, in the Middle Ages, and in most primitive painting and relief. The fact that it occurs in modern children's drawings and in the drawings of untrained adults suggests that it belongs to a universal primitive level of representation. But it should be observed that this is also the method of illustration in the most advanced scientific work in the past and today.

This fact does not mean that representation is wholly without expressive personal features. A particular treatment of the "empty" background may become a powerful expressive factor. Careful study of so systematic a method of representation as geometrical perspective shows that within such a scientific system there are many possible choices; the position of the eye-level, the intensity of convergence, the distance of the viewer from the picture plane—all these are expressive choices within the conditions of the system. Moreover, the existence of the system itself presupposes a degree of interest in the environment which is already a cultural trait with a long history.

The fact that an art represents a restricted world does not allow us to infer, however, a corresponding restriction of interests and perceptions in everyday life. We would have to suppose, if this were true, that in Islam people were unconcerned with the human body, and that the present vogue of "abstract" art means a general indifference to the living.

An interesting evidence of the limitations of the assumed identities of the space or time structure of works of art and the space or time experience of individuals is the way in which painters of the thirteenth century represented the new cathedrals. These vast buildings with high vaults and endless vistas in depth are shown as shallow structures, not much larger than the human

beings they inclose. The conventions of representation provided no means of re-creating the experience of architectural space, an experience that was surely a factor in the conception of the cathedral and was reported in contemporary descriptions. (It is possible to relate the architectural and pictorial spaces; but the attempt would take us beyond the problems of this paper.) The space of the cathedrals is intensely expressive, but it is a constructed, ideal space, appealing to the imagination, and not an attempt to transpose the space of everyday life. We shall understand it better as a creation adequate to a religious conception than as one in which an everyday sentiment of space has been embodied in architecture. It is an ideological space, too, and, if it conveys the feelings of the most inspired religious personalities, it is not a model of an average, collective attitude to space in general, although the cathedral is used by everyone.

The concept of personality in art is most important for the theory that the great artist is the immediate source of the period style. This little-explored view, implicit in much historical research and criticism, regards the group style as an imitation of the style of an original artist. Study of a line of development often leads to the observation that some individual is responsible for the change in the period form. The personality of the great artist and the problems inherited from the preceding generation are the two factors studied. For the personality as a whole is sometimes substituted a weakness or a traumatic experience which activates the individual's will to create. Such a view is little adapted to the understanding of those cultures or historical epochs that have left us no signed works or biographies of artists; but it is the favored view of many students of the art of the last four centuries in Europe. It may be questioned whether it is applicable to cultures in which the individual has less mobility and range of personal action and in which the artist is not a deviant type. The main difficulty, however, arises from the fact that similar stylistic trends often appear independently in different arts at the same time; that great contemporary artists in the same field—Leonardo, Michelangelo, Raphael—show a parallel tendency of style, although each artist has a personal form; and that the new outlook expressed by a single man of genius is anticipated or prepared in preceding works and thought. The great artists of the Gothic period and the Renaissance constitute families with a common heritage and trend. Decisive changes are most often associated with original works of outstanding quality; but the new direction of style and its acceptance are unintelligible without reference to the conditions of the moment and the common ground of the art.

These difficulties and complexities have not led scholars to abandon the psychological approach; long experience with art has established as a plausible principle the notion that an individual style is a personal expression; and continued research has found many confirmations of this, wherever it has been possible to control statements about the personality, built upon the work, by referring to actual information about the artist. Similarly, common traits in the art of a culture or nation can be matched with some features of social life, ideas, customs, general dispositions. But such correlations have been of single elements or aspects of a style with single traits of a people; it is rarely a question of wholes. In our own culture, styles have changed very rapidly, yet the current notions about group traits do not allow sufficiently for corresponding changes in the behavior patterns or provide such a formulation of the group personality that

one can deduce from it how that personality will change under new conditions.

It seems that for explanation of the styles of the higher cultures, with their great variability and intense development, the concepts of group personality current today are too rigid. They underestimate the specialized functions of art which determine characteristics that are superpersonal. But we may ask whether some of the difficulties in applying characterological concepts to national or period styles are not also present in the interpretation of primitive arts. Would a psychological treatment of Sioux art, for example, give us the same picture of Sioux personality as that provided by analysis of Sioux family life, ceremony, and hunting?

VIII

We turn last to explanations of style by the forms of social life. The idea of a connection between these forms and styles is already suggested by the framework of the history of art. Its main divisions, accepted by all students, are also the boundaries of social units—cultures, empires, dynasties, cities, classes, churches, etc.—and periods which mark significant stages in social development. The great historical epochs of art, like antiquity, the Middle Ages, and the modern era, are the same as the epochs of economic history; they correspond to great systems, like feudalism and capitalism. Important economic and political shifts within these systems are often accompanied or followed by shifts in the centers of art and their styles. Religion and major world views are broadly coordinated with these eras in social history.

In many problems the importance of economic, political, and ideological conditions for the creation of a group style (or of a world view that influences a style) is generally admitted.

The distinctiveness of Greek art among the arts of the ancient world can hardly be separated from the forms of Greek society and the city-state. The importance of the burgher class, with its special position in society and its mode of life, for the medieval and early Renaissance art of Florence and for Dutch art of the seventeenth century, is a commonplace. In explaining Baroque art, the Counter-Reformation and the absolute monarchy are constantly cited as the sources of certain features of style. We have interesting studies on a multitude of problems concerning the relationship of particular styles and contents of art to institutions and historical situations. In these studies ideas, traits, and values arising from the conditions of economic, political, and civil life are matched with the new characteristics of an art. Yet, with all this experience, the general principles applied in explanation and the connection of types of art with types of social structure have not been investigated in a systematic way. By the many scholars who adduce piecemeal political or economic facts in order to account for single traits of style or subject matter, little has been done to construct an adequate comprehensive theory. In using such data, scholars will often deny that these "external" relationships can throw any light on the artistic phenomenon as such. They fear "materialism" as a reduction of the spiritual or ideal to sordid practical affairs.

Marxist writers are among the few who have tried to apply a general theory. It is based on Marx's undeveloped view that the higher forms of cultural life correspond to the economic structure of a society, the latter being defined in terms of the relations of classes in the process of production and the technological level. Between the economic relationships and the styles of art intervenes the process of ideological construction, a complex imaginative transposition of class roles and needs, which affects the special field—religion, mythology, or civil life—that provides the chief themes of art.

The great interest of the Marxist approach lies not only in the attempt to interpret the historically changing relations of art and economic life in the light of a general theory of society but also in the weight given to the differences and conflicts within the social group as motors of development, and to the effects of these on outlook, religion, morality, and philosophical ideas.

Only broadly sketched in Marx's works, the theory has rarely been applied systematically in a true spirit of investigation, such as we see in Marx's economic writings. Marxist writing on art has suffered from schematic and premature formulations and from crude judgments imposed by loyalty to a political line.

A theory of style adequate to the psychological and historical problems has still to be created. It waits for a deeper knowledge of the principles of form construction and expression and for a unified theory of the processes of social life in which the practical means of life as well as emotional behavior are comprised.

BIBLIOGRAPHY

Adama van Scheltema, F. 1923. *Die altnordische Kunst*. Berlin: Mauritius-Verlag.

Boas, F. 1927. *Primitive Art*. Cambridge: Harvard University Press.

Coellen, L. 1921. *Der Stil in der bildenden Kunst*. Darmstadt: Arkadenverlag.

Dilthey, W. 1922. *Einleitung in die Geisteswissenschaften* (1883). In: *Gesammelte Schriften*, Vol. I. Leipzig: B. G. Teubner.

Dvořák, M. 1924. *Kunstgeschichte als Geistesgeschichte*. Munich: R. Piper & Co.

FOCILLON, H. 1934. *La Vie des formes.* Paris: Librairie E. Leroux. English translation: *The Life of Forms in Art.* New York: Wittenborn, Schultz, 1948.

FRANKL, P. 1938. *Das System der Kunstwissenschaft.* Brünn and Leipzig: R. M. Rohrer.

FREY, D. 1929. *Gotik und Renaissance als Grundlagen der modernen Weltanschauung.* Augsburg: B. Filser Verlag.

FRY, R. 1920. *Vision and Design.* London: Chatto & Windus.

HAUSER, A. 1951. *The Social History of Art.* New York: A. A. Knopf.

LÖWY, E. 1900. *Die Naturwiedergabe in der älteren griechischen Kunst.* English translation: *The Rendering of Nature in Early Greek Art.* London: Duckworth & Co., 1907.

NOHL, H. 1920. *Stil und Weltanschauung.* Jena: Diederichs.

RIEGL, A. 1893. *Stilfragen: Grundlegungen zu einer Geschichte der Ornamentik.* Berlin: G. Siemens Verlag.

———. 1901. *Die spätrömische Kunstindustrie.* Vienna: Osterreichische Staatsdruckerei. 2d ed., 1927.

SCHAEFER, H. 1922. *Von ägyptischer Kunst.* Leipzig: J. C. Hinrichs.

SEMPER, G. 1860. *Der Stil in den technischen und tektonischen Künsten.* Munich: F. Bruckmann.

SPENGLER, O. 1919. *Der Untergang des Abendlandes.* English translation: *The Decline of the West.* New York: A. A. Knopf, 1926–28. Also a French translation.

WEISBACH, W. 1921. *Der Barock als Kunst der Gegenreformation.* Berlin: P. Cassirer.

WÖLFFLIN, H. 1915. *Kunstgeschichtliche Grundbegriffe.* Munich: F. Bruckmann. Also an English translation.

———. 1931. *Italien und das deutsche Formgefühl.* Munich: F. Bruckmann.

———. 1940. *Gedanken zur Kunstgeschichte.* Basel: B. Schwabe & Co.

WORRINGER, W. 1908. *Abstraktion und Einfühlung: Ein Beitrag zur Stilpsychologie.* Munich: R. Piper & Co.

———. 1912. *Formprobleme der Gotik.* Munich: R. Piper & Co. English translation: *Form Problems of the Gothic.* New York: G. E. Stechert & Co., 1920. Also a French translation.

Universal Categories of Culture[1]

By CLYDE KLUCKHOHN

THERE ARE two interrelated problems: Are there fairly definite limits within which cultural variation is constrained by panhuman regularities in biology, psychology, and the processes of social interaction? Do these limits and also the accompanying trends toward similarities in form and content make for categories of culture which are universal in the sense of being both invariant points of reference for description and comparison and, perhaps, substantive uniformities or near-uniformities? This paper will move back and forth between these two slightly different, but closely connected, frames of reference. First, various aspects of the two problems and their implications must be stated in slightly more expanded form.

There is a certain paradox in recent and contemporary anthropological thinking. Radcliffe-Brown and other British anthropologists have characterized social anthropology as "comparative sociology." American anthropologists of late have stressed the cross-cultural approach, and some of us have justified our sometimes rather imperialistic claims to being the *scientia scientiarum* of human studies on the grounds that only anthropologists transcend the limitations of the categories of their own cultures. Yet genuine comparison is possible only if nonculture-bound units have been isolated.[2]

In fact, linguistics alone of the branches of anthropology has discovered elemental units (phonemes, morphemes, and the like) which are universal, objective, and theoretically meaningful. Even physical anthropology, which deals with the biological givens in a single order, is just beginning to grope its way beyond common-sense concepts such as "nose," "young," "middle-aged," and "old." The whole history of science shows that advance depends upon going beyond "common sense" to abstractions that reveal unobvious relations and common properties of isolable aspects of phenomena. Anthropologists, above all, should realize this because "sense" becomes "common" only in terms of cultural convention, particularly in terms of the conventions of implicit culture.

Cultural anthropology has followed two paths, neither of which makes possible a true and complete comparison. A few anthropologists have organized their descriptions largely along the dimensions recognized by the culture being described. The categories chosen

1. The research assistance of Nathan Gould is gratefully acknowledged.

2. The broad tripartite classification of "cultural" (relation of man to nature, man to man, and "subjective aspects"), upon which there has been a large measure of convergence, does not help us much for comparative purposes. For a detailed discussion see Kroeber and Kluckhohn (1952). Perhaps the "seven major facets" of culture elements used in the 1950 edition of Murdock *et al.*, *Outline of Cultural Materials*, see pp. xix ff., takes us a bit further.

are those which appear explicitly in the native language. This method, in the favorable case, gives a view of experience as it appears consciously to the people studied and avoids the distortions that inevitably result when a culture is dismembered and reassembled arbitrarily according to the classifications familiar to Western thought. On the other hand, no approach which neglects the tacit premises and crypto-categories of the implicit culture really presents a unique cultural world in its totality. Moreover—and more to the point for the present discussion—this path represents untrammeled cultural relativism at its extreme. Each distinct culture becomes, indeed, a self-contained monad which can in the nature of the case be compared with others only vaguely, "intuitively," "artistically."

The second path is the one followed, with numerous variations and compromises, by the overwhelming majority of ethnographers. The selected categories are the well-known ones of the "standard" monograph, typically: physical environment; techniques, economic and technological, for coping with this environment; social organization; religion; sometimes language; more recently, "life-cycle" or methods of childhood training and the like. In the first instance these were common-sense concepts corresponding to nineteenth-century Western notions of the all-pervasive framework of human life. They have been slightly modified in accord, on the one hand, with the empirical generalizations summed up under Wissler's "universal culture pattern" and, on the other hand, with changing theoretical fashions (for example, recent attention to nursing habits, toilet training, etc.).

On the whole, these categories have been crudely serviceable and have made certain meaningful comparisons possible. In broad form, though not in content, they represent rough empirical universals into which descriptive data can conveniently be grouped. Comparative analysis is aided by more truly scientific concepts, purposefully created by anthropologists: Linton's "item," "trait," and "activity"; his "form," "function," "use," and "meaning"; his "universals," "alternatives," and "specialties"; Kroeber's three types of patterns; Opler's "themes"; and Herskovits' "focus." But the data obtained in the field which must serve as our materials for a comparative science continue to be perverted, slightly or greatly, by the prescientific nature of our basic categories. The technical processes of farming or weaving (though not the symbolic accretions of these activities) can be compared with relatively little distortion because of their objectivity and of the limiting "givens" of nature. Our concepts, however, of "economics," "religion," and "politics" have a large element of cultural arbitrariness. Probably the main reason that anthropologists have written so little about "political behavior" is the circumstance that they have felt intuitively uncomfortable, unable to isolate in many cultures an order of phenomena strictly comparable to our category of "government."

In cultural anthropology we are still too close to the phase in linguistics when non-European languages were being forcibly recast into the categories of Latin grammar. We can discover and recognize similarities due to historical connection, but nonhistorically derived similarities, other than the most gross and obvious ones, elude us because our frame is too culture-bound and so insufficiently abstract that we can compare only in terms of specific content. The Human Relations Area Files are admirable in intent and decidedly useful in many ways as they stand. Yet it is the testimony of many who have worked intensively with these materials that the Files bring together much which is conceptually distinct, and separate much that ought to be together. An altogether adequate organization of comparative data must await a better working-out of the theory of the universal categories of culture,[3] both structural principles and content categories. Present methods obtain, organize, and compare in ways that beg questions which are themselves at issue. This is the contemporary paradox of the so-called "comparative" science of cultures.

The present paper cannot hope to resolve this paradox. It can at best state the problem more clearly, focus the central issues, indicate some clues as to the lines along which resolution may eventually take place. First, the state of affairs in a sample of recent monographs will be briefly summarized. There will follow a short historical sketch of anthropological thinking about universal categories. Finally, some aids from biology, psychology, and sociology will be mobilized.

An examination was made of the tables of contents of ninety ethnographic monographs published in English within the last twenty years. Of these, four were works on the cultures of contemporary industrial societies. Studies limited to or focused upon single topics were not examined. Rather, the sample was restricted to general accounts of a people and their culture.

Findings may be summarized as follows: There is a stereotyped scheme with numerous but comparatively mi-

nor variations upon it; genuine innovation is exceedingly rare; reports in the second decade of our sample tended strongly to show more conscious theoretical orientation. Variations reflect, in part, shifting conceptual fashions, in part the interests and presumably the temperaments of individual workers.[4]

Avoidance of explicit theoretical frames of reference is particularly marked in certain series, such as *Anthropological Records* and the Bishop Museum publications. However, the majority of studies which have appeared since World War II exhibit a striving toward problem-centered research and toward (sometimes strained) theoretical sophistication. There is also a greater awareness of the dangers of imposing the categories of the anthropologist's culture upon cultures outside the Western tradition. Honigmann, for example, uses "ideational culture" and avoids "religion" in his treatment of the Kaska.

Expectably, comparability is best where description treats of the satisfaction of basic physical needs or por-

3. Murdock *et al.* (1950, p. xix), state that "they have attempted to group inherently related categories in the same section and they have arranged the sections in an order that is not wholly without logic. Beyond this, however, they insist that the classification is wholly pragmatic. . . . Through trial and error . . . the categories have come to represent a sort of common denominator of the ways in which anthropologists, geographers, sociologists, historians, and non-professional recorders of cultural data habitually organize their materials."

4. Commenting on the comparability of community studies of contemporary societies, Steward (1950, p. 25) states: "In a *comparative approach* to contemporary communities, the problems which are studied in one community—or at least the cultural perspectives acquired in any study—are utilized in the investigation of other communities. Ideally, there is some comparability of research projects that have common purposes, problems, and methods. The widely differing characteristics of communities naturally dictate some differences in approach; but individual interests, purposes, and methods have produced even greater differences, and community studies have little in common beyond the fact that they purport to use a cultural approach."

Commenting on the "more purely ethnographic studies," Steward (1950, p. 26; see illustrations of this, pp. 26–27) states: "These show considerable disparity of emphasis because of varied individual interests. The general chapter headings may be more or less similar, but there is a great difference in purpose and problem."

trays customs directly related to the life-cycle or departs from other biologically or physically given points of reference. The proportion of space given to various topics reflects, of course, theoretical orientation and personal interests.[5] In general, the distribution of attention appears somewhat more "objective" or better balanced in the monographs of the pre–World War II period when theory was less explicit. Reading of prefaces and introductions makes it clear that exigencies of the field situation were also important in influencing the kind and amount of data collected. Finally, there are the technical problems and limitations which Herskovits has discussed.[6]

In short, careful examination confirms an initial impression that the data recorded in recent anthropological monographs are only roughly, loosely, and for certain purposes comparable. About 1939 Malinowski began to publish what he later called his "universal

institutional types."[7] What is substantially a revision of this has recently been presented by Nadel (1951, pp. 135 ff.). However, no ethnography has yet been published which organizes its materials in accord with this theoretical system. Similarly, Leslie White has discussed universal categories of a Morgan-Engels-Marx sort, but his published studies of cultures follow the traditional pattern. The situation remains as Evans-Pritchard described it (1940, p. 261): "These weighty volumes generally record observations in too haphazard a fashion to be either pleasant or profitable reading. This deficiency is due to absence of a body of scientific theory in Social Anthropology."

---

5. Steward (1950, p. 28), who analyzed the relative amount of space accorded different subjects in community studies to determine differences of emphasis, states in summary: "The amount of space devoted to a subject depends somewhat, of course, upon its functional importance in the community. *Nonetheless, even substantially similar communities are given quite unlike treatment, which reflects individual purposes and methods even more than differences in facts*" (my italics). Discussing "the more purely ethnographic studies" of community life, Steward states that "even these show considerable disparity of emphasis because of varied individual interests. The general chapter headings may be more or less similar, but there is a great difference in purpose and problem. The Lynds' studies of Middletown [1929, 1937] are concerned with how economic factors and changes affect community life, which is described in most of its aspects. West's *Plainville* [1945], Yang's Chinese Village [1945], and Hsu's study of a Chinese community [1948] are interested in the interrelation of culture and personality, and following the current approach to this problem, they accord considerable space to the 'life cycle'—the development

of the individual in the culture. Parsons' Mexican [1936] and Ecuadorian [1945] studies have the very different purpose of determining the native Indian and Spanish elements in the culture of her communities. Redfield's study of Yucatan [1941], though dealing with folk cultures not unlike those recorded by Parsons, is preoccupied with the transformation of folk societies under urbanizing influences. And Fei's monographs on Chinese peasants [e.g., Fei and Chang, 1945], through reporting on people who are similar to those studied by Yang and Hsu, are concerned with rural economy in its relationship to community types and show no interest in culture and personality."

6. "It is impossible for any study of a culture . . . to describe more than a portion of the aspects of the life of a single people. Even those whose aim is to give the most rounded portrayal possible find certain limits which, for technical reasons of time, space and competence they cannot exceed. In practice, language is left to the specialist, and so is music. If any attempt is made to include expressions of the literary arts, this material must commonly be reserved for separate treatment because of its bulk. Some aspects of culture are rarely studied as such; forms of dramatic expression, for instance, since in non-literate societies drama is customarily a part of ritual. The dance, also, has too rarely been analyzed, because of the technical difficulties it presents in the way of valid recording" (1948, p. 238).

7. For his final version see *A Scientific Theory of Culture* (1944, pp. 62 ff.).

Many of the earlier anthropologists were certain that there were universal categories[8] for culture or universal categories which underlay all cultures. Witness the "stages" of the evolutionists and the "elementary ideas" of Bastian. Boas[9] called chapter VI of the 1911 edition of *The Mind of Primitive Man* "The Universality of Culture Traits" and says:

We may therefore base our further considerations on the theory of the similarity of mental functions in all races. Observation has shown, however, that not only emotions, intellect, and will-power of man are alike everywhere, but that much more detailed similarities in thought and action occur among the most diverse peoples.

But, in general, from about this time on, the attention of anthropologists throughout the world appears to have been directed overwhelmingly to the distinctiveness of each culture and to the differences in human custom as opposed to the similarities. The latter, where recognized, were explained historically rather than in terms of the common nature of man and certain invariant properties of the human situation. In the case of the United States, there was the added factor of the anti-theoretical bias of American anthropologists for at least a generation.

Between roughly 1910 and roughly 1940 the only significant anthropological advance[10] in formulating the basic principles upon which all cultures rest appears to be represented by Wissler's discussion of the universal culture pat-

tern, in 1923.[11] However, workers in other disciplines were attempting to establish regularities in human response which transcended cultural difference. Durkheim, Mauss, and other French sociologists propounded their famous principles of collective representations, reciprocity, and the like. Simmel looked for social regularities of a somewhat different type. Birkhoff in his *Aesthetic Measure* tried to develop panhuman canons of artistic response.[12] Zipf discovered the k-constant, applied the harmonic principle to social behavior, and, a little later, enunciated his so-called "law of least effort." The psychoanalysts tried to show the universality of the Oedipus complex, sibling rivalry, and certain sorts of fantasy and symbolic processes. Human geography, in France and elsewhere, abandoned simplist "environmental determinism" in favor of the view that there was a high correlation between certain aspects of culture, especially types of social organization, and certain ecological situations.

These and other movements had an impact upon anthropology. There was probably also within the profession an increasing skepticism of the tautology that culture alone begets or determines culture and of the proposition that culture is purely and solely the precipitate

8. For brief discussions of the history of theories of the universal culture pattern see Murdock (1945) and Herskovits (1948).

9. In the 1938 edition of the same work Boas (p. 195) says: "There is no reason why we should accept Bastian's renunciation. The dynamic forces that mould social life are the same now as those that moulded life thousands of years ago. We can follow the intellectual and emotional drives that actuate man at present and that shape his actions and thoughts."

10. Linton's *Study of Man* (1936) did significantly advance some theoretical aspects. For example, he discusses "the universal reactions of man," such as the dependence of human beings upon emotional responses from one another—a factor to which William James had directed attention.

11. In a sense, as Mr. Gould has pointed out to me, enumerative definitions of culture, of which Tylor's is the classical illustration, may be viewed as statements of the categories of the universal pattern.

12. Cf. a recent statement by Raymond Firth (1951): "I believe that there are universal standards of aesthetic quality, just as there are universal standards of technical efficiency." Such standards are based on "similar psychological impulses."

of the accidents of history.[13] At all events Radcliffe-Brown led off an anthropological search for "universal social laws" in the English-speaking world. Chapple and Arensberg, stimulated alike by Simmel, Radcliffe-Brown, and Malinowski, attempted to establish quantitatively invariant properties of social interaction. Murdock, departing from the Sumner-Keller sociological tradition and from Wissler and other American anthropologists, likewise initiated quantitative work with the aim of factoring out the specifically historical and establishing cross-cultural trends and tendencies. His founding of the Cross-cultural Survey in the thirties appears to have been largely a means

13. The most impressive theoretical statement by an anthropologist signalizing a return to universal processes and factors is contained in A. V. Kidder's paper "Looking Backward" (1940):

"In both hemispheres man started from cultural scratch, as a nomadic hunter, a user of stone tools, a palaeolithic savage. In both he spread over great continents and shaped his life to cope with every sort of environment. Then, in both hemispheres, wild plants were brought under cultivation; population increased; concentrations of people brought elaboration of social groupings and rapid progress in the arts. Pottery came into use, fibres and wools were woven into cloth, animals were domesticated, metal working began—first in gold and copper, then in the harder alloy, bronze. Systems of writing were evolved.

"Not only in material things do the parallels hold. In the New World as well as in the Old, priesthoods grew and, allying themselves with temporal powers, or becoming rulers in their own right, reared to their gods vast temples adorned with painting and sculpture. The priests and chiefs provided for themselves elaborate tombs richly stocked for the future life. In political history it is the same. In both hemispheres group joined group to form tribes; coalitions and conquests brought preeminence; empires grew and assumed the paraphernalia of glory.

"These are astonishing similarities. And if we believe, as most modern students do, that the Indians' achievement was made independently, and their progress was not stimulated from overseas, then we reach a very significant

to this end.[14] Roheim and other psychoanalytically oriented anthropologists put Freudian theory to the test of field work. Leighton, an anthropologically experienced psychiatrist, formulated, in *The Governing of Men* and *Human Relations in a Changing World,* some principles about raw or subcultural human nature. Forde, Richards, and others in British anthropology and Steward and others in American anthropology put the search for the environmental determinants of culture upon a new and more sophisticated basis. Steward's 1938 paper, "Ecological Aspects of Southwestern Society," was a particularly notable demonstration of certain relationships between forms of social organization and geographical situation.

Two cross-disciplinary papers in which each team of writers included an anthropologist attempted to sketch out the more abstract foundations for a system of categories that would permit true cross-cultural comparability. A quotation from the first of these is appropriate because the present paper represents essentially a modification and a development of the same point of view:[15]

conclusion. We can infer that human beings possess an innate urge to take certain definite steps toward what we call civilization. And that men also possess the innate ability, given proper environmental conditions, to put that urge into effect. In other words, we must consider that civilization is an inevitable response to laws governing the growth of culture and controlling the man-culture relationship."

14. In "The Cross-cultural Survey" (1940, p. 366), Murdock remarks: "To the extent that culture is ideational, we may conclude all cultures should reveal certain similarities, flowing from the universal laws governing the symbolic, mental processes, e.g., the worldwide parallels in the principles of magic."

15. Lynd (1939, p. 124) provides the same clue: ". . . the error lies in seeking to derive the laws of social science from study of sequences observed in a single set of historically conditioned *institutions, qua institutions,* rather than from study of the *full range of*

The following model is intended to cut across ... specialized and narrow abstractions. It does not rest on ... assumptions about "human nature" but abstracts immediately from the concrete behavior of men in social systems. ... Variations in the patterning of different social systems are indefinitely numerous. The principle on which the present outline has been built up is, however, that these variations are grouped about certain *invariant points of reference*. These are to be found in the nature of social systems, in the biological and psychological nature of the component individuals, in the external situations in which they live and act, in the nature of action itself, in the necessity of its coordination in social systems. In the orientation of individuals these "foci" of structure are never ignored. They must in some way be "adapted to" or "taken account of." The ... three main classes of patterns [situational, instrumental, and integrative] are coherently grouped because of their relation in each case to a related group of these foci of patterning. In the first case it is certain facts about the situation in which men are placed, their biological nature and descent, their psychological nature. In the second it is the content of the differentiated functional roles by virtue of which a system of interdependent units becomes possible. In the third, finally, it is certain necessities of the coordinated functioning of a social system as a whole.[16]

The second paper, "The Functional Prerequisites of a Society" (Aberle *et al.*, 1950), refines and elaborates one aspect of the conceptual scheme just referred to. The theoretical takeoff is as follows:

A comparative social science requires a generalized system of concepts which will enable the scientific observer to compare

---

behavior around the functional cores these institutions express."

16. J. F. Dunlop, M. P. Gilmore, C. Kluckhohn, T. Parsons, and O. H. Taylor, "Toward a Common Language for the Area of Social Science" (mimeographed, 1941). The above quotation appears in the portion of the complete memorandum printed in T. Parsons (1949).

and contrast large bodies of concretely different social phenomena in consistent terms. A promising social analysis is a tentative formulation of the functional prerequisites of a society. Functional prerequisites refer broadly to the things that must get done in any society if it is to continue as a going concern, *i.e.*, the generalized conditions necessary for the maintenance of the system concerned. The specific structural arrangements for meeting the functional prerequisites differ, of course, from one society to another and, in the course of time, change in any given society. Thus all societies must allocate goods and services somehow. A particular society may change from one method, say business enterprise, to another, say a centrally planned economy, without the destruction of the society as a society but merely with a change in its concrete structures.

Florence Kluckhohn (1950), combining sociological and anthropological thinking and conclusions, has provided a frame for comparing the profiles exhibited by different cultures with respect to their premises, tacit and overt, about five universal human problems: "what are the innate predispositions of man? what is the relation of man to nature? what is the significant time dimension? what is the direction in time of the action process? what type of personality is to be most valued? what is the dominant modality of the relationship of man to other men?" Assuming that "all societies find a phraseology within a range of possible phraseologies of basic human problems," she notes: "The problems as stated are constant; they arise inevitably out of the human situation. The phraseology of them is variable but variable only within limits."

Human biology sets limits, supplies potentialities and drives, provides clues which cultures neglect or elaborate.[17] This is standard anthropological doctrine at present, and it may turn out that this is about all there is to it. Yet

17. For a recent review see Bergman (1952).

when one learns that the introduction of an electric needle into a certain cortical area of one species of monkey results in these monkeys thereafter defecating upon their own kind, whereas previously they would defecate only upon strangers, one wonders if, after all, there may not be specific biological bases for certain of our social habits.[18] At all events, there is general recognition of the social and cultural implications of such elementary biological facts as the existence of two sexes, the ordinary human life-span, the dependency of human infants (of which the psychoanalysts have made so much). Those features of human cultures such as family life which have their counterparts in lower primates and other mammals presumably have a rather definite biological base. This assumption has recently been discussed by Marston Bates (1950, p. 162 and *passim*) and by Ford and Beach (1951, pp. 3 ff.). Allee's (1951) studies of patterns of social co-operation among animals are also highly suggestive both for biological and for social determinants of universal categories of culture.

The biological leads easily into the psychological. The ways, for instance, in which biological dependency is transformed into psychological dependency have often been discussed. Dreaming, which has surely given rise to many cultural parallels, is both a biological and a psychological process. And the biological nature of man plus his

18. Current experiments at the Orange Park primate laboratory are also interesting. Give chimpanzees an incomplete circle, and they will fill it in, and they will draw a cross to complete the symmetry of a design. This and Schiller's work on perceptual completion suggest a specific biological basis, shared by humans and other primates, for certain tendencies toward closure manifested in human cultures. The facts are well established that such behavior as nursing and walking are dependent more on the myelination of the relevant nerve tracts and less on sociocultural factors than had previously been thought.

psychological capabilities and predispositions interact with certain universalities in man's social interactions and other features of his environing situation. As Bates and others have shown, the sheer territorial dimension of human existence has its effects upon culture. In various studies Steward has generalized some of these. Given the principle of limitation of possibilities, independent parallel developments have occurred again and again. As Steward (1949) says, for example:

In densely settled areas, internal needs will produce an orderly interrelationship of environment, subsistence patterns, special groupings, occupational specializations, and overall political, religious, and perhaps military integrating factors. These interrelated institutions do not have unlimited variability, for they must be adapted to the requirements of subsistence patterns established in particular environments; they involve a cultural ecology.

In psychological language the generalization is that human beings are so constituted that, particularly under conditions of extreme stress, they will often react in roughly similar ways to the same pressures. Nativistic movements constitute a case much studied of late by anthropologists. Details vary widely in accord with the pre-existing cultures, but the broad patterns are very much alike. Marie Bonaparte (1947) has demonstrated that at the time of the fall of France in 1940 a tale with the same general theme ("the myth of the corpse in the car") was told over widely separated areas within such a brief period that the possibility of diffusion must be ruled out. There is considerable evidence of parallelisms in fantasy productions arising over long periods and under "normal" conditions among peoples who cannot be presumed to have had direct or indirect historical contact within a relevant time range. Rank (1914), for instance, has demonstrated remarkable similarities in widespread myths of heroes. In spite of the fact that many psychoanalytic writers have run Freudian theories of panhuman sexual symbolism into the ground, there remain arresting and irreducible resemblances among such symbolisms in the most historically diverse cultures.

Throughout, one can recognize the empirical convergences without necessarily accepting the psychoanalytic interpretations. Thus one can pay due regard to Bonaparte's data without allegiance to her "human sacrifice" explanation. Nevertheless I should like to repeat what I have recently written about psychoanalysis and anthropology (Kluckhohn and Morgan, 1951):

I still believe that some of the cautions uttered by Boas and others on the possible extravagances of interpretations in terms of universal symbolism, completely or largely divorced from minute examination of cultural context, are sound. But the facts uncovered in my own field work and that of my collaborators have forced me to the conclusion that Freud and other psychoanalysts have depicted with astonishing correctness many central themes in motivational life which are universal. The styles of expression of these themes and much of the manifest content are culturally determined, but the underlying psychologic drama transcends cultural difference.

This should not be too surprising—except to an anthropologist overindoctrinated with the theory of cultural relativism—for many of the inescapable givens of human life are also universal. Human anatomy and human physiology are, in the large, about the same the world over. There are two sexes with palpably visible differences in external genitalia and secondary sexual characteristics. All human infants, regardless of culture, know the psychological experience of helplessness and dependency. Situations making for competition for the affection of one or both parents, for sibling rivalry can be to some extent channeled this way or that way by a culture but they cannot be eliminated, given the universality of family life. The trouble has been —because of a series of accidents of intel-lectual and political history—that the anthropologist for two generations has been obsessed with the differences between peoples, neglecting the equally real similarities—upon which the "universal culture pattern" as well as the psychological uniformities are clearly built.

A. V. Kidder[19] some time ago put the general case cautiously but wisely:

The question . . . is: does culture, although not biologically transmitted, develop and function in response to tendencies—it is perhaps too connotative to call them law—that are comparable to those controlling biological evolution? There seems to be evidence that, in some degree at least, it does. All over the world and among populations that could apparently not possibly have come into contact with each other, similar inventions have been made and have been made in a seemingly predetermined order. Extraordinary similarities are to be observed in the nature and order of appearance among widely separated peoples of certain social practices and religious observances.

These are likenesses, not identities; history, to reverse the proverb, never repeats itself; different environments and differing opportunities have seen to that. But they do seem to indicate that there are definite tendencies and orderlinesses, both in the growth of this compelling force and in man's responses thereto. It is therefore the task of the disciplines concerned with man and his culture—genetics, history, archaeology, sociology, the humanities—to gather and to correlate information which may enable us more fully to understand these now dimly perceived trends and relationships.

Anthropologists have been rightly criticized by sociologists and certain psychologists for neglecting the universalities in interaction processes, the common elements in the structuring of social action. To some extent, as suggested earlier, this has been corrected in recent years by the work of the Brit-

19. Mimeographed document from the Carnegie Institution, quoted in Steward (1950, p. 118).

ish social anthropologists and such Americans as Chapple and Arensberg. It does appear that groups as such have certain basic properties. One may instance Lewin's concept of quasi-stationary equilibrium (cf. Wilson, 1951). A philosopher (Riezler, 1950) has just published a penetrating study of the constant and the variable in human social life which raises many issues too often overlooked by anthropologists.

My colleague, Professor George Homans, has investigated, with the aid of his seminar, the relations between mother's brother and sister's son, father's sister and her brother's son, and brothers and sisters in a considerable range of nonliterate societies. Homans operates upon the hypothesis that there are discoverable structural laws for social conduct in all human societies, but he informs me that this investigation only partially bore out this hypothesis. For the first two relationships there appeared to be patterns that transcended cultural differences. These relationships evidenced considerable regularity, but the relations between brothers and sisters were irregular in the same societies. In some, stringent avoidance was enjoined; in others, brothers and sisters were permitted to be what Lévi-Strauss has called "chaste companions of the bed." The difference seemed to be traceable not to principles of social structure but rather to cultural values, specifically the varying emphasis upon internal as opposed to external controls for moral behavior. I suspect that this work of Homans[20] may represent a broader paradigm: some aspects of culture take their specific forms solely as a result of historical accidents; others are tailored by forces which can properly be designated as universal.

20. Homans has been strongly influenced by Chapple, Arensberg, and other anthropologists who have tried to limit themselves to observable social interaction analyzed in terms of a few simple concepts (cf. 1950).

It is possible, of course, to follow Kroeber (1949)[21] and regard cross-cultural likenesses as being subcultural—as the limits and conditions of culture:

Such more or less recurrent near-regularities of form or process as have to date been formulated for culture are actually mainly sub-cultural in nature. They are limits set to culture by physical or organic factors. The so-called "cultural constants" of family, religion, war, communication, and the like appear to be biopsychological frames variably filled with cultural content, so far as they are more than categories reflecting the compartments of our own Occidental logico-verbal culture. Of processes, diffusion and socialization are both only psychological learning, imitation, and suggestion under special conditions. Custom is psychobiological habit on a social scale and carrying cultural values.

But the universals are part of cultures in the sense that they are incorporated and socially transmitted. Moreover, the "so-called 'cultural constants'" are not mere empty frames. In the case of language, for instance, there are also striking resemblances within the frame. Every phonology is a system, not a random congeries of sound-classes. The differentiating principles of a phonetic system are applied with some consistency to sounds produced in more than one position. In a study just published Jakobson and others (1952) assert: "The inherent distinctive features which we detect in the languages of the world and which underlie their entire lexical and morphological stock amount to twelve binary oppositions." All languages are made up of "vowels" and "consonants." Meaningful utterances in all languages arise from combining morphemes, and there are certain other generalized properties of morphophonemics. All languages exhibit a high degree of flexibility with

21. For a reply to Kroeber's often expressed view that categories, like "sacrifice," are "fake universals" see Lévi-Strauss, *Twentieth Century Sociology,* pp. 523 ff.

respect to the meanings that can be expressed. The subject-predicate form of expression is universal so far as extended and connected discourse is concerned. Possession or the genitive is expressed in all languages. This list could be considerably extended.[22]

It can be argued that even these congruences in content reflect subcultural "limits." That is, the facts that the range of number of phonemes in human languages is narrow and that all languages appear to embrace between five and ten thousand morphemes can be interpreted as reflecting only certain limits of human anatomy and physiology which, assuming the principle of economy or "least effort," make a language based upon forty thousand combinations of two phonemes most unlikely (since the human nervous system is not equipped to "code" and "decode" that fast). The same argument can be advanced as regards the limited range of variation in number of kinship terms and the fundamental contrasts in principles of kinship systems which Murdock has published. However, it is not important whether these phenomena be regarded as universal categories *of* culture or universal categories *for* the comparison of cultures. They reflect, admittedly, "limits" or "conditions" and are in this sense "subcultural."

But it should be noted in passing that features which no one would dispute as cultural are also limiting conditions to other aspects of culture. Thus Boas (1940) has said: "We may . . . consider exogamy as the condition on which totemism arose." Fortes (1949) and Firth (1951) have asserted:

The hypothesis that all kinship institutions derive from the facts of sex, procreation, and child-rearing is acceptable if the emphasis is laid not on their biological and utilitarian value but on the moral values attached by society to these facts, and perpetuated through the social relationships brought into being by their conjunction. . . . The existence of a social system necessitates, in fact, a moral system for its support.

In any case, the crucial point is this: *biological, psychological, and sociosituational universals afford the possibility of comparison of cultures in terms which are not ethnocentric, which depart from "givens," begging no needless questions.*

Most anthropologists would agree that no constant elemental units like atoms, cells, or genes have as yet been satisfactorily established with culture in general.[23] Many would insist that within one aspect of culture, namely, language, such constant elemental units have been isolated: phonemes[24] and morphemes. It is arguable whether such units are, in principle, discoverable in sectors of culture less automatic than speech and less closely tied (in some ways) to biological fact.[25]

22. While most of the points in this and the following paragraph have been familiar to me and used in my lectures for some years, this statement in its present form owes much to a lecture delivered by Dr. Joseph Greenberg in April, 1952, to the staff of the Laboratory of Social Relations, Harvard University. I am grateful to Dr. Greenberg for this help and stimulation.

23. Much of the remaining portion of this paper is drawn, in slightly modified form, from a monograph (*Culture* ["Papers of the Peabody Museum of Harvard University"], in press) by A. L. Kroeber and C. Kluckhohn. While most of the paragraphs utilized here were originally drafted by Kluckhohn, they have been improved by Dr. Kroeber, to whom gratitude is expressed for permission to reuse in this form.

24. R. Jakobson (1949) remarks: "Linguistic analysis with its concept of ultimate phonemic entities signally converges with modern physics which revealed the granular structure of matter as composed of elementary particles."

25. Wiener (1948) and Lévi-Strauss (1951) also present contrasting views on the possibilities of discovering lawful regularities in anthropological data. Wiener argues (*a*) that the obtainable statistical runs are not long enough and (*b*) that observers modify the

Kroeber feels that it is highly unlikely that any such constant elemental units will be discovered. Their place is on lower, more basic levels of organization of phenomena. Here and there suggestions have been ventured that there are such basic elements: the culture trait, for instance, or the small community of face-to-face relations. But no such hints have been systematically developed by their proponents, let alone accepted by others. Culture traits can obviously be divided and subdivided and resubdivided at will, according to occasion or need. Or, for that matter, they are often combined into larger complexes which are still treatable, in *ad hoc* situations, as unitary traits and are, in fact, ordinarily spoken of as traits in such situations. The face-to-face community, of course, is not actually a unit of culture but the supposed unit of *social* reference or frame for what might be called a "minimal culture." At that, even such a social unit has in most cases no sharply defined actual limits.

As for the larger groups of phenomena like religion that make up "the universal pattern"—or even subdivisions of these such as "crisis rites" or "fasting" —these are recurrent indeed, but they are not uniform. Anyone can make a definition that will separate magic from religion; but no one has yet found a definition that all other students ac-

cept: the phenomenal contents of the concepts of religion and magic simply intergrade too much. This is true even though almost everyone would agree in differentiating large masses of specific phenomena as respectively religious and magical—supplicating a powerful but unseen deity in the heavens, for instance, as against sticking a pin into an effigy. In short, concepts like religion and magic have an undoubted heuristic utility in given situations. But they are altogether too fluid in conceptual range for use either as strict categories or as units from which larger concepts can be built up. After all, they are in origin common-sense concepts, like "boy," "youth," "man," "old man," which neither physiologists nor psychologists will wholly discard but which they will also not attempt to include among the elementary units and basic concepts upon which they rear their sciences.

This conclusion of Kroeber's is akin to what Boas said about social-science methodology in 1930: "The analysis of the phenomena is our prime object. Generalizations will be more significant the closer we adhere to definite forms. The attempts to reduce all social phenomena to a closed system of laws applicable to every society and explaining its structure and history do not seem a promising undertaking" (Boas, 1930, p. 268). The significance of generalizations is proportional to the definiteness of the forms and concepts analyzed out of phenomena—in this seems to reside the weakness of the uniformities in culture heretofore suggested; they are *indefinite*.

A case on the other side is put as follows by Julian Steward (1949) in his important paper: "Cultural Causality and Law: A Trial Formulation of the Development of Early Civilization":

It is not necessary that any formulation of cultural regularities provide an ultimate

---

phenomena by their conscious study of them. Lévi-Strauss replies that linguistics at least can meet these two objections and suggests that certain aspects of social organization can also be studied in ways that obviate the difficulties. It may be added that Wiener has remarked in conversation with one of us that he is convinced of the practicability of devising new mathematical instruments which would permit of satisfactory treatment of social-science facts. Finally, note Murdock's (1949, p. 259) finding: "Cultural forms in the field of social organization reveal a degree of regularity and of conformity to scientific law not significantly inferior to that found in the so-called natural sciences."

explanation of culture change. In the physical and biological sciences, formulations are merely approximations of observed regularities, and they are valid as working hypotheses despite their failure to deal with ultimate realities. So long as a cultural law formulates recurrences of similar inter-relationships of phenomena, it expresses cause and effect in the same way that the law of gravity formulates but does not ultimately explain the attraction between masses of matter. Moreover, like the law of gravity, which has been greatly modified by the theory of relativity, any formulation of cultural data may be useful as a working hypothesis, even though further research requires that it be qualified or reformulated.

Cultural regularities may be formulated on different levels, each in its own terms. At present, the greatest possibilities lie in the purely cultural or superorganic level, for anthropology's traditional primary concern with culture has provided far more data of this kind. Moreover, the greater part of culture history is susceptible to treatment only in superorganic terms. Both sequential or diachronic formulations and synchronic formulations are superorganic, and they may be functional to the extent that the data permit. Redfield's tentative formulation that urban culture contrasts with folk culture in being more individualized, secularized, heterogeneous, and disorganized is synchronic, superorganic, and functional. Morgan's evolutionary schemes and White's formulation concerning the relationship of energy to cultural development are sequential and somewhat functional. Neither type, however, is wholly one or the other. A time-dimension is implied in Redfield's formulation, and synchronic, functional relationships are implied in White's. . . .

The present statement of scientific purpose and methodology rests on a conception of culture that needs clarification. *If the more important institutions of culture can be isolated from their unique setting so as to be typed, classified, and related to recurring antecedents or functional correlates, it follows that it is possible to consider the institutions in question as the basic or constant ones, whereas the features that lend uniqueness are the second-ary or variable ones.* For example, the American high civilizations had agriculture, social classes, and a priest-temple-idol cult. As types, these institutions are abstractions of what was actually present in each area, and they do not take into account the particular crops grown, the precise patterning of the social classes, or the conceptualization of deities, details of ritual, and other religious features of each culture center.

There are, admittedly, few genuine uniformities in culture content unless one states the content in extremely general form—e.g., clothing, shelter, incest taboos, and the like. There are mainly what Kidder has called "likenesses rather than identities." The seventy-two items listed by Murdock (1949, p. 124) "which occur, so far as the author's knowledge goes, in every culture known to history or ethnography" are mainly blanket categories of the "universal ground plan," though a few, such as "modesty concerning natural functions," approach a certain kind of specificity. This list could doubtless be extended. Hallowell[26] in an unpublished paper has suggested self-concepts. Even the most exhaustive list, however, would have to be purged of culture-bound or partially culture-bound categories before it could serve more than the rough heuristic utility suggested by Herskovits' (1948, p. 239) comment on the organization of a "rounded study of a culture":

The assumptions that underlie the progression of topics in such a presentation is that of most descriptive studies. They derive from a logic that proceeds from the consideration of those aspects that supply the physical wants of man, to those that order social relations, and finally to the aspects which, in giving meaning to the universe, sanction everyday living, and in their aesthetic manifestations afford men

26. "The Self and Its Behavioral Environment." To appear in: GEZA ROHEIM (ed.), *Psychoanalysis and the Social Sciences*, Vol. IV.

some of the deepest satisfactions they experience.

A few rather specific content universals have been mentioned earlier. A few others could also be mustered. As Murdock has shown, the nuclear family is universal either as the sole prevailing form or as the basic unit from which more complex familial forms are compounded. Boas (1911) remarked that "the three personal pronouns—I, thou, and he—occur in all human languages."[27] Unilateral preferential cross-cousin marriage takes rather consistently different forms in matrilateral than in patrilateral societies. Institutionalized female homosexuality appears to be largely, if not completely, absent in matrilateral societies.

But, in general, one, *of course*, expects uniqueness in detail—this follows from the very essence of culture theory. As Steward remarks in the passage just quoted, the secondary or variable features of culture naturally exhibit distinctiveness. After all, the *content* of different atoms and of different cells is by no means identical. These are constant elemental units of *form*. Wissler, Murdock, and others have shown that there are a considerable number of categories and of structural principles found in all cultures. Fortes (1949) speaks of kinship as an "irreducible principle of Tale social organization." It appears to be an irreducible principle of all cultures, however much its elaboration and the emphasis upon it may vary. When Fortes also says that "every social system presupposes such basic axioms," he is likewise pointing to a constant elemental unit of each and every culture.

The inescapable fact of cultural relativism does not justify the conclusion that cultures are in all respects utterly disparate monads and hence strictly noncomparable entities. If this were

27. For a fuller discussion of the implications of this and related facts, see Riezler (1950).

literally true, a comparative science of culture would be *ex hypothesi* impossible. It is, unfortunately, the case that up to this point anthropology has not solved very satisfactorily the problem of describing cultures in such a way that objective comparison is possible. Most cultural monographs organize the data in terms of the categories of our own contemporary Western culture: economics, technology, social organization, and the like. Such an ordering, of course, tears many of the facts from their own actual context and loads the analysis. The implicit assumption is that our categories are "given" by nature—an assumption contradicted most emphatically by these very investigations of different cultures. A smaller number of studies have attempted to present the information consistently in terms of the category system and whole way of thought of the culture being described. This approach obviously excludes the immediate possibility of a complete set of common terms of reference for comparison. Such a system of comparable concepts and terms remains to be worked out and will probably be established only gradually.

In principle, however, there is a generalized framework that underlies the more apparent and striking facts of cultural relativity. All cultures constitute so many somewhat distinct answers to essentially the same questions posed by human biology and by the generalities of the human situation. These are the considerations explored by Wissler under the heading of "the universal culture pattern" and by Murdock under the rubric of "the least common denominators of cultures." Every society's patterns for living must provide approved and sanctioned ways for dealing with such universal circumstances as the existence of two sexes; the helplessness of infants; the need for satisfaction of the elementary biological requirements such as food, warmth, and sex;

the presence of individuals of different ages and of differing physical and other capacities. The basic similarities in human biology the world over are vastly more massive than the variations. Equally, there are certain necessities in social life for this kind of animal, regardless of where that life is carried on or in what culture. Co-operation to obtain subsistence and for other ends requires a certain minimum of reciprocal behavior, of a standard system of communication, and, indeed, of mutually accepted values. The facts of human biology and of human gregariousness supply, therefore, certain invariant points of reference from which cross-cultural comparison can start without begging questions that are themselves at issue. As Wissler pointed out, the broad outlines of the ground plan of all cultures are and have to be about the same because men always and everywhere are faced with certain unavoidable problems which arise out of the situation "given" by nature. Since most of the patterns of all cultures crystallize around the same foci, there are significant respects in which each culture is not wholly isolated, self-contained, disparate but rather related to and comparable with all other cultures.

Valid cross-cultural comparison could best proceed from the invariant points of reference supplied by the biological, psychological, and sociosituational "givens" of human life. These and their interrelations determine the likenesses in the broad categories and general assumptions that pervade all cultures because the "givens" provide foci around which and within which the patterns of every culture crystallize. Hence comparison can escape from the bias of any distinct culture by taking as its frame of reference natural limits, conditions, clues, and pressures. Cultural concepts are human artifacts, but the conceptualization of nature is enough bound by stubborn and irreducible fact so that

organisms having the same kind of nervous system will at the very least understand one another, relatively free from arbitrary convention. Hartmann, Kris, and Lowenstein (1951, pp. 13–14) have well joined the various kinds of determinants in this statement from a (tempered) psychoanalytic viewpoint:

The "ubiquity" of certain symbols, particularly of sexual symbols, seems accountable if we keep in mind how fundamentally similar every human infant's situation in the adult world is; how limited the number of meaningful situations is which the infant invests with affect; how typical and invariant the infant's anxieties are, and finally how uniform some of his basic perceptions and bodily sensations are bound to be. The fact that most sexual symbols are related to parts of the body and their function has repeatedly been pointed out. These functions are familiar from a large number of experiences of the child and these experiences themselves are organized in the image of the body, one of the apparatus of the ego. However far the differentiation of human behavior by environmental influences may go, the basic relationship of precepts to parts of the body, of movements to the impulses to caress or hurt, to eliminate or to include, to receive or to retain—at least to these—not only form the basis for the formation of symbols but are equally the basis for the universality of nonverbal communication . . . not only the body is "human"; the fact that the personality is structured, that verbalization is part of the function of the apparatus of all men, that the transition from primary to secondary processes in the child's development, etc., are universal, is bound to influence the formation of symbols. . . . We expect to find "limits" of ubiquity and cultural variations and superimposed symbolic meanings around an ubiquitous core.

. . . Propositions dealing with the oedipus complex imply similar assumptions: the fetalization of the human and the extraordinary dependence of the infant on adult (maternal) care and protection, the development of impulses of a genital order at a time when the child lives among adults, is attached to them and at the same time still totally dependent on them, is the nucleus of a conflict situation which we believe to be universal.

The next step is to organize data and write an ethnography within the framework of the invariant points of reference. The first serious trial will not be easy, but it should be rewarding.

In conclusion, it should be explicitly recognized that this procedure, like any other scientific method, has its cost as well as its gain. In this case, however, the cost would not be greater than in most current practice. This involves abstraction and relative neglect of how the events or patterns described appear or "feel" from the standpoint of participants (cf. Riezler, 1950). It is a question of what MacLeod (1947)[28] has

28. Quoted in Hallowell, *op. cit.*

called "the sociological bias," analogous to the stimulus-receptor bias in the field of perception:

This bias in its most common form involves the acceptance of the structures and processes of society as defined by the sociologist as the true coordinates for the specification of behavior and experience. From this point of view, *e.g.*, the church or the political party in which the individual possesses membership, is regarded as an institution of society, possessing the manifold properties and functions which a many-sided sociological investigation reveals, rather than as the church or political party as it is apprehended and reacted to by the individual. The process of social adjustment, of socialization or of attitude formation thus becomes defined in terms of a set of norms which have reality for the scientific observer, but not necessarily for the individual concerned.

REFERENCES

ABERLE, D.; COHEN, A.; DAVIS, A.; LEVY, M.; and SUTTON, F. 1950. "The Functional Prerequisites of a Society," *Ethics*, LX, No. 2, 100–111.

ALLEE, W. C. 1951. *Cooperation among Animals: With Human Implications.* New York: Henry Schuman.

BATES, MARSTON. 1950. *The Nature of Natural History.* New York: Charles Scribner's Sons.

BERGMAN, R. A. M. 1952. "The Biological Foundations of Society," *Civilisations*, II, No. 1, 1–15.

BOAS, FRANZ. 1911. *Mind of Primitive Man.* New York: Macmillan Co.

———. 1940. "The Origin of Totemism." In his *Race, Language, and Culture*, pp. 316–23. New York: Macmillan Co.

BONAPARTE, MARIE. 1947. *Myths of War.* London: Imago Publishing Co.

EVANS-PRITCHARD, E. E. 1940. *The Nuer.* Oxford: Clarendon Press.

FEI HSIAO-TUNG and CHANG CHIH-I. 1945. *Earthbound China: A Study of Rural Economy in Yünnan.* Chicago: University of Chicago Press.

FIRTH, RAYMOND. 1951. *Elements of Social Organization.* New York: Philosophical Library.

FORD, CLELLAN S., and BEACH, FRANK A. 1951. *Patterns of Sexual Behavior.* New York: Harper & Bros.

FORTES, MEYER. 1949. *The Web of Kinship among the Tallensi.* London: Oxford University Press, for the International African Institute.

HARTMANN, HEINZ; KRIS, ERNST; and LOWENSTEIN, RUDOLPH M. 1951. "Some Psychoanalytic Comments on 'Culture and Personality.'" In *Psychoanalysis and Culture*, pp. 3–31.

HERSKOVITS, MELVILLE. 1948. *Man and His Works.* New York: A. A. Knopf.

HOMANS, GEORGE. 1950. *The Human Group.* New York: Harcourt, Brace & Co.

HSU, FRANCIS L. K. 1948. *Under the Ancestors' Shadow: Chinese Culture and Personality.* New York: Columbia University Press.

JAKOBSON, R. 1949. "On the Identification of Phonemic Entities," *Travaux du Cercle linguistique de Copenhague*, V, 205–13.

JAKOBSON, R.; FANT, C.; and HALLE, M. 1952. *Preliminaries to Speech Analysis.* ("MIT Acoustics Laboratory Technical Reports," No. 13.)

KIDDER, A. V. 1940. "Looking Backward," *Proceedings of the American Philosophical Society,* LXXXIII, No. 4, 527–37.

KLUCKHOHN, CLYDE, and MORGAN, WILLIAM. 1951. "Some Notes on Navaho Dreams." In *Psychoanalysis and Culture,* pp. 120–31.

KLUCKHOHN, FLORENCE. 1950. "Dominant and Substitute Profiles of Cultural Orientations," *Social Forces,* XXVIII, 376–93.

KROEBER, ALFRED L. 1949. "The Concept of Culture in Science," *Journal of General Education,* III, 182–88.

KROEBER, A. L., and KLUCKHOHN, C. 1952. *Culture,* Part III. ("Papers of the Peabody Museum of Harvard University.")

LÉVI-STRAUSS, C. 1951. "Language and the Analysis of Social Laws," *American Anthropologist,* n.s., LIII, No. 2, 155–63.

LINTON, RALPH. 1936. *The Study of Man.* New York: Appleton-Century-Crofts, Inc.

LYND, R. S. 1939. *Knowledge for What?* Princeton: Princeton University Press.

LYND, ROBERT S. and HELEN M. 1929. *Middletown.* New York: Harcourt, Brace & Co.

———. 1937. *Middletown in Transition: A Study in Cultural Conflicts.* New York: Harcourt, Brace & Co.

MACLEOD, ROBERT B. 1947. "The Phenomenological Approach to Social Psychology," *Psychological Review,* LIV, 193–210.

MALINOWSKI, BRONISLAW. 1944. *A Scientific Theory of Culture.* Chapel Hill: University of North Carolina Press.

MURDOCK, G. P. 1940. "The Cross-cultural Survey," *American Sociological Review,* V, No. 3, 361–70.

———. 1945. "The Common Denominator of Cultures." In LINTON, R. (ed.), *The Science of Man in the World Crisis,* pp. 123–42. New York: Columbia University Press.

———. 1949. *Social Structure.* New York: Macmillan Co.

MURDOCK, G. P., *et al.* 1950. *Outline of Cultural Materials.* New Haven: Human Relations Area Files, Inc.

NADEL, S. F. 1951. *The Foundations of Social Anthropology.* Glencoe, Ill.: Free Press.

PARSONS, ELSIE C. 1936. *Mitla: Town of the Souls, and Other Zapoteco-speaking Pueblos of Oaxaca, Mexico.* Chicago: University of Chicago Press.

———. 1945. *Peguche, Canton of Otavalo, Province of Imbabura, Ecuador: A Study of Andean Indians.* Chicago: University of Chicago Press.

PARSONS, T. 1949. *Essays in Sociological Theory.* Glencoe, Ill.: Free Press.

RANK, OTTO. 1914. *The Myth of the Birth of the Hero.* New York: Journal of Nervous and Mental Disease Publishing Co.

REDFIELD, ROBERT. 1941. *The Folk Culture of Yucatan.* Chicago: University of Chicago Press.

RIEZLER, K. 1950. *Man Mutable and Immutable: The Fundamental Structure of Social Life.* Chicago: Henry Regnery.

STEWARD, JULIAN. 1949. "Cultural Causality and Law: A Trial Formulation of the Development of Early Civilization," *American Anthropologist,* n.s., LI, No. 1, 1–27.

———. 1950. *Area Research: Theory and Practice.* (Social Science Research Council Bull. 63.)

WEST, JAMES. 1945. *Plainville, U.S.A.* New York: Columbia University Press.

WIENER, N. 1948. *Cybernetics.* New York: Technology Press, John Wiley & Sons.

WILSON, A. T. M. 1951. *Some Aspects of Social Process.* (*Journal of Social Issues,* Supplementary Ser., No. 5.)

YANG, MARTIN C. 1945. *A Chinese Village: Taitou, Shantung Province.* New York: Columbia University Press.

Social Structure

By CLAUDE LÉVI-STRAUSS

THE TERM "social structure" refers to a group of problems the scope of which appears so wide and the definition so imprecise that it is hardly possible for a paper strictly limited in size to meet them fully. This is reflected in the program of this symposium, in which problems closely related to social structure have been allotted to several papers, such as those on "Style," "Universal Categories of Culture," "Structural Linguistics." These should be read in connection with the present paper.

On the other hand, studies in social structure have to do with the formal aspects of social phenomena; therefore, they are difficult to define, and still more to discuss, without overlapping other fields pertaining to the exact and natural sciences, where problems are similarly set in formal terms or, rather, where the formal expression of different problems admits of the same kind of treatment. As a matter of fact, the main interest of social-structure studies seems to be that they give the anthropologist hope that, thanks to the formalization of his problems, he may borrow methods and types of solutions from disciplines which have gone far ahead of his own in that direction.

Such being the case, it is obvious that the term "social structure" needs first to be defined and that some explanation should be given of the difference which helps to distinguish studies in social structure from the unlimited field of descriptions, analyses, and theories dealing with social relations at large, confounding themselves with the whole scope of social anthropology. This is all the more necessary, since some of those who have contributed toward setting apart social structure as a special field of anthropological studies conceived the former in many different manners and even sometimes, so it seems, came to nurture grave doubts as to the validity of their enterprise. For instance, Kroeber writes in the second edition of his *Anthropology*:

"Structure" appears to be just a yielding to a word that has a perfectly good meaning but suddenly becomes fashionably attractive for a decade or so—like "streamlining"—and during its vogue tends to be applied indiscriminately because of the pleasurable connotations of its sound. Of course a typical personality can be viewed as having a structure. But so can a physiology, any organism, all societies and all cultures, crystals, machines—in fact everything which is not wholly amorphous has a structure. So what "structure" adds to the meaning of our phrase seems to be nothing, except to provoke a degree of pleasant puzzlement" [Kroeber, 1948, p. 325].[1]

Although this passage concerns more particularly the notion of "basic personality structure," it has devastating implications as regards the generalized use of the notion of structure in anthropology.

1. Compare with the statement by the same author: ". . . the term 'social structure' which is tending to replace 'social organization' without appearing to add either content or emphasis of meaning" (1943, p. 105).

Another reason makes a definition of social structure compulsory: from the structuralist point of view which one has to adopt if only to give the problem its meaning, it would be hopeless to try to reach a valid definition of social structure on an inductive basis, by abstracting common elements from the uses and definitions current among all the scholars who claim to have made "social structure" the object of their studies. If these concepts have a meaning at all, they mean, first, that the notion of structure has a structure. This we shall try to outline from the beginning as a precaution against letting ourselves be submerged by a tedious inventory of books and papers dealing with social relations, the mere listing of which would more than exhaust the limited space at our disposal. In a further stage we will have to see how far and in what directions the term "social structure," as used by the different authors, departs from our definition. This will be done in the section devoted to kinship, since the notion of structure has found in that field its main applications and since anthropologists have generally chosen to express their theoretical views also in that connection.

I. DEFINITION AND PROBLEMS OF METHOD

Passing now to the task of defining "social structure," there is a point which should be cleared up immediately. The term "social structure" has nothing to do with empirical reality but with models which are built up after it. This should help one to clarify the difference between two concepts which are so close to each other that they have often been confused, namely, those of *social structure* and of *social relations*. It will be enough to state at this time that social relations consist of the raw materials out of which the models making up the social structure are built, while social structure can, by no means, be reduced to the ensemble of the social relations to be described in a given society.[2] Therefore, social structure cannot claim a field of its own among others in the social studies. It is rather a method to be applied to any kind of social studies, similar to the structural analysis current in other disciplines.

Then the question becomes that of ascertaining what kind of model deserves the name "structure." This is not an anthropological question, but one which belongs to the methodology of science in general. Keeping this in mind, we can say that a structure consists of a model meeting with several requirements.

First, the structure exhibits the characteristics of a system. It is made up of several elements none of which can undergo a change without effecting changes in all the other elements.

In the second place, for any given model there should be a possibility of ordering a series of transformations resulting in a group of models of the same type.

In the third place, the above properties make it possible to predict how the model will react if one or more of its elements are submitted to certain modifications.

And, last, the model should be constituted so as to make immediately intelligible all the observed facts.[3]

2. The same idea appears to underlie E. R. Leach's remarkable study, "Jinghpaw Kinship Terminology" (1945).

3. Compare Von Neumann: "Such models (as games) are theoretical constructs with a precise, exhaustive and not too complicated definition; and they must be similar to reality in those respects which are essential to the investigation at hand. To recapitulate in detail: The definition must be precise and exhaustive in order to make a mathematical treatment possible. The construct must not be unduly complicated so that the mathematical treatment can be brought beyond the mere formalism to the point where it yields complete numerical results. Similarity to reali-

These being the requirements for any model with structural value, several consequences follow. These, however, do not pertain to the definition of structure but have to do with the main properties exhibited by, and problems raised by, structural analysis when contemplated in the social and other fields.

A) OBSERVATION AND EXPERIMENTATION

Great care should be taken to distinguish between the observation and the experiment levels. To observe facts and elaborate methodological devices permitting of constructing models out of these facts is not at all the same thing as to experiment on the models. By "experimenting on models," we mean the set of procedures aiming at ascertaining how a given model will react when submitted to change and at comparing models of the same or different types. This distinction is all the more necessary, since many discussions on social structure revolve around the apparent contradiction between the concreteness and individuality of ethnological data and the abstract and formal character generally exhibited by structural studies. This contradiction disappears as one comes to realize that these features belong to two entirely different planes, or rather two stages of the same process. On the observational level, the main—one could almost say the only—rule is that all the facts should be carefully observed and described, without allowing any theoretical preconception to decide whether some are more important and others less. This rule implies, in turn, that facts should be studied in relation to themselves (by what kind of concrete process did they come into being?) and in relation to

the whole (always aiming to relate each modification which can be observed in a sector to the global situation in which it first appeared).

This rule together with its corollaries has been explicitly formulated by K. Goldstein (1951, pp. 18–25) in relation to psychophysiological studies, and it may be considered valid for any kind of structural analysis. Its immediate consequence is that, far from being contradictory, there is a direct relationship between the detail and concreteness of ethnographical description and the validity and generality of the model which is constructed after it. For, though many models may be used as convenient devices to describe and explain the phenomena, it is obvious that the best model will always be that which is *true*, that is, the simplest possible model which, while being extracted exclusively from the facts under consideration, also makes it possible to account for all of them. Therefore, the first task is to ascertain what those facts are.

B) CONSCIOUSNESS AND UNCONSCIOUSNESS

A second distinction has to do with the conscious or unconscious character of the models. In the history of structural thought, Boas may be credited with having introduced this distinction. He made clear that a category of facts can more easily yield to structural analysis when the social group in which they are manifested has not elaborated a conscious model to interpret or justify them (e.g., 1911, p. 67). Some readers may be surprised to find Boas' name quoted in connection with structural theory, since he was often described as one of the main obstacles in its path. But this writer has tried to demonstrate that Boas' shortcomings in matters of structural studies were not in his failure to understand their importance and significance, which he did, as a matter of fact, in the most prophetic way. They

---

ty is needed to make the operation significant. And this similarity must usually be restricted to a few traits deemed 'essential' *pro tempore* —since otherwise the above requirements would conflict with each other" (Von Neumann and Morgenstern, 1944).

rather resulted from the fact that he imposed on structural studies conditions of validity, some of which will remain forever part of their methodology, while some others are so exacting and impossible to meet that they would have withered scientific development in any field (Lévi-Strauss, 1949*a*).

A structural model may be conscious or unconscious without this difference affecting its nature. It can only be said that when the structure of a certain type of phenomena does not lie at a great depth, it is more likely that some kind of model, standing as a screen to hide it, will exist in the collective consciousness. For conscious models, which are usually known. as "norms," are by definition very poor ones, since they are not intended to explain the phenomena but to perpetuate them. Therefore, structural analysis is confronted with a strange paradox well known to the linguist, that is: the more obvious structural organization is, the more difficult it becomes to reach it because of the inaccurate conscious models lying across the path which leads to it.

From the point of view of the degree of consciousness, the anthropologist is confronted with two kinds of situations. He may have to construct a model from phenomena the systematic character of which has evoked no awareness on the part of the culture; this is the kind of simpler situation referred to by Boas as providing the easiest ground for anthropological research. Or else the anthropologist will be dealing, on the one hand, with raw phenomena and, on the other, with the models already constructed by the culture to interpret the former. Though it is likely that, for the reason stated above, these models will prove unsatisfactory, it is by no means necessary that this should always be the case. As a matter of fact, many "primitive" cultures have built models of their marriage regulations which are much more to the point than models built by professional anthropologists.[4] Thus one cannot dispense with studying a culture's "home-made" models for two reasons. First, these models might prove to be accurate or, at least, to provide some insight into the structure of the phenomena; after all, each culture has its own theoreticians whose contributions deserve the same attention as that which the anthropologist gives to colleagues. And, second, even if the models are biased or erroneous, the very bias and types of errors are a part of the facts under study and probably rank among the most significant ones. But even when taking into consideration these culturally produced models, the anthropologist does not forget—as he has sometimes been accused of doing (Firth, 1951, pp. 28–31)—that the cultural norms are not of themselves structures. Rather, they furnish an important contribution to an understanding of the structures, either as factual documents or as theoretical contributions similar to those of the anthropologist himself.

This point has been given great attention by the French sociological school. Durkheim and Mauss, for instance, have always taken care to substitute, as a starting point for the survey of native categories of thought, the conscious representations prevailing among the natives themselves for those grown out of the anthropologist's own culture. This was undoubtedly an important step, which, nevertheless, fell short of its goal because these authors were not sufficiently aware that native conscious representations, important as they are, may be just as remote from the unconscious reality as any other (Lévi-Strauss, 1951).

C) STRUCTURE AND MEASURE

It is often believed that one of the main interests of the notion of structure is to permit the introduction of meas-

4. For examples and detailed discussion see Lévi-Strauss (1949*b*, pp. 558 ff.).

urement in social anthropology. This view was favored by the frequent appearance of mathematical or semimathematical aids in books or articles dealing with social structure. It is true that in some cases structural analysis has made it possible to attach numerical values to invariants. This was, for instance, the result of Kroeber's studies of women's dress fashions, a landmark in structural research (Richardson and Kroeber, 1940), as well as of a few other studies which will be discussed below.

However, one should keep in mind that there is no necessary connection between *measure* and *structure*. Structural studies are, in the social sciences, the indirect outcome of modern developments in mathematics which have given increasing importance to the qualitative point of view in contradistinction to the quantitative point of view of traditional mathematics. Therefore, it has become possible, in fields such as mathematical logic, set-theory, group-theory, and topology, to develop a rigorous approach to problems which do not admit of a metrical solution. The outstanding achievements in this connection—which offer themselves as springboards not yet utilized by social scientists—are to be found in J. von Neumann and O. Morgenstern, *Theory of Games and Economic Behavior* (1944); N. Wiener, *Cybernetics* (1948); and C. Shannon and W. Weaver, *The Mathematical Theory of Communication* (1950).

D) MECHANICAL MODELS AND
STATISTICAL MODELS

A last distinction refers to the relation between the scale of the model and that of the phenomena. According to the nature of these phenomena, it becomes possible or impossible to build a model, the elements of which are on the same scale as the phenomena themselves. A model the elements of which are on the same scale as the phenomena will be called a "mechanical model"; when the elements of the model are on a different scale, we will be dealing with a "statistical model." The laws of marriage provide the best illustration of this difference. In primitive societies these laws can be expressed in models calling for actual grouping of the individuals according to kin or clan; these are mechanical models. No such distribution exists in our own society, where types of marriage are determined by the size of the primary and secondary groups to which prospective mates belong, social fluidity, amount of information, and the like. A satisfactory (though yet untried) attempt to formulate the invariants of our marriage system would therefore have to determine average values—thresholds; it would be a statistical model. There may be intermediate forms between these two. Such is the case in societies which (as even our own) have a mechanical model to determine prohibited marriages and rely on a statistical model for those which are permissible. It should also be kept in mind that the same phenomena may admit of different models, some mechanical and some statistical, according to the way in which they are grouped together and with other phenomena. A society which recommends cross-cousin marriage but where this ideal marriage type occurs only with limited frequency needs, in order that the system may be properly explained, both a mechanical and a statistical model, as was well understood by Forde (1941) and Elwin (1947).

It should also be kept in mind that what makes social-structure studies valuable is that structures are models, the formal properties of which can be compared independently of their elements. The structuralist's task is thus to recognize and isolate levels of reality which have strategic value from his point of view, namely, which admit of representation as models, whatever their kind. It often happens that the same data may be considered from different perspectives embodying equal strategic values, though the resulting models will be in some cases mechanical and in others statistical. This situation is well known in the exact and natural sciences; for instance, the theory of a small number of physical bodies belongs to classical mechanics, but if the number of bodies becomes greater, then one should rely on the laws of thermodynamics, that is, use a statistical model instead of a mechanical one, though the nature of the data remains the same in both cases.

The same situation prevails in the human and the social sciences. If one takes a phenomenon like, for instance, suicide, it can be studied on two different levels. First, it is possible by studying individual situations to establish what may be called mechanical models of suicide, taking into account in each case the personality of the victim, his or her life-history, the characteristics of the primary and secondary groups in which he or she developed, and the like; or else one can build models of a statistical nature, by recording suicide frequency over a certain period of time in one or more societies and in different types of primary and secondary groups, etc. These would be levels at which the structural study of suicide carries a strategic value, that is, where it becomes possible to build models which may be compared (1) for different types of suicides, (2) for different societies, and (3) for different types of social phenomena. Scientific progress consists not only in discovering new invariants belonging to those levels but also in discovering new levels where the study of the same phenomena offers the same strategical value. Such a result was achieved, for instance, by psychoanalysis, which discovered the means to lay out models in a new field, that of the psychological life of the patient considered as a whole.

The foregoing should help to make clear the dual (and at first sight almost contradictory) nature of structural studies. On the one hand, they aim at isolating strategic levels, and this can be achieved only by "carving out" a certain family of phenomena. From that point of view, each type of structural study appears autonomous, entirely independent of all the others and even of different methodological approaches to the same field. On the other hand, the essential value of these studies is to construct models the formal properties of which can be compared with, and explained by, the same properties as in models corresponding to other strategic levels. Thus it may be said that their ultimate end is to override traditional boundaries between different disciplines and to promote a true interdisciplinary approach.

An example may be given. A great deal of discussion has taken place lately about the difference between history and anthropology, and Kroeber and others have made clear that the time-dimension has very little importance in this connection. From what has been stated above, one can see exactly where the difference lies, not only between these two disciplines but also between them and others. Ethnography and history differ from social anthropology and sociology, inasmuch as the former two aim at gathering data, while the latter two deal with models constructed from these data. Similarly, ethnography and social anthropology correspond to two different stages in the same research, the ultimate result of which is to construct mechanical models, while history (together with its so-called "auxiliary" disciplines) and sociology end ultimately in statistical models. This is the reason why the social sciences, though having to do—

all of them—with the time-dimension, nevertheless deal with two different categories of time. Anthropology uses a "mechanical" time, reversible and non-cumulative. For instance, the model of, let us say, a patrilineal kinship system does not in itself show whether or not the system has always remained patrilineal, or has been preceded by a matrilineal form, or by any number of shifts from patrilineal to matrilineal and vice versa. On the contrary, historical time is "statistical"; it always appears as an oriented and nonreversible process. An evolution which would take back contemporary Italian society to that of the Roman Republic is as impossible to conceive of as is the reversibility of the processes belonging to the second law of thermodynamics.

This discussion helps to clarify Firth's distinction between social structure, which he conceives as outside the time-dimension, and social organization, where time re-enters (1951, p. 40). Also in this connection, the debate which has been going on for the past few years between followers of the Boasian antievolutionist tradition and of Professor Leslie White (1949) may become better understood. The Boasian school has been mainly concerned with models of a mechanical type, and from this point of view the concept of evolution has no operational value. On the other hand, it is certainly legitimate to speak of evolution in a historical and socio-logical sense, but the elements to be organized into an evolutionary process cannot be borrowed from the level of a cultural typology which consists of mechanical models. They should be sought at a sufficiently deep level to insure that these elements will remain unaffected by different cultural contexts (as, let us say, genes are identical elements combined into different patterns corresponding to the different racial [statistical] models) and can ac-cordingly permit of drawing long statistical runs.

A great deal of inconvenience springs from a situation which obliges the social scientist to "shift" time, according to the kind of study he is contemplating. Natural scientists, who have got used to this difficulty, are making efforts to overcome it. Very important in this connection is Murdock's contention that while a patrilineal system may replace, or grow out of, a matrilineal system, the opposite process cannot take place (1949, pp. 210–20). If this were true, a vectorial factor would for the first time be introduced on an objective basis into social structure. Murdock's demonstration was, however, challenged by Lowie (1948a, pp. 44 ff.) on methodological grounds, and for the time being it is impossible to do more than to call attention to a moot problem, the solution of which, when gen-erally accepted, will have a tremendous bearing upon structural studies, not only in the field of anthropology but in other fields as well.

The distinction between mechanical and statistical models has also become fundamental in another respect: it makes it possible to clarify the role of the comparative method in structural studies. This method was greatly em-phasized by both Radcliffe-Brown and Lowie. The former writes (1952, p. 14):

Theoretical sociology is commonly re-garded as an inductive science, induction being the logical method of inference by which we arrive at general propositions from the consideration of particular in-stances. Although Professor Evans-Pritch-ard . . . seems to imply in some of his statements that the logical method of in-duction, using comparison, classification and generalization, is not applicable to the phenomena of human social life . . . I hold that social anthropology must depend on systematic comparative studies of many so-cieties.

Writing about religion, he states (1945, p. 1):

The experimental method of social religion ... means that we must study in the light of our hypothesis a sufficient number of diverse particular religions or religious cults in relation to the particular societies in which they are found. This is a task not for one person but for a number.

Similarly, Lowie, after pointing out (1948a, p. 38) that "the literature of anthropology is full of alleged correlations which lack empirical support," insists on the need of a "broad inductive basis" for generalization (1948a, p. 68). It is interesting to note that by this claim for inductive support these authors dissent not only from Durkheim (1912, p. 593): "when a law has been proved by a well performed experiment, this law is valid universally," but also from Goldstein, who, as already mentioned, has lucidly expressed what may be called "the rules of structuralist method" in a way general enough to make them valid outside the more limited field in which they were first applied by their author. Goldstein remarks that the need to make a thorough study of each case implies that the amount of cases to be studied should be small; and he proceeds by raising the question whether or not the risk exists that the cases under consideration may be special ones, allowing no general conclusions about the others. He answers (1951, p. 25): "This objection completely misunderstands the real situation . . . an accumulation of facts even numerous is of no help if these facts were imperfectly established; it does not lead to the knowledge of things as they really happen. . . . We must choose only these cases which permit of formulating final judgments. And then, what is true for one case will also be true for any other."

Probably very few anthropologists would be ready to support these bold statements. However, no structuralist study may be undertaken without a clear awareness of Goldstein's dilemma: either to study many cases in a superficial and in the end ineffective way; or to limit one's self to a thorough study of a small number of cases, thus proving that, in the end, one well-done experiment is sufficient to make a demonstration.

Now the reason for so many anthropologists' faithfulness to the comparative method may be sought in some sort of confusion between the procedures used to establish mechanical and statistical models. While Durkheim's and Goldstein's position undoubtedly holds true for the former, it is obvious that no statistical model can be achieved without statistics, i.e., by gathering a large amount of data. But in this case the method is no more comparative than in the other, since the data to be collected will be acceptable only in so far as they are all of the same kind. Therefore, we remain confronted with only one alternative, namely, to make a thorough study of one case. The real difference lies in the selection of the "case," which will be patterned so as to include elements which are either on the same scale as the model to be constructed or on a different scale.

After having thus clarified these basic questions revolving around the nature of studies in social structure, it becomes possible to make an inventory of the main fields of inquiry and to discuss some of the results achieved so far.

II. SOCIAL MORPHOLOGY OR GROUP STRUCTURE

In this section, "group" is not intended to mean the social group but, in a more general sense, the way according to which the phenomena under study are grouped together.

The object of social-structure studies is to understand social relations with the aid of models. Now it is impossible to conceive of social relations outside a common frame. Space and time are the two frames we use to situate social relations, either alone or together. These space- and time-dimensions are not the same as the analogous ones used by other disciplines but consist of a "social" space and of a "social" time, meaning that they have no properties outside those which derive from the properties of the social phenomena which "furnish" them. According to their social structure, human societies have elaborated many types of such "continuums," and there should be no undue concern on the part of the anthropologist that, in the course of his studies, he may temporarily have to borrow types widely different from the existing patterns and eventually to evolve new ones.

We have already noticed that the time-continuum may be reversible or oriented in accordance with the level of reality embodying strategical value from the point of view of the research at hand. Many other possibilities may arise: the time-dimension can be conceived of as independent from the observer and unlimited or as a function of the observer's own (biological) time and limited; it may be considered as consisting of parts which are, or are not, homologous with one another, etc. Evans-Pritchard has shown how such formal properties underlie the qualitative distinctions between the observer's life-span, history, legend, and myth (1939, 1940). And his basic distinctions have been found to be valid for contemporary societies (Bernot and Blancard, MS).

What is true of the time-dimension applies equally well to space. It has been Durkheim's and Mauss's great merit to call attention for the first time to the variable properties of space which should be called upon in order to understand properly the structure of several primitive societies (1901–2). In this undertaking they received their inspiration from the work of Cushing, which it has become fashionable in recent years to belittle. However, Cushing's insight and sociological imagination make him deserving of a seat on Morgan's right, as one of the great forerunners of social-structure studies. The gaps and inaccuracies in his descriptions, less serious than the indictment of having "over-interpreted" some of his material, will be viewed in their true proportions when it is realized that, albeit in an unconscious fashion, Cushing was aiming less at giving an actual description of Zuni society than at elaborating a model (his famous seven fold division) which could explain most of its processes and structure.

Social time and space should also be characterized according to scale. There is in social studies a "macro-time" and a "micro-time"; the same distinction applies also to space. This explains how social structure may have to do with prehistory, archeology, and diffusion processes as well as with psychological topology, such as that initiated by Lewin or by Moreno's sociometry. As a matter of fact, structures of the same type may exist on quite different time and space levels, and it is far from inconceivable that, for instance, a statistical model resulting from sociometrical studies might be of greater help in building a similar model in the field of the history of cultures than an apparently more direct approach would have permitted.

Therefore, historicogeographical concerns should not be excluded from the field of structural studies, as was generally implied by the widely accepted opposition between "diffusionism" and "functionalism."[5] A functionalist may be far from a structuralist, as is clearly

5. Never accepted by Lowie; see the Preface in Lowie (1920).

shown by the example of Malinowski. On the other hand, undertakings such as those of G. Dumézil,[6] as well as A. L. Kroeber's personal case of a highly structure-minded scholar devoting most of his time to distribution studies, are proofs that even history can be approached in a structural way.

Since synchronic studies raise fewer problems than diachronic ones (the data being more homogeneous in the first case), the simplest morphological studies are those having to do with the qualitative, nonmeasurable properties of social space, that is, the way according to which social phenomena can be situated on a map and the regularities exhibited in their configurations. Much might have been expected from the researches of the so-called "Chicago school" dealing with urban ecology, and the reasons for the gradual loss of interest along this line of research are not altogether clear. It has to do mostly with ecology, which was made the subject of another paper in this symposium. However, it is not inappropriate to state at this point what kind of relationship prevails between ecology, on the one hand, and social structure, on the other. Both have to do with the spatial distribution of phenomena. But social structure deals exclusively with those "spaces" the determinations of which are of a purely sociological nature, that is, not affected by natural determinants, such as geology, climatology, physiography, and the like. This is the reason why so-called "urban ecology" should have held great interest for the social anthropologist; the urban space is small enough and homogeneous enough (from every point of view except the social one) for all its differential qualitative aspects to be assigned mostly to the action of internal forces accessible to structural sociology.

It would perhaps have been wiser, instead of starting with complex com-

6. These researches were summarized by their author in Dumézil (1949).

munities hard to isolate from external influences, to approach first—as suggested by Marcel Mauss (1924–25)—those small and relatively isolated communities with which the anthropologist usually deals. A few such studies may be found (e.g., Firth, 1936; Steward, 1938; Nadel, 1947; Forde, 1950), but they rarely and then reluctantly go beyond the descriptive stage. There have been practically no attempts to correlate the spatial configurations with the formal properties of the other aspects of social life.

This is much to be regretted, since in many parts of the world there is an obvious relationship between the social structure and the spatial structure of settlements, villages, or camps. To limit ourselves to America, the camp shapes of Plains Indians have for long demanded attention by virtue of regular variations connected with the social organization of each tribe; and the same holds true for the circular disposition of huts in Gê villages of eastern and central Brazil. In both cases we are dealing with relatively homogeneous cultural areas where important series of concomitant variations may be observed. Another kind of problem results from the comparison of areas where different types of village structures may be compared to different types of social relations, e.g., the circular village structure of the Gê and the parallel-layers structure of the Pueblo. The latter could even be studied diachronically with the archeologist's help, which would raise questions such as the eventual linkage of the transition from semicircular structures to parallel ones, with the shift of village sites from valley to mesa top, of structural distribution of clan houses suggested by many myths to the present-day statistical one, etc.

These few examples are not intended to prove that spatial configuration is the mirror-image of social organization but to call attention to the fact that, while among numerous peoples it would be extremely difficult to discover any such relation, among others (who must accordingly have something in common) the existence of a relation is evident, though unclear, and in a third group spatial configuration seems to be almost a projective representation of the social structure. But even the most striking cases call for a critical study; for example, this writer has attempted to demonstrate that, among the Bororo, spatial configuration reflects not the true, unconscious social organization but a model existing consciously in the native mind, though its nature is entirely illusory and even contradictory to reality.[7] Problems of this kind (which are raised not only by the consideration of relatively durable spatial configurations but also in regard to recurrent temporary ones, such as those shown in dance, ritual, etc.) offer an opportunity to study social and mental processes through objective and crystallized external projections of them.

Another approach which may lead more directly to a mathematical expression of social phenomena starts with the numerical properties of human groups. This has traditionally been the field of demography, but it is only recently that a few scholars coming from different horizons—demography, sociology, anthropology—have begun to elaborate a kind of qualitative demography, that is, dealing no longer with continuous variations within human groups selected for empirical reasons but with significant discontinuities evidenced in the behavior of groups considered as wholes and chosen on the basis of these discontinuities. This "socio-demography," as it was called by one of its proponents (De Lestrange, 1951), is

7. C. Lévi-Strauss, "Les Structures sociales dans le Brésil central et oriental," in Sol Tax (ed.), *Indian Tribes of Aboriginal America: Selected Papers of the XXIXth Congress of Americanists* (Chicago: University of Chicago Press, 1952).

"on a level" with social anthropology, and it is not difficult to foresee that in the very near future it will be called upon to provide firm grounds for any kind of anthropological research. Therefore, it is surprising that so little attention was paid in anthropological circles to the study by a demographer, L. Livi, of the formal properties characteristic of the smallest possible size of a group compatible with its existence as a group (1940–41, 1949). His researches, closely connected with G. Dahlberg's, are all the more important for anthropologists, in that the latter usually deal with populations very near Livi's minimum. There is an obvious relation between the functioning and even the durability of the social structure and the actual size of the population (Wagley, 1940). It is thus becoming increasingly evident that formal properties exist which are immediately and directly attached to the absolute size of the population, whatever the group under consideration. These should be the first to be assessed and taken into account in an interpretation of other properties.

Next come numerical properties expressing not the group size taken globally but the size and interaction of subsets of the group which can be defined by significant discontinuities. Two lines of inquiry should be mentioned in this connection.

There is, first, the vast body of researches deriving from the famous "rank-size rule" for cities, which has proved to be applicable in many other social fields, though the original rule remains somewhat controversial (see Davis, 1947; Stewart, 1947; Zipf, 1949).

Of a much more direct bearing on current anthropological research is the recent work of two French demographers, who, by using Dahlberg's demonstration that the size of an isolate (i.e., a group of intermarrying people) can be computed from the frequency of marriages between cross-cousins (Dahlberg, 1948), have succeeded in computing the average size of isolates in all French *departements*, thus throwing open to anthropological investigation the marriage system of a complex modern society (Sutter and Tabah, 1951). The average size of the French isolate varies from less than 1,000 to over 2,800 individuals. This numerical evaluation shows that, even in a modern society, the network of people united by kinship ties is much smaller than might be expected, of about the same size as in primitive groups. The inference is that, while the absolute size of the intermarrying group remains approximately on the same scale in all human societies (the proportion of the French types in relation to the average primitive types being about 10 to 1), a complex society becomes such not so much because of an expansion of the isolate itself as on account of an expansion of other types of social links (economic, political, intellectual); and these are used to connect a great number of isolates which, by themselves, remain relatively static.

But the most striking result of this research is the discovery that the smallest isolates are found not only in mountain areas, as was expected, but also (and even more) in areas including a large urban center; the following *departements:* Rhône (Lyon), Gironde (Bordeaux), and Seine (Paris) are at the bottom of the list, with the size of their isolates respectively 740, 910, and, 930. In the Seine *departement*, which is practically reduced to Paris and suburbs, the frequency of consanguineous marriages is higher than in any of the fifteen rural *departements* which surround it (Sutter and Tabah, 1951, p. 489).

It is not necessary to emphasize the bearing of such studies on social structure; the main fact, from the point of view of this paper, is that they at the same time make possible and call for an immediate extension on the anthropological level. An approach has been found which enables one to break down a modern complex society into smaller units which are of the same nature as those commonly studied by anthropologists; on the other hand, this approach remains incomplete, since the absolute size of the isolate is only a part of the phenomenon, the other one, equally important, being the length of the marriage cycles. For a small isolate may admit of long marriage cycles (that is, tending to be of the same size as the isolate itself), while a relatively large isolate can be made up of shorter cycles. This problem, which could be solved only with the help of genealogies, points the way toward close cooperation between the structural demographer and the social anthropologist.

Another contribution, this time on a theoretical level, may be expected from this co-operation. The concept of isolate may help to solve a problem in social structure which has given rise to a controversy between Radcliffe-Brown and Lowie. The former has labeled as "a fantastic reification of abstraction" the suggestion made by some anthropologists, mostly in America, that anthropology should be defined as the study not of society but of culture. To him, "European culture is an abstraction and so is the culture of an African tribe." All that exists is human beings connected by an unlimited series of social relations (Radcliffe-Brown, 1940*b*, pp. 10–11). This, Lowie says, is "a factitious quarrel" (1942, pp. 520–21). However, the misunderstandings which lie at its root appear to be very real, since they were born all over again on the occasion of the publication of a book by White (1949) and its criticism by Bidney (1950, pp. 518–19; see also Radcliffe-Brown, 1949*b*).

It seems that both the reality and the

autonomy of the concept of culture could better be validated if culture were, from an operational point of view, treated in the same way as the geneticist and demographer do for the closely allied concept of "isolate." What is called a "culture" is a fragment of humanity which, from the point of view of the research at hand and of the scale on which it is being carried out, presents, in relation to the rest of humanity, significant discontinuities. If our aim is to ascertain significant discontinuities between, let us say, North America and Europe, then we are dealing with two different cultures; but should we become concerned with significant discontinuities between New York and Chicago, we would be allowed to speak of these two groups as different cultural "units." Since these discontinuities can be reduced to invariants, which is the goal of structural analysis, one sees that culture may, at the same time, correspond to an objective reality and be a function of the kind of research undertaken. Accordingly, the same set of individuals may be considered to be parts of many different cultural contexts: universal, continental, national, provincial, parochial, etc., as well as familial, professional, confessional, political, etc. This is true as a limit; however, anthropologists usually reserve the term "culture" to designate a group of discontinuities which has significance on several of these levels at the same time. That it can never be valid for all levels does not prevent the concept of "culture" from being as fundamental for the anthropologist as that of "isolate" for the demographer. Both belong to the same epistemological family. On a question such as that of the positive character of a concept, the anthropologist can rely on a physicist's judgment; it is Niels Bohr who states (1939, p. 9) that "the traditional differences of [human cultures] in many ways resemble the dif-ferent equivalent modes in which physical experience can be described."

III. SOCIAL STATICS OR COMMUNICATION STRUCTURES

A society consists of individuals and groups which communicate with one another. The existence of, or lack of, communication can never be defined in an absolute manner. Communication does not cease at society's borders. These borders, rather, constitute thresholds where the rate and forms of communication, without waning altogether, reach a much lower level. This condition is usually meaningful enough for the population, both inside and outside the borders, to become aware of it. This awareness is not, however, a prerequisite for the definition of a given society. It only accompanies the more precise and stable forms.

In any society, communication operates on three different levels: communication of women, communication of goods and services, communication of messages. Therefore, kinship studies, economics, and linguistics approach the same kinds of problems on different strategic levels and really pertain to the same field. Theoretically at least, it might be said that kinship and marriage rules regulate a fourth type of communication, that of genes between phenotypes. Therefore, it should be kept in mind that culture does not consist exclusively of forms of communication of its own, like language, but also (and perhaps mostly) of *rules* stating how the "games of communication" should be played both on the natural and on the cultural level.

The above comparison between the fields of kinship, economics, and linguistics cannot hide the fact that they refer to forms of communication which are on a different scale. Should one try to compute the communication rate involved, on the one hand, in the intermarriages and, on the other, in the exchange of messages going on in a given society, one would probably discover the difference to be of about the same magnitude as, let us say, that between the exchange of heavy molecules of two viscous liquids through a not too permeable film, and radio communication. Thus, from marriage to language one passes from low- to high-speed communication; this comes from the fact that what is communicated in marriage is almost of the same nature as those who communicate (women, on the one hand, men, on the other), while speakers of language are not of the same nature as their utterances. The opposition is thus one of *person* to *symbol*, or of *value* to *sign*. This helps to clarify economics' somewhat intermediate position between these two extremes—goods and services are not persons, but they still are values. And, though neither symbols nor signs, they require symbols or signs to succeed in being exchanged when the exchange system reaches a certain degree of complexity.

From this outline of the structure of social communication derive three important sets of considerations.

First, the position of economics in social structure may be precisely defined. Economics in the past has been suspect among anthropologists. Even in this symposium, no paper was explicitly assigned to economic problems. Yet, whenever this highly important topic has been broached, a close relationship has been shown to prevail between economic pattern and social structure. Since Mauss's pioneer papers (1904–5, 1923–24) and Malinowski's book on the *kula* (1922)—by far his masterpiece—every attempt in this direction has shown that the economic system provides sociological formulations with some of their more fundamental invariants (Speck, 1915; Richards, 1932, 1936, 1939; Steward, 1938;

Evans-Pritchard, 1940; Herskovits, 1940; Wittfogel and Goldfrank, 1943).

The anthropologist's reluctance originated in the condition of economic studies themselves; these were ridden with conflicts between bitterly opposed schools and at the same time bathed in an aura of mystery and conceit. Thus the anthropologist labored under the impression that economics dealt mostly with abstractions and that there was little connection between the actual life of actual groups of people and such notions as value, utility, profit, and the like.

The complete upheaval of economic studies resulting from the publication of Von Neumann and Morgenstern's book (1944) ushers in an era of closer co-operation between the economist and the anthropologist, and for two reasons. First—though economics achieves here a rigorous approach—this book deals not with abstractions such as those just mentioned but with concrete individuals and groups which are represented in their actual and empirical relations of co-operation and competition. Next—and as a consequence—it introduces for the first time mechanical models which are of the same type as, and intermediate between, those used in mathematical physics and in social anthropology—especially in the field of kinship. In this connection it is striking that Von Neumann's models are borrowed from the theory of games, a line of thought which was initiated independently by Kroeber when he compared social institutions "to the play of earnest children" (1942, p. 215). There is, true enough, an important difference between games of entertainment and marriage rules: the former are constructed in such a way as to permit each player to extract from statistical regularities maximal differential values, while marriage rules, acting in the opposite direction, aim at establishing statistical regularities in spite of the differential values existing between individuals and generations. In this sense they constitute a special kind of "upturned game." Nevertheless, they can be treated with the same methods. Besides, such being the rules, each individual and group tries to play it in the "normal" way, that is, by maximizing his own advantages at the expense of the others (i.e., to get more wives or better ones, whether from the aesthetic, erotic, or economic point of view). The theory of courtship is thus a part of formal sociology. To those who are afraid that sociology might in this way get hopelessly involved in individual psychology, it will be enough to recall that Von Neumann has succeeded in giving a mathematical demonstration of the nature and strategy of a psychological technique as sophisticated as bluffing at the game of poker (Von Neumann and Morgenstern, 1944, pp. 186–219).

The next advantage of this increasing consolidation of social anthropology, economics, and linguistics into one great field, that of communication, is to make clear that they consist exclusively of the study of *rules* and have little concern with the nature of the partners (either individuals or groups) whose play is being patterned after these rules. As Von Neumann puts it (*op. cit.*, p. 49): "The game is simply the totality of the rules which describe it." Besides that of game, other operational notions are those of play, move, choice, and strategy. But the nature of the players need not be considered. What is important is to find out when a given player can make a choice and when he cannot.

This outlook should open the study of kinship and marriage to approaches directly derived from the theory of communication. In the terminology of this theory it is possible to speak of the information of a marriage system by the number of choices at the observer's disposal to define the marriage status of an individual. Thus the information is unity for a dual exogamous system, and, in an Australian kind of kinship typology, it would increase with the logarithm of the number of matrimonial classes. A theoretical system where everybody could marry everybody would be a system with no redundancy, since each marriage choice would not be determined by previous choices, while the positive content of marriage rules constitutes the redundancy of the system under consideration. By studying the percentage of "free" choices in a matrimonial population (not absolutely free, but in relation to certain postulated conditions), it would thus become possible to offer numerical estimates of its entropy, both absolute and relative.

As a consequence, it would become possible to translate statistical models into mechanical ones and vice versa, thus bridging the gap still existing between population studies, on the one hand, and anthropological ones, on the other, thereby laying a foundation for foresight and action. To give an example, in our own society the organization of marriage choices does not go beyond (1) the prohibition of near kin, (2) the size of the isolate, and (3) the accepted standard of behavior, which limits the frequency of certain choices inside the isolate. With these data at hand, one could compute the information of the system, that is, translate our loosely organized and highly statistical marriage system into a mechanical model, thus making possible its comparison with the large series of marriage systems of a "mechanical" type available from simpler societies. Similarly, a great deal of discussion has been carried on recently about the Murngin kinship system, which has been treated by different authors as a 7-class system, or less than 7, or 4, or 32 (Warner, 1930–31; Lévi-Strauss, 1949*b*; Lawrence and Murdock, 1949; Radcliffe-Brown, 1951; Elkin, personal correspondence). By getting a good statistical run of actual marriage choices among other excluded possibilities, one could get at a "true" solution. This conception of a class system as a device to reduce the amount of information required to define several hundred kinship statuses was clearly outlined at first by Professor Lloyd Warner (1937b).

In the preceding pages an attempt has been made to assess the bearing of some recent lines of mathematical research upon anthropological studies. We have seen that their main contribution was to provide anthropology with a unifying concept—communication—enabling it to consolidate widely different types of inquiry into one and at the same time providing the theoretical and methodological tools to further knowledge in that direction. The question which should now be raised is: To what extent is social anthropology ready to make use of these tools?

The main feature of the development of social anthropology in the past years has been the increased attention to kinship. This is, indeed, not a new phenomenon, since it can be said that, with his *Systems of Consanguinity and Affinity of the Human Family*, Lewis Morgan's genius at one and the same time founded social anthropology and kinship studies and brought forward the basic reasons for attaching such importance to the latter: permanency, systematic character, continuity of changes (1871). The views outlined in the preceding pages may help to explain this fundamental interest in kinship, since we have considered it as the anthropologist's own and privileged share in the science of communication. But, even if this interpretation were not accepted by all, the fact of the enormous development of kinship studies cannot be denied. It has recently been assessed in various works (Lowie, 1948a;

Murdock, 1949; Spoehr, 1950). The latest to appear (Radcliffe-Brown and Forde, 1950) has brought together a tremendous wealth of information. Chapters such as Forde's and Nadel's have added the final stroke to unilineal interpretations. However, one may be permitted to regret that the different outlooks of the contributors, their failure to get together and try to extract from their data a small set of significant variations, might become responsible for discouraging potential field workers instead of clearly showing them the purpose of such studies.

Unfortunately, the amount of usable material in relation to that actually collected remains small. This is clearly reflected in the fact that, in order to undertake his survey, Murdock found it possible to retain information concerning no more than about 250 societies (from our point of view, a still overindulgent estimate) out of the 3,000 to 4,000 distinct societies still in existence (Ford and Beach, 1951, p. 5); an attempt to add material valid on a diachronic level would considerably increase the last number. It is somewhat disheartening that the enormous work devoted in the last fifty years to the gathering of ethnographic material has yielded so little, while kinship has been one of the main concerns of those undertaking them.

However, it should be kept in mind that what has brought about this unhappy result is not a lack of coverage—on the contrary. If the workable material is small, it is rather on account of the inductive illusion: it was believed that as many cultures as possible should be covered, albeit lightly, rather than a few thoroughly enough to yield significant results. Accordingly, there is no lack of consistency in the fact that, following their individual temperaments, anthropologists have preferred one or the other of the alternatives imposed by the situation. While Radcliffe-Brown,

Eggan, Spoehr, Fortes, and this writer have tried to consider limited areas where dense information was available, Murdock has followed the complementary (but not contradictory) path of widening the field even at the expense of the reliability of the data, and Lowie (1948a) has tried to pursue a kind of middle road between the two approaches.

The case of the Pueblo area is especially striking, since for probably no other area in the world is there available such an amount of data and of such controversial quality. It is almost with despair that one comes to realize that the voluminous material accumulated by Voth, Fewkes, Dorsey, Parsons, and, to some extent, Stevenson is practically unworkable, since these authors have been feverishly piling up information without any clear idea of what it meant and, above all, of the hypotheses which it should have helped to check. The situation changed with Lowie's and Kroeber's entering the field, but the lack of statistical data on marriage choices and types of intermarriages, which could have been gathered for more than fifty years, will probably be impossible to overcome. This is much to be regretted, since Eggan's recent book (1950) represents an outstanding example of what can be expected from intensive and thorough study of a limited area. Here we find a new instance of the demonstration made under similar conditions by the same author (1937a, b) and elaborated upon by Spoehr, namely, as the latter puts it, "kinship system does preserve the characteristics of a 'system' despite radical changes in type" (1942, 1947, p. 229). The more recent study of the Pueblo's kinship systems by Eggan confirms the results of these earlier, purely diachronic inquiries. Here we observe closely connected forms, each of which preserves a structural consistency, although they present, in relation to one another, discontinuities which become significant when compared to homologous discontinuities in other fields, such as clan organization, marriage rules, ritual, religious beliefs, etc.

It is by means of such studies, exhibiting a truly "Galilean" outlook,[8] that one may hope to reach a depth where social structure is put on a level with other types of mental structures, particularly the linguistic one, as suggested by this writer (1951). To give an example: it follows from Eggan's survey that the Hopi kinship system requires no less than three different models for the time-dimension: there is, first, an "empty" time, stable and reversible, illustrated by the father's mother's and mother's father's lineage, where the same terms are consistently applied throughout the generations; second, a progressive, nonreversible time, as shown in Ego's (female) lineage with the sequence: grandmother $\rangle$ mother$\rangle$ sister $\rangle$ child $\rangle$ grandchild; and, third, an undulating, cyclical, reversible time, as in Ego's (male) lineage with the indefinite alternation between sister and sister's child. On the other hand, these three "straight" frames are clearly distinct from the "curved" frame of Zuni Ego's (female) lineage, where four terms: mother's mother (or daughter's daughter), mother, daughter, are disposed in a kind of ringlike arrangement, this conceptual grouping being accompanied, as regards the other lineages, by a greater poverty both of terms inside the acknowledged kin and of kin acknowledgment. Since time aspects belong also to linguistic analysis, the questions can be raised whether or not there is a correlation between these fields; if so, at what level; etc. More

8. That is, aiming to determine the law of variation, in contradistinction to the "Aristotelian" outlook mostly concerned with inductive correlations; for this distinction, fundamental to structural analysis, see Lewin (1935).

general problems, though of a similar kind, were raised by L. Thompson (1950) in reference to Whorf's linguistic treatment of Hopi.

Progress in this and other directions would undoubtedly have been more substantial if general agreement had existed among social anthropologists on the definition of social structure, the goals which may be achieved by its study, and the methodological principles to be applied at the different stages of research. Unfortunately, this is not the case, but it may be welcomed as a promising factor that some kind of understanding can be reached, at least on the nature and scope of these differences. This seems an appropriate place to offer a rapid sketch of the attitude of the main contributors to social-structure researches in relation to the working assumptions which were made at the beginning of this paper.

The words "social structure" are in many ways linked with the name of A. R. Radcliffe-Brown. Though his contribution does not limit itself to the study of kinship systems, he has stated the goal of these studies in terms which every scholar in the same field would probably be ready to underwrite: the aim of kinship studies, he says, is (1) to make a systematic classification; (2) to understand particular features of particular systems (*a*) by revealing the particular feature as a part of an organized whole and (*b*) by showing that it is a special example of a recognizable class of phenomena; (3) to arrive at valid generalizations about the nature of human societies. And he concludes: "To reduce this diversity (of 2 or 300 kinship systems) to some sort of order is the task of analysis. . . . We can . . . find . . . beneath the diversities, a limited number of general principles applied and combined in various ways" (1941, p. 17). There is nothing to add to this lucid program besides pointing out that this

is precisely what Radcliffe-Brown has done in his study of Australian kinship systems. He brought forth a tremendous amount of material; he introduced some kind of order where there was only chaos; he defined the basic operational terms, such as "cycle," "pair," and "couple." Finally, his discovery of the Kariera system in the region and with the characteristics inferred from the study of the available data and before visiting Australia will forever remain one of the great results of sociostructural studies (1930–31). His masterly Introduction to *African Systems of Kinship and Marriage* may be considered a true treatise on kinship; at the same time it takes a step toward integrating kinship systems of the Western world (which are approached in their early forms) into a world-wide theoretical interpretation. Another capital contribution by the same scholar, about the homologous structure of kinship terminology and behavior, will be dealt with later on.

However, it is obvious that, in many respects, Radcliffe-Brown's conception of social structure differs from the postulates which were set up at the outset of the present paper. In the first place, the notion of structure appears to him as a means to link social anthropology to the biological sciences: "There is a real and significant analogy between organic structure and social structure" (1940*b*, p. 6). Then, instead of "lifting up" kinship studies to put them on the same level as communication theory, as has been suggested by this writer, he has lowered them to the same plane as the phenomena dealt with in descriptive morphology and physiology (1940*b*, p. 10). In that respect, his approach is in line with the naturalistic trend of the British school. In contradistinction to Kroeber (1938, 1942, pp. 205 ff.) and Lowie (1948*a*, chap. iv), who have emphasized the artificiality of kinship, he agrees with Malinowski that biological ties are, at one and the same time, the origin of and the model for every type of kinship tie (Radcliffe-Brown, 1926).

These principles are responsible for two consequences. In the first place, Radcliffe-Brown's empirical approach makes him very reluctant to distinguish between *social structure* and *social relations*. As a matter of fact, social structure appears in his work to be nothing else than the whole network of social relations. It is true that he has sometimes outlined a distinction between *structure* and *structural form*. The latter concept, however, seems to be limited to the diachronic perspective, and its functional role in Radcliffe-Brown's theoretical thought appears quite reduced (1940*b*, p. 4). This distinction was thoroughly discussed by Fortes, who has contributed a great deal to the distinction, quite foreign to Radcliffe-Brown's outlook, between "model" and "reality" (see above): "structure is not immediately visible in the 'concrete reality.'... When we describe structure ... we are, as it were, in the realm of grammar and syntax, not of the spoken word" (Fortes, 1949, p. 56).

In the second place, this merging of social structure and social relations induces him to break down the former into the simplest forms of the latter, that is, relations between two persons: "The kinship structure of any society consists of a number of ... dyadic relations.... In an Australian tribe, the whole social structure is based on a network of such relations of person to person ..." (1940*b*, p. 3). It may be questioned whether such dyadic relations are the materials out of which social structure is built, or whether they do not themselves result from a preexisting structure which should be defined in more complex terms. Structural linguistics has a lot to teach in this respect. Examples of the kind of analysis commended by Radcliffe-Brown may be found in the works of Bateson and Mead. However, in *Naven* (1936), Bateson has gone a step further than Radcliffe-Brown's classification (1941) of dyadic relations according to order: he has attempted to place them in specific categories, an undertaking which implies that there is something more in social structure than the dyadic relations, i.e., the structure itself. This was a significant step toward the communication level (Ruesch and Bateson, 1951). Since it is possible to extend, almost indefinitely, the string of dyadic relations, Radcliffe-Brown has shown some reluctance toward the isolating of social structures conceived as self-sufficient wholes (in this respect he disagrees with Malinowski). His is a philosophy of continuity, not of discontinuity; this accounts for his hostility toward the notion of culture, already alluded to, and his avoiding the teachings of structural linguistics and of modern mathematics.

All these considerations may explain why Radcliffe-Brown, though an incomparable observer, analyst, and classifier, has sometimes proved to be disappointing when he turned to interpretations. These, in his work, often appear vague or circulative. Have marriage prohibitions really no further function than to help perpetuate the kinship system (Radcliffe-Brown, 1949*b*)? Are all the peculiar features of the Crow-Omaha systems satisfactorily accounted for when it has been said that they emphasize the lineage principle (Radcliffe-Brown, 1941)? These doubts, as well as many others, some of which will find their place later on in this paper, explain why the work of Radcliffe-Brown, to which nobody can deny a central place in social-structure studies, has often given rise to bitter arguments.

For instance, Murdock has called the kind of interpretation to which Radcliffe-Brown seems to be addicted: "mere verbalizations reified into causal forces (1949, p. 121)," and Lowie expressed himself in similar terms (1937, pp. 224–25). As regards Murdock, the lively controversy which has been carried on lately between him and W. H. Lawrence (Lawrence and Murdock, 1949), on the one hand, and Radcliffe-Brown (1951), on the other, may help to clarify the basic differences in their respective positions. This was about the so-called "Murngin type" of kinship system, a focal point in social-structure studies not only because of its many intricacies but because, thanks to Lloyd Warner's book and articles (1930–31, 1937a), we possess a thorough and extensive study of this system. However, Warner's study leaves some basic problems unanswered, especially the way in which marriage takes place on the lateral borders of the system. For Radcliffe-Brown, however, there is no problem involved, since he considers any kind of social organization as a mere conglomerate of simple person-to-person relations and since, in any society, there is always somebody who may be regarded as one's mother's brother's daughter (the preferred spouse among the Murngin) or as standing in an equivalent relation. But the problem is elsewhere: it lies in the fact that the natives have chosen to express these person-to-person relations in a class system, and Warner's description of this system (as acknowledged by himself) makes it impossible in some cases for the same individual to belong simultaneously to the right kind of class and to the right kind of relation. Under these circumstances, Lawrence and Murdock have tried to invent some system which would fit with the requirements of both the marriage rules and a system of the same kind as the one described by Warner. They invented it, however, as a sort of abstract game, the result being that, while their system meets some of the difficulties involved in Warner's account, it also raises many

others. One of the main difficulties implied in Warner's system is that it would require, on the part of the natives, an awareness of relationships too remote to make it believable. Since the new system adds a new line to the seven already assumed by Warner, it goes still further in that direction. Therefore, it seems a good hunch that the "hidden" or "unknown" system underlying the clumsy model which the Murngin borrowed recently from tribes with completely different marriage rules is simpler than the latter and not more complicated.

One sees, then, that Murdock favors a systematic and formal approach, different from Radcliffe-Brown's empirical and naturalistic one. But he remains, at the same time, psychologically and even biologically minded, and he can comply with the resulting requirements only by calling upon other disciplines, such as psychoanalysis and behaviorist psychology. Thus he succeeds in unloading from his interpretations of kinship problems the empiricism which still burdens Radcliffe-Brown's work, though, perhaps, at the risk of leaving them uncompleted or having to be completed on a ground foreign to anthropology, if not contradictory to its goals. Instead of seeing in kinship systems a sociological means to achieve a sociological result, he rather treats them as sociological results deriving from biological and psychological premises (1949, pp. 131–32).

Two parts should be distinguished in Murdock's contribution to the study of social structure. There is, first, a rejuvenation of a statistical method to check assumed correlations between social traits and to establish new ones, a method already tried by Tylor but which Murdock, thanks to the painstaking efforts of his Yale Cross-cultural Survey and the use of a more complex and exacting technique, was able to carry much further than had his predecessor. Everything has been said on the manifold difficulties with which this kind of inquiry is fraught (Lowie, 1948*a*, chap. iii), and, since nobody more than its author is aware of them, it is unnecessary to dwell upon this theme. Let it only be recalled that, while the uncertainty involved in the process of "carving out" the data will always make any alleged correlation dubious, the method is quite efficient in a negative way, that is, to explode false correlations. In this respect Murdock has achieved many results which no social anthropologist can permit himself to ignore.

The second aspect of Murdock's contribution is a scheme of the historical evolution of kinship systems. This suggests a startling conclusion, namely, that the so-called "Hawaiian type" of social organization should be placed at the origin of a much greater number of systems than has generally been admitted since Lowie's criticism of Morgan's similar hypothesis (Lowie, 1920, chap. iii). However, it should be kept in mind that Murdock's scheme is not based upon the consideration of individual societies taken as historicogeographical units or as co-ordinated wholes, but on abstractions and even, if one may say so, on abstractions "twice-removed": in the first place, social organization is isolated from the other aspects of culture (and sometimes even kinship systems from social organization); next, social organization itself is broken up into disconnected elements which are the outcome more of the traditional categories of ethnological thought than of the concrete analysis of each group. This being understood, the method for establishing a historical scheme can only be ideological; it proceeds by extracting common elements belonging to each stage in order to define a previous stage and so on. Therefrom it is obvious that systems placed at the beginning can be only those which exhibit the more general features, while systems with special features must occupy a more remote rank. In order to clarify this, a comparison may be used, though its oversimplification makes it unfair to Murdock: it is as though the origin of the modern horse were ascribed to the order of vertebrates instead of to *Hipparion.*

Regardless of the difficulties raised by his approach, Murdock's book should be credited with presenting new material and raising fascinating problems, many of which are new to anthropological thought. It is not doing him an injustice, then, to state that his contribution consists more in perfecting a method of discovering new problems than in solving them. Though this method remains "Aristotelian," it is perhaps unavoidable in the development of any science. Murdock has at least been faithful to the best part of the Aristotelian outlook by demonstrating convincingly that "cultural forms in the field of social organization reveal a degree of regularity and of conformity to scientific law not significantly inferior to that found in the so-called natural sciences" (1949, p. 259).

In relation to the distinctions made in the first section of this paper, it can be said that Radcliffe-Brown's work expresses a disregard for the difference between observation and experimentation, while Murdock shows a similar disregard for the difference between mechanical and statistical models (since he tries to construct mechanical models with the help of a statistical method). Conversely, Lowie's work seems to consist entirely in an exacting endeavor to meet the question (which was acknowledged as a prerequisite for any study in social structure): *What are the facts?* When he became active in research as well as in theoretical ethnology, the latter field was fraught with philosophical prejudices and an aura of sociological mysticism; therefore, his paramount contribution toward assessing the subject matter of social anthropology has sometimes been misunderstood and thought of as wholly negative (Kroeber, 1920). But, although this situation made it imperative at that time to state, in the first place, what the facts were *not*, the creative energy liberated by his merciless disintegration of arbitrary systems and alleged correlations has furnished, to a very large extent, the power consumed by his followers. His own positive contributions are not always easy to outline on account of the extreme modesty of his thought and his aversion to any kind of wide-scope theoretical claim. He himself used the words "active skepticism" to outline his position. However, it is Lowie who, as early as 1915, stated in modern terms the role of kinship studies in relation to social behavior and organization: "Sometimes the very essence of social fabric may be demonstrably connected with the mode of classifying kin" (1915, 1929c). In the same paper he was able to reverse the narrow historical trend which, at that time, was blinding anthropological thinking to the universal action of structural forces: exogamy was shown to be a scheme defined by truly genetic characters and, whenever present, determining identical features of social organization, without calling for historicogeographical relations. When, a few years later, he exploded the "matrilineal complex" (1919), he achieved two results which are the fundamentals of social-structure studies. In the first place, by dismissing the notion that every so-called "matrilineal" feature was to be understood as an expression or as a vestige of the complex, he made it possible to break it up into several variables. In the second place, the elements thus liberated could be used for a permutative treatment of the differential features of kinship systems

(Lowie, 1929a). Thus he was laying the foundation for a structural analysis of kinship on two different levels: that of the terminological system, on the one hand, and, on the other, that of the correlation between the system of behavior and terminology, showing the path which, later on, was to be followed by others (Radcliffe-Brown, 1924; Lévi-Strauss, 1945).

Lowie should be credited with many other theoretical contributions: he was probably the first one to demonstrate the true bilateral nature of most of the so-called "unilineal" systems (1920, 1929b). He made clear the impact of residence on filiation (1920). He convincingly dissociated avoidance customs from incest prohibition (1920, pp. 104-5); his care to interpret social organization not only as a set of institutionalized rules but also as the outcome of individual psychological reactions, which sometimes contradicted or inflected the rules, led to the strange result that the same scholar who was so much abused for his famous "shreds and patches" statement on culture was able to offer some of the most thorough and well-balanced pictures we have of cultures treated as wholes (1935, 1948a, chaps. xv, xvi, xvii). Finally, Lowie's role as a promoter and exponent of South American social anthropology is well known; either directly or indirectly through guidance and encouragement, he has contributed toward breaking a new field.

IV. SOCIAL DYNAMICS: SUBORDINATION STRUCTURES

a) ORDER OF ELEMENTS (INDIVIDUALS OR GROUPS) IN THE SOCIAL STRUCTURE

According to this writer's interpretation, which does not need to be expounded systematically, since (in spite of efforts toward objectivity) it probably permeates this paper, kinship systems, marriage rules, and descent groups constitute a co-ordinated ensemble, the function of which is to insure the permanency of the social group by means of intertwining consanguineous and affinal ties. They may be considered as the blueprint of a mechanism which "pumps" women out of their consanguineous families to redistribute them in affinal groups, the result of this process being to create new consanguineous groups and so on. This view results from Linton's classical distinction between "conjugal" and "consanguineous" family (1936, pp. 159–63). If no external factor were affecting this mechanism, it would work indefinitely and the social structure would remain static. This is not the case, however; hence the need to introduce into the theoretical model new elements to account for the diachronic changes of the structure, on the one hand, and, on the other, for the fact that kinship structure does not exhaust social structure. This can be done in three different ways.

As always, the first step consists in ascertaining the facts. Since the time when Lowie expressed regret that so little had been done by anthropologists in the field of political organization (1920, chap. xiii), some progress has been made; in the first place, Lowie himself has clarified the issue by devoting most of his recent book to problems of that sort and by regrouping the facts concerning the American area (1927, 1948a, chaps. vi, vii, xii–xiv, 1948b). A recent work has brought together significant data concerning Africa (Fortes and Evans-Pritchard, 1940). To this day, the best way to organize the still much confused material remains Lowie's basic distinctions (1948a) between social strata, sodalities, and the state.

The second type of approach would be an attempt to correlate the phenom-

ena belonging to the order first studied, i.e., kinship, with phenomena belonging to the new order but showing a direct connection with the former. This approach raises, in turn, two different problems: (1) Can the kinship structure by itself result in structures of a new type (that is, dynamically oriented)? (2) How do *communication structures* and *subordination structures* interact on each other?

The first problem should be related to education, i.e., to the fact that each generation plays alternately a submissive and a dominant part in relation to the preceding and to the following generation. This aspect has been dealt with chiefly by Margaret Mead;[9] its discussion will probably find a more appropriate place in other papers.

Another side of the question lies in the important attempt to correlate a static position in the kinship structure (as defined by terminology) with a dynamic behavior expressed, on the one hand, in rights, duties, obligations, and, on the other, in privileges, avoidance, etc. It is impossible to go into the discussion of these problems to which many writers have contributed. Especially significant is a protracted controversy between Radcliffe-Brown and others (Radcliffe-Brown, 1935, 1940a, 1949a; Opler, 1937, 1947; Brand, 1948) about the kind of correlation which exists, if any, between kin terminology and behavior.

According to Radcliffe-Brown's well-known position, such a correlation exhibits a high degree of accuracy, while his opponents have generally tried to demonstrate that this is neither absolute nor detailed. In contrast to both opinions, this writer has tried to establish that the relation between terminology and behavior is of a dialectical nature. The modalities of behavior between relatives express to some extent

9. In connection with this paper's approach, see particularly Mead (1949).

the terminological classification, and they provide at the same time a means to overcome difficulties and contradictions resulting from this classification. Thus the rules of behavior result from an attempt to overcome contradictions in the field of terminology and marriage rules; the functional unwedging—if one may say so—which is bound to exist between the two orders causes changes in the former, i.e., terminology; and these, in turn, call for new behavior patterns, and so on indefinitely.

The second problem confronts us with the kind of situation arising when the kinship system does not regulate matrimonial exchanges between equals but between members of a hierarchy (either economic or political). Under that heading come the problems of polygamy which, in some cases at least, may be shown to provide a bridge between two different types of guarantees, one collective and political, the other individual and economic (Lévi-Strauss, 1944); and that of hypergamy. This deserves much more attention than it has received so far, since it is the doorway to the study of the caste system (Hocart, 1938; Davis, 1941; Lévi-Strauss, 1949*b*, chaps. xxiv–xxvii) and hence to that of social structures based on race and class distinctions.

The third and last approach to our problem is purely formal. It consists in an a priori deduction of the types of structure likely to result from relations of domination or dependency as they might appear at random. Of a very promising nature for the study of social structure are Rapoport's attempts to make a mathematical theory of the pecking order among hens (1949). It is true that there seems to be a complete opposition between, let us say, the pecking order of hens, which is intransitive and cyclical, and the social order (for instance, the circle of kava in Polynesia), which is transitive and noncyclical (since those who are seated at the far

end can never sit at the top). But the study of kinship systems shows precisely that, under given circumstances, an intransitive and cyclical order can result in a transitive and noncyclical one. This happens, for instance, in a hypergamous society where a circulative marriage system with mother's brother's daughter leaves at one end a girl unable to find a husband (since her status is the highest) and at the other end a boy without a wife (since no girl has a lower status than his own). Thus, with the help of such notions as transitivity, order, and cycle, which admit of mathematical treatment, it becomes possible to study, on a purely formal level, generalized types of social structure where both the communication and the subordination aspects become fully integrated. It is also possible to enlarge the field of inquiry and to integrate, for a given society, actual and potential types of order. For instance, in human societies the actual forms of social order are practically always of a transitive and noncyclical type: if A is above B and B above C, then A is above C; and C cannot be above A. But most of the human "potential" or "ideological" forms of social order, as illustrated in politics, myth, and religion, are conceived as intransitive and cyclical; for instance, in tales about kings marrying lasses and in Stendhal's indictment of American democracy as a system where a gentleman takes his orders from his grocer.

b) ORDER OF ORDERS

Thus anthropology considers the whole social fabric as a network of different types of orders. The kinship system provides a way to order individuals according to certain rules; social organization is another way of ordering individuals and groups; social stratifications, whether economic or political, provide us with a third type; and all these orders can themselves be put in order by showing the kind of relationships which exist between them, how they interact on one another on both the synchronic and the diachronic levels. Meyer Fortes has successfully tried to construct models valid not only for one type of order (kinship, social organization, economic relations, etc.) but where numerous models for all types of orders are themselves ordered inside a total model (1949).

When dealing with these orders, however, anthropologists are confronted with a basic problem which was taken up at the beginning of this paper, i.e., to what extent does the manner according to which a society conceives its orders and their ordering correspond to the real situation? It has been shown that this problem can be solved in different ways, depending on the data at hand.

All the models considered so far, however, are "lived-in" orders: they correspond to mechanisms which can be studied from the outside as a part of objective reality. But no systematic studies of these orders can be undertaken without acknowledging the fact that social groups, to achieve their mutual ordering, need to call upon orders of different types, corresponding to a field external to objective reality and which we call the "supernatural." These "thought-of" orders cannot be checked against the experience to which they refer, since they are one and the same thing as this experience. Therefore, we are in the position of studying them only in their relationships with the other types of "lived-in" orders. The "thought-of" orders are those of myth and religion. The question may be raised whether, in our own society, political ideology does not belong to the same category.

After Durkheim, Radcliffe-Brown has contributed greatly to the demonstration that religion is a part of the social structure. The anthropologist's task is to discover correlations between different types of religions and different types of social organization (Radcliffe-Brown, 1945). Radcliffe-Brown failed, however, to achieve significant results for two reasons. In the first place, he tried to link ritual and beliefs directly to sentiments; besides, he was more concerned with giving universal formulation to the kind of correlation prevailing between religion and social structure than in showing the variability of one in relation to the other. It is perhaps as a result of this that the study of religion has fallen into the background, to the extent that the word "religion" does not even appear in the program of this symposium. The field of myth, ritual, and religion seems nevertheless to be one of the more fruitful for the study of social structure; though relatively little has been done in this respect, the results which have been obtained recently are among the most rewarding in our field.

Great strides have been taken toward the study of religious systems as co-ordinate wholes. Documentary material, such as Radin's *The Road of Life and Death* (1945) or Berndt's *Kunapipi* (1951), should help in undertaking, with respect to several religious cults, the kind of ordering of data so masterfully achieved by Gladys Reichard for the Navaho (1950). This should be completed by small-scale comparative studies on the permanent and nonpermanent elements in religious thought as exemplified by Lowie.

With the help of such well-organized material it becomes possible, as Nadel puts it (1952), to prepare "small-scale models of a comparative analysis ... of an analysis of 'concomitant variations' ... such as any inquiry concerned with the explanation of social facts must employ." The results thus achieved may be small; they are, however, some of the most convincing and rigorous in the entire field of social organization. Nadel himself has proved a correlation between shamanism and some aspects of psychological development (1946); using Indo-European comparative material borrowed from Iceland, Ireland, and the Caucasus, Dumézil has interpreted an enigmatic mythological figure in relation to specific features of social organization (1948); Wittfogel and Goldfrank have shown how significant variations in mythological themes can be related to the socioeconomic background (1943). Monica Hunter has established beyond doubt that the structure of the magical beliefs may vary in correlation with the structure of the society itself (Hunter-Wilson, 1951). These results, together with some others, on which space prevents our commenting, give hope that we may be close to understanding not only what kind of function religious beliefs fulfil in social life (this has been known more or less clearly since Lucretius' time) but how they fulfil this function.

A few words may be added as a conclusion. This paper was started by working out the notion of "model," and the same notion has reappeared at its end. Social anthropology, being in its incipient stage, could only seek, as model for its first models, among those of the simplest kind provided by more advanced sciences, and it was natural enough to seek them in the field of classical mechanics. However, in doing so, anthropology has been working under some sort of illusion since, as Von Neumann puts it (Von Neumann and Morgenstern, 1944, p. 14), "an almost exact theory of a gas, containing about 10^{25} freely moving particles, is incomparably easier than that of the solar system, made up of 9 major bodies." But when it tries to construct its models, anthropology finds itself in a case which is neither the one nor the other: the objects with which we deal—social roles and human beings—are considerably more numerous than those dealt with in Newtonian mechanics and, at the same time, far less numerous than would be required to allow a satisfactory use of the laws of statistics and probability. Thus we found ourselves in an intermediate zone: too complicated for one treatment and not complicated enough for the other.

The tremendous change which was brought about by the theory of communication consists precisely in the discovery of methods to deal with objects—signs—which can be subjected to a rigorous study despite the fact that they are altogether much more numerous than those of classical mechanics and much less than those of thermodynamics. Language consists of morphemes, a few thousand in number; significant regularities in phoneme frequencies can be reached by limited counts. The threshold for the use of statistical laws becomes lower, and that for operating with mechanical models higher, than was the case when operating on other grounds. And, at the same time, the size-order of the phenomena has become significantly closer to that of anthropological data.

Therefore, the present conditions of social-structure studies can be summarized as follows: phenomena were found to be of the same kind as those which, in strategics and communication theory, were made the subject of a rigorous approach. Anthropological facts are on a scale which is sufficiently close to that of these other phenomena as not to preclude their similar treatment. Surprisingly enough, it is at the very moment when anthropology finds itself closer than ever to the long-awaited goal of becoming a true science that the ground seems to fail where it was expected to be the firmest: the facts themselves are lacking, either not numerous enough or not collected under conditions insuring their comparability.

Though it is not our fault, we have

been behaving like amateur botanists, picking up haphazardly heteroclite specimens, which were further distorted and mutilated by preservation in our herbarium. And we are, all of a sudden, confronted with the need of ordering complete series, ascertaining original shades, and measuring minute parts which have either shrunk or been lost. When we come to realize not only what should be done but also what we should be in a position to do, and when we make at the same time an inventory of our material, we cannot help feeling in a disheartened mood. It looks almost as if cosmic physics was set up to work on Babylonian observations. The celestial bodies are still there, but unfortunately the native cultures where we used to gather our data are disappearing at a fast rate, and what they are being replaced by can only furnish data of a very different type. To adjust our techniques of observation to a theoretical framework which is far more advanced is a paradoxical situation, quite opposite to that which has prevailed in the history of sciences. Nevertheless, such is the challenge to modern anthropology.

REFERENCES

BATESON, G. 1936. *Naven.* Cambridge: At the University Press.

BERNDT, R. A. 1951. *Kunapipi.* New York: International Universities Press.

BERNOT, L., and BLANCARD, R. MS: "Nouville: Un Village français." UNESCO.

BIDNEY, D. 1950. Review of WHITE, L. A. *The Science of Culture,* in *American Anthropologist,* LII, No. 4, Part I, 518–19.

BOAS, F. (ed.). 1911. *Handbook of American Indian Languages.* (Bureau of American Ethnology Bull. 40 [1908], Part I.) Washington, D.C.: Government Printing Office.

BOHR, N. 1939. "Natural Philosophy and Human Culture," *Nature,* CXLIII, 268–72.

BRAND, C. S. 1948. "On Joking Relationships," *American Anthropologist,* L, 160–61.

CUSHING, F. H. 1896. "Outlines of Zuni Creation Myths," *Bureau of American Ethnology, 13th Annual Report, 1891–1892,* pp. 325–447. Washington, D.C.: Government Printing Office.

———. 1920. *Zuni Breadstuff.* ("Indian Notes and Monographs, Museum of the American Indian, Heye Foundation," Vol. VIII.) New York.

DAHLBERG, G. 1948. *Mathematical Methods for Population Genetics.* London and New York: Interscience Publishers.

DAVIS, K. 1941. "Intermarriage in Caste Societies," *American Anthropologist,* XLIII, 376–95.

———. 1947. *The Development of the City in Society: Proceedings of the 1st Conference on Long Term Social Trends, Social Science Research Council.*

DUMÉZIL, G. 1948. *Loki.* Paris: G. P. Maisonneuve.

———. 1949. *L'Heritage indo-européen à Rome.* Paris: Gallimard.

DURKHEIM, E. 1912. *Les Formes élémentaires de la vie religieuse.* ("Bibliothèque de philosophie contemporaine.") Paris: F. Alcan.

DURKHEIM, E., and MAUSS, M. 1901–2 (1903). "De quelques formes primitives de classification: Contribution à l'étude des représentations collectives," *Année sociologique,* VI, 1–72.

EGGAN, F. 1937a. "Historical Changes in the Choctaw Kinship System," *American Anthropologist,* XXXIX, 34–52.

———. (ed.). 1937b. *Social Anthropology of North American Tribes.* Chicago: University of Chicago Press.

———. 1950. *Social Organization of the Western Pueblos.* Chicago: University of Chicago Press.

ELWIN, V. 1947. *The Muria and Their Ghotul.* Oxford: Oxford University Press.

EVANS-PRITCHARD, E. E. 1939. "Nuer Time Reckoning," *Africa,* XII, 189–216.

———. 1940. *The Nuer.* Oxford: Clarendon Press.

FIRTH, R. 1936. *We, the Tikopia.* London and New York: G. Allen & Unwin.

———. 1946. *Malay Fishermen.* London: Kegan Paul, Trench, Trubner & Co.

———. 1951. *Elements of Social Organization.* London: Watts & Co.

FORD, C. S., and BEACH, F. A. 1951. *Patterns of Sexual Behavior.* New York: Harper & Bros.

FORDE, D. 1941. *Marriage and the Family among the Yakö in S.E. Nigeria.* ("Monographs in Social Anthropology," No. 5.) London: London School of Economics and Political Science.

———. 1950. "Double-Descent among the Yakö." In RADCLIFFE-BROWN, A. R., and FORDE, D. (eds.), *African Systems of Kinship and Marriage.* London: Oxford University Press, for the International African Institute.

FORTES, M. (ed.). 1949. *Social Structure: Studies Presentéd to A. R. Radcliffe-Brown.* Oxford: Clarendon Press.

FORTES, M., and EVANS-PRITCHARD, E. E. 1940. *African Political Systems.* Oxford: Oxford University Press, for the International Institute of African Languages and Cultures.

GOLDSTEIN, K. 1951. *Der Aufbau des Organismus.* French translation. Paris: Gallimard.

HERSKOVITS, M. J. 1940. *The Economic Life of Primitive Peoples.* New York: Alfred A. Knopf.

HOCART, A. M. 1938. *Les Castes.* ("Annales du Musée Guimet bibliothèque du vulganisation," Vol. LIV.) Paris.

HUNTER-WILSON, M. 1951. "Witch Beliefs and Social Structure," *American Journal of Sociology,* LVI, No. 4, 307–13.

KROEBER, A. L. 1920. Review of LOWIE, R. H., *Primitive Society,* in *American Anthropologist,* XXII, No. 4, 377–81.

———. 1938. "Basic and Secondary Patterns of Social Structure," *Journal of the Royal Anthropological Institute,* LXVIII, 299–309.

———. 1942. "The Societies of Primitive Man," *Biological Symposia,* VIII, 205–16.

———. 1943. "Structure, Function, and Pattern in Biology and Anthropology," *Scientific Monthly,* LVI, 105–13.

———. 1948. *Anthropology.* New ed. New York: Harcourt, Brace & Co.

LAWRENCE, W. E., and MURDOCK, G. P. 1949. "Murngin Social Organization," *American Anthropologist,* LI, No. 1, 58–65.

LEACH, E. R. 1945. "Jinghpaw Kinship Terminology," *Journal of the Royal Anthropological Institute,* LXXV, 59–72.

LESTRANGE, M. DE. 1951. "Pour une méthode socio-démographique," *Journal de la Société des Africanistes,* Vol. XXI.

LÉVI-STRAUSS, C. 1944. "The Social and Pyschological Aspects of Chieftainship in a Primitive Tribe: The Nambikuara," *Transactions of the New York Academy of Sciences,* Series II, VII, No. 1, 16–32.

———. 1945. "L'Analyse structurale en linguistique et en anthropologie," *Word,* I, No. 1, 33–53.

———. 1949a. "Histoire et ethnologie," *Revue de métaphysique et de morale,* LIV, Nos. 3–4, 363–91.

———. 1949b. *Les Structures élémentaires de la parenté.* Paris: Presses universitaires de France.

———. 1951. "Language and the Analysis of Social Laws," *American Anthropologist,* LIII, No. 2, 155–63.

LEWIN, K. 1935. *A Dynamic Theory of Personality.* New York: McGraw-Hill Book Co.

LINTON, R. 1936. *The Study of Man.* New York: D. Appleton–Century Co.

LIVI, L. 1940–41. *Trattato di demografia.* Padua: Cedam.

———. 1949. "Considérations théoriques et pratiques sur le concept de 'minimum de population,'" *Population,* IV, No. 4, 754–56.

LOWIE, R. H. 1915. "Exogamy, and the Classificatory Systems of Relationship," *American Anthropologist,* Vol. XVII, No. 2.

———. 1919. "The Matrilineal Complex," *University of California Publications in American Archaeology and Anthropology,* XVI, No. 2, 29–45.

———. 1920. *Primitive Society.* New York: Horace Liveright.

———. 1927. *The Origin of the State.* New York: Harcourt, Brace & Co.

———. 1929a. "Notes on Hopi Clans," pp. 303–60. ("American Museum of Natural History, Anthropological Papers," Vol. XXX, Part VI.)

———. 1929b. "Hopi Kinship," pp. 361–88. ("American Museum of Natural History, Anthropological Papers," Vol. XXX, Part VII.)

———. 1929c. "Relationship Terms." In *Encyclopaedia Britannica,* pp. 84–89. 14th ed. 1948. Chicago, London, and Toronto: Encyclopaedia Britannica, Inc.

———. 1935. *The Crow Indians*. New York: Farrar & Rinehart.

———. 1937. *The History of Ethnological Theory*. New York: Farrar & Rinehart.

———. 1942. "A Marginal Note to Professor Radcliffe-Brown's Paper on 'Social Structure,'" *American Anthropologist*, XLIV, No. 3, 519–21.

———. 1948a. *Social Organization*. New York: Rinehart & Co.

———. 1948b. "Some Aspects of Political Organization among American Aborigines (Huxley Memorial Lecture)," *Journal of the Royal Anthropological Institute*, LXXVIII, 11–24.

MALINOWSKI, B. 1922. *Argonauts of the Western Pacific*. London: George Routledge & Sons, Ltd.

MAUSS, M. 1904–5 (1906). "Essai sur les variations saisonnières dan les sociétés Eskimos: Étude de morphologie sociale." *Année sociologique*, IX, 39–132.

———. 1923–24. "Essai sur le don, forme archaïque de l'échange," *ibid.*, n.s., I, 30–186.

———. 1924–25. "Division et proportion des divisions de la sociologie," *ibid.*, n.s., II, 98 ff.

———. 1950. *Sociologie et anthropologie.* Paris: Presses universitaires de France.

MEAD, M. 1949. "Character Formation and Diachronic Theory." In FORTES, M. (ed.), *Social Structure: Studies Presented to A. R. Radcliffe-Brown*, pp. 18–34. Oxford: Clarendon Press.

MORGAN, L. H. 1871. *Systems of Consanguinity and Affinity of the Human Family*. ("Smithsonian Institution Contributions to Knowledge," Vol. XVII, No. 218.) Washington, D.C.

MURDOCK, G. P. 1949. *Social Structure*. New York: Macmillan Co.

NADEL, S. F. 1946. "Shamanism in the Nuba Mountains," *Journal of the Royal Anthropological Institute*, LXXVI, Part I, 25–38.

———. 1947. *The Nuba*. London and New York: Oxford University Press.

———. 1952. "Witchcraft in Four African Societies: An Essay in Comparison," *American Anthropologist*, LIV, Part I, 18–29.

NEUMANN, J. VON, and MORGENSTE.. ,. 1944. *Theory of Games and Economic Behavior*. Princeton, N.J.: Princeton University Press.

OPLER, M. E. 1937. "Apache Data Concerning the Relation of Kinship Terminology to Social Classification," *American Anthropologist*, XXXIX, No. 2, 201–12.

———. 1947. "Rule and Practice in the Behavior Pattern between Jicarilla Apache Affinal Relatives," *American Anthropologist*, XLIX, No. 3, 453–62.

RADCLIFFE-BROWN, A. R. 1924. "The Mother's Brother in South Africa," *South African Journal of Science*, XXI, 542–55.

———. 1926. "Father, Mother, and Child," *Man*, Vol. XXVI, Art. 103, pp. 159–61.

———. 1930–31. "The Social Organization of Australian Tribes," *Oceania*, I, No. 1, 34–63; No. 2, 206–46; No. 3, 322–41; No. 4, 426–56.

———. 1935. "Kinship Terminology in California," *American Anthropologist*, XXXVII, No. 3, 530–35.

———. 1940a. "On Joking Relationships," *Africa*, XIII, No. 3, 195–210.

———. 1940b. "On Social Structure," *Journal of the Royal Anthropological Institute*, LXX, 1–12.

———. 1941. "The Study of Kinship Systems," *ibid.*, LXXI, 1–18.

———. 1945. "Religion and Society (Henry Meyers Lecture)," *ibid.*, LXXV, 33–43.

———. 1949a. "A Further Note on Joking Relationships," *Africa*, XIX, No. 2, 133–40.

———. 1949b. "White's View of a Science of Culture," *American Anthropologist*, LI, No. 3, 503–12.

———. 1951. "Murngin Social Organization," *ibid.*, LIII, No. 1, 37–55.

———. 1952. "Social Anthropology, Past and Present," *Man*, Vol. LII, Art. 14.

RADCLIFFE-BROWN, A. R., and FORDE, D. (eds.). 1950. *African Systems of Kinship and Marriage*. Oxford: Oxford University Press, for the International African Institute.

RADIN, P. 1945. *The Road of Life and Death*. New York: Pantheon Books, Inc.

RAPOPORT, A. 1949. "Outline of Probabilistic Approach to Animal Sociology," *Bulletin of Mathematical Biophysics,* XI, 183–96, 273–81.

REICHARD, G. A. 1950. *Navaho Religion: A Study in Symbolism.* 2 vols. ("Bollingen Series," No. XVIII.) New York: Pantheon Books, Inc.

RICHARDS, A. I. 1932. *Hunger and Work in a Savage Tribe.* London: G. Routledge & Sons.

——. 1936. "A Dietary Study in Northeastern Rhodesia," *Africa,* IX, No. 2, 166–96.

——. 1939. *Land, Labour and Diet in Northern Rhodesia.* Oxford: Oxford University Press, for the International Institute of African Languages and Cultures.

RICHARDSON, J., and KROEBER, A. L. 1940. "Three Centuries of Women's Dress Fashions: A Quantitative Analysis," *Anthropological Records,* V, No. 2, 111–54.

RUESCH, J., and BATESON, G. 1951. *Communication: The Social Matrix of Psychiatry.* New York: W. W. Norton & Co.

SHANNON, C. E., and WEAVER, W. 1950. *The Mathematical Theory of Communication.* Urbana: University of Illinois Press.

SPECK, F. G. 1915. *Family Hunting Territories and Social Life of Various Algonkian Bands of the Ottawa Valley.* (Canada Department of Mines, Geological Survey Mem. 70, "Anthropological Series," No. 8.) Ottawa: Government Printing Bureau.

SPOEHR, A. 1942. *Kinship System of the Seminole,* pp. 29–113. ("Anthropological Series, Field Museum of Natural History," Vol. XXXIII, No. 2.)

——. 1947. *Changing Kinship Systems,* pp. 153–235. ("Anthropological Series, Field Museum of Natural History," Vol. XXXIII, No. 4.)

——. 1950. "Observations on the Study of Kinship," *American Anthropologist,* LII, No. 1, 1–15.

STEWARD, J. H. 1938. *Basin-Plateau Aboriginal Sociopolitical Groups.* (Bureau of American Ethnology, Smithsonian Institution Bull. 120.) Washington, D.C.: Government Printing Office.

STEWART, J. Q. 1947. "Empirical Mathematical Rules Concerning the Distribution and Equilibrium of Population," *Geographical Review,* XXXVII, No. 3, 461–85.

SUTTER, J., and TABAH, L. 1951. "Les Notions d'isolat et de population minimum," *Population,* VI, No. 3, 481–89.

THOMPSON, L. 1950. *Culture in Crisis: A Study of the Hopi Indians.* New York: Harper & Bros.

WAGLEY, C. 1940. "The Effects of Depopulation upon Social Organization as Illustrated by the Tapirapé Indians," *Transactions of the New York Academy of Sciences,* Series 2, III, No. 1, 12–16.

WARNER, W. L. 1930–31. "Morphology and Functions of the Australian Murngin Type of Kinship System," *American Anthropologist,* XXXII, No. 2, 207–56; XXXIII, No. 2, 172–98.

——. 1937a. *A Black Civilization: A Social Study of an Australian Tribe.* New York: Harper & Bros.

——. 1937b. "The Family and Principles of Kinship Structure in Australia," *American Sociological Review,* II, 43–54.

White, L. A. 1949. *The Science of Culture.* New York: Farrar, Straus & Co.

Wiener, N. 1948. *Cybernetics.* Paris: Herman et Cie; New York: John Wiley & Sons, Inc.

WITTFOGEL, K. A., and GOLDFRANK, E. S. 1943. "Some Aspects of Pueblo Mythology and Society," *Journal of American Folklore,* LVI, 17–30.

ZIPF, G. K. 1949. *Human Behavior and the Principle of Least Effort.* Cambridge, Mass.: Addison-Wesley Press, Inc.

Culture, Personality, and Society

By A. IRVING HALLOWELL

HISTORICALLY VIEWED, specialized interest in and systematic investigation of problems in the area most familiarly labeled "personality and culture" are a twentieth-century development in anthropology.[1] Although it is chiefly

1. Since major sources in the form of books, contributions in periodicals, and two volumes of reprinted articles are easily accessible, this footnote is offered as a brief but direct guide to this literature. Furthermore, since it appeared impractical to review the full range of concrete contributions in a limited space and the symposium itself is concerned with an over-all and integrated view of anthropology, emphasis has been given to the wider rather than the narrower implications of personality and culture studies, their relation to the interests of general anthropology as well as to those of closely related disciplines.

For historical perspective see Lowie (1937, "Retrospect and Prospect"); Volkart (1951, for the "Outline of a Program for the Study of Personality and Culture" prepared by W. I. Thomas and submitted to the Social Science Research Council in 1933); Margaret Mead (1937, Introduction); Betty J. Meggers (1946, for a rather dim view of the newer trends); Clyde Kluckhohn (1944, on the influence of psychiatry on anthropology in America); Clyde Kluckhohn and Henry A. Murray (1948, Introduction).

Reprintings of two series of selected articles in the area of personality and culture studies, embodying a large amount of concrete data as well as theoretical discussion, are to be found in Kluckhohn and Murray (1948) and Haring (1949, rev. ed.). In this latter volume will be found an extensive and alphabetically arranged bibliography, which, together with the bibliographical references in Kluckhohn and Murray, lead directly to the source material. Since the writings of Bateson, Benedict, DuBois, Erikson, Fromm, Gillin, Gorer, Hallowell, Henry, Kardiner, Kluckhohn, LaBarre, Linton, Mead, Roheim, Sapir, Sullivan, etc., are listed in the Haring volume, it seems unnecessary to repeat them all in the bibliography of this article. Attention may be called to the fact, however, that a volume of the *Selected Writings of Edward Sapir* was edited by D. Mandelbaum and published in 1949. Since that time, a lengthy and extremely valuable review article by Z. S. Harris (1951), systematically expounding Sapir's views, has appeared. A bibliography of the writings of Margaret Mead is to be found in *Psychiatry*, X (1947), 117–20. Subsequently published books include *Male and Female* (1949), *Soviet Attitudes toward Authority* (1951), and *Growth and Culture* (Mead and Macgregor, 1951). Among the items not included in, or published subsequent to, Haring's bibliography, attention is particularly directed to the following: *Proceedings of an Interdisciplinary Conference on Culture and Personality*, ed. Sargent and Smith (1949), held under the auspices of The Viking Fund in 1947; the review of personality and culture studies from a psychoanalytic point of view by Roheim (1950), the annual series edited by him, "Psychoanalysis and the Social Sciences" (beginning 1947), and the *Essays* in his honor, ed. Wilbur and Muensterberger, under the title *Psychoanalysis and Culture* (1951); Erik H. Erikson's *Childhood and Society* (1950); the *Proceedings of the American Psychopathological Association* (1948), devoted to the general topic "Psychosexual Development in Health and Disease," ed. Hoch and Zubin (1949) and to which Ford, Hallowell, Henry, Mead, and Murdock contributed papers; and the general review of human sexual patterns of behavior by Ford and Beach (1951), and the monograph of the Berndts on the Australians (1951); studies of individual Navaho by Dyk (1947) and by the Leightons (1949), a Hopi by Aberle (1951), and an Indian of the Plains by Devereux (1951), L. K. Frank (1951), Honigmann (1949).

American anthropologists who have made this area their own, as early as 1923, in England, the topic of C. G. Seligman's presidential address to the Royal Anthropological Institute was the relations of anthropology and psychology,[2] and Lévi-Strauss, in the Introduc-

2. Seligman, 1924. Subsequent articles showing his continuing interest were published in 1928, 1929, and 1932. In 1936, Seligman wrote an Introduction to J. S. Lincoln's *The Dream in Primitive Cultures*, in which he said: "Today the Anthropologist must be aware of current psychological theory; he must make up his mind how far his researches should be directed by this, and on what class of material he should particularly focus his attention in order not only to test the theories of psychologists but also to further his own science. To put it briefly, how can a profitable give and take relationship between psychology and anthropology best be established at the present time?

"This is a problem to which the writer of this Introduction has given much thought of recent years. Brought up in the main in the Tylorian (comparative) School of Anthropology, having thereafter gained some knowledge of and made use of the Historical School of Rivers, and of late years watched the development of the functional method, the writer has become convinced that the most fruitful development—perhaps indeed the only process that can bring social anthropology to its rightful status as a branch of science and at the same time give it the full weight in human affairs to which it is entitled—is the increased elucidation in the field and integration into anthropology of psychological knowledge. That we have not progressed further than in fact we have is probably only in part due to the relatively scant amount of material available or to any inherent difficulty which Anthropologists should find in handling it. The writer hopes he is not being unfair to his colleagues, but cannot help considering that this failure is far more due to a lack of eclecticism, a determination of each exponent and adherent of a particular school to show little interest in the technique and conclusions of others."

Aside from the interest shown by S. F. Nadel, who acknowledges a debt to Gestalt psychologists (*Foundations* [1951], Vol. VI), the relations between psychology and anthropology envisioned by Seligman do not seem to have been realized, despite the fact that, on the psychological side, Sir F. C. Bartlett (1937, p. 419) suggested that "if the Anthropologist could tighten up his work and give it

tion to a posthumous reprinting of a volume of articles by Marcel Mauss (1950), has called attention to the manner in which the latter, at about the same time, seems to have anticipated certain later developments.

Despite the somewhat misleading nature of the dichotomy[3] implied by the label "personality *and* culture," a significant historical fact should not be overlooked. The differentiation in subject matter and point of view which, beginning in the Enlightenment, subsequently led to the crystallization of the separate disciplines and subdisciplines that we now know as the social and psychological sciences, while advancing knowledge in highly specialized areas, has by no means provided all the final answers to many perennial questions regarding the nature and behavior of man. Some of these questions inevitably remain of common concern to more than one discipline, so that cross-fertilization is not only inevitable but may be extremely fruitful. The Freudian conception of human nature, particularly the model of personality theory which has had an immense impact upon both psychological and social disciplines in this century, was developed independently not only of experimental psychology but likewise of the culture concept as developed in anthropology. The very conjunction, then, of the terms "personality" and "culture" provides an implicit clue to one of the major characteristics of the

a more definite direction by a judicious application of psychological methods, and if the psychologist could learn to humanize his experiments by a study of anthropological material, there would, I believe, be speedy and genuine advance on both sides."

3. Kluckhohn and Murray, for example, characterize "the bipolarity between 'personality and culture' as false or at least misleading in some important senses" (1948, p. xi); cf. Spiro. There have been other dichotomies (mind-matter, nature-man, body-mind, individual-society) which have had to be reordered with reference to some more inclusive unity.

studies pursued under this caption. What they have done is to refocus attention upon problems central to a deeper understanding of the nature of man, his behavior, and the primary significance of culture, at a more inclusive level of integration. In terms of the organization of knowledge today, this necessarily involves an interdisciplinary perspective.

Learning theory as developed in recent decades by psychologists, quite independently of the personality theories of psychoanalysis or psychiatry, may be cited as another example of specialized knowledge which is becoming more pertinent for anthropology at the same level of integration. Although culture, ever since the classical definition of Tylor, has been assumed to be a phenomenon that rests upon a learning process, without the intensive research of psychologists it is impossible to advance beyond the simplest kind of hypotheses in our own discipline. Only a few years ago Professor Kroeber, discussing "what culture is" and the use of such terms as "social heredity" and "social tradition," very pertinently remarked (1948, p. 253) that "perhaps *how it comes to be* is really more distinctive of culture than what it *is*." It is to *how* questions that much of personality and culture study is directed. Sophisticated knowledge of *how* a human being is groomed for the kind of adult life and social participation that prepares him for one kind of culture rather than for another, and likewise for passing it on, necessarily involves a learning theory as well as personality theory, in addition to any evaluation of the cultural determinants involved. A well-developed learning theory is relevant to promoting further knowledge of the whole process of cultural transmission as well as the processes involved in acculturation and culture change. Integrated knowledge of this order can hardly fail to be of interest

to all the social sciences. It should ultimately lead to formulations of greater predictive power than statements that "culture is always acquired by human individuals" or that culture is our "social inheritance" passed on from generation to generation by a process of conditioning, in contrast to our biological heritage transmitted through the "germ plasm." Today the latter term seems antiquated because we now know a great deal about the genes and how they operate. Relatively, we still know much less about the actual transmission of culture. One cannot fail to recall one of the central problems of anthropology as Boas conceived it. According to Benedict,[4] "he himself often said that this problem was the relation between the objective world and man's subjective world as it had taken form in different cultures." The actual processes and mechanisms of human adjustment which make this unique relationship possible in our species involve knowledge that transcends the descriptive facts of culture.

Today many reciprocal lines of interest have developed between anthropologists and those working in the psychological disciplines (psychoanalysts, psychiatrists, specialists in learning theory, perception, and social psychology, etc.), as well as with sociologists and other social scientists. Relations with those in the former group in particular have emerged mainly on the basis of the potentialities discerned in personality and culture studies rather than from any body of organized knowledge and theory now extant. It seems likely that these areas of reciprocal interest will be further developed and intensified. It is out of such an interchange that there may emerge a solid core of knowledge and theory that is directly relevant to all the disciplines that are now concerned with human be-

4. This is to Kroeber, Benedict, *et al.*, *Franz Boas* (1943).

havior, personality, and social relations.[5]

All the social and psychological disciplines must make some assumptions about the nature of man, society, culture, and personality,[6] no matter what areas of specialized research are undertaken. Among other things, some attitude must be adopted toward man's position in the natural universe and the necessary and sufficient conditions[7] or prerequisites, of a human existence as compared with a subhuman existence. It is the absence of such a core of generally accepted knowledge and theory which makes cross-disciplinary reference still difficult in many respects. Because anthropology has always maintained a perspective which has dealt with the evolutionary facts concerning

5. Cf. Murdock (1949), who "with tongue in cheek," has coined "lesocupethy" (from the two initial letters of learning, society, culture, personality, theory) points out that "there is as yet no general agreement as to an appropriate name for the emerging unified science. Such terms as 'human relations' and 'social relations' slight the psychological components and, to some, suggest application rather than theory. The 'science of human behavior' carries too strong a connotation of behaviorism and too weak an implication of important social and cultural factors. The general term 'social science' seems to exclude psychology." See also, Parsons and Shils (1951).

6. G. Gordon Brown in a recent article (1951) rejects the term "culture" "in the interests of clarity." He says: "I do not necessarily expect the concurrence of fellow anthropologists in thus slighting one of our most sacred terms but have personally found it expedient to think without it."

7. Cf. the remarks of J. H. Randall, Jr. (1944, pp. 355 ff.). Whitehead (1930, p. 99) has asserted: "It is a false dichotomy to think of Nature *and* Man. Mankind is that factor *in* Nature which exhibits in its most intense form the plasticity of Nature. Plasticity is the introduction of novel law. The doctrine of the Uniformity of Nature is to be ranked with the contrasted doctrine of Magic and Miracle, as an expression of partial truth, unguarded and uncoordinated with the immensities of the Universe. Our interpretations of experience determine the limits of what we can do with the world."

our species, on the one hand, and with the constancies and the widely varying aspects of cultural data, on the other, it should continue to be among the chief contributors to a developing science of man.

Society, culture, and personality may, of course, be conceptually differentiated for specialized types of analysis and study.[8] On the other hand, it is being more clearly recognized than heretofore that society, culture, and personality cannot be postulated as completely independent variables.[9] Man as an organic species, evolved from a primate ancestry, constitutes our basic frame of reference, and we find ourselves confronted, as observers, with the complexities of the human situation that have resulted from this process. Here I wish to consider man as the dynamic center of characteristic modes and processes of adjustment that are central to a human existence, in order to emphasize the integral reality of society, culture, and personality structure as human phenomena. It is this integral reality that constitutes the human situation as our unique subject matter. Our abstractions and constructs, which may be ordered in different ways and for different purposes and which may vary in their heuristic value, are derived from observations of the same integral

8. Nadel (1951, pp. 79 ff.) gives explicit references to the conceptual differences between "society" and "culture" that have been stressed by various anthropologists. "In recent anthropological literature," he observes, "the terms 'society' and 'culture' are accepted as referring to somewhat different things or, more precisely, to different ways of looking at the same thing."

9. Cf. Parsons and Shils (1951, p. 22): "Cultural patterns when internalized become constitutive elements of personalities and of social systems. *All concrete systems of action, at the same time, have a system of culture and are a set of personalities* (or sectors of them) and a social system or sub-system. Yet all three are conceptually independent organizations of the elements of action."

order of phenomena. And to it certain of our generalizations must eventually be directed. Instead of being primarily concerned, therefore, with definitions and with divergencies in point of view, I shall try to stress central issues and indicate the kind of basic assumptions and generalizations that seem reasonable to make if psychological data are considered integrally with sociocultural data.

Considered in purely material terms, man's constitution contains no chemical elements that are not found in other animals, rocks, and even distant nebulae.[10] Biologically, man is also continuous with other living things in nature. At the same time, he is morphologically distinct from his nearest animal kin. But a human mode of existence is dependent upon more than this. In evolutionary perspective, the level of functioning inherent in the human organism embodies novel possibilities of adaptation. Among these, and perhaps central, are inherent potentialities of a psychological order.[11] However, the

realization of these potentialities is contingent upon conditions outside the organism. One of the necessary conditions of psychological structuralization is association of the human individual with others of his species. Physical, social, or sensory isolation makes any full realization of these inherent potentialities impossible. That is, the development of a characteristically *human* psychological structure (mind or personality) is fundamentally dependent upon socially mediated experience in interaction with other persons. Inherent in the same condition is the concomitant development of a human social order and a cultural heritage. A human society, by minimal definition, requires organized relations, differentiated roles,[12] and patterns of social interaction, not simply an aggregation of people.[13] Since the

10. Cf. Shapley (1930), who essays a cosmic survey of the material universe known to us. "Our studies of the universe," he says, "show the uniformity of its chemical structure and generally of its physical laws. We are colloids. Our very bodies consist of the same chemical elements found in the most distant nebulae and our activities are guided by the same universal rules. The recent analyses of the chemical constitution of man, beast, rock and star have brought to light the remarkable uniformity of all chemical composition. Little as we human beings are, so temporary in time and space, yet the chemical elements of which we are composed are also the predominant elements in the crust of the earth and are prominent components in the structure of the fiery and gaseous stars. We are, chemically, made of nothing unusual or exotic."

11. Schneirla contrasts the "psycho-social" level of adaptation in human societies with the "bio-social" level of insect societies. "The individual learning capacity of insects, stereotyped and situation-limited as it is, plays a subordinate (facilitating) role in individual socialization and shows its greatest elaboration in

the foraging act (i.e., outside the nest). The various individuals make reproductive or nutritive contributions to colony welfare, and no individual learning that occurs can change the standard pattern of the species in lasting ways. The society is bio-social in the sense that it is a composite resultant of individual biological characteristics dominating group behavior.

"In contrast, human societies may be termed psycho-social, in that cultural processes dominate which are the cumulative and non-genetically transmitted resultants of experience and learning, under the influence of human needs and desires interacting variably with the procedures of labor or conflict, reasoning or routine."

12. Cf. Parsons and Shils (1951) on role as the unit of social systems. H. S. Jennings, discussing the differentia of social organization among infra-human animals, writes: "... only if the individuals play different functional roles is there social organization" (1942, p. 105).

13. Aberle, Cohen, *et al.* (1950, p. 101) define a society as "a group of human beings sharing a self-sufficient system of action which is capable of existing longer than the life-span of an individual, the group being recruited at least in part by the sexual reproduction of the members." As functional prerequisites to a society, i.e., *what* must get done, not *how* it is done, the authors list the following: (*a*) provision for adequate relationship to the envi-

structure represented by the organized relations of its component individuals is a function of their capacity for social adjustment through learning, even a superficial analysis indicates that a human society is dependent upon psychological processes. Since the persistence of any human social order over any considerable period of time involves the replacement of its personnel, the crucial importance of psychological processes is obvious. The maintenance of any particular form of human social organization not only requires provision for the addition of new individuals by reproduction but ways and means of structuralizing the psychological field of the individual in a manner that will induce him to act in certain predictable ways. From whatever angle we look at the situation, the psychological potentialities of man are integral to the maintenance of a social order. No natural boundary can be drawn between the individual and society when the latter is conceptualized as an identifiable unit with an observable structure that persists in time.

Viewed from the standpoint of the individual, a socialization process is the psychological concomitant of the process of physical maturation with which it is integrated in varying ways.[14] At

---

ronment and for sexual recruitment, (*b*) role differentiation and role assignment, (*c*) communication, (*d*) shared cognitive orientation, (*e*) a shared, articulated set of goals, (*f*) the normative regulation of means, (*g*) the regulation of affective expression, (*h*) socialization, (*i*) the effective control of disruptive forms of behavior.

Although not directly concerned with explicit relations between society, culture, and personality structure, it is obvious, I think, that in answer to the question "*How* are these functional prerequisites mediated?" a necessary assumption is that the individual members of a society must become psychologically structured in a manner that will tend to maintain a socio*cultural* system and, at the same time, afford a satisfactory personal adjustment to life.

birth the human individual is prepared for only a very limited sphere of action because the neonate is undeveloped and dependent upon others. Psychological maturation is dependent upon the organization of inherent potentialities, in order that the individual may be prepared for autonomous action in the larger sphere that includes much more than the roles and patterns of social interaction that characterize his society. The socialization process *may* be viewed functionally as a necessary condition for the continuity of a social structure. But this structure is an abstraction from a larger reality. A human society requires the continuously motivated behavior of human beings in a culturally constituted behavioral environment that is cognitively structured with reference both to the nature of the cosmos as well as to the self, in which traditional meanings and values play a vital role in the organization of needs and goals, and in which the reorganization and redirection of experience, expressed in discovery, invention, and culture change, are potentially present. The psychological core of being human involves a level of integration that implies much more than a set of roles and habit patterns, important as these are.

Even though a chimpanzee may learn to ride a bicycle, all the motivations connected with such a performance and the needs and goals that may be connected with it are, for him, not of the same order as those of a human being. Even as an object it cannot be a bicycle to him. Although he may be-

14. See Margaret Mead (1951) for a "study of the way in which human growth rhythms are patterned within human cultures." Three areas of research are defined: "(1) the nature of the human growth process, (2) the degree of individuality within the human growth process and (3) the way in which these growth processes, the generally human and the idiosyncratic, are interwoven in the process of learning to be a human being in a given culture" (p. 14).

come highly skilled in performance and respond adequately to the authoritative directions of a human being, the fact that he has learned to ride a bicycle does not qualify a chimp as a member of a human society. All he has learned are certain signs and skills. The level of psychological organization that is characteristic of the chimpanzee permits a great deal of learning, but under no conceivable conditions would it be possible for a chimp to invent a bicycle.[15] Men, given certain motivational conditions and technological knowledge, have been able to invent bicycles as well as ride them. One of the major conditions typical of, and a crucial implement in, the socialization process in man is a novel means of communication. Neither a human society nor a human personality can be conceived in functional terms apart from systems of symbolic communication.

At the level of human adjustment the *representation* of objects and events of all kinds plays as characteristic a role in man's total behavior as does the direct *presentation* of objects and events in perception. Thus skill in the manipulation of symbols is directly involved with the development of man's rational and creative capacities. But symbolization is likewise involved with all other psychic functions—attention, perception, interest, memory, dreams, imagination, etc. Representative processes are

15. The remarkably vivid account of Viki, adopted and brought up in the home of Dr. and Mrs. Hayes (see Hayes, 1951), dramatizes the inherent psychobiological limitations of the chimpanzee under optimum conditions of systematic motivation from infancy, designed to exploit the animal's full potentialities for comparison with children reared under comparable circumstances. The range of the imitative responses of the chimpanzee in all spheres *except* language has never been more sharply demonstrated. Within three years Viki *did* become "socialized" in the human sense; her responses did become appropriately conditioned to culturally defined situations; even her food habits were not "culture free"; she became a "carrier" of culture—but only up to a point.

at the root of man's capacity to deal with the abstract qualities of objects and events, his ability to deal with the possible or conceivable, the ideal as well as the actual, the intangible along with the tangible, the absent as well as the present object or event, with fantasy and with reality. Every culture as well as the personal adjustment of each individual gives evidence of this, both at the level of unconscious as well as conscious processes. Then, too, symbolic forms and processes color man's motivations, goals, and his affective life in a characteristic way. They are as relevant to an understanding of his psychopathological as to his normal behavior. [16]

Symbolic communication is the basis on which a common world of meanings and values is established and transmitted in human societies. Communication at this new level is a necessary condition for the operation of human societies in their characteristic form.

Since even a most highly evolved primate, like the chimpanzee, cannot master a human language and there is no evidence that at any subhuman level the graphic and plastic arts exist, extrinsic symbolic systems as media of communication are an exclusively human creation. They provide man with the central vehicle that has been used to build up culturally constituted modes of existence for himself. The transmission of culture, either generically or specifically conceived, is the over-all unifying factor in the temporal continuity of man from generation to generation. And, since man has been able to develop, live by, and transmit different images of the nature of the world and himself, rather than adapt himself to some given existential reality in an "objective" sense, distinct cultural traditions become the differential attributes of discrete human societies.

16. Hallowell (1950a, pp. 165–66). Cf. Cassirer (1944). Nissen (1951) discusses symbolization in phylogenetic perspective as a novel instrumentality of special significance in the human primate.

Consequently, there can be no natural cleavage, from the standpoint of the dynamics of human adjustment, between the psychological organization of the individual, culture, and society. While a human mind has long been assumed to be a necessary psychological substratum of a human existence and implicitly, if not explicitly, of culture and although Dewey pointed out many years ago that a "social" existence was a necessary condition for the development of a human mind in the individual,[17] it is no longer satisfactory to

speak of human societies as constituted of individuals with human minds, and let it go at that. We need to know what the integral relations are between mind, society, and culture. But we are still handicapped in our thinking by these familiar categorical terms; especially so since, being traditionally associated with disciplines approaching man from different points of view, mind, society, and culture have from time to time been given substantive definition.

From the psychological point of view the concept of "personality structure" would appear to mark a conceptual transition from an earlier period to now. This concept and the theoretical constructs back of it force us to think in terms of how the human individual is specifically organized psychodynamically. It orients us toward the conditions under which psychological structuralization takes place and the relations between differences in personality organization and behavioral differences. The Freudian model of personality structure and its derivative formulations has provided the most useful constructs so far but not necessarily the final ones.[18]

Historically, there is some analogy to the situation in physics at the end of the nineteenth century. Up until that time, physics had gotten along very well on the assumption that the atom was something very small, hard, possibly spherical, and of more or less uniform constitution throughout. The atom, in short, was conceived essentially as an ultimate particle of matter. It was not supposed that it possessed a structure and that a deeper knowledge of this structure would revolutionize our conception of matter.

---

17. Dewey (1917) drew attention to what he considered to be a very fruitful conception of Gabriel Tarde, far ahead of his time. This, writes Dewey, was the idea that "all psychological phenomena can be divided into the physiological and the social, and that when we have relegated elementary sensation and appetite to the former head, all that is left of our mental life, our beliefs, ideas and desires fall within the scope of social psychology." More recent developments, continues Dewey, have provided "an unexpected confirmation of the insight of Tarde that what we call 'mind' means essentially the working of certain beliefs and desires, and that these in the concrete—in the only sense in which mind may be said to exist—are functions of associated behavior, varying with the structure and operation of social groups." Thus, instead of being viewed as "an antecedent and ready-made thing, 'mind' represents a reorganization of original activities through their operation in a given environment. It is a formation, not a datum, a product and a cause only after it has been produced. Now, theoretically, it is possible that the reorganization of native activities which constitute mind may occur through their exercise within a purely physical medium. Empirically, however, this is highly improbable. Consideration of the dependence in infancy of the organization of the native activities into intelligence upon the presence of others, upon sharing in joint activities and upon language, makes it obvious that the sort of mind capable of development through the operation of native endowment in a non-social environment is of the moron order, and is practically, if not theoretically, negligible." The fact that Dewey makes use of neither the term "culture" nor the term "personality" makes the clarity of his statement all the more interesting and significant in historical perspective.

18. See Mullahy (1948) for an exposition of psychoanalytic personality theories and the relevant literature. Cf. Bronfenbrenner (1951) and the "Symposium on Theoretical Models and Personality Theory" in the *Journal of Personality*, Vol. XX, No. 1 (1951), to which psychologists are the main contributors.

The generic concept of "mind" when applied to "individuals" as the "units" of "society" and as the "bearers" of "culture" may have been useful in relation to certain orders of abstraction in the past, but we can now see more clearly the limitations imposed by this kind of conceptualization.

Furthermore, structural concepts have already supplanted the older concept of "society" in many areas of sociological analysis. And the "pattern" concept is the most obvious cultural analogy (cf. Weakland, 1951, p. 59). The concept of personality structure belongs to the same conceptual trend. Unlike the concept "mind" of an older tradition, the concept of personality structure *assumes* a sociocultural matrix as an essential condition of ontogenetic development. It involves a systematic examination of the influence of the relevant factors that constitute this matrix, considered as independent variables with reference to the kind of personality structure that is produced and to which characteristic patterns of conduct, considered as dependent variables, are related. In terms of such a paradigm the structure of personality is conceived as being rooted in part in an organized system of intervening variables.[19]

To say that culture, viewed as an independent variable in relation to the human organism, "determines" or "conditions" *behavior* is to conceive the problem much too narrowly, if not inadequately. While it is quite true that the acquisition of motor skills and other habits of this order may be rather simply related to culture, what has impressed many psychologists as a more important contribution of anthropology is the demonstrable relations between cultural variability and the motivational systems of human individuals, that is, the differential organization of drives, needs, emotions, attitudes, and so on, which lie at the core of relatively enduring *dispositions* to act in a predictable manner. As Else Frenkel-Brunswik has expressed it (Adorno, Frenkel, Brunswik, *et al.*, 1950, pp. 5 ff.):

Personality is a more or less enduring organization of forces within the individual. These persisting forces of personality help to determine response in various situations, and it is thus largely to them that consistency of behavior—whether verbal or physical—is attributable. But behavior, however consistent, is not the same thing as personality; personality lies *behind* behavior and *within* the individual. The forces of personality are not responses but *readiness* for response; whether or not a readiness will issue in overt expression depends not only upon the situation of the moment but upon what other readiness stands in opposition to it. Personality forces which are inhibited are on a deeper level than those which immediately and consistently express themselves in overt behavior. . . .

Although personality is a product of the social environment[20] of the past, it is not, once it has developed, a mere object of the contemporary environment. What has developed is a *structure* within the individual something which is capable of self-initiated action upon the social environment and of selection with respect to varied impinging stimuli; something which though always modifiable is frequently very resistant to fundamental change. This conception is necessary to explain consistency of behavior in widely varying situations, to explain the persistence of ideological trends in the face of contradictory facts and radically altered social conditions, to explain why people in the same sociological situation have different or even conflicting views on social issues, and why it is that people whose behavior has been changed through psychological manipulation lapse into their old ways as soon as the agencies of manipulation are removed.

19. For a simple diagram representing motives, attitudes, etc. as intervening variables see Newcomb (1950, p. 31). E. C. Tolman sets forth a model in which intervening variables constitute the crucial construct in Parsons and Shils (1951, Part 3).

20. "Cultural" may be substituted.

The conception of personality structure is the best safeguard against the inclination to attribute persistent trends in the individual to something "innate" or "basic" or "racial" within him.

The concept of personality structure has proved particularly useful because, in addition to providing an effective intellectual means for examining the factors underlying the psychodynamics of individual adjustment, it has been found possible to express the major central tendencies that are characteristic of a series of individuals who belong to a single society, tribal group, or nation, in more or less equivalent terms.[21] This does not mean, of course, that there are no idiosyncratic variations in the personality structure of such a series of individuals. On the contrary, this must be expected. What is assumed is that membership in a given sociocultural system, or subsystem, subjects human beings to a common set of conditions that are significant with reference to the personality organization of these individuals. As Kluckhohn and Murray phrase it (1948, p. 39):

The members of any organized enduring group tend to manifest certain personality traits more frequently than do members of other groups. How large or how small are the groupings one compares depends on the problem at hand. By and large, the motivational structures and action patterns of Western Europeans seem similar when contrasted to those of the Near East or to Eastern Asiatics. Most white citizens of the United States, in spite of regional,

21. Although the terminology employed has varied somewhat both with respect to semantic content as well as to linguistic expression, nevertheless similar phenomena have been brought to a focus in what has been characterized, e.g., as "basic personality structure" (Kardiner, 1939, 1945a); "modal personality structure" (DuBois, 1944); "communal aspects of personality" (Kluckhohn and Mowrer, 1944); "social character" (Fromm, 1941); and "national character" (see the survey of the literature by Klineberg, 1950). Cf. Honigmann's tabulation of "Some Concepts of Ethos" (1949, Appendix B, pp. 357–59).

ethnic, and class differences, have features of personality which distinguish them from Englishmen, Australians or New Zealanders. In distinguishing group-membership determinants, one must usually take account of a concentric order of social groups to which the individual belongs, ranging from large national or international groups down to small local units. One must also know the hierarchical class, political or social, to which he belongs within each of these groups. How inclusive a unit one considers in speaking of group-membership determinants is purely a function of the level of abstraction at which one is operating at a given time.

In this connection the question also arises: To what kind of cultural unit are personality data to be related? Can we assume that our cultural classifications, as, for example, well-established areal differences, necessarily have a one-to-one correspondence with differences in modal personality type? Devereux has argued (1951, p. 38) that

in many respects the segment or aspect of the basic personality which is determined by the areal ethos is, functionally at least, a far more important component of the total personality of a given Plains Indian, than is the segment determined by the culture pattern of his own particular tribe. In fact, it might even be argued that the *specific manner* in which, e.g., a Crow Indian differs from a Cheyenne Indian, is entirely different from the *specific manner* in which *either* of the two differs from a Pueblo Indian, and that these two distinctive types of intra-areal, respectively inter-areal, differences are also determined primarily by the influence which the respective areal ethoses exert upon the personality of the Plains Indian, and upon that of the Pueblo Indian.

On the basis of observations contained in seventeenth- and eighteenth-century documents the writer inferred a constellation of psychological characteristics which he generalized for the Indians of the Eastern Woodland area, despite the well-known linguistic and cultural difference between Algonkian peoples and the Iroquois (Hallowell, 1946). Later, Fenton (1948, pp. 505–10) expressed essential agreement that most of these traits seemed reasonably applicable to the modern Iroquois. Wallace (in press), on the basis of a sample of Rorschach protocols representing a highly acculturated Tuscarora community, demonstrated a core of personality characteristics common to these people and the Ojibwa, as well as differences which seemed congruent with cultural differences.

On the other hand, Rorschach data (unpublished) from the Hopi, Navaho, Zuni, and Papago suggest quite marked tribal differences, so far as psychological adjustment is concerned. No one has studied this material, however, with a view to determining both similarities and differences. At the same time, Kroeber (1947), reviewing autobiographical and dream material, was impressed with "the rather striking similarity of the untutored, unguided self-depiction of a particular Navaho and a particular Walapai," and he raises the question whether the likeness is a "coincidence," which, he says, he does not believe, "or mainly due to a regional though super tribal resemblance of culture; or whether perhaps it is generally expectable in folk cultures, as a recurrent type definable in socio-psychological terms, although varying somewhat in its outer cultural dress."

Perhaps it is not possible to give conclusive answers to such questions at the present time but only to view them as research problems still open for investigation. A closely related question would be whether or not there are definable psychological characteristics which, say in North America, may even transcend the cultural areas that have been defined and typify "Indians," as contrasted with Europeans or Melanesians (cf. Kroeber, 1948, p. 587).

Another question, of a different type, has been raised by Kroeber (1948, p.

597 n.; cf. p. 587), namely, "the possibility that cultures of unlike content can be alike psychologically; or their contents may be similar but their psychology dissimilar." In regard to the first possibility, a most suggestive psychological analogue has been drawn by Goldschmidt[22] between Yurok-Hupa, on the one hand, and emergent capitalistic Europe, on the other, i.e., two spatially distant and historically unconnected peoples. Goldschmidt's thesis is that, in both instances, "the structural character of the society is one which rewards certain personality configurations so that they dominate the social scene and set the patterns. It also creates a configuration of demands and tensions which are transmitted through child rearing to successive generations." Typical personality characteristics stressed are "a compulsive concern over asceticism and industriousness, patterns of personal guilt, as well as tendencies toward hostility, competition and loneliness."

What specific factors, or patterns of determinants, are the most crucial for the structuring of the personality, how and when and by what means they become psychologically effective in the socialization of the individual, have been objects of specific researches in the culture and personality area.

Ethnographic knowledge on a worldwide comparative scale, including observable differences in modes of child-training, value systems, and goals, together with the traditional emphasis upon the fact that culture is acquired by the individual, stimulated anthropologists to develop hypotheses concerning the relation of personality structure to cultural variables, once some of them became aware of the newer developments in personality theory. Be-

22. 1951, pp. 521–22; H. E. Erickson, approaching the Yurok material from the standpoint of child training, developed a somewhat different interpretation of their culture.

sides this, anthropologists, as contrasted with other social scientists and psychologists, were accustomed to doing field work in other cultures, so it was possible to test hypotheses in the field and to exploit the significant cross-cultural data as well. We may say, I think, that the general hypothesis underlying culture and personality studies has been confirmed. Moot points, such as how early personality structure is set, what reorganization is possible after the initial years of childhood, and what are the most crucial determining factors involved, concern personality theory itself rather than the fundamental hypothesis.[23] That human personality structure is a product of experience in a socialization process and that the resulting structure varies with the nature and conditions of such experience can scarcely be doubted.[24]

Reinforcement is now coming from psychologists through a renewed interest in the study of perception. Although long conceptualized as a basic function of the "mind" and chiefly investigated at the level of psychophysics, more recent studies have clearly shown the need of taking personality variables into account.[25] It is rapidly becoming a psychological commonplace that human beings groomed under different conditions may be expected to vary in perceptual experience, functionally related to needs, which, in turn, are in part defined by a culturally constituted order of reality. The properties of a universal objective order of reality, once reputed to be mediated to us directly through

cognitive processes, are now conceded to involve more complex determinants and intervening variables, related to noncognitive experiences of the human organism.[26]

The importance of this hypothesis for a deeper understanding of the nature of the integral relations that exist between personality, culture, and society is far-reaching. Since perception is fundamental to all human adjustment in the sense that it is made the basis of judgment, decision, and action, to experience the world in common perceptual terms must be considered a prime unifying factor in the integration of culture, society, and the functioning person. Indeed, through the operation of culturally derived constituents, perception in man may be said to have acquired an overlaid *social* function. Among other things, it becomes one of the chief psychological means whereby beliefs in reified images and concepts as integral parts of a culturally constituted reality may become substantiated in the experience of individuals.[27] Different world views as described in our ethnographic monographs take on a deeper significance when considered in relation to the functioning of perception in man. We are on our way to a better grasp of the significance of culture as *lived* rather than as described.[28]

26. This by no means implies an "absolute" relativism in perception. Recognition of this fact simply helps to define the real problem. A completely relativistic hypothesis would be as inadequate as a purely absolute one (see Gibson, 1950a).

27. See Hallowell (1951a); Dennis has a related chapter in Blake and Ramsey (1951).

28. Lewin (1948) has pointed out that "experiments dealing with memory and group pressure on the individual show that what exists as 'reality' for the individual is, to a high degree, determined by what is socially accepted as reality. This holds even in the field of physical fact: to the South Sea Islander the world may be flat; to the European it is round. 'Reality,' therefore, is not an abso-

23. See the critique by Orlansky (1949).

24. A highly representative example in which the conceptual frame of reference adopted and the hypotheses employed are clearly set forth in DuBois (1944).

25. See Blake and Ramsey (1951). Hilgard has a chapter on "The Role of Learning in Perception"; Bruner discusses "Personality Dynamics and the Process of Perceiving"; Miller, "Unconscious Processes and Perception"; etc.

As anthropologists, we may acquire a very detailed and thoroughgoing knowledge of the belief system, the social organization, as well as all the other aspects of a culture. We may learn to act with propriety, to sing a song or two, to dance, or to draw a bow. We may be bursting with empathy. We may even learn to speak the language. We may be aware of culture patterns and subtle relations that escape the people themselves. But the culture we study is not part of us. Our perceptions are not structured in the same mold. The very fact that our approach is objective, that we want to grasp it in its totality, is an index to the fact that we do not belong. We are not motivated to learn about another culture in order to live it but in order to talk or write about it, describe it, analyze it, seek out its history. The meaning of culture that emerges for us is a function of *our* background, interests, aims. In terms of this approach, substantive conceptualizations of culture rather than psychological or functional ones are almost inescapable. But culture may likewise be conceived as

lute. It differs with the group to which the individual belongs.

"This dependence of the individual on the group for a determination of what does and what does not constitute 'reality' is less surprising if we remember that the individual's own experience is necessarily limited. In other words, the probability that his judgment will be right is heightened if the individual places greater trust in the experience of the group, whether or not this group experience tallies with his own. This is one reason for the acceptance of the group's judgment, but there is still another reason. In any field of conduct and belief, the group exercises strong pressure for compliance on its individual members. We are subject to this pressure in all areas—political, religious, social—including our belief of what is true or false, good or bad, right or wrong, real or unreal. Under these circumstances it is not difficult to understand why the general acceptance of a fact or a belief might be the very cause preventing this belief or fact from even being questioned."

meaningful in terms of the psychological adjustment of the human being to his world of action and to concrete living, not as abstracted by an outsider. A psychological approach to culture, in the sense that what we wish to find out is the structural basis of the varying ways in which man has built up distinctive modes of life for himself, not only throws light upon the nature of man and the necessary conditions of a human existence but upon the substratum of particular cultures as descriptively generalized.

The psychological substratum of culture has been partially obscured until recently, because, in addition to the lack of effective theories of personality structure, development, and functioning, theories of learning adequate for handling this complicated process at the human level were not sufficiently developed. To some extent this is still true. Only a few years ago, Hilgard pointed out that sometimes psychologists have given the impression that "there are no differences, except quantitative ones, between the learning of lower animals and primates, including man." He goes on to say, however, that, "while this position is more often implied than asserted, it is strange that the opposite point of view is not more often made explicit—that at the human level there have emerged capacities for retaining, reorganizing, and foreseeing experiences which are not approached by the lower animals, including the other primates. No one has seriously proposed that animals can develop a set of ideals which regulate conduct around long-range plans, or that they can invent a mathematics to help them keep track of their experiences. Because a trained dog shows some manifestations of shame, or a chimpanzee some signs of cooperation, or a rat a dawning concept of triangularity, it does not follow that these lower organisms, clever as they are, have all the richness of human mental activity."[29]

The learning process when considered in relation to culture has often been conceptualized too simply in the past, among other reasons because it has not been considered in relation to the development of a personality structure and likewise to the potentialities for readjustment and creativity that this level of psychological organization in man permits, with appropriate motivation.

We now know that to say *merely* that the individual acquires culture through learning in a socialization process is only a confession of ignorance as to what this process actually involves. We know at least that culture as systematically described and topically organized by the ethnographer is not what is directly presented to and learned by the individual at any point in this process. We know that the socialization process from the very beginning is mediated by close personal relations of the child with adults and that there are important affective components involved. We know that mediation through symbolic modes of communication plays a role. We know that the individual beginning at a level of dependence must achieve the capacity for independent and autonomous action. We know that the individual must achieve some kind of patterned integration that we call "personality structure." We know that, while this structure may take different forms, there are likewise constant elements that are characteristic of a *human* personality structure in a generic sense. We know

29. Ernest R. Hilgard (1948, pp. 329–30). Cf. Miller and Dollard (1941) and Gibson's outline of what he considers to be desirable features of a theory of social learning in man (1950*b*). Whiting (1941), using the Hull model of learning theory, systematically analyzes the acquisition of Kwoma culture by the child. The chapter on "Inculcation of Supernatural Beliefs" is of special interest.

that, concretely viewed, culture becomes part of the individual. If this were not so, he could not live it nor could he hand it on.[30] Beliefs viewed abstractly as part of a culture objectively described become his beliefs; values are incorporated into his motivational system; his needs and goals, although culturally constituted, function as personal needs and goals. A culture as lived is not something apart from the individuals who live it or separable from the societal organization through which group living functions, any more than the characteristic features of an animal's morphology are something

30. Tolman (see Parsons and Shils, 1951, p. 359) has remarked that "psychology is in large part a study of the internalization of society and of culture within the individual human actor"; and Newcomb (1950, p. 6) speaks of the individual as having "somehow got society inside himself. Its ways of doing things become his own." Cf. Miller and Hutt (1949), who point out that "the interiorization of social values is only a relatively recent area of investigation."

Such statements, coming from psychologists in particular, are highly relevant for cultural anthropology. In so far as some anthropologists have given the impression, even if they have not always systematically defended the view, that, fundamentally, culture is to be considered as something apart from or outside the individual rather than as an integral part of him, some basic dichotomy between personality and culture is implied. An extreme statement of this position is embodied in the remark of White (1947) that, "as a matter of fact, the most effective way to study culture scientifically is to proceed as if the human race did not exist." Spiro has brought this problem to a focus in his 1951 article. "What cultural realists have failed to realize," he says, "is that once something is learned it is no longer external to the organism, but is 'inside' the organism; and once it is 'inside,' the organism becomes a biosocial organism, determining its own behavior as a consequence of the modifications it has undergone in the process of learning. But the individual-culture dichotomy accepted by the realists prevents them from acknowledging this most elementary point and, as a consequence, they think in terms of a superorganic culture determining the behavior of an organic adult."

apart from the gene system that is their substratum. A living, functioning culture is not, existentially, dependent upon a group of interacting human beings, abstractly considered, but upon the manner in which such individuals are psychologically structured. A culture may be said to be just as much the *expression* of their mode of human psychodynamic adjustment as it is a *condition* for the grooming of successive generations of individuals in this mode.

Fromm has pointed out (1949, pp. 5–6, 10):

Modern, industrial society, for instance, could not have attained its ends had it not harnessed the energy of free men for work in an unprecedented degree. He had to be moulded into a person who was eager to spend most of his energy for the purpose of work, who acquired discipline, particularly orderliness and punctuality, to a degree unknown in most other cultures. It would not have sufficed if each individual had to make up his mind consciously every day that he wanted to work, to be on time, etc., since any such conscious deliberation would have led to many more exceptions than the smooth functioning of society can afford. Threat and force would not have sufficed either as motive for work since the highly differentiated work in modern industrial society can only be the work of free men and not of forced labor. The *necessity* for work, for punctuality and orderliness had to be transformed into a *drive* for these qualities. This means that society had to produce such a social character in which these strivings were inherent.

Human beings, in other words, have to become psychologically structured in such a way that they "*want to act as they have to act* [author's italics] and at the same time find gratification in acting according to the requirements of the culture." According to Fromm, there must be some nuclear character structure "shared by most members of the same culture," i.e., "social character," the functioning of which is essential to the functioning of the culture as a going concern.[31] Child-training, viewed in the context of social structure, is "one of the key *mechanisms of transmission of social necessities into character traits* [author's italics]."

The behavioral manifestations upon which we depend for constructing our substantive pictures of cultures are always rooted in the personality structure of individuals. The only way in which a culture may be said to perpetuate itself is through the characteristic psychological structuralization of a group of individuals. It is only through organized personalities, not "individuals" or "minds," that human societies and culture attain living reality. In so far as a culture may in any sense be conceived abstractly, it is *our* abstraction, a convenience adapted to the kind of analysis we wish to make of the problems we wish to pursue. Culture can hardly be an abstraction for those to whom it is an intellectually unexamined mode of life. Human beings have died in defense of concrete beliefs, which, abstractly viewed, may be characterized as a part of their culture but which, psychologically considered, take on the kind of palpable reality that motivates actual behavior. I suspect that there still may linger in the minds of some a faint aura of an earlier day, when psychology meant psychophysics, or primarily a study of the mechanisms of behavior or the investigation of the properties of mind

31. Cf. the statement of Goldschmidt (*op. cit.*, p. 522): "The individualized pattern of social action, the internalized demands for personal success with its road theoretically open to all, the absence of fixity of social position and security in group solidarity, and the importance of property for social advancement and hence satisfaction of the *ego*—all these combine to support such traits of character as aggressiveness, hostility, competitiveness, loneliness and penuriousness. *Indeed, it is hard to see how a Hupa or Yurok could operate effectively in his society without these traits*" (italics ours).

in the most generic and abstract sense, and little else. In contrast, the rich and varied content of cultures appeared to be in another phenomenal dimension. Today, in some areas of social anthropology, abstract relations and patterns are given prime consideration. On the other hand, for an understanding of personality structure, its development, and relationship to a typically human mode of existence, cultural content in its full range and depth cannot be ignored.

Although the child requires socialization in order to achieve the psychological status that marks him as a human being, it is not necessary that he develop the particular personality structure that characterizes societies A, C, or N; B, D, or Z will provide the necessary conditions that are functionally equivalent. What we have to assume—and there is empirical evidence for this—is that there are generic attributes of human personality as well as provincial and variable kinds of organization. There is an obvious analogy with human speech. A necessary condition for socialization in man is the learning and use of a language. But different languages are functionally equivalent in this respect, and one language is comparable with another because human speech has certain common denominators.

While a human individual, therefore, on account of his inherent organic potentialities, can adjust himself to life under a variety of conditions, a particular culture, in so far as we assume it to be dependent upon a characteristic psychological organization of a group of individuals, cannot maintain its existence unless this condition is satisfied.[32] In terms of this hypothesis, man's

potentialities for readjustment and creativity are thrown into sharp relief as constant human phenomena. Particular cultures may rise, flourish, and disappear, but other modes of life take their place. While viewed in a provincial setting and in limited temporal perspective, it may seem adequate to speak of individuals as the "carriers" of a culture or the "creatures" of culture, this does not take into account *all* that we know about the nature of man. If we fail to give due weight to man's potentialities as creator and re-creator of the kind of life that is his most distinctive attribute, how are we to account for the emergence of a cultural mode of existence in the first place?[33] Surely, we must assume that it has been through the development of his own potentialities that man has made the

---

32. Newcomb (1950, p. 448) has generalized this point, emphasizing childhood experiences as the "essential link" in temporal continuity: "Childhood experiences provide the essential link in the chain by which the culture of any society and the common personality characteristics of its members are bound together and continue to be bound together over succeeding generations.... There would be neither common personality characteristics within a society nor a continuing culture were it not for common childhood experiences."

33. Bidney (1947, p. 395) postulates a "human nature" that "is logically and genetically prior to culture since we must postulate human agents with psychobiological powers and impulses capable of initiating the cultural process as a means of adjusting to their environment and as a form of symbolic expression. In other words, the determinate nature of man is manifested functionally through culture but is not reducible to culture." In another article (1949, p. 347) he points out: "In the development of modern cultural anthropology one may discern two major 'themes.' On the one hand there is the theme derived from the naturalistic, positivistic, evolutionary tradition of the Nineteenth Century that cultural reality represents an autonomous, superorganic, superpsychic level of reality subject to its own laws and stages of development or evolution. On the other hand, there is the recurring theme, which dates back to the humanistic tradition of the Renaissance and the rationalism of the Eighteenth Century philosophers of the Enlightenment, that human culture is the product of human discovery and creativity and is subject to human regulation."

world intelligible to himself in livable terms. Whatever form these images may have taken, they have emerged out of human experience, transmuted into symbolically articulated terms. Since creativity in the individual human being, in so far as we know anything about it, involves unconscious processes, we may assume that equivalent factors have been among those operative throughout man's history. If, therefore, we examine the relation between the individual and culture only with regard to the manner in which he becomes groomed as a participator in a static provincial and continuing mode of life, we may *avoid*, but never solve, the more perplexing problems that arise if we keep man as a whole constantly in view. When we do this, culture change, acculturation, and personal readjustment come into the foreground.

We know too little as yet about the psychological consequences of acculturation to make any broad generalizations. But we assume that changes in any established mode of life that eventuate in new or varied culture patterns imply readjustment in the habits, attitudes, and goals of the individuals concerned, that such processes of readjustment must be motivated, and that learning is involved.[34] The crucial question, however, turns upon the psychological depth of such readjustments. And this question, in turn, depends upon a number of situational variables: the time span covered, the rate of acculturation, the manner in which the relations between individuals of the interacting groups are structured, qualitative factors, etc. All the processes of social interaction involved are matched in complexity by those of a psychological nature.[35] We certainly cannot assume, even in an acculturation situation where

one group is dominant over the other and the pressures on the subordinate group are severe, that the latter can acquire a new personality structure by the same process or in terms of the same motivations which lead to the acquisition of new tools, house types, or a new language. In my own investigations of the Ojibwa, I believe I have secured sufficient evidence to demonstrate that considerable acculturation can occur without any profound effect upon the "modal" or "communal" aspects of personality. On the other hand, the same data indicate that, in one group at least, conditions exist that have greatly accelerated the breakdown of the aboriginal personality structure that has persisted in other groups despite a considerable degree of acculturation.[36]

If we wish to understand more about the potentialities of human beings for psychological reorganization and a reconstruction of their culture, a close examination of what happens under various conditions of acculturation will be fruitful. In one type of situation, it is

34. See Hallowell (1945) for a preliminary consideration of the problem.

35. See, in particular, Spindler and Goldschmidt (1952). Their research design is "oriented toward the understanding of the processes of change within a society [the Menomini Indians of Wisconsin] under the impact of modern American civilization, and is particularly concerned with the adoption of outward manifestations of cultural and social behavior in their relation to changes in the individual personality characteristics of its personnel, without for the present, treating either as the independent variable in the situation." The results of this particular investigation are being prepared for publication by George Spindler.

Adams (1951) discussed the hypothesis advanced by H. G. Barnett in "Personal Conflicts and Cultural Change" (1941) with reference to his own data.

36. The major summarization of data and conclusions may be found in Hallowell (1951b). Cf. Hallowell (1950b) and the brief presentation in *Acculturation in the Americas: Proceedings and Selected Papers of the XXIXth International Congress of Americanists*, ed. Sol Tax (1952).

true, a whole group of individuals may be forced back on their psychological heels, so to speak. But it would be interesting to know more about the conditions under which a positive psychological reorganization might take place. One would like to know which are the most important factors that might contribute to the latter outcome. I suspect that a crucial variable may be the kind of personality structure of the people undergoing acculturation.

Here I think we have one of the crucial points of human adjustment, considered from the standpoint of man's group living and the perpetuation of a particular cultural tradition. The type of personality structure that prepares the individual for group living in *one* set of cultural terms does not prepare him for a successful adjustment to life in *any* set of cultural terms. Nevertheless, the people of one society may have the kind of personality organization that, under given conditions, enables them to adjust more readily to a new mode of life than the people of some other society. Fully to understand the dynamics of acculturation, we need to take psychological, as well as cultural, facts into account.

Changes in the cultural patterning of existence are always possible to man so long as certain generic psychological conditions, prerequisite for the maintenance of *any* human society, are met. Evans-Pritchard (1951), for example, in discussing what is implied by the term "social structure," points out that "it is evident that there must be uniformities and regularities in social life, that a society must have some sort of order, or its members could not live together," and then goes on to say: "It is only because people know the kind of behavior expected of them, and what kind of behavior to expect from others, in the various conditions of social life, and coordinate their activities in sub-

mission to rules and under the guidance of values that each and all are able to go about their affairs. They can make predictions, anticipate events, and lead their lives in harmony with their fellows because every society has a form or pattern which allows us to speak of it as a system, or structure, within which, and in accordance with which, its members live their lives." It is evident in this passage that the writer is assuming that the human individual is capable of self-awareness, is aware of self-other relations, and consciously relates traditional values to his own conduct. What is assumed, without comment, is a level of psychological functioning that is characterized by self-awareness, one basic facet of human nature and the human personality (Hallowell, 1950a). Self and society may be considered as aspects of a single whole. This whole has been designated by Cottrell (1942) as the "self-other" system. Phrased in this way, explicit recognition is given to the self as a constant factor in the human personality structure, intrinsic to the operation of human societies and all situations of social interaction.

The attribute of self-awareness, which involves man's capacity to discriminate himself as an object in a world of objects other than himself, is as central to our understanding of the prerequisites of man's social and cultural mode of adjustment as it is for the psychodynamics of the individual. A human social order implies a mode of existence that has meaning for the individual at the level of self-awareness. A human social order, for example, is always a moral order. If the individual did not have the capacity for identifying the conduct that is his own and, through self-reflection, appraising it with reference to values and social sanctions, how would a moral order function in human terms? If I cannot assume moral responsibility for my conduct, how can guilt or shame arise? What conflict can there be between impulse and standards if I am unaware of values or sanctions? It is man's capacity for and development of self-awareness that makes such unconscious psychological mechanisms as repression, rationalization, and so on of adaptive importance for the individual. They would have no function otherwise. They allow the individual to function without full self-knowledge. They enable him to function in a moral order with something less than a perfect batting average.

Self-awareness, like gravity, was long taken for granted before it was subjected to analysis, genetically and functionally. We now know that it is one of the attributes of a generic personality structure that has to be built up in the individual in every human society during the socialization process. This has been one of the contributions of modern personality psychology. From the anthropological side we know that there are varying traditional concepts of the self in different societies that must contribute to the self-image of the individual. How far variables in self-concepts are related to differences in the needs and goals of the individual and consequently to behavioral differences needs further investigation.[37] However, both the generic and the specific aspects of the self with particular reference to variability in culturally derived content and the organization of the total personality are among the topics that need further clarification if social anthropology is to have a firm psychological foundation. Self-awareness is as inherent in the human situation as are social structure and culture.

37. Further elaboration of this topic will be found in my forthcoming paper, "The Self and Its Behavioral Environment," to be published in *Psychoanalysis and the Social Sciences*, Vol. IV.

Man, unlike his animal kin, acts in a universe that he has discovered and made intelligible to himself as an organism not only capable of consciousness but also of self-consciousness and reflective thought. But this has been possible only through the use of speech and other extrinsic symbolic means that have led to the articulation, communication, and transmission of culturally constituted worlds of meanings and values. An organized social life in man, since it transcends purely biological and geographic determinants, cannot function apart from communally recognized meanings and values, or apart from the psychological structuralization of individuals who make these their own. Learning a culture and the roles on which the persisting patterns of social structure depend is not equivalent to learning a set of habits or skills but involves a higher order of psychological integration. In order for this unique level of integration to be achieved in man, such unconscious mechanisms as conflict, repression, identification, etc., are intrinsic to the socialization process and consequently form a part of the psychodynamics of human adjustment. They are as inherent in the emergence and functioning of human societies as they are relevant to a full understanding of how the personality structure of the individuals exposed to a given cultural situation differs from, or is similar to, that of another set of individuals.

Personality, culture, and society form systems of relations that function as integral wholes in a wider universe of other-than-human reality. Considered from an integral point of view, they have no independent existence apart from the social adjustment of the individuals involved and the organization of human experience, in a manner that typifies the human situation.

REFERENCES

ABERLE, DAVID FRIEND. 1951. *The Psychosocial Analysis of a Hopi Life-History.* ("Comparative Psychological Monographs," Vol. XXI, No. 107.)

ABERLE, D. F.; COHEN, A. K.; DAVIS, A. K.; LEVY, M. J., JR.; and SUTTON, F. X. 1950. "The Functional Prerequisites of a Society," *Ethics*, LX, 100–111.

ADAMS, RICHARD N. 1951. "Personnel in Culture Change: A Test of a Hypothesis," *Social Forces*, XXX, 185–89.

ADORNO, T. W.; FRENKEL-BRUNSWIK, ELSE; LEVINSON, D. J.; and SANFORD, R. N. 1950. *The Authoritarian Personality.* New York: Harper & Bros.

BARNETT, HOMER G. 1941. "Personal Conflicts and Culture Change," *Social Forces*, XX, 160–71.

BARTLETT, F. C. 1937. "Psychological Methods and Anthropological Problems," *Africa*, X, No. 4, 401–19.

BATESON, GREGORY. 1942. "Social Planning and the Concept of 'Deutero-Learning.'" In BRYSON, L., and FINKELSTEIN, L. (eds.), *Science, Philosophy, and Religion: Second Symposium*, pp. 81–97. New York.

———. 1944. "Cultural Determinants of Personality." In HUNT, J. McV. (ed.), *Personality and the Behavior Disorders*, II, 714–35. New York: Ronald Press Co.

BERNDT, RONALD M. and CATHERINE H. 1951. *Sexual Behavior in Western Arnhem Land.* ("Viking Fund Publications in Anthropology," No. 16.) New York.

BIDNEY, DAVID. 1947. "Human Nature and the Cultural Process," *American Anthropologist*, XLIX, 375–99.

———. 1949. "The Concept of Meta-anthropology and Its Significance for Contemporary Anthropological Science." In NORTHROP, F. S. C. (ed.), *Ideological Differences and World Order*, pp. 323–55. New Haven: Yale University Press.

BLAKE, ROBERT R., and RAMSEY, GLENN W. (eds.). 1951. *Perception: An Approach to Personality.* New York: Ronald Press Co.

BRONFENBRENNER, URIE. 1951. "Toward an Integrated Theory of Personality." In BLAKE, ROBERT R., and RAMSEY, GLENN W. (eds.), *Perception: An Approach to Personality*, pp. 206–57. New York: Ronald Press Co.

BROWN, G. GORDON. 1951. "Culture, Society, and Personality: A Restatement," *American Journal of Psychiatry*, CVIII, 173–75.

CASSIRER, ERNST. 1944. *An Essay on Man.* New Haven: Yale University Press.

COTTRELL, LEONARD S., JR. 1942. "The Analysis of Situational Fields in Social Psychology," *American Sociological Review*, VII, 370–82.

DENNIS, WAYNE. 1951. "Cultural and Developmental Factors in Perception." In BLAKE, ROBERT R., and RAMSEY, GLENN W. (eds.), *Perception: An Approach to Personality*, pp. 148–69. New York: Ronald Press Co.

DEVEREUX, GEORGE. 1951. *Reality and Dream: Psychotherapy of a Plains Indian.* Prefaces by KARL A. MENNINGER and ROBERT H. LOWIE. Psychological tests edited and interpreted by ROBERT R. HOLT. New York: International Universities Press.

DEWEY, JOHN. 1917. "The Need for a Social Psychology," *Psychological Review*, XXIV, 266–77.

DOLLARD, J., and MILLER, N. 1950. *Personality and Psychotherapy: An Analysis in Terms of Learning, Thinking, and Culture.* New York: McGraw-Hill Book Co., Inc.

DUBOIS, CORA. 1944. *The People of Alor.* Minneapolis: University of Minnesota Press.

DYK, WALTER. 1947. *A Navaho Autobiography.* ("Viking Fund Publications in Anthropology," No. 8.) New York.

ERIKSON, ERIK H. 1950. *Childhood and Society.* New York: W. W. Norton & Co., Inc.

EVANS-PRITCHARD, E. E. 1951. *Social Anthropology.* London: Cohen & West, Ltd.

FENTON, WILLIAM N. 1948. "The Present Status of Anthropology in Northeastern North America: A Review Article," *American Anthropologist*, L, 494–515.

FORD, CLELLAN S., and BEACH, FRANK A. 1951. *Patterns of Sexual Behavior.* New York: Harper & Bros., and Paul B. Hoeber.

FROMM, ERICH. 1941. *Escape from Freedom*. New York: Farrar & Rinehart.

——. 1947. *Man for Himself: An Inquiry into the Psychology of Ethics*. New York: Rinehart & Co.

——. 1949. "Psychoanalytic Characterology and Its Application to the Understanding of Culture." In SARGENT, S. S., and SMITH, M. W. (eds.), *Culture and Personality*, pp. 1–12. New York: Viking Fund.

FRANK, L. K. 1949. *Society as the Patient*. New Brunswick, N.J.: Rutgers University Press.

——. 1951. *Nature and Human Nature*. New Brunswick, N.J.: Rutgers University Press.

GIBSON, J. J. 1950a. *The Perception of the Visual World*. Boston: Houghton Mifflin Co.

——. 1950b. "The Implications of Learning Theory for Social Psychology." In MILLER, JAMES GRIER (ed.), *Experiments in Social Process: A Symposium on Social Psychology*. New York: McGraw-Hill Book Co., Inc.

GOLDSCHMIDT, WALTER. 1951. "Ethics and the Structure of Society: An Ethnological Contribution to the Sociology of Knowledge," *American Anthropologist*, LIII, 506–24.

HALL, J. K.; ZILBOORG, G.; and BUNKER, H. A. (eds.). 1944. *One Hundred Years of American Psychiatry*. New York: Columbia University Press.

HALLOWELL, A. IRVING. 1945. "Sociopsychological Aspects of Acculturation." In LINTON, RALPH (ed.), *The Science of Man in the World Crisis*, pp. 171–200. New York: Columbia University Press.

——. 1946. "Some Psychological Characteristics of the Northeastern Indians." In JOHNSON, FREDERICK (ed.), *Man in Northeastern North America*, ·pp. 195–225. ("Papers of the R. S. Peabody Foundation for Archeology," Vol. III.) Andover, Mass.

——. 1950a. "Personality Structure and the Evolution of Man," *American Anthropologist*, LII, 159–73.

——. 1950b. "Values, Acculturation, and Mental Health," *American Journal of Orthopsychiatry*, XX, 732–43.

——. 1951a. "Cultural Factors in the Structuralization of Perception." In

ROHRER, J. H., and SHERIF, M. (eds.), *Social Psychology at the Crossroads*, pp. 164–95. New York: Harper & Bros.

——. 1951b. "The Use of Projective Techniques in the Study of Sociopsychological Aspects of Acculturation," *Journal of Projective Techniques*, XV, 26–44.

HARING, DOUGLAS G. (ed.). 1949. *Personal Character and Cultural Milieu: A Collection of Readings*. Rev. ed. Syracuse, N.Y.: Syracuse University Press.

HARRIS, ZELLIG S. 1951. "Review of Selected Writings of Edward Sapir," *Language*, XXVII, 288–333.

HAYES, CATHY. 1951. *The Ape in Our House*. New York: Harper & Bros.

HILGARD, ERNEST R. 1948. *Theories of Learning*. New York: Appleton-Century.

HOCH, PAUL H., and ZUBIN, JOSEPH. 1949. *Psychosexual Development in Health and Disease: Proceedings of the 38th Annual Meeting of the American Psychopathological Association, 1948*. New York: Grune & Stratton.

HONIGMANN, JOHN J. 1949. *Culture and Ethos of Kaska Society*. ("Yale University Publications in Anthropology," No. 40.) New Haven: Yale University Press.

HUNT, J. McV. (ed.). 1944. *Personality and the Behavior Disorders*. 2 vols. New York: Ronald Press Co.

JENNINGS, H. S. 1942. "The Transition from the Individual to the Social Level." In REDFIELD, ROBERT (ed.), *Levels of Integration in Biological and Social Systems*, pp. 105–19. ("Biological Symposia," Vol. VIII.) Lancaster, Pa.: Jacques Cattell Press.

KARDINER, ABRAM. 1939. *The Individual and His Society*. New York: Columbia University Press.

——. 1945a. *The Psychological Frontiers of Society*. (With the collaboration of RALPH LINTON, CORA DuBOIS, and JAMES WEST.) New York: Columbia University Press.

——. 1945b. "The Concept of Basic Personality Structure as an Operational Tool in the Social Sciences." In LINTON, RALPH (ed.), *The Science of Man in the World Crisis*, pp. 107–22. New York: Columbia University Press.

KARDINER, ABRAM, and OVERSEY, LIONEL. 1951. *The Mark of Oppression: A Psy-*

chological Study of the American Negro. New York: W. W. Norton & Co.

KLINEBERG, OTTO. 1950. *Tensions Affecting International Understanding: A Survey of Research.* (Social Science Research Council Bull. 62.) New York: Social Science Research Council.

KLUCKHOHN, CLYDE. 1944. "The Influence of Psychiatry on Anthropology in America during the Past One Hundred Years." In HALL, J. K., and OTHERS (eds.), *One Hundred Years of American Psychiatry,* pp. 489–618. New York: Columbia University Press.

———. 1949. *Mirror for Man.* New York: McGraw-Hill Book Co., Inc.

KLUCKHOHN, CLYDE, and MOWRER, O. H. 1944. "Culture and Personality: A Conceptual Scheme,",*American Anthropologist,* XLVI, 1–29.

KLUCKHOHN, CLYDE, and MURRAY, H. A. (eds.). 1948. *Personality in Nature, Society, and Culture.* New York: Alfred A. Knopf.

KROEBER, A. L. 1947. "A Southwestern Personality Type," *Southwestern Journal of Anthropology,* III, 108–13.

———. 1948. *Anthropology.* New York: Harcourt, Brace & Co.

KROEBER, A. L.; BENEDICT, RUTH; EMENEAU, MURRAY B.; *et al.* 1943. *Franz Boas, 1858–1942. (American Anthropologist,* Vol. XLV, No. 3, Part II.)

LEIGHTON, ALEXANDER and DOROTHEA C. (With the assistance of CATHERINE OPLER.) 1949. *Gregorio, the Hand-Trembler: A Psychobiological Personality Study of a Navaho Indian.* ("Papers of the Peabody Museum of American Archeology and Ethnology, Harvard University," Vol. XL, No. 1.) Boston.

LEWIN, KURT. 1948. *Resolving Social Conflicts: Selected Papers on Group Dynamics.* Edited by GERTRUD WEISS LEWIN. New York: Harper & Bros.

LINTON, RALPH. 1945. *The Cultural Background of Personality.* New York: Appleton-Century-Crofts, Inc.

LOWIE, ROBERT H. 1937. *The History of Ethnological Theory.* New York: Farrar & Rinehart.

MANDELBAUM, DAVID G. (ed.). 1949. *Selected Writings of Edward Sapir in Language, Culture, and Personality.* Berke-

ley and Los Angeles: University of California Press.

MAUSS, MARCEL. 1950. *Sociologie et anthropologie.* Introduction à l'œuvre de Marcel Mauss par C. LÉVI-STRAUSS. Paris: Presses universitaires de France.

MEAD, MARGARET. 1937. *Cooperation and Competition among Primitive Peoples.* New York and London: McGraw-Hill Book Co., Inc.

———. 1949. *Male and Female.* New York: William Morrow & Co.

———. 1951. *Soviet Attitudes toward Authority.* New York: McGraw-Hill Book Co., Inc.

MEAD, MARGARET, and MACGREGOR, FRANCES COOKE. 1951. *Growth and Culture.* (A photographic study of Balinese childhood based upon photographs by GREGORY BATESON and analyzed in Gesell categories.) New York: G. P. Putnam's Sons.

MEGGERS, BETTY J. 1946. "Recent Trends in American Ethnology," *American Anthropologist,* XLVIII, 176–214.

MILLER, DANIEL K., and HUTT, MAX L. 1949. "Value Interiorization and Personality Development," *Journal of Social Issues,* V, 2–30.

MILLER, N., and DOLLARD, J. 1941. *Social Learning and Imitation.* New Haven: Yale University Press.

MOWRER, O. H., and KLUCKHOHN, CLYDE. 1944. "Dynamic Theory of Personality." In HUNT, J. McV. (ed.), *Personality and the Behavior Disorders,* pp. 69–135. New York: Ronald Press Co.

MULLAHY, PATRICK. 1948. *Oedipus: Myth and Complex: A Review of Psychoanalytic Theory.* Introduction by ERICH FROMM. New York: Heritage Press.

MURDOCK, GEORGE P. 1949. "The Science of Human Learning, Society, Culture, and Personality," *Scientific Monthly,* LXIX, 377–81.

MURPHY, G. 1947. *Personality: A Biosocial Approach to Origins and Structure.* New York: Harper & Bros.

MURRAY, H. A. 1938. *Exploration in Personality.* New York: Oxford University Press.

NADEL, S. F. 1937a. "The Typological Approach to Culture," *Character and Personality* (now *Journal of Personality*), V, 267–84.

——. 1937b. "Experiments on Culture Psychology," *Africa*, X, 421–35.

——. 1937c. "A Field Experiment in Racial Psychology," *British Journal of Psychology*, XXVIII, 195–211.

——. 1951. *The Foundations of Social Anthropology.* Glencoe, Ill.: Free Press.

NEWCOMB, THEODORE M. 1950. *Social Psychology.* New York: Dryden Press.

NEWCOMB, THEODORE M.; HARTLEY, E. L.; et al. (eds.). 1947. *Readings in Social Psychology.* New York: Henry Holt & Co.

NISSEN, HENRY W. 1951. "Phylogenetic Comparisons." In STEVENS, S. S. (ed.), *Handbook of Experimental Psychology*, chap. xi. New York: John Wiley & Sons.

ORLANSKY, H. 1949. "Infant Care and Personality," *Psychological Bulletin*, XLVI, 1–48.

PARSONS, TALCOTT, and SHILS, EDWARD A. (eds.). 1951. *Toward a General Theory of Action.* Cambridge: Harvard University Press.

RANDALL, JOHN HERMAN, JR. 1944. "Epilogue: The Nature of Naturalism." In KRIKORIAN, Y. H. (ed.), *Naturalism and the Human Spirit*, pp. 354–82. New York: Columbia University Press.

ROHEIM, GEZA. 1943. *The Origin and Function of Culture.* ("Nervous and Mental Disease Monograph Series," No. 63.) New York.

——. 1950. *Psychoanalysis and Anthropology: Culture, Personality, and the Unconscious.* New York: International Universities Press.

ROHRER, JOHN H., and SHERIF, MUZAFER (eds.). 1951. *Social Psychology at the Crossroads.* New York: Harper & Bros.

SAPIR, EDWARD. See MANDELBAUM and HARRIS.

SARGENT, S. STANSFELD, and SMITH, MARIAN W. (eds.). 1949. *Culture and Personality: Proceedings of an Interdisciplinary Conference Held under the Auspices of the Viking Fund, November 7 and 8, 1947.* New York: Viking Fund.

SCHNEIRLA, T. C. 1951. "The 'Levels' Concept in the Study of Social Organization in Animals." In ROHRER, J. H., and SHERIF, M. (eds.), *Social Psychology*

at the Crossroads, pp. 83–120. New York: Harper & Bros.

SELIGMAN, C. G. 1924. "Anthropology and Psychology," *Journal of the Royal Anthropological Institute*, LIV, 13–46.

——. 1928. "The Unconscious in Relation to Anthropology," *British Journal of Psychology*, XVIII, 374–87.

——. 1929. "Temperament, Conflict and Psychosis in a Stone-Age Population," *British Journal of Medical Psychology*, IX, 187–202.

——. 1932. "Anthropological Perspective and Psychological Theory (Huxley Memorial Lecture for 1932)," *Journal of the Royal Anthropological Institute*, LXII, 193–228.

——. 1936. Introduction to LINCOLN, J. S, *The Dream in Primitive Cultures.* London: Cresset Press, n.d. Baltimore: Williams & Wilkins.

SHAPLEY, HARLOW. 1930. *Flights from Chaos.* New York: McGraw-Hill Book Co., Inc.

SLOTKIN, J. S. 1951. *Personality Development.* New York: Harper & Bros.

SPINDLER, GEORGE, and GOLDSCHMIDT, WALTER. 1952. "Experimental Design in the Study of Culture Change," *Southwestern Journal of Anthropology*, VIII, 68–83.

SPIRO, MELFORD E. 1951. "Culture and Personality: The Natural History of a False Dichotomy," *Psychiatry*, XIV, 19–46.

STEVENS, S. S. (ed.). 1951. *Handbook of Experimental Psychology.* New York: John Wiley & Sons, Inc.

SULLIVAN, H. S. 1947. *Conception of Modern Psychiatry.* Washington, D. C.: William Alanson White Psychiatric Foundation.

VOLKART, EDMUND H. (ed.). 1951. *Social Behavior and Personality.* ("Contributions of W. I. Thomas to Theory and Social Research.") New York: Social Science Research Council.

WALLACE, ANTHONY F. C. 1952. *The Modal Personality Structure of the Tuscarora Indians, as Revealed by the Rorschach Test.* (Bureau of American Ethnology Bull. 150.) In press.

WEAKLAND, JOHN HART. 1951. "Method in Cultural Anthropology," *Philosophy of Science*, XVIII, 55–69.

WHITE, LESLIE A. 1925. "Personality and Culture," *Open Court*, XXXIX, 145–49.

———. 1947. "The Locus of Mathematical Reality: An Anthropological Footnote," *Philosophy of Science*, XIV, 289–303.

WHITEHEAD, A. N. 1930. *Adventures of Ideas*. Cambridge: At the University Press.

WHITING, JOHN W. M. 1941. *Becoming a Kwoma: Teaching and Learning in a New Guinea Tribe*. New Haven: Yale University Press.

WILBUR, GEORGE B., and MUENSTERBERGER, WARNER (eds.). 1951. *Psychoanalysis and Culture: Essays in Honor of Geza Roheim*. New York: International Universities Press, Inc.

Acculturation

By RALPH BEALS

THIS SURVEY of acculturation is presented within the following restricted framework: (1) it is almost wholly confined to the work of anthropologists of the British Commonwealth, the United States, and Latin America; (2) in so far as it is possible to do so, problems of application are excluded from this paper, although this is difficult to do in British studies; and (3) especially in British writings the term "culture contact" is considered broadly synonymous with "acculturation."

I. HISTORICAL SURVEY

The recency and rapid proliferation of acculturation studies have resulted in the employment of widely differing definitions and methodologies. Theory and conceptualization likewise appear still to be in a formative stage. Some of these points seem best illustrated by a brief historical survey of the subject. The attempt to trace the origins and growth of a concept such as acculturation in the United States or the parallel usage of "culture contact" by British anthropologists is an instructive exercise for the student of culture change. Although early sporadic interest in the phenomena of contact situations may be found which resembles modern approaches rather than the traditional diffusionist discussions, one is driven to the employment of surmise and hypothetical reconstruction to account for the development of special terms and concepts.

The term "acculturation" is generally credited to American anthropologists. The occasional British student to refer to the word may concede its convenience but regards it with some horror. Paul Kirchhoff, however, has stated in conversation that the term was used in Germany by Walter Krickeberg in lectures somewhere in the mid-1920's to refer to the progress of development of a common basic culture among the tribes of diverse origin found on the upper Rio Xingu.[1] In a rather cursory examination of German literature I have found no appearance of the word in print, but it is of interest that Thurnwald was the earliest writer to use the word in the title of an article in English. This lends some support to a possible German origin for the term. Drawing upon an uncertain memory, it is clear that extended discussion and argument long preceded the first appearance of the term "acculturation" in the literature in the United States. My own memories place the appearance of the term at the level of graduate student

1. Since writing the above, R. H. Lowie has called my attention to the following passage by Krickeberg in the first (1910) edition of Buschan's *Illustrierte Völkerkunde* (pp. 97 f.): "Das beständige durcheinanderfluten ursprünglich heterogener Stamme brachte einen weitgehenden *kulturellen Ausgleich* (Akkulturation) zustande, durch den die Kultur in dem ganzen gewaltigen Dreieck zwischen Anden, Orinoko, Rio Negro und Madera ein sehr einheitliches Gepräge erhielt." This conforms to the ideas reported by Kirchhoff for a later date.

discussion somewhere about 1928 under circumstances which suggest it already had diffused widely from its point of origin. Who first used the term and attempted to conceptualize the field, and who were parties to the earliest discussions, would require reconstruction of a "memory" culture, the now partially vanished anthropological culture of the United States in the 1920's.[2]

Interest in acculturation studies in the United States probably originated in part as a reaction against these very reconstructions of "memory" cultures. The emphasis of the early part of the century upon studying or recovering the memory of "unmodified" cultures became increasingly difficult and of diminishing fruitfulness in the 1920's. At the same time, students became increasingly aware of the existence of contemporary cultures of no less interest for the elucidation of cultural principles.

Interest in contact phenomena in Great Britain and elsewhere may have had a similar origin, although it would appear that functionalism was the major reaction in Great Britain to the study of memory cultures. Rather I would tentatively suggest that the origin of interest in culture contact in Great Britain stemmed from two sources, namely, the increasing urgency of practical applications of anthropol-

2. A partial survey of United States textbooks in anthropology suggests the recency of the subject. No discussion appears in F. Boas and others, *General Anthropology* (1938); R. Lowie, *Introduction to Cultural Anthropology* (1st ed., 1934); E. Chapple and C. Coon, *Principles of Anthropology* (1942); or A. Goldenweiser, *Anthropology* (1937). In the second edition of Lowie (1940) there are five references in the Index to statements concerning cases of change through contact and a definition (p. 525) as "assimilation to an alien culture." J. Gillin, *The Ways of Men* (1948), and M. J. Herskovits, *Man and His Works* (1948), each contains a chapter on the subject.

ogy in colonial areas and in part as a reaction against certain limitations inherent in the more formal functionalist systems. This is not the place to argue the merits of formal functionalist systems; nevertheless, the more classical schemes seem to many to run into difficulties over the problem of culture change. Studies of culture contact offered the opportunity of applying the best of the functionalist approaches, as within a dynamic framework of change. Moreover, the rapidity of change in the colonial situation was such that classical functionalists like Malinowski could at least pretend that the time dimension did not exist, a pretense which extended only to their theoretical positions and not, as we shall see, to their methodological procedures.

The obvious utility of acculturation studies for the solution of practical problems was also a factor in their early popularity. The beginnings of interest in contact situations in Great Britain, France, and Holland coincided with the rise of a new sense of responsibility toward colonial peoples, while in the United States the great development of acculturation studies coincided with the depression era and its accompanying widespread concern with social problems. External cultural forces, then, may well have played an important part in the rise of acculturation studies.

Full acceptance of acculturation as a field of anthropological study is quite recent in the United States, if, indeed, it has yet been achieved. Thus at the annual meeting of the American Anthropological Association for 1936 the editor of the *American Anthropologist*, Leslie Spier, inquired in his annual report:

The question has also arisen how far we should go in printing material on the culture of natives who participate in civilized life. I refer here to the so-called acculturation studies. It is maintained on the one hand that studies of such hybrid cultures are best left to sociological or other journals concerned with aspects of modern life; on the other, that they belong in the *American Anthropologist*. Since your wishes should be followed, I would like an expression of your opinion of what we should include.

Following the editor's report, we find:

It was moved and seconded: It is the sense of the American Anthropological Association that papers in the field of acculturation lie within the interests of anthropology, and that, at the Editor's discretion, they be not discriminated against in the *American Anthropologist*. It was voted that the motion be tabled without prejudice [*Proceedings of the American Anthropological Association for 1936, p.* 322].

There is no record that this motion was ever removed from the table. Nevertheless, the editor apparently had no qualms, for acculturation is referred to six times in the volume index. Two articles by Herskovits (1937*a*, 1937*b*) in Volume XXXIX deal with acculturation, the word appearing in the title of one. Other references are to book reviews, one of which is Benedict's (1937) review of Redfield's *Chan Kom.* Another, Beals's (1939) review of Parson's *Mitla,* is the first review in this journal to discuss the problem of acculturation by name. Other references are to the merest mention of European contact. Gerhard Lindblom's (1937) review of Monica Hunter's *Reaction to Conquest* in the same volume remarks that the book "seems to me . . . first and foremost of sociological importance, but here I propose to regard it from an exclusively ethnological point of view." While recognizing the significance of this pioneering work, Lindblom evidently was reluctant to consider the new field to be anthropological. Apparently the editor interpreted the lack of action by the association as giving him a free hand. In the General Index for 1929–38, published under his direction,

seven additional items in Volume XXXIX are indexed under "acculturation," including every mention, however slight, to effects of European contact.

To trace the intellectual development which led to the earlier use of the term is difficult. Herskovits (1948, p. 523) notes a use by J. W. Powell in 1880 to refer to culture borrowing. W. J. McGee later speaks of "piratical acculturation," accounting for the only appearance of the word in the General Index of the *American Anthropologist* for 1888–1928. In the same period the term "culture contact" is indexed not at all. The term "acculturation" next appears in the program of the annual meeting for 1928 (p. 326), which lists a paper by M. J. Herskovits, "The Coto-Missies of Suriname: A Study in Acculturation." Presumably this paper used acculturation in the modern sense. Other papers may have been delivered at earlier annual meetings, but not all the programs were published. In the General Index for 1929–38 the earliest reference to acculturation is to Robert Redfield's (1929) "The Material Culture of Spanish-Indian Mexico." Although the problems are clearly acculturational, the word is not used in the article. Neither is the term "culture contact" employed. While the mixed character of the Spanish-Indian culture of Mexico is discussed, there is no emphasis on process.

The earliest article to be indexed under the term "culture contact" is Leslie Spier's (1929) "Problems Arising from the Cultural Position of the Havasupai." Emphasis in the article is on the dynamics of culture growth in relation to culture contacts on an aboriginal level. Significantly, while this and Redfield's article are indexed under "culture contact" and "acculturation," respectively, in the General Index, they are not so indexed in the Annual Index for the volume. Thus we may surmise a growing preoccupation with the problems of contact between 1929 and 1938 and, in the general handling of the 1929–38 General Index, an effort on the part of the editor, Leslie Spier, to apply "acculturation" solely to examples of European contacts and "culture contact" to those contacts occurring on an aboriginal level. The next reference in the General Index is to "Aboriginal Survivals in Mayo Culture," by Ralph L. Beals (1932). A considerable part of the article is devoted to discussion of contact problems, and it is the first article in the *American Anthropologist* to use the term "acculturation," except for McGee's much earlier usage. Later in the same year appears the first article with the word "acculturation" in the title: Richard Thurnwald's (1932) "The Psychology of Acculturation." This article is noteworthy for two things: it is the first to show interest in the psychological problems of acculturation and the first to attempt a systematic analysis of the concept and the processes involved.

In this same year Margaret Mead published her *Changing Culture of an Indian Tribe* (1932), the earliest major work in the United States devoted primarily to the effects of culture contact. The term "acculturation" is used only once in reference to degrees of acculturation. The following year, Elsie Clews Parsons (1933) used the term in "Some Aztec and Pueblo Parallels." While some subsequent articles discuss acculturational problems, notably Robert Redfield's (1934) "Cultural Changes in Yucatan," and, while even the most trivial references to European contact are indexed in the General Index, the next actual use of the term is in the "Memorandum for the Study of Acculturation" by Robert Redfield, Ralph Linton, and Melville J. Herskovits (1936).

A more hasty survey of British jour-nals suggests that the appearance and use of the term "culture contact" roughly paralleled in time the United States use of the term "acculturation."

Malinowski wrote, on the need of studying the changing native as early as 1929: "A new branch of anthropology must sooner or later be started: the anthropology of the changing Native. Nowadays, when we are intensely interested, through some new anthropological theories, in problems of contact and diffusion, it seems incredible that hardly any exhaustive studies have been undertaken on the question of how European influence is being diffused into native communities" (p. 22). Malinowski clearly regarded this as a practical study and felt that the changing native was a result of European contact. The implication that no change existed before such contact is surprising, although he suggested the value of contemporary studies for understanding the process of diffusion.

The first systematic recognition of culture contact seems to have been in the "Five Year Plan of Research" in *Africa* (1932). This memorandum is clearly oriented toward practical administrative problems and the problems of culture change, although the term "culture contact" is not employed. Change as it is discussed is clearly concerned with the results of European contact. However, stemming from the work initiated under the "Five Year Plan," two years later L. P. Mair (1934) published "The Study of Culture Contact as a Practical Problem" in the same journal. This was the first of a series of articles by various authors which were later gathered together in *Memorandum XV* of the International Institute of African Languages and Cultures (1938). The year 1935 saw publication of the Redfield-Linton-Herskovits memorandum in *Man*, a year earlier than its publication in the United States.

Implicit in most of the British work both in the developmental period and later is a close relation between "practical" anthropology and culture contact studies and definition of culture contact as referring to European native contacts with special emphasis on administrative problems. Malinowski referred to French, Dutch, and German anthropologists as students of culture change and practical anthropology. Thus, after such a review, Malinowski (1945, p. 5) concludes:

Finally, in Great Britain and the United States, interest in culture change has of late become dominant. The names of W. H. R. Rivers and of Captain G. H. L. F. Pitt-Rivers head the list among early British scholars. The work of the Departments of Anthropology at Sydney and Capetown, under the initiative of A. R. Radcliffe-Brown; the teaching and research at Cambridge, London and Oxford; the special interest shown in culture change and applied anthropology by the Royal Anthropological Institute—all have started almost simultaneously with the American initiative associated with the names of Wissler, Redfield, Parsons, Herskovits, and Radin; as well as P. H. Buck (Te Rangi Hiroa) and Felix Keesing working at Honolulu. The International Institute of African Languages and Cultures has, since its foundation in 1926, made an attempt to take the question beyond national boundaries and, avoiding all political issues, has organized research on problems of contact in all African colonies, with the cooperation of science, missionary enterprise, and the administrative agencies of all the countries concerned.

This summary includes many names, both British and American, to say nothing of other national groups, which are not mentioned in my own historical summary. Reasons for this discrepancy are twofold. On the one hand, the directive for my memorandum recommended the omission of problems of application; on the other, I have endeavored to confine myself very largely to the authors who have been concerned with conceptualization and definition of the field and with the development of methodology. As an example one might cite B. Schrieke (ed.), *The Effect of Western Influence on Native Civilizations in the Malay Archipelago* (Batavia, 1929), an almost completely descriptive work except for some discussion of administrative policy.

In the subsequent sections of this survey I propose to discuss what seem to me major problems and issues raised by work in acculturation rather than to review the work of particular individuals or groups of individuals. The treatment will be concerned, first, with problems of conceptualization and definition and, second, with problems of methodology. In a final section I shall attempt some general appraisal of the present status of acculturation studies and point out some areas of needed investigation. In these succeeding sections I trust I will not be accused of cultural imperialism if for convenience I use the term "acculturation" as synonymous with "culture contact" as the latter is used in the British Commonwealth.

II. PROBLEMS OF DEFINITION AND USAGE

The earliest writers to employ the term "acculturation" apparently did not attempt a definition of the term; usage, nevertheless, is often clear. Parsons' Mitla study (1936) is described by the author as "concerned with acculturation, with what the Indian culture took from the Spanish." Acculturation to Parsons clearly meant only cases of syncretization and obvious cases of Spanish borrowing. Although pointing out that the product of Spanish-Indian contact in Mexico is a new and changing blend, she does not consider as acculturation those aspects of the blend which have no identifiable European component. Indian survivals or new organizations or relationships emerging as an indirect result of the blend are excluded. This same interpretation occurs earlier in Parsons (1933). A somewhat broader interpretation is suggested by Beals (1932), in which the entire set of processes involved in acceptance, rejection, and reorganization are considered to be acculturation.

The first systematic definition is that by Redfield, Linton, and Herskovits (1936): "Acculturation comprehends those phenomena which result when groups of individuals having different cultures come into continuous first-hand contact, with subsequent changes in the original cultural patterns of either or both groups." While widely criticized and modified by later writers, including the authors, this remains the most used definition, although full understanding of it requires consideration of the entire memorandum. Points in this definition which appear to have caused most difficulty are the following: (1) What is meant by "continuous first-hand contact"? (2) What is meant by "groups of individuals"? (3) The relation of acculturation to the concepts of culture change and diffusion. (4) What is the relation between acculturation and assimilation? (5) Is acculturation a process or a condition?

Among the striking problems raised is that of modifications of culture arising through intermittent contacts with missionaries or traders, who in some cases are bearers of a culture other than their own. Although there is little difficulty in considering acculturation as a special case of culture change, such cases as those referred to raise difficulty in distinguishing between acculturation and diffusion. Both represent culture change as the result of transmission of culture between groups. Herskovits (1948, pp. 523 ff.) solves this problem by considering diffusion to be "achieved

cultural transmission," while acculturation is "cultural transmission in process." This viewpoint he modifies to include those instances in which documentation of transmission by ethnohistorical methods is possible, as opposed to cases in which diffusion must be inferred or its history reconstructed by inferential methods. In this position Herskovits is very close to that of Malinowski, who wrote as early as 1939 of "The Dynamics of Contemporary Diffusion." On the other hand, in the *Dynamics of Culture Change* (1945, p. 1) Malinowski remarks: "It [culture change] may be induced by factors and forces spontaneously arising within the community, or it may take place through the contact of different cultures. In the first instance it takes the form of *independent invention;* in the second it constitutes that process which in anthropology is usually called *diffusion.*" Clearly, however, Malinowski's whole interest is in what in the United States would today without hesitation be called acculturation; moreover, it is almost wholly with the study of acculturative processes as these arise in connection with practical problems related to colonial administration and with the impact of European culture upon native culture.

Although few discussions have reached print, some United States anthropologists have discussed the role of force, broadly conceived, as perhaps providing the proper distinction between diffusion and acculturation. In such discussions, force is broadly treated to include not only overt or naked force but pressures resulting from deprivations, introduction of compelling new goals, or psychological pressures arising from sentiments of inferiority and superiority. A corollary type of approach is the suggestion that acculturation be confined to situations in which one of the groups in contact, for whatever reason, loses complete freedom of choice or freedom to accept or reject new cultural elements. Such restrictions for the term "acculturation" would be rejected by others, who would, indeed, extend the term beyond its present usage. These divergent points of view will receive treatment below.

The fourth and fifth points above have received relatively little attention and have perhaps troubled sociologists more than they have anthropologists. In the main the literature of acculturation stresses dynamic aspects. Acculturation is seen by most writers as important because process is rapid and easily observable. Such rapidity of process is seen to afford abundant opportunities for comparison and an approach to laboratory conditions. Thurnwald (1932, p. 557) opens his article on the psychology of acculturation with the sentence, "Acculturation is a process, not an isolated event." By implication, rather than by direct statement, he is clearly dealing with the acquisition of cultural elements by one culture from another and says: "This process of adaptation to new conditions of life is what we call acculturation." Later (1938, pp. 179–80), he says: "For 'contact' is not a single event but implies the turning on of a switch which sets in motion an almost endless series of happenings; it is a process, but with different stages." Mair (1934) likewise recognizes the value of using contact studies to discover rules governing process of culture change, while Fortes (1936, p. 53) remarks: "Culture contact has to be regarded, not as a transference of elements from one culture to another, but as a continuous process of interaction between groups of different culture."

Without multiplying examples, one can assert confidently that acculturation studies are generally seen as dynamic in character and concerned with process. Such understandings are not, however, universal, nor, indeed, is recogni-

tion of the field of study itself. Thus, in a study many would consider at least partially acculturational, DuBois wrote: "Patterning and acculturation might be practically synonymous. However, acculturation seems to have been given special meaning. It is used most frequently to describe minimal cases of patterning; that is, cases in which dislocations accompanying the absorption of foreign features exceed integrations. More specifically, it seems to have been used to describe the manner in which a shattered aboriginal culture makes the best of a bad bargain. . . . The difference between patterning which represents integration and acculturation which represents at best only partial integration is not always obvious in cultural phenomena" (1939, p. 137). This might be ignored if the same author in 1951 in a useful short discussion of the dynamics of culture contact had not remarked: "Acculturation that was in vogue among anthropologists some fifteen or twenty years ago has since then been recognized as a dangerously fragmented phrasing of more inclusive inquiries into the nature of cultural and social dynamics" (1951, p. 32). Writers on acculturation will have some difficulty recognizing their subject in these terms.

Despite the general recognition of the dynamic aspect of acculturation studies, it is common, particularly in the United States, to speak of "degrees of acculturation" and of "partially or wholly acculturated individuals." In the case of a wholly acculturated individual, clearly the acculturative process has terminated and we are speaking of a condition. Moreover, it is difficult to see how this differs from sociological usages of the term "assimilation." The Redfield, Linton, and Herskovits definition, indeed, is modified by a note that "acculturation is to be distinguished from. . . *assimilation*, which is at times a phase of acculturation." Possibly what is generally meant is that assimilation is that form of acculturation which results in groups of individuals wholly replacing their original culture by another (as opposed to groups reformulating a "mixed" culture). Usage is far from consistent or clear, and the frequent reference to acculturated individuals (rather than groups) seems particularly ambiguous in terms of most of the formal definitions. In part these differences reflect emphasis upon institutional or sociocultural approaches, on the one hand, and upon individual and psychological approaches, on the other. Finally, field studies of acculturation frequently are essentially descriptive; we are given the results of acculturation rather than an attempt to discover its dynamics.

In terms of the Redfield, Linton, and Herskovits definition, acculturation should be viewed as a two-way process, affecting both groups in contact. Beyond an occasional suggestion that the culture of Europeans (mainly missionaries, traders, and administrators) undergoes some change as a result of contact or that Spanish culture in the New World was modified by Indian culture, only lip service has been paid to this aspect of acculturation. Fernando Ortiz (1940) has proposed the term "transculturation" to emphasize the reciprocal character of most contact situations. In his Preface to the work, Malinowski is enthusiastic about the new term, but one finds no serious consideration of the reciprocal aspects of culture contact in any of his own publications. "Transculturation" has had some use by Latin-American writers, and, were the term "acculturation" not so widely in use, it might profitably be adopted.

Most British discussions and definitions of culture contact are entirely concerned with the impact of European cultures upon native cultures. Fortes (1936, p. 54) is almost alone in raising the question of why African contact

agents, such as Hausa, Mosi, Dagomba, and Fulani, have been less influential than European contacts. Wagner (1936, p. 317) similarly points out the theoretical importance of Asian contacts with Africa. In the United States general discussions are usually carefully phrased to cover all types of culture contact. In actual practice, however, most United States and virtually all Latin-American studies of acculturation are, in fact, concerned with the impact of European upon non-European cultures. Scattered references could be found to pre-European acculturation situations, but specific studies or analyses are either of very minor scope or nonexistent. Perhaps the most notable examples of papers on acculturation in which European culture is not involved are Lindgren's (1938) "An Example of Culture Contact without Conflict: Reindeer Tungus and Cossacks of Northwestern Manchuria"; Ekvall's (1939) "Cultural Relations on the Kansu-Tibetan Border"; and Greenberg's (1941) "Some Aspects of Negro-Mohammedan Culture Contact among the Hausa."

A number of other studies, notably those of Robert Redfield, have centered about the problem of urban influence upon folk or rural cultures. Although Redfield is chary of applying the word "acculturation" to this situation, I believe most American scholars would so classify his studies.

Quite different in character are the studies of Herskovits on the Negro in the Americas. Avowedly considered acculturation studies by the author, in strict terms the situation does not represent "groups of individuals" in the same sense as do many of the British studies in Africa. Rather, uprooted individuals are moved out of their society and cultural setting and placed in a new culture. This usage is followed by many students in the American field, including such Latin-Americans as Arthur Ramos (1947). Of the same type are

Emilio Willems' studies of the acculturation of Germans and Japanese in Brazil. Sociologists also use the term increasingly in the same way to refer to the adaptations of immigrants. More recently Beals (1951) has suggested that not only can other immigrant groups in the United States be studied from the standpoint of acculturation but also the whole process of urbanization, whether dealing with the extension of urban influence to the rural populations or the migration of rural populations to the city, presents an acculturative situation. This point was made by Gregory Bateson (1935) with respect to contacts between groups within a culture, although he did not project it against a situation within a European-type culture.

This brief review clearly suggests that both definitions and usage of the term "acculturation" (or "culture contact") are varied and unsatisfactory. At the same time it must be recognized that a very large core of studies is easily and generally recognized today as being acculturational. The difficulties lie mainly at the fringes of the field and at least in part are logical rather than actual. While it may be asserted that acculturation studies should not be confined to situations involving European-type cultures, it is, in fact, extremely difficult to find situations where European-type cultures are not involved. Nevertheless, it seems clear that a re-examination of the subject is in order, particularly with respect to the reciprocal aspects of acculturation, its relation to the problem of assimilation, and the propriety of extending the term to studies of contact between groups within a culture and to studies of migrant groups.

III. PROBLEMS OF METHOD

Problems of method in the study of acculturation fall into two major categories: formal organized memoranda or schemes for study, and general discussions of specific problems, together with actual research studies. In the first category we find some six schemes presented: those of Thurnwald (1932), the Redfield, Linton, and Herskovits memorandum (1935, 1936), Bateson (1935), Linton (1940), Malinowski (1945), and Ramos (1947).

Despite its title and its emphasis upon the role of the individual, the Thurnwald article is primarily concerned with process. In this earliest memorandum we may note the following points, by now familiar to all students of acculturation: change of function; variable rates of acceptance for different traits; selection of traits, depending in part upon the conditions of contact; unforeseen consequences of adoption of new traits; attitudes and relationships between groups often determinant; group traditions important; circumstances of contact must be considered; occurrence of stages of reaction to contact which may include withdrawal from the strange or unknown, uncritical acceptance, complete assimilation, formation of new cultural entities, and rejection.

The Redfield, Linton, Herskovits memorandum merits somewhat more detailed treatment. The following discussion in outline form parallels the memorandum but is confined to the more critical issues:

1. Definition. This has been previously discussed.

2. Approach to the problem. Under subheading C, "Techniques Employed in the Studies Analyzed," we find "direct observation," "recent acculturation studied through interviews with members of acculturated groups," "use of documentary evidence," and "deductions from historical analyses and reconstructions." The authors thus clearly envisioned historical approaches as a proper part of the study of acculturation.

3. Analysis of acculturation. Under this heading the authors include de-

tailed subheadings concerning the types of contacts, the kinds of situations, and the processes involved. Such matters as contact only between selected or specialized groups from one or another culture, whether contacts are friendly or hostile, differences in size and complexity of groups, existence of force, and equality or inequality are among those included under the first two subheadings. Under "processes," the authors clearly consider significant such matters as order of selection of traits, manner of presentation of traits, resistances and the reasons therefore, and the way traits are integrated into the accepting culture, suggesting such factors as time, conflict arising out of new traits, and processes of adjustment.

4. Psychological mechanisms. The authors here consider the part played by the individual, and such problems as class, role, status, and personality differences.

5. The results of acculturation. These are defined as *Acceptance,* i.e., taking over the greater portion of another culture and assimilating both to behavior patterns and to inner values of the new culture; *Adaptation,* combining original and foreign traits either in a harmonious whole or with retention of conflicting attitudes which are reconciled in everyday behavior according to specific occasions; *Reaction,* where a variety of contra-acculturative movements arise, with emphasis on the psychological factors involved.

Bateson's paper is in part a critique of the memorandum, suggesting that it is premature to attempt to set up a system of categories before the basic problems have been clearly defined. He also suggests that the authors have been unduly influenced by the kinds of questions asked by administrative officers. As noted, he also suggests extension of the term "acculturation" to cover contacts between differentiated groups within a single culture and even for the acquisition of culture by the child (a common use by psychologists for which the term "enculturation" has more recently been used by a number of writers). Bateson then attempts to outline a series of problems, phrased in a combination of behavioral, psychiatric, and functional terms. Although points of considerable interest are made in this memorandum, apparently it has had little direct influence in actual acculturation studies.

Malinowski's "Method for the Study of Culture Contact" is essentially a rather mechanical organization of data for analytical purposes; his major headings are (A) white influences, interests, and intentions; (B) process of culture contact and change; (C) surviving forms of tradition; (D) reconstructed past; and (E) new forces of spontaneous African reintegration or reaction. The discussion and illustrations utilized adhere rigidly to Malinowski's classical functionalist approach, save for a slight and grudging bow to time elements in the category of the "reconstructed past." The "method" is also focused directly upon Africa and upon administrative or colonial problems, although the value of practical studies for the development of theory is stressed.

Both the Linton and the Ramos treatments essentially are refinements of the original Redfield, Linton, and Herskovits memorandum. The Ramos memorandum is much simpler, taking for granted many points spelled out in detail in the earlier document. Both writers, in different ways, lay greater stress upon psychological factors.

Aside from formal memoranda or outlines, there have been a considerable number of both explicit and implicit treatments of method centering around various phases of acculturation studies. In addition, a number of specialized emphases have made their appearance. In the following paragraphs I will attempt to summarize both discussions and field work with respect to the following points: (*a*) the use of historical data and approaches, (*b*) the comparative approach, (*c*) the "trait list" versus the holistic approach, (*d*) the role of the individual and psychological approaches, (*e*) linguistic acculturation studies, (*f*) the major cultural processes, and (*g*) quantification and indices.

a) THE USE OF HISTORICAL DATA AND APPROACHES

In the main, the use of historical data and approaches has been accepted, even by the majority of functionalist-trained scholars. Thus Richards writes (1935, p. 21):

> But what, in concrete terms, does it mean to study a society as it "actually functions"? In most parts of Africa cultural changes are taking place so rapidly that the anthropologist cannot study what is, without studying what was. As Miss Hunter writes in a previous article in this series: "Any culture can only be fully understood in its historical context, and when the culture under consideration has undergone revolutionary changes within a generation the relative importance of the historical context is very much greater than when the culture has been comparatively static." Thus, paradoxically enough, it is just those anthropologists who have turned their backs most resolutely on "antiquarianism," to whom "history" of some kind or other is of greatest value.

L. P. Mair (1934, pp. 416–17) writes:

> The central object of the inquiry [of the Baganda] seemed to be to find out how a working system of social cooperation had been affected by the various European influences to which it had been subjected for some years, and in particular to discover the respects in which there was more or less serious maladjustment. This required as its starting point a reconstruction of the system....
>
> It is obvious that such a reconstruction can never have the same factual value as the results of observation.... Nevertheless it seems essential for this type of inquiry. The functional theory of anthropology in general stresses the importance of studying native life as it is actually lived, and rejects the appeal to historical origins to explain peculiarities of social configuration. In a native society which has not recently suffered violent disturbance such explanations are unnecessary, and since they usually attempt to follow out a hypothetical course of evolution, they nearly always mislead.... Most native societies are now undergoing a process of rapid and forcible transformation, comparable only to the violent changes of revolution, and entirely distinct from the gradual, almost imperceptible, process of adaptation in which the normal evolution of human cultures consists. For this reason a straightforward description of such a society as the ethnologist finds it would not do justice to the crucial problems of the existing situation, which arose just where the traditional system has been forcibly wrenched away.... This does not mean that it is necessary to look for the "original" native culture.

Miss Mair later suggests that studies of historical sequences of change will be of little value and considers the crucial problem to be the study of the sum total of changes from the "zero point of what can be discovered of the independent native system." In interpreting Miss Mair's meaning it should be borne in mind that she is here emphasizing practical rather than theoretical significance.

Malinowski, on the whole, remained intransigent to the end concerning history, despite his inclusion of a column for the "Reconstructed Past" in his outline tables. This indeed he really viewed not as a "reconstructed past" but as the "past remembered" (1945, p. 29). The importance of the latter no one will quarrel with, but even his disciples today hardly will go as far as he does in criticizing Mair's suggestions. Thus he remarks (p. 30): "The ethnographer working on the reconstructed past would have to appear before the practical man with, at the best, 'damaged goods' in the line of practical advice and theoretical insight." In part, Malinowski's objections to history (and he had no objection to history in what he conceived to be its proper role and place) stem from a pervading feeling of its unscientific character, in part from his particular understanding of both science and history, and in part from his definition of culture change as resulting only from European contact. Thus in 1929 he manages clearly to convey the impression that change is only the result of European contact. Of course, Malinowski did not really believe this intellectually, for he has mentioned diffusion and change in other contexts frequently. Nevertheless, the aspect of European influence dominated his thinking and forms the basis for his objection to Mair's suggestion that one should seek a zero point for studies of culture change.

Fundamentally, Malinowski conceived of the zero point as a point at which culture change began. The implication clearly is that, before European contact, no change existed and the zero point must be at the first instant of European contact, a view that few other writers have sustained. Rather, if I understand Mair, she proposed establishing a zero point on the best and most convenient base line with respect to a specified series of changes permitted by the data and the situation. The most historical-minded would ask no more. And, indeed, the entire discussion may hinge primarily upon concepts of history and the occasional attempt to oppose history and science. Malinowski himself points out that this is futile and that the functional method "introduces the time element, at first on a smaller scale, but nonetheless in the real historical sense." If we accept time as a necessary dimension in a scientific approach (as it certainly is in modern physics), the old dichotomy largely disappears except for considerations of the proper employment of the time dimension.

Certainly, in a number of fields and more particularly in the work of American students of acculturation, historical data are used whenever possible. The approach of Herskovits and others with respect to the Negro in the New World makes the fullest possible use of historical materials. The same is true of most students in the Latin-American field. Thus in *Heritage of Conquest* by Sol Tax and others (1952), historical reference appears constantly in the discussions by a group of scholars of most diverse specific interests linked primarily by their concern with Middle America. It would seem, therefore, that the fundamental point of divergence is not in the use of history but in the type of problem and in the kind and extent of historical data used. There is more than a hint in the literature, especially in the writings of Malinowski, that historical interests are antiquarian rather than scientific, although clearly what is often meant is that historical interests are not "practical."

British writers likewise reveal what seems to many Americans either a curious unawareness of the nature of historical studies or a preoccupation with evolutionary approaches of a bygone century. Thus Miss Mair in the quotation above says that, since historical explanations "usually attempt to follow out a hypothetical course of evolution, they nearly always mislead." A similar attitude is expressed by Fortes (1936, p. 53):

I have indicated what I consider to be the limitations of a retrospective approach which treats the present state of affairs as an accomplished fact standing in contrast to a hypothetical "untouched" tribal culture. This is not rejecting history as a source of sociological data. Verifiable history, documenting the whole period of change, is indispensable to the student of social change. But history of the "before the deluge" kind does not, to my mind, illuminate the real problem, of which the problems raised by culture contact form but a part, namely, what are the causes of social change?

Earlier, though, he writes (1935, p. 6):

Ideally this method requires a temporal extension, continuous observation over a period of years, or repeated observations at intervals to yield definitive information on the causes of social change. But few anthropologists are likely to be in the position to satisfy this ideal; and this is where accurate history can step into the breach.

Wagner (1936, pp. 317–20) writes more concretely:

First it is necessary to obtain as concise a picture as possible of native culture prior to the contact. Secondly the nature of the various contact agencies must be determined. The third problem will be the functional analysis of the present stage of the cultural process that is resulting from the contact. A knowledge of this contact process as a whole . . . can only be gained by following all three approaches. An analysis dealing merely with the phase of the process in evidence at the time of investigation, which disregarded the basis from which it started and the variety of causes that set it in motion and still keep it going, would be suspended in the air. It would miss the very essence of the problem which is to give an insight into the response of a culture to foreign influences. It is obvious that one cannot study the response alone without knowing in some detail what is responding and what it is that provokes the response. . . .

To determine the basis from which the contact process started it is not always necessary or even desirable to go back to the beginning of the contact process as a whole . . . but only to the situation before a particular set of contact influences became effective.

Schapera (1935, p. 316) is likewise specific in stating that analysis of culture contact calls for knowledge of the original culture and of the forces bearing upon it at various times. The first step he envisions is to reconstruct as far as possible a picture of the old culture before Europeans came upon the scene, utilizing the best methods possible. The second step is the study of the history and nature of contact, including not merely a chronology of events or institutions but also motives, interests, and personalities. A third step is to seek explanations of change either through tracing changes in specific elements of native culture, for example, religion, or through tracing the influence of specific elements or agencies.

Hunter (1934, pp. 336–37), after describing situations she could not understand, states:

I have given this very obvious example of the impossibility of understanding existing institutions without a knowledge of the past. It might be paralleled by examples from every aspect of the culture. Any culture can only be fully understood in its historical context, and when the culture under consideration has undergone revolutionary changes within a generation the relative importance of the historical context is very much greater than when the culture has been relatively static. (a) . . . I decided . . . the most possible method of gauging the changes resulting from the contact was to compare areas subject to different contact influences, and that the study would be simplified if I began in the most conservative areas, that is, the one least affected by contact influences.

Hunter both studied four areas and also made a reconstruction of the older culture. She then made a comparison, with the result that she was much better able both to understand present cultures and the significance of culture change and to predict crucial points when changes occurred. Urging use of journals and other documents, she also says (pp. 343–44):

I am not concerned with origins as such, or with tracing the spread of particular elements of culture whether material elements like tobacco, soap, or a complex of beliefs, but I am concerned to discover the reactions of Pondo culture to European culture, and to discover these reactions it is necessary as far as possible to distinguish elements borrowed from European culture from those which were a part of Pondo culture before the coming of the European.

b) THE COMPARATIVE APPROACH

Comparative approaches fall into two categories. The first consists of studies of groups with the same or similar original cultures which have been exposed to different degrees of the same contact situation, perhaps beginning at different times. The purpose here is to understand the steps by which the group with the most modified culture has arrived at its present situation.

The method is . used by Hunter (1934), Richards (1935), and Culwick (1935), among British anthropologists, and also has been employed by American anthropologists, especially Hallowell (1949) and Redfield (1941). Essentially, the purpose is the reconstruction of past stages of acculturation, with the hope of gaining insight into processes. Few scholars, including users of the method, seem to have recognized that this is historical reconstruction by use of the basic age-area hypothesis; hence its employment has escaped the criticisms leveled at more avowedly historical approaches. Nevertheless, it must be grouped with other methods for reconstructing the past.

The second comparative approach is still almost unemployed in any systematic fashion: the comparison of various acculturative situations for the purpose of extracting generalizations about contact situations. It is true that a good many similar processes and end-results have been observed to occur in many different acculturative situations. An excellent summary is given by Herskovits (1948, p. 534). What is lacking still are detailed comparative analyses. As Fortes has said (1936, p. 26), a comparative sociology of culture contact is needed "without which we can never hope to perceive the causes of social change."

c) THE "TRAIT LIST" VERSUS THE HOLISTIC APPROACH

There is little discussion of the differences between the two approaches. British anthropologists, with their predominantly functionalist approach, tend to insist upon the importance of studying cultural wholes and occasionally have criticized efforts to study segments or parts of culture. In general, however, they dismiss the matter by essentially *ex cathedra* statements concerning the functional interrelatedness of cultures. In point of fact, however, no one has yet demonstrated a method by which cultures may be studied in their entirety. And, as Herskovits (1948) has pointed out, many significant studies have been accomplished by utilizing either an aspect of culture or through a frank dissection into traits as in the case of Parsons' *Mitla*. Indeed, the Malinowski method of study fundamentally involves listing elements of a culture. While he insists upon listing institutions, this is likewise a method involving temporary fragmentation of a culture, even though the fragments be somewhat larger than those of Parsons. The matter becomes more significant in connection with the discussion of quantification and indices.

d) THE ROLE OF THE INDIVIDUAL AND PSYCHOLOGICAL APPROACHES

Essentially, two different problems are involved here. The first emerges from studies concerned with the detailed mechanics of acculturation and centers about the role of specific individuals either in the donor or in the receiving culture. Thus Hunter (1934, pp. 347–49) discusses the importance of understanding the contact agents and their personalities (referring here to overt attitudes and behavioral patterns). Thurnwald (1935) likewise emphasizes the need to understand not only the agents of acculturation and their motivations but the changes which take place in the agents as a result of the contact situation. A great many studies in the United States likewise devote considerable attention to the role of specific individuals in contact situations. This is particularly marked in the numerous studies of revivalistic and nativistic cults.

Of a different order are investigations of personality structure and personality change in connection with acculturation situations. Perhaps the most active and consistent worker in this field has been A. Hallowell, whose writings range from broad analyses of general psychological processes (1945) to highly systematic investigations utilizing projective techniques. Based upon the general assumption of some relationship between a given culture and the personality of the individual culture bearers, most investigations have been devoted to exploring the problem of the amount and rapidity of personality change under conditions of culture contact and the relationships between personality and acceptance or rejection of culture change. The rather voluminous but scattered literature is closely related to the literature of the "culture-personality" approach in general. Also of considerable interest are studies employing personal documents, myth, and song to reveal psychological problems and characteristics (cf. Thurnwald, 1935; Barnouw, 1950).

Sociologists have also paid some attention to this problem, particularly in connection with structural-functional analysis. Both some sociologists (e.g., Merton, 1949, p. 53) and some anthropologists have tended to assign an independent causal status to the psychological or personality variables, a view sharply criticized by DuBois (1951). Others have merely considered sociocultural and psychological variables to be in dynamic relationship. An important recent statement of the problem is Spindler and Goldschmidt's (1952) "Experimental Design in the Study of Culture Change," which attempts to isolate social and psychological variables and delineates a method for examining their interrelations.

e) LINGUISTIC ACCULTURATION

Although the similarity of linguistic and cultural change has been long recognized in general terms, few concrete studies dealing with the problem have emerged. George Herzog, Edward Spier, Jean Bassett Johnson, and Dorothy Lee all published articles in 1941 and 1943 dealing with specific examples of linguistic acculturation among North American Indian tribes. More recently George Barker (1947) has worked on the same problem with relation to Mexicans in the United States.

Studies thus far published are relatively preliminary and have included few theoretical statements. Generally, stress has been laid upon the interrelationship between sociocultural and linguistic factors in change. Despite some suggestion that linguistic studies could provide indices for acculturation, the field is little developed and is mentioned here merely because it appears to offer unexplored potentialities.

f) IDENTIFICATION OF MAJOR CULTURAL PROCESSES

Although the identification of processes is perhaps the ultimate theoretical objective of acculturation studies, relatively little empirical investigation which permits of adequate generalization has taken place. Such work or speculation as has taken place has perhaps been primarily done by United States anthropologists, although there are notable exceptions, the most recent being Elkin (1951). But most British anthropologists seem to follow Miss Hunter (1934, p. 335) when she says:

"My interest in culture contact is primarily practical. . . . The nature and extent of the changes taking place in the Bantu community are my first concern, the mechanism of change a secondary one."

In very broad terms there are agreements among students of culture contact as to some of the possible results. Virtually all discussions point out acceptance, syncretism, and reaction as being possible results of culture contact, with the recognition that in most cases all three effects may occur, with emphasis varying according to the conditions of contact as well as through time as the contact situation continues. Acceptance, without modification by other attitudes, ultimately leads to complete assimilation to the contact culture. Even if other responses intervene, assimilation may in some cases ultimately result. Syncretism is a frequent result of contact and has been well documented, especially in the studies of Latin-American Indian cultures and in the studies of the Negro in the New World. Less frequently mentioned in the various memoranda for study, but prominent in some of the actual studies both in the New World and in Africa, is the occurrence of spontaneous reformulations which often result in the modification of elements from either of the cultures in contact or produce entirely new structures. While the totality of the emergent culture may be regarded in some measure as a syncretism, large areas of the social structure may be essentially new. Perhaps the most thoroughly studied of the primary areas of phenomena is that of reaction. Clearly to be included in this category are the various revivalistic and nativistic movements. Not only has Linton (1943) given us a useful typology for organizing studies of such movements, but there are numerous analyses of special movements, such as the studies of the Peyote cult, the Ghost Dance, and related movements in North America; Williams' studies in New Guinea; and various others. Although often undertaken without being placed in an acculturational framework, they provide valuable materials for analysis.

Beyond these rather general terms, processual analysis does not seem adequately conceptualized. The majority of existing discussions of process are heavily psychological and essentially deal with the role of the individual in change or the impact of change upon the individual. Few explanations in sociological or cultural terms have been developed. Even those attempts made are often somewhat specialized in character, especially in studies with practical objectives. Thus Miss Hunter (1934, p. 350) says:

What administrator, missionary, and commercial man alike are really concerned to discover is what were the sanctions for social behavior under tribal conditions, and how these sanctions are being affected by contact with Europeans. The social sanctions, the bonds integrating the society, are only to be understood by studying the work and the interrelation of the institutions of the society, and it is the change in the working and interrelation of institutions resulting from European contact which we must discover.

One cannot quarrel with Miss Hunter's objectives and proposals, which are in line with her avowed preoccupation with practical problems, but one must suggest that they do not provide adequate conceptualizations for enlarging the theoretical framework, nor does she really suggest in any very profound way techniques for arriving at analysis of the processes of change. In this respect Redfield's studies offer considerably more in the way of theoretical formulation in his use of such concepts as secularization, individualization, and so on; but they are admittedly confined to those aspects of the contact situation which are related to the change from folk to urban. Fortes (1936) has pointed out that culture contact must be viewed as a continuous process of interaction. Despite his recognition of the importance of a comparative sociology of culture contact, he offers little in more concrete terms. Beyond very broad concepts, then, little progress has been made in accurate conceptualization of processes or their empirical identification, particularly in broad theoretical contexts. Perhaps the most important contribution in recent years is Elkin (1951), who has presented an analytical discussion of native reaction in Australia which deserves critical appraisal and testing in other areas and situations.

g) QUANTIFICATION AND INDICES

British anthropologists have been especially insistent upon the necessity of collecting quantified information. In situations of change, it becomes particularly important to know what proportions of a given population conform to various of the changing norms. Richards especially (1935) has emphasized the village census as a technique, but she is not unique in its use. Many problems of sampling and of reliability of data have not been adequately dealt with as yet. Wagner (1936) has pointed out the unreliability of data obtained by schedules and the impossibility of using them for house-to-house interviews or in any sort of random sampling, where problems of rapport are involved. He makes an ingenious suggestion for utilizing a genealogical method to get quantitative data which raises important sampling problems.

The use of quantitative approaches has also been suggested for developing indices of acculturation. Interesting proposals in this direction, as well as on the use of quantified data to meas-

ure relative rates of change as between different segments of a given culture and to make acculturation studies more directly comparable, were made by Leonard Broom in two short articles in 1939 and 1945, but this lead has never been followed up. Spindler (unpublished manuscript) and Spindler and Goldschmidt make use of quantified data to establish classes or strata representing (presumably) levels of acculturation within a group. Although there is considerable growth in quantification of data, there is little development of consistent methodologies or sophistication in statistical treatments which could contribute to growth in theoretical understanding.

IV. CONCLUSION

The survey and discussion here presented represent an inadequate coverage of the growing literature on acculturation. The work of anthropologists, both British and United States, in the Pacific area has been largely omitted from consideration for reasons of time. Moreover, there may appear to be an overemphasis on earlier literature. Nevertheless, there is some justification for such an emphasis.

Despite the fact that the interest in acculturation has reached a point where an entire volume on the subject may be organized from the papers presented at the Congress of Americanists or that a symposium on Middle American ethnology can be presented as a volume on acculturation (Tax *et al.*, 1951), recent literature has in the main been either descriptive in character, concerned with specialized problems, such as the psychological approaches, or has been frankly applied in nature. Most recent studies have followed lines laid down in the earlier literature and have made little theoretical contribution. One finds refinements of method and of field techniques, but one does not find great sharpening of concepts or the development of firm theoretical structures. Despite its bulk, the literature of acculturation does not seem to be cumulative in character.

Such a review as the present suggests strongly the need for serious stocktaking and reformulation of the field of acculturation. There is an urgent necessity to re-examine our conceptual apparatus and to reach agreement on objectives and methods which will produce more comparability in studies and which will develop a series of really significant hypotheses.

It would seem that such a re-examination could best take place within the framework of the broader problem of culture change. As Robert Nesbit has said (unpublished manuscript), the functionalists in sociology and anthropology have made a major contribution by emphasizing the *statics* of culture. Only recently has functionalist theory become interested again in change, an interest which clearly requires some modification of functionalist theory. Most particularly, it is necessary to introduce the time dimension if the dynamic situation is to receive adequate treatment.

If, as Julian Huxley (1952, p. 16) has said, "a study of the mechanism of cultural transmission and variation may be as important for anthropology as the study of genetics has been for biology," then there are few more important tasks in our field. Within the area of culture change, acculturation seems to offer the best possibilities for getting at an important part of the "genetics" of culture change. Nevertheless, to attempt to develop acculturation studies without reference to the total problem of cultural transmission and variation would seem to be undesirable.

This is not the place to attempt to define the directions which reformulations of acculturation should take. Nevertheless, a few comments may be in order. Apart from the basic task of

sharpening our concepts and revising our theoretical structure, the following seem some of the needed steps:

1. It should be made clear that the study of acculturation is primarily concerned with the study of process. As process must in the main be inferred, we need clarification of the methods of inference.

2. Without in any way belittling the importance of psychological problems related to acculturational situations, a clear understanding of and division between sociocultural and psychological phenomena and explanations should be established.

3. Dynamic situations, as the physicists have long recognized, require the use of time as a dimension. New techniques and standards are called for.

4. Various specialized approaches need further exploration, especially the field of linguistics.

5. Quantification should be extensively developed. Quantification should not be developed for its own sake but to provide techniques for objectively determining relative rates of acculturation between various aspects of culture and between individuals in a given society, to establish types and classes, and to provide better comparative methods. Quantification should be developed in close relation to the advance of structural and functional types of analysis. Without this, quantification may result in unrealistic fragmentation of cultures without means of reintegrating the results.

6. Studies should aim increasingly at comparability. Emphasis must be given to the discovery of uniformities in culture processes and to research designs which will produce additive results.

7. It is of the utmost importance that both theoretical and empirical studies give adequate consideration to the reciprocal nature of acculturation and to instances of acculturation which do not involve European cultures.

8. There is need to explore the relation of acculturation to the broader problems of culture change and to such concepts as assimilation, syncretization, disorganization, and dysfunction. While in such theoretical exploration it is perhaps not too important that we define the limits of the field of acculturation with precision at this time, it is important that we explore the utility of typologies, the possible existence of continua, the usefulness of polar concepts, and the validity of using the acculturation approach in connection with migration phenomena and urbanism where contacts may be between individuals rather than organized social groups. Because of the relatively greater number of anthropologists in the United States and the relatively less strong pressure upon them for applied studies, the development of theory and method is perhaps a particular responsibility of scholars in the United States. This statement is not an attempt to set up a "reserved area," upon which others should not poach, but rather a recognition of actualities and an assertion of special responsibilities. Finally, although further review perhaps should precede a decision, the time seems ripe for a new committee representing a variety of interests to re-examine the field and perhaps prepare a new research memorandum.

REFERENCES AND BIBLIOGRAPHY

The following does not pretend to be a complete bibliography of acculturation. Rather it represents only works cited in this paper plus a few others included either because of their historical significance or as representing important collections of papers.

AMERICAN ANTHROPOLOGICAL ASSOCIATION. 1937. "Proceedings of the Annual Meeting for 1936," *American Anthropologist,* XXXIX, 316–27.

BARKER, GEORGE. 1947. "Social Functions of Language in a Mexican-American Community," *Acta Americana,* V, 185–202.

BARNOUW, VICTOR. 1952. *Acculturation and Personality among the Wisconsin Chippewa.* ("American Anthropological Association Memoirs," No. 72.)

BATESON, GREGORY. 1935. "Culture Contact and Schimogenesis," *Man,* Art. 199.

BEALS, RALPH L. 1932. "Aboriginal Survivals in Mayo Culture," *American Anthropologist,* XXXIV, 28–39.

——. 1937. Review of PARSONS, E. C., *Mitla: Town of the Souls, ibid.,* XXXIX, 681–82.

——. 1951. "Urbanism, Urbanization and Acculturation," *ibid.,* LIII, 1–10.

BENEDICT, RUTH. 1937. Review of REDFIELD, R., and VILLA, A. R., *Chan Kom: A Maya Village, American Anthropologist,* XXXIX, 340–42.

BOAS, FRANZ, *et al.* 1938. *General Anthropology.* New York: D. C. Heath & Co.

BROOM, LEONARD. 1939. "The Cherokee Clan: A Study in Acculturation," *American Anthropologist,* XLI, 266–68.

——. 1945. "A Measure of Conservatism," *ibid.,* XLVII, 630–35.

BUSCHAN, G. 1910. *Illustrierte Völkerkunde.* 2 vols. Stuttgart: Strecker.

CHAPPLE, E., and COON, C. 1942. *Principles of Anthropology.* New York: Henry Holt & Co.

——. 1943. "Centenary of the American Ethnological Society," *American Anthropologist,* XLV, 181–243.

CULWICK, A. T. and G. M. 1935. "Culture Contact on the Fringe of Civilization," *Africa,* VIII, 163–70.

DuBois, CORA. 1939. *The 1870 Ghost Dance.* ("Anthropological Records," Vol. III, No. 1.)

——. 1951. "The Use of Social Science Concepts To Interpret Historical Materials: Comments on the Two Preceding Articles," *Far Eastern Quarterly,* XXI, 31–34.

EKVALL, ROBERT B. 1939. *Cultural Relations on the Kansu-Tibetan Border.* Chicago: University of Chicago Press.

ELKIN, A. P. 1932. "Five Year Plan of Research," *Africa,* V, 1–13.

ELKIN, A. P. 1951. "Reaction and Inter-action: A Food Gathering People and European Settlement in Australia," *American Anthropologist*, LIII, 164–86.

FORTES, MEYER. 1936. "Culture Contact as a Dynamic Process," *Africa*, IX, 24–55.

GILLIN, JOHN. 1948. *The Ways of Men.* New York: D. Appleton–Century Co., Inc.

GOLDENWEISER, ALEXANDER. 1937. *Anthropology.* New York: F. S. Crofts & Co.

GREENBERG, JOSEPH H. 1941. "Some Aspects of Negro-Mohammedan Culture Contact among the Hausa," *American Anthropologist*, XLIII, 51–61.

HALLOWELL, A. I. 1945. "Sociopsychological Aspects of Acculturation." In LINTON, R. (ed.), *The Science of Man in the World Crisis*, pp. 171–200. New York: Columbia University Press.

———. 1949. "Ojibwa Personality and Acculturation." In TAX, SOL (ed.), *Acculturation in the Americas: Proceedings and Selected Papers of the XXIXth International Congress of Americanists*, pp. 105–14. Chicago: University of Chicago Press.

HERSKOVITS, MELVILLE. 1937a. "The Significance of the Study of Acculturation for Anthropology," *American Anthropologist*, XXXIX, 259–64.

———. 1937b. "African Gods and Catholic Saints in New World Negro Belief," *ibid.*, pp. 635–43.

———. 1938. *Acculturation: The Study of Culture Contact.* New York: J. J. Augustin.

———. 1948. *Man and His Works.* New York: A. A. Knopf.

HERZOG, GEORGE. 1941. "Culture Change and Language: Shifts in the Pima Vocabulary." In NEWMAN, STANLEY; SPIER, LESLIE; and HALLOWELL, A. I. (eds.), *Language, Culture, and Personality: Essays in Memory of Edward Sapir*, pp. 66–74. Menasha, Wis.: Sapir Memorial Publication Fund.

HUNTER, MONICA. *See* WILSON, MONICA HUNTER.

HUXLEY, JULIAN. 1952. "Biological Evolution and Human History," *American Anthropological Association News Bulletin*, VI, 16.

INTERNATIONAL CONGRESS OF AMERICANISTS. 1952. *Acculturation in the Americas: Proceedings and Selected Papers of the XXIXth International Congress of Americanists.* Chicago: University of Chicago Press.

INTERNATIONAL INSTITUTE OF AFRICAN LANGUAGES AND CULTURES. 1938. *Memorandum XV.* London.

JOHNSON, JEAN BASSETT. 1943. "A Clear Case of Linguistic Acculturation," *American Anthropologist*, XLV, 427–34.

LEE, DOROTHY. 1943. "The Linguistic Aspect of Wintu Acculturation," *American Anthropologist*, XLV, 435–40.

LINDBLOM, GERHARD. 1937. Review of HUNTER, MONICA, *Reaction to Conquest*, *American Anthropologist*, XXXIX, 688–90.

LINDGREN, ETHEL JOHN. 1938. "An Example of Culture Contact without Conflict: Reindeer Tungus and Cossacks of Northwestern Manchuria," *American Anthropologist*, XL, 605–21.

LINTON, RALPH (ed.). 1940. *Acculturation in Seven North American Indian Tribes.* New York: D. Appleton–Century Co.

———. 1943. "Nativistic Movements," *American Anthropologist*, XLV, 230–39.

LOWIE, ROBERT H. 1934. *Introduction to Cultural Anthropology.* 2d ed. New York: Farrar & Rinehart, Inc., 1940.

MAIR, L. P. 1934. "The Study of Culture Contact as a Practical Problem," *Africa*, VII, 415–22.

MALINOWSKI, B. 1929. "Practical Anthropology," *Africa*, II, 22–38.

———. 1939. "The Dynamics of Contemporary Diffusion." Summary in *Proceedings of the International Congress of Historical and Ethnological Sciences.* Copenhagen.

———. 1945. *The Dynamics of Culture Change: An Inquiry into Race Relations in Africa.* New Haven: Yale University Press.

MEAD, M. 1932. *The Changing Culture of an Indian Tribe.* New York: Columbia University Press.

MERTON, ROBERT. 1949. *Social Theory and Social Structure.* Glencoe, Ill.: Free Press.

ORTIZ, FERNANDO. 1940. *Contrapunteo del tobaco y el azucar.* Havana: J. Montero.

PARSONS, E. C. 1933. "Some Aztec and Pueblo Parallels," *American Anthropologist,* XXXV, 611–31.

——. 1936. *Mitla: Town of the Souls.* Chicago: University of Chicago Press.

RAMOS, ARTHUR. 1947. *Intradução à antropologia brasileira.* Vol. II. Rio de Janeiro.

REDFIELD, ROBERT. 1929. "The Material Culture of Spanish-Indian Mexico," *American Anthropologist,* XXXI, 602–18.

——. 1934. "Culture Changes in Yucatan," *ibid.,* pp. 57–69.

——. 1941. *The Folk Cultures of Yucatan.* Chicago: University of Chicago Press.

REDFIELD, R.; LINTON, R.; and HERSKOVITS, M. J. 1936. "Memorandum on the Study of Acculturation," *American Anthropologist,* XXXVIII, 149–52. (Also published in *Man, Africa,* and *Oceania.*)

RICHARDS, AUDREY I. 1935. "The Village Census in the Study of Culture Contact," *Africa,* VIII, 20–33.

SCHAPERA, I. 1935. "Field Methods in the Study of Modern Culture Contacts," *Africa,* VIII, 315–26.

SCHRIEKE, B. (ed.). 1929. *The Effect of Western Influence on Native Civilizations in the Malay Archipelago.* Batavia: G. Kolff & Co.

SPICER, EDWARD. 1943. "Linguistic Aspects of Yaqui Acculturation," *American Anthropologist,* XLV, 410–26.

SPIER, LESLIE. 1929. "Problems Arising from the Cultural Position of the Havasupai," *American Anthropologist,* XXXI, 213–22.

SPINDLER, GEORGE C., and GOLDSCHMIDT, WALTER. 1941. "Symposium on Acculturation," *American Anthropologist,* XLIII, 1–61.

——. 1952. "Experimental Design in the Study of Culture Change," *Southwestern Journal of Anthropology,* VIII, 68–83.

TAX, SOL, et al. 1951. *Heritage of Conquest: The Ethnology of Middle America.* Glencoe, Ill.: Free Press.

THURNWALD, RICHARD. 1932. "The Psychology of Acculturation," *American Anthropologist,* XXXIV, 557–69.

——. 1935. *Black and White in East Africa.* London: Humanities Press.

——. 1938. "The African in Transition: Some Comparisons with Melanesia," *Africa,* XI, 174–86.

WAGNER, GUNTER. 1936. "The Study of Culture Contact and the Determination of Policy," *Africa,* IX, 317–31.

WILSON, MONICA HUNTER. 1934. "Methods in the Study of Culture Contact," *Africa,* VII, 335–50.

——. 1936. *Reaction to Conquest.* London: H. Milford.

National Character*

By MARGARET MEAD

NATIONAL CHARACTER studies are a recent development in anthropological research on problems of personality and culture. They take both their form and methods from the exigencies of the post-1939 world political situation.[1] Although the national-character approach utilizes the premises and methods of the personality and culture field, historically it has had two distinguishing features: the group of persons with a shared social tradition whose culture is studied is selected because they are the citizens or subjects—the "nationals" —of a sovereign political state, and the society *may* be so inaccessible to direct field observation that less direct methods of research have to be used. These contemporary national character studies of culture at a distance resemble attempts to reconstruct the cultural character of societies of the past (Mead, 1951*b*) in which the study of documents and monuments has to be substituted for the direct study of individuals interacting in observable social situations. However, they differ from historical reconstruction in that, whether they are done at a distance or through field work in the given nation, they are based primarily on interviews with and observation of living human beings.

National character studies, like all culture and personality studies, are focused on the way human beings embody the culture they have been reared in or to which they have immigrated. These studies attempt to delineate how the innate properties of human beings, the idiosyncratic elements in each human being, and the general and individual patterns of human maturation are integrated within a shared social tradition in such a way that certain regularities appear in the behavior of all members of the culture which can be described as a *culturally* regular character. In this sense, "cultural character" is an abstraction which anthropologists use when their conceptual apparatus is devised to include assumptions about intra-psychic structure. A statement like "In culture X, married men must avoid their wives' mothers" is a cultural statement. "In culture X, the mother-in-law avoidance is enforced through a sense of shame" is an inexplicit culture and personality statement in which "sense of shame," a construct about intra-psychic behavior, is invoked without analysis or supporting psychological theory. But, "In culture X the mother-in-law avoidance is maintained through a sense of shame; the individual learns to associate exposure of certain parts of the body with social disapproval, so that he responds to the presence of his mother-in-law as he would to physical exposure" is a (still very simple) statement in which the words "learns to associate" involve a psychological theory of learning. A cul-

* In the preparation of this paper in its final form, I have been very much indebted to Professor David Mandelbaum's detailed criticism.

1. This development is summarized in Mead (1951*c*); also in French edition (see "Selective Bibliography").

ture and personality approach may use as one part of its conceptual apparatus a relatively simple tentative psychological scheme such as simple associationalism; the rounded-out system of Hullian learning theory (Hilgard and Marquis, 1940; Dollard and Miller, 1950), Gestalt perceptual theory (Kofka, 1935), and Freudian theories of character formation (see esp. Fromm, 1941; Kardiner, 1945; Erikson, 1950); the eclectic constructs of social psychology (Murphy, 1947); or others. Whether the type of psychological theory drawn upon is one that relies on detailed assumptions about the nature of innate drives and phylogenetically determined perceptual mechanisms or one that simply assumes that social behavior is learned and that the way it is learned is significant for the understanding of a culture, it is the *presence* of psychological theory, that is, the inclusion of intra-psychic processes in the descriptions of members of a society, that differentiates the culture and personality approach.

Once a theoretical scheme accepting intra-psychic behavior as investigable and relevant is used, some psychological theory is involved. This includes even such a scheme as Radcliffe-Brown used in his study of the Andaman Islands (1922), in which he utilized the psychological construct of "sentiments" as a signpost to indicate how far he meant to go in involving theories about intra-psychic behavior in his study of this culture, or Franz Boas' use of the explanatory phrase "automatic behavior." The tendency to characterize some anthropological works as involving "culture and personality" and others as not is really an attempt to draw an artificial dividing line at some point in the formulation of the problem. Actually, there is a continuum, at one end of which formal ethnographic work—like most social history—dodges the issue with statements like "Murder was much more frequent among the coastal tribes"

or "During the next century the times became much more unsettled, and robbery and murder were rife," without posing the problem of what correlates of the changed incidence of violence there were in the intra-psychic organization of individuals (Ware, 1940).

Practically speaking, it is possible to distinguish culture and personality studies from simple descriptive studies by determining the proportion of clusters of information on single individuals with which the anthropologist works. In a cultural study, it is theoretically possible to collect each item of information about the culture from a different individual, cross-checking only in order to guard against pathology or extreme idiosyncrasy of response. In a culture and personality study, actual studies of identified individuals must be undertaken by ongoing observation, retrospective life-histories (Dollard, 1935; Gottschalk, Kluckhohn, and Angell, 1945; Mead, 1949*b*, Introd.), or the use of projective tests (Henry, 1947; Abel, 1948); at the very least, the items of information about interpersonal behavior—especially that involved between young persons or immigrants and the older members of the society—must be organized *as if* these details of interpersonal interaction were occurring among individuals with specifiable characteristics of constitution, temperament, sex, degree of maturation, previous experience (Kardiner, 1939), and so forth. If, for example, having only the information that the vision experience required of young men in a certain culture is expressed in accounts of what is *seen* during the "vision" and that no "hearings" of any sort are allowed for, we consider this piece of information together with the possibility that some individuals in every culture may be primarily "auditory" in type and therefore will be handicapped when it comes to "seeing" visions, then we are proceeding *as if* it were possible to study identifiable individuals within that culture pattern. We have material on the cultural hope expressed by the Cheyenne that young men will be brave (Grinnell, 1923), and we have material on the assumption of a transvestite position by some Cheyenne, who refuse to assume the warrior role; if we attempt to explain these transvestites by assuming that they possess individual characteristics of timidity or negativism or have experienced a closer-than-usual tie with their mothers or unusual strictness from their fathers, these speculations (valuable, in the absence of field research, only for the construction of hypotheses and the identification of problems) are nevertheless within the culture and personality field. When it is possible to study the actual characteristics of individuals who are choosing or have chosen the transvestite role and the order of birth or the relative age and status of the actual children who show discrepant amounts of aggressiveness, our work becomes full culture and personality research.

Just as culture and personality research draws upon the developing conceptual schemes of psychology (principally upon learning theories, psychoanalytic psychology, and Gestalt psychology), so studies of national character draw upon the developing conceptual schemes of the culture and personality field (Sapir, 1934; Gorer, 1943b; Bateson, 1944; Mead, 1946b; Frank, 1948; Haring, 1948; Kluckhohn and Murray, 1948; Sargent and Smith, 1949). Conclusions drawn from detailed field work that has involved the use of psychological constructs on living, identified, observable groups of human beings are used as the conceptual background of national character studies (Gorer, 1938; Bateson and Mead, 1942; Kluckhohn and Leighton, 1946, 1947) of complex societies where no such complete field studies are possible. Fairly sharp distinctions can be

drawn between the direct application of particular psychological schemes to the behavior of members of a society (which, without the "mediating variable" of "culture," results in oversimplified statements about a nation's members being "paranoid" [Brickner, 1943] or "regressed") and the explicit invoking of field studies to specify the kind of steps in cultural learning or unlearning which may lead to behavior that is characteristically paranoid or schizophrenic in many respects but that must be referred to cultural patterns rather than to any particular individual's idiosyncratic defect in "reality testing" (Mead, 1952). One of the difficulties encountered by students of national character is their dependence for this "mediating variable" upon a relatively new branch of anthropology that is not widely known to either anthropologists or psychologists.

The simplest meaning of the "mediating variable" can be discovered by examining the differences between the caricature statement, *Swaddling them as infants makes Russians incapable of freedom,* and the national-character statement, *The prolonged and very tight swaddling to which infants are subjected in Russian child-rearing practice is one of the means by which Russians communicate to their infants a feeling that a strong authority is necessary.*[2] The first statement assumes that swaddling, as an experience of certain human infants, somehow produces an attitude in adult Russians, independently of the entire history of Russia; the second insists that it is when Russians (who themselves embody their whole culture) handle their own children (who are in the process of learning to be Russians) in a particular way that this way of handling becomes a form of

2. For bibliography surrounding this controversy, see Endleman (1949); Gorer (1949); Orlansky (1949); Goldman (1950); Shub (1950); Mead (1951d, e); and Wolfe (1951).

communication between parent and child in which the child learns something the adult has already learned, not necessarily by the same means. The mediating variable used here is "culture." A second "mediating variable" is represented by the phrase "child-rearing practice," which invokes our entire systematic knowledge of infant growth and development and of the connections which clinical work has traced in individual cases between child-rearing practice and personality. Such a view of culture assumes, furthermore, that each member of a society is systematically representative of the cultural pattern of that society, so that the treatment accorded infant or immigrant, pupils or employees or rulers, is indicative of the culturally regular character-forming methods of that society (Bateson, 1942a; Mead, 1948; Joffe, 1949).

From the systematic invocation of this conceptual framework, we are able to say that a change in the pattern of interpersonal contact will be accompanied by a change in the response system of both parties—parent and child, native and stranger, employer and employee. Such changes may be merely temporary adjustments to a changed situation, but, if continued long enough, they may become part of the "character" of both members of the interacting pair. When such changes occur throughout a social system (as when, for example, equalitarian patterns of relationship are substituted for hierarchical patterns), an alteration in "cultural character" may be expected to occur as the intra-psychic correlate of what is usually called "social change" (Mead, 1940, 1947a, 1949c).

Professor Hallowell has outlined in an earlier paper, "Culture, Personality, and Society," some of the basic premises of the culture and personality approach. With Professor Hallowell's general approach to the field of personality and culture, particularly as exemplified in his field work and detailed papers on

aspects of the problem, I am very much in agreement, although I would not use the particular units or entities he used in presenting his analytical discussion. As the field of national character is derivative from the field of personality and culture, it will be necessary to rephrase very briefly some of the points that Professor Hallowell has discussed.

Culture and personality theory depends upon systematic studies of culture which have demonstrated that the culture of any people is learned and can be altered through such processes as borrowing, resistance, invention, and so forth; that cultural forms are not related in any demonstrable way to racial characteristics, except that, when certain cultural characteristics are attributed to certain physically identifiable members of a society, they may then learn them (Warner, Junker, and Adams, 1941); that the developing child shows patterns of regularity of maturation from fetal life through physical maturation (Gesell, 1945). It depends also upon systematic experimental studies of learning and perception (Hilgard and Marquis, 1940; Bateson, 1942b), systematic sociological studies of such correspondences as that between social status and differences in learning within a society (Davis and Havighurst, 1947), and clinical studies of individual children and individual adults (Fries, 1947; Adorno et al., 1950; Erikson, 1950).

Against the background of such systematic investigations, culture and personality studies on primitive peoples have been made, and the clarity of their psychocultural formulations has increased as the young disciplines of child development, learning psychology, Gestalt psychology, and psychoanalysis have been able to provide formulations more applicable cross-culturally, partly in response to the use which anthropologists have made of such formulations in the field. Systematic culture and personality field studies among primitive peoples where the cultural and societal conditions were appropriate for intensive work have, in turn, provided the background for work in national character—for the attempt to delineate the regularities in character among the members of a national group attributable to the factors of shared nationality and the accompanying institutional correlates—nation-wide linguistic usages, legal codes, economic activities, educational forms, and so forth.

Perhaps the most frequent misconception (Endleman, 1949; Orlansky, 1949; Goldman, 1950; Lindesmith and Strauss, 1950; Little, 1950; Shub, 1950; Wolfe, 1951) about work on national character has been the belief that students of national character used the *same methods* to study German or English or Japanese character that were used for the study of the Alorese, the Navaho, or the Pukapukans. In addition to the objection that these methods of observation would have been seriously misapplied had they been used to study societies not accessible to observation, the legitimate objection has been made that methods applicable to small primitive societies of relatively simple organization are not applicable to nation-states of many millions, since the very difference in size introduces qualitative differences in the possible methods of research. This misunderstanding was fostered somewhat by those of us who began the work in the field, because we stressed the usefulness of the anthropological training which enabled us to use the verbal reports and postural responses of living individuals (or their written or artistic work treated as living behavior) as our primary subject matter. Thus an anthropological skill learned in field work among primitive peoples— the skill of evaluating an individual informant's place in a social and cultural whole and then recognizing the formal patterns, explicit and implicit, of his culture expressed in his spontaneous verbal statements and his behavior—became identified as the single contribution the anthropologist could make to the study of contemporary cultures.

It would be less misleading to say that the study of national character is a form of anthropology in which the anthropologist draws upon experience with and knowledge of the findings of the body of pure research materials resulting from field work in culture and personality, but uses new methods (Mead, 1951a). Experience in the training of skilled members of the psychological disciplines to apply their psychological skills directly to cultural materials, either primitive or complex modern, indicates that the presence of the cultural anthropologist who has a command of personality and culture research methods and theory is essential if studies of national character, as distinct from studies of projections or attitudes or descriptions of social perception patterns, are to result. Original personality and culture studies of the particular culture on which members of the psychological disciplines are working may, of course, be substituted for the physical presence of an anthropologist on a working team.[3]

Studies of national character make the following assumptions, based on the types of research enumerated above:

1. There are no known differences among races of men which either interfere with or facilitate the learning of cultural forms (psychic unity of mankind).

2. There are wide individual differences among human beings which must be taken into account; these may be grouped with varying degrees of probable correctness as attributable to sex, temperament, constitutional type, or other repetitive genetic factors.

3. Cultures—the abstraction used by

3. See use of data from West's *Plainville* (1945) in Kardiner's *The Psychological Frontiers of Society* (1945).

anthropologists to apply to historically developed, shared, learned behavior of members of a society—have systematic aspects which can be referred to the biologically given characteristics of their human characters, such as maturational sequences, hand-eye co-ordination, capacity for symbolic behavior, etc.

4. Cultures have other systematic aspects that can be referred to other regularities in nature; a cultural handling of the calendar, for example, can be referred to, and understood in terms of, our independently verified astronomical knowledge.

5. Human cultures may be seen as historically patterned systems of communication between individuals, within individuals, and between individuals and the nonhuman environment, which codify and give meaning to the child's, or the immigrant's, proprioceptive and exteroceptive experience (e.g., a lump in the throat comes to be experienced as sorrow, a tingling in the big toe as fear, the color red as a signal of danger, a circle as a sign of unity, the stars in the Great Bear as a constellation indicating the northern sky, and so forth).

6. Human cultures have certain holistic characteristics which may be referred to the comparable biologically given capacity of human beings to systemize experience and to the circumstance that a culture is shared by members of a *society*—itself organized as a whole in such a way that changes in one part have reverberations in other parts of the society.

7. The culture of each society has unique characteristics which may be referred in an infinite regression to antecedent conditions. No formulation on the basis of an analysis under points 3, 4, 5, and 6 should be expected to account for these unique characteristics without recourse to a known sequence of historical events.

8. Each culture may be expected to change concomitantly with impinging events which were hitherto outside the system—an invasion from a hitherto unknown people, an earthquake, an epidemic arising outside the society, and so on. Such changes should not contradict formulations made on the basis of points 3, 4, 5, and 6; but formulations based on these assumptions should not be expected to predict the occurrence of such changes but only to establish the limits within which such cultural change is likely to fall, if externally precipitated.

9. Cultures are carried by successive generations in such a way that each member of each generation, from infancy to old age, contributes to the perpetuation and reinterpretation of the cultural forms. Changes in the behavior of any member may be expected to set up repercussions within the society; changes in the behavior of a category of members may be expected to result in changes within the whole system.

10. Cultures, although individually unique, may be expected to show comparable features when cross-cultural categories (amount of capital goods, caste, class, size of primary groups, degree of segmentation, and so forth) are applied to them in such a way that the unique pattern of organization of each culture is also taken into account.

11. The version of the wider cultural pattern manifested by the members of any subgroup in a culture may be expected to be systematically related to the wider cultural pattern. But the reverse is not true; the wider pattern need not include any of the features which are *distinctive* of the particular pattern of the subgroup. In the United States, for example, wide patterns of common American behavior may be expected to recur in the behavior of Kentucky mountaineers, Texas ranchers, New England mill workers, second-generation Italian wine growers, and Pennsylvania farmers of German extraction;

and from an examination of several such groups it should be possible to delineate patterns which would be found, in different and distinctive form, among the others. But the nation-wide pattern so delineated would not provide a basis for predicting the version of the culture distinctive of Texas ranchers or New England mill workers without additional information on these particular groups.

12. Any member of a group, provided that his position within that group is properly specified, is a perfect sample of the group-wide pattern on which he is acting as an informant. So a twenty-one-year-old boy born of Chinese-American parents in a small upstate New York town who has just graduated *summa cum laude* from Harvard and a tenth-generation Boston-born deaf mute of United Kingdom stock are equally perfect examples of American national character, *provided that their individual position and individual characteristics are taken fully into account.*

13. Any cultural statement must be made in such a way that the addition of another class of informants previously unrepresented will not change the nature of the statement *in a way which has not been allowed for in the original statement.* So the representativeness of the informants used should be included in the statement, as, for example, "These statements are made about the culture prevailing in the rural south among people living in communities of less than twenty-five hundred people." Then further interviewing of a group of people in the rural South (women, for example) should not change the statement; if women were not properly represented, the anthropologist should have said "among men" instead of "among people" in the original statement of applicability.[4] (That is, the anthropologist samples in terms of structure of the group he is studying, and he is responsible for building a

sufficiently good model of that structure to enable him to place each informant within it and describe accurately the deficiencies of his material.)

We may now examine the present field of anthropological research defined as the application of the methods and findings of culture and personality research to the identification of culturally regular behavior in members of modern nation-states.

All citizens of modern nation-states are exposed to institutional patterns that have regularities attributable to the state of nationhood—national systems of government, taxation, money, criminal and civil law, transportation regulation, military service, systems of mass communication, and so forth. The degree of uniformity and central control differs from one nation to another, and statements about national character must take into account the degree of local government, regionalization, and so on, which will, in turn, be embodied in the national character of each member of the nation, in proportion to the distinctiveness of the participation of the particular subgroup to which they belong. For example, although gypsies may refuse to send their children to school, the devices they use to keep their children out of school in the United States or in the United Kingdom will be related to the state-administered standards of school attendance and may include crossing internal boundaries periodically to avoid state or local truant officers. Thus many patterns of the wider culture will be represented in institutionalized forms in the versions that subgroups display, in the very ways that members of subgroups avoid conformity or bend the institutions to local purposes. This is equally true of a pattern which may be stated as "the

4. For a careful statement of the limitations of the informant see Gorer and Rickman's *The People of Great Russia* (1949 and 1950), sec. 6, p. 116.

house in American culture is characterized by the presence of opaque walls,
a roof, hinged doors that can be closed,
and translucent windows." Houses may
be found that do not meet any of these
criteria, but they will be classified as
being to that degree special; an "open
doorway" between dining room and
living room is an open space where
otherwise a door would be—a version
of a door, not merely a version of an
entrance. People who have houses with
glass walls still reflect the cultural form,
as in a recent instance in the state of
Connecticut where the residents of a
glass house, in order to warn trespassers
off the grounds and away from the
transparent walls, put up a sign reading, "This house is now occupied. Please
respect the privacy of the occupants."

Statements applying to a whole nation cannot be made until the pattern
of differentiation is known, even though
the detail may not be. Thus in a study
of British culture it would be expected
that every type of informant capable of
expressing any political knowledge of
the sort would indicate somehow the
fact that Scotland is still in many respects a special administrative unit
within the United Kingdom. They may
speak of "getting married in Scotland"
or say that "the chart of meat cuts they
had for rationing during the war was
different in Scotland" or that "the minis-
try allowed them to build *brick* child-
welfare centers in Scotland," and so
forth. Such comments are enough to
indicate to the anthropologist the existence of some sort of special administrative treatment of Scotland. Such a clue
can then be followed up until its representation in the special versions of the
culture characteristic of subgroups can
be abstracted. This is not, however, a
method of studying the administrative
structure of the United Kingdom or of
any other literate society about which
it is possible to get both written documents and expert assistance. It is simply

a method of insuring the inclusion in
statements about the culture of the way
individuals who characterize themselves
as "British" will include in their self-
image some statement of the type of
relationship existing *between* Scotland
and England *within* Britain. Further
research would be necessary to establish whether the best commonwealth-
wide statement would be: to be "British" is to be also a member of a group
having a distinctive culture of its own
with which one is also identified (e.g.,
English, Welsh, Scottish), and the term
"British" will be preferred to the terms
"English," "Welsh," "Scottish," in those
contexts in which the entire British
political system is contrasted with
or distinguished from other national
groups. But, in order to make this statement, sufficient work would have to be
done to know, for instance, whether
Singhalese will use "British" in this
same way, and, if this is not known,
the anthropologist may have to limit his
statements to the United Kingdom or
to the British Commonwealth, exclusive
of those countries where the majority
of the population is not of United Kingdom derivation, and so forth.

So statements about the manifestations of national institutional patterns
may be limited to a series of subgroups.
One may speak of the New England
version of the American national culture by specifying the systematic responses of New Englanders to national
institutions and indicating by the retention of the qualifying regional adjective
"New England" that information on
those aspects of the regional pattern
that are assumed to be nation-wide is
limited to information collected from
New England informants and New
England materials. The assumption that
other regions will show manifestations
of "American national character" would
be based upon our knowledge of cultures. The New England study would
provide us with a *specific* set of ex-

pectations as to which measures of the United States government had a standardizing effect throughout the nation—e.g., income tax administration, pure food and drug acts, defense measures, federal communication regulations, currency controls—and which areas would demonstrate local differentiation, as, for example, marriage and divorce laws, public education, real estate taxes, and so on.

Additional types of selection may enter into a study of national culture, depending upon the accessibility of the society being studied and the particular political and class structure of the society at the moment of study. When a group now classified as a subgroup, a unit within the larger society that we are attempting to handle as a whole, has played or is playing a particularly decisive role in the definition of national policy (either inter- or intra-nationally), special attention may be given to the culturally regular character of this subgroup and to its version of the culture. For example, special studies might be made of the public school–educated Englishman in discussing British foreign policy; of Clydeside and the industrial areas of the north of England in discussing trade-unionism; of Polish culture in delineating the development of the Soviet secret police; of Texans in discussing the United States air force; of Cossacks in Russia and Sikhs in India in discussing military police; and so forth. Such emphases would be determined by the nature of the problem. Applied studies have to keep close to specific situations and be as contemporaneous as possible. If the stamp of Dsjerzhinsky, the Polish designer of the Soviet secret police, is still such that behavior within the contemporary MVD can best be understood after an investigation of the standards of asceticism and self-discipline expected from Polish saints, this will be included, especially if information on the functioning of the Soviet Union's political police is meager. But if we are making a study of the regular army in the United States, it may be most economical to utilize strictly contemporary material on the attitudes of today's army on the subjects of honor, patriotism, and so forth, in spite of the fact that the question might well be approached through a delineation of the special southern American regional variation on these themes because of the importance of the large number of regular army officers of southern regional origin. Or, if we wish to know something about the kind of political expectations that have developed out of an experience of the administrative system of the old Austro-Hungarian empire, we might start by making an intensive study of several representative Gallician communities which, except for having been on opposite sides of the old Austro-Hungarian border, shared a common or closely related local cultural tradition; or we might proceed by making an intensive study of the premises and practices of the Austro-Hungarian bureaucracy as revealed in documentary sources, including biographies and diaries. For the elucidation of some particular problem, it may be necessary to concentrate on exploring some small particular segment of a society and only a special aspect of its culture. In World War II, for example, some of the friction that arose between Americans and the British could be traced to the varying meanings they placed on their "partnership," and, in order to explain these particular disagreements, it was necessary to concentrate on British sports behavior and the sports ideals of the great public schools (from which the major coloring of the British handling of the word "partnership" was found to come) and on American business culture with a predominantly middle-class coloring (the source of American expectations about the "partnership" relation).

So far I have discussed studies of national *culture* and of aspects of national culture rather than studies of national *character*, a special form of the study of national culture which normally should follow, not precede, studies of a national culture. Although in emergency situations the direct study of national character by a highly trained anthropologist, who can take culture systematically into account while concentrating on certain culturally regular intra-psychic dynamics of a segment of the population, may be resorted to, it remains an emergency solution, as, for instance, in Geoffrey Gorer's initial work on the Japanese (1943*b*). The Columbia University Research in Contemporary Cultures study of the culture of the eastern European small towns is an example of the more ideal sequence in which culture is studied before character, and formulations about the intra-psychic dynamics follow. In certain instances, trained anthropologists are able to use their "native" knowledge of their own culture and/or long participant experience of another culture as a sufficient cultural background from which to proceed directly to a delineation of the character structure of the members of that society (Mead, 1942; C. and F. Kluckhohn, 1947; Gorer, 1948). A special elaboration of this technique of using knowledge of own culture as a background for material on national character studies is the method of using expert informants—psychiatrists, psychologists, political scientists —who can both provide primary observations and annotate them themselves, using some systematic theoretical approach.

Furthermore, certain types of research may be used both to provide a cultural description in which the intra-psychic dynamics are not spelled out and to describe character. Child-rearing practices, for example, may be used as a key to the values of a society, and they may also be used as one essential part of a study of character formation. An analysis of the plots of films or popular novels may serve to document consciously recognized themes (such as *success* in the United States or *self-control* in Britain) along the lines originally developed by Madariaga in his *Englishmen, Frenchmen and Spaniards* (1928) or by Ruth Benedict in *The Chrysanthemum and the Sword* (1946*c*), in which differences in values are stated without any explicit psychological apparatus; an examination of plots (with the apparatus of Freudian psychology, for example) may also be used as a way of exploring covert themes assumed to be part of a national character, as Wolfenstein and Leites have done (1950). Even projective test protocols can be used to delineate elements of cultural content, although to do so would be extremely wasteful and clumsy. So if French Rorschach protocols are found to contain a large number of references to exotic and mythological figures, this may be analyzed from the point of view of French attitudes toward the exotic, or of the distinctively French way of handling certain types of threatening situations by distantiation (Abel, 1948).

National character studies attempt to trace the way in which the identified cultural behavior is represented in the intra-psychic structure of the individual members of the culture, combining cultural theory and psychological theory (principally learning theory, Gestalt psychology, Freudian psychology, and child-development studies) into a new psychocultural theory to explain how human beings embody the culture, learn it, and live it. For example, once the areas of approved and disapproved behavior have been descriptively outlined, the mechanisms which the individual uses in conforming may be analyzed in terms that show in detail how approved behavior is rewarded by praise, allotment of greater freedom, material gifts from parents, child nurses, servants, joking relations; how disapproved behavior is punished; and how in the course of experiencing these types of reward and punishment the individual not only learns to engage in or refrain from certain activities but also—over time and particularly during early developmental stages—establishes certain patterns of conformity involving identifiable emotions such as fear, shame, pride, guilt (Mead, 1950), etc., which will be systematically manifested by members of that society in the various situations where the questions of conforming to approved social behavior and avoiding disapproved behavior arise.

Explorations along such lines as these, undertaken in both primitive and contemporary societies, have provided material for the construction of interpretative schemes, such as Erikson's "tasks" (1950) or Riesman's types of orientation (1950, 1952). Thus material gathered within a contemporary society (in Erikson's case, clinical studies of American children; in Riesman's, masses of verbatim material from American adults carefully specified as to position in the society) can be used in combination with the theoretical schemes of personality and culture research to amplify the personality and culture conceptualizations by intensive elaboration of theory from other sources.

The anthropological approach to the study of contemporary culture makes the following definite contributions, in addition and complementary to traditional methods of studying contemporary complex societies:

1. It provides a way of analyzing the culture of a society as a whole. The study of cultural wholes was originally a historical development based upon the expectation that individual anthropologists would be the only students of a vanishing culture and upon the accompanying requirement that as many categories of articulate scientific inquiry as possible be included within the observational scheme. With the new field methods developed during the last thirty years of research on living cultures, there has been added to this historical situation the intensive study of small primitive communities within which every individual could be known and the actual network of interrelationships mapped and studied. As soon as anthropological methods were applied to modern cultures, even in the form used in *Middletown* (R. S. and H. M. Lynd, 1929), it became clear that different methods of treating the culture would have to be devised. The methods so far developed have included various adaptations of sociological sampling methods suitable for the study of large communities, so large that their members cannot all be studied individually; positional studies in which small complex parts of the total structure are carefully localized and intensively studied, as when the organization of one of the several shops in a factory is studied (Chapple, 1949); and one specifically anthropological method of cross-checking on the precision with which findings on any segment of cultural material is actually representative of the whole culture (Bateson and Mead, 1942). This anthropological method consists of the intensive analysis of segments of the culture which are unsystematically related to each other and overlap in a variety of ways—the analysis of such segments, for example, as Soviet novels, the proceedings of party congresses, leadership in Soviet agriculture, controls in Soviet industry, the records of the Great Trials, a year's cartoons in *Krokodil*, and Komsomol organization (Mead, 1951d). These segments of material are chosen in such a way that the regularities found in the analysis of one segment can be checked against those found in another

segment; they must be congruent if the analysis is correct, because some of the same individuals are involved in different ways in a number of the segments —as officials, readers, workers, party members, and so forth. A variety of such segments providing comparable cross-checks but using organizational material and interviews were utilized in the "Yankee City" studies (Warner *et al.*, 1941–47).

2. The anthropological approach provides for the disciplined use of the primitive small society as a conceptual model. The anthropologist's small community model differs from the use of models—in engineering, for example— in which the model is constructed according to already known specifications, so that its use, while facilitating the process of conceptualization and permitting the use of developed analytical methods, is still limited to the state of knowledge of those who built it. The anthropologist, on the other hand, does not build his model—he finds it, in a living historical setting, and then analyzes it in such a way as to obtain types of information hitherto unobtainable. When studying complex societies, the historically given model, the biography of a single individual, the role played by a family in the industrial development of a region, the study of a single community or institution—all may function in this same way (see, e.g., Wiener, 1948; Lamb, 1950). The use of living models has the additional advantage that the unanalyzed and even unguessed-at complexities of human beings may be carried along within the model, increasing the probabilities that the derivations which are made will be "true to life."

3. The anthropological approach provides categories of analysis which have been developed comparatively and are thus freer from cultural bias. When the culture and personality approach is used and the concept of national character is added to the concept of national culture, it provides a way of incorporating into descriptions of contemporary behavior a specification of the way in which the individual organism embodies this culture. Such psychobiological specifications, whether based on studies of maturation, perception, or learning, fill in the gaps in the models used by historians, economists, and formal sociologists.

4. The culture and personality approach to the study of complex contemporary cultures has made and may be expected to continue to make one further contribution: it provides a particularly congenial atmosphere for interdisciplinary cross-stimulation and teamwork. This appears to be related to the circumstance that the whole culture and personality field is itself the product of interdisciplinary co-operation. We might use such scientific fields as optics or acoustics as examples. Thus the optical or acoustical engineer is dependent upon pure scientific work, which is a co-operative effort of physicists, physiologists, biochemists, and psychologists and which continues to be a field out of which cross-disciplinary insights arise. Formal linguistics can be integrated with the neurological study of brain lesions and processes of maturation and aging. Similarly, the anthropologically oriented study of modern cultures provides a flexible medium within which the methods of literary criticism (Armstrong, 1946; Spurgeon, 1935), architectural history (Garvan, 1951), equilibrium theory (Bateson, 1949; Lamb, 1951), content analysis (Lasswell, 1949*a*, *b*), biophysics, cybernetics,[5] sociometry, topological psychology, and so forth, can be integrated

5. H. von Foerster (ed.), *Cybernetics: Transactions of the Seventh Conference, March 23–24, 1950* (New York: Josiah Macy, Jr., Foundation, 1951), and *Transactions of the Eighth Conference, March 15–16, 1951* (New York: Josiah Macy, Jr., Foundation, 1952).

and used. It will be noted that most of these approaches were also the result of cross-stimulation between two or more disciplines rather than—as is the case with the core disciplines, which rigidly delimit their boundaries—of an attempt to establish a separate and valid "science." It may even be possible to suggest that this hospitality to other methods may be directly related to the persistent and stubborn attempt of anthropologists to keep together, despite extreme centrifugal pressures, the original cluster of anthropological sciences—ethnology, linguistics, physical anthropology, and archeology—as four ways of approaching the study of man.

I propose to discuss problems of criticism and methods of validation together, because they are at present inextricably linked. Criticism of the approach falls under the following main headings:

1. The methods that were suitable for the study of small, pre-literate societies are not suitable for the study of modern complex societies encompassing millions of people. With this statement the anthropologist working on modern cultures agrees and replies that neither are the methods suitable for studying fish in an aquarium suitable for studying fish in the environment of a large lake or sea—the ecologist does not take out of the laboratory his thermostatic controls but rather the *conceptual scheme* for observing the behavior of fish which observation within a small, controlled situation has given him. He may also take *categories of observation* and *habits of observation of fish behavior*. The criticism that the anthropologist uses the same *methods* for the study of both very small and very large societies is simply based on a misunderstanding. (There are other aspects of this criticism—the insistence that primitive man and modern man are different in kind, that large societies are qualitatively different from

small ones in ways that make them incomparable, that noble Caucasians cannot be studied in the same terms as Africans and Mongolians—which are based on a difference in fundamental assumptions between anthropologists and many historians, economists, and members of other disciplines; these criticisms are of another order, and they necessitate going back to fundamental anthropological rejections of such matters as the fixity of evolutionary sequences, assumed racial inferiority, prelogical thought, and so forth.)

2. Anthropological methods are not appropriate to the study of large modern societies because of the sampling problem. In this criticism, the accuracy of studies of the Gallup Poll variety that use large statistically manageable groups of respondents specified only in respect to a few categories, such as age, sex, socio-economic status, and religious affiliation, is contrasted with the anthropological use of intensive work with individual informants. This criticism stems primarily from sociologists (Lindesmith and Strauss, 1950; Merton, 1951). A comparable criticism comes from social psychologists (Klineberg, 1944) concerned about distributions of attitudes and more interested in knowing *how many* middle-aged men will express dissatisfactions with their jobs than *how* job dissatisfaction and satisfaction are integrated within the cultural character. These criticisms have been stimulated further by the attempts of nonanthropologists to establish ideas like that of modal personality structure which imply a statistical model.

Part of this criticism can be met by a clarification of method, another part by the clarification of aims. Anthropological sampling is not a poor and inadequate version of sociological or sociopsychological sampling, a version where *n* equals too few cases. *It is simply a different kind of sampling,* in which the validity of the sample depends not so much upon the number of cases as upon the proper specification of the informant, so that he or she can be accurately placed, in terms of a very large number of variables—age, sex, order of birth, family background, life-experience, temperamental tendencies (such as optimism, habit of exaggeration, etc.), political and religious position, exact situational relationship to the investigator, configurational relationship to every other informant, and so forth. Within this very extensive degree of specification, each informant is studied as a perfect example, an organic representation of his complete cultural experience. This specification of the informant grew up historically as a way of dealing with the few survivors of broken and vanished cultures and is comparable to the elaboration with which the trained historian specifies the place of a crucial document among the few and valuable documents available for a particular period, or experiments in medicine in which a *large* number of measurements are made on a small number of cases.

The second misunderstanding centers around a differential interest in pattern. The sociologist or social psychologist who questions the anthropologist by saying, "But you don't know what the distribution of resistance to paternal authority is," is interested in *how much* of measurable quantities of an entity called "resistance to paternal authority" can be found to be distributed in the total population. But the anthropologist is interested in the *pattern* of resistances and respect, neutralities and intensities, in regard to parents and grandparents and siblings, and the way in which this pattern can be found in other sets of relationships between employer and employee, writer and reader, and so on. The difference in emphasis may be illustrated from linguistics: if one wants to know the grammatical structure of a language, it

is sufficient to use very few informants about whom the necessary specified information has been collected; if one wants to know how many people use a certain locution or a particular word in preference to another, then sampling of the wider type is necessary, although probably not sufficient. The statement that *to be* is an auxiliary verb in English will not be improved or altered by the collection of more and more samples of English speech, but the use of English-speaking informants from Ireland, the American West, and Tasmania may provide different dialect versions of its use. In dealing with culture, the anthropologist makes the same assumptions about the rest of a culture that the linguist makes about the language—that he is dealing with a system which can be delineated by analysis of a small number of very highly specified samples. The decision as to *how many* informants are needed is primarily a structural decision. In linguistic texts, if the customary way of telling folk tales includes *ratio recta*, charms, recipes, chants, and esoteric language, then a collection of folk-tale texts may be adequate for delineating the entire syntax of the language, with a full complement of forms. But if all folk tales in a particular culture are told in a stereotyped narrative style, with conversation in *ratio obliqua*, samples of these other kinds of material will have to be gathered separately. The question of adding informants is, in the same way, a matter of the way a society is structured, the degree of representativeness which is shared among members of both sexes, different ages, classes, generations, and so forth. Those social sciences that use the gas laws as their models, rather than the methods of structural biology, do not stress configuration. The transformation of the statement, "In American culture the dwelling house has opaque walls," into quantitative statements about how many Americans live in such houses—about how many members of a society act *directly* in terms of a cultural stereotype—actually makes it a statement of a different order. All the members of a society may recognize that the correct form of marriage is for a man to marry his mother's father's mother's father's sister's son's daughter's son's daughter, but actually no such marriage may exist at the moment of observation (Mead, 1935; Harris, 1951). The determination of the prevalence and incidence of any piece of behavior requires detailed observation of a large sample of individuals, in primitive societies by studying the entire community, in large complex societies by using elaborate sampling methods of the sociological sort.

3. A third criticism is that there is no way of *replicating* the observations; each anthropologist reports something different because individual informants cannot be treated like respondents on a questionnaire or test. This criticism, too, fails to take into account the element of pattern. No two texts of the same folk tale told by the same informant are absolutely identical; but, if a given method of linguistic analysis has been applied correctly to one set of texts, it is expected that a second set examined within the same framework will show the same pattern. The statement that "the people want children" is relatively meaningless, and the finding cannot be replicated; however, if answers to questions as to how many children there are per family, what is considered to be the ideal size for a family, how many adoptions there are, and how adoptions are phrased show that married couples say they have fewer children than they want and make an effort to persuade others to give children to them and that others give up their children reluctantly and as a great favor, then such findings, taken together, present a picture which

can be replicated. Similarly, the statement that "these are a very oral people" is interpretive if taken alone, but if it is supported with detailed descriptions of type of oral play, with photographs of such play, and with text and observational material, the descriptive term "oral," which refers to a definite theoretical framework, and the comparative word "very," which refers to the other peoples on which that particular anthropologist has experience or data, can be given explicit meaning. Any field record containing sufficiently detailed material is subject to this type of cross-check against comparable material collected either by another investigator or at a different date or by a split-halves handling of the single corpus. There have been instances in the personality and culture field in which all the detailed material has been thrown away, as in the presentation of interpretations of Rorschach records without the protocols. This, however, is a comment upon the procedure of particular field workers, not on the possibilities of studying culture in such a way that adequate replication is obtainable.

There is a variety of other criticisms which stem from various prejudices of the critics: that it is inappropriate for an anthropologist to study materials on which he is bound to have bias (which is equally applicable to his studies of primitive peoples); that the method ignores history (which is simply not true); that the stating of regularities in national character is a new kind of racism (which is also quite incorrect, as the whole approach is based on the premise that differences in national cultural behavior are learned).

It is, however, possible to deal with problems of method and validation from an anthropological standpoint, and this involves questions germane to the approach, not questions based on various sorts of cross-disciplinary failures in communication. The peculiar problems that face the student of national culture may be discussed under the following heads:

1. Against what comparative range of cultural behavior is the behavior identified for any national group to be placed? This involves the establishment of culture areas, the development of cross-cultural categories appropriate for cultures of complex societies which are comparable in level of abstraction with those which are used for pre-literate cultures, and ways of specifying the groups of cultures to which any statement of presence or absence, more or less, can be referred. The conventional anthropological base—*all recorded primitive cultures*—is much more difficult to use when making statements about historical cultures on which there is a great wealth of documentation. A precise insistence upon an enumerative background—"all cultures which have been studied by this method," "all folklores which have been recorded and analyzed," "the existing body of culturally differentiated projective test protocols"—seems the best present device for dealing with this difficulty.

2. What changes in the observer-observed ratio should be introduced in order to deal with the greater complexity and still preserve the essential anthropological method by which a cultural system which owes its regularities to the regularities of the human mind is analyzed by passing a large amount and variety of raw material through a single human mind? The complexity of material in a modern nation-state, the need to collect materials from both sexes, different classes, and occupations, and a variety of the cultural versions of regional subgroups obviously calls for a team; but the anthropological requirement of integration of all the material within a single analysis calls for teamwork of a special sort. It should be arranged that all data collected by any member of the team are shared, not merely in the sense of "made available," but actually read by, or looked at (in the case of visual records), or listened to (in the case of aural records), by each member of the team. This requirement obviously limits the amount of data that can be used, but the study of national culture does not involve documentary obligations of a historical, large statistical, or survey nature; the task is to delineate pattern. A smaller amount of material shared by the entire group assures an integration which is comparable but not identical with that obtained by the single field worker (see the discussion of method in Mead, 1951*d*).

The question of the composition of the team has many facets. The importance of having both sexes and different kinds of minds and experience represented is obvious. The desirability of interdisciplinary membership is primarily a function of the need to use special skills (such as projective testing or psychiatric interviews), or special areas of competence (as in providing historical depth or tapping bodies of existing economic or political analyses). These two kinds of diversity—diversity of age, sex, and temperament and diversity of disciplinary training—can cross-cut each other. Mixed national origin, including trained members of the culture being studied and representatives of at least two other national cultures, is practically a *sine qua non*. In the particular case of applied studies of cultures at a distance which have been undertaken since World War II to meet urgent practical needs, the team serves a different function, a real interacting group of human beings focused on small amounts of data becoming a model in reverse of the field situation, in which a single individual or a husband-and-wife pair respond to a whole community interacting before their observing eyes.

3. How are the anthropologists' methods of using the sought and guided spoken interview to be inte-

grated with the methods of historians
who depend upon analysis of documents which were produced in some
context other than that for which they
are later used? Although a considerable
amount of cross-disciplinary understanding can be provided by simply
working together on records of the past
—especially unpublished autobiogra-
phies and diaries—the most complete
bridge is provided here when regularities of human psychology—such mechanisms as condensation, displacement, fig-
ure-and-ground relationships—are used
systematically to analyze both the anthropological interview and the historical document.

4. What use can the anthropologists
working on national character make of
the findings of other disciplines to validate their findings?

a) *Validation from other data.*—Bodies of organized data which have been
collected for a quite different purpose
or within some other frame of reference
(the materials in *The American Sol-
dier*,[6] for example, or in *Fortune* surveys[7]) may be used as checks on the
hypotheses which have been developed.
Or some new collection of unorganized
cultural materials, as, for instance, the
collection of selections from *Yank* or
the *American Song Bag*, the findings of
a British Royal Commission, a collection of French political speeches, and
so forth, may be used subsequently as
a testing ground for hypotheses developed on the basis of other materials.
Use of this method involves acceptance
of the good faith of the anthropologist
—as does any other validating experiment—but this is so much less often
accorded to anthropological work that
it seems necessary to give it special
mention.

b) *Validation from other bodies of*

6. *Studies in Social Psychology in World
War II* (4 vols.; Princeton: Princeton University Press, 1949–50).

7. As used by G. Gorer in *The American
People* (1948).

theory.—If the anthropologist is working
within a specific theoretical framework,
his results can be tested in terms of
that framework in two ways—for fit and
for a nonfit which can be treated systematically. Whiting's *Kwoma* (1941) and
DuBois's *Alor* (1944) are examples of
testing for fit; Muensterberger's article
on Chinese character (1951) is an example of emphasis on fit, the organization of field material in terms of a theory developed within a different culture, which demonstrates that the new
material can be fitted into the old
structure. Bateson's discussion of the
frustration-aggression hypothesis is an
example of looking at new material
(Balinese) and using a culturally limited theoretical formulation as a way
of systematizing the Balinese material
(1941). Extension of the Gesell maturational framework originally based on
the sequence observed in American
middle-class children in New Haven—
frogging, creeping, all fours, standing,
then squatting—by analysis of the Balinese sequence—frogging, very little
creeping, sitting, squatting, then standing (Mead and Macgregor, 1951)—is
another example of expanding a theoretical framework, in its own terms, by
the introduction of cross-cultural behavior. This procedure inevitably results in expanding the original theoretical framework, and the requirements of
the method are that any discrepancy or
incongruity between the analysis of the
new material and the previous theoretical formulation should be such that
this discrepancy can be handled by expanding the theoretical framework.
Erikson's zonal-modal chart[8] has both
served as a theoretical framework and
been modified and expanded through
this use, as was Kurt Lewin's theory of
the relationship of success and failure
to effort (Lewin, 1948).

Thus, to the extent that the student

8. For successive publications see Homburger (1937); Mead (1946a); Erikson
(1950).

of national character relies on psychobiological theoretical frameworks, the extra-anthropological aspects of such frameworks provide a way of validating the direction of his research. When the psychocultural theories which he uses can be definitely related to biological data which are ascertained by different methods and within a quite different framework (if, for example, a theory of the function of rhythmic mourning can be related to findings on epileptics,[9] or a theory of the way anger is organized in a given national character can be related to teething behavior), this is convincing cross-disciplinary validation and also tends to direct the national character theories involved into a more systematic framework—in contrast to cultural approaches resembling those of Ruth Benedict and Malinowski, in which the biological substratum was initially derived from a comparative study of cultures and then used as a point of reference in explaining them (Mead, 1946b).

c) However, the most convincing validation still remains one of pattern, of the testing of the hypothesis for intra-cultural and intra-psychic fit. Every piece of cultural behavior is so overdetermined in its systematic relationship to every other piece that any discrepancy within the material should immediately demand a revision of the delineation hypothesis established so far. Just as the experienced field anthropologist works with congruencies and discrepancies, and each discrepancy or contradiction means that the whole pattern is still not understood, so any body of reliable observations which challenges the present formulations of national culture calls for their re-examination. If an attempt is made to delineate national character in addition to the national culture, then the criterion of internal consistency has to

be invoked in relation to some psychocultural theory of personality. For example, the statements that in certain Moslem countries women respond with deep inferiority to the articulate lament present in the culture to the birth of a girl and that women do not rebel against their lot or appear to manifest any envy of the male role present a challenge to existing psychoanalytic personality theory which is sufficiently important to justify a demand for further explanation. When it is recognized that the male whose birth is so loudly celebrated carries a very strong load of fear and need for self-validation, so that the father's role as contrasted with the mother's is one of unenviable insecurity and vulnerability, the mechanism by which the daughter identifies contentedly with the more secure parent becomes clearer and less subject to challenge. While the student of national culture must primarily meet the challenge of internal congruity in terms of cultural materials, the student of national character must meet this double challenge of cultural and psychological consistency. This requirement should be read, of course, not as a demand for uniformities in culture or in character, but as a demand for the delineation of regularities which are systematically explicable in terms of our knowledge of the history of the culture and of the society and the biological nature of man.

d) One further form of validation is prediction, and this can be of two types: (1) a prediction of the form that events in the future will take, especially of the limits within which the predicted set of events will fall, and (2) the systematic relating of two completed series of events within the same society in terms of the description of the culture. Predictions can only be expected to state probabilities, and, like predictions from the laboratory to the real world, they cannot specify events belonging to a differently functioning

9. H. von Foerster (ed.), *Cybernetics: Transactions of the Ninth Conference, March 20–21, 1952* (in preparation).

system from that included in the studies of culture. For example, it should be easier to predict the possibilities of a dictatorship ending by assassination or by natural death than by accidental death, but it should not be expected that the actual assassination could be predicted any more than the date of natural death can be assigned. When an assassination occurs, however, the national pattern which has been delineated should be capable of explaining the patterns of an attack on a head of state, as, for example, the recent instance in which Puerto Rican malcontents launched attacks against buildings even when it was not certain that their intended victim was in them. A set of hypotheses about Japanese culture which could not explain the bombing of Manila after it had been declared an open city would have to be declared faulty; if the Japanese had continued isolated resistances in large numbers at the end of World War II in spite of the fact that the emperor was retained as the head of the state, then the hypotheses about Japanese culture on the basis of which it had been predicted that the decree of the emperor would be obeyed would have had to be re-examined.

For proof of the sort demanded in the experimental sciences, it is necessary to construct experiments in which the cultural membership of experimental groups is systematically varied and the hypotheses about their behavior systematically tested. Very few attempts of this sort have yet been made, and most of them have been partly accidental by-products of the Lewinian school of group-dynamics experimentation: French's (1944) findings on the behavior of his Italian-American group as compared with Harvard students (which could also be interpreted in terms of subgroup cultural difference), and the confirmation in the Bavelas (Lewin, 1943; Mead, 1943) test findings on Iowa children of the formula-

tions about the place of food in American character are examples of this sort of validations.

In attempting to evaluate cultural hypotheses made by individuals who, no matter how great their training in the use of cross-cultural categories, are never free from unrecognized cultural bias in all the areas of culture which have not yet been made articulate, blind interpretations by members of the same culture are not useful. Such methods as the use of blind Rorschachs (DuBois, 1944), in which Rorschach protocols are read blind and then tested against the judgment of the field workers on the same individuals and on the culture as a whole, are tests of *reliability*, but are not validations, as both the Rorschach specialist and the anthropologist share the same cultural approach and the same general theoretical frame of reference.

Methods of research developed in the study of national character may have important results in developing research bridges between anthropology and the other social sciences (particularly history). The study of national character has been, to date, in its references to contemporary political units primarily an applied science. We have studied national character not as the best setting within which to trace the correspondences between political forms and individual character formation—for very possibly a much smaller unit, such as the New England town or the Swiss canton, would be a far better locus for pure research—but because, in today's world, nation-states are of paramount political significance, and a great many activities of individuals and groups, both in domestic and in international settings, are conducted in terms of national values. For this reason, almost all the work in this field has been conducted in connection with national enterprises, either of problems of domestic morale or of the conduct of war or peace. The most extensive work has been done in the United States on Japan in wartime, with certain peacetime follow-ups on the spot;[10] on Germany, with special reference to postwar problems (Schaffner, 1945, 1948); on relationships between British and Americans during World War II (for bibliog., see Mead, 1949a, pp. 457–59; Métraux, 1951, pp. 210–13); on the Soviet Union (Gorer and Rickman, 1949; Mead, 1951d), with international participation in teams which have been financed in the United States. All these major researches have been initially conducted at a distance, and in the case of the Soviet Union no follow-up field work has been possible. Without field work, it is impossible to describe the society, and the proportions in which any given trait is manifested cannot be ascertained; in fact, all questions that depend upon statistical sampling or upon detailed mapping of interpersonal networks have to be begged. France,[11] Britain (Mead, 1947b; Gorer, 1950), Czechoslovakia,[12] and Poland[13] represent cases where work done at a distance has been followed or accompanied by field studies. China,[14] Syria,[15] Rumania (Benedict, 1946a), and, to a very partial degree Italy have been studied only at a dis-

tance, using isolated individuals and enclaves. There has been an exploratory field study of Norway,[16] without any formulations in regard to the dynamics of Norwegian character. Field work is now going on in Holland,[17] preceded by unpublished preliminary work at a distance. The four UNESCO field studies in France, Australia, India, and Sweden,[18] with a primarily social-psychological focus, are now approaching publication. Burma (Gorer, 1943a; Hanks, 1949) and Thailand (Benedict, 1946b) and Greece were all tentatively analyzed during the war, and there have been follow-up field studies in Thailand and Burma. No work has been reported for any Latin-American country as a whole or on Denmark, Belgium, Ireland, Bulgaria, Hungary, Yugoslavia, Portugal, Spain, Indo-China, Pakistan, or on any of the Near Eastern countries except Syria, or on any of the countries of the British Commonwealth except the United Kingdom —as wholes, although there is a variety of valuable studies of particular communities or subgroups which have not been specifically oriented to problems of national culture and national character. In addition to these attempts to delineate whole cultures and the dynamics of the character, seen nationally, there has been a variety of studies of attitudes toward health, nutrition, military service, agriculture, visual and auditory mass communication, and so forth, in which partial attempts have been made to place problems of relief, technical assistance, psychological warfare, and others within a total national cultural setting.[19]

10. See series of articles on "The Problems Raised by *The Chrysanthemum and the Sword,*" *Japanese Journal of Ethnology* (published at 132, Shimohoya Hoya-machi, Tokyo), XIV, No. 4 (1949), 1–35.

11. M. Mead and R. Métraux, chapter in a volume on France, edited by Saul Padover and others (in preparation).

12. D. Rodnick and E. Rodnick, "Czechs, Slovaks, and Communism" (unpublished MS).

13. Unpublished field work by Dr. Sula Benet.

14. R. Bunzel, "Explorations in Chinese Culture" (unpublished report prepared for the Office of Naval Research); Weakland (1950); Abel and Hsu (1949).

15. Unpublished field work, Columbia University Research in Contemporary Cultures.

16. By David and Elizabeth Rodnick (1950–51).

17. By Dorothy Keur.

18. "UNESCO Community Studies" (in preparation).

19. *Culture Patterns and Technical Change: A Manual Prepared by the World Federation for Mental Health for UNESCO* (1951) (in press).

The status of the subject may be best dramatized by saying that, if a world organization were to be formed in which the constituent units were not the present nation-states but larger regional or smaller subnational units, the interest in "national character" would shift; reference to the old national units would become a matter of historical research, and they would be of only contemporary interest to the extent that individuals still bore the imprint of the national institutions within which they had been reared in some way which could be invoked to explain their contemporary behavior. So, in analyzing contemporary Polish national behavior, it is sometimes useful to refer in retrospect to the experience of groups of Poles still living who were once part of the nation-states of czarist Russia, imperial Germany, and the Austro-Hungarian Empire; and, from other points of view, the present position of Poles as part of the Soviet sphere of influence with its increasingly standardized political institutions may have to be invoked. In each case the problem and the context within which it is being discussed will determine which of these political units and their representations within the character of Poles should be invoked.

It is useful to divide the study of national character into a series of steps:

(1) developing initial hypotheses in which any material which is highly patterned can be used (Gorer, 1943*b*; Gorer and Rickman, 1949; Mead, 1951*d*); (2) subjecting these hypotheses to systematic scrutiny in the light of selected bodies of materials; (3) the determination by extensive sampling techniques of the prevalence and incidence of the behavior which have been identified; (4) validation of the findings through prediction and experiment. Where a society is inaccessible, step 3 is impossible, except in a very specialized form, such as extensive interviewing of either a skewed sample, like Soviet defectors, or of a disrupted society, like the scattered members of a single community. The very exigencies of the present world situation, which are responsible for directing research into this field, also often limit the conditions within which full-length field studies can be undertaken. Further development of this approach waits upon field studies within accessible complex modern states, involving systematic cooperation with historians and members of other disciplines who work on aspects of modern culture, on the one hand, and upon the further development of theory—from culture and personality research conducted within the more favorable settings of small primitive communities—on the other.

REFERENCES

ABEL, T. M. 1948. "The Rorschach Test in the Study of Culture," *Rorschach Exchange and Journal of Projective Techniques,* XII, No. 2, 79–93.

ABEL, T. M., and HSU, F. L. K. 1949. "Some Aspects of Personality of Chinese as Revealed by the Rorschach Test," *Rorschach Research Exchange and Journal of Projective Techniques,* XIII, No. 3, 285–301.

ADORNO, T. W.; FRENKEL-BRUNSWIK, E.; LEVINSON, J.; and SANFORD, R. N. 1950. *The Authoritarian Personality.* ("Studies in Prejudice Series.") New York: Harper & Bros.

ARMSTRONG, E. A. 1946. *Shakespeare's Imagination: A Study of the Psychology of Association and Inspiration.* London: Lindsay Drummond.

BATESON, G. 1941. "The Frustration-Aggression Hypothesis," *Psychological Review,* XLVIII, No. 4, 350–55. Reprinted in NEWCOMB, T. M.; HARTLEY, E. L.; *et al.* (eds.), *Readings in Social Psychology,* pp. 267–69. New York: Henry Holt & Co., 1947.

——. 1942*a*. "Morale and National Character." In WATSON, G. (ed.), *Civilian Morale*, pp. 71–91. Boston: Houghton Mifflin Co.

——. 1942*b*. "Social Planning and the Concept of Deutero Learning." In BRYSON, L., and FINKELSTEIN, L. (eds.), *Science, Philosophy, and Religion, Second Symposium*, pp. 81–97. New York: Conference on Science, Philosophy, and Religion. Also in NEWCOMB, T. M.; HARTLEY, E. L.; *et al.* (eds.), *Readings in Social Psychology*, pp. 121–38. New York: Henry Holt & Co., 1947.

——. 1944. "Cultural Determinants of Personality." In HUNT, M. (ed.), *Personality and the Behavior Disorders*, Vol. II. New York: Ronald Press Co.

——. 1949. "Bali: The Value System of a Steady State." In FORTES, M. (ed.), *Social Structure: Studies Presented to A. R. Radcliffe-Brown*, pp. 35–53. Oxford: Clarendon Press.

BATESON, G., and MEAD, M. 1942. *Balinese Character: A Photographic Analysis*. ("Special Publications of the New York Academy of Sciences," Vol. II.) New York.

BENEDICT, R. 1946*a*. "Rumanian Culture and Behavior." New York: Institute for Intercultural Studies. Mimeographed.

——. 1946*b*. "Thai Culture and Behavior." New York: Institute for Intercultural Studies. Mimeographed. Re-mimeographed as "Data Paper, South East Asia Program," Cornell University, 1951.

——. 1946*c*. *The Chrysanthemum and the Sword*. Boston: Houghton Mifflin Co.

BRICKNER, R. 1943. *Is Germany Incurable?* Philadelphia: J. B. Lippincott Co.

CHAPPLE, E. C. 1949. "The Interaction Chronograph: Its Evaluation and Present Application," *Personnel*, XXV, No. 4, 295–307.

DAVIS, W. A., and HAVIGHURST, R. J. 1947. *Father of the Man*. Boston: Houghton Mifflin Co.

DOLLARD, J. 1935. *Criteria for the Life History*. New Haven: Yale University Press. Reprinted, New York: Peter Smith, 1949.

DOLLARD, J., and MILLER, N. E. 1950. *Personality and Psychotherapy: An Analysis in Terms of Learning, Thinking, and Culture*. New York: McGraw-Hill Book Co., Inc.

DuBois, C. 1944. *The People of Alor: A Socio-psychological Study of an East Indian Island*. Minneapolis: University of Minnesota Press.

ENDLEMAN, R. 1949. "The New Anthropology and Its Ambitions," *Commentary*, VIII, No. 3, 284–91.

ERIKSON, E. 1950. *Childhood and Society*. New York: W. W. Norton & Co.

FRANK, L. K. 1948. *Society as the Patient*. New Brunswick, N.J.: Rutgers University Press.

FRENCH, J. R. P. 1944. *Organized and Unorganized Groups under Fear and Frustration*, pp. 231–308. ("Iowa University Series in Child Welfare," Vol. XX, Part V.)

FRIES, M. 1947. "Diagnosis of the Child's Adjustment through the Age Level Test," *Psychoanalytic Review*, XXXIV, 1–31.

FROMM, E. 1941. *Escape from Freedom*. New York: Farrar & Rinehart.

GARVAN, A. 1951. *Architecture and Town Planning in Colonial Connecticut*. New Haven: Yale University Press.

GESELL, A. 1945. *Embryology of Behavior* New York: Harper & Bros.

GOLDMAN, I. 1950. "Psychiatric Interpretations of Russian History: A Reply to Geoffrey Gorer," *American Slavic and East European Review*, IX, No. 3, 151–61.

GORER, G. 1938. *Himalayan Village*. London: Michael Joseph.

——. 1943*a*. "Burmese Personality." New York: Institute for Intercultural Studies. Mimeographed.

——. 1943*b*. "Themes in Japanese Culture," *Transactions of the New York Academy of Sciences*, Series 2, V, No. 5, 106–24.

——. 1948. *The American People*. New York: W. W. Norton & Co.

——. 1949. "Some Aspects of the Psychology of the People of Great Russia," *American Slavic and East European Review*, VIII, No. 3, 155–66.

——. 1950. "Some Notes on the British Character," *Horizon*, XX, 369–79.

GORER, G., and RICKMAN, J. 1949. *The People of Great Russia*. London: Cresset

Press; New York: Chanticleer Press, 1950.

GOTTSCHALK, L.; KLUCKHOHN, C.; and ANGELL, R. 1945. *The Use of Personal Documents in History, Anthropology, and Sociology.* (Social Science Research Bull. 53.) New York.

GRINNELL, G. B. 1923. *The Cheyenne Indians.* New Haven: Yale University Press.

HANKS, L. M. 1949. "The Quest for Individual Autonomy in the Burmese Personality," *Psychiatry*, XII, No. 3, 285–300.

HARING, D. (ed.). 1948. *Personal Character and Cultural Milieu.* Syracuse: Syracuse University Press.

HARRIS, Z. S. 1951. *Methods in Structural Linguistics.* Chicago: University of Chicago Press.

HENRY, W. E. 1947. "The Thematic Apperception Technique in the Study of Culture-Personality Relations," *Genetic Psychology Monographs*, XXXV, No. 1, 3–135.

HILGARD, E. R., and MARQUIS, D. G. 1940. *Conditioning and Learning.* New York: Appleton-Century-Crofts.

HOMBURGER, E. 1937. "Configurations in Play—Clinical Notes," *Psychoanalytical Review*, XXII, 139–214.

JOFFE, N. 1949. "The Dynamics of Benefice among East European Jews," *Social Forces*, XXVII, No. 3, 238–47.

KARDINER, A. 1939. *The Individual and His Society.* New York: Columbia University Press.

——. 1945. *The Psychological Frontiers of Society.* New York: Columbia University Press.

KLINEBERG, O. 1944. *A Science of National Character.* (Society for the Psychological Study of Social Issues Bull. 19.)

KLUCKHOHN, C. and F. 1947. "American Culture: Generalized and Class Patterns." In *Conflicts of Power in Modern Culture: 1947 Symposium of the Conference on Science, Philosophy and Religion*, pp. 106–82. New York.

KLUCKHOHN, C., and LEIGHTON, D. 1946. *The Navaho.* Cambridge: Harvard University Press.

——. 1947. *Children of the People.* Cambridge: Harvard University Press.

KLUCKHOHN, C., and MURRAY, H. A. (eds.). 1948. *Personality in Nature, Society, and Culture.* New York: A. A. Knopf.

KOFKA, K. 1935. *Principles of Gestalt Psychology.* New York: Harcourt, Brace & Co.

LAMB, R. K. 1950. "Entrepreneurship in the Community," *Explorations in Entrepreneurial History*, II, No. 3, 114–27.

——. 1951. "Political Elites and the Process of Economic Development" (paper presented at the 27th annual Harris Institute, University of Chicago, June 20). In HOSELITZ, B. F. (ed.), *The Progress of Underdeveloped Areas*, pp. 30–53 ("Harris Foundation Lectures.") Chicago: University of Chicago Press, 1952.

LASSWELL, H. D. 1949a. "The Language of Power." In LASSWELL, H. D., and LEITES, N. (eds.), *Language and Politics*, pp. 3–19. New York: George Stewart.

——. 1949b. "Style and the Language of Politics." In LASSWELL, H. D., and LEITES, N. (eds.), *Language and Politics*, pp. 20–39. New York: George Stewart.

LEWIN, K. 1943. "Forces behind Food Habits and Methods of Change." In *The Problem of Changing Food Habits*, pp. 35–65. (National Research Council Bull. 108.)

——. 1948. *Resolving Social Conflicts: Selected Papers on Group Dynamics, 1935–1946.* Edited by G. W. LEWIN. New York: Harper & Bros.

LINDESMITH, A. R., and STRAUSS, A. L. 1950. "A Critique of Culture-Personality Writings," *American Sociological Review*, XV, No. 5, 587–600.

LITTLE, K. L. 1950. "Methodology in the Study of Adult Personality," *American Anthropologist*, LII, No. 2, 279–82.

LYND, R. S. and H. M. 1929. *Middletown.* New York: Harcourt, Brace & Co.

MADARIAGA, S. DE. 1928. *Englishmen, Frenchmen, Spaniards: An Essay in Comparative Psychology.* London: Oxford University Press.

MEAD, M. 1935. *Sex and Temperament in Three Primitive Societies*, Part II. New York: William Morrow & Co.

———. 1940. "Social Change and Cultural Surrogates," *Journal of Educational Sociology*, XIV, No. 2, 92–110.

———. 1942. *And Keep Your Powder Dry*. New York: William Morrow & Co.

——. 1943. "Anthropological Approach to Dietary Problems," *Transactions of the New York Academy of Sciences*, Series 2, V, No. 7, 177–82.

———. 1946a. "Research on Primitive Children." In CARMICHAEL, L. (ed.), *Manual of Child Psychology*, pp. 667–706. New York: John Wiley & Sons; London: Chapman & Hall, 1946.

———. 1946b. "Personality, The Cultural Approach to." In HARRIMAN, P. L. (ed.), *Encyclopedia of Psychology*. New York: Philosophical Library.

———. 1947a. "The Implications of Culture Change for Personality Development," *American Journal of Orthopsychiatry*, XVII, No. 4, 633–46.

———. 1947b. "The Application of Anthropological Techniques to Cross-national Communication," *Transactions of the New York Academy of Sciences*, Series 2, IX, No. 4, 133–52.

———. 1948. "A Case History in Cross-national Communication." In BRYSON, L. (ed.), *The Communication of Ideas*, pp. 209–29. New York: Institute for Religious and Social Studies.

———. 1949a. *Male and Female*. New York: William Morrow & Co.

———. 1949b. *The Mountain Arapesh*. V. *The Record of Unabelin with Rorschach Analyses*. ("Anthropological Papers of the American Museum of Natural History," Vol. XLI, Part III.) New York.

———. 1949c. "Character Formation and Diachronic Theory." In FORTES, M. (ed.), *Social Structure: Studies Presented to A. R. Radcliffe-Brown*, pp. 18–34. Oxford: Clarendon Press.

———. 1950. "Some Anthropological Considerations concerning Guilt." In REYMERT, M. L. (ed.), *Feelings and Emotions: The Mooseheart Symposium*, pp. 362–73. New York: McGraw-Hill Book Co., Inc.

———. 1951a. "Columbia University Research in Contemporary Cultures." In GUETZKOW, H. (ed.), *Groups, Leadership, and Men*, pp. 106–18. Pittsburgh, Pa.: Carnegie Press.

———. 1951b. "Anthropologist and Historian: Their Common Problems," *American Quarterly* (spring), pp. 3–13.

———. 1951c. "The Study of National Character." In LERNER, D., and LASSWELL, H. (eds.), *The Policy Sciences*, pp. 79–85. Stanford, Calif.: Stanford University Press.

———. 1951d. *Soviet Attitudes toward Authority*. New York: McGraw-Hill Book Co., Inc.

———. 1951e. "What Makes Soviet Character?" *Natural History*, LX, No. 7, 296–303, 336.

———. 1952. "Some Relationships between Social Anthropology and Psychiatry." In ALEXANDER, F., and ROSS, H. (eds.), *Dynamic Psychiatry*, pp. 401–48. Chicago: University of Chicago Press.

MEAD, M., and MACGREGOR, F. C. 1951. *Growth and Culture: A Photographic Analysis of Balinese Childhood*. New York: G. P. Putnam's Sons.

MERTON, R. K. 1951. "Selected Problems of Field Work in the Planned Community," *American Sociological Review*, XII, No. 3, 304–17.

MÉTRAUX, R. (ed.). 1951. "A Report on National Character." Prepared for the Working Group on Human Behavior under Conditions of Military Service, Research and Development Board. Unpublished.

MUENSTERBERGER, W. 1951. "Orality and Dependence: Characteristics of Southern Chinese." In ROHEIM, G., *et. al.* (eds.), *Psychoanalysis and the Social Sciences*, III, 95–108. New York: International Universities Press.

MURPHY, G. 1947. *Personality: A Biosocial Approach to Origins and Structure*. New York: Harper & Bros.

ORLANSKY, H. 1949. "Infant Care and Personality," *Psychological Bulletin*, XLVI, No. 1, 1–48.

RADCLIFFE-BROWN, A. R. 1922. *The Andaman Islanders*. Cambridge: At the University Press; new ed. Glencoe, Ill.: Free Press, 1948.

RIESMAN, D. 1950. *The Lonely Crowd*. New Haven: Yale University Press.

———. 1952. *Faces in the Crowd*. New Haven: Yale University Press.

SAPIR, E. 1934. "The Emergence of the Concept of Personality in a Study of Cultures," *Journal of Social Psychology,* V, 408–15.

SARGENT, S. S., and SMITH, M. W. (eds.). 1949. *Culture and Personality: Proceedings of an Interdisciplinary Conference.* New York: Viking Fund.

SCHAFFNER, B. 1945. "Round Table, 1945: Germany after the War," *American Journal of Orthopsychiatry,* Vol. XV, No. 3.

———. 1948. *Father Land.* New York: Columbia University Press.

SHUB, B. 1950. "Soviets Expose a Baby," *New Leader* (June 17), pp. 11–12.

SPURGEON, C. 1935. *Shakespeare's Imagery and What It Tells us.* Cambridge: At the University Press.

WARE, C. F. (ed.). 1940. *The Cultural Approach to History.* New York: Columbia University Press.

WARNER, W. L., *et al.* 1941–47. "Yankee City Series," Vols. I–IV. New Haven: Yale University Press.

WARNER, W. L.; JUNKER, B. H.; and ADAMS, W. A. 1941. *Color and Human Nature.* Washington, D.C.: American Council on Education.

WEAKLAND, J. 1950. "The Organization of Action in Chinese Culture," *Psychiatry,* XIII, No. 3, 361–70.

WEST, J. 1945. *Plainville, U.S.A.* New York: Columbia University Press.

WHITING, J. 1941. *Becoming a Kwoma.* New Haven: Yale University Press.

WIENER, N. 1948. *Cybernetics, or Control and Communication in the Animal and the Machine.* New York: John Wiley & Sons, Inc.

WOLFE, B. D. 1951. "The Swaddled Soul of the Great Russians," *New Leader* (January 29), pp. 15–18.

WOLFENSTEIN, M., and LEITES, N. 1950. *Movies: A Psychological Study.* Glencoe, Ill.: Free Press.

A SELECTIVE BIBLIOGRAPHY

BATESON, GREGORY. "Morale and National Character." In WATSON, GOODWIN (ed.), *Civilian Morale: Second Yearbook of the Society for the Psychological Study of Social Issues,* pp. 71–91. New York, 1942.

BENEDICT, RUTH. *The Chrysanthemum and the Sword: Patterns of Japanese Culture.* Boston: Houghton Mifflin Co., 1946.

ERIKSON, ERIK H. *Childhood and Society.* New York: W. W. Norton & Co., Inc., 1950.

GORER, GEOFFREY. *The American People.* New York: W. W. Norton & Co., Inc., 1948. English edition, *The Americans* (London, 1948).

———. "The Concept of National Character," *Science News,* No. 18. Hammondsworth, Middlesex, England: Penguin Books, 1950.

———. "Themes in Japanese Culture," *Transactions of the New York Academy of Sciences,* Series 2, V, No. 5, 106–24.

GORER, GEOFFREY, and RICKMAN, JOHN. *The People of Great Russia.* London: Cresset Press, 1949; New York: Chanticleer Press, 1949.

HARING, DOUGLAS. "Aspects of Personal Character in Japan," *Far Eastern Quarterly,* VI, 12–22. Reprinted in HARING, D. G. (ed.), *Personal Character and Cultural Milieu: A Collection of Readings,* pp. 355–65. Syracuse: Syracuse University Press, 1948.

KARDINER, ABRAM. *The Psychological Frontiers of Society.* New York: Columbia University Press, 1945.

KLINEBERG, OTTO. "A Science of National Character," *Journal of Social Psychology,* XIX (1944), 147–62.

KLUCKHOHN, CLYDE and FLORENCE. "American Culture: Generalized and Class Patterns." In *Conflicts of Power in Modern Society: 1947 Symposium of the Conference on Science, Philosophy, and Religion,* pp. 106–28. New York, 1948.

MEAD, MARGARET. *And Keep Your Powder Dry.* New York: William Morrow & Co., 1942. English edition, *The American Character* (London, 1944). Austrian edition, *Und halte dein Pulver trocken* (Vienna, 1947). German edition, *Und haltet euer Pulver trocken!* (Munich, 1946).

——. "Columbia University Research in Contemporary Cultures." In GUETZKOW, HAROLD (ed.), *Groups, Leadership and Men: Human Relations Research Sponsored by the United States Navy*, pp. 106–18. Pittsburgh, Pa.: Carnegie Press, 1951.

——. "The Study of National Character." In LERNER, D., and LASSWELL, H. D. (eds.), *The Policy Sciences: Recent Developments in Scope and Method*, pp. 70–85. Stanford, Calif., 1951. French edition, "L'Étude du caractère national." In *Les Sciences de la politique aux États-Unis*. ("Cahiers de la Fondation Nationale des Science Politiques," No. 19.) Paris, 1951.

MEAD, MARGARET, and MÉTRAUX, RHODA. *Research in Contemporary Cultures: A Manual on Theory and Practice in the Study of Culture at a Distance by Interdisciplinary Groups*. Prepared for the Human Relations Branch, Office of Naval Research. (To be published in 1953.)

ROHEIM, GEZA. *Psychoanalysis and Anthropology*. New York: International Universities Press, 1950.

SCHAFFNER, BERTRAM. *Father Land*. New York: Columbia University Press, 1948.

ZBOROWSKI, MARK, and HERZOG, ELIZABETH. *Life Is with People: The Jewish Little-Town of Eastern Europe*. New York: International Universities Press, 1952.

Cultural Values

By F. S. C. NORTHROP

CONTEMPORARY LEGAL science provides a convenient basis for giving an inventory of representative anthropological theories of cultural values. Law, like personal ethics, is concerned with norms. Since norms express the ethos of a culture, different theories of legal norms take one to the heart of the problem of cultural values.

Roughly contemporary legal theories of cultural norms fall into five groups: (1) legal positivism, (2) pragmatic legal realism, (3) neo-Kantian and Kelsenian ethical jurisprudence, (4) functional anthropological or sociological jurisprudence, and (5) naturalistic jurisprudence. Each group contains different subspecies and varieties.

LEGAL POSITIVISM

Legal positivism is the theory that cultural values are to be found and understood solely in terms of the positive legal constitutions, statutes, codes, and institutions themselves, perhaps supplemented by police power or force. The main representative of this theory of legal values is the British jurist, John Austin. The designation of this theory of cultural values as "positivism" is not an accident. It arises from the fact that this is the legal theory of traditional Anglo-American culture and that the philosophy of this culture is British empiricism, which is positivistic in its theory of scientific knowledge. Cultural values are positivistic in character when the meaning of the words "good" or "valuable" is given as a particular, inductively through the senses. This excessive emphasis on induction has the consequence also of making each science an independent science. Hence the restriction of legal education in any culture whose values are positivistic, such as modern England and pre-1932 United States, to nothing but the positive institutions, statutes, codes, and decisions contained in the books in the law-school libraries. No further study of the relation of law to society is required. Law, like ethics, on this positivistic theory of cultural values, is an autonomous science; knowledge of economics, sociology, or anthropology is quite unnecessary. To this Austin added the necessity of police power or force to give the law sanctions. The decisions and the constitutional norms were not law unless police power was added. Here again a factor derived from British empirical philosophy entered, namely, the materialistic power-politics philosophy of Hobbes.

Our designation of the first theory of cultural values in our inventory has revealed an additional fact. This theory is not merely culture-bound but also philosophy-bound. It holds only for that portion of Anglo-American culture which derives from British empirical philosophy.

PRAGMATIC LEGAL REALISM

The concepts selected to express the program of this conference, which place

422

the inventory of cultural values under the category of "Problems of Process," is an anthropological illustration of the legal philosophy of pragmatic realism. According to this theory, cultural values are not given in the positive legal norms used to decide in a given dispute whether the conduct involved is to be permitted or prohibited; these norms of decision, the constitutional codes and statutes, are instead merely instruments for social change. Thereby positive legal norms and cultural values are transformed from ends into means. Furthermore, instead of the positive cultural norm, as expressed in a code, statute, or constitutional principle, being the measure of the conduct, the solution of the dispute is made the measure of the norm. If traditional norms prevent disputes from being resolved or merely generate new disputes when they are applied, then they are instrumentally demonstrated to be bad. "Problems of process" become the key to cultural values. At bottom, what this means is that cultural values center not in norms or propositions but, instead, in the problematic situation presented by men in society and in the process which brings the diverse competing and conflicting items in the social situation to a synthesis which produces equilibrium. The word "synthesis" is not a misnomer in this connection, since this legal and anthropological theory derives from the American philosopher, John Dewey. The last philosopher to influence Dewey before he created his instrumental pragmatism was Hegel.

It is not irrelevant to point out that the Yale Law School has been a center of this theory of law and that when students with law degrees coming from Asiatic and Continental European law schools are confronted with this legal philosophy for the first time, they are shocked. The shock arises not merely from the conflict with their European or Asian training but also because they

come from areas where dictators have been rampant, and they fear a theory of law which makes cultural values an instrument of the decision-maker rather than a constitutional control of him. In any event, we see that the problems of process theory of cultural values is both culture- and philosophy-bound. This theory is seriously considered largely in the United States and derives from its pragmatic instrumental philosophy.

At bottom, this theory of cultural values makes the solution of the problem in what Dewey calls "the problematic situation" the criterion of the good. Or, to put the matter more precisely, it makes the bringing to equilibrium of the diverse competing elements in the social situation the criterion of the good and of cultural value. But with a dictator in the social situation and with law made his instrument rather than a fixed norm to control him and with equilibrium made more easy by dictatorial than by democratic parliamentarian methods, what factor is there in this pragmatic instrumental theory of cultural values to insure that the cheap and easy way to equilibrium will not be taken?

The answer to this question as given by American pragmatists is that only that solution is a "true" solution which results from sensitivity to, rather than dictatorial blotting out of, all factors and interests in the problematic situation. This amounts, however, to the admission (a) that all values are not in process and (b) that there must be at least one constant noninstrumental norm even in an instrumental philosophy of cultural norms, the noninstrumental norm of objective sensitivity to every factor in the situation.

Even if this be granted, certain questions remain. To read the literature of the American proponents of this theory is to move in an aura of optimism.

Values in process and problem-solving become uncritically identified with progress. In Europe and Asia, to set norms and values in flux is all too often to create problems rather than to solve them and to produce demoralization and confusion rather than progress, whatever that vague word may mean. In short, outside the United States, this problem of process instrumental philosophy of cultural values has an aura of optimism which makes it seem culturally false and artificial.

The outstanding fact of our contemporary world is that its problematic international situation is shot through with conflicts between rival ideologies which are logically incompatible and hence not resolvable by the facile injunction to be sensitive to all the factors in the situation. Moreover, one major nation in the world has its explicit answer to the present problematic situation. Merely to counter with emphasis on problem-solving is not enough. The situation calls for a specification of what the answer is. But to specify an answer will be to specify the cultural norms according to which the decision-maker must operate. Again one has norms controlling the decision-maker rather than norms which are mere instruments of the decision-maker. Moreover, the question arises: What are these norms which solve the problem in the contemporary international problematic situation? To answer this question, it is necessary to go beyond instrumental pragmatism and legal realism.

Even so, this theory of cultural values has been necessary. We are living in a world in which the traditional norms are being reconstructed or giving place to new. Pragmatic legal realism is the necessary instrument for breaking from those values of one's part which are outmoded.

NEO-KANTIAN AND KELSENIAN ETHICAL JURISPRUDENCE

Kelsen and the neo-Kantians have one assumption in common concerning the nature of cultural values. This assumption is that values always involve an "ought" which cannot be derived from any "is." Put positively, this means that the basic norm of a culture cannot be found empirically but must be assumed a priori as the presupposition of any ethical or legal judgment whatever. Empiricism in culture or legal science merely gives the materials upon which the value judgment is based, but not the value norm itself, according to this theory.

In the United States Morris and Felix Cohen represent the neo-Kantian position. The difference between Kelsen and the neo-Kantians centers merely in the degree to which the a priori ethical norm of a society, which Kelsen calls "imputation," applies to the legal and social order as a whole. For Kelsen most of the law is given inductively in positive legal codes and statutes. To these codes and statutes of positive law, Kelsen adds but one *Grundnorm,* which is basically ethical and a priori in character. This *Grundnorm* is the a priori assumption that the positive laws given inductively ought to be. It is, according to Kelsen, only because of this ought, given as an ethical a priori by imputation, that the judge has the authority to use the inductively given positive law to send a violator of the law to the electric chair. Kelsen believes that the codes themselves do not give this ought. With the Kantian and neo-Kantians, not merely one solitary *Grundnorm* at the background and basis of the inductively given positive law but every proposition and statute in the entire positive law and in every instance of its application presuppose a continuous contribution of the presuppositions of the a priori ethical moral judgment.

That every culture is not merely the inductively given is of the behavior of the people in that culture but also the culture itself, through its leaders, passing normative judgment upon that behavior in the light of certain norms which express an ought rather than a mere is, cannot be denied. It is clear that man in society is not merely acting but also acting in the light of and under the control of both a personal and a social norm. There is, to be sure, the is of social action, but this is, if scientifically complete, includes the behavior of the murderer as well as the behavior of those who do not violate the ethos of the society. Clearly, therefore, the ought which defines the ethos is true only of a part of what is and requires something more than the is for its own definition. To this extent, therefore, the Kantians and the Kelsenian positivists are correct when they say that a scientific account of cultural values cannot be determined in any given society by the inductive description of the is of that society. Otherwise, any behavior whatever in that society would be good, and there would be no need whatever for norms, legal institutions, and the citizen's sense of having to reconcile what he can do inductively with what he ought to do. Upon this point everyone, including even the instrumental pragmatists when they resort to sensitivity to all the factors in the problematic situation, must agree. The cultural ought for any society is not to be identified with its inductively given is.

Kantian and Kelsenian ethical jurisprudence has one other characteristic: No conduct is ethical, embodying an ought, unless it is the kind of conduct which can be generalized for all men in the form of a determinate universal law. This is the point of Kant's categorical imperative.

Here modern a priori ethical jurisprudence holds a thesis in common with classical Greek and Roman Stoic nat-ural-law jurisprudence. Both affirm that moral man and just man is universal man. By this they mean that to be moral and to stand for the ethos of one's culture means to stand for certain determinate commandments, codes, or principles which hold for all men. Any society which takes as its ethos the thesis that all men are equal under the law is one holding this Kantian, a priori, and ethical, or the classical Greek and Stoic Roman natural-law, theory of cultural values as values expressed in determinate universal laws.

This concept of cultural values has its basis in a particular conception of the method of scientific knowledge, namely, the method of deductively formulated scientific theory. The reason for this is that, in such a scientific method, no fact is ever supposed to be anything more than an enigma still to be scientifically accounted for, if it is to be given merely inductively. Before it can take on the status of a scientific fact, it must, according to this deductive theory of scientific method, be embodied in a deductively formulated theory. In other words, it must be shown to be an instance of a universal, determinate law. It is not an accident that Kelsen conceives of positive law as deductively formulated or that Kant, who is the author of the categorical imperative, was a physicist who had mastered the deductively formulated mathematical physics of Galileo and Newton before he wrote his moral philosophy. In fact, it is only in Kant's philosophy of mathematical physics, with its theory of any individual as an instance of a determinate universal law, that he can find the basis for his categorical imperative.

This theory of cultural values as things expressed in terms of determinate statutes and laws is also culture-bound. It characterizes the entire legal history of the Western world since the creation of Western law by the Roman Stoic philosophers. This concept of law, these lawyers tell us, derived straight through Greek philosophy from Greek physics. In fact, it was in ancient Greek physics that, for the first time, men on this earth arrived at the conception of man and nature in which every individual event and thing is thought of as scientifically known, only when it is imbedded in an abstractly constructed, deductively formulated theory.

To be sure, before this there had been codes expressing the cultural values of different societies in the world, but these codes were not technically formulated. They were expressed in concrete, inductively given language, and they were codes which restricted citizenship under the law to membership in a patriarchal joint family or to membership in a village community of elders or to membership in a blood-bound tribe.

Only following the discovery by the ancient Greek mathematical physicists of a new way of knowing man and nature as an instance of universal laws having nothing to do with inductively given family or tribal relations, did the concept of cultural values expressed in terms of abstractly constructed constitutions interpreted by means of a technical legal terminology arise. As the student of ancient law, Sir Henry S. Maine, has put the matter, the shift was made "from Status to Contract." The significance of his meaning becomes clear if we express it as the shift from inductively given family or tribe to theoretically constructed status under universal law in a deductively formulated, contractually written, constitution or theory. Upon this conception of cultural values as things expressed in universal, theoretically constructed, determinate laws, the Greek and Roman natural-law jurists and Kantian and Kelsenian ethical jurists are in agreement.

But this conception of cultural values is restricted largely to the cultures of the West and to Islam, in so far as it has drawn on Greek science and philosophy. In pre-Western Confucian Chinese culture, for example, there are, to be sure, codes, but they are of the inductive, natural-history, concrete type. Furthermore, they are used only as a last resort. Instead of being the good way to settle disputes, required by the ethos of their culture, they are used only when the good way prescribed by the ethos of a Confucian culture is not accepted by the disputants. The proper procedure for dispute-handling in a Confucian Chinese culture is not recourse to codes, after the manner of the Western concept of justice, but the softening of the insistence upon codified rights through the intervention of a mediator. Again we see the degree to which any theory of cultural values is bound both to a given culture and to the philosophy of that culture.

Notwithstanding the correctness of its thesis that the ought expressed in the ethos of any culture cannot be identified with the inductively given is of the total behavior of people in that culture, the Kantian ethics, with its absolute insistence upon the impossibility of deriving the ought from the is, has turned out to be incomplete and at bottom inadequate. This becomes evident the moment a judge in a Western court tries to use it. To tell him that he has to use an ought and that this ought must have the property of being expressible as a universal law is of little use to him in deciding a case; for the decision turns around whether this determinate, universal, propositionalized ought is to have one content rather than another. To be more precise, is it to be given the content of a laissez faire, a nationalized Socialistic, a Thomistic Roman Catholic, or a Communistic communal ethos? To such a crucial question Kelsenian and Kantian ethical legal and cultural science can give no answer. In practice, therefore, it leaves judicial decision completely relativistic and arbitrary. It also leaves anthropological legal and cultural science generally with nothing whatever to say with respect to the solution of the normative conflicts of the contemporary world.

FUNCTIONAL ANTHROPOLOGICAL OR SOCIOLOGICAL JURISPRUDENCE

The essence of functional anthropological or sociological jurisprudence is that a distinction must be drawn between the positive law and the living law. By "positive law" is meant the inductively given constitution, codes, and institutions and cases of Austin's and Kelsen's positivistic jurisprudence. By "living law" is meant the underlying inner order of the behavior of people in society, apart from the universal statutes, codes, and cases of the positive law. The thesis of sociological jurisprudence is that the good norm for the positive law to be used by the judge in making his decision is to be found by identifying it with the inner order of the anthropologically and sociologically given is of men in the society in question. Positive law is good if it corresponds to the underlying inner order of society as given by sociology or anthropology; it is bad if it does not so correspond. Since the inner order of society has content and varies often from one society to another, this theory of cultural values has the merit of giving to the judge who is operating his positive legal institutions a norm possessing content. He is not left with merely an abstract, vacuous, empty universal concept of justice, after the manner of the follower of the Kantian or Kelsenian autonomous ethical jurisprudence.

It is to be noted that this sociological jurisprudential theory completely rejects the thesis of Kant and Kelsen that the ought can never be identified with any is. Sociological jurisprudence shows the sense in which the neo-Kantian doctrine is true and the sense in which it is false. The truth of the doctrine consists in the fact that the ought of the positive law cannot be derived from the is of positive law. The mere fact of the Constitution of the United States, with its particular norms and positive legal institutions, is no justification for the ought of that constitution and its institutions. The Kantian and Kelsenian jurisprudence is correct, therefore, in the thesis that the ought of a given subject cannot be derived from the is of that same subject. Thus an ought for positive law cannot be derived from the is of the positive law. But it does not follow from this that the ought of positive law cannot be derived from the is of something else.

It is at this point that the a priori Kelsenian and Kantian theory of cultural values committed the error which left it with nothing but an abstract, empty a priori. To get content, one must go to some subject matter. The pure abstract a priori notion of a universal norm can never give specific content. Specific content, by its very nature, has to be provided by an is. This means that the ought presupposes an is.

Nor does this present any difficulty. Clearly, it presents difficulty only for a person who insists upon restricting cultural values to an autonomous science of ethics or law. Then, clearly, the ought for the subject matter of that science cannot be identified with its is, and the Kantian-Kelsenian theory holds true. But why suppose that the ethical character of society lives in hothouse isolation from the rest of society and culture? Why assume that the positive law must be separated from the living law of the inner order of the society to which it refers?

To put the matter positively, let us assume that positive law can be constructed in terms of universal norms by any kind of positive hypothesis for society that the imaginations of men can construct. Clearly, the ought for any one of these hypotheses cannot be derived from the positive hypothesis itself. Thus, in this sense, the impossibility of deriving the ought of the positive law from the is of any inductively given positive law holds. But this does not prevent the criterion of the ought for the positive law from being derived from the inductively given is of the inner order of the behavior of people in society, quite apart from any given present or proposed positive law.

Prohibition legislation in the United States some few decades ago provides an instance. This legislation was legally passed. Hence, so far as positive law was concerned, it was an is. It happened, however, that it failed to correspond to the living-law habits of the people of the community. Hence it became a dead letter and was repudiated. Here the is of positive law was measured against the is of living law and found wanting. Thus sociological and anthropological jurisprudence teaches us that any adequate theory of cultural values must both distinguish the ought from the is and identify the ought with the is. This presents no contradiction or difficulty whatever, provided that one distinguishes between the different social manifestations of the is: one, the is of positive legal constitutions, codes, and institutions, and the other the is of the *de facto* inner order of the behavior of people in a specific society, independent of the positive law. To identify the is of the positive law with its ought is clearly a fallacy. But this in no way prevents the definition of the ought of the positive law in terms of the is of the living law. Put more concretely, this means that that positive law ought to be which corresponds to the living law of the society to which it refers; that positive law ought not to

be which does not so correspond. In contemporary anthropology one finds this theory of cultural values exhibited in the functional anthropology of Malinowski. It is also illustrated in the anthropology of cultural patterns of Kroeber and Benedict.

In practice, however, this sociological or anthropological jurisprudence and the anthropology and sociology of which it is the expression have turned out to be harder to put into practice than to write about in theory. This weakness is not discovered by the sociologists or anthropologists who hold the theory, since they never become the judges who have to apply it. In the Yale Law School, however, holders of this theory have been forced to bring it down to concrete application. One person who has done this is the late Professor Underhill Moore. In practice, he found no two sociological jurists to agree upon what the inner order or pattern of a given society was, which the judge is to use in judging the positive law. All too often, as Underhill Moore showed, they identified the inner order of the sociological is with their own particular, pet theory of political and social reform. One suspects also that the intuitive pattern which one anthropologist "finds" in Japanese culture might not be that found by another.

As a result, Underhill Moore found himself forced to determine the inner order of society of the sociological and anthropological is, which the jurist is to use to judge whether his positive-law universal norms are good or bad, by throwing away the intuitive, synoptic method of describing society of the traditional anthropologists and sociologists, who emphasized pattern, and by introducing an analytic, objective method grounded in the behavioristic psychology of Professor Clark Hull. He did this because he found, when he used the traditional method, that no two observers describing the same social pattern came out with the same description. To overcome this difficulty of the classical anthropological and sociological theory of cultural values, he introduced purely objective spatiotemporal descriptive concepts. When this was done, he found that different observers gave the same account of the inner order of the society which they investigated.

There is not time to go into the details of his system here. Suffice it to say that it consisted in defining the inner order of society as the high-frequency portion of the objectively observed spatiotemporal total behavior of society. This provided a truly objective criterion of the inner order of the sociological is, which is to be used by the lawyer to judge whether the positive law ought or ought not to be. That positive law which corresponds to the high-frequency behavior of the total behavior of people in society is, on this theory of cultural values of sociological and anthropological jurisprudence, the positive law that ought to be; the positive law that does not so correspond is the one that ought not to be. We have in this theory, therefore, the thesis that the ought of one kind of law, i.e., positive law, cannot be derived from the is of that law, but can be derived from the is of the underlying, empirically determinable, living law of an anthropological or sociological jurisprudence which uses an analytic objective method.

Underhill Moore saw, however, that even this is not enough to provide an adequate theory of cultural values. It is necessary, but it is not sufficient. In any society it is necessary to judge and to reform not merely the positive law but also the high-frequency behavior which is the inner order of the underlying living law. This is easy to see in the case of a foreign culture. The fact that the Germans, with an overwhelming, spontaneous enthusiasm, embraced and followed Hitler in their living-law behavior will not be taken by most social scientists as a scientific justification for the thesis that such high-frequency behavior and the cultural norms which it embodied ought to be. In short, just as it is necessary to judge the is of the positive law against an ought beyond itself, so also it is necessary to judge the high-frequency behavior which is the is of the living law against an ought beyond itself.

Moreover, any society is not merely expressing its high-frequency living-law behavior but also reforming it. An adequate theory, therefore, of legal and cultural norms must provide meaning for judging the is of the living law to be bad or in need of reform. This calls for something beyond the living law itself. At this point, therefore, anthropological and sociological jurisprudence points beyond itself. The is which it provides cannot pass the judgment which must be passed upon itself. Beyond society and culture, only one thing remains, namely, nature.

NATURALISTIC JURISPRUDENCE

The thesis of naturalistic jurisprudence is that, just as the positive law cannot find the meaning for its ought in the is which is the positive law itself but must be judged as to its ought against the is of the living law of anthropological and sociological jurisprudence, so similarly the living law of anthropological and sociological jurisprudence cannot find the criterion for its ought in the is which is the living law or pattern of culture itself but can be judged only from the standpoint of the is of something beyond itself, namely, the inner order of nature as revealed by natural science. We have already found an illustration of this theory in the account of the concept of moral man as an instance of a universal law, as formulated by Roman Stoic lawyers and given to them through Greek philosophy by Greek natural science. Put more concretely, the theory is that, just as the ought for positive-law legal codes is the is of the inner order of society as specified by anthropological and sociological science, so the ought toward which this inner order of society is to be changed is the is of the inner order of natural man and nature as determined by the philosophically analyzed and articulated, empirically verified, knowledge of nature. It was, we have noted, the discovery by Greek mathematical physicists that true knowledge of any individual object or event involves understanding it as an instance of determinate universal laws in a deductively formulated theory that gave rise to the Western concept of moral and legal man as a citizen of nature rather than as a citizen of a patriarchal joint family or of a tribe, which, in turn, generated Western Roman legal universalism, with its thesis that all men, regardless of family, color, race, or religion, are equal under the law. This is something novel in the cultures of the world.

Asian cultures, to be sure, also achieve universalism, but it is of a different kind, relating all men to nature by intuitive immersion rather than by technically constructed constitutions in which all men are equal under the universal determinate codes. Because this Asian way of conceiving nature is verified empirically, it is as much a scientific theory as are the theories of the West. Whether the moral or legal classics of a given culture do or do not describe its sages as physicists has little, if anything, to do with the question as to whether its values are verified by appeal to nature. The Chinese classics make little or no reference to scientists. Nevertheless, as Needham and others have shown recently, the Chinese cultural values refer to nature for their source and verification.

A major consideration leading to this naturalistic theory of cultural values is the failure of recent attempts to find the ought for judging the high frequency of the living law of anthropological and sociological jurisprudence within the latter type of jurisprudence itself. Such attempts tried to identify the ought for judging today's scientifically determined inner order or pattern of culture with the is of tomorrow's inner order. To make such a theory succeed, it is necessary to be able today to determine what the inner order of tomorrow's society will be. For this, a historical social determinism is necessary. This is the reason, for example, why the Marxist theory of cultural values employs and requires a deterministic theory of social evolution. Underhill Moore also attempted such a theory. Both attempts, however, fail, as Underhill Moore in his case recognized.

The Communists' attempt consisted in using what they call the "dialectical deterministic theory of history." The necessity for this, if the evolution of Western civilization is to be explained, is obvious. The inner order of society as conceived by the ethos of the Holy Roman Empire, for example, is quite different from the inner order of society as conceived by the laissez faire ethos of nineteenth-century United States. The latter ethos is, in turn, different from that of the recent British Labour government or of the Marxist Soviet Russians. Such antitheses convinced Hegel and the Marxists following Hegel that historical evolution cannot proceed according to the traditional logic of identity. No logic of identity can deduce, from a given set of premises, the contradictory or antithesis of those premises. For example, from the thesis which designates the norms of the ethos of the Holy Roman Empire, one cannot, by the formal logic of identity, deduce the ethos of nineteenth-century laissez faire United States, nor can one from this ethos deduce that of the British Labour government, to say nothing about that of the Marxist Communists. The propositions which would describe these four inner orders of society are clearly, on certain basic points, mutually contradictory. Hegel and the Communists following him conclude, therefore, quite correctly, that, if there is a historical determinism in society, it must proceed by the logic of negation and not by the logic of identity. A process governed by negation is, by definition, dialectical. Hence, the Hegelian and Marxist dialectical determinism.

But calling dialectical evolution "deterministic" does not make it so. In fact, an evolution of culture which is dialectical clearly cannot be deterministic. To be dialectically deterministic, the negation of a thesis in time must generate one and only one antithesis. The negation of a given thesis, however, does not give rise to one and only one antithesis. One can negate the basic legal norms of the Holy Roman Empire in many different ways. It follows automatically, therefore, that a cultural evolution which is dialectical cannot be deterministic. Thus the Hegelian and Marxist attempt to find the ought for judging the inner order of today's society in the is, determinable today, of the inner order of tomorrow's society fails.

Underhill Moore's attempt rested on the logic of identity. He took physical science as his model at this point. Physical science does have a determinism in the sense that, given its postulates and a determination of the values of the present state of a physical system, T_1, one can at the present time, T_1, logically deduce the inner order of that same system at any later time, T_2—tomorrow, the day after tomorrow, or ten years from tomorrow. Underhill Moore, therefore, attempted, by the use of Clark Hull's behavioristic psychology, to set up a deductively formulated theory of anthropological and sociological jurisprudence, from which, given the high-frequency behavior of today's society, he could deduce that for tomorrow. He found that he was able to make the deduction only if he assumed the norms for tomorrow's order. In short, the deterministic method of connecting the inner order of the present state to the inner order of future states in cultural systems presupposes tomorrow's norms and hence cannot define them. Thus this method of finding a meaning within the cultural sciences alone for the ought to be used to judge the is of today's inner order or value pattern also fails.

It is to be noted in this connection that the most exact of the social sciences that we have today, namely, economics, has never been able to achieve a theoretical dynamics. In other words, it has not been able to deduce tomorrow's state of the economic system from today's. There are basic theoretical reasons why this must be the case. The attempt, therefore, to find the criterion for judging and reforming the inner order of today's society must be found in an is with content outside today's society. This is why the sociological and anthropological theory of cultural values leads inevitably into the naturalistic theory.

This does not mean that anthropology and sociology can be dispensed with. Quite the contrary. It means, instead, that there will be no adequate anthropological or sociological theory of cultural values and of the cultural methods for judging such values until anthropological and sociological science pays as much attention to the way in which members of any society know and conceptualize nature as it has given in the past to the inner order of social relations, which, as we shall see, is in major part the result of the conceptualization of nature.

Some sociological and anthropological scientists have recently come to this same conclusion. It will be fruitful to approach their work from that of the sociologist of law, Underhill Moore. His method of determining the inner order of society even at the present time, T_1, of the system, by observing the spatio-temporal total high-frequency behavior of people in society is unworkable for a total culture. He applied it to simple cultural phenomena, such as parking on a restricted block on a street in New Haven, Connecticut. To determine the inner order of the behavior of four hundred million Chinese in this manner is out of the question, and to do it for all the different cultures is even more impracticable. The same is roughly true of most of the other inductive methods of other schools of anthropological and sociological science, since they tend to be either so intuitive in their methods for determining the inner order of society that there is, as Underhill Moore noted, not sufficient agreement among them on what it is, or else their methods are so inductively piecemeal that the inner order of society is not exhibited.

At this point the cultural anthropology of Kluckhohn is exceedingly important. He found in his study of the Navaho Indians that no amount of inductive observation, however complete, gave him an understanding of their value system or their legal norms. It was not until he conceptualized the inductive facts which he saw in terms of the concepts which the Navahos themselves used to conceptualize these facts that their cultural values became evident and that the norms which they use for settling disputes followed logically and naturally. Furthermore, he found that, when their concepts were brought out into the open, he had a complete philosophy on his hands. Without this philosophy, the facts which he saw were not understood as the Navaho understood them, and the norms which

they use for settling disputes were not grasped, nor did they make sense.

Sorokin found the same thing earlier in sociology. He showed that the inner order which defines the *de facto* living law of any society is determined by the philosophy of the people in that society. This is the point of Sorokin's thesis —that causality in the cultural sciences is logico-meaningful rather than merely mechanical, as in natural science. The meanings which its people bring to the raw data of their experience are what determine the inner order or pattern of any particular culture. In fact, there are no objective bonds between people observable from an airplane which give their culture a pattern. The word "pattern" is merely a figure of speech. Only when many people conceptualize the raw data of their experience with the same basic, consistently related concepts, i.e., the same philosophy, does an "inner order" between them arise.

In other words, norms arise from knowledge, and knowledge involves conceptualizing and propositionalizing the experience that is known. Now philosophy is nothing but the name for the basic minimum and complete number of consistent concepts and propositions necessary to conceptualize the inductive data of experience. It appears, therefore, that the values of a culture are the fruits of living according to the basic philosophical assumptions used by a people in conceptualizing the raw data of their experience.

In short, the inner order of a given society is put upon an objectively determinable basis only when anthropological and sociological scientists not merely observe in the field as many facts as possible but also discover the philosophy used by the people in the culture in question to conceptualize those facts. If, moreover, at bottom, as in the Hindu and Moslem communities in a village of India, two different philosophies are used, then to that extent one is confronted with two cultures rather than with one.

It may be asked immediately: But how can one determine the philosophy of a culture in an objective way? To this the answer is twofold. First, the philosophy of the Navaho discovered and specified by Kluckhohn involves concepts quite foreign to those of the non-Navaho American culture from which he came. In this sense the philosophy of a culture other than one's own is surprisingly objective. Second, most cultures have their philosophy already present objectively in the basic treatises of the culture. Those of pre-Western Chinese philosophy are objectively present in the classics of Confucius and Mencius. Chiang Monlin has recently shown, through a description of his own childhood, the degree to which this Confucian philosophy infiltrated every nook and cranny of his early life. It appears, therefore, that an objective, workable, anthropological, and sociological science which can define the inner order or ethos of any culture must be not merely inductive with respect to the facts but also inductive with respect to the philosophical concepts used by the people in the society being studied for the conceptualization of those facts. In short, scientific anthropology and sociology must be an empirically verified, philosophical sociology and anthropology.

Kluckhohn and others demonstrate also that the inductive method must be that which supplements mere induction with deductively formulated theory. This is necessary because philosophical anthropology and sociology exhibit different cultures as different postulate sets for conceptualizing the raw data of experience.

But this philosophical sociological and anthropological science of cultural values leads straight over into natural-law jurisprudence and the philosophy of natural science as a criterion of cul-

tural values. This comes out when Sorokin and Kluckhohn reveal that the concepts which the people in a given society use to define their legal and ethical norms and to generate their creatively constructed values arise from and are essentially connected with their inductive, empirically verified theories for conceptualizing nature.

If, for example, in the conceptualization of merely natural facts, quite apart from cultural and social phenomena, a people restrict themselves only to those meanings given through the senses, then the cultural values of that people tend to be those of what Sorokin calls "a sensate culture." If, on the other hand, in the conceptualization of natural phenomena they resort to what we today call "constructs" or to what Plato and Aristotle called "ideas" which are universals, that is, to concepts of individuals which have no meaning apart from universal scientific laws or postulates, then a people tend to free themselves from family- or tribally centered values of the more natural-history mode of knowing nature of a more sensate or of a more Asian intuitive culture. Similarly, Florence Kluckhohn, in her attempt to find a scientific principle for classifying the diverse cultural values of the many different cultures, finds herself forced to use the concepts of space and of time. Now these concepts are clearly concepts of natural science. More concrete examples can be given if one approaches nature by restricting one's self largely to what is given purely impressionistically, or by what Chiang Monlin, describing Chinese mentality, calls "naïve observation." Then what impresses one is the sequence from darkness of night through dawn to the brightness of day, through dusk to the blackness of night again, the sequence of the seasons and of the cycles of human existence. Thus one is led by one's empirically verified, and hence scientific, theory to a cyclical theory of time, in which time is regarded, not as something made quantitatively exact by astronomical measurements and calculations, but as something intuitively and impressionistically vague. Then appointments are rarely kept in social relations with the precision that occurs in the United States. Also this impressionistic cyclical theory of time in nature tends also to make the improvement of society pointless, since reform and improvement merely hasten the time when what is different from today becomes identical with what one has today.

This inevitable intrusion of the empirically verified concepts of nature used by a people into their values and norms for culture appears in our own time in another way. The Marxists and countless others have pointed out the manner in which the social and political and other values of society change with a change in technological instruments. But what is this but the effect of man's scientifically verified abstract theories of nature upon the norms and inner ordering relations of culture?

It appears, therefore, that an inventory of the major theories of cultural values as exhibited in contemporary legal, sociological, and anthropological science leads to the conclusion that each one of these theories has something to say for itself and that none alone is the whole truth. Unless cultural values are expressed in the positive law, the anthropological and sociological jurisprudential theory of cultural values can never be brought to bear in the concrete legal dispute or case. But, unless the positive law is referred to the living law of sociological jurisprudence, there is no criterion enabling the jurist to choose between one content of the positive law rather than another in his judging of any dispute. And unless sociological jurisprudence becomes philosophical and its philosophy in turn is tested against the concepts used by a people to know, integrate, and envisage themselves and nature, there is no criterion for judging or reforming the living law of anthropological and sociological jurisprudence. To inventory in a way that gives the meaning of what is inventoried is also to integrate.

BIBLIOGRAPHY

For the bibliography of the legal theories see the works indicated below. Since the corresponding anthropological theories of cultural values are well known to anthropologists, the bibliography of them is not included here.

POUND, ROSCOE. 1943. *Outlines of Lectures on Jurisprudence.* Cambridge: Harvard University Press.

FRIEDMANN, W. 1949. *Legal Theory.* 2d ed. London: Stevens & Sons, Ltd.

NORTHROP, F. S. C. (ed.). 1949. *Ideological Differences and World Order.* New Haven: Yale University Press.

———. 1952. "Contemporary Jurisprudence and International Law," *Yale Law Journal* (May), pp. 623–54.

NEEDHAM, JOSEPH. 1951. *Human Law and the Laws of Nature in China and the West.* London: Oxford University Press.

MAINE, SIR HENRY S. 1908. *Ancient Law.* London: John Murray.

KELSEN, HANS. 1946. *General Theory of Law and State.* Cambridge, Mass.: Harvard University Press.

EHRLICH, EUGEN. 1936. *Fundamental Principles of the Sociology of Law.* Cambridge, Mass.: Harvard University Press.

MOORE, UNDERHILL, and CALLAHAN, CHARLES C. 1943. *Law and Learning Theory: A Study in Legal Control.* New Haven: Yale Law Journal Co., Inc.

CHIANG MONLIN. 1947. *Tides from the West.* New Haven: Yale University Press.

COHEN, FELIX. 1935. *Ethical Systems and Legal Ideals: An Essay on the Foundation of Legal Criticism.* New York: Falcon Press.

———. 1937–38. "The Problems of a Functional Jurisprudence," *Modern Law Review,* I, 5.

COHEN, MORRIS R. 1931. *Reason and Nature,* pp. 333–457. New York: Harcourt, Brace & Co.

———. 1932. "Philosophy and Legal Science," *Colorado Law Review,* XXXII, 1103.

———. 1933. *Law and the Social Order* New York: Harcourt, Brace & Co.

The Concept of Value in Modern Anthropology

By DAVID BIDNEY

MODERN ANTHROPOLOGISTS have been so concerned with establishing the claim that their science is a natural, as well as a social, science that they have tended until recently to overlook the problem of values. As natural scientists, anthropologists were supposed to deal with facts and laws and to leave values to the philosophers and humanists. A historical survey of anthropological thought reveals that this attitude is a comparatively modern development and was not at all characteristic of the founders of anthropological science.

I. MODERN RATIONALISM AND THE IDEA OF PROGRESS

The concept of the continuity of culture history, involving progressive development from a lower to a higher degree of culture, was not original with Tylor and may be traced back to the rationalists of the age of Enlightenment. Their characteristic doctrine of the perfectibility of man in time implied that cultural progress was dependent upon man's rational efforts to perfect himself and his institutions. Culture or civilization was recognized as the instrument evolved by man, under divine providence, for the perfecting of humanity. Man was conceived as the creator of his cultural destiny, and there were thought to be no limits to his ability to transform the inherited, historical-cultural order in the light of newly emerging moral ideals. By living in harmony with the fixed laws of human nature and the order of cosmic nature, man could regulate his individual and social life in accordance with the dictates of reason so as to promote universal peace and the general happiness of mankind. Rousseau notwithstanding, the arts and sciences were appreciated as instruments for the progress of humanity rather than as impediments which corrupt and hinder human intelligence. In Germany, in particular, the concept of culture (*Cultur* or *Kultur*) was contrasted with Rousseau's deification of nature and the cult of sophisticated primitivism.

This humanistic conception of man as the creator and transformer of his culture implied a distinction between the fixed order of nature and the variable order of human culture. While nature herself was conceived as increasing in perfection through divine creativity in time, this meant only a gradual increment of forms of being, but no essential transformation in the order of nature as a whole. But in the sphere of human culture, which was man-made, there was continuous progress and transformation in the very organization of human life and society, as well as in the number and variety of human inventions and discoveries.

Once it became apparent that culture was a natural process and that man was, by nature, a self-perfecting, culture-producing animal, then philosophers and historians attempted to describe the "natural history" of man from "rudeness" to civilization. The concept of natural history, as originally utilized by Vico, Herder, Rousseau, and Ferguson, involved the assumption of the continuity of cultural development from savagery to civilization. Culture history was progressive precisely because it was continuous and did not involve any radical breaks with the past. This meant also that time was an essential factor in the evolution of human culture and that time made for progress.

The idea of progress which the eighteenth-century of philosophers generally accepted was also combined with an antithetical theory of history which assumed the essential discontinuity of history and the comparatively stationary character of time. As rationalists, they glorified their own age of Enlightenment and prophesied an even greater era of human progress in the future, while deploring the vice, ignorance, and superstition of the past, such as the Middle Ages. Man was indeed perfectible, but progress was not inevitable and required eternal vigilance and constantly renewed effort, lest the opposing forces of darkness and deception gain the ascendancy once more. Gibbon had demonstrated in his *Decline and Fall* how civilization had declined from the high point it had reached in the second century and how long and difficult had been the task of recovering from the triumph of barbarism and superstition. The constant factor in history was human nature, and it was conceived to be the task of the historian to demonstrate the universal principles of human nature as they manifest themselves in the course of historical experience.

In agreement with their rationalistic, Aristotelian, and Stoic interpretation of the state of man's nature as being an ideal rational state conforming to the dictates of common sense and morality, the eighteenth-century philosophers could reinterpret the concept of natural history. Following the Stoic maxim that to live in conformity with nature is to live in accord with the dictates of reason, one may argue that natural history is rational history. Natural history, morality, and reason coincide, so that the historian may differentiate those historical processes and institutions which are "natural," in the sense of being in accord with the requirements of human nature and reason, from those which he designates as "unnatural," because he evaluates them as being contrary to human nature and reason. In this way the philosopher-historian can moralize about "progress" and "retrogression" in culture history and can appeal to history for justification of his moral principles. Thus, in place of the old dichotomy of the "state of nature" versus the state of civilization, there is introduced the duality of natural cultural history and "natural laws," on the one hand, and arbitrary, "unnatural" cultural conventions which interfere with, or contravene, natural law and natural history, on the other.

This mode of thought may be exemplified by Adam Smith's discussion of "the natural progress of opulence" in his *Wealth of Nations*. Smith was prepared to generalize that the natural course of things invariably led to similar stages of economic development from agriculture, through manufacturing, to foreign trade in every society. Natural necessity and the natural inclinations of man combined to produce this rational economic sequence, but governments tend to interfere with this natural order and to produce an unnatural, retrograde order which gives precedence to manufactures and foreign trade. Thus we have the beginning of what Dugald Stewart called "theoretical or conjectural history" which deduces the probable stages of culture history from a psychological analysis of the normal lines of development for rational men. This comparative-historical method of historical reconstruction was developed systematically by the nineteenth-century cultural anthropologists. The thesis that natural history is also rational history was taken over by the cultural evolutionists, and this accounts for their preoccupation with the fixed and necessary stages of cultural development from the simple and irrational to the complex and rational.

On the whole, the predominant tendency of eighteenth-century anthropological thought was to emphasize the discontinuities of culture history and to abstract historical experiences in order to demonstrate their various theoretical analyses. The chronological order of events and actual historical origins were not essential, and hypothetical history would do where actual records were not available. The ultimate objective was a normative, moral, cultural science of man, based upon inductive generalizations concerning the nature of man, which would prescribe the ideal conditions of human virtue and happiness suitable to the "proper state of man's nature."

II. POSITIVISM AND THE ORIGIN OF THE SOCIAL SCIENCES

With the advent of the Darwinian theory of biological evolution and with the introduction of new archeological evidence bearing upon the antiquity of man, the quest for human origins was revived. Unlike the seventeenth- and eighteenth-century thinkers, the nineteenth-century culture historians and ethnologists were interested in the natural history of cultural development as an end in itself. Ethnology, as Tylor, Lubbock, Maine, and Morgan understood it, was essentially a historical discipline and was that part of culture history especially concerned with the culture of pre-literate peoples.

Under the influence of the positivistic philosophy of science deriving from Comte, evolutionary ethnologists professed an interest in discovering the psychological laws underlying the culture history of mankind. That is, the nineteenth-century ethnologists, unlike the eighteenth-century social philosophers, did not appeal directly to the empirical and introspective evidence of individual psychological phenomena or to selected records of history for inductive generalizations of human nature. Like Comte, their approach was primarily historical and social, and they hoped to arrive at a knowledge of man's nature through a comparative study of culture history. Psychological laws were to be discovered as the final product of the study of comparative culture history, and they were not to be regarded as the presuppositions of historical study. Man was to be known through a study of culture history, not culture history through a study of man.

Furthermore, the evolutionary ethnologists sought to evaluate the natural history of culture and the stages of cultural progress. They were interested not only in the mental and spiritual development of mankind but also in the comparative development of the arts, customs, and social institutions in historical societies. While Tylor still spoke of ethnology as essentially a reformer's science, just as the eighteenth-century philosophers had thought, his proximate interest was in theory rather than in practice. The first objective of the ethnologist was to describe and evaluate the stages of cultural evolution and the historical sequence of modes of thought and action in the various types of culture. In the course of his historical researches, Tylor came upon cultural phenomena which he termed "survivals" of a previous age in which they had ethno-functional significance. This meant that the ethnologist could, after all, exercise an indirect, practical function by indicating the ethno-historical origins of extant folkloristic myths, superstitions, and obsolete customs. By making people conscious of the anachronistic character of these cultural survivals, the way would be prepared for eventual cultural reform. But the cultural anthropologist considered himself primarily a natural scientist interested in the cultural evolution of man and in the mental laws underlying cultural development.

Modern ethnological thought has been built largely upon the foundations of Comtean positivism. Tylor was much influenced by Comte's conception of a natural history of mankind, subject to laws of growth comparable to those of physics. Tylor felt, however, that in the present state of knowledge the data were insufficient for the construction of a general philosophy of history, although he admitted in principle the possibility of a natural science of human culture history. If law was anywhere, it was everywhere.

Thus the laws of nature as manifested in culture history replaced the wisdom of man and the providence of God as the conditions of human evolution and progress. Like the Stoics of old, the social scientists urged man to conform to nature, but the nature they asked man to conform to was a historical nature, not one fixed and eternal. By conforming to the laws of history and to the rational, scientific ideals indicated therein, man would be certain of achieving the ultimate goal of civilization as a self-conscious agent of nature. Their guiding principle was that of a progressive development in history, in contrast to any theory of degeneration from a more advanced to a less advanced stage.

III. EVOLUTIONARY POSITIVISM AND THE EVALUATION OF PROGRESS

As was mentioned previously, modern ethnological thought has been greatly influenced by the positivistic philosophy of science of Comte. It remains to indicate how positivism affected the evaluation of the idea of progress itself.

While the eighteenth-century philosophers did indeed speak of progress and of the perfectibility of man, progress was, for them, measured by the growth of rationalism in all phases of culture. Hence they were opposed to the authority of tradition, especially that of the Christian church, and all forms of supernaturalism and myth. Everything had to be within the limits of reason. They were not opposed to theology and metaphysics as such, provided that they were in accord with the evidence of the senses and the arguments of natural reason.

According to positivism, the concept of progress had to be sharply redefined and re-evaluated. Intellectual progress was measured by the Comtean law of the three stages, namely, from theology, through metaphysics, to positive science. This meant that progress was evaluated as a linear process from a primitive to a final stage of civilization, in the course of which man evolved out of theology and metaphysics. The stage of positive science was thought to be incompatible with theological and metaphysical thought. Culture history was interpreted as essentially a rational process, involving development from prescientific to scientific thought. The institutions of a culture were held to correspond to the mental stage achieved by a given society.

Thus, in taking over the positivistic philosophy of science and philosophy of culture history, the evolutionary ethnologists also assumed the value theory which positivism presupposed. This may be illustrated by Frazer's thesis that the development of primitive thought was from magic, through religion, to science. Frazer differed from Comte only in his suggestion that science was not necessarily the final stage of mental development and that some new, and as yet unknown, mental stage was possible and conceivable.

IV. TYLOR AND THE EVALUATION OF RELIGION

The positivistic value theory presupposed in evolutionary ethnology is perhaps best exemplified in Tylor's analysis of the origin and evolution of religion. In his *Primitive Culture* Tylor maintained that animism, the belief in spiritual beings, was the primary form of religion. He assumed that primitive man arrived at this dualistic philosophy of religion through observing the difference between the living organism and the corpse and inferring that there must be some vital entity in the former which was lacking in the latter. Furthermore, the savage's experience of dreams might provide another source from which he could derive the notion of souls as being ethereal images of bodies. Tylor suggested that primitive man combined, or associated, the two types of experience into the idea of a ghost-soul common to man, animals, and some objects.

The significant point in Tylor's interpretation of religion in primitive culture is that he bases religious belief upon a psychological delusion and mistaken logical inference. Primitive man is said to confuse subjective and objective reality, ideal and real objects. The evolution of religious thought from pluralistic animism, or even from pre-animism as Marett suggested, to the monotheism of civilized peoples is therefore based on an initial delusion concerning the objective reality of souls independent of bodies. On this premise,

religion is incompatible with a genuinely realistic, scientific mentality. While there is progressive evolution within religion itself from the primitive amoral spirits, demons, and nature-powers up to the moral deity of civilized peoples, the rational course of cultural development indicates, as Frazer so clearly realized, that religion is a passing phase of human culture destined to be superseded by the scientific antimetaphysical mentality of the future. Man evolves out of religion and into science, or whatever the stage which may supersede science.

It is of interest to note in this connection that the evolutionary ethnologists differentiated rather sharply between religious belief and moral values. In accordance with their positivistic thesis, they assumed that religion was essentially a delusion, though having pragmatic value in enabling primitive and prescientific man to face the crises of life; but moral values were held to be objective and to provide a valid criterion for measuring and evaluating progress in culture. Thus Tylor speaks of progress and degeneration in civilization and of the partial deterioration of moral virtues in urban life. The positive science of man in society called for a science of moral laws and for the moral evaluation of culture history.

When Andrew Lang (1909) and, later, Father Schmidt (1931) objected to Tylor's thesis of the unilinear development of religion from animism and pointed out that the concept of a high god was to be found in the most primitive cultures, Tylor replied that such notions must have been derived through acculturation and as a result of contact between natives and civilized individuals, such as missionaries, since his evolutionary theory precluded such beliefs at the primitive level. For Tylor, the more coherent and nobler ideals had to develop out of the less coherent and morally deficient beliefs. Lang and

Schmidt, on the other hand, were prepared to grant that the concept of a supreme deity or high god may have originated as a direct result of primitive man's reflections upon the order of nature and that the evolution of religion may have been subject in many instances to a process of degeneration rather than of progress. The methodological significance of Lang's theory is that he derived faith in a high god from metaphysical, intellectual contemplation of nature and held this faith to be independent of the belief in spirits and ghosts which he, in agreement with Tylor, derived from animistic psychological experiences. This meant that for Lang and Schmidt the validity of faith in a supreme deity did not depend upon the psychological delusions of animistic thought, since the origin of the former was independent of the latter.

On the whole, I find that contemporary cultural anthropologists have been inclined to accept the Marett-Tylor-Frazer evolutionary interpretation of religion and to explain the origin and development of religion from a stage of pre-animism, through pluralistic animism, to monotheistic thought. Religion and mythology are, therefore, closely linked, since myths are but traditional rationalizations used to validate religious ritual—a thesis developed by Robertson-Smith in *The Religion of the Semites* and made current in modern ethnology by Boas and Malinowski. It is little wonder that contemporary cultural anthropologists find that religion is largely a lost cause and that its adherents in contemporary life are fighting a losing battle against the advance of science. In all fairness it may be said that modern cultural anthropology has contributed in large measure to this negative evaluation of religion. Religion is usually treated in the textbooks of anthropology as a branch of culture which is very significant for the study of primitive cultures and in the folklore

of all peoples but of little importance for the scientific anthropologists themselves, who have no need of such hypotheses. How to find substitutes for traditional religion, which will promote the feeling of solidarity and peace of mind which religion formerly produced, remains an unresolved ethnological problem.

V. CULTURAL PLURALISM AND THE AESTHETIC EVALUATION OF CULTURE PATTERNS

With the advent of the twentieth century, the thesis of the cultural evolutionist, that cultural development was always from the simple to the complex and from the amoral to the moral and that there were definite, fixed stages of cultural evolution making for cultural progress, was subjected to devastating criticism, especially by British and American ethnologists, such as Rivers and Boas. Boas, in particular, reacted rather sharply to the tendency of the evolutionists to set up scales of cultural progress applicable to all mankind and was, therefore, inclined to limit himself in practice to the study of particular cultures and to the diffusion of culture traits over given areas. Anthropology was understood as the study of particular cultures conceived as functional, integrated wholes rather than as the study of the evolution of the culture of mankind as a whole. In contrast to the monistic theory of cultural evolution involving mankind as a whole, Boas and his followers in America preferred a pluralistic theory of the history of cultures. The notion, accepted by Tylor, that our western European civilization represents the highest point of cultural development seemed to him obviously ethnocentric, and he therefore preferred the alternative of cultural pluralism and cultural relativity.

So far as the concept of progress was concerned, Boas admitted that there had been progress in technological achievements, as well as refinement and clarification in conceptual thought, but he denied that there had been any linear progress in the sphere of the arts, religion, and morality. In contrast to the certainty of the eighteenth-century rationalists and the nineteenth-century evolutionists that there was a rational norm of cultural progress, Boas and his followers were not all certain that there was any such rational and empirical criterion. According to *The Mind of Primitive Man*: "The evaluation of intellectual coordination of experience, of ethical concepts, artistic form, religious feeling is so subjective in character that an increment of cultural values cannot readily be defined." Progress was said to be relative to a special ideal, and absolute progress was denied. Boas was afraid that the tendency to value our own form of civilization as higher than that of the rest of mankind —a tendency which he equated with the ethnocentric actions of primitive man— would lead to nationalistic arrogance. Instead of laying down categorically a fixed scale of cultural values, he concluded that "the general theory of valuation of human activities, as developed by anthropological research, teaches us a higher tolerance than the one we now profess." In this respect, the attitude of American anthropologists coincided strikingly with the liberal and democratic climate of opinion of their culture.

While American anthropologists were critical of the theory of cultural progress, they continued, nevertheless, to think in terms of a positivistic, inductive philosophy of science and had little sympathy with philosophical systematization of culture history and with metaphysical concepts and norms. In practice, they carried on their field investigations and applied their cultural knowledge on the romantic assumption of an irreducible plurality of types of culture, each of which had an intrinsic value of its own, and therefore made no attempt, on principle, at a comparative evaluation of cultures.

Ruth Benedict's *Patterns of Culture* gave articulate expression to the accepted ethnological mode of thinking. Given historic cultures, whether literate or pre-literate, were regarded as aesthetic patterns or configurations, each of which is a legitimate expression of the potentialities of human nature. There is, it was held, no absolute normality or abnormality of social behavior; the abnormal is only that which is divergent from the cultural pattern of the community. For Benedict, as for Boas, a frank recognition of cultural equality and tolerance for the coexisting patterns of culture provide the only scientific basis for intercultural harmony. Her basic assumption is that there is a kind of Leibnitzian pre-established harmony of cultures which makes it possible for all to coexist together. This was essentially a pluralistic cultural world rather than the "one world" of which we hear so much nowadays. Although each culture was thought to be an integrated whole, revealing distinct patterns, such as the Apollonian and Dionysian patterns which she discerned in some native cultures, she did not think of the culture of humanity as constituting a possible integrated whole.

In retrospect, it appears that American anthropologists continued to reflect the prevailing attitude of their democratic society. As liberals and democrats, they merely accentuated tendencies inherent in their culture but professed to have derived their "higher tolerance" from a comparative study of primitive cultures. They uncritically assumed the value of cultural differences and their mutual compatibility. The idea of an "ethics of violence" (Sorel, 1925 and 1941) and of perpetual crises brought about through the conflict of social classes and national interests, which Marx and Sorel taught, did not enter into their peaceful scientific perspective at all. Had they thought in terms of the possible incompatibility and conflict of ideologies and of the doctrine of social revolution rather than of social evolution, they would not have labored under the naïve optimism of cultural laissez faire. It has taken the impact of the second World War to shake this romantic cultural optimism and to awaken anthropologists to the reality of cultural crises and to the need for cultural integration on a world scale.

VI. CULTURAL RELATIVISM AND THE TRANSVALUATION OF VALUES

In time, this aesthetic, romantic, and liberal attitude toward the variety of culture systems led to explicit avowal of a doctrine of cultural relativism. The sociologist Sumner gave classic expression to this thesis in his *Folkways* (1940, p. 79), when he stated that "the goodness or badness of mores consists entirely in their adjustment to the life conditions and the interests of the time and place." Among contemporary cultural anthropologists, Herskovits in particular has articulated the thesis of cultural relativism most explicitly. In *Man and His Works* he devotes an entire chapter to "The Problem of Cultural Relativism" and attempts to meet current criticism of this position. I shall, therefore, summarize briefly his main arguments in behalf of cultural relativism, with a view to indicating his basic presuppositions.

Ethnocentrism is defined as "the point of view that one's own way of life is to be preferred to all others" (Herskovits, 1948, p. 68). In so far as ethnocentrism is associated with a liberal, tolerant perspective which respects the rights of others to their own cultural values, it is apparently highly commendable; it becomes reprehensible when it is associated with intolerance of other culture systems.

From a philosophical perspective, it is extremely interesting to note that Herskovits, in common with "metalinguists" such as Whorf, adopts the thesis of historical idealism and quotes Cassirer with approval to corroborate his view that "experience is culturally defined" (Herskovits, 1948, p. 27). Reality as known is a function of culture. "Even the facts of the physical world are discerned through the enculturative screen so that the perception of time, distance, weight, size and other 'realities' is mediated by the conventions of any given group" (1948, p. 63). It is because Herskovits explicitly adopts the epistemological thesis of historical idealism that he is so uncompromising in his advocacy of cultural relativism. For him there is literally no other reality than cultural reality, and hence he maintains quite logically that the perspective of an individual is culturally conditioned by his cultural environment and that the only values which are acceptable to the individual are those which are relatively valid for his society at a given time. His basic thesis is that "evaluations are relative to the cultural background out of which they arise" (1948, p. 63).

Thus Herskovits maintains that the term "primitive" is not to be taken in the sense in which the evolutionary anthropologists understood it, namely, as an evaluative term implying the judgment that the culture of native peoples is inferior in quality to that of historic civilizations. If used at all, the term "primitive" should be employed descriptively as a synonym for nonliterate (1948, p. 75).

Herskovits distinguishes between cultural absolutes and cultural universals. There are cultural universals in the formal sense that there are universal types of institutions, such as the family and systems of morality—a thesis which Wissler and Malinowski had previously discussed. But the content of any given system of morality is conditioned by the historical-cultural experience of a society and hence is to be explained as a function of a given culture system. As Herskovits puts it: "Morality is a universal, and so is enjoyment of beauty, and some standard of truth. The many forms these concepts take are but products of the particular historical experience of the societies that manifest them" (1948, p. 76). That is why there can be no absolutes in the sense of fixed standards which admit of no variations. There are, for Herskovits, no concrete universal norms or values because there are no objective absolute values. There are only abstract, formal, cultural universals whose content varies historically with cultural experience and social change.

As a liberal and a democrat, Herskovits, like Boas, asks us to show a high degree of tolerance and respect for cultural differences in the name of cultural relativism. While each individual is to abide by the social code of his society and time—since otherwise there would be no social discipline—he must respect the right of others to conform to their social codes also. The difficulty which some find in accepting the doctrine of cultural relativism is attributed to "an enculturative experience wherein absolutes are stressed" (1948, p. 77). It is only in a puritanical culture such as ours, wherein cultural absolutes are presupposed, that cultural relativism is difficult to comprehend. Once we learn to discount our ethnocentric biases, we will emerge from "the ethnocentric morass in which our thinking about ultimate values has for so long bogged down" (1948, p. 78).

Thus we are told to transcend our ethnocentrism in the name of cultural relativism. "Cultural relativism" is used as a value-charged term denoting a positive, praiseworthy attitude, while "ethnocentrism" denotes a negative value incompatible with an unbiased, objective approach. Herskovits does not explain how it is theoretically possible to have cultural relativism without ethnocentrism, in view of the fact that cultural conditioning necessarily leads the members of any given society to prefer their own value system above all others. What he apparently has in mind is a culture system which inculcates the relative validity of its own values for its own adherents, together with recognition of the equal value of other value systems. He implies, therefore, an ideal cultural relativism totally different from the real cultural relativism of historic cultures, which recognize the absolute validity of their values and deny equal recognition to other value systems. A major source of confusion in Herskovits' thesis is that he fails to differentiate clearly between this implicit ideal cultural relativism which he advocates and the real, historic-cultural relativism which he posits to account for the variety of actual value systems. As an idealist and romanticist, Herskovits respects cultural differences as an absolute good, notwithstanding his disavowal of any absolute standards in the name of cultural relativism.

There are, apparently, two kinds of ethnocentrism—a vicious and a benign kind. The vicious kind of ethnocentrism involves belief in objective absolute values and hence intolerance of other codes. The benign kind involves preference for one's own value system, as well as mutual respect for those of other societies. How it is possible to transcend ethnocentrism of the intolerant variety, if there is no objective standard of comparison, is not explained. Furthermore, it is not at all clear why one should prefer his own system of cultural values rather than some other system, provided that the cultural blinkers which have been imposed on him do not prevent him from envisaging some other system. It may be expedient to adhere to a given social code at a given time and place, but it is difficult to see why one should adhere to it exclusively or exercise moral restraint in the presence of other culture systems. The fact of cultural relativism in historic cultures does not logically imply the absolute value of cultural differences and the obligation to respect them. The "is" of cultural relativism does not imply the "ought." To derive the ought from the is of culture is to commit what I have elsewhere termed "the positivistic fallacy" (Bidney, 1944).

As an axiological position, the doctrine of cultural relativism involves what Nietzsche has termed "the transvaluation of values." The absolute values of truth, goodness, and beauty which men profess are thought to have only a limited, relative, historical validity for a given society and culture. All so-called "absolute" values are really "relative absolutes," whose validity is recognized only within the context of a given culture. We must distinguish, however, sociological relativism from cultural relativism. According to sociological relativism, cultural values are a function of social organization and vary with its modes. That is, the sociological relativist explains the origin of particular values by reference to the society and the class interests which it fosters. Thus Nietzsche evaluated moral values by reference to two social classes, the masters and the slaves, engaged in a conflict of wills to power, and Marx evaluated moral values as reflecting the economic interests of classes, such as capitalists and workers. By contrast, the cultural relativist does not explain the origin of social values but accepts them as given. Philosophically, some contemporary ethnologists apparently find historical-cultural idealism most congenial and postulate cultural reality as a reality *sui generis* which renders all the phenomena of experience intelligible. At most, we are informed that cultural relativism is a fact of ethnographic ex-

perience and is a necessary product of cultural conditioning. Values are said to be conditioned by culture, but culture itself must be taken as given and as self-explanatory. This is what is meant by the statement that culture is a closed system.

This relativistic transvaluation of values is incompatible with the idea of absolute progress. Cultural relativism was partly a direct consequence of the opposition of contemporary anthropologists to the doctrine of linear evolution and cultural progress. Evolutionary cultural progress has been hastily dismissed as a reflection of narrow ethnocentrism and nationalistic bias in favor of Western culture.

I find it difficult, therefore, to follow Kroeber when he states in his revised *Anthropology* (1948, p. 265) that the idea of progress as advocated by nineteenth-century anthropologists was "favorable to attitudes of relativity, instead of fixity or a perfection already achieved." The cultural evolutionists were, indeed, opposed to fixity and static perfection, but this did not imply a doctrine of cultural relativity, since the latter negated the idea of absolute progress. In so far as ethnologists recognized the relativity of morals, they did so in spite of the theory of evolutionary progress, not because of it. The cultural evolutionists were convinced that, with the advance of scientific intelligence and moral experience, the relativity of epistemic and moral evalution which springs from prescientific mythological thought would tend to be superseded by rational, scientific norms of universal validity. That was why the evolutionary ethnologists looked upon ethnology as a reformer's science, intolerant of the "survivals" of superstition in their own culture. They looked for rational social laws and moral norms of universal validity as the final product of a science of man in society and were far from content with a romantic interest in cultural pluralism and cultural relativism. The latter sophistic attitude was characteristic of Sumner and of the romantic, sentimental followers of Boas, who no longer took the idea of cultural progress seriously.

The issue as interpreted by the cultural relativists apparently turns on two alternatives: either one accepts a doctrine of fixed absolute values, or else one denies objective norms in favor of historic relativity and relative validity of values. I do not think, however, that we are necessarily limited to these two alternatives. In the sphere of natural science there is a cumulative advance in man's knowledge of nature, notwithstanding the continuous re-evaluation of beliefs and postulates. The scientist does not argue that, because some former truth values are rejected as a result of new, objective evidence, there is therefore no objective criterion of truth in the sense of verified knowledge. On the contrary, it is because of his faith in an objective order of nature amenable to gradual human discovery that he is prepared constantly to question his assumptions and generalizations and to alter them in accordance with his empirical evidence. The natural scientist does not use objective evidence to discredit objective truth values. Similarly, in the sphere of moral truth values, it is not logical to reject objective moral norms simply because some alleged objective moral norms are seen to have a purely subjective validity within a given cultural context. Subjectivity and objectivity are correlatives in all spheres of value, and both aspects are required for an adequate evaluation of the cultural situation. There is no reason why there may not be a cumulative increment in our knowledge and achievement of moral ideals comparable to our advance in the attainment of truth values in the natural sciences. Murder and theft are examples of negative moral values which are, even now, con-

crete ethnological universals, even though there is considerable disparity as regards the area of their application in different cultures.

The cultural relativists perceive that social culture determines the ideological perspective of its adherents and hence can see no common measure in cultural values. There are, for them, only historic "relative absolutes," since each culture system claims to be absolutely valid. Relativity is then regarded as identical with subjectivity. What is overlooked by the relativists is the important consideration 'to which Kant drew attention in his essay "Idea for a Universal History with Cosmopolitan Intent," namely, that "in man those mature faculties which aim at the use of reason shall be fully developed in the species, not in the individual" (1949, p. 118). That is, man has a capacity for reason which is historically developed in the history of human society but not in the experience of the individual, since the life of the individual is far too short to achieve complete rationality. Mankind has the potentiality for developing rationality to its fullest extent, and rationality is therefore a universally valid ideal. In the meantime, a beginning may be made by visualizing such potentially universal rational ideals as are suggested by the available accumulation of knowledge and experience and by attempting to realize them in practice. Thus, if society through its culture is responsible for warping the perspective of the individual through its relative absolutes, it is also the only means for achieving in time whatever degree of objectivity and universality man is capable of attaining. Similarly, if it is true that the perspective of the individual is a product of his culture, it is also true that individuals may, in turn, affect the cultural perspective of their society in the direction of greater rationality and objectivity.

VII. CULTURAL RELATIVISM AND THE "STATEMENT ON HUMAN RIGHTS"

The doctrine of cultural relativism is apparently regarded as one of the major achievements of contemporary ethnology by many American anthropologists, although there have been some notable exceptions, such as Cooper, Hallowell (1952), Kluckhohn (1949), and Mead (1950), and there have been indications of a growing appreciation of humanistic values. It appears to be an essential element in that "Copernican revolution" which anthropologists attribute to their science. This impression is strengthened by the "Statement on Human Rights" which Herskovits (1947) drafted on behalf of the executive board of the American Anthropological Association in 1947 and submitted to the United Nations Commission on Human Rights. In this statement the author submits three basic propositions: (1) The individual realizes his personality through his culture; hence respect for individual differences entails a respect for cultural differences. (2) Respect for differences between cultures is validated by the scientific fact that no technique of qualitatively evaluating cultures has been discovered. (3) Standards and values are relative to the culture from which they derive, so that any attempt to formulate postulates that grow out of the beliefs or moral codes of one culture must to that extent detract from the applicability of any Declaration of Human Rights to mankind as a whole.

Here again Herskovits reiterates his distinction between universals and absolutes in human culture and reaffirms his thesis of the relative, historical validity of so-called "absolutes" on the ground that every people regards its own values as "eternal verities" because they have been taught to regard them as such. There is, he maintains, no means of evaluating cultural values comparatively, since any attempt at comparative evaluation presupposes an ethnocentric perspective. To avoid ethnocentric judgments, one must, therefore, suspend judgment altogether and try to act and regard other culture systems as if they were of equal validity with one's own, even though it may be difficult to believe that they really are equal but different.

The only absolute right which the cultural relativist recognizes is the negative right to be different and to adhere to one's own culture. There can be no absolute, positive rights, since "what is held to be a human right in one society may be regarded as anti-social by another people" (Herskovits, 1947, p. 542). For example, standards of freedom and justice are to be regarded as cultural universals whose actual content will vary with different cultures. Hence, in practice, one must not interfere or intervene in the affairs of another society, no matter how their behavior affects one's sensibilities, since to do so would be to infringe on their right to be different. The cultural relativist is so afraid of ethnocentrism and possible intolerance that he is prepared, in theory at least, to tolerate any violation of his cultural standards by members of another society, on the assumption that, no matter what the consequences may be for others, they would still be in accord with the principle of the relativity of values.

Nevertheless, Herskovits does concede that in instances where political systems deny citizens the right of participation in their government or seek to conquer weaker peoples, "underlying cultural values may be called on to bring the peoples of such states to a realization of the consequences of the acts of their governments, and thus enforce a brake upon discrimination and conquest" (Herskovits, 1947, p. 543). In effect, he is urging citizens to oppose their governments when they embark upon discrimination and conquest, assured that there will probably be found universal, latent values which might serve as a justification for such opposition. He is assuming that "the people" of a given state are bound to oppose discrimination and conquest, once they understand the true consequences of such policies. That is, discrimination and conquest are assumed to be objective, universal, negative values and not merely relative, ethnocentric "absolutes" of a given culture.

In practice, extreme liberalism and extreme conservativism tend to converge upon a common policy. Extreme cultural relativists are opposed to a declaration of objective universal rights of man for fear of infringing upon the freedom and cultural values of given societies. Extreme conservatives, together with nondemocrats who would safeguard the interests of the "elite," are opposed to a declaration of universal rights because they are against any policies which tend to equalize effective social standards at the expense of special interests. Both parties prefer the status quo.

My general impression is that cultural relativists are so concerned to safeguard cultural differences that they fail to appreciate the polar requirement of a common core of objective cultural values. There can be no mutual respect for differences where there is no community of values also. I suspect that, on the whole, there are more concrete similarities and identities in the cultural values of different societies than the cultural relativist has so far explicitly recognized. Otherwise, even the degree of co-operation in world affairs which mankind has so far attained would not have been possible.

Finally, the cultural relativists fail to see that cultural ideologies are effective precisely because they are believed and acknowledged to have absolute value by their adherents, and not only for their adherents. If a given value system were not accepted as objectively valid, it would soon lose its effectiveness as a motivation for conduct. That is why pragmatic sociologists, such as Sorel (1941, pp. 142–45) and Pareto (1935, p. 1300; Degre, 1943, pp. 45–50), regard social myths as indispensable for social action, regardless of their truth value. What is important is that the myth should be believed and serve as an inspiration for heroic action.

The practical alternatives are not cultural absolutism versus cultural relativism, as contemporary anthropologists are inclined to hold, but rather rational norms with a potentiality for universal acceptance and realization versus mythological absolutes destined to lead to perpetual crises and conflicting political policies. Far from resolving our international problems, cultural relativism leads to conflicting political and social mythologies. The only effective alternative to a mythical relative absolute is a better, more rational, and more objective ideal of conduct and belief, capable of overcoming the limitations of the former.

VIII. FUNCTIONALISM AND THE BIOLOGICAL EVALUATION OF VALUES

The distinction between cultural universals and cultural absolutes is one which received its most explicit expression through the work of Malinowski. Approaching culture from a biogenetic perspective, Malinowski was concerned to demonstrate the function of cultural institutions in satisfying primary and derived human impulses, needs, and requirements. There are, he pointed out, basic human needs and universal cultural responses, organized into institutions designed to satisfy these needs. Hence arise universal "instrumental imperatives of culture" (1944a), leading to economic institutions, social control through morality and law, education, and political organization.

There are cultural universals because

there are universal human needs, biological, derived, and integrative. But the actual empirical content of a culture varies with the social context in relation to a given geographical environment. To explain a given cultural institution is to indicate its social function in promoting the existence and welfare of a given society; beyond that one cannot go. No one has insisted more emphatically than Malinowski upon the necessity for evaluating cultural traits with reference to the sociocultural context and upon the falsification which results when traits are abstracted from their context. This approach he carried to the extreme of denying the validity of comparative and historical analysis of culture forms apart from functions. In effect, this meant an insistence upon the relativity of all cultural traits and symbols to their sociocultural context and the instrumental, utilitarian nature of all cultural values. The only absolute value implicit in Malinowski's theory is survival value, all other cultural values being understood as means to this end.

Malinowski's functionalistic approach led him to re-evaluate primitive mythology and religion (1948, pp. 72–124). As against previous scholarly attempts to interpret myths intellectualistically as primitive man's philosophy of nature, he maintained that myths were to be understood as motivated by a practical concern to face the crises of life. The function of myth was to validate the cultural institutions, customs, and rites of a culture, not to explain them intellectually, and to provide a common bond of social solidarity through a common faith. Thus myth was evaluated positively as having a functional, pragmatic value for a given society in facing the crises of life. So understood, myth was not merely primitive man's superstitions and delusions but his constructive response to overcome his natural fears and perplexities in adjusting to his environment. The function exer-

cised by myth in primitive societies continues to be exercised by religion in contemporary civilized societies. Unlike the positivists, Malinowski does not regard religion as something to be evolved out of and superseded in the course of scientific progress, but rather as something which continues to fulfil a necessary function in contemporary life which scientific knowledge to date has failed to achieve. Contemporary ethnologists, under the influence of psychoanalytical throught, are now beginning to adopt a similar functionalistic approach to the evaluation of religion.

In his posthumous work, *Freedom and Civilization*, Malinowski (1944b) revealed himself as a democrat and a liberal passionately concerned with individual liberty and with transcultural, international ideals. He was outspoken in his denunciation of totalitarian tyranny, notwithstanding his professed position that human freedom is a relative function of culture and is to be understood by reference to some cultural context. He finally distinguished between "intrinsic constraints" and "arbitrary constraints" which involve an abuse of power, thereby postulating transcultural values having objective validity by which to evaluate social systems. I know of no better example in contemporary anthropology of the disparity of ethnological theory and practice under critical conditions. In the end, Malinowski, too, was prepared to justify the very ideals of a democratic society for which his scientific theory of cultural relativism failed to account.

IX. FUNCTIONALISM AND THE SOCIOLOGICAL EVALUATION OF CULTURE

The functionalism of Radcliffe-Brown differs from that of Malinowski, inasmuch as the former tends to adopt a comparative sociological approach in interpreting the data of primitive culture. Social anthropology is for Radcliffe-Brown, as it is for his followers among British anthropologists, concerned with the comparative study of the relation of cultural phenomena to social structure and is said to differ from ethnology, which is devoted to the historical study of cultural processes and events (1952). According to this sociological approach, moral and religious values are products of social life and are to be understood in terms of their functions in promoting the solidarity and welfare of a given society. Cultures are viewed as functioning wholes, all the parts of which are closely interrelated. To evaluate any given institution, one must indicate its place in the culture as a whole and the special function it performs in promoting the existence of the society in which it is found. The ultimate, absolute value for Radcliffe-Brown is the survival value of the society, all other cultural values being subservient as means or instruments to this end.

As an indication of the transvaluation of values implicit in this type of sociocultural theory, it is of interest to bear in mind that in *The Elementary Forms of the Religious Life* Durkheim identifies the object of religious worship with society. If society is the ultimate reality *sui generis,* then indeed society is what the classical philosophers and theologians have meant by God, even though they were not aware of it. Religion is said to be, not a system of ideas and beliefs corresponding to some determinate object, such as nature or the infinite, but a system of actions and sentiments whose objective cause is society itself. Religion is simply the concentrated expression of the whole collective life. "The idea of society is the soul of religion" (1926, p. 419). For Durkheim, religion is not a delusion, and to this extent he finds himself in agreement with William James. He differs from James in that he assigns the objective cause, as distinct from the subjective belief of the believers, to society rather than to some metaphysical entity. In religion, man worships himself and his ideals collectively. All the traditional formulas of religion are now transferred to this god of the sociologist, whom mankind apparently have always worshiped and called by a variety of names, without understanding his true nature. The problem of the social scientist in our times is, as Durkheim sees it, to create new symbols of religion capable of evoking a new faith for all mankind. What form these symbols would take was, for him, "something which surpasses the human faculty of foresight" (1926, p. 428). That mankind would continue to worship and be inspired by the mythological constructs of their own imaginations is something which Durkheim assumes as a matter of course, just as cultural relativists, in general, tend to assume that men would continue to adhere to, and respect, their cultural values, even after they were convinced by the ethnologists that their so-called "absolute" and "universal" values were but subjective delusions.

X. APPLIED ANTHROPOLOGY AND THE PROBLEM OF CULTURAL UNIVERSALS

Cultural anthropology, like the older discipline of sociology, has now become an applied science, as well as a "pure" science devoted to empirical knowledge gained by field investigations. A significant reason for the popularity of the functional, dynamic approach to the study of cultural processes has been the insight it has provided into the evaluation of primitive institutions. Malinowski in particular was conscious of the need for applied anthropology devoted to the study of the acculturated native as he exists rather than the "uncontaminated" native as he was before contact with

Western man (1945). The task of the anthropologist has now been interpreted as being, in part, that of advising governments, missionaries, and commercial interests concerning native needs and the means to be employed in obtaining native co-operation in alien enterprises.

The evils of ethnocentrism become most apparent in the contacts between races and cultures. To impose by force of arms customs and institutions which are alien to a native society and to punish natives for failing to conform to these impositions are now recognized as an uncivilized procedure which is detrimental to the true interests of both parties. As a result, many anthropologists have come to the conclusion that the primary message of their discipline is that of the higher tolerance of cultural relativism, the recognition that all so-called "absolutes" have only a relative, historical validity, and that there is no justification for imposing our own ethnocentric absolutes upon other peoples with different cultural traditions and customs.

An older generation of anthropologists, who thought in terms of a theory of progressive cultural evolution, recommended a policy of humane tolerance of native cultures on other grounds. It was thought to be the white man's responsibility to assist natives in achieving the goal of civilization. The native was not to be despised for the primitiveness of his culture but counseled and guided in overcoming his deficiences. Evolutionary applied anthropology saw cultural evolution as a necessary but slow process which might be accelerated through acculturation and indoctrination.

By contrast, the modern cultural relativist adopts a romantic attitude toward native cultures, insisting upon the intrinsic value of the variety of native cultures and questioning the wisdom of interference, no matter how well in-

tentioned. The natives, they advise, should be assisted to develop the potentialities of their own cultures and to lead lives of their own, rather than to acquire our Western culture, which they cannot understand or appreciate adequately. Laura Thompson's *Culture in Crisis* (1950) is an eloquent exposition of this point of view. The case is made even stronger by pointing out, as many have done, that to impose our own mode of living upon natives without the corresponding rights and privileges has resulted in detribalized, demoralized natives who have lost their self-respect and will to live.

The problem is undoubtedly a difficult one, and there is no easy solution. But I do think it is important that we clarify further the principles on which we may act and the goals we may set before us. I would like to stress the point once more that it is a falsification of the issue to contrast cultural absolutism with cultural relativism and to attribute all the virtues to the latter and all the vices to the former.

All absolutes are not necessarily ethnocentric, and all cultural ideologies are not of equal value. Belief in transcultural absolutes, in rational norms and ideals which men may approximate in time but never quite realize perfectly, is quite compatible with a humane policy of tolerance of cultural differences. If cultural progress is a valid and objective ideal, it is the duty of the anthropologist as a student of culture history and of comparative cultural dynamics to co-operate in the common task by indicating some of the conditions for its realization in our own and other cultures. To urge cultural laissez faire because of the ethnocentric follies and crimes of the past is a counsel of despair which fails to face the real issues which confront mankind. If there is danger of nondemocratic procedures in imposing ethnocentric ideals and institutions upon the adherents of alien cultures, there is equally the danger that the liberal advocates of cultural laissez faire may fail to correct gross injustices committed by those who recognize no common human rights and values. In practice, it is frequently necessary to choose between the greater good and the lesser evil rather than between an absolute good and an absolute evil. And there are times when the evil and injustice which require correction are far more obvious than the possible harm which may result from some ethnocentric predilections. The second World War and the crimes of genocide have provided a superabundance of instances which may illustrate this point.

XI. MODERN ANTHROPOLOGY AND THE COMPARATIVE STUDY OF VALUES

As I see it, the most important and difficult task which confronts the cultural anthropologist is that of making a critical and comparative study of values. The choice is no longer between a romantic cultural pluralism and a fixed evolutionary absolutism but rather between a world in perpetual crisis and a world order based on rational principles capable of winning the adherence of the nations of the world.

In their anxiety to avoid and obviate the evils of national ethnocentrism, especially when allied with the quest for power and domination over weaker peoples, modern and contemporary anthropologists have unwittingly tended to substitute serial ethnocentrism for the static ethnocentrism and absolutism which they abhor. By "serial ethnocentrism" I mean the attitude of viewing each culture from its own perspective only, as if that were the primary and sole virtue of the objective anthropologist. So timid and wary has the modern anthropologist become, lest he commit the fallacies of the comparative evolutionary ethnologist of the nineteenth century, that the very thought of comparative analysis, of "the comparative method," strikes him with terror. We are reminded repeatedly, by functionalists and nonfunctionalists alike, that each culture must be viewed as an integrated whole and that no culture traits or institutions may be understood apart from a given cultural context. Thus comparative studies are viewed as unscientific adventures reminiscent of an outmoded era in cultural anthropology.

As against this extreme attitude, I maintain that comparative studies of cultures and their values are indispensable if anthropology is to approximate its objectives as a science of man. So long as anthropology remains at the descriptive stage, which is the first stage of empirical science, anthropologists may rest content with cultural pluralism, on the ground that they do not wish to overstep the bounds of scientific fact. But if anthropology is to attain the stage of making significant generalizations concerning the conditions of the cultural process and the values of civilization, then comparative studies of cultures and their values must be made with a view to demonstrating universal principles of cultural dynamics and concrete rational norms capable of universal realization. Hitherto the task of suggesting and prescribing normative ideals and goals has been left, for the most part, to utopian philosophers and to cynical sociologists who equated social ideals with myths. I suggest that it is high time that anthropology came of age and that anthropologists show their respect for human reason and science by co-operating with other social scientists and scholars with a view to envisaging practical, progressive, rational ideals worthy of winning a measure of universal recognition in the future.

REFERENCES

BIDNEY, DAVID. 1944. "On the Concept of Culture and Some Cultural Fallacies," *American Anthropologist*, XLVI, 30–44.

DEGRE, GERARD L. 1943. "Society and Ideology." Ph.D. thesis, Columbia University, New York.

DURKHEIM, ÉMILE. 1926. *The Elementary Forms of the Religious Life.* New York: Macmillan Co.

HALLOWELL, A. I. 1952. "The Self and Its Behavioral Environment." In ROHEIM, GEZA (ed.), *Psychoanalysis and the Social Sciences,* Vol. IV.

HERSKOVITS, MELVILLE. 1947. "Statement on Human Rights," *American Anthropologist,* XLIX, 539–43.

——. 1948. *Man and His Works.* New York: A. A. Knopf.

KANT, IMMANUEL. 1949. *The Philosophy of Kant.* Edited by FRIEDRICH. ("Modern Library.") New York: Random House.

KLUCKHOHN, C. 1949. *Mirror for Man.* New York: Whittlesey House, McGraw-Hill Book Co., Inc.

KROEBER, ALFRED L. 1948. *Anthropology.* New York: Harcourt, Brace & Co.

LANG, ANDREW. 1909. *The Making of Religion.* 3d ed. London: Longmans, Green & Co.

MALINOWSKI, B. 1944a. *A Scientific Theory of Culture and Other Essays.* Chapel Hill: University of North Carolina Press.

——. 1944b. *Freedom and Civilization.* New York: Roy Publishers.

——. 1945. *The Dynamics of Culture Change.* New Haven: Yale University Press.

——. 1948. *Magic, Science, and Religion and Other Essays.* Glencoe, Ill.: Free Press.

MEAD, MARGARET. 1950. "The Comparative Study of Cultures and the Purposive Cultivation of Democratic Values, 1941–1949." (Paper submitted to Tenth Conference on Science, Philosophy, and Religion, held in New York City in 1950.)

PARETO, VILFREDO. 1935. *The Mind and Society.* New York: Harcourt, Brace & Co.

RADCLIFFE-BROWN, A. R. 1952. "Historical Note on British Social Anthropology," *American Anthropologist,* LIV, 275–77.

SCHMIDT, WILHELM. 1931. *The Origin and Growth of Religion.* London: Methuen & Co.

SOREL, GEORGE. 1941. *Reflections on Violence.* New York: P. Smith. 1st ed., London: Allen & Unwin, 1925.

SUMNER, WILLIAM GRAHAM. 1940. *Folkways.* Boston: Ginn & Co. (Also 1907, 1911.)

THOMPSON, LAURA. 1950. *Culture in Crisis.* New York: Harper & Bros.

Relations of Anthropology to the Social Sciences and to the Humanities

By ROBERT REDFIELD

INTRODUCTION

As a "background" or "inventory" paper, this contribution is written for the eye rather than the ear and so without summaries or graces of rhetoric. For convenience in discussion, each section bears a title and each paragraph a number. The topic is treated from the viewpoint of an American anthropologist. British anthropology is in view, to lesser degree; other anthropology very little. The treatment derives from understanding of the subject that has been provided by Kroeber in a long series of his publications; indeed, there is no fundamental idea that I can find to add to his.

THE SOCIAL AND THE METHODO-LOGICAL RELATIONS BETWEEN DISCIPLINES

1. An academic discipline is at once a group of men in persisting social relations and a method of investigation. "Anthropology" is both the professors and other practitioners of that discipline and the problems characteristic of it, with the ways of going to work upon them. The relations between anthropology and any other discipline are, accordingly, of two sorts: social (societal and personal), on the one hand,

and logical or methodological, on the other. The societal relations appear in such institutions as professional organizations and departmental arrangements; the personal relations appear in the attitude and sentiments characteristic of anthropologists with regard to the representatives of other disciplines, and vice versa. The methodological relations exist in the resemblances and differences between anthropology and another discipline as to assumptions made, as to choice of subject matter and questions asked, as to concepts employed, and as to operations followed, from the abstractions achieved by the mind to the concrete and particular devices of field or laboratory.

2. The two kinds of relations, social and methodological, are mutually influential, but neither determines the other. Where a methodological relationship is discovered, as recently between some anthropologists and some practitioners of "depth psychology," closer social relations also develop. Nevertheless, as societies, the disciplines are within the general society and are influenced by attitudes characterizing the general society; for this reason the social relations between anthropology and another discipline do not correspond precisely to

the methodological relations between them. As a way of work, anthropology at Columbia is substantially the same as anthropology at Chicago, and sociology in the one institution is very similar to sociology in the other; the difference in social relations between the two disciplines as seen at the two universities is to be explained by events in social, not methodological, relations. Viewing the whole United States, one sees that the social relations between sociology and anthropology are closer than those between anthropology and political science; this is partly due to greater similarity in ways of work. On the whole, again, sociology has taken a lead in introducing anthropology into academic respectability; yet the rapid success of anthropology here tends now to color the attitudes directed toward anthropology by sociology or other social sciences with those directed in society generally to the *arriviste*. These commonplaces illustrate the influence of societal attitudes upon the relations between our disciplines. Methodological relations are accordingly helped or hindered.

3. Considering the relations of anthropology to the natural sciences, on the one hand, and to the humanities, on the other, one may recognize the effects of both methodological and societal influences. The social relations of anthropology to the natural sciences are closer than they are to the humanities, and closer than are the relations of other social sciences to the natural sciences. In universities anthropology is rarely grouped with literature and the arts, and the professional connections which anthropology enjoys in the Social Science Research Council, the National Research Council, and the American Association for the Advancement of Science are valued, by anthropologists, more highly and are more energetically exploited than are the relations with the humanities that are

provided by the American Council of Learned Societies. With psychology, anthropology is admitted by natural scientists to special grouping in the NRC and the AAAS, and chapters of Sigma Xi admit anthropologists where other social scientists may be refused. Both the degree of welcome given anthropology by the natural sciences and the relative weakness of anthropological connections with the humanities are undoubtedly in large part expressions of the fundamental conception which anthropology long ago formed of itself and still realizes in important degree: as a discipline interested in the phenomena and the forces of nature as they are, and how they have come to be, "without preconceptions and without primary ulterior motives of existing philosophy, theology, politics, or philanthropy" (Kroeber, 1948, p. 841). At the same time, the orientation of anthropology toward the sciences rather than toward the humanities may be seen as an aspect of a general societal phenomenon: the arrangement of the disciplines in a hierarchy of status wherein the "harder" natural sciences occupy the uppermost positions and the humanist is the man farthest down. The point that will now be developed is that, while anthropology is pulled toward realization of a methodology like that of the natural sciences by both the attractiveness of superior status and its own fundamental conception of its nature, there is, nevertheless, in the very way of work which anthropology has developed, a strong check upon this pull, so that anthropology is held back from science toward a substantial, if not wholly recognized, connection with the humanities.

THE POLARITIES OF THE ANTHROPOLOGICAL FIELD

4. The existence, within anthropology, of two major centers of interest is

simply apparent in the opposition of physical anthropology to cultural anthropology. Other separations made within the discipline are secondary to this one: the attempted emphasis on generalizing, "synchronic" method as against "diachronic" history already assumes a cultural anthropology separated from physical anthropology, and both archeology and linguistics reach toward connections with other ways of understanding man as a human being rather than as an animal. The deeplying and persisting determination of anthropologists to see all man, animal and human, as a whole keeps together the several subdisciplines or ways of work in spite of their differences; yet it is physical anthropology alone that is truly biological and so most separable.

5. Kroeber has identified the two polar fields as "first, man viewed as any other animal; and second, man's culture as an extraordinary product, that powerful exudate, influential above all on himself, which is peculiar to man and sets him off from all other animals" (1948, p. 840). Several circumstances suggest a restatement of this pair of foci. First, there is the continuing uncertainty as to whether the central substantive concept of the one subfield is to be culture or society or social relations, and even whether it is necessary to choose. Second, there is the recently developed interest among anthropologists in personality, which is not culture but another aspect of that aspect of mankind which culture also expresses. And, third, there is a return in our times of a conscious concern, as yet unprovided with dependable methods of work, with human nature. This term, replacing a misconceived "psychic unity," may be understood to refer to the characteristics of all human beings as acquired in whatever society. The conception of universal human qualities has reappeared, among other places, in the recognition recently given

by such men as Firth and Kluckhohn to the existence of moral values universal in all cultures because necessary conditions for these values are present in all societies.

6. The alternative statement of the two polarities of anthropology is, then, that anthropology is organized around an interest in man seen as something with the characteristics of all life, and around an interest in man seen as something human—a quality not shared, or very little shared, with other forms of life. The quality that induces the second polarity—humanity—is manifest in three basic forms: as it appears in individuals (personality), in persisting social groups or societies (culture), and in all socialized members of our species (human nature). It is this humanity, subject matter of that part of the anthropological field organized around the second polarity, that links anthropology, in spite of the powerful pulls toward natural science, with the disciplines which bear the name of that subject matter: "the humanities."

THE AMBIGUITY OF THE ANTHROPOLOGICAL METHOD

7. By "method" may here be meant the logical character of the problems set and of the arrangements of propositions in the more ultimate written product: "a science" is a different kind of book from "a history." For long it has been recognized that a second methodological polarity provides tensions within the anthropological effort: that which seeks the writing of histories and that which seeks the writing of sciences, or possibly a science. Following Kroeber (1936), Rickert, and Windelband, one identifies the effort toward the making of histories with that toward "descriptive integration," the reconstructive effort to preserve reality within its contexts of unique positions in time, space, and quality, and the

test of validity by the degree of the fit of the phenomena reported within the totality of conceptual findings. The history which arranges its descriptive integration in chronological order is, by this view, but one form of history. One identifies "science" with the transmutation of phenomena into abstract concepts that provide understanding away from the particular phenomena, with the explication of process, and with the building of competent general precise propositions (theories).

8. Anthropologists must then "do history" in presenting to a reader a culture or a personality, especially where it is presented in discharge of a felt responsibility to present "all of it." They may or may not "do history" or "do science" in the comparisons and other arrangements of more widely drawn facts. It is possible, as in much of the work of Boas or Nordenskiöld, to preserve a spirit more scientific than historical without writing either much science or much history, and the work of G. Elliott Smith suggests that it is possible to write a good deal of history without maintaining a spirit essentially historical. The prevailing orientation of anthropology since its beginning has probably been more strongly directed toward science than toward history, but the proposition will be challenged. In the nineteenth century, at least in England, the choice of orientations was not forced, for the logical character of the major propositions—generalizations as to the way in which things always or usually develop through time—seemed to serve both history and science. The influences of developing natural science and of positivism in respect to human society helped to push anthropologists toward the making of a conscious decision as to their method, and some (W. D. Strong, very recently Evans-Pritchard, and others) pronounced anthropology a history; others, notably Radcliffe-Brown, declared it a generalizing science; while others found it unnecessary to say. The sense of tension as to the goal set persists and is one of the disturbing and stimulating aspects of anthropology.

9. Again, as in the case of any other society, the conceptions which the members hold of themselves and their ideals influence, but do not determine, the conduct of anthropologists with respect to history and science. The scientific bent of Radcliffe-Brown is more apparent in his statements as to what anthropology should be and in his limited use of generalizing concepts as guides for research than in any more nearly ultimate part-science that he has written for us. In his Marett lecture Evans-Pritchard rejects the scientific models, "natural systems," "general principles or laws," and adopts explicitly models provided by history and even art. Nevertheless, as Forde and others have remarked, the details of his program—and probably his practice—provide for comparisons in separated societies for the discovery of "general patterns" and for the advancing of new hypotheses that can be broken down as field-work problems. The approach is surely far less explicitly scientific than is that of Radcliffe-Brown, but the outcome is not likely to be so different as to deserve another nomenclature for the discipline.

THE PARTIAL CORRELATION BETWEEN FIELD AND METHOD

10. In the old concepts of *Geisteswissenschaften* and *Naturwissenschaften* the two polarities of subject matter and of method were consistently aligned: history was seen as concerned with human events and values in an individualizing way, and science with subhuman phenomena in a generalizing way. The whole later (and characteristically American) development of social science in the image of the natural

sciences denies the necessity of the alignment, and few would attempt to hold it now. Nevertheless, in Kroeber's words, "the history of the sciences as a whole shows some sort of objective or partial correlation to exist between material and objective" (1936, p. 317). As Kroeber arranged subject matter into four levels of phenomena and four "approaches" (of which scientific and historical concern us now), he found that there "is something . . . which invites the historical approach in the uppermost level . . . and the scientific in the lowest" (1936, p. 328). It is somehow easier to be scientific in treating matter or life-forms and harder to do this as one goes toward humanity. Kroeber could not find very much to fill in the pigeonhole in his scheme representing the scientific treatment of the superorganic. There is, in some degree, an inherent consistency between the method of descriptive integration and humanity, on the one hand, and the method of generalizing science and the nonhuman, on the other.

THE "HOLISTIC" NATURE OF HUMANITY

11. The subject matter, humanity, provides one of the two polarities of the anthropological field. The nature of this subject matter exerts the influence that brings it about that the human is more easily treated by the method of descriptive integration than by that of generalizing science. And this nature also, correspondingly, checks the effort of anthropology, otherwise directed strongly in the direction set by examples from the natural sciences, and helps maintain a connection with the humanities thus inherent in our discipline.

12. What is this relevant nature of the subject matter, humanity? It is the fact that it is the nature of humanity, in its three forms, to cease to be itself in so far as it is decomposed into parts or elements. What is in this respect true of

stone or oyster is yet more true of culture, personality, and human nature. The effort of the scientific mind to reduce the reality to elements amenable to analysis, comparison, and even mensuration early results in a distortion or in the disappearance of the subject matter as common sense knows it. A culture or a personality is "known" in the first place and convincingly by an effort of comprehension which is not analytic, which insists on a view of the whole as a whole. When more is known of human nature, the same is likely to be said of that. The attempts of anthropological and other science to represen* a culture by a list, a formula of structural relationships, or a single underlying pattern are resisted and corrected by the insistence of the reality itself which is so much more than any of these. This "more" is the whole apprehended without resolution into elements. The same assertion may be made of a personality.

EFFECTS OF THE HUMAN REALITY UPON ANTHROPOLOGY

13. Of all scientifically oriented students of man in society, the anthropologist is most accustomed to viewing the human reality "holistically." The small community of which he has characteristically been the sole responsible investigator has been seen by him in its entirety and as a whole. A complex community viewed in the same way is commonly identified as viewed "from the anthropological approach" (*Middletown*). So with respect to the more specialized social sciences the influence of the anthropologist is to correct and enlarge the understanding achieved by more segmental and analytical approaches through consideration of the entirety. This entirety, seen as social structure, a system of social relations, or more commonly as culture, is again offered by the anthropologist in correction and amplification of the analytic,

experimentally conceived science of psychology. And the more integrated view of the human personality taken by psychoanalysis is congenial to the anthropologist, while yet it, too, requires from him the context of culture which he supplies to these students of the human individual also. To that recent restatement of the more scientifically oriented study of man which now appears under the name of "the behavioral sciences," the anthropologist makes his contribution, but characteristically so as to demand that account be taken of culture and of personality seen as a whole. The very simplicity of the anthropologist's concepts, especially with regard to culture and particularly with regard to personality, leaves him free to return easily to the immediately apprehended real whole.

14. The complete identification of anthropology with "the behavioral sciences" is also checked by the necessity that the anthropologist, in understanding a culture or a personality, be guided by projection of his own human qualities into the situation to be understood. The anthropologist's own human nature is an instrument of work. In this respect the position of the anthropologist is like, on the one hand, that of the psychoanalyst; on the other, it is like that of the humanists of the Western tradition, at least since the Renaissance. A psychoanalyst, examining his science or his healing, has recently written: "We first give free rein to the imagination, in order to sense how the situation looks to the patient, and then we examine the situation carefully, to test the intuitive impressions thus gained" (French, p. 29). The psychoanalyst's intuitions and the anthropologist's also are provided with content by what each apprehends about his own and his neighbor's human qualities. And when Ruth Benedict wrote in her presidential address that the great tradition of the humanities "is distinguished by command of vast detail about men's thinking and acting in different periods and places, and in the sensitivities it has consequently fostered to the qualities of men's minds and emotions" (1948, p. 588), her words applied as well to anthropological students of culture, society, and personality.

THE VARIETY OF MODELS IN ANTHROPOLOGICAL THINKING[1]

15. These ideas may be reviewed in terms of the conception of alternative models for achieving knowledge or for organizing knowledge so as to communicate understanding and to provide foresight. The models of overwhelming influence in our times are those provided by the natural sciences. As a pattern to follow in achieving new knowledge, the natural science model conceives of a number of necessarily related steps: activities that begin with a problem seen and conclude with a theory tested. Such a model for work has been described recently by Donald G. Marquis (1948), who regards the social sciences as each separately developing one or a few of the steps necessary to make up a science; anthropology, by this view, already achieves careful observation and description but requires more effort in the direction of testable theory. Among models for the organization of achieved knowledge, the causal model is prominent in the natural sciences: in this model, classes of phenomena are arranged in the form of general causal laws which would make it possible for an ideal observer to predict all future states of a system from conditions at a given time. It is represented in the field of human society by the Marxian theory of history and by Pareto's general equilibrium theory. A recent example of thinking that approximates this model is provided by Kardiner's theory of

1. The assistance of Milton Singer in connection with this section is acknowledged.

basic personality, in which general causal relations are said to connect the
"primary" institutions of a culture with
the personalities of its carriers and the
"secondary" institutions. The causal
model may be developed by conceiving
a system of universal relationships out
of the observation of one or a few cases,
as in the instance just given, or it may,
in a somewhat weaker form, be developed more inductively from statistical
intercorrelations of traits and trait complexes, as in Murdock's *Social Structure*
and in other studies from the cross-
cultural files at Yale University. A moderate statement of the causal model,
contenting itself with "tendencies rather than universal principles," more
characteristic of many anthropologists,
is made by Firth (1944).

16. The other model, also in part
derived from examples in the natural
sciences, which influences anthropology
is the functional model. In this a culture or a society is seen as an organization of means designed to achieve certain ends. "The ends may be attributed
to individuals, to associations of individuals, or, in some sense to the culture as a whole" (personal communication from Singer). These ends may be
found in needs or impulses more or
less biologically rooted or (as in art
and religion as viewed by Malinowski)
as acquired ends to some extent defined by culture. The means may be
found in almost anything interior or
exterior to the culture society. The functional model, familiar in physiology, in
anthropology is characteristically associated with Malinowski but may be
illustrated by work done by Kluckhohn,
among others; and a functional model
strongly associated with conceptions of
structure is apparent in the work of
more than one British anthropologist
and, in sociology, in the work of Talcott
Parsons and his associates.

17. While these models that receive
support from their success in the natural sciences are paramount in anthropology as in much other social science,
having recently exerted influence upon
the developing conception of "the behavioral sciences," they have not been
unchallenged. Evans-Pritchard is one
who has recently denounced the adoption of those models as an error of anthropology and called for models drawn
from history—albeit a history more comparative than some (1950). There hover
about anthropological thinking other
models than the causal and the functional. In the studies of Whorf and
others as to the relationships of linguistic categories to modes of thought,
there may be detected a logical model
wherein the major premises of a culture might be discovered and from
them be deduced much of the rest of
the culture. The relations between the
elements of an integrated culture are
then seen as those of logical consistency. Sorokin's characterizations of cultural types probably represent this
model. And from the point of view of
the immediate interest in relations of
anthropology to the humanities it is
well to recognize the influence of an
aesthetic model. It is possible to read
many an anthropological account of a
culture, and perhaps more particularly
some of those provided by M. Mead, as
a constructed work of art. According
to this model, a culture might be conceived in terms also appropriate to
works of art: theme, plot, phrasing,
style, classic, or romantic. In Benedict's
Patterns of Culture the emphasis on
rites and ceremonials gives some plausibility to a dramatic interpretation of
the cultures she there compares: in
this view each culture is a play written
by the past for the present, each individual an actor of a role. And Benedict
herself told us of the influence upon
her of Santayana's study of three great
Western poets as "contrasting studies

of the genius of three great civiliza-tions" (1948, p. 591). By this road one may arrive at attempts to distinguish national or tribal character by concep-tions more familiar to the history of humanistic learning than to those of the behavioral sciences. Indeed, it may be possible to identify among models for the organization of conceptions of cul-ture a fifth model still farther away from the models of natural science and also identifiable with the arts: the sym-bolic model. In such a model a culture is conceived as represented in its char-acteristic properties as a whole by certain symbolic representations—epic, dance form, allegory, etc. The symbols may be transformations of the reality represented and of the impulses pro-jected of perhaps quite fantastic nature: assumed is the capacity of symbol-creating and imaginative beings to frame meanings for themselves. Cas-sirer has told us about the relations of symbolic representations to culture. The symbolic model may be illustrated by Warner's concept of symbol sys-tem; in this case the reality conceived to be represented is emphatically the social structure. Other symbolic models, emphasizing religious conceptions or ideal behavior as that which is sym-bolized, may also be seen in recent studies of the mythology of primitive and other peoples.

18. The dominance in anthropology of models associated with the natural sci-ences is not matched by corresponding success in executing studies based on these models. Anthropological formula-tions of knowledge do not serve as bases of prediction comparable with those provided for prediction in the natural sciences. The literature does not show competent general propositions appli-cable to all cases within precisely de-fined classes and allowing of exact pre-dictive application. Though exceptions may be recognized (as in the predic-tion of linguistic change according to phonemic pattern), the success of an-thropology in prediction takes place chiefly as a consequence of understand-ing gained of particular cases—the an-thropologist studies the Indian tribe in transition, the social movement among Japanese-Americans in confinement, the discontents of colonialized peoples—and foresees, more clearly than do most who lack his special knowledge, what will occur. Even where anthropological knowledge about the behavior of peo-ple and the expected consequences upon them of courses of action is framed in the form of general proposi-tions, as in Leighton's *The Governing of Men*, the usefulness of the proposi-tions suggests comparison rather with the formulated wisdom of a humane man than with the tables and formulas of the electrical engineer. Moreover, the validity of a characterization of a culture by any of the models employed, but especially those which approximate the aesthetic, logical, or symbolic models, is not today established (what-ever may develop in the future) by ex-perimental or any other precise proof such as is demanded in many fields of the natural sciences. Rather it may be said that the reader of an account of a culture or system of social institutions is satisfied as to the truth of what he reads only in part by the correspond-ences between the more comprehensive propositions and the documentation offered. In part the proof, if proof it be, seems to issue from the conviction brought upon the reader as to the con-gruence of the parts within a whole conceived. It is as if, in the establish-ment of "truth" about a culture or a personality, a part is played by an act of apprehension of the totality on the part of him who accepts the presenta-tion as true. And such an act of appre-hension is characteristic of the under-

standing of a work of art and plays a part also in humanistic activity.

ANTHROPOLOGY AS "FREEDOM IN TENSION"

19. One might speak of anthropology as enjoying and also as suffering from the consequences of the polarities and ambiguities of its subject matter and its method. The coherence of the discipline is threatened by the variety of attachments which anthropologists make to problems and fields of inquiry that, though linked to anthropology, are far apart from one another. But the very tensions within anthropology, the disposition to become concerned with questions marginal to any sector of the immense and variegated study of man, make anthropology the freest and most explorative of the sciences.

20. Anthropology is thus provocatively undecided as to whether its subject matter is mankind *in toto* or man as a cultural being: "social anthropology" is taught in some places as a discipline by itself. It is unclear as to whether it moves toward the writing of a science (or perhaps separable sciences of social relations and of culture) or toward the writing of histories. Its views as to such histories as it does write vary from the more humanistic impressions of aboriginal history and of Indian personalities, as in the work of Radin, toward histories compared and reduced to generalizations about developments, cycles, transformations. It finds common cause with students of the behavior of rats in mazes, of human neuroses, of economic history, geography, geology, or the half-life of radioactive elements; and it also finds that it shares interests with Burckhardt, James Henry Breasted, Santayana, and the great works of Shakespearean criticism.

21. Experiencing such pulls toward disintegration, anthropology remains integrated by a number of centripetal forces. There is, first, the deeply established commitment toward viewing mankind, this creature both unique and yet one among all other creatures, objectively, completely, as all nature is looked at by all naturalists. This commitment holds together the two polarities of subject matter. It is helped to this end by the conception of the societal, for society, in the wide sense, may be and perhaps must be studied in all life-forms in which individuals maintain relations with one another from the *Paramecia* onward. It is helped also by the establishment of all societies on the land or on the sea; ecological problems are unifying. Both as history and as science, mankind may be viewed as one of many life-forms. And now anthropology, the years having established its university chairs, its associations, and its founding fathers, is helped to maintain its unity through the fact that it is itself a society, one of the societies of the greater society of scholars and scientists.

22. On the other hand, in so far as mankind is viewed as a unique realm of nature made up of persons and traditions, of moral life, self-consciousness, and creative activity directed by ideals, anthropology is not one thing but two: a science and history of that animal which is man; and a history and perhaps also a science or two of that special subject matter, humanity. In this direction anthropology becomes an influence upon the other social sciences to recognize, in their work, the holistic reality of humanity. And in this direction it is drawn toward interests shared with the humanities.

THE DEVELOPING RELATIONS OF ANTHROPOLOGY

23. Current trends suggest that anthropology will, at least in the near future, continue to extend and to deepen its connections with other disciplines without losing its character as a distinct discipline in itself. It will par-

ticipate in the renewed effort to realize the causal model in the study of man that appears in "the behavioral sciences." This will affect anthropology by stimulating more formal and precise designs of research, while the essential commitment of anthropology to the humane reality will hold back the behavioral sciences from becoming mechanical and meaningless. And the experience of anthropology in examining the general propositions of the other social sciences in the light of knowledge of widely different societies and cultures will continue to exert another kind of corrective and expansive influence on social science. From other social or biological sciences anthropology receives frequent and varied stimulus. The recent influence on anthropology, in the United States especially, of "depth psychology" is undeniable and far-reaching; the influence of learning theory on anthropology is claimed but is not fully demonstrated; the influence of sociological theory has become great in the work of many recent anthropologists. Anthropology is a creature and a creator of many frontiers.

24. In the future the interests which anthropology shares with humanistic learning are likely to deepen and to become more fully recognized. At least four developments taking place in anthropology move it in this direction. One is the attempt to characterize "as wholes" the ways of life of both national and tribal peoples: the studies of national character, of fundamental value systems, of themes and basic culture patterns. As suggested above (par. 17), such characterizations have long been made by historians, philosophers of history, and students of literature and the other arts, and the holistic apprehension is itself perhaps an aesthetic mode of thought. At any rate, the help that Benedict found she got from humanists is likely to be drawn upon more fully by anthropologists as they explore the literature and the methodology of studying American, French, or Siamese character.

25. The very extension of the field of anthropology to include civilized peoples, and especially those civilized peoples whose civilization is an outgrowth of an indigenous tribal and peasant culture, tends to bring the anthropologist together with the humanist in such a study. "Regional studies" may have one development into a study not so much of a region as of a culture: a single localized long-standing way of life composed of a Little Tradition of the nonliterate and illiterate and a Great Tradition of the literate and philosophic few. These two aspects of the one reality are to be found, respectively, in the community study of the anthropologist and in the study of the art and literature by the humanist. The two traditions have made each other—in the Far East and the Near East—and anthropologists are likely to join with Sinologists and other specialists of literature and history in the complete study of these culture-civilizations.

26. A third tendency in anthropology draws anthropologists into new connections, on the one hand, with science, and, on the other, with humanistic studies—the developing interest in personalities. Conceived as a "modal personality" or as a problem in the causation of a human type by reason of customs of child-training or of some other sort, this field of study is scientific. Yet here again it is the anthropologist who characteristically holds back (as exemplified in M. Mead's recent statements on the relations among child-training, social institutions, and personality as wholes of interdependent parts) from strictly deterministic forms of explanation of personality formation or of the relations of attitudes to type of personality. And as anthropologists have come to look more intensively at particular personalities, they have come

to produce discussions of the interrelations of individual and society, personality and culture, which parallel the works of literary people. Biographies of Indians or of Africans, presented in relation to ethnographic accounts, evoke comparison with the biographies of the historians and, indeed, with the work of novelists. The division of labor in developing understanding of Newburyport between W. Lloyd Warner and J. P. Marquand is not altogether clear. Furthermore, an interest appears in some anthropologists (as in the work of Radin on the creative individual in the formation of mythology and that of Bunzel on Pueblo potters) in the human individual as modifier and creator of his culture; at this point anthropology has moved over into a field more often identified with the humanities: the study of the producers and the creative products of humanity.

27. Finally, the developing explicit concern with values moves anthropology into developing relationship with the humanities. In the first place, there is the current anthropological interest in exploration of the concept of "value," as value is represented in those human beings who are the objects of anthropological study. Anthropologists have always studied values, for the attitudes of preference that are connected with acts and material objects are centrally characteristic of culture and personality; but now the conception is examined, its sources investigated, its varieties looked into, and its validations developed. This links the anthropologist with the philosopher. And also the anthropologist is drawn to value in another aspect: to value as it appears in the anthropologist himself. How do the anthropologist's own values affect his work? The earlier assumption that his own values are entirely removable as factors of consequence in anthropological research now comes to be questioned. The conception of anthropology as a purely theoretical part of natural history is now qualified by the recognition of applied anthropology, of "action anthropology," and of the responsibility of anthropologists in Point 4 and related programs. These engagements seem to make difficult or perhaps even impossible anthropology as a pure science alone. In advising men of action, in participating in social change—indeed, in being themselves agents of social change in acculturated societies—anthropologists come to entertain the question: What, then, is the good life?

REFERENCES

BENEDICT, RUTH. 1948. "Anthropology and the Humanities," *American Anthropologist*, n.s., L, No. 4, Part I, 585–93.

EVANS-PRITCHARD, E. E. 1950. "Social Anthropology, Past and Present," *Man*, L, No. 198, 118–24.

FIRTH, RAYMOND. 1944. "The Future of Social Anthropology," *Man*, XLIV, No. 8, 19–22.

FRENCH, THOMAS M. 1952. *The Integration of Behavior*, Vol. I. Chicago: University of Chicago Press.

KROEBER, A. L. 1936. "So-called Social Science," *Journal of Social Philosophy*, I, No. 4, 317–40.

———. 1948. *Anthropology*. New York: Harcourt, Brace & Co.

MARQUIS, DONALD G. 1948. "Scientific Methodology in Human Relations," *Proceedings of the American Philosophical Society*, XCII, No. 6, 411–16.

Contributors

ERWIN H. ACKERKNECHT

Dr. Ackerknecht is professor of the history of medicine and biology at the University of Zurich, Switzerland. He was formerly professor of the history of medicine at the University of Wisconsin, a research fellow at the Johns Hopkins University, and assistant curator at the American Museum of Natural History in New York. His writings include *Medizinalreform von 1848* (1932) and *Malaria in the Upper Mississippi Valley, 1760–1900* (1945).

MARSTON BATES

Dr. Bates, formerly of the Rockefeller Foundation, where he was special assistant to the president, has been professor of zoölogy at the University of Michigan since 1952. He is author of *The Natural History of Mosquitoes* (1949), *The Nature of Natural History* (1950), and *Where Winter Never Comes: A Study of Man and Nature in the Tropics* (1952), *The Prevalence of People* (1955), *The Darwin Reader* (with P. S. Humphrey, 1957), *Coral Island* (with D. P. Abbott, 1958), *The Forest and the Sea* (1960), and *Man in Nature* (1961).

RALPH BEALS

Dr. Beals is professor of anthropology and sociology at the University of California at Los Angeles. He was the organizer and for a time chairman of the Department of Anthropology and Sociology at UCLA. He was president of the American Anthropological Association (1950), fellow of the Center for Advanced Study in the Behavioral Sciences (1955–56), and Guggenheim fellow (1958–59). He carried on extensive field studies in Latin America. His publications include *Cherán: A Sierra Tarascan Village* (1946), *No Frontier to Learning* (1957), and *An Introduction to Anthropology* (with H. Hoijer, 1954).

WENDELL C. BENNETT

Dr. Bennett was professor of anthropology and chairman of the Department of Anthropology at Yale University, New Haven, Connecticut. He was president (1952) of the American Anthropological Association. He conducted numerous archeological research projects in Mexico, Bolivia, Venezuela, Chile, Peru, Colombia, and Ecuador. Dr. Bennett died September 6, 1953.

DAVID BIDNEY

Dr. Bidney is professor of anthropology and philosophy at Indiana University. He was a Guggenheim fellow in anthropology (1950). He is author of *The Psychology and Ethics of Spinoza* (1940) and *Theoretical Anthropology* (1953).

WILLIAM C. BOYD

Dr. Boyd is professor of immunochemistry at the School of Medicine, Boston University, Massachusetts. He received a Fulbright Award to study anthropology and human genetics in Pakistan during 1952. Dr. Boyd was president of the American Association of Immunologists in 1958 and during 1959 was a lecturer in the U.S.S.R. (at the request of the U.S. State Department). He is the author of *Blood Grouping Technic* (with F. Schiff, 1942), *Fundamentals of Immunology* (1947), *Genetics and the Races of Man* (1950), and *Biochemistry and Human Metabolism* (with B. S. Walker and I. Asimov, 1952).

ALFONSO CASO

Dr. Caso has been director of the Instituto Nacional Indigenista in Mexico City since 1949. He holds honorary membership in the Société des Americanistes of Paris, the Academy of Sciences in New York, and the Instituto de Ciencias y Artes del Estado de Oaxaca. He is an honorary fellow of the Royal Anthropological Institute of Great Britain and Ireland. He holds membership in the American Anthropological Association and the American Philosophical Society. In 1952 Dr. Caso was recipient of the Wenner-Gren Foundation's Viking Medal for Archeology. In 1939 he was president of the XXVIIth International Congress of Americanists, and in 1956 he represented the Mexican government at the XXXIId International Congress of Americanists in Copenhagen, Denmark. He is author of *The Zapotec Estelae* (1928), *The Exploration in Oaxaca* (1936), and *The Religion of the Aztecs* (1937).

V. GORDON CHILDE

Dr. Childe was professor of prehistoric European archeology and director of the Institute of Archaeology of the University of London, England. He was president (1938) of Section H of the British Association for the Advancement of Science. His publications include *What Happened in History* (1942), *Progress and Archaeology* (1944), *The Dawn of European Civilization* (1946), *Man Makes Himself* (1951), and *Social Evolution* (1951). Dr. Childe died October 19, 1957.

J. GRAHAME D. CLARK

Dr. Clark is Disney Professor of Prehistoric Archaeology at Cambridge University, England. He has been editor of the *Proceedings* of the Prehistoric Society of England since 1935 and has participated in field trips to most parts of Europe. He is author of *The Mesolithic Age in Britain* (1932), *The Mesolithic Settlement of Northern Europe* (1936), *Archaeology and Society* (1939), *Prehistoric England* (1940), *Prehistoric Europe: The Economic Basis* (1952), *Excavations at Star Carr* (1954), and *World Prehistory: An Outline* (1961).

JOSEPH H. GREENBERG

Dr. Greenberg is professor of anthropology at Columbia University, New York. His field research includes both ethnological and linguistic research in Nigeria. He is the author of works on African ethnology and African and general linguistics, including *The Influence of Islam on a Suda-*nese Religion (1946), *Studies in African Linguistic Classification* (1955), and *Essays in Linguistics* (1957).

A. IRVING HALLOWELL

Dr. Hallowell is professor of anthropology at the University of Pennsylvania in Philadelphia and professor of anthropology in psychiatry in the medical school. He was chairman of the Division of Anthropology and Psychology, National Research Council (1946–49), and is a member of the National Academy of Sciences. He is a past president of the American Anthropological Association (1949), the American Folklore Society (1940–41), and the Society of Projective Techniques (1950–51). He was editor of the Viking Fund Monographs in Anthropology (Wenner-Gren Foundation for Anthropological Research, 1950–55) and the recipient of the Viking Medal and Award in General Anthropology for 1955. He is author of *Bear Ceremonialism in the Northern Hemisphere* (1926), *The Role of Conjuring in Saulteaux Society* (1942), and *Culture and Experience* (1955).

HARRY HOIJER

Dr. Hoijer is professor of anthropology at the University of California at Los Angeles. He was president (1946) of the Southwest Anthropological Association, "Memoirs" editor (1948) of the American Anthropological Association, president (1959) of the Linguistic Society of America, and chairman of the Joint Committee on American Native Languages (1948——). He is author of *Chiricahua and Mescalero Apache Texts* (1938), *Linguistic Structures of Native America* (with others, 1946), *An Introduction to Anthropology* (with R. L. Beals, 1953, 1959), and *Language in Culture* (editor, 1954).

CLYDE KLUCKHOHN

Dr. Kluckhohn was professor of anthropology in the Department of Social Relations and director of the Russian Research Center at Harvard University, and curator of southwestern ethnology at the Peabody Museum of Ethnology and Archaeology, Cambridge, Massachusetts. He was the recipient of the Viking Fund Medal in General Anthropology (1950). He was co-chief of the Joint Morale Survey of the Office of War Information and president (1947) of the American Anthropological Association. His publications include *To the Foot of the Rainbow* (1927), *Mirror for Man* (1949), and, as editor with Henry Murray, *Personality in Nature, Society, and Culture* (1948). Dr. Kluckhohn died July 29, 1960.

CLAUDE LÉVI-STRAUSS

Dr. Lévi-Strauss is professor at the Collège de France, Paris. He has carried on field research in the Mato Grosso region of Brazil and the southern Amazon. He is author of *Les Structures élémentaires de la parenté* (1949), *Tristes Tropiques* (1955), *Anthropologie Structurale* (1958), *Le Totémisme aujourd'hui* (1962), *La Pensée Sauvage* (1962).

MARGARET MEAD

Dr. Mead is associate curator of ethnology, American Museum of Natural History, New York City, and adjunct professor of anthropology, Columbia University, New York City. She has held National Research Council (1925) and Social Science Research Council (1928–29) fellowships, has been president of the Society for Applied Anthropology (1949–50), president of the American Anthropological Association (1960), and president of the World Federation for Mental Health. She is presently secretary of the Institute for Intercultural Studies, and a fellow of the American Association for the Advancement of Science (also member of the Board of Directors since 1955), the American Ethnological Society, and the American Orthopsychiatric Association. She is visiting professor of anthropology in the Department of Psychiatry, University of Cincinnati (since 1957) and visiting professor at the Menninger Foundation, Topeka, Kansas (since 1959). In 1957–58, she was the recipient of the Viking Medal in General Anthropology, awarded by the Wenner-Gren Foundation for anthropological research. Some of her principal works are *Coming of Age in Samoa* (1928), *Growing Up in New Guinea* (1930), *Sex and Temperament in Three Primitive Societies* (1935), *Balinese Character* (with Gregory Bateson, 1942), *Cooperation and Competition among Primitive Peoples* (editor, 1937), *And Keep Your Powder Dry!* (1942), *Male and Female* (1949), *Soviet Attitudes toward Authority* (1951), *Growth and Culture* (with Frances Cooke Macgregor, 1951), *New Lives for Old* (1956), *An Anthropologist at Work* (1959), and *People and Places* (1959).

HALLAM L. MOVIUS, JR.

Dr. Movius is professor of anthropology in the Department of Anthropology and curator of paleolithic archeology in the Peabody Museum, Harvard University, Cambridge, Massachusetts. In 1949 he was recipient of the Viking Fund Medal for Archeology. He is a member of the National Academy of Sciences. He has done archeological field work on various aspects of the Old World paleolithic and mesolithic cultures in Czechoslovakia (1930), western and central Europe (1931), Palestine (1932), Ireland (1932–36), Burma and Java (1937–38), eastern France (1948), western Europe (1949), and at Les Eyzies in the classic Dordogne region of southwestern France (1953 and 1958–61). His Ph.D. thesis on *The Irish Stone Age* was published in 1942 by the Cambridge University Press. He is also author of *Early Man and Pleistocene Stratigraphy in Southern and Eastern Asia* (1944), *The Lower Paleolithic Cultures of Southern and Eastern Asia* (1949), and *The Rock-Shelter of La Colombière* (with Sheldon Judson, 1956), as well as more than seventy other scientific papers dealing with various aspects of prehistoric archeology in the Old World.

F. S. C. NORTHROP

Dr. Northrop is Sterling Professor of Philosophy and Law, Yale University Law School, New Haven, Connecticut. He was chairman (1947) of Section L of the American Association for the Advancement of Science and was president of the Eastern Division of the American Philosophical Association (1952). His published works include *Science and First Principles* (1932), *The Meeting of East and West* (1946), *The Logic of the Sciences and the Humanities* (1947), *The Taming of the Nations: A Study of the Cultural Bases of International Policy* (1952), *European Union and United States Foreign Policy* (1952), *Complexity of Legal and Ethical Experience* (1959), and editor of *Ideological Differences and World Order* (1949).

ROBERT REDFIELD

Dr. Redfield was professor of anthropology and chairman of the Department of Anthropology at the University of Chicago. He was dean (1934–46) of the Division of Social Sciences at the University of Chicago and research associate (1930–46) in charge of ethnological field work in Yucatan and Guatemala with the Carnegie Institution of Washington. His works include *Tepoztlán: A Mexican Village* (1930), *Chan Kom: A Maya Village* (with Alfonso Villa Rojas, 1934), *The Folk Culture of Yucatan* (1941), and *A Village That Chose Progress* (1950). Dr. Redfield died October 16, 1958.

IRVING ROUSE

Dr. Rouse is professor of anthropology and chairman of the Department of Anthropology at Yale University, New Haven, Connecticut. He was president (1952–53) of the Society for American Archaeology and was formerly editor of *American Antiquity*. His publications include *Prehistory in Haiti: A Study in Method* (1939), *A Survey of Indian River Archeology, Florida* (1951), *Porto Rican Prehistory* (1952), and *An Archeological Chronology of Venezuela* (with J. M. Cruxent, 1958–59).

MEYER SCHAPIRO

Dr. Schapiro is professor of fine arts and archeology, Columbia University, New York. He was a Carnegie fellow (1926–28) and a Guggenheim fellow (1939–40) and is on the board of editors of the *Journal of the History of Ideas*. His works include *Van Gogh* (1950) and *Cézanne* (1952), many studies of early Christian, Byzantine, medieval, and modern art, and a work on

Leonardo and Freud (*Journal of the History of Ideas*, XVII [1956]).

WILLIAM L. STRAUS, JR.

Dr. Straus is professor of anatomy and physical anthropology at the Johns Hopkins University. He was a National Research Council fellow (1926–27), a Guggenheim Memorial fellow (1937–38), and the recipient of the Viking Fund Medal in Physical Anthropology for 1952. He was coeditor (with C. G. Hartman) of *The Anatomy of the Rhesus Monkey* (1933).

PIERRE TEILHARD DE CHARDIN

Dr. P. Teilhard was a research associate of the Wenner-Gren Foundation, a member of the French Académie des Sciences, and director of research of the Centre National de la Recherche in Paris. He was also an adviser to the National Geological Survey of China. His field research included trips to China, India, Java, Burma, and South Africa. Dr. Teilhard died April 10, 1955.

HENRI V. VALLOIS

Dr. Vallois is director of the Institut de Paléontologie Humaine, Paris, France. He was director of the Musée de l'Homme and professor at the Muséum national d'Histoire naturelle (1941–60) and chargé de cours of physical anthropology at the Faculté des Sciences (1948–60). He is also general secretary of the Société d'Anthropologie de Paris and editor of the *Bulletins et Mémoires* of the Société d'Anthropologie and of *L'Anthropologie* and *Archives* of the Institut de Paléontologie Humaine. He was the recipient of the Huxley Memorial Medal of the Royal Anthropological Institute (1954) and of the Viking Fund Medal in Physical Anthropology (1958). Some of his publications are *L'Anthropologie de la population française* (1942), *La Place de l'homme dans la nature* (1944), *Les Races humaines* (5th ed.; 1960), *Les Hommes fossiles: éléments de paléontologie humaine* (with M. Boule) (4th ed.; 1952; English transl., 1957), *L'Ordre des Primates* (1955).

S. L. WASHBURN

Dr. Washburn is professor of anthropology at the University of California at Berkeley. He was president (1951–52) of the American Association of Physical Anthropologists and was editor of the *American Journal of Physical Anthropology* (1955–57). He has done research in Ceylon, Thailand, Borneo, and Africa.

GORDON R. WILLEY

Dr. Willey is Bowditch Professor of Central American and Mexican Archeology and Ethnology at Harvard University, Cambridge, Massachusetts. He was formerly field supervisor for the Institute of Andean Research in Peru and anthropologist with the Bureau of American Ethnology, Smithsonian Institution, Washington, D.C. Dr. Willey received the Wenner-Gren medal for Archeology in 1953, was elected to the National Academy of Sciences in 1960, and was president of the American Anthropological Association in 1961. He has directed archeological field work in British Honduras (1953–56), in Guatemala (1958–61), and in Nicaragua (1959 and 1961). His published works include *Archaeology of the Florida Gulf Coast* (1949) and *Prehistoric Settlement Patterns in the Virú Valley, Peru* (1952), and *Method and Theory in American Archeology* (with Philip Phillips, 1957).

Index

PHOENIX BOOKS
in Anthropology

PHOENIX BOOKS
in Archeology

PHOENIX BOOKS
in History